T0257342

High-Performance Computing on Complex Environments

**WILEY SERIES ON PARALLEL
AND DISTRIBUTED COMPUTING**

Series Editor: Albert Y. Zomaya

High-Performance Computing on Complex Environments

Emmanuel Jeannot

Inria

Julius Žilinskas

Vilnius University

Copyright © 2014 by John Wiley & Sons, Inc. All rights reserved.

Published by John Wiley & Sons, Inc., Hoboken, New Jersey.
Published simultaneously in Canada.

No part of this publication may be reproduced, stored in a retrieval system, or transmitted in any form or by any means, electronic, mechanical, photocopying, recording, scanning, or otherwise, except as permitted under Section 107 or 108 of the 1976 United States Copyright Act, without either the prior written permission of the Publisher, or authorization through payment of the appropriate per-copy fee to the Copyright Clearance Center, Inc., 222 Rosewood Drive, Danvers, MA 01923, (978) 750-8400, fax (978) 646-8600, or on the web at www.copyright.com. Requests to the Publisher for permission should be addressed to the Permissions Department, John Wiley & Sons, Inc., 111 River Street, Hoboken, NJ 07030, (201) 748-6011, fax (201) 748-6008.

Limit of Liability/Disclaimer of Warranty: While the publisher and author have used their best efforts in preparing this book, they make no representations or warranties with respect to the accuracy or completeness of the contents of this book and specifically disclaim any implied warranties of merchantability or fitness for a particular purpose. No warranty may be created or extended by sales representatives or written sales materials. The advice and strategies contained herin may not be suitable for your situation. You should consult with a professional where appropriate. Neither the publisher nor author shall be liable for any loss of profit or any other commercial damages, including but not limited to special, incidental, consequential, or other damages.

For general information on our other products and services please contact our Customer Care Department with the U.S. at 877-762-2974, outside the U.S. at 317-572-3993 or fax 317-572-4002.

Wiley also publishes its books in a variety of electronic formats. Some content that appears in print, however, may not be available in electronic format.

Library of Congress Cataloging in Publication Data:

Jeannot, Emmanuel.
   High performance computing on complex environments / Emmanuel Jeannot, Julius Zilinskas.
      pages cm
   Includes bibliographical references and index.
   ISBN 978-1-118-71205-4 (cloth)
   1. High performance computing. I. Žilinskas, J. (Julius), 1973- II. Title.
   QA76.88.J43 2014
   004.1'1–dc23

2013048363

High-Performance Computing on Complex Environments / Emmanuel Jeannot and Julius Žilinskas
Printed in the United States of America.

10 9 8 7 6 5 4 3 2 1

To our colleague Mark Baker

Contents

7. Effective Data Access Patterns on Massively Parallel Processors   **115**

Gabriele Capannini, Ranieri Baraglia, Fabrizio Silvestri, and Franco Maria Nardini

8. Scalable Storage I/O Software for Blue Gene Architectures   **135**

Florin Isaila, Javier Garcia, and Jesús Carretero

**11. Heterogeneous Parallel Computing Platforms and Tools for
Compute-Intensive Algorithms: A Case Study**   **193**

Daniele D'Agostino, Andrea Clematis, and Emanuele Danovaro

Contributors

ALEJANDRO ÁLVAREZ-MELCÓN, Technical University of Cartagena, Cartagena, Spain

HAMID ARABNEJAD, Universidade do Porto, Porto, Portugal

HENRI E. BAL, VU University, Amsterdam, The Netherlands

RANIERI BARAGLIA, National Research Council of Italy, Pisa, Italy

JORGE G. BARBOSA, Universidade do Porto, Porto, Portugal

ROBERT BASMADJIAN, Passau University, Passau, Germany

GABRIELE CAPANNINI, D&IT Chalmers, Göteborg, Sweden

JESÚS CARRETERO, Universidad Carlos III of Madrid, Madrid, Spain

RAIMONDAS ČIEGIS, Vilnius Gediminas Technical University, Vilnius, Lithuania

DAVID CLARKE, University College Dublin, Dublin, Ireland

ANDREA CLEMATIS, IMATI CNR, Genoa, Italy

GEORGES DA COSTA, Toulouse University, Toulouse, France

DANIELE D'AGOSTINO, IMATI CNR, Genoa, Italy

EMANUELE DANOVARO, IMATI CNR, Genoa, Italy

MATJAŽ DEPOLLI, Jožef Stefan Institute, Ljubljana, Slovenia

KIRIL DICHEV, University College Dublin, Dublin, Ireland

NIELS DROST, Netherlands eScience Center, Amsterdam, The Netherlands

JOSE J. FERNANDEZ, National Centre for Biotechnology, National Research Council (CNB-CSIC), Madrid, Spain

MARC E. FRINCU, West University of Timisoara, Timisoara, Romania

JAVIER GARCIA, Universidad Carlos III of Madrid, Madrid, Spain

ESTER M. GARZON, University of Almería, Almería, Spain

DOMINGO GIMÉNEZ, University of Murcia, Murcia, Spain

ARTURO GONZALEZ-ESCRIBANO, Universidad de Valladolid, Valladolid, Spain

TORSTEN HOEFLER, ETH Zürich, Zürich, Switzerland

JOSÉ IGNACIO AGULLEIRO,   University of Almería, Almería, Spain

ALEKSANDAR ILIC,   Technical University of Lisbon, Lisbon, Portugal

FLORIN ISAILA,   Universidad Carlos III of Madrid, Madrid, Spain

EMMANUEL JEANNOT,   Inria Bordeaux Sud-Ouest, Talence, France

KONSTANTINOS KARAOGLANOGLOU,   Aristotle University of Thessaloniki, Thessaloniki, Greece

HELEN KARATZA,   Aristotle University of Thessaloniki, Thessaloniki, Greece

GABOR KECSKEMETI,   University of Innsbruck, Innsbruck, Austria

ATTILA KERTESZ,   MTA SZTAKI Computer and Automation Research Institute, Budapest, Hungary

TIMO VAN KESSEL,   VU University, Amsterdam, The Netherlands

GREGOR KOSEC,   Jožef Stefan Institute, Ljubljana, Slovenia

LUKASZ KUCZYNSKI,   Czestochowa University of Technology, Czestochowa, Poland

ALEXEY LASTOVETSKY,   University College Dublin, Dublin, Ireland

LAURENT LEFEVRE,   INRIA, LIP Laboratory, Ecole Normale Superieure of Lyon, Lyon, France

DIEGO R. LLANOS,   Universidad de Valladolid, Valladolid, Spain

DIMITAR LUKARSKI,   Uppsala University, Uppsala, Sweden

JASON MAASSEN,   Netherlands eScience Center, Amsterdam, The Netherlands

SIDI A. MAHMOUDI,   University of Mons, Mons, Belgium

PIERRE MANNEBACK,   University of Mons, Mons, Belgium

ATTILA CS. MAROSI,   MTA SZTAKI Computer and Automation Research Institute, Budapest, Hungary

GUILLAUME MERCIER,   Bordeaux Polytechnic Institute, Talence, France; Inria Bordeaux Sud-Ouest, Talence, France

FRANCO MARIA NARDINI,   National Research Council of Italy, Pisa, Italy

ZSOLT NEMETH,   MTA SZTAKI Computer and Automation Research Institute, Budapest, Hungary

MAYA NEYTCHEVA,   Uppsala University, Uppsala, Sweden

ARIEL OLEKSIAK,   Poznan Supercomputing and Networking Center, Poznan, Poland

HECTOR ORTEGA-ARRANZ,   Universidad de Valladolid, Valladolid, Spain

ERENCAN OZKAN,   Ankara University, Ankara, Turkey

OZCAN OZTURK,   Bilkent University, Ankara, Turkey

CARLOS PÉREZ-ALCARAZ,   University of Murcia, Murcia, Spain

DANA PETCU,   West University of Timisoara, Timisoara, Romania

JOSÉ-GINÉS PICÓN,   University of Murcia, Murcia, Spain

JEAN-MARC PIERSON,   Toulouse University, Toulouse, France

FERNANDO D. QUESADA,   Technical University of Cartagena, Cartagena, Spain

ANTONIO J. PLAZA,   University of Extremadura, Caceres, Spain

TOMÁS RAMÍREZ,   University of Murcia, Murcia, Spain

VLADIMIR RYCHKOV,   University College Dublin, Dublin, Ireland

FRANK J. SEINSTRA,   Netherlands eScience Center, Amsterdam, The Netherlands

FABRIZIO SILVESTRI,   National Research Council of Italy, Pisa, Italy

LEONEL SOUSA,   Technical University of Lisbon, Lisbon, Portugal

FRÉDÉRIC SUTER, IN2P3 Computing Center, CNRS, IN2P3, Lyon-Villeurbanne, France

YURI TORRES, Universidad de Valladolid, Valladolid, Spain

SULEYMAN TOSUN, Ankara University, Ankara, Turkey

ROMAN TROBEC, Jožef Stefan Institute, Ljubljana, Slovenia

GHISLAIN LANDRY TSAFACK CHETSA, INRIA, LIP Laboratory, Ecole Normale Superieure of Lyon, Lyon, France

NATALIJA TUMANOVA, Vilnius Gediminas Technical University, Vilnius, Lithuania

FRANCISCO VAZQUEZ, University of Almería, Almería, Spain

MARCIN WOZNIAK, Czestochowa University of Technology, Czestochowa, Poland

ROMAN WYRZYKOWSKI, Czestochowa University of Technology, Czestochowa, Poland

ZIMING ZHONG, University College Dublin, Dublin, Ireland

JULIUS ŽILINSKAS, Vilnius University, Vilnius, Lithuania

Preface

High-performance computing (HPC) is an important domain of the computer science field. For more than 30 years, it has allowed finding solutions to problems and enhanced progress in many scientific and industrial areas, such as climatology, biology, geology, and drug design, as well as automobile and aerospace engineering. However, new technologies such as multicore chips and accelerators have forced researchers in the field to rethink most of the advances in the domain, such as algorithms, runtime systems, language, software, and applications.

It is expected that a high-end supercomputer will be able to deliver several hundreds of petaflops (1 petaflop is 10^{15} floating-point operations per second) in 5 years from now. However, this will require mastering several challenges, such as energy efficiency, scalability, and heterogeneity.

Better and efficient parallel computers will enable solving problems at a scale and within a timeframe that has not been reached so far. These modern hierarchical and heterogeneous computing infrastructures are hard to program and use efficiently, particularly for extreme-scale computing. Consequently, none of the state-of-the-art solutions are able to efficiently use such environments. Providing tools for the whole software stack will allow programmers and scientists to efficiently write new program that will use most of the available power of such future complex machines.

COST Action IC0805 "Open European Network for High-Performance Computing on Complex Environments" (ComplexHPC) was devoted to heterogeneous and hierarchical systems for HPC, and is aimed at tackling the problem at every level (from cores to large-scale environments) and providing new integrated solutions for large-scale computing for future platforms. The duration of ComplexHPC Action was May 2009–June 2013. The goal of COST Action was to establish a European research network focused on high-performance heterogeneous computing to address the whole range of challenges posed by these new platforms, including models, algorithms, programming tools, and applications. Indeed, some of the most active research groups in this area are in Europe. The network has contributed to exchanging information, identifying synergies, and pursuing common research activities, thereby reinforcing the strength of these groups and the leadership of Europe in this field. This book presents the results of COST Action. The chapters are written by expert participants of the Action.

This book is intended for scientists and researchers working in the field of HPC. It will provide advanced information for the readers already familiar with the basics of parallel and distributed computing. It may also be useful for PhD students and early stage researchers in computer science and engineering. It will also be of help to these young researchers to get a deep introduction to the related fields.

This book would not have been possible without the efforts of the contributors in preparing the respective chapters, and we would like to thank them for timely submissions and corrections. We would also like to thank Prof. Albert Zomaya for giving us the opportunity to publish this book in the "Wiley Series on Parallel and Distributed Computing." We would also like to thank Simone Taylor, Director, Editorial Development, John Wiley & Sons, Inc., and the editorial team for their patience and guiding us through the publication of this book. We would also like to thank COST for the support that enabled the publication.

Delft, Netherlands   E. JEANNOT AND J. ŽILINSKAS
May, 2013

ESF provides the COST Office through an EC contract

COST is supported by the EU RTD Framework programme

COST–the acronym for European Cooperation in Science and Technology–is the oldest and widest European intergovernmental network for cooperation in research. Established by the Ministerial Conference in November 1971, COST is presently used by the scientific communities of 36 European countries to cooperate in common research projects supported by national funds.

The funds provided by COST–less than 1% of the total value of the projects–support the COST cooperation networks (COST Actions) through which, with EUR 30 million per year, more than 30 000 European scientists are involved in research having a total value which exceeds EUR 2 billion per year. This is the financial worth of the European added value which COST achieves.

A "bottom up approach" (the initiative of launching a COST Action comes from the European scientists themselves), "à la carte participation" (only countries interested in the Action participate), "equality of access" (participation is open also to the scientific communities of countries not belonging to the European Union) and "flexible structure" (easy implementation and light management of the research initiatives) are the main characteristics of COST.

As precursor of advanced multidisciplinary research COST has a very important role for the realisation of the European Research Area (ERA) anticipating and complementing the activities of the Framework Programmes, constituting a "bridge" towards the scientific communities of emerging countries, increasing the mobility of researchers across Europe and fostering the establishment of "Networks of Excellence" in many key scientific domains such as: Biomedicine and Molecular Biosciences; Food and Agriculture; Forests, their Products and Services; Materials, Physical and Nanosciences; Chemistry and Molecular Sciences and Technologies; Earth System Science and Environmental Management; Information and Communication Technologies; Transport and Urban Development; Individuals, Societies, Cultures and Health. It covers basic and more applied research and also addresses issues of pre-normative nature or of societal importance.

Web: http://www.cost.eu

Neither the COST Office nor any person acting on its behalf is responsible for the use which might be made of the information contained in this publication. The COST Office is not responsible for the external websites referred to in this publication.

PART I

Introduction

1

Summary of the Open European Network for High-Performance Computing in Complex Environments

Emmanuel Jeannot
Inria Bordeaux Sud-Ouest, Talence, France

Julius Žilinskas
Vilnius University, Vilnius, Lithuania

In this chapter, we describe the COST Action IC0805 entitled "Open European Network for High-Performance Computing on Complex Environments." This Action had representation from more than 20 countries and lasted from 2009 to 2013. We outline the scientific focus of this Action, its organization, and its main outcomes. The chapter concludes by presenting the structure of the book and its different chapters.

High-Performance Computing on Complex Environments, First Edition.
Edited by Emmanuel Jeannot and Julius Žilinskas.
© 2014 John Wiley & Sons, Inc. Published 2014 by John Wiley & Sons, Inc.

1.1   INTRODUCTION AND VISION

In recent years, the evolution and growth of the techniques and platforms commonly used for high-performance computing (HPC) in the context of different application domains has been truly astonishing. While parallel computing systems have now achieved certain maturity thanks to high-level libraries (such as ScaLAPACK) or runtime libraries (such as MPI), recent advances in these technologies pose several challenging research issues. Indeed, current HPC-oriented environments are extremely complex and very difficult to manage, particularly for extreme-scale application problems.

At the very low level, the latest generation CPUs are made of multicore processors that can be general-purpose or highly specialized in nature. On the other hand, several processors can be assembled into a so-called symmetrical multiprocessor (SMP) which can also have access to powerful specialized processors, such as graphics processing units (GPUs), that are now increasingly being used for programmable computing resulting from their advent in the video-game industry, which has significantly reduced their cost and availability. Modern HPC-oriented parallel computers are typically composed of several SMP nodes interconnected by a network. This kind of infrastructure is hierarchical and represents a first class of heterogeneous system in which the communication time between two processing units is different, depending on whether the units are on the same chip, on the same node, or not. Moreover, current hardware trends anticipate a further increase in the number of cores (in a hierarchical way) inside the chip, thus increasing the overall heterogeneity, even more toward building extreme-scale systems.

At a higher level, the emergence of heterogeneous computing now allows groups of users to benefit from networks of processors that are already available in their research laboratories. This is a second type of infrastructure where both the network and the processing units are heterogeneous in nature. Specifically, here the goal is to deal with networks that interconnect a (often high) number of heterogeneous computers that can significantly differ from one another in terms of their hardware and software architecture, including different types of CPUs operating at different clock speeds and under different design paradigms, and also different memory sizes, caching strategies, and operating systems.

At the high level, computers are increasingly interconnected together throughout wide area networks to form large-scale distributed systems with high computing capacity. Furthermore, computers located in different laboratories can collaborate in the solution of a common problem. Therefore, the current trends of HPC are clearly oriented toward extreme-scale, complex infrastructures with a great deal of intrinsic heterogeneity and many different hierarchical levels.

It is important to note that all the heterogeneity levels mentioned above are tightly linked. First of all, some of the nodes in computational distributed environments may be multicore SMP clusters. Second, multicore chips will soon be fully heterogeneous with special-purpose cores (e.g., multimedia, recognition, networking) and not only

GPUs mixed with general-purpose ones. Third, these different levels share many common problems such as efficient programming, scalability, and latency management. Hence, it is very important to conduct research targeting the heterogeneity at all presented hardware levels. Moreover, it is also important to take special care of the scalability issues, which form a key dimension in the complexity of today environment. The extreme scale of this environment comes from every level:

1. *Low Level*: number of CPUs, number of cores per processor;
2. *Medium Level*: number of nodes (e.g., with memory);
3. *High Level*: distributed/large-scale (geography dispersion, latency, etc.);
4. *Application*: extreme-scale problem size (e.g., calculation-intensive or data-intensive).

In 2008, the knowledge on how to efficiently use program or scale applications on such infrastructures was still vague. This was one of the main challenges that researchers wanted to take on. Therefore, at that time, we decided to launch the COST Action for high-performance and extreme-scale computing in such complex environments entitled "*Open European Network for High-Performance Computing in Complex Environments*." The main reasons were as follows:

- There was a huge demand in terms of computational power for scientific and data-intensive applications;
- The architectural advances offered the potential to meet the application requirements;
- None of the state-of-the-art solutions in HPC at that time allowed exploitation to this potential level;
- Most of the research carried out in this area was fragmented and scattered across different research teams without any coordination.

COST[1] was indeed an appropriate framework for the proposed Action. The main goal of this Action was to overcome the actual research fragmentation on this very hot topic by gathering the most relevant European research teams involved in all the scientific areas described above (from the CPU core to the scientific applications) and coordinate their research.

Summarizing, this project within the COST framework allowed us to expect some potential benefits such as high-level scientific results in the very important domain of high-performance and extreme-scale computing in complex environment; strong coordination between different research teams with significant expertise on this subject; a better visibility of the European research in this area; and a strong impact on other scientists and high-performance applications.

---

[1] European Cooperation in Science and Technology: http://www.cost.eu.

1.2   SCIENTIFIC ORGANIZATION

1.2.1   Scientific Focus

The expected scientific impacts of the project were to encourage the specific community to focus research on hot topics and applications of interest for the EU, to propagate the collaboration of research groups with the industry, to stimulate the formation of new groups in new EU countries, and to facilitate the solution of highly computationally demanding scientific problems as mentioned above. For this, the groups involved in this Action collaborated with several scientific and industrial groups that could benefit from the advances made by this Action, and prompted the incorporation of new groups to the network.

To achieve the research tasks, different leading European research teams participated in the concrete activities detailed in Section 1.3.

1.2.2   Working Groups

Four working groups were set up to coordinate the scientific research:

- numerical analysis for hierarchical and heterogeneous and multicore systems;
- libraries for the efficient use of complex systems with emphasis on computational library and communication library;
- algorithms and tools for mapping and executing applications onto distributed and heterogeneous systems;
- applications of hierarchical-heterogeneous systems.

It is important to note that these working groups targeted vertical aspects of the architectural structure outlined in the previous section. For instance, the Action's goal was to carry out work on numerical analysis at the multicore level, at the heterogeneous system level, as well as at the large-scale level. The last working group (Applications) was expected to benefit from research of the other three groups.

1.3   ACTIVITIES OF THE PROJECT

To achieve the goal of this Action, the following concrete activities were proposed. The main goal was to promote collaboration through science meetings, workshops, schools, and internships. This allowed interchange of ideas and mobility of researchers.

1.3.1   Spring Schools

The goal was to provide young researchers with a good opportunity to share information and knowledge and to present their current research. These schools contributed to the expansion of the computing community and spread of EU knowledge.

1.3.2   International Workshops

The goal of these meetings was to take the opportunity during international conferences to meet the attendees and other researchers by co-locating workshops.

1.3.3   Working Groups Meetings

The scientific work plan was divided among different working groups. Each working group had substantial autonomy in terms of research projects. A leader nominated by the Management Committee led each working group. Members of a given working group met once or twice a year to discuss and exchange specific scientific issues and problems.

1.3.4   Management Committee Meetings

These meetings were devoted to the organization of the network and ensured the scientific quality of the network.

1.3.5   Short-Term Scientific Missions

The goal of short-term scientific missions (STSMs) was to enable visits by early stage researchers to foreign laboratories and departments. This was mainly targeted at young researchers to receive cross-disciplinary training and to take advantage of the existing resources. The goal was to increase the competitiveness and career development of those scientists in this rapidly developing field through cutting-edge collaborative research on the topic.

1.4   MAIN OUTCOMES OF THE ACTION

We believe that this COST Action was a great success. It gathered 26 European countries and 2 non-COST countries (Russia and South Africa). We have held 12 meetings and 2 spring schools. Fifty-two STSMs have been carried out. We have a new FP7 project coming from this Action (HOST). We have edited a book, and more than 100 papers have been published thanks to this Action.

We have set up an application catalog that gathers applications from the Action members. Its goal is to gather a set of HPC applications that can be used as test cases or benchmarks for researchers in the HPC field. The applications catalog is available at https://complexhpc-catalogue.bordeaux.inria.fr.

In total, the Action gathered more than 250 participants over the four years of the project.

We have sent a survey to the Action members. From this survey, it clearly appears that one of the greatest successes of the Action is the continuous strengthening of the network for many of its members both in terms of research teams and research domains. Many STSMs have been done through new network connections. Spring schools are seen as a major success, as they helped many young researchers to share and exchange knowledge and gain new connections. Many PhD theses have been defended during the course of the Action, and some of the management committee members have been invited on the defense board of some of these PhDs. Moreover, many presentations given during the meeting are considered very useful and have opened new research directions for other attendees.

We had four goals in this Action:

1. to train new generations of scientists in high-performance and heterogeneous computing;
2. to overcome research fragmentation, and foster HPC efforts to increase Europe's competitiveness;
3. to tackle the problem at every level (from cores to large-scale environment);
4. vertical integration to provide new integrated solutions for large-scale computing for future platforms.

Goal 1 has exceeded our expectations. The spring schools have been a great success. We had many STSMs, and the number of early stage researchers attending the meeting was always very high. We had great response from young researchers.

Goal 2 has also been achieved satisfactorily. Thanks to the Action, many joint researches have been carried out, and we have created a nice network of researchers within our Action. Moreover, many top-level publications have been made thanks to the Action.

Goal 3 has also been achieved. We have scientific results that cover the core level and the distributed infrastructure, as well as results that cover the intermediate layers. This is due to the fact that the consortium was made of researchers from different areas. This was very fruitful.

Goal 4 has not been achieved. The main reason is the fact that providing integrated solutions requires more research and development than a COST Action can provide. It goes far beyond the networking activities of COST Action.

1.5   CONTENTS OF THE BOOK

This book presents some of the main results, in terms of research, of the COST Action presented in this chapter. We are very proud to share this with the interested reader. We have structured the book according to the following parts in order to have a good balance between each part:

1. Numerical Analysis for Heterogeneous and Multicore Systems (Chapters 2, 3, and 4);
2. Communication and Storage Considerations in High-Performance Computing (Chapters 5, 6, 7, and 8);
3. Efficient Exploitation of Heterogeneous Architectures (Chapters 9, 10, 11, and 12);
4. CPU + GPU coprocessing (Chapters 13, 14, and 15);

5. Efficient Exploitation of Distributed Systems (Chapters 16 and 17);
6. Energy Awareness in High-Performance Computing (Chapters 18, 19, and 20);
7. Applications of Heterogeneous High-Performance Computing (Chapters 21, 22, and 23).

Chapter 2 discusses the redesign of the iterative solution algorithm in order to efficiently execute them on heterogeneous architectures. Chapter 3 studies the performance of a meshless numerical partial differential equation (PDE) solver, parallelized with OpenMP. The results depend on the way the computations are distributed and the way the cache is used. Chapter 4 presents the development of three parallel numerical algorithms for the solution of parabolic problems on graphs with a theoretical and experimental study of their scalability.

Chapter 5 surveys different techniques for mapping processes to computing units in order to optimize communication cost and reduce execution time. Chapter 6 offers a comprehensive overview of how to implement topology- and performance-aware collective communications. Chapter 7 analyzes the many-core architecture using a new model (K-model) in order to estimate the complexity of a given algorithm designed for such an architecture. Chapter 8 presents a scalable I/O storage system for the hierarchical architecture of Blue Gene computers featuring buffering and asynchronous I/O.

Chapter 9 describes algorithmic techniques for offline scheduling of independent workflows in order to satisfy user's quality of service. Chapter 10 investigates the advantage of using modern heterogeneous architecture for the efficient implementation of the Reed–Solomon erasure code. Chapter 11 analyzes the factors that enable the development of efficient parallel programs on modern many-core parallel architecture. Chapter 12 studies efficient solutions for electromagnetism applications in clusters of CPU + GPU nodes.

Chapter 13 describes how the functional performance model can be used to optimize the performance of scientific applications for heterogeneous and hierarchical platform. Chapter 14 presents algorithms for multilevel load-balancing on multicore and multi-GPU environments. Chapter 15 faces the all-pair shortest path problem for sparse graph. Different scheduling strategies are studied to efficiently solve such problems on heterogeneous systems.

Chapter 16 surveys different resource management systems and scheduling algorithms for HPC for clouds. Chapter 17 discusses different approaches for performing resource discovery in large-scale distributed systems.

Chapter 18 focuses on how to optimize and adapt software solution to improve energy efficiency in the context of HPC application. Chapter 19 studies energy-aware scheduling policies for three scenarios of federated cloud dealing with energy awareness. Chapter 20 explores the use of heterogeneous chip multiprocessors for network security and strategy to improve energy consumption in such contexts.

Chapter 21 describes the "jungle computing paradigm," which consists in gathering a complex hierarchical collection of heterogeneous computing hardware with an application to hyperspectral remote sensing. Chapter 22 presents a new model for image and video processing based on parallel and heterogeneous platforms in order to improve the performance of the application when dealing with high-definition images. Chapter 23 applies load-balancing techniques to efficiently execute tomographic reconstruction using hybrid GPU + CPU systems.

As you can see, this covers a large spectrum of results and topics on HPC and heterogeneous systems.

We wish you a fruitful and enjoyable time with this book.

ACKNOWLEDGMENT

This publication is supported by COST.

PART II

Numerical Analysis for Heterogeneous and Multicore Systems

2

On the Impact of the Heterogeneous Multicore and Many-Core Platforms on Iterative Solution Methods and Preconditioning Techniques

Dimitar Lukarski and Maya Neytcheva

Uppsala University, Uppsala, Sweden

Computer simulations are now broadly recognized as a third branch of research, complementing theory and experimental work. The significant increase of available computing power has enabled tackling very large scale, challenging, real-life problems and opening new possibilities for revolutionary breakthrough results in science and engineering. At the same time, the complexity of the computer architecture has risen to levels where it is possible to achieve its full computing power only after careful redesigning of existing algorithms and developing novel computational and

High-Performance Computing on Complex Environments, First Edition.
Edited by Emmanuel Jeannot and Julius Žilinskas.
© 2014 John Wiley & Sons, Inc. Published 2014 by John Wiley & Sons, Inc.

communication strategies. In this chapter, we discuss this issue for a class of methods, broadly used in scientific computations—the iterative solution methods.

2.1 INTRODUCTION

For many years, the potential of available, serial as well as parallel, computer resources has been growing hand in hand with the need to numerically solve increasingly larger models of real-life problems. During the past decades, it has been recognized that, together with theoretical development and laboratory or field experiments, computation has become a third branch of research. Scientific computing is today's driving force behind the progress in the most challenging and demanding problems we attempt to solve. As examples, we mention turbulent combustion with complex chemistry, atmospheric dynamics, laser fusion, medical imaging, detailed modeling of the human heart, and artificial brain simulation with over a million neurons, to name a few.

In recent years, we have been witnessing a change in the means to increase the computational power which has a strong impact on how that power should be utilized via the algorithms used in scientific computations. Therefore, we briefly describe the phases in performing numerical simulations. Consider a complex physical phenomenon, described as a set of, usually coupled, processes that develop in space and time, which we want to study, analyze, and predict. It is assumed that the simulation requires a large amount of computer resources in terms of memory and computation.

The process of performing the numerical simulations can be split into the following steps:

I Mathematical model: Describes the phenomenon continuously in time and space in terms of mathematical relations, most often as coupled ordinary or partial differential equations. These equations depend on various problem parameters, such as thermal conductivity, capacitance, material properties, and so on.

II Discrete model: Because of the high complexity of the continuous model, analytical solutions are in general not available. Therefore, we pose the task to compute the solution in a number of discrete points in time and space, thus discretizing the mathematical model. This can be accomplished using various techniques. Space discretization can be done using finite differences, finite elements, finite volumes, boundary elements, and so on. Similarly, in time, various explicit or implicit time-stepping procedures can be utilized. In addition to the model parameters, here additional discretization parameters are introduced, usually denoted as h in space and τ in time. The discrete model is expressed in terms of linear or nonlinear algebraic systems of equations which have to be solved. Depending on the problem, but also on the discretization techniques, the matrices associated with the algebraic systems can be dense or sparse, symmetric or nonsymmetric, and so on. As nonlinear systems are most often solved via linearization, we consider from now on only linear systems that are also large and sparse.

III The linear systems arising in Step II have to be solved by a proper solution method—direct or iterative. Because of the targeted large-sized problems and the lesser demands on computer resources, we consider iterative solvers only. The iterative methods may introduce yet other method parameters which increase further the dimension of the parameter space.

IV Computer implementation: To enable computer simulations, the numerical methods have to be implemented on some computer platform.

V Visualization and verification: This step is also of importance, but it is not considered here any further.

When performing numerical simulations, we deal with two major concerns. The first concern is *robustness* with respect to model, discretization, and method parameters. Robustness is understood in the sense that the numerical efficiency of the iterative method chosen in Step III should not depend on changes in the parameters. For example, the number of iterations should not increase uncontrollably when h decreases. The *numerical efficiency*, related to fast convergence rate, can be seen also as an element of the robustness of the method. The second concern is the *efficiency of the implementation* in Step IV. It is based on a programming model (such as shared or distributed memory model), programming language, and a particular computer platform.

It has been recognized that, in order to achieve fast, accurate, and reliable results from computer simulations, sufficient knowledge is required for all the above steps, in particular Steps II, III, and IV, and awareness of the interplay among them. By choosing one or another discretization method, we may influence the structure and the properties of the arising matrices; by choosing a particular solution method we may ensure robustness with respect to the various problem, discretization, and method parameters; but we may sacrifice the amount of internal parallelism. Knowledge about the computer architecture on which the simulations are to be run may influence the choice of the solution method, which in turn has to be combined with the requirements of accuracy and robustness.

With the ongoing radical shift in the computer architecture toward multicore and many-core computational units, the importance of the above arguments becomes even stronger. The new technology based on multicore and many-core devices provides higher performance capabilities both in terms of computational power (GFlop/s) and memory bandwidth (GB/s). The available and easily accessible power enables scientists to tackle larger problems with higher resolution, providing in this way a better understanding of the world.

The radical shift is clearly seen when we compare the supercomputers available 10 years ago with the personal computers of today. All supercomputers in 2003 contained less than 10,000 cores[1]. By the end of 2004, the situation was still the

---

[1] Top500 http://www.top500.org/statistics/efficiency-power-cores/.

same, with two exceptions. At present, the computer landscape is very different. Not only the Top500 leaders have over 500,000 cores. Currently, NVIDIA delivers GPU (graphical processing unit) cards with more than 2500 cores per device (see GPU NVIDIA K20X[2]). With an improved power supply, four of these cards can be installed in a standard personal computer and thus one can obtain a system with more than 10,000 cores, which is a commodity at our desktop.

In order to achieve fast and reliable performance of the iterative methods, it becomes crucial to reconsider and redesign the implementation of well-known algorithms as well as to gain a deeper insight into what the expected performance is of the most common solution techniques on multicore heterogeneous computer platforms.

The focus of this chapter is to show how iterative methods can be performed efficiently on highly parallel, heterogeneous platforms. We present various methods and examples to show how this can be done, which includes mathematical description, as well as hardware-specific aspects.

2.2   GENERAL DESCRIPTION OF ITERATIVE METHODS AND PRECONDITIONING

We briefly discuss basic iterative techniques as well as two of the most often used projection-based methods—the conjugate gradient (CG) method [1], the generalized minimal residual (GMRES) method [2], and the multigrid (MG) method [3]. We also describe the defect-correction technique [4] as an illustration of an approach particularly suitable for solving linear systems on heterogeneous computers.

2.2.1   Basic Iterative Methods

Consider the solution of the linear system

$$Ax = b, \tag{2.1}$$

where $A \in \mathbb{R}^{n \times n}$ is a nonsingular matrix, so Equation (2.1) has a unique solution. The matrix A is large and sparse, and therefore the number of nonzero elements, $nnz(A)$, is proportional to the size of the matrix, n; that is, $nnz(A) = O(n)$.

Finding the solution to Equation (2.1) is equivalent to finding the root of the equation

$$\mathbf{b} - A\mathbf{x} = \mathbf{0}. \tag{2.2}$$

One straightforward way to introduce simple iterative methods is to rewrite (2.2) as a fixed-point iteration, namely

for some given $\mathbf{x}^{(0)}$, iterate

$$\mathbf{x}^{(k+1)} = \mathbf{x}^{(k)} + (\mathbf{b} - A\mathbf{x}^{(k)}), \quad k = 0, 1, \ldots \text{ until convergence.} \tag{2.3}$$

---

[2]NVIDIA K20 specification http://www.nvidia.com/object/tesla-servers.html

The computational procedure (2.3) defines a basic stationary iterative method. The computation cost per iteration involves one matrix–vector multiplication and two vector updates, and is clearly $O(n)$. Such a method, however, usually exhibits too slow a convergence, which manifests itself in unacceptably many iterations. In some cases, convergence may not even be achieved.

Aiming at accelerating the convergence of the iterative process has led to the idea to involve some method parameter, replacing the simple iteration (2.3) by

$$\mathbf{x}^{(k+1)} = \mathbf{x}^{(k)} + \tau \mathbf{r}^{(k)}, \quad \text{or} \quad \mathbf{x}^{(k+1)} = \mathbf{x}^{(k)} + \tau_k \mathbf{r}^{(k)}, \tag{2.4}$$

where $\mathbf{r}^{(k)} = \mathbf{b} - A\mathbf{x}^{(k)}$ is the *residual* at the kth iteration and τ or τ_k are some properly chosen method parameters. In Equation (2.4), the method parameters to tune are scalars. Of course, nothing prevents us from replacing them with a properly chosen matrix, referred to in the sequel as P; thus we consider

$$\mathbf{x}^{(k+1)} = \mathbf{x}^{(k)} + P^{-1}\mathbf{r}^{(k)}, \ k = 0, 1, \ \dots \ \text{untill convergence.} \tag{2.5}$$

As will be discussed later, P can also vary during the iterative process. For simplicity, now we consider that it is some explicitly given nonsingular matrix.

It is easy to see that Equation (2.5) is obtained by replacing the original system $A\mathbf{x} = \mathbf{b}$ by the transformed system

$$P^{-1}A\mathbf{x} = P^{-1}\mathbf{b},$$

and applying the fixed-point scheme to it. In this case, the iterative scheme becomes

$$\begin{vmatrix} \mathbf{r}^{(k)} = \mathbf{b} - A\mathbf{x}^{(k)}, \\ P\mathbf{d}^{(k)} = \mathbf{r}^{(k)}, \\ \mathbf{x}^{(k+1)} = \mathbf{x}^{(k)} + \mathbf{d}^{(k)}. \end{vmatrix} \tag{2.6}$$

The scheme (2.6) has a higher computational complexity than that of Equation (2.4), since a solution of a system with the matrix P is required at each iteration. Clearly, the achieved decrease in the number of iterations must be significant enough to compensate for the extra cost per iteration.

We see from Equation (2.6) that the choice $P = A$ would lead to a procedure that converges within one iteration. However, the computational cost would be unacceptably high, similar to that of a direct solution method. Clearly, P should satisfy some conditions so that we can achieve faster convergence, keeping at the same time the overall computational costs of the whole iterative method as low as possible.

The matrix P is referred to as a *preconditioner* to A. We consider next some well-known choices of P, leading to a family of classical iterative methods which are based on the so-called matrix splitting technique.

Intuitively, P has to be related to A. Consider the following splitting of A,

$$A = P - R,$$

where P is nonsingular and R can be seen as an error matrix. Then,

$$P^{-1}A = P^{-1}(P - R) = I - P^{-1}R,$$

where I is the identity matrix of proper order.

The matrix $B = P^{-1}R$ is referred to as the *iteration matrix* and is used in theoretical derivations to show the convergence of the corresponding iterative method, as well as to estimate its rate of convergence (see [5] for details). Using the splitting, we rewrite Equation (2.5) as follows:

$$\mathbf{x}^{(k+1)} = \mathbf{x}^{(k)} + P^{-1}(\mathbf{b} - A\mathbf{x}^{(k)}) = P^{-1}\mathbf{b} + P^{-1}R\mathbf{x}^{(k)}$$

or

$$P\mathbf{x}^{(k+1)} = R\mathbf{x}^{(k)} + \mathbf{b}.$$

Let A be represented in the following way, $A = D - L - U$ where D, L, and U are the diagonal, the strictly lower triangular, and the strictly upper triangular part of A, respectively. Table 2.1 shows some classical iterative schemes, based on the latter splitting of A.

For more details on the convergence of these methods, refer to [5].

The common characteristic of these methods is the simplicity of their implementation. Here, P is a diagonal or a triangular matrix, and the degree of parallelism is related to the sparsity structure of the underlying matrices.

The bottleneck of these methods is their slow convergence. Their importance has not been lost, however. Today, they are mostly used as subsolvers in more advanced iterative techniques described in Sections 2.2.2 and 2.5. Because of their low arithmetic cost and ease of implementation, they are important ingredients in the so-called projection methods.

2.2.2 Projection Methods: CG and GMRES

The idea behind the projection methods is that the original problem of huge dimension (easily of tens or even hundreds of millions of degrees of freedom) is projected over a subspace of much smaller dimension. An approximate solution is sought in that smaller subspace and then projected back to the original large space. When the

TABLE 2.1 Classical Iterative Schemes Based on Matrix Splitting

Method	P	R	Scheme
Jacobi iteration	D	$L + U$	$D\mathbf{x}^{(k+1)} = (L + U)\mathbf{x}^{(k)} + \mathbf{b}$
Gauss–Seidel backward	$D - U$	L	$(D - U)\mathbf{x}^{(k+1)} = L\mathbf{x}^{(k)} + \mathbf{b}$
Gauss–Seidel forward	$D - L$	U	$(D - L)\mathbf{x}^{(k+1)} = U\mathbf{x}^{(k)} + \mathbf{b}$
SOR	$D - \omega L$	$\omega U + (1 - \omega)D$	$(D - \omega L)\mathbf{x}^{(k+1)} =$ $(\omega U + (1 - \omega)D)\mathbf{x}^{(k)} + \mathbf{b}$

projection utilizes some particular subspaces, referred to as *Krylov subspaces*, the corresponding methods are known as the Krylov subspace methods. For detailed derivations and properties of the projection methods, refer, for example, to [1].

We present the most popular representatives of the Krylov subspace methods, namely, the CG method, used for solving linear systems with symmetric and positive-definite matrices, and the GMRES method, which is suitable for general nonsymmetric matrices. The presentation of the algorithms follows [1]:

Algorithm 2.1

```
Preconditioned CG method: Given x⁰
1: Compute r⁰ = b − Ax⁰, d⁰ = r⁰,
   q⁰ = P⁻¹r⁰
2: For k = 1,2,...until convergence Do:
3:      τₖ = (rᵏ,qᵏ) / (dᵏ,Adᵏ)
4:      xᵏ⁺¹ = xᵏ + τₖdᵏ
5:      rᵏ⁺¹ = rᵏ − τₖAdᵏ
6:      qᵏ⁺¹ = P⁻¹rᵏ⁺¹
7:      β = (rᵏ⁺¹,qᵏ⁺¹) / (rᵏ,qᵏ)
8:      dᵏ⁺¹ = qᵏ⁺¹ + βdᵏ
9: EndDo
```

The notation $\mathbf{q} = P^{-1}\mathbf{r}$ should be interpreted as a solution of a system with the preconditioner P.

The arithmetic complexity per CG iteration includes one matrix–vector multiplication, three vector updates, two scalar products, and solution of a system with P. Provided that A is sparse, the arithmetic cost per iteration, excluding that to solve a system with P, is linear in the number of degrees of freedom.

Algorithm 2.2

```
Preconditioned GMRES method: Given x⁰ and dimension m
1: Arnoldi process: compute r⁰ = b − Ax⁰, β = ‖r⁰‖₂, v¹ = r⁰/β
2: define a matrix Hₘ = hᵢⱼ of size (m + 1) × m and set Hₘ = 0
3: For j = 1,2,...,m Do:
4:      Compute zʲ = P⁻¹vʲ
5:      Compute wʲ = Azʲ
6:      For i = 1,2,...,j Do:
7:          hᵢⱼ = (wʲ,vⁱ)
8:          wʲ = wⁱ − hᵢⱼvⁱ
9:      EndDo
10:     hⱼ₊₁,ⱼ = ‖wʲ‖₂. If hⱼ₊₁,ⱼ = 0, set m = j and go to 12
11:     vʲ⁺¹ = wʲ/hⱼ₊₁,ⱼ
12: EdnDo
13: Compute xᵐ as xᵐ = x⁰+P⁻¹Vₘyᵐ, where yᵐ is the minimizer
    of βe¹−Hₘxᵐ, e¹=[1,0,...,0]ᵀ and Vₘ = [vʲ], j = 1,...,m.
```

In contrast to CG, the arithmetic cost per GMRES iteration increases with the number of iterations. We see that we need to keep an increasing number of vectors $\mathbf{v}^i$, as well as the vectors $A\mathbf{z}^j$. We have to do more scalar products at each iteration, and also solve a small least-squared problem with the matrix H_m, which is also of growing dimension.

If we assume that the preconditioner P is such that the number of CG or GMRES iterations is kept small and bounded independently of the problem size, we see that the major ingredients of the iterative methods are matrix–vector multiplications, vector updates, and scalar products. Parallelization of these operations is well studied, and efficient computational libraries are available (e.g., [6, 7] etc.).

The crucial element when applying iterative solution methods on parallel computer architectures is the preconditioning step. Experience shows that the most numerically efficient preconditioners are among the most difficult to parallelize efficiently. As we will discuss in the next sections, a compromise is usually made in order to optimize the overall performance of the iterative solver.

2.3   PRECONDITIONING TECHNIQUES

Among the first who coined the term *preconditioning* in its modern sense were D.J. Evans and O. Axelsson in the late 1960s and early 1970s (5, 8). Preconditioning is usually understood as an auxiliary matrix, P, that would improve the condition number of the product (the preconditioned matrix) $P^{-1}A$ and thus enhance the convergence.

We note that the preconditioner may be available in an explicit matrix form, but it can also be implicitly defined by some procedure, denoted as $[P]$, that implements the action of a preconditioner on a vector or the solution of a system with it. We mention further that the best known preconditioners so far are implicitly defined. These include MG methods [3], algebraic multigrid (AMG) methods [9], algebraic multilevel iteration (AMLI) methods [10, 11], and some domain decomposition (DD) preconditioners [12].

The preconditioner may be an approximation of A, and during the preconditioning step we solve a system with it. However, P may be some (sparse) approximation of A^{-1}, and then the action of P on a vector is one matrix–vector multiplication. Last but not least, we mention that, as for the nonstationary simple iterative methods, we may allow a preconditioner that changes (varies) during the iterations. This technique may be very useful. To ensure convergence, it imposes some additional conditions for the iterative method. We refer to [13] and [14] for some theoretical and practical details.

To achieve the so-called optimal preconditioner, P has to be such that the cost to solve systems with it is proportional to the number of the degrees of freedom and that the number of iterations is bounded independently of the problem size. We give below examples of such preconditioners. For most of the commonly used preconditioners, the number of iterations grows as $O(n^\alpha)$ for some $\alpha > 1$.

There are various ways to construct a preconditioner to a given matrix A. These can be classified in two groups:

- *"Given-the-matrix" Approach*: In this case, only the matrix is given and the preconditioner is based on some algebraic manipulations of A and its structure.

The resulting preconditioners are generally applicable. Their efficiency could be, however, limited. Typical representatives of this class are the preconditioners based on some incomplete factorization of A.

- *"Given-the-problem" Approach*: In this case, when constructing P, we use some additional information about the problem from which the matrix has been obtained—the discretization mesh and or the element matrices in an FEM (finite element method) context, and so on. The resulting preconditioners are problem dependent. They can be very efficient for the corresponding class of problems, and are of limited or no applicability in general.

2.4 DEFECT-CORRECTION TECHNIQUE

Recall the preconditioned fixed-point iteration (2.5)

$$\mathbf{x}^{(k+1)} = \mathbf{x}^{(k)} + P^{-1}(\mathbf{b} - A\mathbf{x}^{(k)}). \tag{2.7}$$

To proceed, we first compute the residual $\mathbf{r}^k = \mathbf{b} - A\mathbf{x}^k$, then solve the so-called residual system $P\mathbf{y}^k = \mathbf{r}^k$, and finally update the iterative solution.

The general idea of defect correction is that we assume to possess two approximations of the original operator A—one of higher accuracy (A_h) and another of lower accuracy (A_l). Clearly, A_h may coincide with A. Then, we compute the residual using A_h and the defect—using A_l, see Algorithm 2.3. For example, $A \equiv A_h$ may represent the discretization operator in double precision, and A_l the same operator computed in single precision.

Another possibility is to achieve the action of A_l using another (inner) iterative method for the defect with a much lower stopping tolerance than the outer solution procedure (2.7).

Algorithm 2.3

```
Defect-correction: Given x⁰
1:  For k = 1,2,...until convergence Do:
2:      rᵏ = b - Aₕxᵏ
3:          Convert to lower precision r₁ := rᵏ
4:              Solve in lower precision A₁y₁ = r₁
5:          Convert to higher precision yₕ := y₁
6:      xᵏ = xᵏ + yₕ
7:  EdnDo
```

The defect-correction technique is widely used in various contexts. For instance, A_h and A_l may correspond to a more accurate or less accurate discretization, respectively, of the original differential equation [4].

2.5   MULTIGRID METHOD

Multigrid algorithms are techniques to construct fast solution methods or optimal order preconditioners, and have been successfully used for linear systems arising in a wide variety of partial differential equation (PDE) models [3, 9, 11].

Fast convergence is achieved by traversing a hierarchy of geometric grids or algebraically constructed levels. For clarity, let us associate the top ("finest") grid/level in this hierarchy with the largest size problem, the one we want to solve. The levels split the degrees of freedom into nested classes of decreasing dimension (top to bottom).

On each of the levels, the algorithm performs auxiliary steps, traversing those levels in some prescribed order. The auxiliary steps are motivated by the observation that some of the components of the finest level error are reduced much more efficiently on lower levels. To do this, a residual equation is formed, transferred to a coarse level, approximated there by solving an auxiliary systems, and transferred back to the finer level, to correct the corresponding approximate solution on that level. The procedure is then applied recursively. The computation on the coarser level is cheaper than that on the finest level, and by balancing the amount of work per level with respect to the number of degrees of freedom on the finest level, we achieve also optimal or near-optimal computational complexity.

The levels are related to a sequence of nested discrete meshes (geometric multigrid) or can be automatically generated on the basis of algebraic information of the problem, namely, the matrix graph (algebraic multigrid).

On each level, simple iteration methods are used, typically a few Jacobi or Gauss–Seidel (GS) steps. The levels can be traversed in various ways. In Algorithm 2.4, we present the so-called V-cycle, where the levels are traversed from top to bottom and back.

Algorithm 2.4

```
V-cycle: Given A_k, x_k, b_k
1:   Pre-smoothing  x_k = Smooth(A_k, x_k, b_k);
2:   Defect-correction  d_k = b_k − Ax_k
3:      Coarse grid mapping  d_{k-1} := R_k^{k-1} d_k
4:        Solve recursively V-cycle (A_{k-1}, g_{k-1}, b_{k-1})
5:      Fine grid mapping  g_k := P_{k-1}^k g^{k-1}
6:   Correction  x_k = x_k + g_k
7:   Post-smoothing  x_k = Smooth(A_k, x_k, b_k);
```

As MG is an active field of research, the related literature is very rich. For more details, refer to the classic work [3].

2.6   PARALLELIZATION OF ITERATIVE METHODS

The above-described iterative methods clearly identify their key components, namely vector–vector operations, which involve vector updates and scalar products;

matrix–vector multiplication; and preconditioning. The parallel execution of an iterative solver boils down to repeatedly performing these components in parallel.

- *Vector–Vector Operations*: Vector updates of type $\mathbf{x} = \alpha\mathbf{x} + \beta\mathbf{y}$, where $\mathbf{x}$ and $\mathbf{y}$ are n-dimensional real or complex vector and α, β are scalars, can straightforwardly be performed in parallel since there are no dependencies among the elements. Reduction operations can also be performed in parallel and using readily available, highly tuned library routines.
- *Sparse Matrix–Vector Multiplication*: Sparse matrices are typically stored in some compressed form based on a special data format. There are many formats to represent efficiently structured and unstructured matrices. The parallel computation can be performed by rows with a sparse scalar product of each row of the matrix and the input vector.
- *Preconditioning*: Solving the preconditioned equation is the most nontrivial task to parallelize. We briefly discuss various techniques for parallelization of some of the most commonly used preconditioners on multicore and many-core devices.

The parallelism that we consider in this chapter is applicable to multicore and many-core devices. We do not focus on distributed memory systems such as clusters.

2.7 HETEROGENEOUS SYSTEMS

Heterogeneous system is a computer platform that combines computational units with different characteristics, special-purpose hardware (accelerator cores or devices), GPU, digital signal processor (DSP), and so on. This means that we have at our disposal computing units that can perform efficiently additional and/or special operations. However, the definition does not reflect the memory structure of the computing system, which is highly heterogeneous and hierarchical itself. To illustrate this, in Figs 2.1 and 2.2 we present two different heterogeneous platforms.

Figure 2.1 represents a single processing unit that contains different types of cores. An example for such architecture is the IBM Cell BE processor,[3] which contains two general-purpose cores (called *PPEs*) and eight special computing units (called *SPEs*). In this setup, typically all cores share the same memory controller.

In the second configuration (Fig. 2.2), the heterogeneity is due to an additional physical device (an accelerator), which contains computing cores and its own memory. The accelerator card is connected to the host via a bus. For example, this could be a host that contains a CPU and a GPU card attached to the system. Because of technological developments, the memory bandwidth and the computing capability of the accelerators are higher than those of the host devices. In most cases, the cores of the accelerator are many but smaller and simpler (in terms of local memory storage

---

[3]IBM Cell BE https://www.research.ibm.com/cell/.

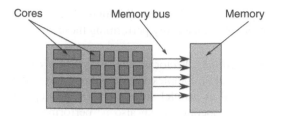

FIGURE 2.1 *Heterogeneous device.*

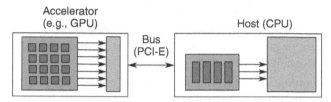

FIGURE 2.2 *Heterogeneous system based on host and an accelerator.*

and additional logic such as Instruction Level Parallelism (ILP) and branch prediction). On the other hand, the memory capacity of the accelerator cards is much smaller than that of the host. This is shown in Fig. 2.2, where the blocks denote the complexity/capacity by their size, and the bandwidth is illustrated by the number of arrows. The setup for the Intel accelerator card based on Xeon Phi[4] is similar.

Typically, the additional cores in a heterogeneous setup are specialized to perform certain operations—mostly vector floating point operations. These are not capable of performing general-purpose operations such as hard disk I/O, network access, and so on.

2.7.1 Heterogeneous Computing

There are two straightforward approaches to explore heterogeneous systems. The first, and the most common, technique is to use the additional computing power (accelerator cards or additional compute cores) to accelerate critical parts in an application, that is, offload those on the accelerator. The second technique is to fully utilize the system by ensuring good load balance and occupying all computing units under the computation.

The speedup obtained by offloading only the critical parts of the application is bound by Amdahl's law. However, this is natural and in many applications cannot be avoided—for example, data needs to be read from a hard disk or has to be communicated over the network.

Utilizing all the compute-capable cores to their full capacity would be the most effective way of using a heterogeneous computer. Unfortunately, this is possible only in some particular cases for special algorithms, as we discuss in later sections.

[4]Intel Many Integrated Core Architecture (MIC) http://www.intel.com/content/www/us/en/processors/xeon/xeon-phi-detail.html.

TABLE 2.2 Computational Intensity for Vector and Matrix Routines

Routine	Flop	Data	CI
Dot product	$2n$	$2n + 1$	1
Vector update	$2n$	$3n$	2/3
Stencil (Laplace 2D)	$6n$	$2n$	3
SpMV (CSR)	$2nnz$	$3n + 2nnz$	< 1
LU substitution (CSR)*	$2nnz$	$3n + 2nnz$	< 1

*Compressed Sparse Row data format

2.7.2 Algorithm Characteristics and Resource Utilization

To quantify the performance, we define a metric called *computational intensity* (*CI*) as

$$CI = \frac{Flop}{Data},$$

where "Flop" stands for the number of floating point operations and "Data" denotes the data needed to perform the routine or the algorithm, measured in Flop per Element (or Byte).

As shown in Section 2.6, the performance of most of the iterative methods depends in a straightforward manner on the efficient execution of the vector–vector routines, sparse matrix–vector multiplication, and graph traversing schemes. In Table 2.2, we present the computational intensity for various vector and matrix routines, where n denotes the size of vectors and nnz denotes the nonzero entries of the sparse matrix.

The same metric can be used to characterize the hardware as the ratio of the peak performance over the memory bandwidth. Thus, by comparing the computational complexity of a particular routine or algorithm, we can roughly estimate the expected performance and whether it is bounded by the theoretical performance of the machine or by the raw memory bandwidth. For the current hardware, we obtain CI = 1TFlop/s/208GB/s for the NVIDIA K20 GPU,[5] CI = 1TFlop/s/320GB/s for the Intel Xeon Phi[6] (MIC architecture), and CI = 172GFlop/s/52GB/s for x86 Intel Xeon E5-2680.[7] More accurate estimations could be obtained on the basis of the measured bandwidth for each routine.

Clearly, the performance of an iterative solver based on some sparse preconditioning technique depends only on the utilization of the bandwidth for regular (vector–vector operations) and irregular memory access patterns (sparse matrix–vector operations). Therefore, all these routines are bounded by the memory speed and utilization on the current and, most likely, on the future hardware, too.

[5]NVIDIA K20 http://www.nvidia.com/object/tesla-servers.html.
[6]Intel MIC http://www.intel.com/content/www/us/en/processors/xeon/xeon-phi-detail.html.
[7]Intel Xeon E5-2600 http://download.intel.com/support/processors/xeon/sb/xeon_E5-2600.pdf.

2.7.3   Exposing Parallelism

The granularity of the parallelism for multicore and many-core devices is very different from that for utilizing large clusters and supercomputers. The parallel algorithms and models for clusters are based on the fact that all data is distributed and each node can communicate with the others. The corresponding paradigm for many-core parallel devices is very different—they all share the same memory and the communication among the cores is either very expensive or can be performed only by a group of cores. For example, the GPU does not provide global synchronization or message-passing mechanisms. These differences lead to the need for new algorithms, or modifying old ones, so that they can better utilize such systems.

Except the preconditioning phase, all routines in most of the iterative solution methods can be straightforwardly performed in parallel. Therefore, we focus on techniques for exposing fine-grained level of parallelism in the preconditioning phase.

Preconditioners based on approximate inverse are naturally parallel, since there is no need to solve the preconditioned equation but only to apply the approximated inverse matrix via matrix–vector multiplication. However, efficient approximate inverses are not very easy to construct. Most of the known techniques require additional information such as eigenvalues, prescribed sparsity pattern, or appropriate drop-off tolerance.

The splitting type of preconditioners (such as GS, SOR, and their symmetric equivalents) can be performed in parallel by multicolored decomposition [1, 15]. Another class of rather numerically efficient preconditioners, based on incomplete factorization, are more difficult to parallelize. After the factorization, we obtain lower-triangular and upper-triangular matrices that are sparse. To perform the forward and backward substitution in parallel, we must first analyze the underlying graphs and then, using the obtained dependencies, perform the graph traversing. This technique is called *level scheduling* [1, 16]. Because of the fill-in entries, the amount of parallelism that can be obtained is low. One way to increase the parallelism is to perform a permutation before the factorization process. In this case, we want to find a permutation that spreads the fill-in entries away from the diagonal in order to obtain a higher degree of parallelism, which is counterintuitive to the most of the well-known ordering techniques, primarily intended to reduce the fill-in. This technique provides a higher degree of parallelism and it is suitable for multicore and many-core platforms, see ILU(p, q) preconditioner based on power(q)-pattern method [15].

2.7.4   Heterogeneity in Matrix Computation

To the best of our knowledge, in the iterative methods or in the preconditioning phase it is not possible to explore parallelism using different levels of granularity accomplished via data movement and reorderings of the code operations only.

In the iterative schemes and in the sparse matrix operations (factorization, substitutions, etc.), there are clear dependencies that cannot be changed and reorganized in a "better" way and scheduled in a different setup. We need to also keep in mind that all operations are bandwidth-bounded. For example in the CG method, we need to follow the algorithm and cannot move some of the operations in order to obtain concurrent parallelism. For instance, an attempt was made to reorder the operations on CG so that the scalar products are executed one after another, in order to perform the global reduction operations more efficiently. This, however, affected the stability of the CG algorithm and convergence could not be guaranteed in general [17]. The same is valid for the LU sweeps based on sparse matrices.

In the next section we present a different setup of heterogeneous solvers, where some critical parts of the solver are offloaded to an accelerator. This is in contrast to the operations on dense matrices, where the dependency graph of the tasks could be scheduled differently taking into account the load of the devices and the task sizes. For example, the StarPU project[8] mixes efficiently PLASMA[9] and MAGMA[10] for performing dense Cholesky factorization.

2.7.5 Setup of Heterogeneous Iterative Solvers

To illustrate the ideas, we consider GMRES and multigrid methods, as well as a defect-correction scheme, which can be used as mixed-precision method.

2.7.5.1 GMRES A GMRES iteration consists of two main parts—constructing the Krylov subspace by the Arnoldi method (Steps 1–12 in Algorithm 2.2), and solving a least-squared problem (Step 13). An efficient heterogeneous configuration is to perform the Arnoldi process on the accelerator, since it requires vector–vector updates and sparse matrix–vector multiplications, and, in the preconditioned case, solving an additional sparse system. During each iteration, the Arnoldi method produces a vector which upgrades a Hessenberg matrix. The least-squared problem based on this Hessenberg matrix can be solved on the host, see Fig. 2.3.

For example, in [15], such a configuration of a GMRES solver has been performed on a CPU–GPU system. The underlying problem is a convection–diffusion equation in two dimensions with finite element discretization based on Q1 and Q2 elements. To achieve parallelism in the GS preconditioner, a multi-colored decomposition is used. The ILU preconditioner is performed with ILU(0,1), and for the two GPU devices a block-Jacobi technique is used.

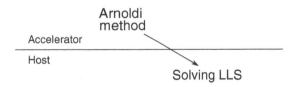

FIGURE 2.3 *Heterogeneous GMRES solver.*

---

[8] StarPU http://icl.cs.utk.edu/projectsfiles/magma/pubs/StarPU_MAGMA_PLASMA.pdf.
[9] PLASMA http://icl.cs.utk.edu/plasma/
[10] MAGMA http://icl.cs.utk.edu/magma/

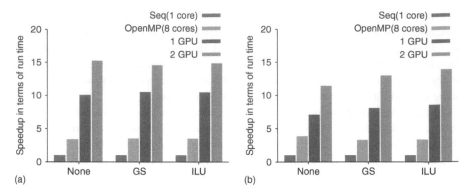

FIGURE 2.4   *Speed-up factors for solving convection–diffusion equations on a heterogeneous platform. 2D convection–diffusion problem with (a) Q1 elements and (b) Q2 elements.*

Fig 2.4a and b show very good utilization of the heterogeneity where the solver can take advantage of the CPU–GPU configuration. The speedup from one to two GPU is less than two because of the ignored couplings in the preconditioned matrix.

2.7.5.2   *Multigrid*   The solution procedure of the multigrid method is based on traversing the problem on several hierarchical grids. We consider here the geometric multigrid. On each grid, the method performs a restriction, an interpolation, and some smoothing steps. When working with unstructured meshes and/or complex geometry, these steps are often represented by matrix–vector operations. On the coarsest possible level, the multigrid method needs to solve a small-sized problem which usually fits in local cache memories. The coarsest mesh system is typically solved by an additional iterative solver (e.g., the Krylov subspace method) or a direct solver.

All steps in the geometrical multigrid method can be performed on an accelerator. However, in practice, the coarsest problem could be too small to fully utilize the accelerators since they are built to provide high performance for large sets of data. Therefore, it is often recommended to compute the coarsest problem (or most of the coarser operations) on the host, see Fig. 2.5. This is especially pronounced when using W-cycles. It has been shown in [15] that, because of the small amount of data, which is inefficient to be performed on GPU devices, the W-cycle (Fig. 2.5, right) does not perform as well as the V-cycle (Fig. 2.5, left).

When the original problem has a complex geometry, and/or an algebraic multigrid is used, the linear system on the coarsest grid can be solved efficiently by a direct method, performed on the host.

In [18], the authors use a BiCGStab [19] solver preconditioned with a multigrid method. Multigrid uses direct LU solvers on the coarsest grid. Apart from that, all other computations are executed on GPU accelerators.

2.7.5.3   *Defect-Correction Schemes*   Because of technological or pure cost restrictions, the currently available accelerator cards can provide partially pipelined double-precision operations. This means that the double-precision operations could

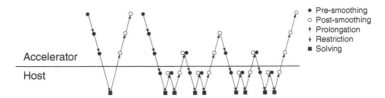

FIGURE 2.5 *Heterogeneous multigrid solver.*

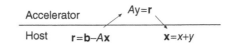

FIGURE 2.6 *Heterogeneous defect-correction solver.*

be more than two times slower compared to single-precision operations. For example, NVIDIA and ATI are releasing GPU cards that have only partial or no support for double-precision operations. These cards are made mainly for visualization and playing games.

Most of the real-life problems require double-precision computation. We can, however, still use accelerator devices with single-precision capabilities to obtain a high accuracy results. One possible way is to use a defect-correction scheme, where we solve the residual equation with a single (or just a lower) precision on an accelerator device and correct the solution on the host in double precision, see Fig. 2.6.

There are some open questions about how to use the defect-correction framework. For instance, when using an iterative method for solving the residual problem, it is unclear as to how to choose the stopping criteria. Another open question is in which cases can the matrix (the linear operator), the solution, and the solution procedure be represented in lower precision.

More details and practical examples can be found in [18, 20].

2.8   MAINTENANCE AND PORTABILITY

Together with the task of achieving high performance and efficient utilization of the computer resources, heterogeneous computing raises the question about portability and reusability of the developed codes and application.

Many application-driven software products go through a long development process. This typically involves applied research in areas of industries such as automobile, aerospace, nuclear, and medical technologies. To ensure the correctness and robustness of the numerical methods, the development phase of such software is long and contains complex verification steps. The development chain could vary from a couple of months to several years. During that time, the processor and accelerator technology could change. For example, in the past five to seven years, the GPU technology has developed from supporting only integer and single-precision operations to

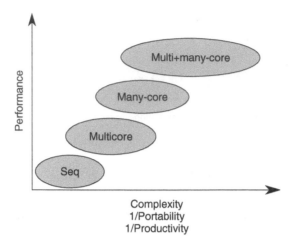

FIGURE 2.7 *Performance versus complexity for heterogeneous programming.*

full double-precision arithmetic and multi-GPU communication mechanisms. Every improvement of this technology provides new features but does not guarantee that the older program can utilize efficiently the newest hardware.

On the other hand, heterogeneous computing could minimize significantly the computational time for many applications.[11] If properly tuned, such applications could provide very high utilization of the underlying hardware and present results that are close to the theoretical peak of the system.

For many years, computer processor manufacturers have been able to increase the performance of the processors in a way fully transparent for the programmers. This has resulted in the so-called "free lunch" for boosting the performance of many applications by just buying the next generation of hardware. Today, to obtain good performance we not only need to get the newest hardware but also to adopt and sometimes fully redesign our algorithms and program implementation in order to utilize the modern systems.

Figure 2.7 presents the relation between performance, Portability, and productivity of the modern multicore and many-core devices.

2.9 CONCLUSION

Heterogeneous systems are becoming more and more common and widespread nowadays. The related technological solutions and architectural details provide a great potential to accelerate critical parts in many scientific applications. Since the iterative methods are among the key components in modern numerical simulations, we presented various techniques to illustrate how the heterogeneous architecture can

---

[11]NVIDIA benchmark report http://www.nvidia.com/docs/IO/122874/K20-and-K20X-application-performance-technical-brief.pdf.

affect their programming implementation. In particular, we discussed how GMRES, multigrid, and defect-correction schemes can be efficiently executed in heterogeneous environments.

For the GMRES method, the heavy computation of the Krylov subspace can be performed on an accelerator while solving the least-squared problem sequentially on the host. Performance results were presented for a CPU–GPU configuration. For the multigrid method, because of the small grid size, traversing the coarser grids becomes more expensive when using many-core devices. In many cases, these operations or, in general, the solution of the coarsest grid problem could be efficiently performed on the host. Mixed-precision methods can be easily implemented via a defect-correction scheme. This technique could be useful for devices with only single-precision support, still allowing us to obtain the solution in double precision.

Furthermore, we discussed aspects not directly related to the performance but to the development processes of software for heterogeneous systems and their maintenance, support, and portability.

A relevant question to pose is: how to look upon heterogeneous computing—as an evolution or a revolution. The answer may depend on the view point of the user but we are certain that the only way to extract performance from those new systems is by efficient and hardware-aware algorithms.

ACKNOWLEDGMENTS

This work was supported by the COST Action IC0805, Open European Network for High-Performance Computing on Complex Environments. In addition, the authors acknowledge the support of the Linnaeus centre of excellence UPMARC, the Uppsala Programming for Multicore Architectures Research Center.

REFERENCES

1. Y. Saad, *Iterative Methods for Sparse Linear Systems*. Philadelphia, PA: Society for Industrial and Applied Mathematics, 2003.
2. Y. Saad and M. H. Schultz, "GMRES: a generalized minimal residual algorithm for solving nonsymmetric linear systems," *SIAM Journal on Scientific and Statistical Computing*, vol. 7, no. 3, pp. 856–869, 1986.
3. W. Hackbusch, *Multi-Grid Methods and Applications, Series in Computational Mathematics*. Berlin: Springer-Verlag, 1985.
4. H. J. Stetter, "The defect correction principle and discretization methods," *Numerische Mathematik*, vol. 29, pp. 425–443, 1978.
5. O. Axelsson, *Iterative Solution Methods*. New York: Cambridge University Press, 1994.
6. E. Anderson, Z. Bai, C. Bischof, L. S. Blackford, J. Demmel, J. J. Dongarra, J. Du Croz, S. Hammarling, A. Greenbaum, A. McKenney, and D. Sorensen, *LAPACK Users' Guide*. Philadelphia, PA: Society for Industrial and Applied Mathematics, 3rd edn, 1999.
7. L. S. Blackford, J. Choi, A. Cleary, E. D'Azeuedo, J. Demmel, I. Dhillon, S. Hammarling, G. Henry, A. Petitet, K. Stanley, D. Walker, and R. C. Whaley, *ScaLAPACK User's Guide*. Philadelphia, PA: Society for Industrial and Applied Mathematics, 1997.

8. C. Brezinski and L. Wuytack, *Numerical Analysis: Historical Developments in the 20th Century*. Elsevier Science Ltd, Amsterdam: The Netherlands, 2001.
9. A. Brandt, "Algebraic multigrid theory: the symmetric case," *Applied Mathematics and Computation*, vol. 19, no. 1-4, pp. 23–56, 1986.
10. O. Axelsson and P. S. Vassilevski, "Algebraic multilevel preconditioning methods. I," *Numerische Mathematik*, vol. 56, no. 2-3, pp. 157–177, 1989.
11. P. S. Vassilevski, *Multilevel Block Factorization Preconditioners: Matrix-Based Analysis and Algorithms for Solving Finite Element Equations*. New York: Springer, 2008.
12. B. F. Smith, P. E. Bjorstad, and W. D. Gropp, *Domain Decomposition: Parallel Multilevel Methods for Elliptic Partial Differential Equations*. Cambridge: Cambridge University Press, 2004.
13. O. Axelsson and P. S. Vassilevski, "A black box generalized conjugate gradient solver with inner iterations and variable-step preconditioning," *SIAM Journal on Matrix Analysis and Applications*, vol. 12, no. 4, pp. 625–644, 1991.
14. Y. Saad, "A flexible inner-outer preconditioned GMRES algorithm," *SIAM Journal on Scientific Computing*, vol. 14, no. 2, pp. 461–469, 1993.
15. D. Lukarski, *Parallel Sparse Linear Algebra for Multi-core and Many-core Platforms—Parallel Solvers and Preconditioners*. PhD thesis, Karlsruhe Institute of Technology, 2012.
16. M. Naumov, "Parallel solution of sparse triangular linear systems in the preconditioned iterative methods on the GPU," Tech. Rep. NVIDIA NVR-2011-001. Santa Clara, CA: NVIDIA, 2011.
17. E. de Sturler and H. A. van der Vorst, "Reducing the effect of global communication in GMRES(m) and CG on parallel distributed memory computers," *Applied Numerical Mathematics*, vol. 18, no. 4, pp. 441–459, 1995.
18. D. Göddeke, *Fast and Accurate Finite-Element Multigrid Solvers for PDE Simulations on GPU Clusters*. PhD thesis, Technische Universität Dortmund, Fakultät für Mathematik, 2010.
19. H. A. Van der Vorst, "Bi-CGSTAB: a fast and smoothly converging variant of Bi-CG for the solution of nonsymmetric linear systems," *SIAM Journal on Scientific and Statistical Computing*, vol. 13, no. 2, pp. 631–644, 1992.
20. H. Anzt, *Asynchronous and Multiprecision Linear Solvers: Scalable and Fault-Tolerant Numerics for Energy Efficient High Performance Computing*. PhD thesis, Karlsruhe Institute of Technology, 2012.

3

Efficient Numerical Solution of 2D Diffusion Equation on Multicore Computers

Matjaž Depolli, Gregor Kosec, and Roman Trobec

Jožef Stefan Institute, Ljubljana, Slovenia

Numerous numerical methods for the solution of partial differential equations (PDEs) are local, meaning that the problem solution in each spatial discretization point is obtained from a few nearest neighbor points only. The local numerical schemes are convenient for parallelization because of the reduced communication with the rest of the domain. We analyze the performance of a parallel implementation of a local meshless numerical method for the solution of the thermal diffusion. This physical phenomenon is modeled by a PDE. The sequential program for the solution procedure is parallelized with OpenMP and run on multicore multiprocessors with hierarchical cache memory architectures. It is confirmed that the parallel execution time depends significantly, not only on the number of cores but also on the problem size and memory architecture. We explain the observed behavior through the analysis of hit rate measurements on the L3 cache level. Some general rules are devised for the determination of an optimal computer architecture which should be tailored to specific application parameters.

High-Performance Computing on Complex Environments, First Edition.
Edited by Emmanuel Jeannot and Julius Žilinskas.
© 2014 John Wiley & Sons, Inc. Published 2014 by John Wiley & Sons, Inc.

3.1 INTRODUCTION

Numerical analysis and computer modeling are becoming basic tools for technological and scientific research because the performance of desktop computers is increasing because of advanced computing architectures that are able to harness many computing cores for the solution of a joint problem. Computing cores communicate and access data from the shared memory, which is organized in several hierarchies regarding their access times [1]. Memory caches are increasing in size and occupy today about 50% of the processors' dies. Cache levels are optimized with respect to their size and access time to the best overall computing performances. However, users are often faced with significant variations in the execution time that are not proportional to the varying system sizes. Demanding high-performance computing (HPC) applications can profit significantly from an appropriate selection of the number of active cores, not only because of more floating point units but also because of a larger size of the cumulative cache space.

Numerous problems, for example, fluid flow, various transport phenomena, weather dynamic, and so on, modeled with partial differential equations (PDEs), can be regarded as HPC applications if solved numerically through a system of linear equations. It is an important advantage if the system matrix is sparse because it can be solved faster. In most numerical simulations, the finite volume method (FVM) [2], the finite difference method (FDM) [3], the boundary element method (BEM) [4], or the finite element method (FEM) [5] is used. However, in the last few years an alternative class of numerical methods, referred to as *meshless methods* [6], is becoming popular. The treatment of complex geometries within the meshless framework is simpler because no topological relations between computational points are required. Several different meshless methods are known [7–9]. This chapter is focused in one of the simplest of them—the point interpolation [10] called *local radial basis function collocation method* (LRBFCM) [11]. The main advantage of local numerical methods is that their system matrix is sparse or banded, which simplifies the solution procedure. In contrast, a global approach [12] might become unstable for increasing number of discretization points, demand a lot of computational resources, and complicate the computer program implementation. Besides being a simpler formulation, a local solution procedure also requires less communication in parallel implementation, which is often a bottleneck of parallel algorithms [13]. Most realistic simulations take vast amounts of time to complete, and therefore numerical approaches have to be implemented with effective parallel implementations on targeted computer architectures.

From the engineering point of view, the computational performance can be increased either by increasing the clock frequency of processor or by increasing the number of processors. Clock frequencies are approaching their physical limits; therefore, the second option—increased number of processing units—is becoming more feasible. Parallel computers, available today in most desktop computers or computer servers, can compensate for the lack of performance of a single computer but only if an efficient parallelization of the computational method is known. Various application programming interfaces (APIs) for parallel programming are used to maximize the performance of parallel systems. Nowadays, the most widely used APIs for parallel programming are OpenMP (aka Open Multi-Processing) for shared-memory systems [14] and MPI (aka *Message Passing Interface*) for distributed-memory systems [15]. Moreover, the use of graphical processing units (GPUs) for solving parallel problems is spreading rapidly. APIs that support parallel programming on GPUs are becoming available, like CUDA (aka *compute unified device architecture*) and OpenCL (aka *open computing language*) [16]. There are several publications regarding the parallelization of different numerical schemes for different applied problems [13, 17–19], mostly based on MPI parallelization, but only a few numerical studies tackle the influence of the cache memory effects on the performance of parallel computations [20]. Cache and main memory latencies in general can form a bottleneck to the computer performance, which is often overlooked [11]. Since the memory hierarchy is composed of several cache layers, main memory, and possibly remote memory, the latency felt by the software is expressed in a complex manner [21, 22].

In this chapter, we explore how the complex memory hierarchy, in particular the L3 cache, affects a parallel program execution of a numerical method. We start by presenting the program—a parallel LRBFCM meshless solution of the classical 2D diffusion test case [23], on a multicore multiprocessor computer architecture. We show that the parallelization of the proposed meshless-based numerical scheme is straightforward on shared-memory systems; only a minor amount of effort and expertise is required to apply OpenMP [24] parallelization if the sequential code is ready. Besides its ease of parallelization, the method also offers other convenient features, such as the ease of implementation, stability, accuracy, and good convergent behavior [23], which have been already successfully confirmed on several demanding nonlinear coupled problems [25–27]. We further demonstrate how the knowledge of the underlying hardware memory hierarchy can be used to maximize the efficiency and, consequently, to achieve lower execution time of the presented parallel meshless solution. All the effects seen from the experimental results are explained by measurements with the performance counter monitor (PCM) library provided by the manufactures of several contemporary processors. The measurements have been performed on numerous executions of the solution method. The results clearly show that caches govern all the discovered effects.

The rest of the chapter is organized as follows. In Section 3.2, the test problem is described. Next, the meshless solution methodology and LBRFCM are briefly presented, followed by the description of parallel program implementation. Section 3.4 is devoted to the analysis and interpretation of the obtained experimental results. The results and their implications are additionally analyzed and discussed in Section 3.5. Section 3.6 summarizes our contribution and lists some important issues that have to be considered by users dealing with complex realistic numerical problems.

3.2 TEST CASE

3.2.1 Governing Equations

We consider a two-dimensional (2D) second-order PDE as a test problem, given by

$$\frac{\partial T}{\partial t} = D\nabla^2 T. \tag{3.1}$$

The performance of numerical implementation is our focus and therefore the coefficient D is set to 1, and a square domain of dimensionless size 1×1 with Dirichlet boundary conditions and uniform initial conditions is considered. The initial dimensionless temperature is set to 1 and at all the boundaries to 0.

$$T\left(\mathbf{p}_\Omega, t = 0\right) = 1,$$
$$T\left(\mathbf{p}_\Gamma, t\right) = 0, \tag{3.2}$$

where $\mathbf{p}_\Omega$ and $\mathbf{p}_\Gamma$ stand for the interior and boundary nodes, respectively. The introduced problem can be also evaluated in a closed form. The solution is presented as

$$T_a\left(\mathbf{p}, t\right) = \sum_n \sum_m \frac{1}{\pi^2} \frac{16}{nm} \sin(\pi n p_x) \sin(\pi m p_y) e^{-\pi^2(n^2 + m^2)t}, \tag{3.3}$$

where m and n are odd integers, and T_a stands for a closed-form solution of the temperature field. The closed-form solution at $t = 0.005$ is presented in Fig. 3.1.

3.2.2 Solution Procedure

The idea behind the local meshless numerical method is the use of a local influence domain for the approximation of a discretized field u, to evaluate the differential operators ($\mathcal{L}$). In this chapter, we use five noded influence domains, that is, the approximation is constructed over the central node where the current computations take place

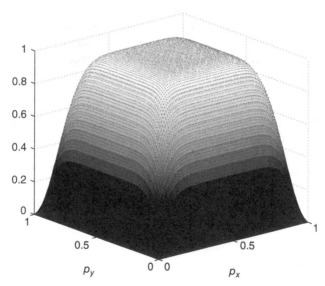

FIGURE 3.1 *Unit square dimensionless domain with uniform initial temperature distribution and Dirichlet boundary conditions (3.2) as calculated from the closed-form solution at $t = 0.005$.*

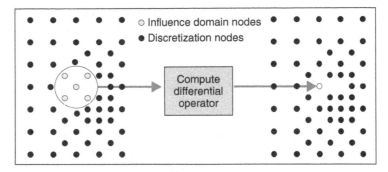

FIGURE 3.2 *Local meshless principle with five noded influence domains.*

and its four closest neighboring nodes. Each node uses its own influence domain for the evaluation of the spatial differential operations, and consequently the domain is discretized with overlapping influence domains. The described principle is presented in Fig. 3.2. The approximation function is introduced as

$$\hat{u}(\mathbf{p}) = \sum_{n=1}^{N} \alpha_n \Psi_n(\mathbf{p}), \qquad (3.4)$$

where $\hat{u}$ is the approximation function, N is the number of basis functions, α_n is the approximation coefficient, $\mathbf{p}(p_x, p_y)$ is the position vector, and Ψ_n is the basis function. The basis could be selected arbitrarily; however, in this chapter only Hardy's multiquadrics (MQs) are used. MQs are defined as

$$\Psi_n(\mathbf{p}) = \sqrt{(\mathbf{p} - \mathbf{p}^n) \cdot (\mathbf{p} - \mathbf{p}^n)/\sigma_C^2 + 1}, \qquad (3.5)$$

where σ_C stands for the free shape parameter and $\mathbf{p}^n$ denotes nth influence domain node. Taking into account all influence domain nodes and 3.4, the approximation system is constructed. The number of basis functions is set to be equal to the number of influence domain nodes $N = 5$. The local approximation simplifies to collocation, which results in a linear system of N equations in each computational node. The matrix formulation of the collocation is thus

$$\boldsymbol{\Psi}\boldsymbol{\alpha} = \boldsymbol{u}. \qquad (3.6)$$

The coefficients α are obtained by solving (3.6). The system (3.6) has to be solved only when the topology of the influence domain changes; accordingly, the computation can be optimized by computing $\boldsymbol{\Psi}^{-1}$ in a preprocessing phase. With the constructed collocation function, the partial differential operator $\mathcal{L}$ can be applied on (3.4):

$$\mathcal{L}\hat{u}(\mathbf{p}) = \sum_{n=1}^{N} \alpha_n \mathcal{L}\Psi_n(\mathbf{p}), \qquad (3.7)$$

which provides a numerical evaluation of $\mathcal{L}u\,(\mathbf{p})$. In this chapter, only five-noded support domains are used and therefore the basis of five MQs is used as well. For the solution of the diffusion equation, second derivatives are required, that is

$$\frac{\partial^2}{\partial p_{x,y}^2}\Psi_n\,(\mathbf{p}) = \frac{1}{\sigma_C^2}\frac{1}{\Psi_n^3\,(\mathbf{p})}. \tag{3.8}$$

Furthermore, the evaluation of α and $\mathcal{L}$ can be combined. All information about numerical operation and the local nodal topology can be stored in a predefined vector. The differential operator vector $(\chi_m^{\mathcal{L}})$ is introduced as

$$\chi_m^{\mathcal{L}}\,(\mathbf{p}) = \sum_{n=1}^{N}\Psi_{nm}^{-1}\mathcal{L}\Psi_n\,(\mathbf{p}). \tag{3.9}$$

The temporal discretization is done through a two-level explicit time stepping given by

$$\frac{\partial\theta}{\partial t} = \frac{\theta - \theta_0}{\Delta t}, \tag{3.10}$$

where the zero-indexed quantities stand for the values at the previous time step and Δt denotes the time step.

One of the most convenient features of the presented meshless spatial discretization is its generality. One can change the number of basis functions, the shape of basis, the size of influence domain, position of computational points, and so on, in order to treat numerical anomalies or problematic parts of the domain, without any kind of special treatment, either of the solution procedure or of the program implementation. All information about the numerical scheme and topology of the computational nodes is stored in differential operator vectors. Such an approach is very suitable for parallel implementation because the computation is completely local. The localization enables the domain to be divided into largely independent parts that can be distributed among multiple computing units. Since the parts are largely independent, only very small amount of communication is required between computing units, with a minor overhead caused by parallel execution.

In order to apply the introduced numerical technique on a problem, first, the discretization nodes have to be created. In this chapter, we use simple orthogonal stationary nodal distribution across the whole domain. After the nodes are positioned, the approximation system in each node is constructed. Since we do not change the topology during the simulation, we precalculate the operator vectors and store them. With the creation of operators, the preprocessing phase is completed and the simulation algorithm continues to the main temporal loop. The temporal loop comprises two spatial loops; in the first one, new temperatures are computed, and in the second one, old temperatures are replaced with the new ones. Both spatial loops are parallelized. The block diagram of the solution procedure is presented in Fig. 3.3.

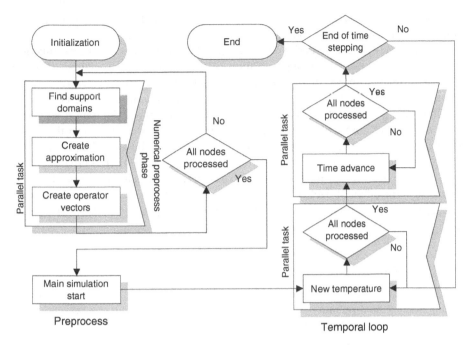

FIGURE 3.3   *Block diagram of the solution procedure.*

3.3   PARALLEL IMPLEMENTATION

3.3.1   Intel PCM Library

Latest architectural designs of processors for desktop computers and workstations provide performance monitoring units (PMUs), a hardware support for counting micro-architectural events of a processor core which are otherwise not explicitly visible to the outside world. In addition, PMUs can collect data form the parts of the processor that are not parts of the core, for example, a memory controller [28]. A wide range of counts is thus accessible, including for hits and misses across the cache hierarchy, number of bytes sent over various system buses, effective and average clock frequencies, and so on. Performance metrics can be calculated using counts of those events over predefined time periods. Either the system or the software performance can then be analyzed and actions can be taken to improve them.

The PCM [29] library comes from Intel and works on Intel processors with Nehalem or newer micro-architectures. The focus of this library is to provide a sample code and give an example on how processor counters can be accessed. Nevertheless, it readily provides access to relevant cache statistics for each core and all cache levels. Its use is very simple, it is light-weight, does not require installation, and can be integrated with the software written in C++, and can thus be readily used in our case. Although it is a part of a package providing also command-line monitoring and extensions for *Windows task manager* and *KDE (K Desktop*

Environment) system monitor (ksysguard), we only use the library part and integrate it into our parallel implementation of the numerical solver code.

To calculate cache statistics, we use the `getSystemCounterState` function before and after the main (temporal) loop of the algorithm and subtract them to get the difference in counters. The function `getSystemCounterState` reads the system-wide counter states, that is, summed up for the all available cores. The accuracy is therefore not optimal in the case of the monitored program running on only a subset of cores, because it unnecessarily takes into account also the background processes, executing on the rest of the cores. On the other hand, since the same overhead is measured no matter how many cores the monitored program actually uses, the runs for various number of cores may be compared without the need to estimate the effect of background processing for each run. To filter out individual counters from the system-wide state, we use functions `getL3CacheMisses` and `getL3CacheHits`.

3.3.2   OpenMP

OpenMP is an API that supports multi-processing programming in C, C++, and Fortran on most shared-memory computer architectures and operating systems including Linux, Mac OS, and Microsoft Windows [19]. OpenMP consists of a set of compiler directives, library routines, and environment variables that influence the run-time behavior. Each section of the code that is designed to run in parallel is marked with a preprocessor directive (`#pragma` in case of C and C++). An OpenMP-enabled program divides the assigned task into disjunct parts and forks into several threads on request, with each thread then processing one or more task parts. After the execution of the parallelized code, the threads join back into the parent process and the program executes sequentially from there on. Fine control is possible over the task division, the number of threads, the synchronization of threads, the management of thread-local and global variables, and so on. OpenMP can implement the task parallelism and data parallelism at the same time. It runs particularly effectively on multicore computer architectures with multilevel memory hierarchy and shared memory caches. The run-time environment allocates the threads to the available processor cores either fully automatically, or it can have thread affinities prescribed on via run-time environment. The code developer is responsible for writing the program in a way that the shared data is processed correctly, for example, managing of data dependencies, balancing data and task distribution. For our case, we use only `parallel for` directive with static scheduling, which divides the problem into equally sized subproblems before a for loop starts, and does not attempt to do any further load balancing. Parallel tasks of the program implementation are shown in Fig. 3.3.

All tests are performed on a computer with four Intel Xeon E4870 processors (Nehalem microarchitecture), each with 10 cores, system clock of 2.80 GHz, 1333 MHz memory bus, and 64 GB of shared main memory. The system has three levels of cache hierarchy: each core has 32 kB of L1 instruction cache and 32 kB of L1 data cache, 256 kB of L2 cache, and shares 30 MB of L3 cache with the other cores of the processor. The typical latencies for accessing data are 4 clock cycles for

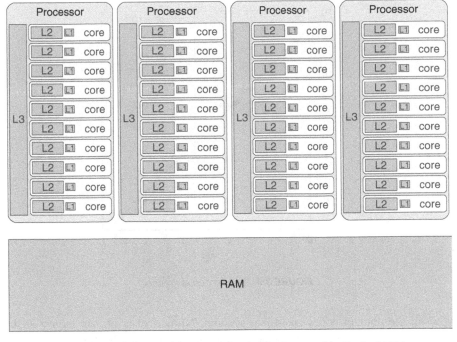

FIGURE 3.4 *Scheme of the computer architecture used for the test case.*

the L1 cache, 10 clock cycles for the L2 cache, 40 clock cycles for the L3 cache, and 120 clock cycles for main memory [32]. The computer architecture is schematically presented in Fig. 3.4.

The tests are run on Nehalem microarchitecture; however, the results are not limited to a specific architecture and thus a similar behavior is expected on all current and future nonuniform memory access (NUMA) processing platforms.

3.4 RESULTS

3.4.1 Results of Numerical Integration

Since the presented diffusion problem has been already analyzed in the past, we focus only on topics related to the present research. However, before we can proceed to the analysis of the execution time, we have to confirm that the presented numerical methodology is suitable for solving PDEs. The presented problem has a closed-form solution, and we can therefore analyze the numerical accuracy very precisely. The numerical accuracy is assessed through the maximal error, defined as

$$E = \max\left(\left|T_a\left(\mathbf{p}_\Omega, t\right) - T\left(\mathbf{p}_\Omega, t\right)\right|\right) \tag{3.11}$$

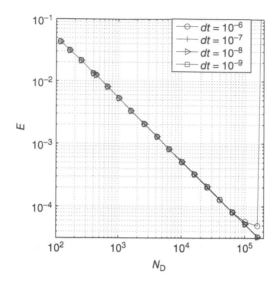

FIGURE 3.5 *Spatial convergence.*

with all the domain nodes taken into account. Numerical errors are largest at the beginning of the simulation when steep gradients occur near the boundaries. However, the error diminishes rapidly with time, and hence a suitable simulation time for the error analysis has to be chosen. To get as much information about the behavior of the method as possible, the dimensionless time $t = 0.005$ is chosen for further analysis. The performance of the numerical method is presented via convergence analysis. In Fig. 3.5, the error with respect to the number of domain nodes N_D for four different time steps is presented. It is evident that the numerical methodology provides adequate results. It can be also seen that the presented meshless method behaves similar to the finite differences method regarding the stability of the numerical integration. The computations with $N_D > 10^5$ and time steps larger than 10^{-6} behave unstably, while $\Delta t < 10^{-7}$ gives stable convergence behavior over the whole analyzed interval.

3.4.2 Parallel Efficiency

Further analysis is focused on the execution efficiency of the presented solution procedure. The efficiency of a parallel program is evaluated through the speedup, defined as

$$S = \frac{t_C^1}{t_C^{N_C}}, \tag{3.12}$$

where $t_C^{N_C}$ stands for the computation time on N_C processor cores. We also measure the L3 cache statistics, including hit rates defined as

$$H_{L3} = \frac{\text{number of L3 hits}}{\text{number of all L3 accesses}}, \tag{3.13}$$

where the subscript defines the considered cache level. The hit rate indicates the relative number of performed memory accesses that can be realized through accessing appropriate cache memory locations. For example, $H_{L3} = 1$ indicates that all the requested memory locations can be found in the L3 or lower cache levels.

Although all the cores are homogeneous regarding their processing capabilities, they have different views on the memory hierarchy. For the presented hardware, the main difference is in the L3 cache. It can either be a same instance for each core, an instance shared among the involved cores, or several instances, each shared by several cores. We observe the computation time, speedup, and L3 cache hit rates for the two extreme cases—either each core has its own cache, or all cores share the same cache. For each case, we perform experiments over a wide range of problem domain sizes $(1 \times 10^2 < N_D < 2 \times 10^5)$ and for one core to the maximum number of cores, 4, for the case where cores have their own caches (computer comprises four processors); and for 10 cores, for the case where all cores share the cache (processor comprises 10 cores).

We start experiments with one core per processor. Binding the solution procedure to one core per processor is performed using OpenMP environment variables. From Fig. 3.6a, it can be seen that the computation time in this case can be separated into three regimes and that its behavior coincides well with the L3 cache hit rate in Fig. 3.6b. As long as the problem fits into the L3 cache (approximately up to $N_D = 3 \times 10^4$), the L3 hit rate remains near 100%, and the computation time increases with the lowest slope. By increasing the dataset, the L3 cache becomes too small to fit the whole problem and consequently the hit rate starts to decline, until it stabilizes at approximately 20%. The first and third regimes are reflected in the computational time linearly dependent on the N_D, but with different slopes. The second regime stands for the transition between them. The slope of the third regime is approximately three times steeper than the slope of the first regime, which corresponds to the ratio between latencies of the main memory and the L3 cache. In the third regime, on average, only one out of five memory locations will be found in the L3 cache. The speedup

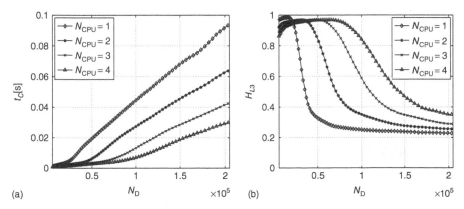

FIGURE 3.6 Solution procedure executing on a single core for $N_{CPU} = 1$–4 processors. (a) Normalized computational time $\tilde{t}_C$, and (b) the corresponding L3 hit rate H_{L3} as functions of the number of domain nodes N_D.

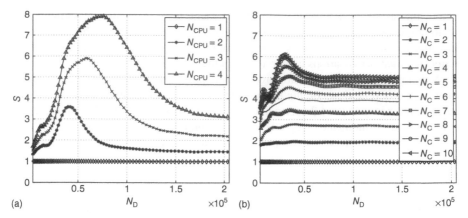

FIGURE 3.7 *Speedup of solution procedure as a function of the number of domain nodes N_D. (a) Executing on a single core for N_{CPU} =1–4 processors. (b) Executing on N_C =1–10 cores of a single processor.*

plotted in Fig. 3.7a reveals that within some specific intervals of the described regimes we get superlinear accelerations with the use of more processors. From Figs 3.6 and 3.7, it is evident that accumulating L3 caches govern the superlinear speedup. In our present analysis, the maximum speedup of $S = 8$ is achieved by running the solution procedure on four cores, each on a different processor.

In Fig. 3.8a, the computational times and corresponding H_{L3} for experiments running on a multiple cores of a single processor are presented. Again, we can identify three regimes that coincide with the H_{L3} regimes in Fig. 3.8b. In the case of a single processor, all cores use the same L3 cache and therefore the hit rate does not depend on the number of involved cores.

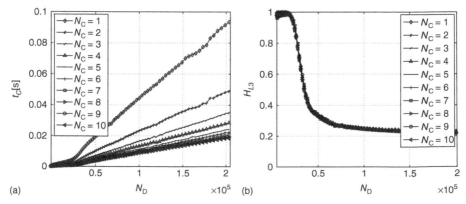

FIGURE 3.8 *Solution procedure executing on N_C =1–10 cores of a single processor. (a) Normalized computational time $\bar{t}_c$, and (b) the corresponding L3 hit rate H_{L3} as functions of the number of domain nodes N_D.*

Speedup measurements, shown in Fig. 3.7b, portray a peculiarity—a peak for high number of processors at approximately $N_D = 3 \times 10^4$. This is not a superlinear speedup as seen in the case with multiple L3 caches, since S is consistently lower than N_C. The peak location coincides with a relatively high L3 cache hit rate $H_{L3} = 0.7$. Comparing the speedups between this and the previous case, we can spot several cases of different behavior. First, speedups on a single processor are much more stable across the N_D interval. This is expected since the cache hit rates are more stable; there is no accumulation of L3 cache and no superlinear speedup. Second and a bit unexpected, speedups on two and three cores are higher on a single processor than on N_C processors for high end of N_D, although the total L3 cache size is smaller and L3 hit rate is lower on a single processor. There is also a difference in speedups on low end of N_D; analogous speedups are higher on the single processor than on the multiprocessor case. The lower H_{L3} on the multiprocessor case for the corresponding N_D explains this difference.

3.5   DISCUSSION

An important lesson can be learned from the presented results. The runtime of OpenMP parallelized programs differs greatly depending on how the threads generated by OpenMP are distributed across available cores. There is no uniformly best distribution, unfortunately, and it is therefore prudent to test several distributions and choose the best one before running very time-consuming programs.

The number of domain nodes N_D can be divided into three disjoint intervals on which the speedup is higher on either a single or multiprocessor case. The multiprocessor case experiences higher speedup only in the interval that corresponds to peak L3 cache hit rate on multiple processors. The speedup in this interval is even superlinear because, in addition to computational resources (cores), the accumulating cache is put to good use. On intervals below and above the peak of L3 cache hit rate, the speedup is higher for the single processor case. On the low side of N_D, the speedup is higher because the L3 cache rate is higher, as pointed out in Section 3.4. On the high side of N_D, the difference in speedups is harder to explain. There is a small difference in L3 cache hit rates, but in the opposite direction of the speedup difference. The reason why the speedup is lower on multiple processors lies in the lower level caches. These require communication when they are caching the same memory block to keep all the caches coherent. In the case of lower level caches, located on different processors, the communication between them takes longer than when they are located on the same processor [21]. Even though the difference in speedups is great, the difference in hit rates of lower level caches can be negligible.

There are also three features left to explain in speedups of experiments on a single processor (Fig. 3.7b)—the convergence of toward 5, as the number of cores increases; the peak around $N_D = 3 \times 10^4$; and the fluctuation preceding the peak. An important part in understanding the first two is the memory bandwidth. At high values of N_D, large amounts of memory are required that cannot be cached, making the memory access the performance bottleneck. The single core demands for memory access are not optimized for the efficient use of the main memory bandwidth. A request for access to a location in the main memory is answered by a block copy from the main memory to the L3 cache. Data locality of the solution procedure then causes the next several requests to find their destinations in L3 cache, which leaves the main memory idle. Only several cores, interleaving their accesses to the main memory, can saturate the main memory bandwidth. Increasing the number of cores even higher brings no speedup since either the main memory or the system bus connecting it to the processors has their bandwidth saturated. The software and hardware combination in our examples seems to saturate the bandwidth at speedup 5.

The reason for the speedup to be able to peak above its saturation value at lower N_D is then quite plain—H_{L3} rate is higher at low N_D, and the number of main memory accesses is lower. While this explains why the speedup can be higher, it does not explain the peak itself. To further explore the peak, we must consider also the parallelization overhead. The parallelization overhead of OpenMP `parallel for` loop consists of time-constant operations: thread creation and management, and loop interval distributions, all independent of the loop interval length. The shorter the loop, the more significant the OpenMP overhead becomes compared to the loop time. Therefore, we get two opposing effects: the relative parallelization overhead that decreases with N_D, and the number of main memory accesses that increases with N_D. The speedup thus peaks at $N_D = 3 \times 10^4$, where the combination of the two limiting effects forms a minimum.

The fluctuation preceding the peak is harder still to explain. It happens in the interval of maximum L3 cache hit rate and appears to be caused by the lower level caches, by an effect similar to the one limiting the speedup on multiple processors. Since cores do not share L2 caches, communication between caches is involved in an effort to keep caches coherent. Fluctuations may happen because the communication between cores of the same processor may occur on various levels, operating at various bandwidths [21]. Depending on the usage pattern, communication may thus sometimes appear faster on average. Every increase in the number of used cores on the same dataset increases the difficulties of keeping the caches coherent, explaining why the fluctuation intensifies as the number of cores increases.

The presented example is among the more humble ones regarding the complexity of memory hierarchy. Modern computer systems often employ much more complicated memory hierarchies. For example, L2 cache is often shared by several but not all cores of a processor. Main memory can also be shared evenly among the processors or can offer larger access speeds to one than to the other processors. If the software executes on a cluster of computers, there are two options for memory sharing. Memory of individual computer may still be made implicitly visible to others but with additional penalty to access speed. Alternatively, memory may only be available upon requests, and computers must communicate with each other explicitly, by the so-called message passing, with the burden of memory management passed from the system to the application. Every level in memory hierarchy can require a different strategy in handling for the computer to perform at its peak. We can learn from the presented example that the level of inefficiency of a flawed design or even just uninformed design is not low but can reach several tens of percent; in the presented case, the peak performance was doubled using the best strategy compared to the worst strategy.

3.6 CONCLUSION

The OpenMP-based parallel implementation of the local meshless solution procedure for solving diffusion problem was implemented on a computer server with four processors, each with 10 cores. In contrast to classical numerical methods, the presented local meshless technique introduced several degrees of freedom over the approximation type, distribution of computational points, the number of support nodes, the shapes of basis functions, and so on. The local differential vector formulation simplified the implementation and understanding of the method but still conserved all the convenient features. Moreover, without a significant additional effort, we could parallelize the sequential code with just a few straightforward #pragma directives. The parallel speedup could be further improved through the optimization of the data structures in order to minimize the communication between cores, but that would require several interferences into the code and hence loss of generality.

Simulation time and speedup measurements were performed for various problem sizes and core use scenarios. In the speedup, several regimes were identified, for which either execution on a single or on multiple processors is favorable. Analysis has been supported by the measurements of CPU performance counters through the low-level performance monitoring. The measurements confirmed the theoretical expectations that the identified regimes are a consequence of complex memory hierarchy, in particular the L3 cache instances. The same measurements also explain the superlinearity, obtained in our test case, with the maximum $S = 8$ on four cores. A detailed analysis explained several smaller effects in speedup measurements, all related to L3 cache instances and also to either lower cache levels or the main memory access.

There are still several unknown factors that have not been explored in full details, for example, motherboard architecture, data and program buses bandwidth, execution and cache policies, and so on. They can influence the results but not change the main messages. Future work should be focused on a more detailed analysis of new architecture-dependent factors and additional diverse software applications.

ACKNOWLEDGMENT

The authors acknowledge the financial support of COST Action IC0805 "Open European Network for High Performance Computing on Complex Environments."

REFERENCES

1. A. Sodan, J. Machina, A. Deshmeh, K. Macnaughton, and B. Esbaugh, "Parallelism via multithreaded and multicore CPUs," *Computer*, vol. 43, no. 3, pp. 24–32, 2010.

2. J. H. Ferziger and M. Perić, *Computational Methods for Fluid Dynamics*. Berlin: Springer-Verlag, 2002.
3. M. N. Özişik, *Finite Difference Methods in Heat Transfer*. Boca Raton, FL: CRC Press, 2000.
4. L. C. Wrobel, *The Boundary Element Method: Applications in Thermo-Fluids and Acoustics*. West Sussex: John Wiley & Sons, 2002.
5. M. Rappaz, M. Bellet, and M. Deville, *Numerical Modelling in Materials Science and Engineering*. Berlin: Springer-Verlag, 2003.
6. S. N. Atluri and S. Shen, *The Meshless Method*. Encino, CA: Tech Science Press, 2002.
7. S. N. Atluri, *The Meshless Method (MLPG) for Domain and BIE Discretization*. Forsyth, GA: Tech Science Press, 2004.
8. W. Chen, "New RBF collocation schemes and kernel RBFs with applications," *Lecture Notes in Computational Science and Engineering*, vol. 26, pp. 75–86, 2002.
9. G. Liu and Y. Gu, *An Introduction to Meshfree Methods and Their Programming*. Dordrecht: Springer, 2005.
10. J. G. Wang and G. R. Liu, "A point interpolation meshless method based on radial basis functions," *International Journal for Numerical Methods in Engineering*, vol. 54, no. 11, pp. 1623–1648, 2002.
11. B. Šarler, J. Perko, and C. S. Chen, "Radial basis function collocation method solution of natural convection in porous media," *International Journal of Numerical Methods for Heat & Fluid Flow*, vol. 14, pp. 187–212, 2004.
12. E. J. Kansa, "Multiquadrics—a scattered data approximation scheme with application to computational fluid dynamics, part I," *Computers & Mathematics with Applications*, vol. 19, pp. 127–145, 1990.
13. R. Trobec, M. Šterk, and B. Robič, "Computational complexity and parallelization of the meshless local Petrov-Galerkin method," *Computers & Structures*, vol. 87, no. 1-2, pp. 81–90, 2009.
14. P. S. Pacheco, *An Introduction to Parallel Programming*. Burlington, MA: Morgan Kaufmann Publishers, 2011.
15. M. Vajteršic, P. Zinterhof, and R. Trobec, "Overview—parallel computing: Numerics, applications, and trends," in *Parallel Computing* (R. Trobec, M. Vajteršic, and P. Zinterhof, eds.), pp. 1–42, London: Springer, 2009.
16. D. B. Kirk and W. W. Hwu, *Programming Massively Parallel Processors*. Burlington, MA: Morgan Kaufmann Publishers, 2010.
17. G. P. Nikishkov, A. Makinouchi, G. Yagawa, and S. Yoshimura, "Performance study of the domain decomposition method with direct equation solver for parallel finite element analysis," *Computational Mechanics*, vol. 19, pp. 84–93, 1996.
18. V. Singh, "Parallel implementation of the EFG method for heat transfer and fluid flow problems," *Computational Mechanics*, vol. 34, pp. 453–463, 2004.
19. L. Zhang, G. J. Wagner, and W. K. Liu, "A parallelized meshfree method with boundary enrichment for large-scale CFD," *Journal of Computational Physics*, vol. 176, no. 2, pp. 483–506, 2002.
20. T. N. Venkatesh, V. R. Sarasamma, S. Rajalakshmy, K. C. Sahu, and R. Govindarajan, "Super-linear speed-up of a parallel multigrid Navier-Stokes solver on Flosolver," *Current Science*, vol. 88, pp. 589–593, 2005.
21. D. Molka, D. Hackenberg, R. Schöne, and M. S. Müller, "Memory Performance and Cache Coherency Effects on an Intel Nehalem Multiprocessor System," *Proceedings of the 18th International Conference on Parallel Architectures and Compilation Techniques, PACT'09*, Raleigh, NC, USA, pp. 261–270, 2009.

22. K. J. Barker, K. Davis, A. Hoisie, D. J. Kerbyson, M. Lang, S. Pakin, and J. C. Sancho, "A performance evaluation of the Nehalem quad-core processor for scientific computing," *Parallel Processing Letters*, vol. 18, no. 4, 2008.

23. R. Trobec, G. Kosec, M. Šterk, and B. Šarler, "Comparison of local weak and strong form meshless methods for 2-D diffusion equation," *Engineering Analysis with Boundary Elements*, vol. 36, no. 3, pp. 310–321, 2012.

24. R. Chandra, L. Dagum, D. Kohr, D. Maydan, J. McDonald, and R. Menon, *Parallel Programming in OpenMP*. San Diego, CA: Academic Press, 2001.

25. E. Divo and A. J. Kassab, "Localized meshless modeling of natural-convective viscous flows," *Numerical Heat Transfer*, vol. B129, pp. 486–509, 2007.

26. G. Kosec, M. Založnik, B. Šarler, and H. Combeau, "A meshless approach towards solution of macrosegregation phenomena," *CMC: Computers, Materials, & Continua*, vol. 580, pp. 1–27, 2011.

27. R. Vertnik and B. Šarler, "Meshless local radial basis function collocation method for convective-diffusive solid-liquid phase change problems," *International Journal of Numerical Methods for Heat & Fluid Flow*, vol. 16, pp. 617–640, 2006.

28. Intel Corporation, "Nehalem performance monitoring unit programming guide." http://software.intel.com/file/30320 (accessed on 02 January 2014).

29. R. Dementiev, T. Willhalm, O. Bruggeman, P. Fay, P. Unger, A. Ott, P. Lu, J. Harris, and P. Kerly, "Intel® performance counter monitor—a better way to measure CPU utilization," 2012.

4

Parallel Algorithms for Parabolic Problems on Graphs in Neuroscience

Natalija Tumanova and Raimondas Čiegis

Vilnius Gediminas Technical University, Vilnius, Lithuania

Three parallel numerical algorithms have been developed for solution of parabolic problems on graphs, suitable for structures containing closed loops. The parallelization of the discrete algorithms is based on the domain decomposition method. Theoretical investigation and the results of numerical and computational experiments show good scalability of all three parallel algorithms.

4.1 INTRODUCTION

Many problems in neuroscience are defined on the so-called arbitrarily branching structures, where the neuron is represented as a set of long, thin dendrites and axon, arising from the cell body, called *soma*, and branching sometimes even hundreds of times. Many neuron models together with thorough biophysical and modeling basis have been given in [1–3]. Physiologically, the most accurate models of excitable cells, based on the Hodgkin–Huxley equations [4], are of the basic form

---

High-Performance Computing on Complex Environments, First Edition.
Edited by Emmanuel Jeannot and Julius Žilinskas.
© 2014 John Wiley & Sons, Inc. Published 2014 by John Wiley & Sons, Inc.

$$C\frac{\partial V}{\partial t} = \frac{a}{2R}\frac{\partial^2 V}{\partial x^2} - \sum_{i=1}^{n} \bar{g}_i(q_1, \dots, q_m)(V - V_i), \tag{4.1}$$

$$\frac{dq_j}{dt} = (1 - q_j)\alpha_j(V) - q_j\beta_j(V), \quad j = 1, \dots, m \tag{4.2}$$

which is supplemented with initial conditions and boundary conditions. Here, $V(x, t)$ is the transmembrane potential, x is a spatial coordinate, t denotes time, and $q_j(x, t)$ are normalized dimensionless functions that describe the kinetics of the ionic currents that depend on V. The main reaction–diffusion equation (4.1) on the compartments is coupled to a set of ordinary differential equations (ODEs) (4.2), forming the so-called conditionally linear system. That means that the voltage equation (4.1) is linear if $q_j(x, t)$ values are known. Also, equations (4.2) are linear if the value of the voltage is known. Employing this property of conditional linearity, the backward Euler method and the Crank–Nicolson method with Picard iterations for nonlinear terms are the most widely used tools for the integration of this type of equations [3]. Also, other methods such as the forward Euler [5, 6], exponential Euler [5], Runge–Kutta, are Gear [3] are also applied by some investigators. Since realistic neural networks involve stiff coupled partial differential equations (PDEs), arising from the integration of individual neurons, the global adaptive time-step integrators IDA and CVODES are used in [7], and a local variable time-step method is investigated in [8].

However, the biggest challenge in this area is modeling of the realistic neural networks, arising from the integration of individual neurons. Equations (4.1) on the compartments are coupled with conjugation conditions, starting from voltage flux conservation equations between the compartments of one neuron to synaptic transmission equations between individual neurons. The most popular method for discretizing branched structures was proposed by Rall [9]. Compartmental modeling is based on the structure splitting into separate parts, whose membranes are isopotential. Changes in the physical properties of the membranes and voltage appear between the compartments. The most popular neurosimulation environments NEURON [7] and GENESIS [5] employ this method.

Hines proposed an implicit method [10] for the tree-like structures without closed loops. The point of the method is the special order of the numbering of compartments, and the resulting matrix of the special form is solved in $\mathcal{O}(N)$ operations, where N is the number of points in the spatial grid. However, recent studies have revealed additional channels for neuronal communication, that is, gap junctions, acting as "electrical synapses" [11–13], which can form closed loops in chains of cells. Mascagni [14] proposed an algorithm based on the superposition principle. In contrast to Hines algorithm, this method allows the investigation of structures with closed loops. The solution of system of equations of the size of branching points is needed, instead.

Predictor–corrector and domain decomposition methods are widely used for the solution of elliptic and parabolic PDEs in multidimensional domains. Such algorithms are well suited for parallel implementation. Some nonstandard domain decomposition methods with overlapping and nonoverlapping domains have been developed by Vabishchevich [15, 16]. Rempe and Chopp [17] and Shi and Liao [18] applied domain decomposition and predictor–corrector methods on graphs.

Another challenge in neuromodeling is the amount of calculations needed for simulation of networks of neurons. Some estimates put the human brain at about 10^{11} neurons and 10^{14} synapses. Modern complex models involve large numbers of ion channels (usually more than 10), and thus parallelization of the algorithms is very important in solving real-world problems; when the amount of computations increases, application of parallel algorithms enables us to reduce essentially the CPU time. Definitely, the explicit methods, for example exponential Euler method (default for GENESIS), are well suited for parallel implementation, provided the loss in stability and restrictions on the integration step are acceptable. In [19], the parallel computations module on MPI basis is developed for NEURON. The provided computation results show almost linear scalability of the algorithm. Another parallel version of Hines algorithm, which can maintain structures with closed loops, was given by Zhuang and Sun [20]. However, this algorithm requires a special domain partitioning to ensure that the subdomains are loop-free. An extensive review on the tools for simulation of networks of neurons, including parallel tools, is given in [21].

The main goal of this chapter is to investigate parallel versions of implicit schemes, based on the superposition principle, and predictor–corrector schemes, which are more stable than explicit methods and suitable for structures with closed loops. We will focus mainly on linear problems in this chapter. A motivation of such a selection depends on two properties. First, due to the conditional linearity property, which is appropriate for this class of excitation models, we can split the initial problems into two linear ones, which can be solved iteratively. Second, the ODE system (4.2) is integrated locally if the voltage value is known. Thus, the amount of local computations is increased and the scalability of the parallel algorithm is improved. In other words, we will investigate the worst case scenario of the given parallel calculations.

The rest of the chapter is organized as follows: The formulation of the mathematical model and the three algorithms are given in Section 4.2; they include the θ-method and two predictor–corrector type algorithms. The parallel versions of the algorithms are given in Section 4.3, where the complexity and scalability analysis is performed. In Section 4.4, we present some results of computation experiments which illustrate the results of theoretical analysis. Finally, conclusions are given in Section 4.5.

4.2 FORMULATION OF THE DISCRETE MODEL

The domain of problem definition can be defined using the terminology of oriented graphs. Let $P = \{p_j, j = 1, \dots, J\}$ be a set of branching points or vertices. Some of these points are joined by individual directed edges, making a set of edges E (or a set of ordered pairs of vertices). Each edge has a direction, and these directions can be selected using any convenient scheme:

$$E = \{e_k = (p_{k_s}, p_{k_f}), p_{k_s}, p_{k_f} \in P, \quad k = 1, \dots, K\},$$

where p_{k_s} is the starting point of the edge e_k, and p_{k_f} is the end point of the same edge.

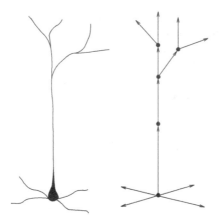

FIGURE 4.1   *Representation of a neuron anatomical structure by graph.*

Let $l_k = |e_k|$ be the length of e_k and let x be the distance along the interval $(0, l_k)$ (Fig. 4.1). On the graph (E, P), we consider a system of parabolic linear problems for a set of functions $\{u^k(x, t)\}$:

$$\frac{\partial u^k}{\partial t} = \frac{\partial}{\partial x}\left(d^k \frac{\partial u^k}{\partial x}\right) - q^k u^k + f^k, \quad 0 < x < l_k, \quad k = 1, \dots, K, \qquad (4.3)$$

$$0 < d_0 \le d^k(x, t) \le d_M, \quad q^k(x, t) \ge 0, \quad f^k = f^k(x, t),$$

$$u^k(x, 0) = u_0^k(x), \quad 0 < x < l_k, \quad k = 1, \dots, K$$

for sufficiently smooth functions d^k, q^k, f^k. At the branch points $p_j \in P$, the fluxes of the solution are conserved:

$$c\frac{\partial u_j}{\partial t} + q_j u_j = \sum_{e_m \in N^-(p_j)} d^m \frac{\partial u^m}{\partial x}\bigg|_{x=0} - \sum_{e_k \in N^+(p_j)} d^k \frac{\partial u^k}{\partial x}\bigg|_{x=l_k} + f_j, \quad \forall p_j \in P, \quad (4.4)$$

where by $N^\pm(p_j)$ we denote the sets of edges having $x = 0$ or $x = l_k$ as an end point of the edge at p_j:

$$N^+(p_j) = \left\{ e_k : \ e_k = (p_{j_s}, p_j) \in E, \ s = 1, \dots, S_j \right\},$$

$$N^-(p_j) = \left\{ e_k : \ e_k = (p_j, p_{j_f}) \in E, \ f = 1, \dots, F_j \right\}.$$

Here we take into account the relaxation time c and a linear sink term q_j; however, this equation can be reduced to the simple case when incoming and outgoing fluxes are conserved:

$$\sum_{e_k \in N^+(p_j)} d^k \frac{\partial u^k}{\partial x}\bigg|_{x=l_k} = \sum_{e_m \in N^-(p_j)} d^m \frac{\partial u^m}{\partial x}\bigg|_{x=0}.$$

At all vertices of the graph, the continuity constraints are satisfied:

$$u_j(t) = u^m(p_j, t), \quad \forall p_j \in P, e_m \in N^{\pm}(p_j).$$

A detailed description of such models is given in [7, 22].

4.2.1 The θ-Implicit Discrete Scheme

On each edge e_k, $k = 1, \ldots, K$, we define a discrete uniform spatial grid

$$\omega_h(k) = \left\{ x_j^k \; : \; x_j^k = jh_k, \quad j = 1, \ldots, N_k - 1 \right\}, \quad x_{N_k}^k = l_k,$$

with the nodes x_j^k and steps h_k. Let ω_τ be a uniform time grid:

$$\omega_\tau = \{t^n \; : \; t^n = n\tau, n = 0, \ldots, N, \quad N\tau = T\},$$

where τ is the time step. On the grids $\omega_h(k) \times \omega_\tau$, we define discrete functions

$$U_j^{k,n} = U^k(x_j, t^n), \quad k = 1, \ldots, K,$$

which approximate the solution $U_j^{k,n}$ on the edge e_k at the time moment t^n. We also define the backward time and the forward and backward space finite differences with respect to t and x:

$$\partial_{\bar{t}} U_j^{k,n} = \frac{U_j^{k,n} - U_j^{k,n-1}}{\tau}, \quad \partial_x U_j^{k,n} = \frac{U_{j+1}^{k,n} - U_j^{k,n}}{h_k}, \quad \partial_{\bar{x}} U_j^{k,n} = \frac{U_j^{k,n} - U_{j-1}^{k,n}}{h_k}.$$

We also introduce the averaging operator

$$A_\theta U_j^n = \theta U_j^n + (1 - \theta) U_j^{n-1},$$

with parameter $\theta \in [0, 1]$.

Using the θ-method, we approximate the differential equations (4.3) by the following finite difference equations:

$$\partial_{\bar{t}} U_j^{k,n} = \partial_{\bar{x}} \left(d_{j+\frac{1}{2}}^{k,n-\theta'} \partial_x A_\theta U_j^{k,n} \right) - q_j^{k,n-\theta'} A_\theta U_j^{k,n} + f_j^{k,n-\theta'},$$

$$x_j \in \omega_h(k), k = 1, \ldots, K, \tag{4.5}$$

where $\theta' = 1 - \theta$.

The flux balance equations (4.4) are approximated by the discrete conservation equations

$$
c\partial_{\bar{t}} U_j^n + q_j^n A_\theta U_j^{n-\theta'} + \sum_{e_k \in N^+(p_j)} \left[d_{N_k - \frac{1}{2}}^{k,n-\theta'} \partial_{\bar{x}} A_\theta U_{N_k}^{k,n} + \frac{h_k}{2} \left(\partial_{\bar{t}} U_{N_k}^{k,n} \right. \right.
$$

$$
\left. + q_{N_k}^{k,n-\theta'} A_\theta U_{N_k}^{k,n} - f_{N_k}^{k,n-\theta'} \right) \Big] - \sum_{e_m \in N^-(p_j)} \left[d_{1/2}^{m,n-\theta'} \partial_x A_\theta U_0^{m,n} \right.
$$

$$
\left. - \frac{h_m}{2} \left(\partial_{\bar{t}} U_0^{m,n} + q_0^{m,n-\theta'} A_\theta U_0^{m,n} - f_0^{m,n-\theta'} \right) \right] = f_j^{n-\theta'}, \quad \forall p_j \in P. \tag{4.6}
$$

At all branch points, the continuity constraints are satisfied:

$$
U_j^n = U^{m,n}(p_j), \quad \forall p_j \in P, e_m \in N^\pm(p_j). \tag{4.7}
$$

The solution of the finite difference scheme (4.5–4.7) is computed efficiently by using a modified factorization algorithm [22], as follows:

- First, using the modified forward factorization algorithm, function $U^{k,n}$ is expressed in the following form:

$$
U_j^{k,n} = \gamma_j^{k,n} V_{k_s}^n + \alpha_j^{k,n} V_{k_f}^n + \beta_j^{k,n}, \quad k = 1, \dots, K, \quad j = 0, \dots, N_k, \tag{4.8}
$$

  where $V_j^n, j = 1, \dots, J$ are unknown values of the discrete solution at the branch points. The complexity of the factorization algorithm is $\mathcal{O}(N_1 + \cdots + N_K)$.
- Second, by substituting equations (4.8) into the discrete flux conservation equations (4.6) and using the continuity conditions (4.7), we obtain a system of linear equations $\mathcal{A}^n \mathbf{V}^n = \mathbf{F}^n$ where $\mathbf{V}^n = (V_1^n, \dots, V_J^n)$ and $\mathcal{A}^n$ is a sparse matrix of dimension $J \times J$. Such systems can be solved very efficiently by direct methods, targeted for linear systems with sparse matrix, or by iterative algorithms, for example, CG (conjugate gradient) type algorithms.
- During the final step, the discrete solution $U^{k,n}$ is computed using (4.8) and values of the vector $\mathbf{V}^n$. The complexity of this step is again $\mathcal{O}(N_1 + \cdots + N_K)$.

Thus, the total complexity of the sequential implicit algorithm is given by

$$
W = W_f + W_s = \mathcal{O}\left(\sum_{k=1}^{K} N_k \right) + \mathcal{O}(\mu \lambda J), \tag{4.9}
$$

where W_f is the complexity of the factorization algorithm, and W_s is the complexity of solving the system of linear equations by using the PCG (preconditioned conjugate gradient) method. The dimension of this system is $J \times J$, λ is the number of nonzero elements per row, and μ is the number of PCG iterations.

The stability and convergence of the θ-implicit scheme is investigated in [23]. The unconditional stability is proved in the L_2, H_1, and maximum norms, and the convergence rate is shown to be $\mathcal{O}(\tau^{\sigma_\theta} + h^2)$, where $\sigma_\theta = 2$ for $\theta = 0.5$ (Crank–Nicolson scheme); otherwise $\sigma_\theta = 1$.

4.2.2 The Predictor–Corrector Algorithm I

Further, we consider two schemes when the graph is decomposed into smaller subgraphs and equations on different subgraphs can be solved in parallel. Both schemes also can be used with the Crank–Nicolson scheme (see detailed description of Algorithm II for Crank–Nicolson in [17]). The first algorithm is based on the sequential discrete algorithm (4.5–4.7) and is developed using the domain decomposition method by dividing some edges of the graph, whereby a set of problems on subgraphs is obtained and these subproblems can be solved efficiently in parallel. For more details on this algorithm, see [24].

4.2.2.1 Graph Decomposition Step The graph is partitioned into subgraphs by dividing some edges of the graph (Fig. 4.2). Let us denote a set of edges that connect vertices belonging to different subdomains by $D = \{e_s \in E, s = 1, \dots, S\}$. Then, each grid $\omega_h(s)$ on these edges is divided into two subgrids by midpoints

$$B = \left\{ x_{j_s} \in \omega_h(s), \quad j_s = N_s/2, \quad s = 1, \dots, S \right\}.$$

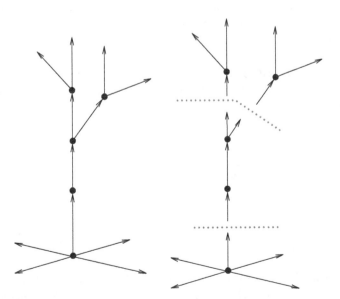

FIGURE 4.2 Domain decomposition scheme for the predictor–corrector Algorithm I.

4.2.2.2 Predictor Step First, we compute in parallel new values of the solution at the splitting points $x_{j_s} \in B$. The explicit Euler approximation is used to discretize the differential equation (4.3):

$$\frac{\widetilde{U}_{j_s}^{s,n} - U_{j_s}^{s,n-1}}{\tau} = \partial_{\bar{x}} \left(d_{j_s+\frac{1}{2}}^{s} \partial_x U_{j_s}^{s,n-1} \right) - q_{j_s}^{n} \widetilde{U}_{j_s}^{s,n} + f_{j_s}^{s,n}, \quad s = 1, \dots, S. \quad (4.10)$$

4.2.2.3 Domain Decomposition Step Second, solutions on each subgraph are computed in parallel using the implicit finite difference scheme (4.5–4.7). The predicted values $\widetilde{U}_{j_s}^{s,n}$ are used as the interface boundary conditions.

4.2.2.4 Corrector Step Third, using the implicit finite difference scheme (4.5) and taking the solution U^n, computed at the second step, we update in parallel the values of the solution at the splitting points.

Using the energy estimates, it is proved in [24] that the predictor–corrector algorithm is unconditionally stable with $\theta = 1$ in the special energy norm. The relation between the space and time steps $\tau = Ch^2$ is still required in order to get the convergence of the discrete solution, since only a conditional approximation $\mathcal{O}(\tau + h^2 + \frac{\tau^2}{h})$ is obtained because of the truncation error introduced at the prediction step.

The total complexity of one time step of the predictor–corrector Algorithm I remains the same as in case of the sequential implicit algorithm (4.9).

4.2.3 The Predictor–Corrector Algorithm II

The second predictor–corrector algorithm is based on the decomposition of the problem into simple one-dimensional problems on each edge, which can be efficiently solved by a factorization algorithm.

4.2.3.1 Predictor Step First, we compute new values of the solution at the branch points. The explicit Euler approximation is used to discretize the flux balance equations (4.4):

$$c\frac{\widetilde{U}_j^n - U_j^{n-1}}{\tau} + q_j^n \widetilde{U}_j^n + \sum_{e_k \in N^+(p_j)} \left[d_{N_k-\frac{1}{2}}^{k} \partial_{\bar{x}} U_{N_k}^{k,n-1} + \frac{h_k}{2} \left(\frac{\widetilde{U}_{N_k}^{k,n} - U_{N_k}^{k,n-1}}{\tau} - f_{N_k}^{k,n} \right) \right]$$
$$\quad (4.11)$$
$$- \sum_{e_m \in N^-(p_j)} \left[d_{\frac{1}{2}}^{m} \partial_x U_0^{m,n-1} - \frac{h_m}{2} \left(\frac{\widetilde{U}_0^{m,n} - U_0^{m,n-1}}{\tau} - f_0^{m,n} \right) \right] = f_j^n, \forall p_j \in P.$$

4.2.3.2 Domain Decomposition Step Second, solutions at each graph edge $e_k \in E$ are computed in parallel using the implicit finite difference scheme (4.5) with the predicted values $\widetilde{U}_s^n$ taken as the interface boundary conditions.

4.2.3.3 Corrector Step The values of the solution at the branch points, computed by the predictor algorithm, are updated using the basic implicit scheme (4.6).

The stability and convergence of this algorithm was investigated in [17] only experimentally. However, the analysis, similar to the one used in [24], shows only conditional convergence rate due to the truncation error introduced at the prediction step (the strict stability and convergence analysis of this scheme is beyond the scope of this chapter).

Since the standard factorization algorithm is implemented for each edge, the complexity of the sequential predictor–corrector algorithm is given by

$$W = \mathcal{O}\left(\sum_k N_k\right) + \mathcal{O}(J).$$

4.3 PARALLEL ALGORITHMS

4.3.1 Parallel θ-Implicit Algorithm

Parallelization of the algorithm (4.5–4.7) is done using the domain decomposition method.

- *Graph Decomposition Step.* To implement the parallel version of the implicit scheme, the edges of the graph are distributed to the processes. The domain decomposition scheme is shown in Fig. 4.3. The constrained load balancing problem should be solved. Its aim is to guarantee that each process has about the

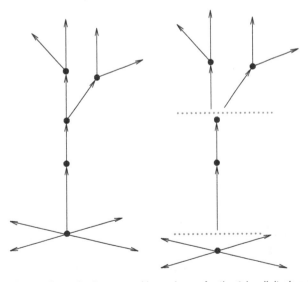

FIGURE 4.3 *Domain decomposition scheme for the θ-implicit algorithm.*

same number of mesh grid points, since this number defines the computational complexity for all parts of the discrete algorithm. At the same time, we want to minimize the number of edges that are cut by the decomposition. Metis tool [25] is applied to distribute the weighted edges of the graph, where the weights are taken as equal to the number of mesh points on the given edge.

- *Forward Factorization Step.* Each process performs locally a forward factorization step on the assigned edges.

- *Solution of the Linear System of Equations.* After the factorization step, processes calculate the local coefficients of the system. The system is solved using the parallel preconditioned conjugate gradient method. After that, processes exchange the solutions on neighbor vertices.

- *Backward Factorization Step.* Using the calculated solution values on vertices and local factorization coefficients, each process performs a backward factorization step locally, thus calculating the solution at each time step.

Since no changes are made in the basic sequential algorithm, the accuracy of approximation and stability of the parallel algorithm coincide with those of the sequential algorithm. It is well known that the convergence rate of the parallel iterative PCG algorithm depends slightly on the rounding errors due to floating point arithmetic and MPI data sending protocols, but the number of iterations is very similar for the parallel and sequential cases.

Let us consider the complexity and efficiency of the parallel algorithm. The modified factorization algorithm (4.8) is fully parallel, and the complexity of this step is $T_{1,p} = W_f/p$, where p is the number of processes and W_f is the complexity of the sequential factorization algorithm.

Now let us evaluate the complexity of the PPCG (parallel preconditioned conjugate gradient) algorithm when the diagonal preconditioner is used. After processing the forward factorization step and calculating local matrix coefficients, processes exchange data on shared vertices. The complexity of this step is $T_{2,p} = \gamma(\alpha + \beta v \lambda)$, where $\gamma = \gamma(p)$ is the largest number of neighbors a process shares vertices with, v is the largest number of vertices shared with the same neighbor, and λ is the number of nonzero elements per row; thus $v\lambda$ is the largest message sent to a neighbor. α is the message startup time, and β is the time required to send one element of data [26]. This estimate evaluates the worst case when the process with the largest number of neighbors sends the largest messages without any optimization of the data communication protocol. In more advanced versions, we use asynchronous data transfer and try to hide the costs of it by maximizing the part of computations with local data before any send or receive operation.

During matrix–vector multiplication, each process exchanges ghost elements of vectors with neighboring processes. The good news is that the structure of the sparse matrix is known and each process sends only a few shared vertices data to its neighbors. This feature reduces the communication costs of the step substantially, compared to the PPCG algorithm for an arbitrary matrix. Thus the complexity of the parallel matrix–vector multiplication is given by

$$T_{3,p} = \lambda \left\lceil \frac{J}{p} \right\rceil + \gamma \left(\alpha + \beta v \right).$$

Parallel computation of the inner product of two vectors requires global communication among all processes during summation of local parts of the product. We use the *MPI_Allreduce* operation, and the complexity of such reduction operation depends on the algorithm used to implement this global reduction operation and the architecture of the computer. Therefore, the cost of broadcasting/reducing one item of data between p processes is estimated by $B_{1,p} = R_B(p)(\alpha + \beta)$.

When the system of linear equations is solved, the neighbor processes exchange values of solutions on neighbor vertices, and the cost of this step is $\gamma(\alpha + v\beta)$.

Summing up the obtained estimates, we compute the complexity of the parallel fully implicit algorithm as

$$T_p = \frac{W_f}{p} \delta + \frac{W_s}{p} \phi \delta + \gamma \left(\alpha + \beta v \lambda \right)$$
$$+ \mu \left(2 R_B(p)(\alpha + \beta) + \gamma \left(\alpha + v\beta \right) \right) + \gamma \left(\alpha + v\beta \right),$$

where $\phi = \phi(p_c) \geq 1$ defines the quality of the load balancing of vertices, and $\delta = \delta(p_c) \geq 1$ is the retardation coefficient, which depends on the maximum number of cores per processor. This coefficient should be taken into account, since the shared-memory structure can become a bottleneck when too many cores try to access the global memory of a node simultaneously. For clusters of computers, the communication start time α is much greater than the time required to send one number β. For the simplest data exchange algorithm and assuming that $\alpha \gg \lambda v \beta$, we obtain the estimate

$$T_p \approx \frac{W_f}{p} \delta + \frac{W_s}{p} \phi \delta + \gamma \alpha \left(\mu + 2 \right) + 2 R_B(p) \mu \alpha. \tag{4.12}$$

It follows from (4.12) that the efficiency of the implicit parallel algorithm $E = \frac{T_0}{p T_p}$ depends on the imbalance of distributed local vertices ϕ. Also, we see that the efficiency of the parallel algorithm should improve for an increased size of the problem, but the effects of worse quality of data distribution ϕ and negative effects of memory usage by cores can change this trend.

Let

$$H(W,p) := p T_p - T_0 = W_f(\delta - 1) + W_s(\phi \delta - 1) + p \gamma \alpha \left(\mu + 2 \right) + 2 p R_B(p) \mu \alpha$$

be the total overhead of a parallel algorithm [26]. Then the isoefficiency function $W = g(p, E)$ is defined by the implicit equation

$$W = \frac{E}{1 - E} H(W, p),$$

where E is a fixed efficiency of the algorithm. After simple calculations, we get

$$W := W_f + W_s = \Theta\left(p(\gamma(p) + R(p))\right).$$

Hence, the scalability of the parallel algorithm depends essentially on the realization of the broadcast operation: $R(p)$ may vary from $\log_2 p$ to p depending on the parallel library implementation and the architecture of the computer.

4.3.2   Parallel Predictor–Corrector Algorithm I

- *Graph Decomposition Step.* The load balancing problem is solved. Because of the stencil of the discretization algorithm, the computational domains of different processes overlap. The information belonging to the overlapped regions should be exchanged among processes. The cost of data exchanges contributes to the additional costs of the parallel algorithm. Thus, a second goal of defining the optimal data mapping is to minimize the overlapping regions.
- *Predictor and Domain Decomposition Steps.* In each time step, processes predict the values on the boundaries of subdomains locally using the formula (4.10). Then they perform the implicit algorithm (4.5–4.7) on the local subdomains in parallel.
- *Corrector Step.* The processes exchange data on the interface of subdomains and then recompute the solution at the splitting points in parallel using formula (4.6).

Let us evaluate the complexity of the given algorithm. When a problem is assigned to p processes, the size of local matrix of coefficients becomes $\frac{J}{p} \times \frac{J}{p}$, since each process gets about $\frac{J}{p}$ vertices of the graph. But the number of nonzero elements λ in the line remains almost the same, since a nonzero element indicates the edge connecting two vertices of the graph. The number of overlapping regions is quite small, thus the number of connections between different edges changes slightly. Consequently, the complexity of the algorithm is estimated as follows:

$$T_p = \frac{W_f}{p}\delta + \frac{W_s}{p}\phi\delta + \gamma(\alpha + \beta)$$

$$\approx \frac{W_f}{p}\delta + \frac{W_s}{p}\phi\delta + \gamma\alpha.$$

The obtained complexity estimate shows that the efficiency of the algorithm mainly depends on the domain partition quality.

The additional costs of the algorithm are

$$H(W, p) = W_f(\delta - 1) + W_s(\phi\delta - 1) + p\gamma\alpha.$$

The isoefficiency function is defined as follows:

$$W := \frac{E}{1 - E}H(W, p) = \Theta\left(p\gamma(p)\right).$$

The main factors that influence the scalability of the algorithm again are the quality of the domain partition and the negative effects of memory usage by cores.

4.3.3 Parallel Predictor–Corrector Algorithm II

In order to minimize the amount of data exchanged among processes, here we split the edges that connect vertices belonging to two different processes (Fig. 4.2). Unlike the predictor–corrector Algorithm I, the subdomains do not overlap in this case. On edges belonging to different processes, the standard factorization algorithm for the solution of systems of linear equations with tridiagonal matrices is modified by the two-side version of this algorithm. Processes should exchange two factorization coefficients during implementation of this parallel version of the factorization algorithm, but the complexity of the algorithm is still $8N$ floating-point operations.

The complexity of the parallel predictor–corrector algorithm is given by (for simplicity of analysis, we assume that $\phi = 1$)

$$T_p = \frac{W}{p}\delta + \gamma(\alpha + 2\beta) \approx \frac{W}{p}\delta + \gamma\alpha.$$

It follows from the obtained formula that the influence of the communication costs is small when the problem size is large enough.

The decrease in the efficiency of the parallel algorithm depends mostly on the retardation coefficient δ. After simple computations, we compute the additional costs of the parallel algorithm $H(W, p)$ and get the following isoefficiency function W:

$$H(W,p) = W(\delta - 1) + p\gamma\alpha, \quad W = \Theta(p\gamma(p)).$$

Thus, if $\gamma(p) \leq \gamma_0$, then the scalability of the parallel algorithm is linear.

4.4 COMPUTATIONAL RESULTS

In this section, we present results of numerical experiments. The parabolic problem was solved on the structure presented in Fig. 4.4. It is an artificial network of seven TTL neurons [27], connected into a ring. The whole structure contains 2310 edges and 1603 branching points. The test structure is not large, and therefore the calculations are performed over a long time interval $T = 1000$ with step $\tau = 0.025$. The lengths of the edges are distributed as $1.1 \leq l_k \leq 233.1, k = 1, \ldots, K$. A uniform mesh with the same space mesh step h for each edge e_k is used. Since the lengths of edges differ by more than 200 times, balancing of the sizes of local tasks becomes a very important issue. We note that the quality of partitions done by Metis is very close to 1.

Computations were performed on a cluster of computers, consisting of nodes with an Intel Core processor i7-860 @ 2.80 GHz and 4 GB RAM. Each of the four cores can complete up to four full instructions simultaneously.

The obtained performance results for the parallel fully implicit ($\theta = 1$) solver are presented in Table 4.1. Here, for each number of processes $p = n \times c$, where n denotes

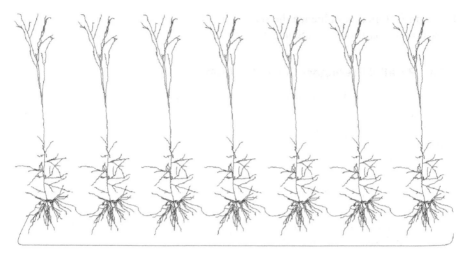

FIGURE 4.4 *Test structure.*

TABLE 4.1 Performance Results for the Parallel Fully Implicit Solver

$p(n \times c)$	1×2	2×1	1×4	2×2	4×1	2×4	4×2	8×1	4×4	8×2	8×4
ϕ	1.02	1.02	1.05	1.05	1.05	1.17	1.17	1.17	1.22	1.22	1.35
$\gamma \times \upsilon$	1×5	1×5	3×3	3×3	3×3	4×4	4×4	4×4	4×7	4×7	5×4
					7 Cells, $h = 1$, $T_0 = 374$						
T_p	193	211	110	121	132	75	89	99	56	69	70
S_p	1.94	1.77	3.40	3.09	2.83	4.99	4.20	3.78	6.72	5.42	5.34
E_p	0.97	0.87	0.85	0.77	0.71	0.62	0.53	0.47	0.42	0.34	0.17
					7 Cells, $h = 0.5$, $T_0 = 686$						
T_p	359	368	203	208	207	119	130	138			81
S_p	1.91	1.86	3.38	3.30	3.31	5.76	5.28	4.97	10.7	10.3	8.47
E_p	0.96	0.93	0.84	0.82	0.83	0.72	0.66	0.62	0.68	0.65	0.26
					14 Cells, $h = 1$, $T_0 = 767$						
ϕ	1.00	1.00	1.02	1.02	1.02	1.08	1.08	1.08	1.18	1.18	1.19
$\gamma \times \upsilon$	1×2	1×2	2×6	2×6	2×6	4×4	4×4	4×4	4×6	4×6	7×8
T_p	393	395	222	212	227	126	140	149	94	112	93
S_p	1.87	1.94	3.45	3.62	3.38	6.09	5.48	5.15	8.16	6.85	8.25
E_p	0.94	0.97	0.86	0.90	0.84	0.76	0.68	0.64	0.51	0.43	0.26

the number of nodes and c the number of cores per node, the coefficients of the algorithmic speedup $S_p = T_0/T_p$ and efficiency $E_p = S_p/p$ are presented. T_p denotes the CPU time required to solve the problem by using p processes. $\gamma \times \upsilon$ denotes the worst case of communications amount: γ is the largest number of neighbors a process shares vertices with, and v the largest number of vertices shared with the same neighbor. This data is supplied for every case of partition.

Two different space steps were used to generate the discrete spatial mesh. First, we present performance results with a spatial step value $h = 1$. The results of the computational experiments agree well with the theoretical model of the complexity of the parallel implicit algorithm. The reduction in efficiency is justified by the worse quality of the load balancing of vertices, the reduced amount of local calculations, and the increased number of neighbors to exchange data with. The degradation of the efficiency of the usage on nodes with less number of cores is due to the PPCG communications costs, which can be crucial in this case.

In the second experiment, computations are performed with half the spatial step value. This increases the amount of local calculations without increasing the communication part, and hence the efficiency also increases, as expected.

In the last series of computations, the influence of costs due to the PPCG algorithm was investigated; therefore, the test structure was doubled by taking 14 cells. The slight increase in efficiency compared to the second series shows that algorithms efficiency can be improved even when a larger system of linear equations is solved with sufficiently good partition quality. This can be explained by fact that the amount of communications is not increased because a larger network is easier to partition.

In Table 4.2, the performance results for the parallel predictor–corrector solver I are presented. We see that the efficiency of the algorithm is higher than that obtained for the parallel implicit algorithm because of the reduced communications between processes. We see some superlinear speedup of the parallel algorithm when more nodes (not cores) are used in the computations. This effect is explained by a better memory caching for smaller subproblems solved on each node. The degradation of the efficiency of the usage of cores for configurations $n \times 2$ and $n \times 4$ is due to the

TABLE 4.2 Performance Results for the Parallel Predictor–Corrector I Solver

$p(n \times c)$	1×2	2×1	1×4	2×2	4×1	2×4	4×2	8×1	4×4	8×2	8×4
					7 Cells, $T_0 = 374$						
ϕ	1.02	1.02	1.06	1.06	1.06	1.17	1.17	1.17	1.26	1.26	1.46
γ	1	1	3	3	3	5	5	5	5	5	7
T_p	188	187	105	96	95	54	50	49	29	27	16
S_p	1.99	2.00	3.56	3.90	3.94	6.92	7.48	7.63	12.9	13.9	23.4
E_p	0.99	1.00	0.89	0.97	0.98	0.87	0.94	0.95	0.81	0.87	0.73
					14 Cells, $T_0 = 767$						
ϕ	1.00	1.00	1.02	1.02	1.02	1.08	1.08	1.08	1.18	1.18	1.22
γ	1	1	2	2	2	3	3	3	4	4	7
T_p	384	373	214	190	188	106	101	95	55	50	29
S_p	2.00	2.06	3.58	4.04	4.08	7.24	7.59	8.07	14.0	15.3	26.4
E_p	1.00	1.03	0.90	1.01	1.02	0.91	0.95	1.01	0.87	0.96	0.83

TABLE 4.3   Performance Results for the Parallel Predictor–Corrector II Solver

$p(n \times c)$	1×2	2×1	1×4	2×2	4×1	2×4	4×2	8×1	4×4	8×2	8×4
					7 Cells, $T_0 = 303$						
γ	1	1	3	3	3	5	5	5	5	5	7
T_p	153	153	86	80	80	44	43	42	24	23	14
S_p	1.98	1.98	3.52	3.79	3.79	6.87	7.05	7.21	12.6	13.2	21.6
E_p	0.99	0.99	0.88	0.95	0.95	0.86	0.88	0.90	0.79	0.82	0.68
					14 Cells, $T_0 = 612$						
γ	1	1	2	2	2	3	3	3	4	4	7
T_p	318	304	176	156	154	87	83	80	45	43	25
S_p	1.93	2.01	3.48	3.92	3.97	7.03	7.37	7.65	13.6	14.2	24.5
E_p	0.96	1.01	0.87	0.98	0.99	0.88	0.92	0.96	0.85	0.89	0.77

memory bus saturation (bottleneck effect). It is interesting to note that the efficiency of the cores is decreased even in a part of investigated cases as the problem size is increased. This trend is opposite to the general scalability result that the efficiency of a parallel algorithm increases when the size of a problem increases for a fixed number of processes. More results on the theoretical and computational analysis of this effect are given in [28, 29]. We note that the bottleneck effect was not observed for this experiment on other clusters consisting of Intel Core 2 processors Quad Q6600 (but the CPU time was longer in this case).

In Table 4.3, the performance results for the parallel predictor–corrector solver II are presented. The super-linear speedup is also observed for a larger problem. In order to test the caching effect, we have solved sequential test problems of sizes N, $N/2$, $N/4$, and $N/8$. We got the following CPU times (in seconds):

$$T_1(N) = 945, T_1(N/2) = 467, T_1(N/4) = 225, T_1(N/8) = 112.$$

These results clearly show the memory caching effect.

4.4.1   Experimental Comparison of Predictor–Corrector Algorithms

The parallel predictor–corrector algorithms show the best performance results and are simpler to implement. Should we recommend them for practical use? The accuracy of the predictor–corrector Algorithm II was investigated experimentally in [17], where the authors presented calculation results showing a convergence rate of $\mathcal{O}(\tau + h^2)$ for the backward Euler underlying scheme and $\mathrm{O}(\tau^2 + h^2)$ for Crank–Nicolson. In [24], we proved the conditional convergence rate of the predictor–corrector algorithm for the linear parabolic problem due to the truncation error $\mathcal{O}(\frac{\tau\sqrt{\tau}}{h^2})$ introduced at the predictor step. Experimental calculations showed that the total convergence rate was slightly better: $\tau + h^2 + \frac{\tau^2}{h}$. Here, we show that the calculation results for the nonlinear problem confirm our assumption on conditional convergence rate in the general case.

For the convergence test, the following nonlinear problem was used:

$$\frac{\partial u^k}{\partial t} = \frac{\partial}{\partial x}\left(d^k \frac{\partial u^k}{\partial x} \right) - q^k u^k + f^k, \quad 0 < x < l_k, k = 1, \dots, K,$$

$$0 < d_0 \le d^k(x) \le d_M, q^k(x, m, n, h) \ge 0, \quad f^k = f^k(x, m, n, h),$$

$$\frac{dm}{dt} = f_1(u^k), \frac{dn}{dt} = f_2(u^k), \frac{dh}{dt} = f_3(u^k),$$

$$u^k(x, 0) = u_0^k(x), \quad 0 < x < l_k, k = 1, \dots, K$$

$$u^k(p_j; t) = \mu_j(t), \quad \forall p_j \in T$$

with known solutions

$$u^k(x, t) = \left(\frac{x}{l_k} \right)^2 \left(1 - \frac{x}{l_k} \right)^2 \exp(t).$$

Functions $f_1(u)$, $f_2(u)$, $f_3(u)$, and $f^k(x, m, n, h)$ were chosen to get the conditionally linear problem

$$d^k(x) = 1 + \frac{x}{l_k}, \quad q^k = m,$$

$$f^k(x, m, n, h) = n + h + -\frac{2t}{l_k^2}\left(8\left(\frac{x}{l_k}\right)^3 - 3\left(\frac{x}{l_k}\right)^2 - 4\left(\frac{x}{l_k}\right) + 1 \right),$$

$$f_1(u^k) = 2u^k + 1, \quad f_2(u^k) = 3(u^k)^2, \quad f_3(u^k) = 2u^k.$$

The lengths of the test structure vary by more than 200 times, and that is why the application of the uniform spatial grid requires a small value of the step h. Experimental calculations show that the same accuracy is obtained by applying a quasi-uniform grid when every edge is divided into N parts.

In Table 4.4, the experimental convergence rates of the predictor–corrector Algorithm II are presented.

The conditional approximation of the predictor–corrector scheme is obvious. The dominating part of the global error in the first column is $\frac{C}{h}$, and in the last one Ch^2. The error in this scheme can be reduced not only by reducing the step τ but also by increasing the spatial step h. The least global error in this experiment got by the latter method was with a value $N = 5$. A higher accuracy requires reducing the step τ. For example, the solution with accuracy 10^{-2} is obtained with $\tau = 0.0125$ per 1 s, exactly as in the case of the fully implicit Euler. The dynamics of the global error of the predictor–corrector method in maximum norm with various fixed τ values is presented in Fig. 4.5. Here, Fig. 4.5a presents the error for quasi-uniform grids, and Fig. 4.5b presents the global error with uniform spatial grid; in fact, the grid

TABLE 4.4 Global Errors of the Solution of a Nonlinear Problem for Predictor–Corrector Scheme in Maximum Norm

N	$\tau = 0.2$	$\tau = 0.1$	$\tau = 0.05$	$\tau = 0.0125$	$\tau = 0.003125$
5	0.1763	0.13090	0.12542	0.12621	0.12705
10	0.19201	0.08783	0.04110	0.03461	0.03588
20	0.28073	0.08783	0.04110	0.00968	0.00960
40	0.47006	0.16544	0.04459	0.00967	0.00260
80	0.66175	0.29959	0.09359	0.00967	0.00238

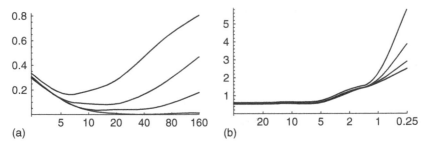

(a) (b)

FIGURE 4.5 *Predictor–corrector error $\|Z(t = 2)\|_\infty$ with a fixed step τ. (a) Quasi-uniform spatial grid (horizontal axis indicates the division number N). (b) Uniform spatial grid (step h). Values of τ are 0.2, 0.1, 0.05, and 0.0125.*

is not actually uniform in this case: the shortest edges with length $l_k < 2h$ are also divided into two parts. The smallest possible absolutely uniform grid is with the step $h = 0.55$; however, because of the conditional approximation, the global error is large in this case.

Besides a very simple implementation and the good parallelization properties of the predictor–corrector Algorithm II, one more advantage is the CPU time, since no system of linear equations need be solved for the vertices. However, while applying the special methods for the sparse matrices (i.e., conjugate gradient method), the complexity of this part is also $\mathcal{O}(J)$ for large, highly branched structures. Considering the conditional convergence rate of the method, we conclude that the traditional implicit Euler and Crank–Nicolson methods are preferable for use in applications.

4.4.2 Numerical Experiment of Neuron Excitation

The numerical experiment of the excitation of the neuron cell was performed using the Crank–Nicolson scheme. We used the realistic model of TTL5 neuron [27], which involves more than a dozen different ionic currents for different types of compartments. This complicates the load balancing task because different ionic channels are intrinsic for different compartments (dendrites, axons, etc.), and hence the update price differs for different types of cell compartments (see [27] for the detailed model). We address this issue by evaluating the coefficients update price for each ionic current and assigning the appropriate weights to the edges of the graph.

TABLE 4.5 Performance Results for the Parallel Crank–Nicolson Solver for the Nonlinear Model

$p(n \times c)$	1×2	2×1	1×4	2×2	4×1	2×4	4×2	8×1	4×4	8×2
ϕ	1.05	1.05	1.31	1.31	1.31	1.75	1.75	1.75	2.24	2.24
$\gamma \times v$	1×5	1×5	3×4	3×4	3×4	3×6	3×6	3×6	4×8	4×8
				7 Cells, $T_0 = 2429$						
T_p	1266	1242	748	666	645	423	386	371	241	221
S_p	1.92	1.96	3.25	3.65	3.77	5.74	6.29	6.55	10.1	11.0
E_p	0.96	0.97	0.81	0.91	0.94	0.72	0.79	0.82	0.63	0.69

The efficiency of the parallel algorithm for a nonlinear problem can be compared with the results for the fully implicit Euler algorithm presented in Table 4.1, because only one iteration is performed. Again, we compare the worst case of a small network. The efficiency is expected to increase because the amount of local calculations increases: calculations of nonlocal coefficients are fully parallelized and the communication part remains the same. The results for the parallel Crank–Nicolson algorithm are presented in Table 4.5.

As expected, the results for the nonlinear problem show higher efficiency.

4.5 CONCLUSIONS

Three parallel numerical algorithms have been developed for the solution of parabolic problems on graphs, suitable for structures containing closed loops. The θ-implicit and two predictor–corrector finite difference schemes were proposed to approximate the differential equation. The parallelization of the discrete algorithms was based on the domain decomposition method. Theoretical investigation and the results of numerical experiments showed good scalability of all algorithms.

The predictor–corrector algorithms based on graph decomposition showed the best performance results. Also, the superlinearity effect due to the memory caching effect was observed. We note that the relation between spatial and time steps is needed for predictor–corrector type algorithms because of the conditional convergence rate.

The θ-implicit algorithm, though not the simplest case for parallelization, imposes no restrictions on the integration steps and also shows good efficiency and scalability results. This algorithm is well scalable on large networks of neurons since a large network can be partitioned efficiently without increasing the number of shared vertices and consequently the communication costs of the PPCG algorithm. We proved that the efficiency reduction occurs mainly because of the memory bus saturation when two or four cores per node are used. As expected, the efficiency of the parallel algorithm is higher for nonlinear problems.

ACKNOWLEDGMENTS

This work was supported by the COST Action IC0805 "Open European Network for High Performance Computing on Complex Environments." Partial support was also provided by the Eureka project E!6799 POWEROPT "Mathematical modelling and optimization of electrical power cables for the improvement of their design rules."

The authors would like to thank the referee for his constructive criticism, which helped to improve the clarity and quality of this chapter.

REFERENCES

1. E. Izhikevich, *Dynamical Systems in Neuroscience*. Cambridge, MA: Computational Neuroscience, MIT Press, 2007.
2. C. Koch, *Biophysics of Computation: Information Processing in Single Neurons*, *Computational Neuroscience Series*, New York: Oxford University Press, 2004.
3. C. Koch and I. Segev, *Methods in Neuronal Modeling: From Synapses to Networks*. Cambridge, MA: A Bradford Book, MIT Press, 1998.
4. A. L. Hodgkin and A. F. Huxley, "A quantitative description of membrane current and its application to conduction and excitation in nerve," *Journal of Physiology*, vol. 117, no. 4, pp. 500–544, 1952.
5. J. Bower and D. Beeman, *The Book of GENESIS: Exploring Realistic Neural Models with the GEneral NEural Simulation System*. New York: TELOS, 1995.
6. M. Hanslien, K. H. Karlsen, and A. Tveito, "A maximum principle for an explicit finite difference scheme approximating the Hodgkin-Huxley model," *BIT Numerical Mathematics*, vol. 45, no. 4, pp. 725–741, 2005.
7. N. T. Carnevale and M. L. Hines, *The NEURON Book*. Cambridge: Cambridge University Press, 2006.
8. W. Lytton and M. Hines, "Independent variable timestep integration of individual neurons for network simulations," *Neural Computation*, vol. 17, pp. 903–921, 2005.
9. W. Rall, "Theoretical significance of dendritic trees for neuronal input-output relations," in *Neural Theory and Modeling* (R. Reiss, ed.), Stanford: Stanford University Press, 1964.
10. M. Hines, "Efficient computation of branched nerve equations," *International Journal of Bio-Medical Computing*, vol. 15, no. 1, pp. 69–76, 1984.
11. T. Fukuda, T. Kosaka, W. Singer, and R. A. W. Galuske, "Gap junctions among dendrites of cortical gabaergic neurons establish a dense and widespread intercolumnar network," *Journal of Neuroscience*, vol. 26, no. 13, pp. 3434–3443, 2006.
12. F. Hamzei-Sichani, N. Kamasawa, W. G. M. Janssen, T. Yasumura, K. G. V. Davidson, P. R. Hof, S. L. Wearne, M. G. Stewart, S. R. Young, M. A. Whittington, J. E. Rash, and R. D. Traub, "Gap junctions on hippocampal mossy fiber axons demonstrated by thin-section electron microscopy and freeze-fracture replica immunogold labeling," *Proceedings of the National Academy of Sciences of the United States of America*, vol. 104, no. 30, pp. 12548–12553, 2007.
13. C. B. McCracken and D. C. S. Roberts, "Neuronal gap junctions: Expression, function, and implications for behavior," in *International Review of Neurobiology* (R. J. Bradley, R. A. Harris, and P. Jenner, eds.), Vol. 73, pp. 125–151, San Diego, CA: Academic Press, 2006.

14. M. Mascagni, "A parallelizing algorithm for computing solutions to arbitrarily branched cable neuron models," *Journal of Neuroscience Methods*, vol. 36, no. 1, pp. 105–114, 1991.

15. P. Vabishchevich, "Domain decomposition methods with overlapping subdomains for the time-dependent problems of mathematical physics," *Computational Methods in Applied Mathematics*, vol. 8, no. 4, pp. 393–405, 2008.

16. P. Vabishchevich, "A substructuring domain decomposition scheme for unsteady problems," *Computational Methods in Applied Mathematics*, vol. 11, no. 2, pp. 241–268, 2011.

17. M. Rempe and D. Chopp, "A predictor-corrector algorithm for reaction-diffusion equations associated with neural activity on branched structures," *SIAM Journal on Scientific Computing*, vol. 28, no. 6, pp. 2139–2161, 2006.

18. H. Shi and H. Liao, "Unconditional stability of corrected explicit-implicit domain decomposition algorithms for parallel approximation of heat equations," *SIAM Journal on Numerical Analysis*, vol. 44, no. 4, pp. 1584–1611, 2006.

19. M. Migliore, C. Cannia, W. Lytton, H. Markram, and M. Hines, "Parallel network simulations with NEURON," *Journal of Computational Neuroscience*, vol. 21, pp. 110–119, 2006.

20. Y. Zhuang and X. Sun, "Stabilized explicit-implicit domain decomposition methods for the numerical solution of parabolic equations," *SIAM Journal on Scientific Computing*, vol. 24, no. 1, pp. 335–358, 2002.

21. R. Brette, M. Rudolph, T. Carnevale, M. Hines, D. Beeman, J. Bower, M. Diesmann, A. Morrison, P. Goodman, J. Harris, C. Frederick, M. Zirpe, T. Natschlger, D. Pecevski, B. Ermentrout, M. Djurfeldt, A. Lansner, O. Rochel, T. Vieville, E. Muller, A. Davison, S. El Boustani, and A. Destexhe, "Simulation of networks of spiking neurons: a review of tools and strategies," *Journal of Computational Neuroscience*, vol. 23, no. 3, pp. 349–398, 2007.

22. R. Čiegis and N. Tumanova, "Finite-difference schemes for parabolic problems on graphs," *Lithuanian Mathematical Journal*, vol. 50, no. 2, pp. 164–178, 2010.

23. R. Čiegis and N. Tumanova, "Stability analysis of implicit finite-difference schemes for parabolic problems on graphs," *Numerical Functional Analysis and Optimization*, vol. 33, no. 1, pp. 1–20, 2012.

24. N. Tumanova and R. Čiegis, "Predictor-corrector domain decomposition algorithm for parabolic problems on graphs," *Mathematical Modelling and Analysis*, vol. 17, no. 1, pp. 113–127, 2012.

25. G. Karypis and V. Kumar, "A fast and high quality multilevel scheme for partitioning irregular graphs," *SIAM Journal on Scientific Computing*, vol. 20, no. 1, pp. 359–392, 1999.

26. R. Trobec, M. Vajteršic, and P. Zinterhof, *Parallel Computing: Numerics, Applications, and Trends*. London: Springer, 2009.

27. E. Hay, S. Hill, F. Schürmann, H. Markram, and I. Segev, "Models of neocortical layer 5b pyramidal cells capturing a wide range of dendritic and perisomatic active properties," *PLoS Computational Biology*, vol. 7, no. 7, pp. 1–18, 2011.

28. R. Čiegis, R. Čiegis, M. Meilūnas, G. Jankevičiutė, and V. Starikovičius, "Parallel numerical algorithms for optimization of electrical cables," *Mathematical Modelling and Analysis*, vol. 13, no. 4, pp. 471–482, 2008.

29. V. Starikovičius, R. Čiegis, and O. Iliev, "A parallel solver for optimization of oil filters," *Mathematical Modelling and Analysis*, vol. 16, no. 2, pp. 326–342, 2011.

Communication and Storage Considerations in High-Performance Computing

5

An Overview of Topology Mapping Algorithms and Techniques in High-Performance Computing

Torsten Hoefler

ETH Zürich, Zürich, Switzerland

Emmanuel Jeannot

Inria Bordeaux Sud-Ouest, Talence, France

Guillaume Mercier

Bordeaux Polytechnic Institute, Talence, France; Inria Bordeaux Sud-Ouest, Talence, France

With the advent of modern hardware architectures of high-performance computers, the way the parallel applications are laid out is of paramount importance for performance. This chapter surveys several techniques and algorithms that efficiently address this issue: the mapping of the application's virtual topology (e.g., its communication pattern) onto the physical topology. Using such a strategy enables the improvement of the applications overall execution time significantly. The chapter concludes by listing a series of open issues and problems.

High-Performance Computing on Complex Environments, First Edition.
Edited by Emmanuel Jeannot and Julius Žilinskas.
© 2014 John Wiley & Sons, Inc. Published 2014 by John Wiley & Sons, Inc.

5.1   INTRODUCTION

High-performance computing (HPC) applications are becoming increasingly demanding in terms of computing power. Currently, this computing power can be delivered by parallel computers only. At the same time, the trends in processors and parallel architecture design lead to an increase in the number of computing cores. Therefore, exploiting efficiently such a complex hardware, that is, bridging the performance gap between the target machine level and the application level, is a challenging issue. Moreover, current and future generations of applications will have to tackle this challenge in order to scale up because of the expected increase in concurrency in the applications and the input data size. As a consequence, the way the application data are organized, accessed, and moved is of paramount importance and should be improved and optimized. This *locality* issue exists at several levels: besides the application data layout, locality issues also stem from the use of multicore nodes (which feature a hierarchical memory organization), as well as network and storage units. Since the time to transfer data between *processing entities* (e.g., processes or threads) of the application depends on both the affinity of these entities and their respective locations, a thorough analysis of the application behavior (datawise) and of the platform on which it is executed is necessary. Given both pieces of information, clever algorithms and techniques can dramatically improve the application communication time by carefully mapping the application processing entities on the various processing units (e.g., CPUs or cores) of the architecture. The goal of this chapter is to provide an overview of this *topology mapping* issue and to present the various techniques and solutions existing in the literature. This chapter is divided into the following six parts: first, we present an overview of the problem in Section 5.2. Then, in Section 5.3 we show a possible formalization of the problem. Section 5.4 presents the existing algorithms that can yield solutions to the topology mapping problem, while Section 5.5 exposes the various techniques that applications can leverage to enforce the mapping computed by the algorithm. Section 5.6 describes the existing software implementing the algorithms and the techniques seen in the previous sections. Lastly, in Section 5.7 we present a set of open problems and research issues that need to be addressed in order to pave the road to Exascale.

5.2   GENERAL OVERVIEW

HPC is more than ever a cornerstone of the development and competitiveness of modern knowledge-based societies and economies. In both fields of science and technology, it is necessary to solve problems requiring tremendous amounts of computing power, memory, and storage. From an industrial perspective, parallel computers are mandatory to reduce the time to market of a large array of products (e.g., cars, drugs, planes), while from a research perspective simulations are required to refine models in order to solve larger problems at longer and finer time scales. Therefore, many scientific domains have already been identified as requiring large amounts of computing power, as for instance by the PRACE research infrastructure [1], which has selected the following five domains: (i) weather, climatology, and solid earth sciences; (ii) astrophysics, high-energy physics, and plasma physics; (iii) materials science, chemistry, and nanoscience; (iv) life sciences and medicine; (v) engineering sciences and industrial applications. Parallel architectures are the only ones that are capable of delivering the much sought-after computing power.

5.2.1 A Key to Scalability: Data Locality

However, to harness the resources of a parallel computer is by no means a trivial undertaking because multiple challenges need to be addressed, one of the hardest being to jump on to the multicore/many-core bandwagon: the size of the machines in terms of number of cores per node is increasing. Exascale computers are expected to feature between hundreds of thousands and millions of nodes, each them integrating between a hundred and tens of thousands of cores. Dealing with such large scales is very challenging. Current generations of machines are already hierarchical, both in terms of network interconnection and memory architecture (cache level, nonuniform access, coherency, etc.), and future generations of machines will feature even deeper hierarchies. As a consequence, the challenge deals with scalability and can be expressed in several ways: how to use maximally the available resources (e.g., CPUs, cores, memory, network) at their full potential, and how to do so with an energy consumption that remains (economically and environmentally) acceptable. One global and practical answer to these questions is to improve the *data locality* of parallel applications, that is, the way the data are placed, accessed, and moved by the multiple hardware processing units of the underlying target architecture.

This is coherent with the behavior of a parallel application that dispatches its workload among *software processing entities* (e.g., tasks, processes, threads) running in parallel on the *hardware processing units* of the target architecture. These processing entities access and exchange data during the application's execution but not necessarily in a regular manner. As a consequence, these data accesses and exchanges can be optimized to fully exploit the hardware. For instance, entities exchanging or sharing lots of data could be placed on hardware processing units physically close to each other. By doing so, the communication costs are reduced, thus decreasing the application's overall execution time, as also, as a consequence, its energy consumption, as emphasized by the IESP roadmap [2]: "*Since much of the power in an Exascale system will be expended moving data, both locally between processors and memory as well as globally, the X-stack must provide mechanisms and APIs for expressing and managing data locality. These will also help minimize the latency of data accesses.*"

5.2.2 Data Locality Management in Parallel Programming Models

One other possible answer to the scalability issue would be to use a new parallel programming paradigm. However, currently, no existing paradigm seems viable, as parallel application developers still rely on proven and widely used tools created years ago. This fact is a consequence of a software inertia as well as the huge number of existing legacy applications.

Nevertheless, data locality has to be taken into account to improve the scalability of present and future parallel applications, regardless of the chosen paradigm. Hence, current existing paradigms can be improved/enhanced to better express this locality management. They indeed offer a simplified view of the architecture: the message passing interface (MPI) relies on a distributed memory model with a flat network, while OpenMP uses a global address space and partitioned global address space (PGAS) languages use, similar to MPI, a flat, partitioned address space. As a consequence, the gap between the underlying hardware and the simple view exposed by the programming model widens. To bridge this gap, paradigm implementations should first be optimized to better reflect the locality management and, second, these paradigms' definition and utilization (locality-wise) should be more specific.

More precisely, the necessary interactions between the applications (relying on paradigm implementations) and the underlying hardware should be explicitly defined and expressed in a synthetic manner. Improving an application's data locality may carry different results, depending on the context and on the programming paradigm used. For instance, in the realm of message-passing-based applications, it may lead to a decrease of the overall communication costs, while for applications based on multithreading the expected results will be a better sharing of the data between the application threads. This implies better use of the underlying hardware: the network, the memory hierarchy, and, of course, the processing units available.

5.2.3 Virtual Topology: Definition and Characteristics

A simple, yet efficient way to improve data locality is to dedicate physical processing units to their specific software processing entities. This means that a *matching* between the applications virtual topology and the target hardware architecture has to be determined. In this chapter, the expression *virtual topology* designates a means to express the existing *dependencies between software processing entities*. For instance, in programming paradigms with explicit communications (e.g., as in message passing), these dependencies are expressed as messages exchanged between processes, while for implicit communications paradigms (e.g., OpenMP) these dependencies are expressed as accesses to common memory locations by the application threads. This virtual topology representation is also tailored for task-based programming environments, as the various tasks depend on each other: indeed, a task can be scheduled only once a set of "previous" tasks is completely executed. Virtual topologies are also often referred to as application *communication patterns*.

Such communication patterns can be either *static* or *dynamic*. Static means that the number of processing entities remains constant during the course of the application and that the dependencies between these entities do not change between consecutive application steps. The pattern can be qualified as dynamic when one of the two above conditions (possibly both) is not fulfilled. For instance, an OpenMP-based application features a dynamic pattern since new threads are created/destroyed when entering/exiting each new parallel section. This communication pattern (or virtual topology) can be considered as a key characteristic of the application [3].

5.2.4 Understanding the Hardware

If, on one hand, understanding the behavior of the application is necessary, on the other, the maximum details regarding the target hardware have to be gathered. Achieving this in a convenient and portable manner is of paramount importance in order to address the largest spectrum possible of parallel architectures. This issue is increasingly complex because of the advent of multicore/many-core CPUs. Indeed, parallel computers used to follow the cluster paradigm that possessed an architectural complexity only at the network level. But multicore CPUs pushed the envelope further because of their intricate and hierarchical memory organization, inducing NUMA (nonuniform memory access) effects. Performance of data accesses and movements between processing units is now heterogeneous. As a consequence, both the physical network topology *and* the multicore node internal structure have to be considered in order to efficiently determine the matching between the virtual and the physical topologies.

As a matter of fact, this matching between the virtual and the physical topologies is achievable in both ways: the virtual topology can be mapped onto the physical one, but the physical topology can also be mapped onto the virtual one. The first case corresponds to a resource allocation problem where the software processing entities have to be mapped onto their hardware processing counterparts. This problem is usually referred to as a *process mapping* issue. In the second case, the hardware can be tailored to fit the application structure (virtual topology). This is feasible with software-reconfigurable networks, for instance.

Hence, the key is to make use of an algorithm/heuristic that yields a satisfactory solution to our topology mapping problem. In the following section, we outline the main algorithms used to compute such mapping as well as environments that application developers can use to apply this mapping.

5.3 FORMALIZATION OF THE PROBLEM

Abstractly seen, the topology mapping problem can be phrased as a minimization problem of various metrics. We will now discuss the static topology mapping problem and later generalize it to a dynamic version that is relevant for task-based environments.

The network is typically modeled by a weighted graph $H = (V_H, \omega_H, \mathcal{R}_H)$, where the set of vertices $V_H \in \mathbb{N}$ represents the execution units and the weighted edges $\omega_H(u, v) \in \mathbb{R}$ with $u, v \in V_H$ represent the weight of the edge between the two vertices u and v. Nonexisting edges can be modeled by the weight zero. The function $\mathcal{R}_H(u, v)$ represents the routing as a probability distribution on the set of simple paths $P(u, v)$ between vertices u and v. Various previous works choose to model the network as a specialized subset of this abstract specification (e.g., the routing function

$\mathcal{R}_H$ is most commonly ignored, and the weights $\omega_H(u, v)$ are often replaced by binary values to indicate the existence of an unweighted edge).

The static application graph is often modeled as a weighted graph $A = (V_A, \omega_A)$, where V_A represents the set of communicating processes and $\omega_A(u, v)$ some metric for the communication between two processes $u, v \in V_A$. There is no general agreement on how application communication is modeled. Some works propose the total message volume of a certain phase of communication, whereas others propose the message size or the number of messages as a model for application communication. Again, almost all previous models fit our general specification.

The topology mapping now considers mappings $\sigma : V_A \rightarrow V_H$, that is, σ assigns each vertex $s \in V_A$ in the application graph a target vertex $t \in V_H$ in the architecture (host) graph. Some works assume σ to be injective or surjective; however, in the general case, it has to be neither (it may map multiple vertices in V_A to the same target vertex in V_H and it may also leave target vertices in V_H unassigned).

Each concrete mapping σ has an associated cost metric, which is typically the target of the optimization (often minimization) problem. As for the communication metrics, there is no general agreement. We distinguish two fundamentally different metrics: dilation and congestion. Informally, dilation is defined as either the maximum or the sum of the pairwise distances of neighbors in A mapped to H. For example, let $d_H(x, y)$ be the shortest distance between vertices $x, y \in V_H$; the weighted sum of the dilation is defined as

$$\sum_{u,v \in V_A} d_H(\sigma(u), \sigma(v)) \times \omega(u, v).$$

We note that the routing function $\mathcal{R}_H$ can increase the dilation if routes are not along the shortest paths. Thus, an algorithm that includes the routing function may find more practical process mappings. The sum (or average) dilation allows a comparison of the number of times packets are transmitted over network interfaces; thus, this metric often correlates strongly with the dynamic energy consumption of the network.

A second fundamental metric is the congestion, which counts how many communication pairs use a certain link. Here, it is necessary to define a routing of messages. However, if $\mathcal{R}_H(u, v)$ is not specified or known, one can always use the shortest path routing between u and v (i.e., all edges on a single shortest path between u and v have routing probability 1, while all other edges have probability 0). Let $p_e(u, v)$ be the probability that any of the routes from u to v crosses an edge $e \in V_H$. Then, we can define the congestion of this edge e as

$$C_e = \sum_{u,v \in V_A} p_e(u, v).$$

Again, we can define various reduction functions to generate an overall measure of congestion across all network links. The most common is a measure for the maximum congestion

$$C_{max} = \max_e C_e,$$

which often correlates strongly with the execution time of bulk-synchronous parallel (BSP) applications.

Optimization algorithms would now strive to minimize any of those metrics in our presented model or a subset thereof. For example, if one was to find a mapping that optimizes dynamic energy consumption, one would strive to minimize dilation, while one would minimize the maximum congestion in order to optimize the completion time of a BSP application.

A simple generalization can be made for tasking systems. Here, the graph A is the data-dependency graph of all active tasks in the system. Static optimizations can be performed as before (we ignore the orthogonal load balancing problem in this regard). If a new task is to be spawned, one could either solve the whole mapping problem from the start with an updated A', or one could place the task heuristically "close" to its neighbors.

5.4 ALGORITHMIC STRATEGIES FOR TOPOLOGY MAPPING

It can be shown that most specific problems of mapping arbitrary A to arbitrary H with regard to any of the metrics are NP-hard. In fact, many of the generic optimization problems can be phrased as a quadratic assignment problem, which belongs, even for highly structured inputs, to the class of strongly NP-hard problems. This means that the problem cannot be approximated well. Using today's solvers, quadratic assignment problems may be solved for very small input instances, but are generally unpractical for data centers or large-scale computing networks.

On the other hand, certain idealized mapping cases can be solved in polynomial time. For example, embedding a $k \times l$ cube (2D torus) into another $k \times l$ cube is simple, or embedding a line of length l into the same cube is simple as well. Numerous works have studied such special and idealized mappings in the past. However, such ideal structures are rarely found in reality. Thus, and because of space constraints, we limit our report to the mapping of arbitrary A to arbitrary H (with some relevant exceptions, such as k-ary n-cubes).

Various heuristics have been developed in the past. This section provides a quick overview of the methods. References to specific works using those methods are provided later. New schemes are invented continuously, making this list a quickly moving target. Such schemes may or may not fit into this classification, but we believe that those classes cover most existing works in the field of topology mapping. Each of those schemes performs well for a certain class of graphs. An exact classification and identification of such graph classes is a subject of ongoing research.

5.4.1 Greedy Algorithm Variants

The probably simplest schemes for mapping are derived from well-known greedy strategies. For example, in a local greedy scheme, one selects two starting vertices $u \in V_H$ and $v \in V_A$, and adds other vertices to the mappings by walking along the neighborhood of both vertices. A global greedy scheme would greedily select the next vertex based on some global property, that is, the weight of all out-edges. One can also mix local and global schemes on the two graphs A and H.

5.4.2 Graph Partitioning

A second general scheme that is often used for topology mapping is graph partitioning. For example, k-way partitioning or its special case bipartitioning (i.e., when k equals 2) can be used to recursively cut both graphs (A and H) into smaller pieces, which are then mapped while unfolding the recursion. A well-known heuristic for bipartitioning is due to Kernighan and Lin [4].

5.4.3 Schemes Based on Graph Similarity

Another class of schemes, first explored in [5], is based on graph similarity. Here, the adjacency lists of the two graphs are permuted into some canonical form (e.g., minimizing the bandwidth of the adjacency matrix using well-known heuristics) such that the two graphs can be mapped on the basis of this similarity.

5.4.4 Schemes Based on Subgraph Isomorphism

Some schemes are based on subgraph isomorphism. For this, we assume that H has more vertices than A, and we try to find a set of target vertices in H to map A to. Several fast algorithms exist for approximating this problem.

5.5 MAPPING ENFORCEMENT TECHNIQUES

In this section, we detail the various techniques that application programmers can use in order to enforce the mapping computed by the dedicated algorithms described in the previous section. We recall that this computation is the outcome of a three-step process:

1. The virtual topology (communication pattern) of the target application is gathered.
2. The physical topology of the target underlying architecture is gathered (or modeled).
3. The matching between both topologies is computed thanks to the relevant algorithm/heuristic, and then applied.

It is worth to be noted that the question of how both pieces of information regarding the topologies are gathered (i.e., the first two aforementioned steps) is out of the scope of this survey which focuses only on the last step. As explained previously, mapping the virtual topology onto the physical one can be achieved by determining the number of the assigned physical processing unit for each of the application's processing elements. As a consequence, enforcing such a mapping comes down to applying a certain *placement policy* for the considered application. In the remainder of this section, we give details about the various techniques that allow a programmer to apply such a placement policy.

5.5.1 Resource Binding

In order to apply the relevant placement policy, one first obvious technique is to bind the processing elements to their dedicated hardware processing units. For instance, in a GNU/Linux-based system, commands such as numactl or taskset fulfill this goal. However, there is no portable solution available across a wide spectrum of systems and architectures. The hardware locality tool (Hwloc) [6] partly solves this problem by providing a generic, system-independent interface that exposes and abstracts the underlying memory hierarchy and processor layout in order to manage the placement of the processing elements. Binding a processing element to its hardware unit is, to some extent, a way of regaining control over the scheduling policy of the operating system. As a matter of fact, when no binding is enforced, the operating system scheduler can swap any processing entity with any processing unit, thus leading to cache misses which may harm performance. Moreover, as the scheduling of processes/threads is not deterministic, the impact on the performance may vary from one run to another: application performance is thus less predictable than in the case of bound entities. For instance, in Table 5.1, we compare the same execution of a Computational Fluid Dynamics application (ZEUS-MP), when either processes are bound to cores or not. We show the mean execution time, the standard deviation, and the coefficient of variation (CV)(i.e., the standard deviation normalized by the mean) for 10 runs and different numbers of iterations. As the means are not equal, only the CV is significant, and we include all data for completeness. We see that in all cases that the CV is lower for the binding case than for the nonbinding case, meaning that binding processes to cores leads to decreased system noise and more stable execution times.

Since it usually relies on commands that are outside the programming paradigm itself (e.g., the process manager in MPI implementations), binding can be performed without any application modifications. However, this induces two issues: first, portability is not guaranteed, as commands may vary from one system to another; second, changing this binding during the course of the application execution can be difficult to achieve in a standard manner.

5.5.2 Rank Reordering

Another technique to enforce the placement policy determined by the matching algorithm is called *rank reordering* [7, 8]. Each processing entity of the parallel application possesses its own identification number. This number can be used, for instance, to exchange data or to synchronize the entities. The rank reordering technique allows the modification of these identification numbers, so as to better reflect the application's virtual topology. Rank reordering does often not rely on external commands/tools of the system and may be part of the programming standard itself (e.g., in MPI). Therefore, legacy applications have to be modified to take advantage of this technique, as

TABLE 5.1   Statistics for 10 Runs of ZEUS-MP/2 CFD Application with 64 Processes (MHD Blast Case) Comparing the Binding Case and the Nonbinding Case[a]

Number of Iterations	No Binding			Binding		
	Mean	Standard Deviation	Coefficient of Variation	Mean	Standard Deviation	Coefficient of Variation
2000	2.8627	0.127	0.044	2.6807	0.062	0.023
3000	4.1691	0.112	0.027	4.0023	0.097	0.024
4000	5.4724	0.069	0.013	5.2588	0.052	0.010
5000	7.3187	0.289	0.039	6.8539	0.121	0.018
10,000	13.9583	0.487	0.035	13.3502	0.194	0.015
15,000	20.4699	0.240	0.012	19.8752	0.154	0.008
20,000	27.0855	0.374	0.014	26.3821	0.133	0.005
25,000	33.7065	0.597	0.018	32.8058	0.247	0.008
30,000	40.6487	0.744	0.018	39.295	0.259	0.007
35,000	46.7287	0.780	0.017	45.7408	0.299	0.007
40,000	53.3307	0.687	0.013	52.2164	0.227	0.004
45,000	59.9491	0.776	0.013	58.8243	0.632	0.011
50,000	66.6387	1.095	0.016	65.3615	0.463	0.007

[a]Courtesy of Jeannot and Mercier.

the scope of these changes varies from one paradigm to another. However, relying on a standard feature ensures portability, transparency, and dynamicity since it can be issued multiple times during an application execution.

However, reordering the ranks is not by itself a sufficient means to improve application performance. Indeed, side effects of poor scheduling decisions (cache misses, etc.) can still apply to applications using only rank reordering. That is why a combined use of resource binding and rank reordering is the most sensible combination of techniques to apply the placement policy. This can be achieved in a two-step process: First, processing entities are bound to processing units when the application is launched. For this step, there is no relevant placement policy to apply, since this binding is enforced just to avoid the scheduling side effects. Then, in a second phase (and during the application execution itself), the ranks of the processing entities are effectively reordered according to the results yielded by the matching algorithm.

5.5.3   Other Techniques

Resource binding and rank reordering are the most prevalent schemes in HPC. However, other fields, such as operating systems and distributed systems, may use different mechanisms. For instance, an operating system may observe memory traffic in a NUMA node and move processes closer to their respective memory banks in order to minimize cross-link traffic [9]. Another example would be optimized network placement algorithms [10]. However, a detailed explanation of such techniques, which is outside the realm of HPC, is beyond the scope of this survey.

5.6 SURVEY OF SOLUTIONS

In this section, we provide an overview of work related to the generic topology mapping problem. As mentioned earlier, we have to omit many specialized solutions (e.g., for certain graph classes) because of space constraints. However, we aim at covering all generic topology mapping schemes at a rather high level, and refer to the original publications for details.

We classify each work as either a purely algorithmic solution or as a software implementation (which may include algorithmic work as well). Works that fall in both categories default to the software solution section.

5.6.1 Algorithmic Solutions

The topology mapping problem is often modeled as a *graph embedding problem*: one formulation of the embedding problem is introduced by Hatazaki [11], while the complexity and an algorithm for the embedding problem are discussed by Rosenberg [12].

Bokhari [13] models the mapping problem as a graph isomorphism problem. However, the strategy described ignores edges that are not mapped. It was shown later that such edges can have a detrimental effect on the congestion and dilation of the mapping. Lee and Aggarwal [14] improve those results and define a more accurate model that includes all edges of the communication graph, and propose a two-stage optimization function consisting of initial greedy assignment and later pairwise swaps. Bollinger and Midkiff [15] use a similar model and simulated annealing to optimize topology mappings.

Sudheer and Srinivasan [16] model the optimization problem for minimizing the weighted average dilation metric (called *hop-byte*) as a quadratic assignment problem. However, the conclusion is that only very small instances can be solved by this approach. A heuristic to minimize the average hop distance has been proposed.

Many practical schemes, which will be described in the next section, use recursive partitioning (or bisection as a special case) for topology mapping. However, Simon and Teng [17] show that recursive bisection does not always lead to the best partitions.

5.6.2 Existing Implementations

In this section, we describe existing software packages that can be used to approach the topology mapping problem. We start with a graph partitioning software that can be employed in conjunction with the recursive partitioning schemes. Then, we discuss specialized solutions and analyses for various network topologies, followed by a description of generic mapping software. Finally, we discuss support for topology mapping in current parallel programming frameworks.

5.6.2.1 Graph Partitioning Software
We now list some graph partitioning software packages. The typical use for those packages is the partitioning of large

graphs for the parallelization of scientific computing problems. The heuristics used in those packages may thus not always be suitable for partitioning small graphs.

Metis [18] and its parallel version ParMetis [19] are among the most used and well-established graph partitioners. The Chaco [20] and Zoltan [21] graph partitioners maintained by Sandia National Laboratories employ a variety of different partitioning schemes. SCOTCH [22] is a graph partitioning framework capable of dealing with tree-structured input data (called tleaf) to perform the mapping. Scotch is based on dual recursive bipartitioning. Other graph partitioners, such as Jostle [23], are available but less commonly used in larger software packages.

5.6.2.2 Mapping for Specific Topologies   The mapping problem is often studied in the context of particular network topologies or technologies. We proceed to give a quick overview of current network technologies: Torus networks are used in different variations in IBM's BlueGene series (BG/L, BG/P [24], and BG/Q [25]), Cray's Gemini network [26], and Fujitsu's K computer [27]. A second large class of topologies is the family of fat tree networks [28–30], which is often used in commodity data centers and high-performance interconnects. Fat trees usually offer higher bisection bandwidth than torus networks. The Dragonfly topology [31] and its variants are used in IBM's PERCS system [31, 32] and Cray's Aries network [33], and promises high bisection bandwidth at lower costs. Those three classes of topologies form the basis of most of today's supercomputer networks. Thus, topology mapping schemes should aim at supporting those topologies.

Some research works thus address only generic application topologies (used to express the communication pattern) but consider only the network physical topology for the hardware aspects. Balaji *et al.* [34], Smith and Bode [35], and Yu *et al.* [36] provide mapping strategies and software for BlueGene systems as target architectures. Subramoni *et al.* [37] discuss how to map processes on InfiniBand networks. Other works, by Rashti *et al.* [38], Träff [39], and Ito *et al.* [40] target specifically multicore networks.

Von Alfthan *et al.* [41] target several classes of architectures such as the Cray XT, the BlueGene/P, and the generic multicore networks. They use a custom, nonstandard interface to build the graph representing the topologies, despite the presence of this functionality in MPI. The network topology is gathered dynamically in the case of Cray and IBM hardware, but is considered flat in case of the generic multicore network.

TREEMATCH [42, 43] is an algorithm and a library for performing topology-aware process placement. Its main target is networks of multicore NUMA nodes. It provides a permutation of the processes to the processors/cores in order to minimize the communication cost of the application. It assumes that the topology is a tree and does not require valuation of the topology (e.g., communication speeds). Therefore, TREEMATCH solution is based only on the structure of the application and the topology and is therefore independent of the way communication speeds are assessed. TREEMATCH also implements different placement algorithms that are switched according to the input size in order to provide a fast execution time, allowing dynamic load balancing for instance.

5.6.2.3 Mapping Frameworks/Libraries LibTopoMap [5] is a generic mapping library that implements MPI-2.2's topology interface [44] using various heuristics such as recursive bisection, k-way partitioning, simple greedy strategies, and Cuthill McKee [45] for graph mapping. It introduces the idea of graph mapping based on similarity metrics (e.g., bandwidth of the adjacency matrices) and offers an extensible framework to implement algorithms on InfiniBand, Ethernet, BlueGene, and Cray networks.

MPIPP [46] is a framework dedicated to MPI applications. Its goal is to reduce the communication costs between groups of processes. The original targets of this work are the meta-cluster architectures, but it could be adapted also in the context of multicore nodes if the node internal topology and organization information were to be gathered, which is currently not the case.

The *resource binding* technique is applied for MPI applications in several works. [47] and [48] use it to reduce communication costs in multicore nodes. Both works rely on the SCOTCH [22] partitioning software to compute the mapping. Also, Rodrigues *et al.* [47] use a purely quantitative approach, while the approach in Mercier and Clet-Ortega [48] is qualitative since it uses the *structure* of the memory hierarchy of a node.

Brandfass *et al.* [7] also strive to reduce the communication costs of CFD MPI applications. It uses a so-called *rank reordering* technique, but it is not the same technique that we described in a previous section of this chapter. Indeed, Brandfass *et al.* [7] reorganize the file containing the nodes' name (a.k.a. the *hosts file*), thus changing the way processes are dispatched on the nodes. By doing so, it manages to regroup physically processes that communicate a lot with each other. However, the processes are not bound to dedicated processing units and the application does not actually rely on the reordering mechanism available in the MPI standard (as shown in the next paragraph).

It is also possible to map several types of processing entities. This case occurs when the so-called hybrid programming paradigm is used (e.g., message passing and multithreading). For instance, Dümmler *et al.* [49] explore the issue of hybrid, MPI + OpenMP application multithreaded process mapping.

In some cases, a thorough knowledge of the application is very helpful. For instance, Aktulga *et al.* [50] discuss works on topology-aware mapping of an eigenvalue solver. They conducted an in-depth study of their application and were able to propose a communication model based on the dilatation, the traffic, and the congestion. They show that minimizing these factors by performing a relevant mapping induces execution time gains of upto a factor of 2.5.

5.6.2.4 Topology Mapping Support in the Message Passing Interface
As seen in the previous section, MPI applications are often the target of topology mapping techniques and frameworks. Actually, both leading free MPI-2 implementations, that is, MPICH2 [51] and Open MPI [52], provide options to bind the MPI processes at launch time thanks to their respective process manager (Hydra and ORTE, respectively). The user can choose from among some predefined placement policies [53].

As for vendor implementations, several offer mechanisms that allow the use to better control its execution environment by binding the MPI processes. Cray's [54, 55], HP's [56], and IBM's [57] MPI versions offer this possibility.

As a matter of fact, the MPI standard itself features several functions dealing with virtual topology building and management. Both Cartesian and generic process topologies can be created at the application level, and several of the functions even possess a `reorder` parameter. However, as Träff [39] explains, the actual implementation of these routines is rather trivial and usually does nothing to reorder the processes, except in the case of a few vendor implementations, such as the one provided by NEC [39].

In revision 2.2 of the MPI standard, more scalable versions of the virtual topology creation and management routines have been introduced. For instance, it is the case of the `MPI_Dist_graph_create` function [44]. Implementations actually performing reordering of this routine are available: Mercier and Jeannot [8] rely on the Hwloc tool to gather hardware information and bind processes, while TREEMATCH is in charge of computing the reordering of MPI process ranks. LibTopoMap [5] also implements this part of the MPI interface with various strategies.

There are also specific parts of the MPI standard that can take advantage of an optimized process placement. I/O operations fall in this category, as the process placement can be performed in order to optimize the pattern of accesses to files between the processes. Venkatesan *et al.* [58] describe an implementation of such feature, which is based on an algorithm called *SetMatch* and is a simplified version of the TREEMATCH algorithm.

5.6.2.5 *Other Programming Models and Standards*

Other programming models also address the issue of virtual topology mapping. For instance, CHARM++ [59, 60] features optimizations for specific topologies [61]. CHARM++ also performs dynamic load balancing of internal objects (chares). Such load balancing is done by the CHARM++ runtime system and does not require the modification of specific parts of the application code. Moreover, the load balancer can be chosen and its parameters set at the beginning of the execution. Thanks to CHARM++ modularity, user-defined load balancers can be easily added to the set of existing ones. There are several criteria to perform load balancing. Among the possible ones, a topology-aware load balancing, called *NucoLB* (nonuniform communication costs load balancer), has recently been proposed [62]. The idea is to gather the topology information and to dynamically monitor the volume of data exchanged by the chares. Then, the NucoLB load balancer migrates the chares according to the topology and their affinity in order to reduce the communication cost of the application among and within compute nodes. Results show improvement up to 20% in execution time.

It is also possible to perform topology-aware mapping in PGAS languages (e.g., UPC [63]). PGAS languages expose a simple two-level scheme (local and remote) for memory affinity which can be used to map the processes depending on the exchanged data and the underlying physical topology. Indeed, in some PGAS programs it is possible to know the communication pattern based on the code and the distribution of the data arrays. With this information, it is natural to apply a process mapping algorithm to carefully map the processes onto the architecture.

5.7 CONCLUSION AND OPEN PROBLEMS

In order for modern parallel machines to deliver their peak performance to applications, it is necessary to bridge the increasing gap between programming models and the underlying architecture. Among the various factors influencing the performance, process placement plays a key role, as it impacts the communication time of the application. This problem has gained huge momentum with the appearance of NUMA architectures, as the communication cost between two processes can vary by several orders of magnitude depending on their location.

In this chapter, we have surveyed different techniques, algorithms, and tools to perform a topology-aware process placement. In all cases, the problem consisted in matching the virtual topology (that may represents communication pattern of the application) to the physical topology of the architecture.

While there exist many solutions to address the topology mapping problem, we can list a set of open problems that are needed to be solved in order to reach larger scale machines.

- The first important issue is the ability to handle very large problems. Some HPC applications feature hundreds of thousands of processes. Mapping these processes onto the architecture requires huge computing power. It is therefore necessary to improve the scalability of the algorithms by reducing their complexity and implementing their costliest parts in parallel.

- Fault tolerance is also an important issue because failures are becoming a "normal" feature of current parallel computers. Computing mappings that are able to cope with failures is therefore of high interest. A way to tackle this problem is to couple the fault-tolerant part and the mapping part of the runtime system in order to take joint decisions when necessary.

- Reducing the communication part has a huge impact on the energy consumption, as between 25% and 50% of the energy spent is due to data movement. However, there is a lack studies about the real gain of topology-aware mapping and energy savings. Moreover, it should also be possible to devise energy-centric metrics for this specific problem.

- Many applications have a communication pattern that varies during the execution (dynamic). It should be interesting to study how the mapping can be adapted according to these changes. Several solutions could be tested, from a global remapping requiring migration of the processes and changes of the internal organization of the application (e.g., MPI communicators) to local remapping within a NUMA node with the advantage of being able to distribute this remapping and doing it transparently, application-wise.

- Extracting the communication pattern is a difficult task. It requires a thorough knowledge of the target application or its monitoring in order to extract its pattern. However, other techniques are possible such as source-code analysis through compilation techniques or software engineering techniques (skeleton, component) which, by design, provides important information of the application behavior.

- Another important research issue is the link between the different aspects of process affinity: within node (cache), between nodes (network), and between node and storage. Each of these aspects may incur contradictory objectives in terms of placement. Therefore, it is required to find compromises or to be able to adapt, at runtime, the mapping according to the dominating factor.

ACKNOWLEDGMENT

This work was supported by the COST Action IC0805 "Open European Network for High Performance Computing on Complex Environments."

REFERENCES

1. PRACE, "Prace scientific case for hpc in europe 2012—2020," 2012. http://www.prace-ri.eu/PRACE-The-Scientific-Case-for-HPC (accessed on 02 January 2014).
2. J. Dongarra *et al.*, "The international exascale software project: a call to cooperative action by the global high-performance community," *International Journal of High Performance Computing Applications*, vol. 23, no. 4, pp. 309–322, 2009.
3. C. Ma, Y. M. Teo, V. March, N. Xiong, I. R. Pop, Y. X. He, and S. See, "An approach for matching communication patterns in parallel applications," in *Proceedings of 23rd IEEE International Parallel and Distributed Processing Symposium (IPDPS'09)*. Rome, Italy: IEEE Computer Society Press, 2009.
4. B. W. Kernighan and S. Lin, "An efficient heuristic procedure for partitioning graphs," *Bell System Technical Journal*, vol. 49, no. 2, pp. 291–307, 1970.
5. T. Hoefler and M. Snir, "Generic topology mapping strategies for large-scale parallel architectures," in *ICS* (D. K. Lowenthal, B. R. de Supinski, and S. A. McKee, eds.), pp. 75–84, ACM, Tucson, Arizona: USA, 2011.
6. F. Broquedis, J. Clet-Ortega, S. Moreaud, N. Furmento, B. Goglin, G. Mercier, S. Thibault, and R. Namyst, "Hwloc: a generic framework for managing hardware affinities in HPC applications," in *Proceedings of the 18th Euromicro International Conference on Parallel, Distributed and Network-Based Processing (PDP2010)*. Pisa, Italia: IEEE Computer Society Press, 2010.
7. B. Brandfass, T. Alrutz, and T. Gerhold, "Rank reordering for MPI communication optimization," *Computer & Fluids*, vol. 80, pp. 372–380, 2013.
8. G. Mercier and E. Jeannot, "Improving MPI applications performance on multicore clusters with rank reordering," in *EuroMPI, Lecture Notes in Computer Science*, Vol. 6960, pp. 39–49. Santorini, Greece: Springer, 2011.
9. T. Ogasawara, "NUMA-aware memory manager with dominant-thread-based copying GC," in *Proceedings of the 24th ACM SIGPLAN Conference on Object Oriented Programming Systems Languages and Applications, OOPSLA '09*, pp. 377–390. New York: ACM, 2009.

10. Q. Yin and T. Roscoe, "VF2x: fast, efficient virtual network mapping for real testbed workloads," in *Testbeds and Research Infrastructure: Development of Networks and Communities, Lecture Notes of the Institute for Computer Sciences, Social Informatics and Telecommunications Engineering* (T. Korakis, M. Zink, and M. Ott, eds.), vol. 44, pp. 271–286. Berlin Heidelberg: Springer, 2012.

11. T. Hatazaki, "Rank reordering strategy for MPI topology creation functions," in *Recent Advances in Parallel Virtual Machine and Message Passing Interface, Lecture Notes in Computer Science* (V. Alexandrov and J. Dongarra, eds.), vol. 1497, pp. 188–195. Berlin/Heidelberg: Springer, 1998.

12. A. L. Rosenberg, "Issues in the study of graph embeddings," in *WG'80*, (*London, UK*), pp. 150–176, 1981.

13. S. Bokhari, "On the mapping problem," *IEEE Transactions on Computers*, vol. 30, no. 3, pp. 207–214, 1981.

14. S.-Y. Lee and J. K. Aggarwal, "A mapping strategy for parallel processing," *IEEE Transactions on Computers*, vol. 36, no. 4, pp. 433–442, 1987.

15. S. W. Bollinger and S. F. Midkiff, "Heuristic technique for processor and link assignment in multicomputers," *IEEE Transactions on Computers*, vol. 40, no. 3, pp. 325–333, 1991.

16. C. Sudheer and A. Srinivasan, "Optimization of the hop-byte metric for effective topology aware mapping," in *19th International Conference on High Performance Computing (HiPC)*, pp. 1–9, Pune: India, 2012.

17. H. D. Simon and S.-H. Teng, "How good is recursive bisection?," *SIAM Journal on Scientific Computing*, vol. 18, pp. 1436–1445, 1997.

18. G. Karypis and V. Kumar, "METIS—unstructured graph partitioning and sparse matrix ordering system, version 2.0," Tech. Rep., 1995.

19. K. Schloegel, G. Karypis, and V. Kumar, "Parallel multilevel algorithms for multi-constraint graph partitioning (distinguished paper)," in *Proceedings from the 6th International Euro-Par Conference on Parallel Processing, Euro-Par '00*. pp. 296–310. London: Springer-Verlag, 2000.

20. B. Hendrickson and R. Leland, "The Chaco user's guide: Version 2.0," Tech. Rep. SAND94–2692. Albuquerque, NM: Sandia National Laboratory, 1994.

21. K. Devine, E. Boman, R. Heaphy, B. Hendrickson, and C. Vaughan, "Zoltan data management services for parallel dynamic applications," *Computing in Science & Engineering*, vol. 4, no. 2, pp. 90–97, 2002.

22. F. Pellegrini, "Static mapping by dual recursive bipartitioning of process and architecture graphs," in *Proceedings of SHPCC'94, Knoxville*, pp. 486–493. Tennessee: IEEE, 1994.

23. C. Walshaw and M. Cross, "JOSTLE: parallel multilevel graph-partitioning software—an overview," in *Mesh Partitioning Techniques and Domain Decomposition Techniques* (F. Magoules, ed.), pp. 27–58, Civil-Comp Ltd., 2007. (Invited chapter).

24. N. R. Adiga, M. A. Blumrich, D. Chen, P. Coteus, A. Gara, M. E. Giampapa, P. Heidelberger, S. Singh, B. D. Steinmacher-Burow, T. Takken, M. Tsao, and P. Vranas, "Blue Gene/L torus interconnection network," *IBM Journal of Research and Development*, vol. 49, no. 2, pp. 265–276, 2005.

25. D. Chen, N. A. Eisley, P. Heidelberger, R. M. Senger, Y. Sugawara, S. Kumar, V. Salapura, D. L. Satterfield, B. Steinmacher-Burow, and J. J. Parker, "The IBM Blue Gene/Q interconnection network and message unit," in *Proceedings of 2011 International Conference for High Performance Computing, Networking, Storage and Analysis, SC '11*, pp. 26:1–26:10. New York: ACM, 2011.

26. R. Alverson, D. Roweth, and L. Kaplan, "The Gemini system interconnect," in *Proceedings of the 2010 18th IEEE Symposium on High Performance Interconnects, HOTI '10*, pp. 83–87. Washington, DC: IEEE Computer Society, 2010.

27. Y. Ajima, S. Sumimoto, and T. Shimizu, "Tofu: a 6D mesh/torus interconnect for exascale computers," *IEEE Computer*, vol. 42, no. 11, pp. 36–40, 2009.
28. C. E. Leiserson, "Fat-trees: universal networks for hardware-efficient supercomputing," *IEEE Transactions on Computers*, vol. 34, no. 10, pp. 892–901, 1985.
29. F. Petrini and M. Vanneschi, "K-ary n-trees: High performance networks for massively parallel architectures," In *Proceedings of the 11th International Parallel Processing Symposium, (IPPS'97)*, pp. 87–93, 1997.
30. S. R. Öhring, M. Ibel, S. K. Das, and M. J. Kumar, "On generalized fat trees," in *IPPS '95: Proceedings of the 9th International Symposium on Parallel Processing*, p. 37. Washington, DC: IEEE Computer Society, 1995.
31. J. Kim, W. Dally, S. Scott, and D. Abts, "Cost-efficient dragonfly topology for large-scale systems," *IEEE Micro*, vol. 29, no. 1, pp. 33–40, 2009.
32. B. Arimilli, R. Arimilli, V. Chung, S. Clark, W. Denzel, B. Drerup, T. Hoefler, J. Joyner, J. Lewis, J. Li, N. Ni, and R. Rajamony, "The PERCS high-performance interconnect," in *Proceedings of 18th Symposium on High-Performance Interconnects (HotI'10)*, Google campus, Mountain View, CA, 2010.
33. G. Faanes, A. Bataineh, D. Roweth, T. Court, E. Froese, B. Alverson, T. Johnson, J. Kopnick, M. Higgins, and J. Reinhard, "Cray cascade: a scalable HPC system based on a Dragonfly network," in *Proceedings of the International Conference on High Performance Computing, Networking, Storage and Analysis, SC '12*, pp. 103:1–103:9. Los Alamitos, CA: IEEE Computer Society Press, 2012.
34. P. Balaji, R. Gupta, A. Vishnu, and P. H. Beckman, "Mapping communication layouts to network hardware characteristics on massive-scale Blue Gene systems," *Computer Science—R&D*, vol. 26, no. 3-4, pp. 247–256, 2011.
35. B. E. Smith and B. Bode, "Performance effects of node mappings on the IBM Blue-Gene/L machine," in *Euro-Par, Lecture Notes in Computer Science* (J. C. Cunha and P. D. Medeiros, eds.), vol. 3648, pp. 1005–1013, Springer, Lisboa: Portugal, 2005.
36. H. Yu, I.-H. Chung, and J. E. Moreira, "Blue Gene system software—topology mapping for Blue Gene/L supercomputer," in *SC*, p. 116, ACM Press, Tampa, Florida: USA, 2006.
37. H. Subramoni, S. Potluri, K. Kandalla, B. Barth, J. Vienne, J. Keasler, K. Tomko, K. Schulz, A. Moody, and D. Panda, "Design of a scalable infiniband topology service to enable network-topology-aware placement of processes," in *Proceedings of the 2012 ACM/IEEE Conference on Supercomputing (CDROM)*, p. 12. Salt Lake City, Utah: IEEE Computer Society, 2012.
38. M. J. Rashti, J. Green, P. Balaji, A. Afsahi, and W. Gropp, "Multi-core and network aware MPI topology functions," in *EuroMPI, Lecture Notes in Computer Science*, vol. 6960 (Y. Cotronis, A. Danalis, D. S. Nikolopoulos, and J. Dongarra, eds.), pp. 50–60, Springer, Santorini: Greece, 2011.
39. J. L. Träff, "Implementing the MPI process topology mechanism," in *Supercomputing '02: Proceedings of the 2002 ACM/IEEE conference on Supercomputing*, pp. 1–14. Los Alamitos, CA: IEEE Computer Society Press, 2002.
40. S. Ito, K. Goto, and K. Ono, "Automatically optimized core mapping to subdomains of domain decomposition method on multicore parallel environments," *Computer & Fluids*, vol. 80, pp. 88–93, 2013.
41. S. von Alfthan, I. Honkonen, and M. Palmroth, "Topology aware process mapping," in *Applied Parallel and Scientific Computing, Lecture Notes in Computer Science* (P. Manninen and P. Öster, eds.), vol. 7782. pp. 297–308. Springer, 2013.
42. E. Jeannot and G. Mercier, "Near-optimal placement of MPI processes on hierarchical NUMA architectures," in *Euro-Par 2010-Parallel Processing* (P. D'Ambra, M. Guarracino, and D. Talia, eds.), pp. 199–210. Berlin, Heidelberg: Springer-Verlag, 2010.

43. E. Jeannot, G. Mercier, and F. Tessier, "Process placement in multicore clusters: Algorithmic issues and practical techniques," *IEEE Transactions on Parallel and Distributed Systems*, vol. 99, PrePrints, issn 1045–9219, 2013, doi http://doi.ieeecomputersociety.org/10.1109/TPDS.2013.104, published by the IEEE Computer Society, Los Alamitos, CA: USA.

44. T. Hoefler, R. Rabenseifner, H. Ritzdorf, B. R. de Supinski, R. Thakur, and J. L. Tracff, "The scalable process topology interface of MPI 2.2," *Concurrency and Computation: Practice and Experience*, vol. 23, no. 4, pp. 293–310, 2010.

45. E. Cuthill and J. McKee, "Reducing the bandwidth of sparse symmetric matrices," in *Proceedings of the 1969 24th National Conference, ACM '69*, pp. 157–172. (New York: ACM, 1969.

46. H. Chen, W. Chen, J. Huang, B. Robert, and H. Kuhn, "MPIPP: an automatic profile-guided parallel process placement toolset for SMP clusters and multiclusters," in *ICS* (G. K. Egan and Y. Muraoka, eds.), pp. 353–360, ACM, Cairns: Australia, 2006.

47. E. Rodrigues, F. Madruga, P. Navaux, and J. Panetta, "Multicore aware process mapping and its impact on communication overhead of parallel applications," in *Proceedings of the IEEE Symposium on Computers and Communication*, pp. 811–817, Sousse (Tunisia), 2009.

48. G. Mercier and J. Clet-Ortega, "Towards an efficient process placement policy for MPI applications in multicore environments," in *EuroPVM/MPI, Lecture Notes in Computer Science*, Vol. 5759, pp. 104–115. Espoo, Finland: Springer, 2009.

49. J. Dümmler, T. Rauber, and G. Rünger, "Mapping algorithms for multiprocessor tasks on multi-core clusters," in *Proceedings of the 2008 37th International Conference on Parallel Processing*, pp. 141–148, Portland, Oregon: USA, 2008.

50. H. M. Aktulga, C. Yang, E. G. Ng, P. Maris, and J. P. Vary, "Topology-aware mappings for large-scale eigenvalue problems," in *Euro-Par 2012 Parallel Processing—18th International Conference, Lecture Notes in Computer Science*, (Christos Kaklamanis, Theodore Papatheodorou and Paul Spirakis, eds). Vol. 7484, pp. 830–842. (Rhodes Island, Greece, 2012.

51. Argonne National Laboratory, "MPICH2," 2004, http://www.mcs.anl.gov/mpi/mpich2 (accessed on 02 January 2014).

52. E. Gabriel, G. E. Fagg, G. Bosilca, T. Angskun, J. J. Dongarra, J. M. Squyres, V. Sahay, P. Kambadur, B. Barrett, A. Lumsdaine, R. H. Castain, D. J. Daniel, R. L. Graham, and T. S. Woodall, "Open MPI: goals, concept, and design of a next generation MPI implementation," in *Proceedings of the 11th European PVM/MPI Users' Group Meeting, (Budapest, Hungary)*, pp. 97–104, 2004.

53. J. Hursey, J. M. Squyres, and T. Dontje, "Locality-aware parallel process mapping for multi-core HPC systems," in *2011 IEEE International Conference on Cluster Computing (CLUSTER)*, pp. 527–531. IEEE, Austin, Texas: USA, 2011.

54. National Institute for Computational Sciences, "MPI tips on Cray XT5." http://www.nics.tennessee.edu/user-support/mpi-tips-for-cray-xt5 (accessed on 02 January 2014).

55. G. B. Justin L. Whitt, and M. Fahey, "Cray MPT: MPI on the Cray XT," 2011. http://www.nccs.gov/wp-content/uploads/2011/03/MPT-OLCF11.pdf (accessed on 02 January 2014).

56. D. Solt, "A profile based approach for topology aware MPI rank placement," 2007. http://www.tlc2.uh.edu/hpcc07/Schedule/speakers/hpcc_hp-mpi_solt.ppt (accessed on 02 January 2014).

57. E. Duesterwald, R. W. Wisniewski, P. F. Sweeney, G. Cascaval, and S. E. Smith, "Method and system for optimizing communication in MPI programs for an execution environment," 2008. http://www.faqs.org/patents/app/20080288957 (accessed on 02 January 2014).

58. V. Venkatesan, R. Anand, E. Gabriel, and J. Subhlok, "Optimized process placement for collective I/O operations," in *EuroMPI, Lecture Notes in Computer Science*. Madrid, Spain: Springer, 2013. to appear.
59. L. Kale and S. Krishnan, "CHARM++: a portable concurrent object oriented system based on C++," in *Proceedings of Object-Oriented Programming, Systems, Languages and Applications (OOPSLA) 93*, pp. 91–108. ACM Press, Washington DC: USA, 1993.
60. A. Bhatelé, L. V. Kalé, and S. Kumar, "Dynamic topology aware load balancing algorithms for molecular dynamics applications," in *ICS '09*, pp. 110–116. New York: ACM, 2009.
61. A. Bhatel and L. V. Kal, "Benefits of topology aware mapping for mesh interconnects," *Parallel Processing Letters*, vol. 18, no. 04, pp. 549–566, 2008.
62. L. L. Pilla, C. P. Ribeiro, D. Cordeiro, C. Mei, A. Bhatele, P. O. Navaux, F. Broquedis, J.-F. Méhaut, and L. V. Kale, "A hierarchical approach for load balancing on parallel multi-core systems," in *41st International Conference on Parallel Processing (ICPP)*, pp. 118–127. IEEE, Pittsburgh, Pennsylvania: USA, 2012.
63. U. Consortium, "UPC language specifications, v1.2," in Lawrence Berkeley National Lab Tech Report LBNL-59208, 2005.

6

Optimization of Collective Communication for Heterogeneous HPC Platforms

Kiril Dichev and Alexey Lastovetsky

University College Dublin, Dublin, Ireland

Communication plays a central role in parallel computing algorithms. For collective communication, significant gains in performance can be achieved by implementing topology- and performance-aware collectives. In this chapter, we offer a comprehensive overview of the existing research in this area. We observe both message passing interface (MPI) collectives as well as alternatives from the distributed computing domain. The existing challenges in analytical and experimental solutions for heterogeneous platforms are presented and discussed.

6.1 INTRODUCTION

This chapter describes the existing methods of optimizing communication for modern platforms. The most basic communication operation is the point-to-point communication involving a sender and a receiver. As a higher level of abstraction, collective

High-Performance Computing on Complex Environments, First Edition.
Edited by Emmanuel Jeannot and Julius Žilinskas.
© 2014 John Wiley & Sons, Inc. Published 2014 by John Wiley & Sons, Inc.

communication, which involves the exchange of data among a group of processes, is fundamental in many areas of computing. Parallel implementations of fundamental mathematical kernels such as dense matrix multiplication [1] or three-dimensional fast Fourier transformation rely on collective operations. More recently, the MapReduce construct [2], widely used by Google for indexing of Web pages, is gaining in popularity, and also requires collective operations.

In this chapter, we cover the different research directions for optimizing collective communication operations. We ask the following seemingly simple questions: What are the best practices of implementing an efficient collective operation for a heterogeneous and/or hierarchical platform? How do they differ from efficient implementations for homogeneous platforms? Can the best practices be classified and presented in a clear way? Is there a trend that shows what is and what is not possible in the area of such optimizations for today's complex platforms?

When answering these questions, we focus both on classical high-performance approaches, which invariably revolve around message passing interface (MPI) collectives, and on more recent and efficient communication libraries. The wide range of collective operations (broadcast, reduce, scatter, etc.) and the efficient algorithms for each of them cannot be covered in detail in this chapter. However, it is helpful to demonstrate the common optimizations for heterogeneous networks based on a use case. In this chapter, we consider the popular broadcast operation as such a use case. In a broadcast, a root process sends the same data to a group of other processes. The broadcast operation is complete when the last process in the group has received the data. The efficiency of the operation is measured by how fast the broadcast is completed.

Even for this fundamental collective operation, there is already a large variety of popular implementations [3]. To name a few, there are the linear tree (or chain or pipeline), the binomial tree, or the flat tree algorithm. In this chapter, our choice is the binomial tree algorithm. We show the broadcast of a message in a trivial binomial tree in Fig. 6.1. The main advantage of such an algorithm is that (as shown in Fig. 6.1b) different point-to-point exchanges can be parallelized. While not always optimal, this algorithm is common for small message broadcasts on trivial networks such as single-switch Ethernet clusters.

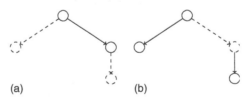

(a)   (b)

FIGURE 6.1 *Broadcast schedule through a binomial tree. (a) In Step 1, the root communicates to its right child. (b) In Step 2, two independent point-to-point exchanges can be performed in parallel to complete the operation.*

6.2   OVERVIEW OF OPTIMIZED COLLECTIVES AND TOPOLOGY-AWARE COLLECTIVES

The general area of communication optimization is very broad and includes a number of different directions. Intuitively, the goal of all such optimization is to reduce the global runtime of the communication operations. But there are different ways to achieve this goal. The vastness of optimizations of MPI collectives has obstructed, rather than helped, any division of the different types of optimizations into categories. For clarity, in this section we specify a few categories of such optimizations in regard to the software layer they are embedded in. MPI [4] is still the most used communication library for high-performance computing (HPC), and we classify all existing approaches in their relation to this library. We present this MPI-centric view in Fig. 6.2. With such a categorization, it is easier to talk of the particular area of interest in this chapter and differentiate it from other works which are also concerned with achieving better performance, but in a different manner.

Optimizations below the MPI layer include tuning of parameters that affect the performance of the underlying protocol. An important example of such tuning [5] demonstrates that the TCP window size has a significant impact on MPI communication on links with a high bandwidth-delay product. Modern grid infrastructures employing fiber optics over very long distances have these properties.

Collective optimizations *within the MPI layer* can be very broad. Some of these are implemented within the MPI library because they require access to hardware-related interfaces. For example, optimizations for Infiniband networks include the use of remote direct memory access calls or multicast calls within MPI [6–8]. Other such optimizations include accessing kernel modules such as CPU affinity to control the migration of MPI processes on cores and others. Also, some protocols such as eager and rendezvous [4], which affect point-to-point and collective operations, are intrinsic to the MPI communication library.

More generic optimized MPI collective algorithms can be implemented *on top of MPI*. The most obvious example is reimplementing a collective based on existing MPI point-to-point calls or MPI collectives.

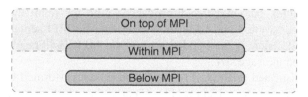

FIGURE 6.2   *Optimizations of collective operations in regard to their relation to MPI — on top, within, or below MPI. In theory, generic optimizations stand above MPI, but in practice their implementation can be either on top of or within the MPI library.*

Still, such generic optimizations are not always implemented on top of MPI, but sometimes are embedded within the MPI layer. The decision to embed an optimization within an MPI implementation in such cases is driven by software development or even political issues rather than strict requirements. For example, some of the optimizations of collectives we list as generic in the next sections are in fact implemented within Open MPI [9].

The main focus of this chapter is as follows:

- *Generic optimizations for collective operations* (Sections 6.6 and 6.7), that is, optimizations not dependent on low-level MPI internals such as hardware or low-level protocol details. As highlighted in Fig. 6.2, they can either be implemented within or on top of the MPI layer.

- *Alternative communication libraries* (Section 6.8) offer interesting optimizations of communication not present, and often not possible, in existing MPI middleware.

In the following section, we present the state of the art in such optimizations of collectives on homogeneous clusters. Then we attempt a structured introduction of the specific area of communication optimizations on heterogeneous networks.

6.3   OPTIMIZATIONS OF COLLECTIVES ON HOMOGENEOUS CLUSTERS

Most optimizations of collective operations on homogeneous clusters focus on finding an efficient algorithm on top of point-to-point primitives. Detailed work analyzing an array of collectives [10] considers the general approaches—analytical (through models) and empirical (through experiments). The model of choice is Hockney (Section 6.7.1), and its point-to-point predictions are used to build prediction formulas for more complex collective operations. However, even seemingly different algorithms often produce predictions of similar time complexity. For this reason, the support of experiments is often needed. The decision-making process is difficult, and depending on the message size and the process number, a range of algorithms can be used for a single collective operation. On the example of the broadcast algorithm, binomial tree broadcast is used for small messages, and a combination of a "scatter" and "allgather" operation (in MPI semantics) for large messages. The decision is hard-coded within the MPICH library[1] based on the process count and message size.

A more sophisticated process of optimization can be performed through a more intelligent, system-specific selection [11]. Clearly, the selection process is good if the selected algorithm is optimal. The optimization consists of the selection from a large set of predefined collective methods. A collective method is considered as the coupling of a particular collective algorithm with a segment size. Formally, a relation

---

[1] MPICH Web page: www.mpich.org

D is defined which maps "the set of all possible collective operation input parameters PIN^c" to the set of available methods M^c while minimizing collective duration:

$$D : PIN^c \rightarrow M^c. \tag{6.1}$$

The author searches for a mapping that selects the fastest collective method for the input parameters on a given platform. Finding such a mapping is extremely difficult in practice. Both analytical solutions (using performance models) and empirical solutions (e.g. graphics encoding schemes or statistical learning methods) are targeted. Both approaches have advantages and drawbacks, and can be used on homogeneous networks.

The empirical solutions have the advantage of being accurate for different platforms. But they have a significant disadvantage—to build a decision map, a number of dimensions need to be examined. Typically, the process number p and the message size m are two orthogonal dimensions of the input. Additionally, different MPI implementations and different platforms make the empirical process very expensive and require some heuristics in most cases.

6.4 HETEROGENEOUS NETWORKS

In recent years, the term "heterogeneity" has been heavily linked with the advent of many-core processors and accelerators such as graphics processing units (GPUs). In this chapter, we consider the network heterogeneity rather than the processor heterogeneity. A variety of examples for network heterogeneity can be found in today's computing platforms. Distributed systems traditionally provide a high level of network heterogeneity—popular examples of such heterogeneous high-performance systems include grid and cloud infrastructures. But even on supercomputers such as the IBM/BlueGene, the torus topology is a heterogeneous network in regard to the latency, with node to node communication depending on the number of hops between the sender and the receiver. On the other hand, supercomputers with thousands of nodes—in which each node consists of many cores and possibly accelerators—can also be clearly characterized as heterogeneous. Communication at different levels shows different properties for these modern resources (e.g., intranode vs. internode communication).

6.4.1 Comparison to Homogeneous Clusters

The most significant challenge in optimization of collectives for heterogeneous networks, compared to homogeneous networks, is in the increase in complexity. If we trivially assume the cost of each communicating pair of nodes i and j to be C_{ij}, then "the problem of finding the optimal broadcast schedule in such a heterogeneous system is NP-complete" [12]. We already observed how analytical and empirical solutions can be used to support the selection of an efficient collective algorithm. With the introduction of this new complexity, the empirical approach becomes more challenging. It is not sufficient to run a set of benchmarks $p_i * m_j$ for a selection of

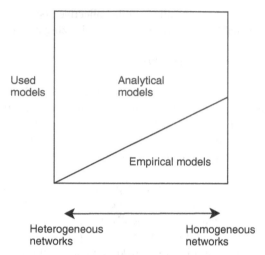

FIGURE 6.3 *While both empirical and analytical solutions are used for homogeneous clusters, analytical solutions are the only option for heterogeneous and more complex networks.*

process counts and message sizes for a handful of fixed communication schedules. For example, on a homogeneous cluster, a binomial tree algorithm would yield the same performance independent of the reordering of processes along the tree. On a heterogeneous cluster, the differing cost per link C_{ij} means that an exponential number of possible binomial trees can be formed, with potentially different total communication cost. This exponential increase in complexity is a challenge both for empirical and analytical solutions, but analytical solutions promise more flexibility in how they can be used, and are very much more efficient than running communication benchmarks. Therefore, analytical solutions seem like the only viable option for optimizations on complex networks. We visualize this limitation in Fig. 6.3. While we can try both empirical and analytical models on homogeneous networks, with increasing network heterogeneity, more empirical, or "lookup table" based solutions, give way to analytical solutions.

6.5   TOPOLOGY- AND PERFORMANCE-AWARE COLLECTIVES

Optimized collectives for heterogeneous networks generally follow two main phases, as shown in Fig. 6.4. In the first phase, a network model is created that characterizes the underlying network in some form and way. In the second phase, this model is used for efficient collective communication.

However, two different categories of collective communication for heterogeneous platforms can be identified—topology-aware and performance-aware collectives (see also [13]).

The now common term *topology-aware* seems to originate from the networking domain [14], where information from routing tables can help reduce the number of hops when transferring packets. The central property of this type of optimization

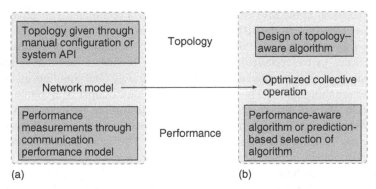

FIGURE 6.4 *General phases of topology- or performance-aware collective communication. (a) A network model represents some properties of the network. (b) The network model is used either in a network-aware algorithm or in a prediction-based selection from a pool of network-unaware algorithms.*

is that it does not rely on actual performance data, but rather on the network topology—which is often synonymous with hierarchy and structure. The network properties for topology-aware communication are configured either manually or automatically.

The other popular direction of optimization is *performance-aware* communication. In this case, network properties are reconstructed with performance measurements. This approach is useful when topology information cannot be provided or is not sufficient to determine the performance.

6.6 TOPOLOGY AS INPUT

Naturally, the first use of topology-aware collectives was through manual configuration. Early work of this kind includes different MPI libraries for distributed computing, where the hierarchy information is provided by the user. The hierarchy in the test cases typically consists of two levels—intra- and intercluster information. Some works reimplement efficiently both the intra- and intercluster communication on top of MPI point-to-point communication [15]. Other works only reimplement the intercluster communication through TCP channels, but rely on the optimized MPI collectives within clusters [16]. Naturally, the main design goal of such middleware is to minimize the expensive cross-site communication for various heterogeneous settings. More recently, with the advent of multicore machines, similar ideas were introduced for topology-aware communication on high-performance clusters. A simple step is a remapping of MPI processes to follow the topology of the resources [17]. More advanced approaches create new collectives with role assignment of processes according to placement [18, 19].

In MPI, collectives are usually implemented through a single spanning tree. However, the use of multiple spanning trees (MSTs) offers performance gains for heterogeneous networks, particularly for large-message collectives. One notable exception in the MPI community is work on optimizing collectives for the meshes/tori topology on the IBM BlueGene supercomputer [20]. On the example of a large-message broadcast, "the basic idea is to find a number of nonoverlapping spanning trees in the rectangular mesh/tori. The broadcast message is split into components, and each component is pipelined separately (and simultaneously) along one of the spanning trees." This approach is also an example of a topology-aware optimization. We will discuss alternative MST optimizations in Section 6.8.

It is worth noting that the often tedious manual configuration of topology or hierarchy has recently given way to useful APIs. This is an important and logical step, since topology in itself—other than performance—rarely changes. A useful API for accessing such topology information gaining popularity in high-performance libraries is *hwloc* [21]. It provides information for the hierarchy and topology within nodes. Automated solutions are emerging also for an internode topology, based, for example, on Infiniband APIs [13].

For further optimizations based on topology, sometimes it is possible to redesign a parallel application to make better use of topology-aware collectives [22].

6.7 PERFORMANCE AS INPUT

Topology is often sufficient to design an efficient collective algorithm. But there are two main cases when topology-aware communication cannot be used. First, with increasing network complexity, the topology might be unknown or difficult to describe. If we book compute resources connected through complex networks, it is not possible anymore to easily represent the network. Second, the topology may only reflect partial performance information—for example, the number of hops, which are related to latency, but unrelated to the bandwidth.

When performance is used to characterize network properties, it is common to use communication performance models. But such performance models face significant challenges. As described in Fig. 6.2, a number of layers exist for the communication library, and components of each layer impact the performance in some way. Therefore, it is unrealistic to look for a "one fits all" model—its complexity and number of parameters would be overwhelming. Instead, it is reasonable to make the assumption that the low-level configuration of software and runtime is optimized, and to focus on the communication as something generic. In many cases, this ideal notion is not possible—for example, misconfiguration of the underlying hardware or software (including MPI) is possible, and then incorporation of additional parameters is necessary. These technicalities are not the subject of this chapter.

A significant advantage of an accurate communication performance model is that it can be efficiently used for a wide range of optimized collective operations. The use of the model consists of two important phases (Fig. 6.4):

- In the first phase, the model parameters are estimated.
- In the second phase, some form of optimization is targeted—either through prediction-based selection or through the design of a new algorithm.

For clarity, each time we introduce a model we will briefly address the above points of estimation, and how the models can be used on the example of a broadcast operation.

6.7.1 Homogeneous Performance Models

The simple Hockney model [23] is the most comprehensive performance model of point-to-point communication, and is the common starting point for modeling collective algorithms. If the latency is α and the reciprocal value of the bandwidth is β, the time T to transfer a message of size m is given as

$$T(m) = \alpha + \beta * m. \tag{6.2}$$

The estimation of model parameters is trivially done with ping-pong benchmarks with different message sizes, and tools such as NetPIPE [24] can be used.

As a simple example of predicting collectives, let us consider the binomial tree broadcast operation. It can be trivially predicted [10] as

$$T(m) = \lceil \log(p) \rceil * (\alpha + m * \beta). \tag{6.3}$$

Numerous early efforts have been made to design efficient collective operations on networks with heterogeneous links with the Hockney model. The common feature of all of them is the use of a heuristic to provide an efficient communication schedule rather than an optimal one. An intuitive idea is to use minimal spanning tree algorithms and modifications thereof, using the communication cost as the edge property [12]. Other heuristics of trees with binomial or other structures also exist, for example, considering overlap of communication [25]. Interestingly, it is not always the case that complex heuristics result in better efficiency—some evidence suggests that even a simple heuristic based on a fixed tree structure with reordering of processes can produce efficient communication trees [26].

A more advanced model is the LogP model [27], which has an upper bound L on latency, overhead o, gap per message g, and the number of processors P. The increase in parameters allows separate contributions for the network and processors at each machine—with g and L being network-dependent and o being processor-dependent. And yet, a number of questions arise. While conceptually we can differentiate between the processor- and network-dependent contributions o and g, it is unclear where to draw the line between these contributions and what benchmarks should be adopted in order to accurately estimate these parameters. This might be unproblematic for point-to-point communication, but it is more important for collectives.

There are also other challenges to these parameters. The gap g and the overhead o parameters overlap in time. Consider for example a trivial broadcast between three processors as shown in Fig. 6.5. The prediction depends on the relation between g and o, since they overlap in time at each node.

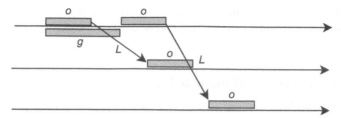

FIGURE 6.5 *LogP example: Even basic predictions for collectives require consideration. Depending on o and g, completion can take either (g + 2 ∗ o + L) or (3 ∗ o + L).*

Let us use this model to predict the familiar binomial tree broadcast for small messages. If we consider that for a small message size m the gap g is small, we make the assumption $g < 2 * o + L$, resulting in:

$$T = \lceil \log(p) \rceil * (2 * o + L). \tag{6.4}$$

An extension of this model—LogGP model [29]—introduces the additional parameter gap per byte G for long messages. The extra parameter accounts for the overhead of sending one long message, where the prediction for a binomial tree broadcast is

$$T(m) = \lceil \log(p) \rceil * (2 * o + L + G * (m - 1)). \tag{6.5}$$

The *PLogP* model [30], or the *parameterized* LogP model, is another model related to LogP/LogGP model. It has the same four parameters, but they capture slightly different properties—we refer to the information provided in the original work for details. An important feature is that the parameters g and o are not constant, but functions—$g(m)$ and $o(m)$, and do not need to be linear but only piecewise linear. This, in principle, allows us to capture nonlinear behavior for varying message sizes, and such nonlinearities are sometimes observed in MPI (e.g., at the switch point between eager and rendezvous protocol).

The developers of the model provide a software tool for estimating its parameters. The original work introducing LogP/LogGP does not provide such software, and only micro benchmarks have been developed for these models. Using the provided *PLogP* software, its parameters can be evaluated, and can in turn be translated into the LogP/LogGP parameters. The estimation of the parameters is much more complex than with simple models such as Hockney. The authors claim that their model can be efficiently evaluated because only $g(0)$ benchmarks need to saturate the network. However, this does not account for the nonlinear behavior of the network when the cost of estimating the parameters increases significantly. In such cases, *PLogP* benchmarks are increased for more message sizes to extrapolate the nonlinear runtime more accurately using $g(m)$ and $o(m)$. For example, the authors acknowledge that $g(m > 0)$ with saturation of a link can take up to 17 times longer per link.

6.7.2 Heterogeneous Performance Models

The motivation for more complex performance models is that predictions for collective operations, when based on traditional point-to-point models, are not sufficiently accurate. Simply put, even if the individual contributing factors can be ignored for point-to-point predictions, these factors are needed when modeling collective communication. Performance models of heterogeneous networks can follow one of two approaches—either homogeneous communication models can be applied separately for each link, or new heterogeneous models can be introduced. To avoid the introduction of an entirely new model, a simple first step is the slight modification of an existing model to represent at least some of the heterogeneity of the used platform. On the example of Log$P$, it has been recognized early that on the sender and the receiver side, contributions can differ for different nodes, and the constant overhead o can be subdivided into separate sender and receiver overheads o_s and o_r [31]. New heterogeneous communication models have been proposed [32, 33] with the idea to have more parameters which give more expressive power and, potentially, better accuracy. Parameters for constant and variable contributions of the network and the sender and the receiver are introduced. Here, we show the point-to-point prediction as given in [32]:

$$T(m) = S_c + S_m * m + X_c + X_m * m + R_c + R_m * m. \tag{6.6}$$

In this formula, the components S_c, X_c, and R_c are the constant parts of the send, transmission, and receive costs, respectively. m is the message size, with S_m, X_m, and R_m being the message-dependent parts. Prediction formulas are provided for various collective operations—but with more expressiveness of different contributions to the runtime than homogeneous models. However, the prediction formulas are significantly more complex. If we consider the binomial tree broadcast, the prediction is

$$T(m) = \max \left\{ T_{\text{recv}}^0(m), T_{\text{recv}}^1(m), \ldots, T_{\text{recv}}^{n-1}(m) \right\} \tag{6.7}$$

with

$$T_{\text{recv}}^i(m) = T_{\text{recv}}^{\text{parent}(i)} + \text{childrank}(\text{parent}(i), i) * \left(S_c^{\text{parent}(i)} + S_m^{\text{parent}(i)} * m \right)$$

$$+ X_m * m + X_c + R_m^I * m + R_c^i, \tag{6.8}$$

where parent(i) is the parent of node i in the broadcast tree, and childrank(parent(i), i) is the order, among its siblings, in which node i receives the message from its parent.

Unfortunately, the maximum operator cannot be eliminated, and a simpler prediction is impossible in such cases. The reason behind this is that it cannot be determined in advance which tree path is overall slower—and dominating the runtime—on heterogeneous networks.

6.7.3 Estimation of Parameters of Heterogeneous Performance Models

A significant challenge when increasing the number of parameters of heterogeneous models is the estimation phase. A model with a large number of parameters capturing separate contributions in communication is useless if the parameters cannot be practically established. After all, in real experiments it is the estimation phase that gives meaning to the model parameters—not an abstract description of what they should represent. There is good reason to be cautious—the presented model in previous section claims that two sets of experiments, ping-pong and consecutive sends, are sufficient to capture all nine parameters. This is not plausible. For example, it is assumed that it is easy to estimate the component S_c in isolation, but how this can be done within a node is not clear. Also, the constant network contribution is sometimes ignored during the estimation phase.

The proper estimation of model parameters is addressed in more recent work [33]. One important requirement is that n model parameters require the estimation phase to provide benchmarks which can be formulated as a system of linear equations with a single unique solution. It is difficult to design an estimation procedure providing such a system of equations. However, under certain assumptions it is feasible and is demonstrated for Ethernet clusters. For a number of collectives, the resulting predictions are shown to be more accurate than simple model predictions.

6.7.4 Other Performance Models

Performance models are not limited to capturing point-to-point or collective operations under "ideal" conditions. Another potential use case for such models is capturing contention and/or congestion. The topic is important, with the increase in networking and memory bus capacity lagging behind the increase of processing units like cores. We only give a short overview of some related work here. Simple approaches suggest introducing a factor to the familiar Hockney model, which slows down performance proportionally to the process number [34]. Other works in this direction introduce more complex extensions to LogP/LogGP to capture network contention [31]. The communication pattern of an application and the underlying network are analyzed. While more accurate for the given applications, the model uses a much larger number of parameters. There are also efforts for new contention models—for example, a simple experiment-oriented model that estimates penalty coefficients for Infiniband [35], or a model capturing the congestion on Ethernet clusters for gather operations [36].

6.8 NON-MPI COLLECTIVE ALGORITHMS FOR HETEROGENEOUS NETWORKS

While communication research in HPC increasingly focuses on the complex hierarchical structure of clusters—consider the presence of cores and accelerators within nodes—the related area of distributed computing is often overlooked. And yet algorithms and ideas from distributed computing have a strong background in optimizing communication for heterogeneous networks. Many of the solutions in this area do not suffer the limitations of MPI. First, we observe a multiple spanning tree algorithm which, unlike the previously presented algorithms, is bandwidth-oriented and not topology-oriented. Then, we focus on adaptive algorithms of distributing data, which are orthogonal to the fixed schedule of communication in MPI. We show two useful applications of such algorithms—efficient alternatives to MPI collectives, or new ways of designing performance models.

6.8.1 Optimal Solutions with Multiple Spanning Trees

A recent work in distributed computing [37] uses MST without the constraints of MPI to implement efficient collective operations. As discussed earlier, the only known MPI solution builds multiple trees following the known network topology.

The problem of finding an optimal set of communication trees is very complex—n^{n-2} different trees exist for n hosts according to Cayley's formula [38]. Naturally, the use of heuristics is required to find a good solution in reasonable time, and the above work uses the following steps:

- Start with a network model to describe the properties of a heterogeneous network—an example is given in Fig. 6.6.
- Generate a good (but not optimal) set of trees for a given network using a heuristic algorithm [39].
- Translate network model and set of trees into a set of constraints.
- Use linear programming algorithm to find maximum throughput.

It is crucial that a heuristic algorithm provides spanning trees for the given problem. These trees can be seen merely as "sensible suggestions." As any heuristic, they have their limitations, which are discussed in detail in related work. In the last steps, the maximum throughput provided by the linear programming is not used for the algorithm design. It serves as a measure of the efficiency of the designed algorithm.

6.8.2 Adaptive Algorithms for Efficient Large-Message Transfer

In middleware like MPI, messages are communicated through a fixed schedule of point-to-point operations. The messages are pushed across the network following this schedule; hence this class of algorithms is called *sender-initiated multicasts*. The orthogonal class of collective operations is called *receiver-initiated multicasts*. In this case, receivers pull the data from senders. A very popular protocol in this category is BitTorrent [40]. While initially more popular in distributed and peer-to-peer computing, BitTorrent has shown promising performance even in the context of high-performance networks with some level of heterogeneity. Experiments on different emulated wide-area networks show that BitTorrent-inspired protocols can perform very well [41]. More surprisingly, even on a hierarchy of

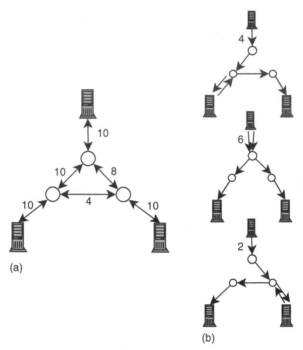

FIGURE 6.6 *A network model [37] and multiple spanning trees for improving throughput. (a) Available bandwidth for each independent link. (b) Three possible spanning trees and predicted throughput for each.*

clusters within a single computing site, broadcasts of very large messages using the original BitTorrent protocol can often outperform state-of-the-art MPI algorithms [42]. Figure 6.7 shows that for message sizes in the range of megabytes, BitTorrent can outperform state-of-the-art MPI implementations on a hierarchy of Ethernet clusters.

While the analysis of BitTorrent communication is not trivial, one fundamental feature of receiver-initiated multicasts is that data can be propagated adaptively. To support this, BitTorrent opens multiple TCP channels in parallel. Early work [43] has also shown that in this case the throughput approaches the maximum. Therefore, there has recently been strong evidence that dynamic and adaptive scheduling of point-to-point communication can be efficient when transferring large data volumes in heterogeneous networks.

6.8.3 Network Models Inspired by BitTorrent

One interesting application of adaptive and dynamic multicast protocols (e.g., BitTorrent) that deserves increased research effort in the future is the generation of a network model. To some extent, this idea has been demonstrated [37] by allowing

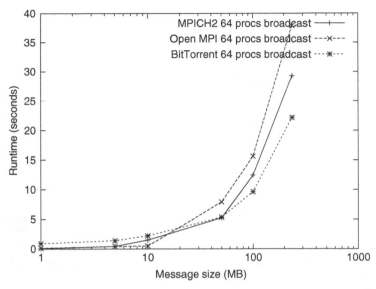

FIGURE 6.7 *Experiments on a hierarchy of three Ethernet clusters within a site in Bordeaux. BitTorrent broadcasts outperform MPI broadcasts for very large messages.*

dynamic stealing of bandwidth within clusters while providing the overall network topology.

Another entirely BitTorrent-based solution is proposed in a network tomography method to identify logical clusters without any *a priori* knowledge of the network [44]. Network tomography is an area of research more related to unknown and uncooperative networks, but in its goal to sufficiently reconstruct a network, it is related to the performance models used in HPC. For the reconstruction in network tomography, only end-to-end measurements are used. Network tomography follows two distinct phases:

- Measurement phase—end-to-end measurements with some level of noise.
- Reconstruction phase—removal of noise through statistical methods.

In its goal, this particular measurement method is quite similar to the estimation of model parameters. But, instead of isolated point-to-point experiments, adaptive BitTorrent-based multicasts are used for network discovery. The multicasts are repeated a number of times until the network properties are reliably reconstructed. In the end, a logical view of the network in the form of bandwidth clusters is built. The resulting accurate clustering of geographically distributed sites according to their bandwidth is shown in Fig. 6.8. The provided clustering can be used as a topology input for any topology-aware collective algorithm.

Furthermore, the presented tomography seems even more suitable for performance-aware collective communication. As shown in Fig. 6.9, such algorithms can provide an entirely performance-based network model, and have the potential

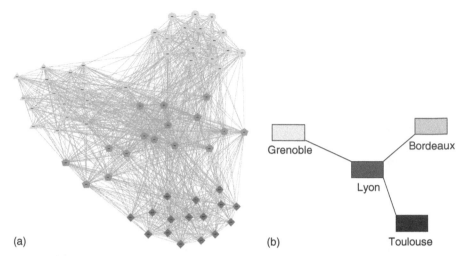

FIGURE 6.8 *Network tomography as proposed in [44]. (a) Reconstructed bandwidth clusters.*
(b) Underlying physical network.

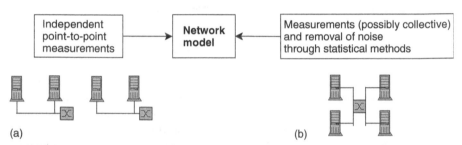

FIGURE 6.9 *Performance-aware network models. (a) Traditionally, a number of isolated point-to-point experiments are used in HPC. (b) Inspired by network tomography, measurements based on collective operations can be performed.*

to replace the traditional performance measurement procedures. The two types of performance measurements differ strongly. Traditional measurement procedures typically use point-to-point operations to reconstruct link model parameters. Each of these measurements needs to be repeated a number of times. On the other side, the measurement procedures inspired by the BitTorrent protocol can be very efficient, and can be entirely based on collective operations such as broadcasts. In a separate phase, the statistical algorithm removes noise and randomness in the measurements till the accuracy levels are good enough. It is significant that collective operations can be used instead of point-to-point operations. This allows for an increased accuracy of the model when targeting predictions of collective operations. For example, it is impossible for point-to-point operations to detect the presence of bottlenecks in most scenarios. However, the use of flexible measurement procedures can detect such bottlenecks [44].

6.9 CONCLUSION

This chapter reviewed the main generic optimization techniques for collective communication. With increasingly heterogeneous networks, empirical approaches to optimizing communication become unfeasible because of the exponential growth of the already huge test space. Therefore, we need some sort of network model. Such a network model can be based on topology or performance. Topology-aware collectives are a relatively straightforward and popular approach to optimization. They offer solid performance gains in case we know the network topology in advance. More advanced network models are based on the performance. In this case, performance communication models are used. While these models strive to capture the network heterogeneity, they are difficult to use. For example, heterogeneous models capturing various contributions produce complex prediction formulas. In addition to that, their parameters are difficult to estimate. More advanced models would be even more complicated to use, and that limits their practical importance. This means that one of the classic cases of using models on homogeneous networks—prediction-based selection of optimal algorithms—is difficult to apply with advanced models for heterogeneous and hierarchical networks. From a scientific point of view, this outcome is not satisfactory. After all, accurate predictions are the only scientific validation of any model. But if we take a more practical approach, even for a "relatively accurate" model, there is a significant potential for designing efficient performance-aware algorithms. The simple Hockney model—even though proven to not always provide accurate predictions—has been successfully used on heterogeneous networks. It has been observed that minimal spanning trees based on the per-link Hockney model provide efficient broadcast for small messages. For larger messages, the same approach can be used successfully for binomial trees broadcasts. For very large messages, receiver-initiated multicasts are gaining popularity in the HPC domain. The adaptive nature of these algorithms makes them suitable even for very complex networks.

ACKNOWLEDGMENTS

This work was supported by the COST Action IC0805 "Open European Network for High-Performance Computing on Complex Environments."

REFERENCES

1. L. S. Blackford, J. Choi, A. Cleary, E. D'Azevedo, J. Demmel, I. Dhillon, J. Dongarra, S. Hammarling, G. Henry, A. Petitet, *et al.*, *ScaLAPACK Users' Guide*, vol. 4. Philadelphia, PA: Society for Industrial and Applied Mathematics, 1987.
2. J. Dean and S. Ghemawat, "MapReduce: simplified data processing on large clusters," *Communications of the ACM*, vol. 51, no. 1, pp. 107–113, 2008.
3. D. Wadsworth and Z. Chen, "Performance of MPI broadcast algorithms," in *International Parallel and Distributed Processing Symposium, IPDPS 2008*, (Miami, FL, USA), pp. 1–7, 2008.

4. W. Gropp, E. Lusk, and A. Skjellum, *Using MPI: Portable Parallel Programming with the Message Passing Interface*, vol. 1. Cambridge, MA: MIT Press, 1999.

5. L. Hablot, O. Gluck, J.-C. Mignot, S. Genaud, and P. V.-B. Primet, "Comparison and tuning of MPI implementations in a grid context," in *IEEE International Conference on Cluster Computing*, (Austin, TX, USA), pp. 458–463, 2007.

6. A. Mamidala, A. Vishnu, and D. Panda, "Efficient shared memory and RDMA based design for MPI_Allgather over InfiniBand," *Recent Advances in Parallel Virtual Machine and Message Passing Interface*, pp. 66–75, 2006.

7. J. Liu, J. Wu, and D. K. Panda, "High performance RDMA-based MPI implementation over InfiniBand," *International Journal of Parallel Programming*, vol. 32, no. 3, pp. 167–198, 2004.

8. T. Hoefler, C. Siebert, and W. Rehm, "A practically constant-time MPI broadcast algorithm for large-scale InfiniBand clusters with multicast," in *International Parallel and Distributed Processing Symposium, IPDPS 2007*, (Long Beach, CA, USA), pp. 1–8, March 2007.

9. E. Gabriel, G. E. Fagg, G. Bosilca, T. Angskun, J. J. Dongarra, J. M. Squyres, V. Sahay, P. Kambadur, B. Barrett, A. Lumsdaine, R. H. Castain, D. J. Daniel, R. L. Graham, and T. S. Woodall, "Open MPI: Goals, concept, and design of a next generation MPI implementation," in *Proceedings, 11th European PVM/MPI Users' Group Meeting*, (Budapest, Hungary), pp. 97–104, 2004.

10. R. Thakur and R. Rabenseifner, "Optimization of collective communication operations in MPICH," *International Journal of High Performance Computing Applications*, vol. 19, pp. 49–66, 2005.

11. J. Pjesivac-Grbovic, *Towards Automatic and Adaptive Optimizations of MPI Collective Operations*. PhD thesis, The University of Tennessee, Knoxville, 2007.

12. P. B. Bhat, C. Raghavendra, and V. K. Prasanna, "Efficient collective communication in distributed heterogeneous systems," *Journal of Parallel and Distributed Computing*, vol. 63, no. 3, pp. 251–263, 2003.

13. H. Subramoni, K. Kandalla, J. Vienne, S. Sur, B. Barth, K. Tomko, R. Mclay, K. Schulz, and D. K. Panda, "Design and evaluation of network topology-/speed- aware broadcast algorithms for InfiniBand clusters," in *IEEE International Conference on Cluster Computing*, (Austin, TX, USA), pp. 317–325, 2011.

14. M. Kwon and S. Fahmy, "Topology-aware overlay networks for group communication," in *12th International Workshop on Network and Operating Systems Support for Digital Audio and Video*, pp. 127–136. New York: ACM, 2002.

15. T. Kielmann, H. E. Bal, and S. Gorlatch, "Bandwidth-efficient collective communication for clustered wide area systems," in *Workshops on Parallel and Distributed Processing, IPDPS 2000*, (Cancun, Mexico), pp. 492–499, 2000.

16. E. Gabriel, M. Resch, T. Beisel, and R. Keller, "Distributed computing in a heterogeneous computing environment," in *Recent Advances in Parallel Virtual Machine and Message Passing Interface*, *LNCS* (V. Alexandrov and J. Dongarra, eds.), vol. 1497, pp. 180–187. Berlin / Heidelberg: Springer, 1998. DOI: 10.1007/BFb0056574.

17. R. Rabenseifner, G. Hager, and G. Jost, "Hybrid MPI/OpenMP parallel programming on clusters of multi-core SMP nodes," in *17th Euromicro International Conference on Parallel, Distributed and Network-Based Processing, 2009*, pp. 427–436. Weimar, Germany: IEEE, 2009.

18. J. Ladd, M. G. Venkata, R. Graham, and P. Shamis, "Analyzing the effects of multi-core architectures and on-host communication characteristics on collective communications," in *40th International Conference on Parallel Processing Workshops, ICPPW 2011*, (Taipei, Taiwan), pp. 406–415, 2011.

19. T. Ma, G. Bosilca, A. Bouteiller, B. Goglin, J. M. Squyres, and J. J. Dongarra, "Kernel assisted collective intra-node MPI communication among multi-core and many-core CPUs," in *International Conference on Parallel Processing, ICPP 2011*, (Taipei, Taiwan), pp. 532–541, 2011.

20. G. Almási, P. Heidelberger, C. J. Archer, X. Martorell, C. C. Erway, J. E. Moreira, B. Steinmacher-Burow, and Y. Zheng, "Optimization of MPI collective communication on BlueGene/L systems," in *International Conference on Supercomputing, ICS 2005*, pp. 253–262. New York: ACM, 2005.

21. F. Broquedis, J. Clet-Ortega, S. Moreaud, N. Furmento, B. Goglin, G. Mercier, S. Thibault, and R. Namyst, "hwloc: a generic framework for managing hardware affinities in HPC applications," in *Euromicro International Conference on Parallel, Distributed and Network-Based Processing, PDP 2010*, (Pisa, Italy), pp. 180–186, 2010.

22. C. Coti, T. Herault, and F. Cappello, "MPI applications on grids: a topology aware approach," in *The 15th International European Conference on Parallel and Distributed Computing, Euro-Par 2009, LNCS*, vol. 5704, pp. 466–477, Berlin / Heidelberg: Springer, 2009.

23. R. W. Hockney, "The communication challenge for MPP: Intel Paragon and Meiko CS-2," *Parallel Computing*, vol. 20, no. 3, pp. 389–398, 1994.

24. Q. O. Snell, A. R. Mikler, and J. L. Gustafson, "NetPIPE: a network protocol independent performance evaluator," in *IASTED International Conference on Intelligent Information Management and Systems*, (Washington, D.C., USA), 1996.

25. J. Hatta and S. Shibusawa, "Scheduling algorithms for efficient gather operations in distributed heterogeneous systems," in *International Conference on Parallel Processing Workshops, ICPPW 2000*, (Toronto, Canada), pp. 173–180, 2000.

26. K. Dichev, V. Rychkov, and A. Lastovetsky, "Two algorithms of irregular scatter/gather operations for heterogeneous platforms," in *17th European MPI Users' Group Meeting Conference on Recent Advances in the Message Passing Interface, vol. 6305 of* LNCS, (Stuttgart, Germany), pp. 289–293, 2010.

27. D. Culler, R. Karp, D. Patterson, A. Sahay, K. E. Schauser, E. Santos, R. Subramonian, and T. von Eicken, "LogP: towards a realistic model of parallel computation," *Fourth ACM SIGPLAN Symposium on Principles in Practices of Parallel Programming*, vol. 28, no. 7, pp. 1–12, 1993.

28. T. Hoefler, L. Cerquetti, T. Mehlan, F. Mietke, and W. Rehm, "A practical approach to the rating of barrier algorithms using the LogP model and Open-MPI," in *International Conference on Parallel Processing Workshops, ICPPW 2005*, pp. 562–569, 2005.

29. A. Alexandrov, M. F. Ionescu, K. E. Schauser, and C. Scheiman, "LogGP: incorporating long messages into the LogP model—one step closer towards a realistic model for parallel computation," in *Proceedings of the Seventh Annual ACM Symposium on Parallel Algorithms and Architectures*, pp. 95–105. Santa Barbara, CA: ACM, 1995.

30. T. Kielmann, H. Bal, and K. Verstoep, "Fast measurement of LogP parameters for message passing platforms," *Workshops on Parallel and Distributed Processing, IPDPS 2000*, pp. 1176–1183, 2000.

31. C. Moritz and M. Frank, "LoGPG: modeling network contention in message-passing programs," *IEEE Transactions on Parallel and Distributed Systems*, vol. 12, no. 4, pp. 404–415, 2001.

32. M. Banikazemi, J. Sampathkumar, S. Prabhu, D. K. Panda, and P. Sadayappan, "Communication modeling of heterogeneous networks of workstations for performance characterization of collective operations," in *8th Heterogeneous Computing Workshop, HCW '99*, pp. 125–133. Washington, DC: IEEE Computer Society, 1999.

33. A. Lastovetsky, V. Rychkov, and M. O'Flynn, "Accurate heterogeneous communication models and a software tool for their efficient estimation," *International Journal of High Performance Computing Applications*, (Barcelona, Spain), vol. 24, pp. 34–48, 2010.

34. L. Steffenel, "Modeling network contention effects on all-to-all operations," in *IEEE International Conference on Cluster Computing, 2006*, pp. 1–10. IEEE, 2006.

35. M. Martinasso and J.-F. Mehaut, "A contention-aware performance model for HPC-based networks: a case study of the InfiniBand network," in *17th International European Conference on Parallel and Distributed Computing, Euro-Par 2011*, (Bordeaux, France), pp. 91–102, 2011.

36. A. Lastovetsky and M. O'Flynn, "A performance model of many-to-one collective communications for parallel computing," in *International Parallel and Distributed Processing Symposium, IPDPS 2007*, pp. 1–8. Long Beach, CA: IEEE, 2007.

37. M. den Burger, *High-Throughput Multicast Communication for Grid Applications*. PhD thesis, Vrije Universiteit Amsterdam, 2009.

38. A. Cayley, "A theorem on trees," *Quarterly Journal of Mathematics*, vol. 23, no. 376-378, p. 69, 1889.

39. R. Izmailov, S. Ganguly, and N. Tu, "Fast parallel file replication in data grid," in *Future of Grid Data Environments Workshop, GGF-10*, 2004.

40. B. Cohen, "Incentives build robustness in BitTorrent," in *1st Workshop on Economics of Peer-to-Peer Systems*, (Berkeley, CA, USA), 2003.

41. M. den Burger and T. Kielmann, "Collective receiver-initiated multicast for grid applications," *IEEE Transactions on Parallel and Distributed Systems*, vol. 22, no. 2, pp. 231–244, 2011.

42. K. Dichev and A. Lastovetsky, "MPI vs BitTorrent: switching between large-message broadcast algorithms in the presence of bottleneck links," in *10th International Workshop on Algorithms, Models and Tools for Parallel Computing on Heterogeneous Platforms, HeteroPar 2012, LNCS* pp. 185–195, vol. 7640. Rhodes Island, Greece: Springer, 2012.

43. P. Rodriguez and E. W. Biersack, "Dynamic parallel access to replicated content in the Internet," *IEEE/ACM Transactions on Networking*, vol. 10, pp. 455–465, 2002.

44. K. Dichev, F. Reid, and A. Lastovetsky, "Efficient and reliable network tomography in heterogeneous networks using BitTorrent broadcasts and clustering algorithms," in *ACM/IEEE International Conference on High Performance Computing, Networking, Storage and Analysis, SC'12*, (Salt Lake City, UT, USA), 2012.

7

Effective Data Access Patterns on Massively Parallel Processors

Gabriele Capannini

D&IT Chalmers, Göteborg, Sweden

Ranieri Baraglia, Fabrizio Silvestri, and Franco Maria Nardini

National Research Council of Italy, Pisa, Italy

The new generation of microprocessors incorporates a huge number of cores on the same chip. Graphics processing units are an example of this kind of architectures. We analyze these architectures from a theoretical point of view using the K-model to estimate the complexity of a given algorithm defined on this computational model. To this end, we use the K-model to derive an efficient realization of two popular algorithms, namely prefix sum and sorting.

7.1 INTRODUCTION

The new generation of microprocessors incorporates a huge number of *cores* on the same chip. This trades single-core performance off for the total amount of work done across multiple threads of execution. Graphics processing units (GPUs) are an example of this kind of architectures. The first generation of GPUs was designed to

High-Performance Computing on Complex Environments, First Edition.
Edited by Emmanuel Jeannot and Julius Žilinskas.
© 2014 John Wiley & Sons, Inc. Published 2014 by John Wiley & Sons, Inc.

support a fixed set of rendering functions. Nowadays, GPUs are becoming easier to program. Therefore, they can be used for applications that have been traditionally handled by CPUs. The reasons of using general-purpose graphics processing units (GPGPUs) in high-performance computations are their raw computing power, good performance per watt, and low costs. However, some important issues limit the wide exploitation of GPGPUs. The main one concerns the heterogeneous and distributed nature of the memory hierarchy. As a consequence, the speed-up of some applications depends on being able to efficiently access the data so that all cores are able to work simultaneously.

This chapter discusses the characteristics and the issues of the memory systems of this kind of architectures. We analyze these architectures from a theoretical point of view using the *K*-model, a model for capturing their performance constraints. The *K*-model is used to estimate the complexity of a given algorithm defined on this model. This chapter describes how the *K*-model can also be used to design efficient data access patterns for implementing efficient GPU algorithms. To this extent, we use the *K*-model to derive an efficient realization of two popular algorithms, namely, *prefix sum* and *sorting*. By means of reproducible experiments, we validate theoretical results showing that the optimization of an algorithm based on the *K*-model corresponds to an actual optimization in practice.

This chapter is organized as follows: Section 7.2 introduces some preliminary details of many-core architectures. Section 7.3 describes the *K*-model in detail. Sections 7.4 and 7.5 analyze the two applications, prefix sum and sorting, by means of the *K*-model. Finally, we present our final remarks in Section 7.6.

7.2 ARCHITECTURAL DETAILS

Processors based on *many-core* architectures are widely available nowadays. This class of processors is specialized for compute-intensive and highly parallel computations. Examples of this kind of architecture are GPUs and Sony Cell/BE. The integration of a massive number of scalar processing units on the same chip organized as an array of single instruction multiple data (SIMD) processors enables the computation of thousands of arithmetic and logical operations at the same time. Each SIMD processor is equipped with a small, private on-chip data memory, while a larger off-chip memory is used to store input and output data.

SIMD architectures widely employ a programming paradigm called *stream processing*. According to this paradigm, a computation consists of a set of operations, called *kernel*, which is mapped in a parallel manner to a set of homogeneous data elements gathered in a *stream*. Each stream element is assigned to one SIMD processor which computes the kernel using its on-chip memory to minimize the communications with the external memory and to share data between its scalar processing elements.

Since SIMD processors cannot synchronize and communicate with each other, and because of the unpredictability of the order in which stream elements are scheduled, their computations cannot exploit reciprocal data dependencies. This approach simplifies software and hardware design by restricting the range of possible computations that can be run on such platforms. In fact, this approach allows these architectures to scale better than multi-core CPUs.

7.3 *K*-MODEL

Designing an efficient kernel is often a hard task for software developers who have to deal with the low flexibility of stream processing as well as the constraints imposed by the hardware. Such constraints concern the exploitation of (i) data parallelism, that is, the possibility to perform a single instruction flow on multiple data simultaneously; (ii) efficient access patterns for sharing data stored in the on-chip memory among the scalar processing elements; and (iii) efficient access patterns for transferring data among SIMD processors and the off-chip memory. Table 7.1 summarizes how existing models deal with the constraints presented above. The *K*-model [1] is the only one able to capture all the constraints characterizing the target architectures.

7.3.1 The Architecture

The *K*-model aims at evaluating the time required to perform a given kernel on a single stream element. To this end, it is designed to be compliant with the stream processing paradigm described in Section 7.2. In particular, the *K*-model simplifies its architecture by exploiting the fact that no data dependencies can occur between two stream elements. As shown in Fig. 7.1, the *K*-model architecture consists of only one SIMD processor equipped with a memory shared among the scalar processors, and an external memory storing input and output data of the overall computation. Note that modeling only one SIMD processor rather than an array does not limit the expressiveness of the stream processing paradigm as it only affects the stream completion time on actual devices.

The *K*-model memory hierarchy consists of an external memory (EM) and an internal memory (IM) made up of σ locations equally divided into k modules IM_i, $i = 1, \ldots, k$. IM is organized so that successive memory positions are assigned to successive memory modules. Let IM_i be one of these modules, and Q_i be the queue that collects the access requests to IM_i.

TABLE 7.1 Architectural Constraints Addressed by Existing Computational Models

Model Name	Data Parallelism	Data Access Pattern	
		On-chip memory	Off-chip memory
PRAM [2]	—	—	—
V-RAM [3]	✓	—	—
(P)BT [4]	—	—	✓
QRQW PRAM [5]	—	✓	—
CO [6]	—	—	✓
K-model	✓	✓	✓

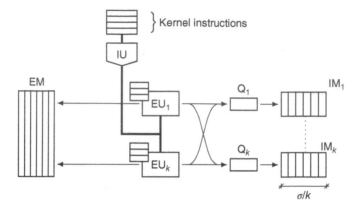

FIGURE 7.1   *Representation of the K-model abstract machine.*

The architecture includes a set of k scalar execution units EU_i, $i = 1, \ldots , k$, that are linked to an instruction unit (IU), which issues the instructions. This characteristic forces the scalar units to work synchronously. As a consequence, the next instruction is not processed until the execution of the current one has been completed and its results have been stored.

When IU issues a load/store instruction accessing IM, up to k memory requests to IM can be issued by the scalar execution units. The IM modules work in parallel, each one providing the accesses for the requests stored in its queue. Since each access is performed in a constant time, the time required to complete the instruction is proportional to the size of queue that collects the highest number of requests.

When a load/store instruction accessing EM is issued, the access is provided by gathering all the requested addresses in the minimum number of k-sized segments of consecutive memory addresses. Each segment is then accessed through a memory transaction in constant time.

7.3.2   Cost and Complexity Evaluation

The K-model provides a function that associates a *cost* with each type of instruction, that is, the time required for its execution. By combining these costs, the execution time of a given kernel can be estimated. In particular, three classes of instructions and the associated cost are defined:

1. instructions accessing IM whose latency is proportional to the contention degree generated among Q_i, $i = 1, \ldots , k$, thus equal to $\max_{1 \leq i \leq k} |Q_i|$;
2. arithmetical instructions whose latency is equal to 1, because they are independently executed by means of private registers of each scalar processor;
3. instructions accessing EM whose latency is defined as the number of memory transactions performed to access all the requested addresses.

Since the time required to access the off-chip memory is one order of magnitude greater than that for executing other types of instructions, the time required for computing a kernel is defined by the two following functions: $T()$ is referred to as the time complexity and denotes the time for computing the instructions executed internally to the SIMD processor, that is, instruction of type 1. and 2.; $G()$ denotes the time required to access the external memory evaluated by counting the total number of memory transactions performed. In the remainder of this chapter, the work measured by the function $T()$ is also referred to as *internal work*. Given an algorithm $\mathcal{A}$ consisting of a set of kernels $\mathcal{K}_1, \ldots, \mathcal{K}_m$, the time required to perform $\mathcal{A}$ on a given input is $\sum_{i=1}^{m} \sum_{\forall s \in S_i} T_i(s) + G_i(s)$, where s denotes an element in the stream S_i related to the kernel $\mathcal{K}_i$.

Resuming, a kernel works efficiently when it is able to exploit data parallelism on k-sized data groups and also when the memory hierarchy is accessed by means of patterns that reduce the costs defined above.

7.3.3 Efficiency Evaluation

The previous section introduced a set of functions for estimating the time required to execute an algorithm made up of a set of kernels by means of the K-model. This section describes two further functions that evaluate the efficiency of a kernel. As the execution of an instruction must be finished before the next one, and since each instruction involves from 1 to k scalar execution units, the total internal work that can be performed in t time intervals is $t \times k$. In fact, in each time interval, k arithmetical instructions can be performed or k positions in IM can be accessed. As a consequence, given an algorithm $\mathcal{A}$ and its $T(\mathcal{A})$, the efficiency of $\mathcal{K}$ is defined as

$$\frac{W(\mathcal{A})}{k \cdot T(\mathcal{A})},$$

where $W(\mathcal{A})$ denotes the total amount of work required to execute the instruction flow issued by IU.

In the same way, we can compute the efficiency of an access to EM. Since the maximum bandwidth is achieved when k memory locations are copied within a memory transaction, the efficiency of accessing m memory locations in EM is

$$\frac{m}{k \cdot G(m)}.$$

Example 7.1 As an example, we analyze the efficiency of an instruction accessing IM. Let $\mathcal{X} = $ "for each $i \in \{1, \ldots, k\}$ do $IM_{i \cdot k} \leftarrow 1$" be the instruction to evaluate at a given time t_0. The total amount of internal work $W(\mathcal{X})$ is k because k operations accessing IM are required. Given that for each $i \in \mathbb{N}$ we have $i \cdot k \equiv 0 \pmod{k}$, the related $T(\mathcal{X})$ is k because all of these accesses imply the use of the same queue (i.e., Q_1 given that indices are shifted of one position), which means performing one operation at a time.

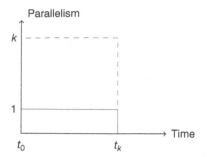

FIGURE 7.2 *Efficiency of $\mathcal{X}$ represented in the Cartesian plane.*

Figure 7.2 depicts the quantities affecting the efficiency of $\mathcal{X}$, which is the ratio of the area surrounded by a solid line over the area surrounded by a dashed line, that is, $\mathcal{X}$ is equal to $k/k^2 = 1/k$. In particular, the area surrounded by a solid line represents $W(\mathcal{X})$ which equals $T(\mathcal{X})$, while the area surrounded by a dashed line corresponds to the maximum amount of work that can be performed in the same amount of time.

7.4 PARALLEL PREFIX SUM

Prefix sum (a.k.a. *scan, prefix reduction,* or *partial sum*) is an important building block that can be efficiently solved by means of parallel computational techniques. Given a list of elements, after a scan operation, each position in the resulting list contains the sum of the items in the list up to its index. Prefix sum operation for any associate operator is defined in [7] as follows:

Definition 1 *Let $\oplus$ be a binary associative operator with identity $\mathcal{I}$. Given an ordered set of n elements*

$$[a_1, a_2, \ldots, a_n],$$

the exclusive scan operation returns the ordered set

$$[\mathcal{I}, a_1, (a_1 \oplus a_2), \ldots, (a_1 \oplus \cdots \oplus a_{n-1})].$$

Because of its relevance, scan has been deeply studied by researchers to devise more efficient parallel solutions for its computation. The rest of the section analyzes the solutions proposed in [8–10] by means of the K-model. The common pattern used by the solutions proposed in [9, 10] to access EM is first discussed. In the second part of this section, we analyze the approaches and the patterns used by the considered solutions for accessing IM once data have been fetched from EM.

The solutions described in [9, 10] are based on visiting a binary tree twice. The first visit consists in a bottom-up visit applied on a tree having as many leaves as the values in the input list; the second visit consists of the same procedure performed in a

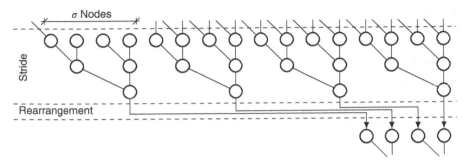

FIGURE 7.3 *Example of a tree-stride committed to a kernel. Given σ = 4, each stream element performs a bottom-up visit on a subtree having four nodes. After the computation, the partial results are rearranged in an auxiliary array stored in EM.*

top-down manner. As a consequence, the following considerations are valid for both the visits. Let us consider the bottom-up visit in the following analysis.

Whenever the input size exceeds $|\text{IM}| = \sigma$, we cannot straightforwardly store the binary tree in IM and, thus, the computation has to be divided into more than one kernel to be executed sequentially. In particular, given σ, the computation of the entire binary tree is divided into sequences of log σ consecutive levels called *strides*. As shown in Fig. 7.3, a stride consists of a set of subtrees with σ leaves and height equal to log σ. Notice that we are working on the assumption that σ elements can be stored in IM. If the condition is violated, a smaller set of values can be allocated in IM, and the height of a subtree computed by a kernel decreases. As a consequence, the number of strides for visiting the entire tree increases by degrading $G()$. Thus, the space complexity of a solution becomes a key point for the overall performance.

Each stride is committed to a kernel, which splits the list of nodes to be computed in σ-sized sequences. Each sequence is treated as a stream element and, once the related subtree has been computed, the result is copied from the subtree root into an auxiliary array in EM. As all these values resulting from the stream computation are stored in consecutive positions, they are efficiently accessed by the next kernel.

Finally, given a n-sized input array, the number of kernels to compute for visiting the entire tree is $f_\sigma(n) = \lceil \log n / \log \sigma \rceil = O(\log_\sigma n)$. Since each kernel accesses all the nodes at the tree level in which its computation starts and the i-th level of a binary tree contains 2^i nodes, the complexity related to the number of memory transactions is

$$G(n,k) = \sum_{i=0}^{f_\sigma(n)-1} \frac{2^{i \log \sigma}}{k} = \frac{1}{k} \sum_{i=0}^{f_\sigma(n)-1} \sigma^i = \frac{1}{k} \cdot \frac{n-1}{\sigma-1} = O\left(\frac{n}{\sigma k}\right).$$

We now evaluate the complexity $T()$ for the presented solutions. In [8], the authors propose a solution inspired by the algorithm described in [11]. Such a solution, depicted in Algorithm 7.1, performs $O(n \log n)$ operations on a list of n values. Since a sequential scan performs $O(n)$ sums, the log n extra factor could have a significant impact on the performance, and hence it cannot be considered work-efficient. Note that the algorithm in [11] is designed for the connection machine architecture [12], which is different from the *K*-model because the execution time is dominated by the number of steps performed rather than the work complexity.

Algorithm 7.1

```
Work-inefficient scan {
    for d ← 1 to log(n) do
        for each k such that 2^d ≤ k < n in parallel do
            A[k] ← A[k] + A[k - 2^(d-1)];
}
```

Algorithm 7.1 performs $\log n$ steps by computing $O(n)$ operations at each step. Such operations can be elaborated k at a time to fully exploit the data parallelism of the architecture. Moreover, they can be implemented to avoid all conflicts on the memory modules by temporarily storing the needed operands fetched from IM into private registers. When all sums have been computed, the results are stored in IM. As a result, the time complexity of the solution is

$$T(n, k) = \frac{O(n \log n)}{k}. \tag{7.1}$$

In [9], a work-efficient scan algorithm that avoids the $\log n$ extra factor is presented. As depicted in Algorithm 7.2, the set of operations is rearranged in a balanced binary tree by exploiting the associativity of the sum operator. The execution consists in visiting twice such a tree. First, a bottom-up visit computes $O(n)$ sums of all the pairs of consecutive nodes at each level of the tree; then it stores the result by replacing one of the operands. Then, a top-down visit redistributes the partial results to the lower levels of the tree.

Algorithm 7.2

```
Work efficient scan {
    for d ← 0 to log(n) - 1 do
        for k ← 0 to n - 1 by 2^(d+1) in parallel do
            i ← k + 2^d - 1;
            A[i + 2^d] ← A[i + 2^d] + A[i];
    A[n-1] ← 0
    for d ← log(n) - 1 down to 0 do
        for k ← 0 to n - 1 by 2^(d+1) in parallel do
            i ← k + 2^d - 1;
            x ← A[i];
            A[i] ← A[i+2^d];
            A[i + 2^d] ← A[i + 2^d] + x;
}
```

Let us now consider only the iterations performing the bottom-up visit (the same considerations are valid also for the second visit). Given $0 \le d < \log(n)$, the number of operations to compute at the level d of the tree is $n/2^{d+1}$ and they are performed k at a time. Considering a k-sized group of operations performed at a level d, the IM modules storing the results are those having index equal to $2^{d+1} \bmod k$. Since the parameter k is usually a power of 2, level by level the contention on IM doubles because the k accesses for storing the results tend to converge to the same queues, and, as a consequence, the latency increases up to a factor k. As a matter of fact, after $\log k$ levels the IU issues k operations to the k scalar processors but the time required to access the data in IM is a multiple of k. In other words, most of the internal work is performed like in the sequential case. The related time complexity is

$$T(n,k) = \frac{1}{k} \cdot \sum_{i=1}^{\log k} n/2^i + \sum_{i=\log k+1}^{\log n} n/2^i. \tag{7.2}$$

Whenever the input size is greater than k, the right-hand side of (7.2) becomes dominant, and then the time complexity is $T(n,k) = O(n)$ with a null speed-up over the sequential case. To face this inefficiency, the authors propose an improvement consisting of a mapping function for arranging data in IM. Given an n-sized input array, the proposed mapping function is $A[i] \mapsto IM[\ i + \lfloor i/k \rfloor\ ]$ with $0 \le i < n$. Such a function periodically interleaves an empty position when allocating the input values, and thus the amount of required memory grows up to $n + \lfloor n/k \rfloor$. This implies an $O(n/k)$ extra space while the first $2 \times \log k$ levels of the tree are efficiently computed. The computation of the remaining levels is still characterized by the inefficiency affecting Algorithm 7.2, which means that most of the accesses to IM exploit one IM module. As a consequence, they are performed sequentially, degrading the internal communication bandwidth by a factor k. The new improved time complexity formula is

$$T(n,k) = \frac{1}{k} \cdot \sum_{i=1}^{2 \cdot \log k} n/2^i + \sum_{i=2 \cdot \log k+1}^{\log n} n/2^i. \tag{7.3}$$

By considering the time complexity of the same computation on a PRAM, we can prove that the lower bound for the time complexity for performing such a visit on a stream element by means of the K-model is $O(n/k)$. We can achieve this result when all the accesses to IM are equally distributed among its modules avoiding conflicts.

Proof: Given a PRAM with a fixed number of processors p, the time complexity of the best known solution for scan is $T_p(n) = 2 \times (\lceil n/p \rceil + \lceil \log p \rceil) = O(n/p + \log p)$. Whenever $n \ge p \log p$, the complexity becomes $O(n/p)$, which is also an optimal speed-up with respect to the sequential case [7]. Since the K-model architecture is equivalent to a PRAM equipped with a fixed number of processors $p = k$ and a set of architectural constraints that can lead to an increase in the time complexity, we can state that $T_k(\cdot) \ge T_p(\cdot)$ where $T_p(\cdot)$ and $T_k(\cdot)$ denote the generic time complexity for PRAM and K-model, respectively.   ∎

Therefore, a solution for prefix sum having a time complexity $T_k(n) = O(n/k)$ in the K-model is optimal because it equals the time complexity $O(n/p)$ on an equivalent PRAM. To reach the complexity $O(n/k)$, a data access pattern, called *leftright*,

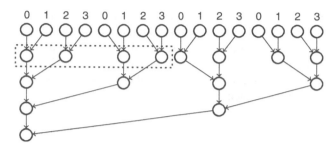

FIGURE 7.4 *Representation of the leftright pattern applied to a tree with n = 16 values allo-cated in IM having k = 4. Numbers on the top denote IM module in which a node is stored. The dotted rectangle gathers a bunch of k operations, namely the atomic unit of the performance analysis.*

is proposed in [10]. It eliminates the memory contention on IM by redirecting the operation results into distinct memory modules for each group of k operations.

As shown in Fig. 7.4, given k operations to execute, the proposed pattern alternatively stores the first $k/2$ results by replacing the values of the operands with smaller indices (i.e., the leftmost positions), and then it stores the remaining $k/2$ results replacing the operands with greater indices (i.e., the rightmost positions). Equation (7.4) formally defines this pattern:

$$LR_m(p, q) = \underbrace{\mathtt{rst}_m(p \cdot 2^q)}_{\text{base}} + \underbrace{\mathtt{cls}_m^q(p)}_{\text{offset}}. \tag{7.4}$$

In particular, $\mathtt{cls}_h^m(x)$ returns the result of computing m times the left circular shift of the h least significant bits of x, and $\mathtt{rst}_h(x)$ resets the h least significant bits of x. For example, $\mathtt{cls}_3^1(12) = \mathtt{cls}_3^1(1100) = \mathtt{cls}_3^1(100) = 001 = 1$ and $\mathtt{rst}_3(13) = \mathtt{rst}_3(1101) = 1000 = 8$. The pseudocode in Algorithm 7.3 shows how the proposed pattern is employed for visiting a tree as in Algorithm 7.2.

Algorithm 7.3

```
Free conflict tree bottom-up visit {
    for d ← 0 to log(n) - 1 do
        for i ← 0 to n/2^(d+1) - 1 in parallel do
            A[LR_log k(i,d + 1)] = A[LR_log k(2i,d)] + A[LR_log k(2i + 1,d)];
}
```

Equation (7.4) defines the proposed pattern. Before proving that it is able to balance the accesses to IM, let us state some preliminary points: (p_1) since the input array A is allocated in a consecutive IM area, each k-sized segment of A is equally distributed among the IM modules; (p_2) Equation (7.4) applies the operator $\mathtt{cls}$ to the least significant $\log k$ bits of the element positions involved in the computation; (p_3) since k is a power of 2, the element at position i is stored in the IM module identified by the $\log k$ least significant bits of i.

Proof: For induction on the level of the tree to visit. According to (p_1), at the first level the operands are equally distributed among the IM modules and no conflicts are generated in accessing them. For each further level to visit, the proposed pattern applies LR to bunches of k pairs of operands in order to define the array positions to replace with the results. According to (p_2) and a set of array positions having distinct values in the $\log k$ least significant bits, the positions obtained by applying the same circular shift to such a set still have distinct values in the last $\log k$ bits. Consequently, from (p_3), these new positions, used for storing the result at the current step, are equally distributed among the IM modules. This avoids conflicts accessing IM during the execution of the current step as well as the next one (note that the result nodes at the current step become operands at the next one).   ∎

As previously argued, this memory access pattern maintains the allocation of the nodes involved in the computation in distinct IM modules so that each access is performed with the minimum latency in a constant time. The corresponding time complexity is

$$T(n,\ k) = \frac{1}{k} \cdot \sum_{i=1}^{\log n} n/2^i = O\left(\frac{n}{k}\right). \tag{7.5}$$

Exploiting the proposed pattern, Algorithm 7.2 has an optimal speed-up over the sequential algorithm, and, as it has the time complexity of an equivalent PRAM, it is optimal.

7.4.1 Experiments

Experiments have been conducted using CUDA SDK 3.1 on the NVIDIA 275GTX video device. Because of the actual size of the on-chip shared data-memory and considering the standard 32-bit word size, each stream element can compute at most 2048 elements.

Figure 7.5 shows the elapsed time of prefix sum computed on input lists that fit in a stream element. The experiment considers only the internal work measured by $T()$.

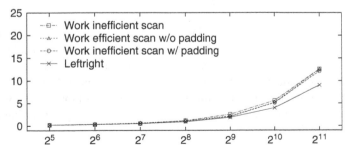

FIGURE 7.5 *Elapsed time (in milliseconds) of the scan operation by varying the size of the input arrays in a range of values that can fit in IM.*

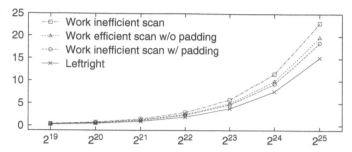

FIGURE 7.6   *Elapsed time (in milliseconds) of the scan operation by varying the size of the input arrays in a range of values that can fit in EM.*

Figure 7.6 shows the elapsed time obtained by computing prefix sum on input lists that do not fit in a stream element. The solution proposed in [10], that is *leftright*, is proven to be up to 25% faster than the competitors. Concerning the computation of large arrays, the benefits of applying the *K*-model-driven data access patterns are less evident, but *leftright* still outperforms the competitors. The main reason of this behavior lies in the increased number of communications with EM that dominates the total computational time.

7.5   BITONIC SORTING NETWORKS

Sorting networks [13] are a mathematical tool consisting of a fixed schema of comparisons exploited to sort a given list of items. The main difference with respect to comparison-based sorting algorithms (e.g., merge sort, quicksort) and other ones (e.g., radix sort) is that the sequence of comparisons is known in advance independently of the input data distribution. A fixed schema of comparisons is particularly suitable for distributed parallel solutions because it permits the study of techniques that balance the workload among the available computational resources. However, the computational cost of this kind of solutions[1] is usually higher (i.e., $O(n \log^2 n)$) than other algorithms, such as quick-sort (i.e., $O(n \log n)$) and radix sort (i.e., $O(n)$).

The analysis of sorting network solutions conducted by means of the *K*-model leads to different results, in particular, regarding the complexity $G()$. The time complexity $T()$ of each solution reaches the maximum speed when dealing with the sequential case, thus leaving unchanged the complexity of the algorithms shown in Table 7.2. The pattern used to access the external memory EM can remarkably influence the computational time of the algorithms. In the following text, we analyze the function $G()$ to devise an efficient pattern for a particular type of sorting networks called *bitonic sorting networks* (BSNs) [15].

---

[1] The best-known sorting network [14] achieves a time complexity $O(n \log n)$. This solution is not feasible in practice because of the large linear constants hidden by the O-notation.

Algorithm 7.4

```
Bitonic sorting network {
    n ← |A|;
    for s ← 1 to log n do
        for c ← s - 1 down to 0 do
            for each 0 ≤ r < n in parallel do
                if r/2^c ≡ r/2^s (mod 2) and A[r] > A[r ⊕ 2^c] then A[r] ⇆ A[r ⊕ 2^c];
}
```

Algorithm 7.4 shows how a BSN performs on an array A of n items (with n equal to a power of 2 for simplifying the notation). For each couple of values c and s, the innermost loop (referred to as a *step*) performs $O(n)$ comparisons between distinct couples of entries. It is done by swapping ($\leftrightarrows$) each pair of entries if they are not in the desired order. Algorithm 7.4 performs $O(log^2 n)$ steps and, as all pairs compared in a step are distinct, each step can be divided in disjoint blocks of k comparisons. The resulting time complexity for computing a single step is then $O(n/k)$ assuming that no conflicts occur when accessing the related entries stored in IM.

Concerning the access to the external memory EM, at each step $A[r]$ is compared with the item stored at position $r \oplus 2^c$ obtained by flipping the c-th bit of r. Consequently, for each sequence of m consecutive steps, it is possible to split A in disjoint subsets of entries to be computed as defined in the following.

Definition 2 *Let $C = \{c_1, \dots, c_m\}$ with $1 \leq m \leq \log n$ being a set of distinct c values computed by Algorithm 7.4, the function $f_C : A \to 2^A$ returns a group of subsets of elements in A whose indices differ only for the bits in positions $c_1, \dots, c_m$.*

From Definition 2, we can claim the following two properties.

Claim 1 *Each subset returned by $f_C(A)$ with $|C| = m$, $|A| = n$, and $1 \leq m \leq \log n$ has 2^m elements.*

Proof: By induction on m. If $m = 1$, then $C = \{c\}$ and each subset returned by $f_C(A)$ is built by matching $A[r]$ versus $A[r \oplus 2^c]$ with $0 \leq r < n$. When $|C| = m + 1$, because values in C are distinct, a new element is added to the subset by flipping the c_{m+1}-th bit of each item inserted in C at the previous step. As a consequence, the number of items doubles, namely it is $2 \cdot 2^m = 2^{m+1}$. ∎

Claim 2 *The function $f_C(A)$ is a partition of A.*

Proof: Let $P = f_C(A)$, where P is a partition of A iff the following three conditions hold: (i) $\emptyset \notin P$. Since $m \geq 1$, each part includes at least two elements, as stated by Claim 1; (ii) let $p_1 \in P$ and $p_2 \in P$ with $p_1 \neq p_2$; then $p_1 \cap p_2 = \emptyset$. From Definition 2, it follows that two elements in A whose indices are equal for the bits in positions not in C are in the same part p. Consequently, if $p_1 \cap p_2 \neq \emptyset$, then there exists $a \in A$ such that $a \in p_1$ and $a \in p_2$ and then $p_1 = p_2$, contradicting the hypothesis $p_1 \neq$

p_2; (iii) $\cup P = A$. Claim 1 states that each partition has exactly 2^m elements and the number of possible combination for the $\log n - m$ bits not in C is $2^{\log n-m}$. As the intersection of any two distinct parts is empty, $|\cup P| = 2^{\log n-m} \cdot 2^m = n$ which is the size of A; then according to the pigeonhole principle, A is entirely covered.   ∎

Therefore, computing a BSN consists in performing all the *steps* each one using the proper value of c. Since each BSN consists of a fixed schema of comparisons, the sequence of values assigned to c in Algorithm 7.4 is fixed as well, and it only depends on the size n of the input. Let $C'(n)$ be the sequence of c values computed by Algorithm 7.4 for an n-sized input array A; then we can rewrite the computation as shown in Algorithm 7.5, where $step(A, c_i)$ denotes the comparisons to perform when $c = c_i$ while $n' = \log n(1 + \log n)/2$ denotes the number of steps to perform. Note that only c determines how the items are paired. As a consequence, s does not affect the analysis of the algorithm complexity.

Algorithm 7.5

```
Bitonic sorting network {
    n ← |A|;
    C' ← [c₁, ...cₙ,];
    for each i ← 1 to n' in parallel do step(A,cᵢ);
}
```

Claim 2 permits us to compute the network as a stream. We can define a kernel for executing a sequence of consecutive steps of the BSN. We arrange the input in a stream of elements using $f_C(A)$ as a pattern to access the external memory EM. As the stream elements are distinct, they can be computed independently, that is, without violating the schema of comparisons stated by Algorithm 7.4.

In [16], the authors propose an algorithm for computing a BSN on GPUs that minimizes the number of kernels to compute. As each kernel computation accesses the entire array A stored in EM, the proposed solution aims at minimizing the overhead of accessing EM by reducing the number of kernel invocations. However, the analysis does not take the memory transaction efficiency into account.

As m steps can be computed within a kernel invocation, and the steps required for sorting n items are $O(\log^2 n)$, the number of kernel to perform is $\lceil O(\log^2 n)/m \rceil$. The upper bound for m depends on the K-model architecture, namely the size of the internal memory IM denoted by σ in Fig. 7.1. In fact, each stream element is computed by the scalar execution units $e_{1,...,k}$ sharing the data stored in IM. As for computing m steps, each stream element needs to store 2^m elements and $2^m \le \sigma$, m is bounded by $\log \sigma$. Therefore, the number of kernels to compute is $\lceil O(\log^2 n)/\log \sigma \rceil$, and Algorithm 7.5 can be rewritten as depicted in Algorithm 7.6, where the invocation of the *step* procedure denotes the computation of a kernel. This way, each stream element p can be independently computed by (i) loading the entries in $p \subseteq A$ from *EM*, (ii) comparing them on the base of the values in C, and (iii) replacing p in EM with the computed permutation.

Algorithm 7.6

```
Bitonic sorting network {
    n ← |A|;
    m ← log σ;
    C' ← [c₁,...,cₙ'];
    for i ← 1 to n' step m do
        C ← {cᵢ,...cᵢ₊ₘ₋₁};
        for each p ∈ f_C(A) in parallel do step(p, c₍ᵢ,...,ᵢ₊ₘ₋₁₎);
}
```

Once the number of kernels is defined, the number of memory transactions to calculate $G()$ can be estimated as defined in Section 7.3. The definition of $f_C(\cdot)$ states that a pair of entries whose indices share the same bit in the positions not occurring in C belong to the same stream element. It follows that the number of memory transactions is related to the range of values returned by $f_C(\cdot)$. In particular, the higher the distance between the values in C with respect to the least significant bit position, the wider the range of the memory area to access as well as its complexity. For example, when C covers the least significant bits, the array entries to copy during the kernel computation are stored at consecutive positions, and then only k-sized segments of EM are addressed during the process. The opposite case is when such a distance is equal to or greater than log k, and consequently the efficiency drops of a factor k. Formally, let the bit in position 0 be the least significant one and, given a set C of values with $c' = \min(C)$, the number of memory transactions to perform grows up to k with $2^{c'}$ factor.

Since the number of kernels to compute is $\lceil O(\log^2 n)/\log \sigma \rceil$ and c is defined in a range $[0, \log n - 1]$, it follows that

$$G(n,k) = O\left(\sigma \cdot \frac{n \log^2 n}{\log \sigma}\right).$$

The formula highlights the underexploitation of the EM bandwidth, namely $1/k$. As $G()$ is more related to the efficiency of each memory transaction, a pattern that forces C to permanently include the values $0, \ldots, \log k - 1$ is proposed in [17]. As a consequence, each stream element is made of subsequences of elements allocated in k-sized segment of EM so as to maximize the efficiency of each memory transaction. On the contrary, as the number of steps performed by a kernel drops from log σ down to log σ − log k, the number of kernel to compute increases. The new complexity is

$$G'(n,k) = O\left(\frac{\sigma}{k} \cdot \frac{n \log^2 n}{\log \sigma - \log k}\right).$$

The previous analysis implicitly requires $IM/k \geq 1$. We can use a stronger assumption, called the *tall-cache assumption* [6], that requires $\sigma = \Omega(k^2)$. According to this assumption, $G()$ and $G'()$, for [16] and [17], respectively, can be written as

$$G(n,k) = O\left(k^2 \cdot \frac{n\log^2 n}{\log k}\right)$$

and

$$G'(n,k) = O\left(k \cdot \frac{n\log^2 n}{\log k}\right),$$

with a speed-up factor of $G'()$ over $G()$ equal to k. Moreover, both solutions have the same $T(n,k) = O((n\log^2 n)/k)$ because $O(n)$ comparisons are performed independently at each step without conflicts accessing IM, as shown in Table 7.2.

The solution above is now compared with the quicksort-based algorithm proposed in [18] and the radixsort-based algorithm proposed in [9].

The quicksort-based solution splits the computation into $\log n$ steps. For each step, it performs three kernels: (i) The first one splits the input array in a given number of stream elements. Each of them counts the number of entries greater or smaller than the global pivot in the given portion of data. (ii) The second one performs two parallel prefix sums on the lists of counters obtained from the previous phase. The lists have as many elements as the stream elements previously defined and, at the end of the current step, they contain the entry points that will be used to rearrange the input in the next phase. (iii) The algorithm copies the input array into a new array in EM by starting from the position computed by the previous kernel.

Concerning the complexity $G()$ of the quicksort-based solution, the first kernel efficiently accesses the input array by addressing k consecutive positions so that the related number of memory transactions is n/k. Then, the counters are flushed and the second kernel starts. Assuming that the number of stream elements is smaller than σ, the prefix sum operations can be performed in parallel. Consequently, each prefix sum needs $O(|stream|/k)$ memory transactions for reading/writing all the counters. Finally, the last kernel efficiently reads the input, and, depending on the distribution of the data, it flushes the elements on EM by requiring $O(n)$ memory transactions.

The first kernel consists in comparing n items, k at a time, with a given pivot. Consequently, the related time complexity is n/k. As the second kernel performs a prefix sum on an input array of size n/k, the time complexity $T()$ of this kernel is $O(\log n/k)$. Moreover, the last kernel performs also in $O(n/k)$ time.

Table 7.3 shows the complexities of the three kernels computed according to the K-model. The complexity of the algorithm can be obtained by multiplying by $\log n$ the sum of the kernel complexities.

TABLE 7.2   Theoretical Evaluation of BSN-Based Solutions According to the K-Model

	$G(n,k)$	$T(n,k)$
Naïve [16]	$O(k^2 \cdot (n\log^2 n)/\log k)$	$O((n\log^2 n)/k)$
K-model [17]	$O(k \cdot (n\log^2 n)/\log k)$	$O((n\log^2 n)/k)$

TABLE 7.3   Theoretical Evaluation of Quicksort-Based Solution According to K-Model

	$G(n, k)$	$T(n, k)$
First kernel	$O(n/k)$	$O(n/k)$
Second kernel	$O(n/k^2)$	$O(\log n/k)$
Third kernel	$O(n)$	$O(n/k)$
Quicksort	$O(n \log n)$	$O\left(\frac{n}{k} \log n\right)$

The radixsort-based solution consists in dividing the n-sized input array into h-sized stream elements and repeating a binary-split kernel on b bit positions at a time. To execute each kernel, blocks of elements are loaded into IM, and then sorted by executing b times a binary-split procedure. Let m be the binary representation size of the elements in memory, and the kernel execution is repeated m/b times. The resulting counters are moved into EM and a prefix sum operation over $\lceil n/h \rceil \cdot 2^b$ values is executed. It is needed for calculating the right position to store the partially sorted data. During the final copy to EM, the sequence of memory addresses accessed is not consecutive as it depends on the input data distribution. The number of memory transactions is $O(2^b)$ and, as for 32-bit words $32/b$ kernels are performed, the total number of memory transactions performed is $O((32/b) \cdot (n/h) \cdot 2^b)$.

Concerning $T()$, radixsort consists of a binary-split procedure which is performed in $O(b \cdot n/k)$. Eventually, complexities of the radixsort-based solution are $G(n, k) = O(n)$ and $T(n, k) = O(n/k)$.

7.5.1   Experiments

Experiments have been conducted using CUDA SDK 3.1 on the NVIDIA 8800GT video device. The input arrays have been generated according to three different distributions: Gaussian, uniform, and zipfian. Because of the size of the physical memory on the device, that is, 512 MB, the maximum size of the array we used is equal to 2^{26}. The experimental results are obtained by averaging the elapsed times resulting from 20 runs per array. Figures 7.7 and 7.8 confirm the theoretical predictions. Radixsort is the fastest solution. This is mainly due to its complexity $G()$, which is dominant with respect to its complexity $T()$.

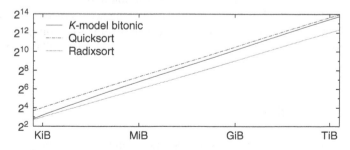

FIGURE 7.7   *Number of memory transactions assuming $k = 16$ (in log scale).*

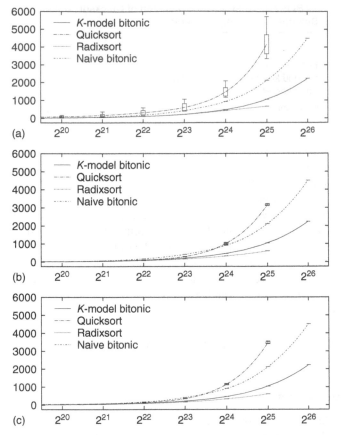

FIGURE 7.8 *Elapsed sorting time (in milliseconds) by varying the size of the array to sort generated with different distributions. Variance, maximum, and minimum of elapsed times are represented with candlesticks. (a) Zipf's distribution. (b) Uniform distribution. (c) Gaussian distribution.*

Furthermore, the quicksort-based solution is the slowest method among the ones analyzed (Fig. 7.8). Results of the BSN designed according to the K-model are comparable with those of the radixsort-based solution and faster than those of the quicksort-based solution. It is due to the enhanced data access pattern which allows the full exploitation of the external memory bandwidth. Regarding the memory usage, as BSNs are an in-place solution, it can devote all the available memory to store the dataset. It is not true for the competitors.

7.6 FINAL REMARKS

Designing algorithms for many cores is a hard task, but the achievable gain in term of speed-up justifies such an effort. This chapter described the K-model, a useful means to design efficient algorithms for this kind of computing architectures. In particular, it focused on data access patterns that constitute the main bottleneck for achieving high performance. The K-model consists of (i) an abstract machine to run stream-based algorithms written with a reduced set of instructions; (ii) a cost function to evaluate the time required for executing each instruction; and (iii) two formulas to compute the overall complexity of a given algorithm. The time required to access the external memory, denoted by $G()$, is usually one order of magnitude higher than the cost sustained to perform the internal work, denoted by $T()$. Generally, $G()$ dominates $T()$, but as the algorithm becomes computationally intensive, $T()$ acquires more importance. To show the feasibility of the K-model, two case studies, namely parallel prefix sum and bitonic sorting networks, were analyzed. They are two important algorithms that can be exploited for building more complex parallel applications. The experiments conducted demonstrated that the K-model could be fruitfully exploited to design efficient algorithms for computational platforms with many cores.

ACKNOWLEDGMENTS

This research was supported by the COST Action IC0805 "Open European Network for High Performance Computing on Complex Environments."

REFERENCES

1. G. Capannini, F. Silvestri, and R. Baraglia, "K-model: a new computational model for stream processors," in *12th IEEE International Conference on High Performance Computing and Communications (HPCC)*, pp. 239–246. Melbourne: IEEE, 2010.
2. S. Fortune and J. Wyllie, "Parallelism in random access machines," in *Proceedings of the Tenth Annual ACM Symposium on Theory of Computing*, pp. 114–118. San Diego, CA: ACM, 1978.
3. G. E. Blelloch, *Vector Models for Data-Parallel Computing*, vol. 75. Cambridge, MA: MIT Press, 1990.
4. A. Aggarwal, A. K. Chandra, and M. Snir, "Hierarchical memory with block transfer," in *28th Annual Symposium on Foundations of Computer Science*, pp. 204–216. Dallas, TX: IEEE, 1987.
5. P. B. Gibbons, Y. Matias, and V. Ramachandran, "The QRQW PRAM: accounting for contention in parallel algorithms," in *Proceedings of the Fifth Annual ACM-SIAM Symposium on Discrete Algorithms*, (Arlington, Virginia), pp. 638–648. Society for Industrial and Applied Mathematics, 1994.
6. M. Frigo, C. E. Leiserson, H. Prokop, and S. Ramachandran, "Cache-oblivious algorithms," in *40th Annual Symposium on Foundations of Computer Science*, pp. 285–297. Washington, DC, IEEE, 1999.
7. G. Blelloch, "Prefix sums and their applications," in *Synthesis of Parallel Algorithms* (J. H. Reif, ed.), pp. 35–60. San Francisco, CA: Morgan Kaufmann, 1990.
8. D. Horn, "Stream reduction operations for GPGPU applications," in *GPU Gems 2*, pp. 573–589. Reading, MA: Addison-Wesley, 2005.

9. M. Harris, S. Sengupta, Y. Zhang, and J. D. Owens, "Scan primitives for GPU computing," in *Proceedings of the 22nd ACM SIGGRAPH/EUROGRAPHICS Symposium on Graphics Hardware*, pp. 97–106. Aire-la-Ville, Switzerland, Switzerland: Eurographics Association, 2007.

10. G. Capannini, "Designing efficient parallel prefix sum algorithms for GPUs," in *IEEE 11th International Conference on Computer and Information Technology (CIT)*, pp. 189–196. Washington, DC: IEEE, 2011.

11. W. D. Hillis and G. L. Steele *Jr.*, "Data parallel algorithms," *Communications of the ACM*, vol. 29, no. 12, pp. 1170–1183, 1986.

12. L. W. Tucker and G. G. Robertson, "Architecture and applications of the connection machine," *Computer*, vol. 21, no. 8, pp. 26–38, 1988.

13. K. E. Batcher, "Sorting networks and their applications," in *Proceedings of the April 30–May 2, 1968, Spring Joint Computer Conference*, pp. 307–314. New York: ACM, 1968.

14. M. Ajtai, J. Komlós, and E. Szemerédi, "An $O(n \log n)$ sorting network," in *Proceedings of the Fifteenth Annual ACM Symposium on Theory of Computing, STOC '83*, pp. 1–9. New York: ACM, 1983.

15. K. E. Batcher, "On bitonic sorting networks," in *Proceedings of the 1990 International Conference on Parallel Processing, vol. 1*, (Syracuse University, NY, USA), pp. 376–379, 1990.

16. G. Capannini, F. Silvestri, R. Baraglia, and F. M. Nardini, "Sorting using BItonic netwoRk wIth CUDA," in *7th Workshop on Large-Scale Distributed Systems for Information Retrieval*, pp. 33–40. Boston, MA: ACM, 2009.

17. G. Capannini, F. Silvestri, and R. Baraglia, "Sorting on GPUs for large scale datasets: a thorough comparison," *Information Processing & Management*, vol. 48, no. 5, pp. 903–917, 2012.

18. D. Cederman and P. Tsigas, "A practical quicksort algorithm for graphics processors," in *Algorithms-ESA 2008*, pp. 246–258. Berlin, Heidelberg: Springer-Verlag, 2008.

8

Scalable Storage I/O Software for Blue Gene Architectures

Florin Isaila, Javier Garcia, and Jesús Carretero

Universidad Carlos III of Madrid, Madrid, Spain

This chapter presents our scalable storage I/O software solution for the hierarchical architecture of Blue Gene supercomputers. At the compute node level, application processes can declare views on the files as hints of potential future accesses, employ collective I/O operations for reducing the number of file system requests, and use asynchronous I/O for overlapping computations and storage I/O. At the I/O node level, our solution provides buffering for further reducing the pressure on the file system and asynchronous I/O for hiding the I/O latency to the compute nodes.

8.1 INTRODUCTION

The architecture of most of today's petascale high-end computing (HEC) systems is hierarchical [1]. For better scalability, computation is performed on a large number of strongly interconnected cores and is segregated from storage I/O functionality, which is delegated to dedicated I/O nodes. The I/O nodes are connected over high-performance networks to file system servers, which are further connected

High-Performance Computing on Complex Environments, First Edition.
Edited by Emmanuel Jeannot and Julius Žilinskas.
© 2014 John Wiley & Sons, Inc. Published 2014 by John Wiley & Sons, Inc.

through storage networks to the back-end storage. In these hierarchies, file access involves pipelining data through several networks with incremental latencies and higher probability of congestion. Furthermore, the current file systems have been designed for scaling to tens of thousands of clients and face increasing challenges as the systems go beyond petascale and approach exascale.

This chapter presents our scalable storage I/O software solution for the hierarchical architecture of Blue Gene supercomputers. At the compute node level, application processes can declare views on the files as hints of potential future accesses, employ collective I/O operations for reducing the number of file system requests, and use asynchronous I/O for overlapping computations and storage I/O. At the I/O node level, our solution provides buffering for further reducing the pressure on the file system and asynchronous I/O for hiding the I/O latency to the compute nodes. The material from this chapter is partially based on our previous work presented in [2–4].

The remainder of the chapter is structured as follows: Section 8.2 provides an overview of the Blue Gene architecture. Our scalable storage I/O architecture for Blue Gene systems is presented in Section 8.3. Finally, we conclude and present future work in Section 8.4.

8.2 BLUE GENE SYSTEM OVERVIEW

This section presents the hardware and software system architecture of Blue Gene.

8.2.1 Blue Gene Architecture

The Blue Gene supercomputer architecture is shown in Fig. 8.1. The architecture segregates compute nodes and I/O nodes. The compute nodes are organized in processing sets called "psets." The compute nodes are interconnected through a high-performance interconnect having a three-dimensional (3D) torus topology in Blue Gene/L and Blue Gene/P and a 5D torus topology in Blue Gene/Q.

I/O functionality of compute nodes is delegated to the I/O nodes. For instance, the compute nodes do not have local storage. Each I/O node acts as a proxy on behalf of the associated compute nodes. The I/O nodes are connected to the compute nodes through a proprietary interconnect with tree topology in Blue Gene/L and Blue Gene/P. On Blue Gene/Q systems, the compute and I/O nodes are interconnected through PCIe 2.0.

The I/O nodes are interconnected to storage nodes running file system servers through 10 Gb Ethernet switches (Blue Gene/P) or 10 Gb Infiniband switches (Blue Gene/Q). Finally, the storage nodes are interconnected to disks through a storage area network such as a fiber channel.

8.2.2 Operating System Architecture

The compute node of Blue Gene can be managed either by a light-weight kernel (LWK) or a full-weight kernel (FWK).

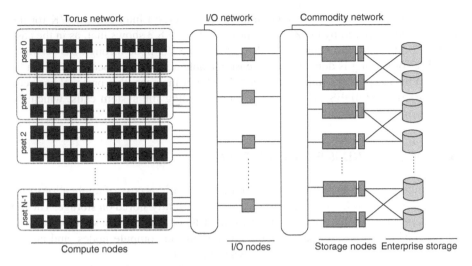

FIGURE 8.1 *Blue Gene architecture overview.*

The IBM solution is an LWK called *compute node kernel* (CNK) [5]. CNK has only basic functionalities such as setting an alarm or getting the time. In order to reduce the noise, CNK lacks much of traditional operating system functionalities such as swapping, local file system support, networking, or dynamic virtual memory translation. As shown in Fig. 8.2, the I/O functionality is delegated to the I/O nodes and is requested through a remote procedure call mechanism denoted I/O forwarding. The I/O nodes act as servers of the I/O functionality. The operating system of the I/O node is a stripped-down LINUX, which lacks the majority of daemons, does not have local storage, and mounts remote file systems. The I/O functionality is provided on the I/O node by a control and I/O daemon (CIOD). CIOD accepts incoming connection from compute nodes and serves them.

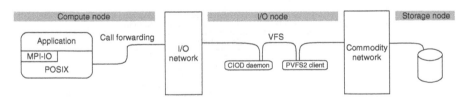

FIGURE 8.2 *File I/O forwarding for IBM solution.*

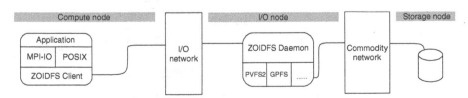

FIGURE 8.3 *File I/O forwarding in ZeptoOS.*

An alternative to the IBM solution is an open-source Linux-based FWK for the compute node offered by the ZeptoOS project.[1] Figure 8.3 shows that, as in the case of CNK, all the I/O functionality is delegated to the I/O node through I/O forwarding. The forwarding is done through a customizable network protocol, which can be handled by a ZeptoOS component called *ZOID*. For instance, this protocol has been customized as ZOIDFS [6], a solution for forwarding file system calls, which we employ in our architecture.

8.3   DESIGN AND IMPLEMENTATION

Our solution targets to optimize the performance of file access of applications running on compute nodes and accessing file data persistently stored on storage. The file access interfaces are the common standards MPI-IO or POSIX. The solution consists of two main modules: a client module running on the compute nodes, and an I/O module running on the I/O nodes as shown in Fig. 8.4.

In the following description, the communication between the application and the compute node caches is implemented in message passing interface (MPI), while the communication between the compute nodes and I/O nodes relies on I/O forwarding provided by ZOID, as discussed in Section 8.2.2. The asynchronous communication between a compute node and an I/O node is managed by an I/O thread running on each aggregator. Similarly, the asynchronous communication between an I/O node and shared file system is managed by an I/O thread running on each I/O node.

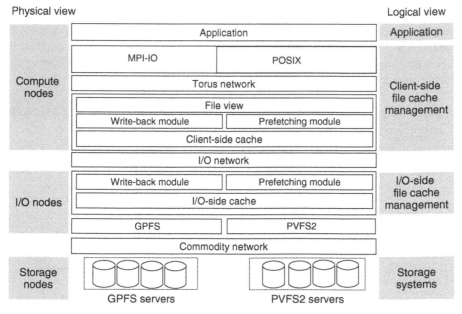

FIGURE 8.4   *Blue Gene storage I/O architecture.*

[1] http://www-unix.mcs.anl.gov/zeptoos/

8.3.1 The Client Module

The client module has the role of improving the performance of transfers between compute nodes and I/O nodes by aggregating small file requests into large requests and reducing the pressure on I/O nodes by absorbing the peak demands into local caches and asynchronously pipelining the transfers. In addition, the client module communicates with the I/O nodes to coordinate the two stages of the pipelined transfer.

The client module consists of four components: a compute node cache component, a file view component, a write-back component, and a prefetching component.

8.3.1.1 The Compute Node Cache The compute node cache is a file cache distributed over a subset of compute nodes called *aggregators*. The subset of the compute nodes can be decided by the application through hints. By default, all compute nodes of an application act as aggregators. A file is distributed over aggregators in a round-robin manner, as can be seen in Fig. 8.5. The cache at each aggregator has a flushing policy based on low/high watermarks, which are expressed as percentages of dirty (modified) page caches. When the number of modified page caches is larger than a high watermark, the aggregator starts to flush dirty pages to I/O node cache until the low watermark is reached. The replacement policy of each aggregator-local cache is least recently used (LRU).

8.3.1.2 The File View Component The file view component contains the implementation of a file view mechanism. A file view is a contiguous window mapped to noncontiguous file regions. Our solution provides a view-based collective I/O implementation. The following steps are performed for a collective file write:

- The application nodes declare in parallel views on a file based on MPI data types. The views are stored on the computed nodes.
- When the views are written, the data is mapped on the file, copies of the file blocks are allocated in the compute node cache, and the data is transferred to these copies.
- The data is transferred from compute node caches to I/O node caches based on the flushing strategy of the compute node cache.
- When the file is closed, all the dirty cache blocks that are still found in the cache are transferred to the I/O node caches. The I/O node caches are also flushed.

A similar mechanism is implemented for collective reads.

As seen above, view-based collective I/O offers mechanisms for improving the file access performance through data aggregation (view data is gathered on compute node caches) and asynchronous transfers between compute nodes and storage.

View-based I/O is an alternative implementation of two-phase collective I/O [7] from ROMIO, one of the most popular MPI-IO distributions. The most important differences between these two implementations can be found in our previous work [2].

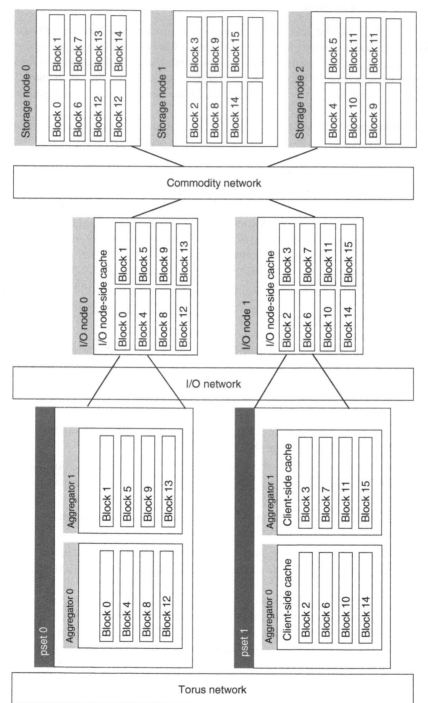

FIGURE 8.5 *Example of file mapping in our system.*

8.3.1.3 The Write-Back Component on the Compute Node The write-back component implements the strategy of flushing the pages from compute node cache to the I/O node cache and the coordination with the I/O node flushing. Different write-back strategies can be enforced by manipulating the high and low water marks of the compute node caches. For instance, a "write-through" behavior can be achieved by setting the high and low watermarks of all aggregators to zero and waiting for the termination of the flush process. On the other hand, setting the high watermark to 100% maximally postpones the flushing until the application finishes writing (or the cache is full).

8.3.1.4 The Prefetching Component on the Compute Node The prefetching component leverages the view information for initiating data prefetching requests from the I/O node cache. In this case, the views are seen as potential future accesses of compute nodes. The user can control the size of the prefetching window through application hints. By default, the prefetching is deactivated. A prefetching request from a compute node initiates a prefetching request on the I/O node. Data is then transferred from storage to the I/O node, and finally to the aggregator node. Subsequently, if a compute node requests the prefetched data, it finds them at the aggregator node.

8.3.2 The I/O Module

The I/O module has the role of improving the performance of transfers between I/O nodes and storage by reducing the pressure on I/O nodes through absorbing the peak demands into local caches and asynchronously pipelining the transfers. In addition, the I/O node module communicates with the compute nodes to coordinate the two stages of the pipelined transfer.

The I/O node module consists of four components: an I/O node cache component, a write-back component, and a prefetching component.

8.3.2.1 The I/O Node Cache The I/O node cache is a file cache distributed over all I/O nodes involved in the compute node partition of an application. A file is distributed to I/O nodes based on the aggregators' mapping, as can be seen in Fig. 8.5: a file block mapped to an aggregator will subsequently be mapped on the I/O node of the aggregator's pset. The cache at each I/O node has a flushing policy based on low/high watermarks, which are expressed as percentages of dirty (modified) page caches. When the number of modified page caches is larger than a high watermark, the I/O node starts to flush dirty pages to the file system until the low watermark is reached. The replacement policy of each I/O node-local cache is LRU.

8.3.2.2 The Write-Back Component on the I/O Node The write-back component implements the strategy of flushing the pages from the I/O node cache to the shared file system and the coordination with the compute node flushing. In the same manner as for compute nodes, different write-back strategies can be enforced by manipulating the high and low watermarks of the I/O node caches.

8.3.2.3   *The Prefetching Component on the I/O Node*   The prefetching component on the I/O node can prefetch data from the file system based on hints received from the compute nodes. These hints can either come from aggregators (in order to coordinate the prefetching policies of the compute node and I/O nodes) or directly from the applications as hints.

8.4   CONCLUSIONS AND FUTURE WORK

This chapter presented a scalable storage I/O solution for Blue Gene systems based on collective I/O optimizations, file views, and pipelined data staging. The data staging is supported by a two-level hierarchical caching system, consisting of an application-close, client-side cache and a storage-close, I/O node-side cache.

In the future, we plan to design novel adaptive data staging policies that address changes in network congestion, I/O node load, and file system response time. In addition, nonvolatile RAM (NVRAM) is considered one of the main memory technologies that will have a significant impact on energy efficiency, performance, access semantics, and resilience of the future exascale systems [1]. For instance, recent studies have focused on the role of NVRAM to absorb I/O bursts of scientific applications [8] and on analyzing the impact of NVRAM on scientific applications [9]. However, the impact of NVRAM technologies on the I/O software stack remains an open problem, as it has direct implications for all I/O stack levels. We plan to study how our solution can be adapted to novel architectural designs including NVRAM and to explore the role of NVRAM in reducing the impact of I/O bursts and increasing the scalability of the I/O stack.

ACKNOWLEDGMENTS

This work was supported in part by Spanish Ministry of Science and Innovation under the project TIN 2007/6309, by the US Department of Energy under Contracts DE-FC02-07ER25808, DE-FC02-01ER25485, and DE-AC02-06CH11357, and NSF HECURA CCF-0621443, NSF SDCIOCI-0724599, and NSF ST-HEC CCF-0444405.

This research used the resources of the Argonne Leadership Computing Facility at Argonne National Laboratory, which is supported by the Office of Science of the US Department of Energy under contract DE-AC02-06CH11357.

This work was also supported by the COST Action IC0805 "Open European Network for High-Performance Computing on Complex Environments."

REFERENCES

1. J. Dongarra, P. Beckman, *et al.*, "The international exascale software roadmap," *International Journal of High Performance Computer Applications*, vol. 25, no. 1, pp. 3–60, 2011.
2. J. G. Blas, F. Isaila, D. E. Singh, and J. Carretero, "View-based collective I/O for MPI-IO," in *CCGRID*, pp. 409–416, 2008.

3. F. Isaila, J. G. Blas, J. Carretero, R. Latham, S. Lang, and R. Ross, "Latency hiding file I/O for Blue Gene systems," in *CCGRID* '09, Shanghai, pp. 212–219, 2009.

4. F. Isaila, J. Garcia Blas, J. Carretero, R. Latham, and R. Ross, "Design and evaluation of multiple-level data staging for Blue Gene systems," *IEEE Transactions on Parallel and Distributed Systems*, vol. 22, no. 6, pp. 946–959, 2011.

5. J. Moreira, *et al.*, "Designing a highly-scalable operating system: the Blue Gene/L story," in *Proceedings of the ACM/IEEE SC 2006 Conference: Tampa*, p. 118, 2006.

6. K. Iskra, J. W. Romein, K. Yoshii, and P. Beckman, "ZOID: I/O-forwarding infrastructure for petascale architectures," in *Proceedings of the 13th ACM SIGPLAN Symposium on Principles and Practice of Parallel Programming, PPoPP '08*, Salt Lake City, pp. 153–162, 2008.

7. R. Thakur and A. Choudhary, "An Extended Two-phase Method for Accessing Sections of Out-of-core Arrays," Sci.Program, vol. 5, no. 4, pp. 301–317, IOS Press, Amsterdam, The Netherlands, 1996.

8. N. Liu, J. Cope, P. H. Carns, C. D. Carothers, R. B. Ross, G. Grider, A. Crume, and C. Maltzahn, "On the role of burst buffers in leadership-class storage systems," in *IEEE 28th Symposium on Mass Storage Systems and Technologies (MSST)*, Pacific Grove, pp. 1–11, 2012.

9. D. Li, J. S. Vetter, G. Marin, C. McCurdy, C. Cira, Z. Liu, and W. Yu, "Identifying opportunities for byte-addressable non-volatile memory in extreme-scale scientific applications," in *Proceedings of the 2012 IEEE 26th International Parallel and Distributed Processing Symposium, IPDPS '12*, pp. 945–956. Washington, DC: IEEE Computer Society, 2012.

PART IV

Efficient Exploitation of Heterogeneous Architectures

9

Fair Resource Sharing for Dynamic Scheduling of Workflows on Heterogeneous Systems

Hamid Arabnejad and Jorge G. Barbosa

Universidade do Porto, Porto, Portugal

Frédéric Suter

IN2P3 Computing Center, CNRS, IN2P3, Lyon-Villeurbanne, France

Scheduling independent workflows on shared resources in a way that satisfies users' quality of service (QoS) is a significant challenge. In this chapter, we describe methodologies for offline scheduling, where a schedule is generated for a set of known workflows, and online scheduling, where users can submit workflows at any moment in time. We consider the online scheduling problem in more detail and present performance comparisons of state-of-the-art algorithms for a realistic model of a heterogeneous system.

High-Performance Computing on Complex Environments, First Edition.
Edited by Emmanuel Jeannot and Julius Žilinskas.
© 2014 John Wiley & Sons, Inc. Published 2014 by John Wiley & Sons, Inc.

9.1 INTRODUCTION

Heterogeneous computing systems (HCSs) are composed of different types of computational units and are widely used for executing parallel applications, predominantly scientific workflows. A workflow consists of many tasks with logical or data dependencies that can be dispatched to different compute nodes in the HCS. To achieve an efficient execution of a workflow and minimize its turnaround time, an effective scheduling strategy that decides when and which resource must execute the tasks of the workflow is necessary. When scheduling multiple, independent workflows that represent user jobs and are thus submitted at different moments in time, the common definition of makespan must be extended to account for the waiting time and execution time of a given workflow. The metric to evaluate a dynamic scheduler of independent workflows must represent the individual execution time instead of a global measure for the set of workflows to reflect the QoS experienced by the users, which is related to the response time of each user application.

The efficient use of any computing system depends on how well the workload is mapped to the processing units. The workload considered in this chapter consists of workflow applications that are composed of a collection of several interacting components or tasks which must be executed in a certain order for the successful execution of the application as a whole. The scheduling operation, which consists in defining a mapping and the order of task execution, has been addressed primarily for single workflow scheduling; that is, a schedule is generated for a workflow and a specific number of processors are used exclusively throughout the workflow execution. When several workflows are submitted, they are considered as independent applications that are executed on independent subsets of processors. However, because of task precedence, not all processors are fully used when executing a workflow, thus leading to low efficiency. One way to improve system efficiency is to consider concurrent workflows: that is, sharing processors among workflows. In this context, there is no exclusive use of processors by a workflow; thus, throughout its execution, the workflow can use any processor available in the system. Although the processors are not used exclusively by one workflow, only one task runs on a processor at any one time.

We first introduce the concept of an application and the heterogeneous system model. Next, the performance metrics that are commonly used in workflow scheduling and a metric for accounting for the total execution time are introduced. Finally, we present a review of concurrent workflow scheduling and an extended comparison of dynamic workflow scheduling algorithms for randomly generated graphs.

9.1.1 Application Model

A typical scientific workflow application can be represented as a directed acyclic graph (DAG). In a DAG, nodes represent tasks and the directed edges represent execution dependencies and the amount of communication between nodes.

A workflow for this application is modeled by the DAG $G = (V, E)$, where $V = \{n_j, j = 1, \dots, v\}$ represents the set of v tasks (or jobs) to be executed and E is a set of e weighted directed edges which represents communication requirements between tasks. Each $edge(i,j) \in E$ represents the precedence constraint that task n_j cannot start before the successful completion of task n_i. *Data* is a $v \times v$ matrix of communication data, where $data_{i,j}$ is the amount of data that must be transferred from task n_i to task n_j.

The target computing environment consists of a set P of p heterogeneous processors organized in a fully connected topology in which all interprocessor communications are assumed to be performed without contention, as explained in Section 9.1.2.

The data transfer rates between the processors, that is, bandwidth, are stored in a matrix B of size $p \times p$. The communication start-up costs of the processors, that is, the latencies, are given in a p-dimensional vector L. The communication cost of the $edge(i,j)$, which transfers data from task n_i (executed on processor p_m) to task n_j (executed on processor p_n), is defined as follows:

$$c_{i,j} = L_m + \frac{data_{i,j}}{B_{m,n}}. \tag{9.1}$$

When both tasks n_i and n_j are scheduled on the same processor, $c_{i,j} = 0$. Typically, the communication cost is simplified by introducing an average communication cost of an $edge(i,j)$ defined as follows:

$$\overline{c_{i,j}} = \overline{L} + \frac{data_{i,j}}{\overline{B}}, \tag{9.2}$$

where $\overline{B}$ is the average bandwidth among all processor pairs and $\overline{L}$ is the average latency. This simplification is commonly considered to label the edges of the graph to allow for the computation of a priority rank before assigning tasks to the processors [1].

Because of heterogeneity, each task may have a different execution time on each processor. Then, W is a $v \times p$ matrix of computation costs in which each $w_{i,j}$ represents the execution time to complete task n_i on processor p_j. The average execution cost of task n_i is defined as follows:

$$\overline{w_i} = \sum_{j=1}^{p} \frac{w_{i,j}}{p}. \tag{9.3}$$

With respect to the communication costs, the average execution time is commonly used to compute the priority ranking for the tasks.

An example is shown in Fig. 9.1, which presents a DAG and a target system with three processors and the corresponding communication and computation costs. In the figure, the weight of each edge represents its average communication cost, and the numbers in the table represent the computation time of each task at each of the three processors. This model represents a general heterogeneous system.

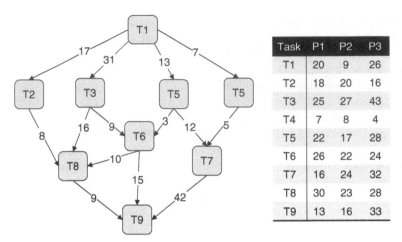

FIGURE 9.1 *Application model and computation time matrix of the tasks in each processor.*

In this section, we present some of the common attributes used in task scheduling, which we will use in the following sections:

- *pred(n_i)*: This denotes the set of immediate predecessors of task n_i in a given DAG. A task with no predecessors is called an *entry* task, n_{entry}. If a DAG has multiple entry nodes, a dummy entry node with zero weight and zero communication edges is added to the graph.

- *succ(n_i)*: This denotes the set of immediate successors of task n_i. A task with no successors is called an *exit* task, n_{exit}. Similar to the entry node, if a DAG has multiple exit nodes, a dummy exit node with zero weight and zero communication edges from current multiple exit nodes to this dummy node is added.

- *makespan or schedule length*: It is the elapsed time from the beginning of the execution of the entry node to the finish time of the exit node in the scheduled DAG, and is defined by

$$makespan = \text{AFT}(n_{exit}) - \text{AST}(n_{entry}), \tag{9.4}$$

where $\text{AFT}(n_{exit})$ is the *actual finish time* of the exit node and $\text{AST}(n_{entry})$ is the *actual start time* of the entry node.

- *level(n_i)*: This is an integer value representing the maximum number of edges composing the paths from the entry node to n_i. For the entry node, the level is $level(n_{entry}) = 1$ and for other tasks it is given by

$$level(n_i) = \max_{q \in pred(n_i)} \{level(q)\} + 1. \tag{9.5}$$

- *Critical path (CP)*: The CP of a DAG is the longest path from the *entry* node to the *exit* node in the graph. The length of this path |CP| is the sum of the computation costs of the nodes and internode communication costs along the path. The |CP| value of a DAG is the lower bound of the schedule length.

- $EST(n_i, p_j)$: This denotes the *earliest start time* of a node n_i on a processor p_j and is defined as

$$EST(n_i, p_j) = \max \left\{ T_{Available}(p_j), \max_{n_m \in pred(n_i)} \{AFT(n_m) + c_{m,i}\} \right\}, \quad (9.6)$$

where $T_{Available}(p_j)$ is the earliest time at which processor p_j is ready. The inner max block in the EST equation is the time at which all data needed by n_i has arrived at the processor p_j. For the entry task, $EST(n_{entry}, p_j) = \max\{T_s, T_{Available}(p_j)\}$, where T_s is the submission time of the DAG in the system.

- $EFT(n_i, p_j)$: This denotes the *earliest finish time* of a node n_i on a processor p_j and is defined as

$$EFT(n_i, p_j) = EST(n_i, p_j) + w_{i,j}, \quad (9.7)$$

which is the *earliest start time* of a node n_i on a processor p_j plus the execution time of task n_i on processor p_j.

The *objective function* of the scheduling problem from the user perspective, a single workflow, is to determine an assignment of tasks of this workflow to processors such that the *schedule length* is minimized. After all nodes in the workflow are scheduled, the schedule length will be the makespan, defined by (9.4).

9.1.2 System Model

Typically, for executing complex workflows, a high-performance cluster or grid platform is used. As defined in [2], a cluster is a type of parallel or distributed processing system which consists of a collection of interconnected stand-alone computing nodes working together as a single, integrated computing resource. A compute node can be a single or multiprocessor system with memory, input/output (I/O) facilities, accelerator devices, such as graphics processing units (GPUs), and an operating system. A cluster generally refers to two or more computing nodes that are connected together. The nodes can exist in a single cabinet or be physically separated and connected via a local area network (LAN). Figure 9.2 illustrates the typical cluster architecture.

The algorithms for concurrent workflow scheduling may be useful when there are a significant number of workflows compared to the computational nodes available; otherwise, the workflows could use a set of processors exclusively without concurrency. Therefore, in the context of the experiments reported in this chapter, we consider a cluster formed by nodes of the same site, connected by a single-bandwidth, switched network. In a switched network, the execution of tasks and communications with other processors can be achieved for each processor simultaneously and without contention. These characteristics allow for the simplification of the communication costs computation in the DAG (Fig. 9.1) by considering the average communication parameters.

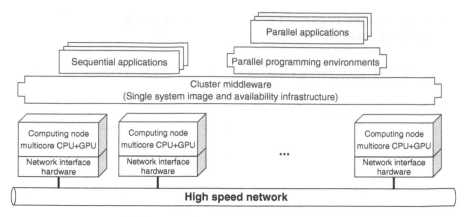

FIGURE 9.2   *Conceptual cluster architecture.*

The target system can be as simple as a set of devices (e.g., central processing units (CPUs) and GPUs) connected by a switched network that guarantees parallel communication between different pairs of devices. The machine is heterogeneous because CPUs can be from different generations and other very different devices, such as GPUs, can be included. Another common machine is the one that results from selecting processors from several clusters at the same site. Although a cluster is homogeneous, the set of processors selected forms a heterogeneous machine. The processor latency can differ in a heterogeneous machine, but such differences are negligible. For low communication-to-computation ratios (CCRs), the communication costs are negligible; for higher CCRs, the predominant factor is the network bandwidth and, as mentioned above, we assume the bandwidth is the same throughout the entire network. In addition, the execution of any task is considered nonpreemptive.

9.1.3   Performance Metrics

Performance metrics are used to evaluate the effectiveness of the scheduling strategy. Because some metrics may conflict with others, any system design cannot accommodate all metrics simultaneously; thus, a balance according to the final goals must be found. The metrics used in this study are described below.

Makespan
> Also referred to as *schedule length*, makespan is the time difference between the application start time and its completion. Most scheduling algorithms use this metric to evaluate their results, and their solutions as compared with other algorithms. A smaller makespan implies better performance.

Turnaround Time
> Turnaround time is the difference between submission and final completion of an application. Different from *makespan*, turnaround time includes the time spent by the workflow application waiting to get started. It is used to measure the performance and service satisfaction from a user perspective.

Turnaround Time Ratio

The turnaround time ratio (TTR) measures the additional time spent by each workflow in the system to be executed in relation to the minimum makespan obtained for that workflow. The TTR for a workflow is defined as

$$TTR = \frac{TurnaroundTime}{\sum_{n_i \in CP} min_{p_j \in P}(w_{(i,j)})}, \tag{9.8}$$

where P is the set of processors of the HCS. The denominator in the TTR equation is the minimum computation cost of the tasks that compose the critical path (CP), which is the lower bound of the execution time for a workflow.

Normalized Turnaround Time

The normalized turnaround time (NTT) is obtained by the ratio of the minimum turnaround time and actual turnaround time for a given workflow G and an algorithm a_i, defined as follows:

$$NTT(G, a_i) = \frac{min_{a_k \in A}\{TurnaroundTime(G, a_k)\}}{TurnaroundTime(G, a_i)}, \tag{9.9}$$

where A is the set of algorithms being compared and $a_i \in A$. For an algorithm a_i, NTT provides the distance that its scheduling solutions are at from the minimum TTR obtained for a given workflow G. NTT is distributed in the interval [0, 1]. The algorithm with a lower spread in NTT with values near 1 is the algorithm that generates more results closer to the minimum, that is, the best algorithm.

Win(%)

The percentage of wins is used to compare the frequency of the best results for turnaround time for the set of workflows being scheduled. The algorithm with a higher percentage of wins implies that it obtains better results from the user perspective, that is, it obtains more frequently the shortest elapsed time from submission to completion of a user job. Note that the sum of this value for all algorithms may be higher than 100%; this is because, when more than one algorithm wins, for a given workflow, it is accounted for all those winning algorithms.

9.2 CONCURRENT WORKFLOW SCHEDULING

Recently, several algorithms have been proposed for concurrent workflow scheduling to improve the execution time of several applications in an HCS system. However, most of these algorithms were designed for offline scheduling or static scheduling, that is, all the applications are known at the same time. This approach, although relevant, imposes limitations on the management of a dynamic system where users can submit jobs at any time. For this purpose, there are a few algorithms that were designed to address dynamic application scheduling. In the following, a review of offline scheduling is presented, followed by a review of online scheduling.

9.2.1   Offline Scheduling of Concurrent Workflows

In offline scheduling, the workflows are available before the execution starts, that is, at compile time. After a schedule is produced and initiated, no other workflow is considered. This approach, although limited, is applicable in many real-world applications, for example, when a user has a set of nodes to run a set of workflows. This methodology is applied by most common resource management tools, where a user requests a set of nodes to execute his/her jobs exclusively.

Several algorithms have been proposed for offline scheduling, where workflows compete for resources and the goal is to ensure a fair distribution of those resources, while minimizing the individual completion time of each workflow. Two approaches based on a fairness strategy for concurrent workflow scheduling were presented in [3]. Fairness is defined on the basis of the slowdown that each DAG would experience (the slowdown is the ratio of the expected execution time for the same DAG when scheduled together with other workflows to that when scheduled alone). They proposed two algorithms: one fairness policy based on finish time, and another fairness policy based on current time. Both algorithms first schedule each DAG on all processors with static scheduling (like HEFT [1] or Hybrid.BMCT [4]) as the pivot scheduling algorithm, save their schedule assignment, and keep their makespan as the slowdown value of the DAG. Next, all workflows are sorted in descending order of their slowdown. Then, until there are unfinished workflows in the list, the algorithm selects the DAG with the highest slowdown and then selects the first ready task that has not been scheduled in this DAG. The main point is to evaluate the slowdown value of each DAG after scheduling a task and make a decision regarding which DAG should be selected to schedule the next task. The difference between the two proposed fairness-based algorithms is that the fairness policy based on finish time calculates the slowdown value of the selected DAG only, whereas the slowdown value is recalculated for every DAG in the fairness policy based on current time.

In [5], several strategies were proposed based on the proportional sharing of resources. This proportional sharing was defined on the basis of the critical path length, width, or work of each workflow. A type of weighted proportional sharing was also proposed that represents a better trade-off between fair resource sharing and makespan reduction of the workflows. The strategies were applied to mixed parallel applications, where each task could be executed on more than one processor. The proportional sharing, based on the work needed to execute a workflow, resulted in the shortest schedules on average but was also the least fair with regard to resource usage, that is, the variance of the slowdowns experienced by the workflows was the highest.

In [6], a path clustering heuristic was proposed that combines the clustering scheduling technique to generate groups (clusters) of tasks and the list scheduling technique to select tasks and processors. Based on this methodology, the authors propose and compare four algorithms: (i) sequential scheduling, where workflows are scheduled one after another; (ii) gap search algorithm, which is similar to the former but searches for spaces between already scheduled tasks; (iii) interleave algorithm, where pieces of each workflow are scheduled in turns; and (iv) group workflows, where the workflows are joined to form a single workflow and then scheduled. The evaluation was made in terms of schedule length and fairness, and it was concluded that interleaving the workflows leads to lower average makespan and higher fairness when multiple workflows share the same set of resources. This result, although relevant, considers the average makespan, which does not distinguish the impact of the delay on each workflow, as compared to exclusive execution.

In [7], the algorithms for offline scheduling of concurrent parallel task graphs on a single homogeneous cluster were evaluated extensively. The graphs, or workflows, that have been submitted by different users share a set of resources and are ready to start their execution at the same time. The goal is to optimize user-perceived notions of performance and fairness. The authors proposed three metrics to quantify the quality of a schedule related to performance and fairness among the parallel task graphs.

In [8], two workflow scheduling algorithms were presented, namely multiple workflow grid scheduling MWGS4 and MWGS2, with four and two stages, respectively. The four-stage version comprises labeling, adaptive allocation, prioritization, and parallel machine scheduling. The two-stage version applies only adaptive allocation and parallel machine scheduling. Both algorithms, MWGS4 and MWGS2, are classified as offline strategies and both schedule a set of available and ready jobs from a batch of jobs. All jobs that arrive during a time interval will be processed in a batch and start to execute after the completion of the last batch of jobs. These strategies were shown to outperform other strategies in terms of the mean critical path waiting time and critical path slowdown.

9.2.2   Online Scheduling of Concurrent Workflows

Online scheduling exhibits dynamic behavior where users can submit the workflows at any time. When scheduling multiple independent workflows that represent user jobs and are thus submitted at different moments in time, the completion time (or turnaround time) includes both the waiting time and execution time of a given workflow, extending the makespan definition for single workflow scheduling [9]. The metric to evaluate a dynamic scheduler of independent workflows must represent the individual completion time instead of a global measure for the set of workflows to measure the QoS experienced by the users related to the finish time of each user application.

Some algorithms have been proposed for online workflow scheduling; they will be described briefly in this section. Three other algorithms were proposed specifically to schedule concurrent workflows to improve individual QoSs. These algorithms, namely online workflow management (OWM), rank hybrid (Rank_Hybd), and fairness dynamic workflow scheduling (FDWS), are described here and compared in the results section. The first two algorithms improve the average completion time of all workflows. In contrast, FDWS focuses on the QoS experienced by each application (or user) by minimizing the waiting and execution times of each individual workflow.

In [10], the min–min average (MMA) algorithm was proposed to efficiently schedule transaction-intensive grid workflows involving significant communication overheads. The MMA algorithm is based on the popular min–min algorithm but uses a different strategy for transaction-intensive grid workflows with the capability of adapting to the change of network transmission speed automatically.

Transaction-intensive workflows are multiple instances of one workflow. In this case, the aim is to optimize the overall throughput rather than the individual workflow performance. Because min–min is a popular technique, we consider one implementation of min–min for concurrent workflow scheduling in our results.

In [11], an algorithm was proposed for scheduling multiple workflows, with multiple QoS constraints, on the cloud. The resulting multiple QoS-constrained scheduling strategy of multiple workflows (MQMW) minimizes the makespan and the cost of the resources and increases the scheduling success rate. The algorithm considers two objectives, time and cost, that can be adapted to the user requirements. MQMW was compared with Rank_Hybd, and Rank_Hybd performed better when time was the major QoS requirement. In our study application, we consider time as the QoS requirement and thus consider Rank_Hybd in our results section.

In [12], a dynamic algorithm was proposed to minimize the makespan of a batch of parallel task workflows with different arrival times. The algorithm was proposed for online scheduling but with the goal of minimizing a collective metric. This model is applied to real-world applications, such as video surveillance and image registration, where the workflows are related and only the collective result is meaningful. This approach is different from the independent workflow execution that we consider in this study.

9.2.2.1 *Rank Hybrid Algorithm*

A planner-guided strategy, the Rank_Hybd algorithm, was proposed by Yu and Shi [13] to address dynamic scheduling of work-flow applications that are submitted by different users at different moments in time. The Rank_Hybd algorithm ranks all tasks using the $rank_u$ priority measure [1], which represents the length of the longest path from task n_i to the exit node, including the computational cost of n_i, and is expressed as follows:

$$rank_u(n_i) = \overline{w_i} + \max_{n_j \in succ(n_i)} \{\overline{c_{i,j}} + rank_u(n_j)\}, \qquad (9.10)$$

where $succ(n_i)$ is the set of immediate successors of task n_i, $\overline{c_{i,j}}$ is the average communication cost of $edge(i,j)$, and $\overline{w_i}$ is the average computation cost of task n_i. For the exit task, $rank_u(n_{exit}) = 0$.

Algorithm 9.1

```
getReadyPool algorithm {
    if (a new workflow has arrived)
        {calculate rank_u for all tasks of the new workflow}
    Ready_Pool ← Read all ready tasks from all DAGs
    multiple ← number of DAGs with ready tasks in Ready_Pool
    if (multiple == 1)
        {Sort all tasks in Ready_Pool in descending order of rank_u}
    else
        {Sort all tasks in Ready_Pool in ascending order of rank_u}
    return Ready_Pool
}
```

In each step, the algorithm reads all the ready tasks from the DAGs and selects the next task to schedule based on their rank. If the ready tasks belong to different DAGs,

Algorithm 9.2

```
Rank Hybrid algorithm {
     while (there are workflows to schedule){
          Ready_Pool ← getReadyPool()
          Resources_free ← get all idle resources
          while (Ready_Pool ≠ φ and Resources_free ≠ φ){
               task_selected ← the first task in Ready_Pool
               resource_selected ← the processor with the lowest Finish
                    Time for task_selected on Resources_free
               Assign task_selected to resource_selected
               Remove resource_selected from Resources_free
               Remove task_selected from Ready_Pool
}}}
```

the algorithm selects the task with the lowest rank; if the ready tasks belong to the same DAG, the task with the highest rank is selected. The Rank_Hybd heuristic is formalized in Algorithm 9.2.

With this strategy, Rank_Hybd allows the DAG with the lowest rank (lower makespan) to be scheduled first to reduce the waiting time of the DAG in the system. However, this strategy does not achieve high fairness among the workflows because it always gives preference to shorter workflows to finish first, postponing the longer ones. For instance, if a longer workflow is being executed and several short workflows are submitted to the system, the scheduler postpones the execution of the longer DAG to give priority to the shorter ones.

9.2.2.2 Online Workflow Management

The online workflow management algorithm (OWM) for the online scheduling of multiple workflows was proposed in [14]. Unlike the Rank_Hybd algorithm which puts all ready tasks from each DAG into the ready list, OWM selects only a single ready task from each DAG, namely the task with the highest rank ($rank_u$). Then, until there are some unfinished DAGs in the system, the OWM algorithm selects the task with the highest priority from the ready list. Then, it calculates the earliest finish time (EFT) for the selected task on each processor and selects the processor that will result in the smallest EFT. If the selected processor is free at that time, the OWM algorithm assigns the selected task to the selected processor; otherwise, the selected task stays in the ready list to be scheduled later. The OWM heuristic is formalized in Algorithm 9.3.

In the results presented by Hsu *et al.* [14], the OWM algorithm performs better than the Rank_Hybd algorithm [13] and the Fairness_Dynamic algorithm (a modified version of the fairness algorithm proposed by Zhao and Sakellariou [3]) in handling online workflows. Similar to Rank_Hybd, the OWM algorithm uses a fairness strategy; however, instead of scheduling smaller DAGs first, it selects and schedules tasks from the longer DAGs first. Moreover, OWM has a better strategy by filling the ready list with one task from each DAG so that all of the DAGs have the chance to be selected in the current scheduling round. In their simulation environment, the number of processors was always equal to the number of workflows so that the scheduler typically has a suitable number of processors on which to schedule the ready tasks. This choice does not expose a fragility of the algorithm that occurs

Algorithm 9.3

```
OWM algorithm {
    while (there are workflows to schedule){
        Ready_Pool ← getReadyPool()
        Resources_free ← get all idle resources
        while (Ready_Pool ≠ φ and Resources_free ≠ φ){
            task_selected ← the first task in Ready_Pool
            resource_selected ← the processor with the lowest Finish
                Time for task_selected on Resources_free
            if (number of free clusters == 1 AND the Finish Time
                on a busy cluster < Finish Time on resource_selected)
                {Keep task_selected for next schedule call}
            else {
                Assign task_selected to resource_selected
                Remove resource_selected from Resources_free
                Remove task_selected from Ready_Pool
}}}}
```

when the number of DAGs is significantly higher than the number of processors, that is, for more heavily loaded systems.

9.2.2.3 *Fairness Dynamic Workflow Scheduling*   The fairness dynamic workflow scheduling (FDWS) algorithm was proposed in [15]. FDWS implements new strategies for selecting the tasks from the ready list and for assigning the processors to reduce the individual completion time of the workflows, for example, the turnaround time, including execution time and waiting time.

The FDWS algorithm comprises three main components: (i) workflow pool, (ii) task selection, and (iii) processor allocation. The workflow pool contains the submitted workflows that arrive as users submit their applications. At each scheduling round, this component finds all ready tasks from each workflow. The Rank_Hybd algorithm adds all ready tasks into the ready pool (or list), and the OWM algorithm adds only one task with the highest priority from each DAG into the ready pool. Considering all ready tasks from each DAG leads to an unbiased preference for longer DAGs and the consequent postponing of smaller DAGs resulting in higher TTR and unfair processor sharing. In the FDWS algorithm, only a single ready task with highest priority from each DAG is added to the ready pool, similar to the OWM algorithm. To assign priorities to tasks in the DAG, it uses an upward ranking, $rank_u$ (9.10).

The task selection component applies a different rank to select the task to be scheduled from the ready pool. To be inserted into the ready pool, $rank_u$ is computed individually for each DAG. To select from the ready pool, $rank_r$ for task n_i belonging to DAG$_j$ is computed, as defined by (9.11), and the task with highest $rank_r$ is selected:

$$rank_r(n_{i,j}) = \frac{1}{\text{PRT}(\text{DAG}_j)} \times \frac{1}{|\text{CP}(\text{DAG}_j)|}. \tag{9.11}$$

The $rank_r$ metric considers the percentage of remaining tasks (PRT) of the DAG and its critical path length ($|$CP$|$). The PRT prioritizes DAGs that are nearly completed and only have a few tasks to execute. The use of the CP length results in a different strategy than the smallest remaining processing time (SRPT) [16]. With SRPT, the application with the smallest remaining processing time is selected and scheduled at each step. The remaining processing time is the time needed to execute all remaining tasks of the workflow. However, the time needed to complete all tasks of the DAG does not consider the width of the DAG. A wider DAG has a shorter |CP| than other DAGs with the same number of tasks; it also has a lower expected finish time. Therefore, in this case, FDWS would give higher priority to DAGs with smaller |CP| values.

In both Rank_Hybd and OWM, only the individual $rank_u$ is used to select tasks into the workflow pool and to select a task from the pool of ready tasks. This scheme leads to a scheduling decision that does not consider the DAG history in the workflow pool.

The processor allocation component considers only the free processors. The processor with the lowest finish time for the current task is selected. In this study, we use the FDWS without processor queues to highlight the influence of the rank $rank_r$ in the scheduling results. The algorithm is formalized in Algorithm 9.4.

9.2.2.4 Online Min–Min and Online Max–Min

The min–min and max–min algorithms have been studied extensively in the literature [17], and therefore we implemented an online version of these algorithms for our problem. In the first phase, min–min prioritizes the task with the minimum completion time (MCT). In the second phase, the task with the overall minimum expected completion time is chosen and assigned to its corresponding resource. In each calling, our online version first collects a single ready task from each available DAG with the highest $rank_u$ value and then puts all of these ready tasks into the ready pool of tasks. It then calculates the MCT value for each ready task. In the selection phase, the task with the minimum MCT value is selected and assigned to the corresponding processor. The calculation of the MCT value for the tasks in the ready pool only considers available (free) processors. The max–min algorithm is similar to the min–min algorithm, but in the selection phase the task with the maximum MCT is chosen to be scheduled on the resource that is expected to complete the task at the earliest time.

Algorithm 9.4

```
FDWS algorithm {
    while (Workflow_Pool ≠ φ ){
        if (new workflow has arrived){
            Compute rank_u for all tasks of the new Workflow
            Insert the Workflow into Workflow_Pool}
        Ready_Pool ← one ready task from each DAG(highest rank_u)
        Compute rank_r (n_i,j) for each task n_i ∈ DAG_j in Ready_Pool
        Resources_free ← get all idle resources
        while (Ready_Pool ≠ φ and Resources_free ≠ φ ){
            task_selected ← the task with highest rank_r from Ready_Pool
            resource_selected ← the processor with the lowest Finish
                Time for task_selected on Resources_free
            Assign task_selected to Resource_selected
            Remove task_selected from Ready_Pool
}}}
```

9.3 EXPERIMENTAL RESULTS AND DISCUSSION

In this section, we compare the relative performance of the Rank_Hybd, OWM, FDWS, min–min, and max–min algorithms. For this purpose, this section is divided into three parts: the DAG structure is described, the infrastructure is presented, and results and discussion are presented.

9.3.1 DAG Structure

To evaluate the relative performance of the algorithms, we used randomly generated workflow application graphs. For this purpose, we use a synthetic DAG generation program.[1] We model the computational complexity of a task as one of the three following forms, which are representative of many common applications: $a \cdot d$ (e.g., image processing of a $\sqrt{d} \times \sqrt{d}$ image); $a \cdot d \log d$ (e.g., sorting an array of d elements); $d^{3/2}$ (e.g., multiplication of $\sqrt{d} \times \sqrt{d}$ matrices), where a is chosen randomly between 2^6 and 2^9. As a result, different tasks exhibit different communication/computation ratios.

We consider applications that consist of 20–50 tasks. We use four popular parameters to define the shape of the DAG: *width*, *regularity*, *density*, and *jumps*. The width determines the maximum number of tasks that can be executed concurrently. A small value will lead to a thin DAG, similar to a chain, with low task parallelism, and a large value induces a fat DAG, similar to a fork joint, with a high degree of parallelism. The regularity indicates the uniformity of the number of tasks in each level. A low value means that the levels contain very dissimilar numbers of tasks, whereas a high value means that all levels contain similar numbers of tasks. The density denotes the number of edges between two levels of the DAG, where a low value indicates few edges and a large value indicates many edges. A jump indicates that an edge can go from level l to level $l + jump$. A jump of one is an ordinary connection between two consecutive levels.

In our experiment, for random DAG generation we consider the number of tasks $n = \{20, \dots, 50\}$, $jump = \{1, 2, 3\}$, $regularity = \{0.2, 0.4, 0.8\}$, $fat = \{0.2, 0.4, 0.6, 0.8\}$, and $density = \{0.2, 0.4, 0.8\}$. With these parameters, we call the DAG generator for each DAG, and it randomly chooses the value for each parameter from the parameter dataset.

9.3.2 Simulated Platforms

We resort to simulation to evaluate the algorithms from the previous section. It allows us to perform a statistically significant number of experiments for a wide range of application configurations (in a reasonable amount of time). We use the SimGrid toolkit[2] [18] as the basis for our simulator. SimGrid provides the required fundamental abstractions for the discrete-event simulation of parallel applications in distributed environments. It was specifically designed for the evaluation of scheduling

---

[1] https://github.com/frs69wq/daggen
[2] http://simgrid.gforge.inria.fr

TABLE 9.1   Description of the Grid 5000 Clusters from Which the Platforms Used in Our Experiments are Derived

Site Name	Cluster Name	Number of CPUs	Power in Gflop/s	Site Heterogeneity
Grenoble	Adonis	12	23.681	$\sigma = 1.12$
	Edel	72	23.492	
	Genepi	34	21.175	
Rennes	Paradent	64	21.496	$\sigma = 2.34$
	Paramount	33	12.910	
	Parapluie	40	27.391	
	Parapide	25	30.130	

algorithms. Relying on a well-established simulation toolkit allows us to leverage sound models of a HCS, such as the one described in Fig. 9.2. In many research papers on scheduling, the authors assume a contention-free network model in which processors can simultaneously send or receive data from as many processors as possible without experiencing any performance degradation. Unfortunately, that model, the *multiport* model, is not representative of actual network infrastructures. Conversely, the network model provided by SimGrid corresponds to a theoretical *bounded multiport* model. In this model, a processor can communicate with several other processors simultaneously, but each communication flow is limited by the bandwidth of the traversed route, and communications using a common network link have to share bandwidth. This scheme corresponds well to the behavior of TCP connections on a LAN. The validity of this network model has been demonstrated in [19].

To make our simulations even more realistic, we consider platforms derived from clusters in the Grid5000 platform deployed in France[3] [20]. Grid5000 is an experimental test bed distributed across 10 sites and aggregating a total of approximately 8000 individual cores. We consider two sites that comprise multiple clusters. Table 9.1 gives the name of each cluster along with its number of processors, processing speed expressed in flop/s, and heterogeneity. Each cluster uses an internal gigabit-switched interconnect. The heterogeneity factor (σ) of a site is determined by the ratio between the speeds of the fastest and slowest processors.

From these five clusters, which comprise a total of 280 processors (118 in Grenoble and 162 in Rennes), we extract four distinct heterogeneous cluster configurations (two per site). For the Grenoble site, we built heterogeneous simulated clusters by choosing 3 and 5 processors for each of the three actual clusters for a respective total of 9 and 15 processors. We apply the same method to the Rennes site by selecting 2 and 4 processors per cluster for a total of 8 and 16 processors. This approach allows us to have heterogeneous configurations in terms of both processor speed and network interconnect that correspond to a set of resources a user can reasonably acquire by submitting a job to the local resource management system at each site.

[3]http://www.grid5000.fr

9.3.3   Results and Discussion

In this section, the algorithms are compared in terms of TTR, percentage of wins, and NTT. We present results for a set of 30 and 50 concurrent DAGs that arrive with time intervals that range from 0% (offline scheduling) to 90% of completed tasks, that is, a new DAG is inserted when the corresponding percentage of tasks from the last DAG currently in the system is completed. We consider a low number of processors compared to the number of DAGs to analyze the behavior of the algorithms with respect to the system load. The maximum load configuration is observed for 8 processors and 50 DAGs.

Figures 9.3–9.6 present results for the Grenoble and Rennes sites for two configurations and two sets of DAGs. For the case of zero time interval, equivalent to offline scheduling, for 8 and 9 processors and 30 and 50 DAGs, FDWS results in a lower distribution for TTR but with similar average values to Rank_Hybd and OWM. The

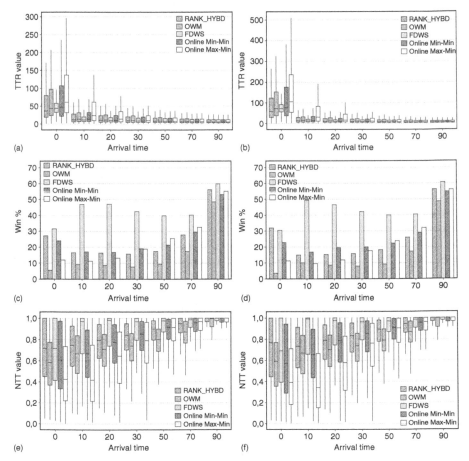

FIGURE 9.3   *Results of TTR, percentage of wins, and NTT on Grenoble site with nine processors. (a),(c),(e) 30 concurrent DAGs. (b),(d),(f) 50 concurrent DAGs.*

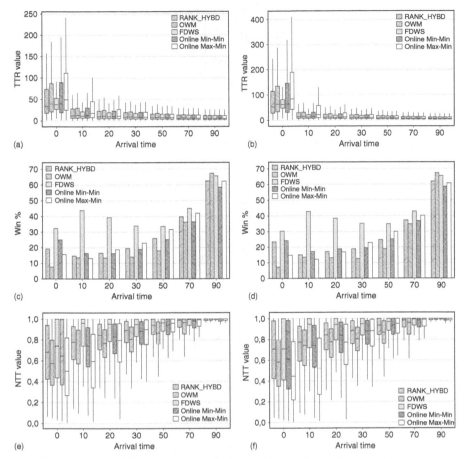

FIGURE 9.4 Results of TTR, percentage of wins, and NTT on Grenoble site with 15 processors.
(a),(c),(e) 30 concurrent DAGs. (b),(d),(f) 50 concurrent DAGs.

small box for FDWS indicates that 50% of the results fall in a lower range of values, and therefore the individual QoS for each submitted job is better. FDWS generated better solutions more often, but from the NTT graphs we conclude that the distance of its solutions to the minimum turnaround time is similar to that of Rank_Hybd. For HCS configurations with more resources (15 and 16 processors for Grenoble and Rennes, respectively), the same behavior is observed for both cases of 30 and 50 concurrent DAGs.

In general, the max–min algorithm yielded poorer results. The min–min algorithm performed the same as Rank_Hybd and performed better than OWM for time intervals of 20 and higher.

For time intervals of 10 and higher, FDWS performed consistently better for higher numbers of concurrent DAGs. For the Rennes site, at 10 time intervals, 30 DAGs, and 8 CPUs, the degree of improvement of FDWS over Rank_Hybd, OWM, min–min,

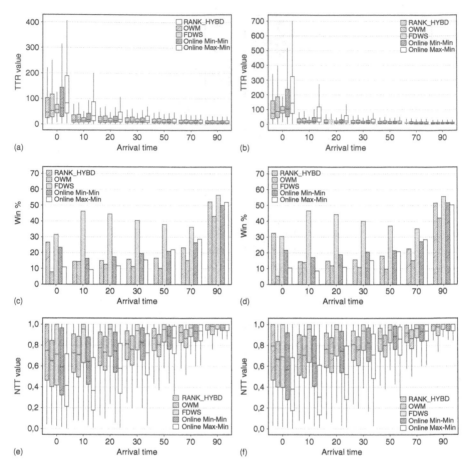

FIGURE 9.5 *Results of TTR, percentage of wins, and NTT on Rennes site for eight processors. (a),(c),(e) 30 concurrent DAGs. (b),(d),(f) 50 concurrent DAGs.*

and max−min is 16.2%, 19.3%, 27.4%, and 63.3%, respectively. On increasing the number of DAGs to 50, the improvements are 17.5%, 23.4%, 31.5%, and 71.0%. Increasing the time intervals between the DAGs' arrival times reduces the concurrency, so the improvements decrease. For the same conditions with 30 DAGs and a time interval of 50, the improvement of FDWS over the others, in the same order, is 5.5%, 11.7%, 4.8%, and 8.9%, respectively. For 50 DAGs and 50 time intervals, the improvements are 5.9%, 13.0%, 3.2%, and 11.1%. For the Grenoble site, with 9 and 15 processors, the improvements are of the same order for the same time intervals and number of DAGs, with 8 and 16 processors in the Rennes site.

With respect to the percentage of wins, FDWS always results in a higher rate of best results for time intervals equal to or higher than 10. The results in the NTT graphs illustrate that FDWS also has a distribution closer to 1, which indicates that its solutions are closer to the minimum turnaround time than the other algorithms.

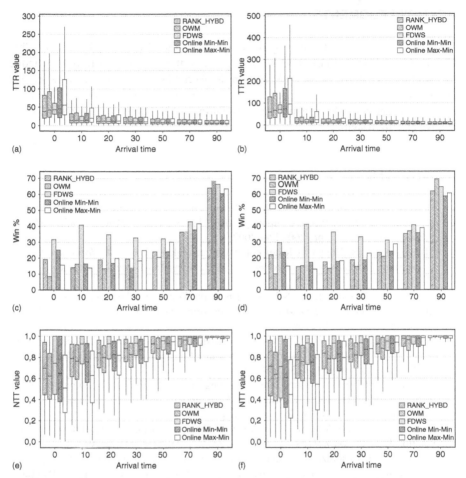

FIGURE 9.6 *Results of TTR, percentage of wins, and NTT on Rennes site with 16 processors. (a),(c),(e) 30 concurrent DAGs. (b),(d),(f) 50 concurrent DAGs.*

9.4 CONCLUSIONS

In this chapter, we presented a review of offline and online concurrent workflow scheduling and compared five algorithms for online scheduling when the goal was to maximize the user QoS defined by the completion time of the individual submitted jobs. The five algorithms are FDWS [15], OWM [14], Rank_Hybd [13], online min–min, and online max–min, which can all handle multiple workflow scheduling in dynamic situations. Based on our experiments, FDWS leads to better performance in terms of TTR, win(%), and NTT, showing better QoS characteristics for a range of time intervals from 10 to 90. For the time interval of zero, which is equivalent to offline scheduling, Rank_Hybd also performed well, but the schedules produced by FDWS had better QoS characteristics.

ACKNOWLEDGMENTS

This work was supported in part by the Fundaç ao para a Ciência e Tecnologia, PhD Grant FCT-DFRH-SFRH/BD/80061/2011. The authors also wish to acknowledge the support given by the COST Action IC0805 "Open European Network for High-Performance Computing on Complex Environments, Working Group 3: Algorithms and tools for mapping and executing applications onto distributed and heterogeneous systems."

REFERENCES

1. H. Topcuoglu, S. Hariri, and M. Wu, "Performance-effective and low-complexity task scheduling for heterogeneous computing," *IEEE Transactions on Parallel and Distributed Systems*, vol. 13, no. 3, pp. 260–274, 2002.
2. M. Bakery and R. Buyya, "Cluster computing at a glance," *High Performance Cluster Computing: Architectures and Systems*, vol. 1, R. Buyya (ed.), Prentice-Hall: Upper Saddle River, NJ, pp. 3–47, 1999.
3. H. Zhao and R. Sakellariou, "Scheduling multiple DAGs onto heterogeneous systems," in *International Parallel and Distributed Processing Symposium (IPDPS)*, Rhodes Island, Greece, pp. 1–14, IEEE, 2006.
4. R. Sakellariou and H. Zhao, "A hybrid heuristic for dag scheduling on heterogeneous systems," in *International Parallel and Distributed Processing Symposium (IPDPS)*, Santa Fe, New Mexico, pp. 111–123, IEEE, 2004.
5. T. N'takpé and F. Suter, "Concurrent scheduling of parallel task graphs on multi-clusters using constrained resource allocations," in *International Symposium on Parallel and Distributed Processing (IPDPS)*, Rome, Italy, pp. 1–8, IEEE, 2009.
6. L. Bittencourt and E. Madeira, "Towards the scheduling of multiple workflows on computational grids," *Journal of Grid Computing*, vol. 8, pp. 419–441, 2010.
7. H. Casanova, F. Desprez, and F. Suter, "On cluster resource allocation for multiple parallel task graphs," *Journal of Parallel and Distributed Computing*, vol. 70, pp. 1193–1203, 2010.
8. A. Carbajal, A. Tchernykh, R. Yahyapour, J. García, T. Röblitz, and J. Alcaraz, "Multiple workflow scheduling strategies with user run time estimates on a grid," *Journal of Grid Computing*, vol. 10, pp. 325–346, 2012.
9. Y. Kwok and I. Ahmad, "Static scheduling algorithms for allocating directed task graphs to multiprocessors," *ACM Computing Surveys*, vol. 31, no. 4, Darlinghurst, Australia, pp. 406–471, 1999.
10. K. Liu, J. Chen, H. Jin, and Y. Yang, "A min-min average algorithm for scheduling transaction-intensive grid workflows," in *Proceedings of the Seventh Australasian Symposium on Grid Computing and e-Research*, pp. 41–48, Australian Computer Society, Inc., 2009.
11. M. Xu, L. Cui, H. Wang, and Y. Bi, "A multiple QoS constrained scheduling strategy of multiple workflows for cloud computing," in *International Symposium on Parallel and Distributed Processing with Applications (ISPA)*, Chengdu, China, pp. 629–634, IEEE, 2009.
12. J. Barbosa and B. Moreira, "Dynamic scheduling of a batch of parallel task jobs on heterogeneous clusters," *Parallel Computing*, vol. 37, no. 8, pp. 428–438, 2011.

13. Z. Yu and W. Shi, "A planner-guided scheduling strategy for multiple workflow applications," in *International Conference on Parallel Processing-Workshops (ICPP-W'08)*, Portland, Oregon, USA, pp. 1–8, IEEE, 2008.

14. C. Hsu, K. Huang, and F. Wang, "Online scheduling of workflow applications in grid environments," *Future Generation Computer Systems*, vol. 27, no. 6, pp. 860–870, 2011.

15. H. Arabnejad and J. Barbosa, "Fairness resource sharing for dynamic workflow scheduling on heterogeneous systems," in *International Symposium on Parallel and Distributed Processing with Applications (ISPA)*, Madrid, Spain, pp. 633–639, IEEE, 2012.

16. D. Karger, C. Stein, and J. Wein, "Scheduling algorithms," *Algorithms and Theory of Computation Handbook*, M. Atallah (Ed.), CRC Press LLC, Florida, 1999.

17. M. Maheswaran, S. Ali, H. Siegal, D. Hensgen, and R. F. Freund, "Dynamic matching and scheduling of a class of independent tasks onto heterogeneous computing systems," in *Proceedings of the Eighth Heterogeneous Computing Workshop*, San Juan, Puerto Rico, pp. 30–44, IEEE, 1999.

18. H. Casanova, A. Legrand, and M. Quinson, "SimGrid: a generic framework for large-scale distributed experiments," in *Proceedings of the Tenth International Conference on Computer Modeling and Simulation*, Cambridge, UK, pp. 126–131, IEEE Computer Society, 2008.

19. P. Velho and A. Legrand, "Accuracy study and improvement of network simulation in the SimGrid framework," in *Proceedings of the 2nd International Conference on Simulation Tools and Techniques (SIMUTools)*, Rome, Italy, 2009.

20. F. Cappello, E. Caron, M. Dayde, F. Desprez, E. Jeannot, Y. Jegou, S. Lanteri, J. Leduc, N. Melab, G. Mornet, R. Namyst, P. Primet, and O. Richard, "Grid5000: a large scale, reconfigurable, controlable and monitorable grid platform," in *Proceedings of the 6th IEEE/ACM International Workshop on Grid Computing*, Seattle, USA, pp. 99–106, 2005.

10

Systematic Mapping of Reed–Solomon Erasure Codes on Heterogeneous Multicore Architectures

Roman Wyrzykowski, Marcin Wozniak, and Lukasz Kuczynski

Czestochowa University of Technology, Czestochowa, Poland

A classical concept of building fault-tolerant systems consists of replicating data on several servers. Erasure codes assume another approach which is based on splitting up the data into blocks, encoding them redundantly, and distributing the blocks over various servers. The use of erasure codes could radically improve the availability of distributed storage in comparison to replication systems with similar storage and bandwidth requirements. The investigation reported in this chapter confirms the advantage of using modern heterogeneous multi/many-core architectures, especially GPUs, for the efficient implementation of the Reed–Solomon erasure codes.

10.1 INTRODUCTION

There has been a rapid increase in sensitive data, such as biomedical records or financial data. Protecting such data while in transit and at rest is crucial [1]. Example are

High-Performance Computing on Complex Environments, First Edition.
Edited by Emmanuel Jeannot and Julius Žilinskas.
© 2014 John Wiley & Sons, Inc. Published 2014 by John Wiley & Sons, Inc.

distributed data storage systems in grids [2] and clouds [3], which have different security concerns than traditional file systems. Rather than being concentrated in one place, data are now spread across multiple hosts. Failure of a single host, or an adversary taking control of a host, could lead to loss of sensitive data and compromise the whole system. Consequently, suitable techniques, for example, cryptographic algorithms and data replication, should be applied to fulfill such key requirements as confidentiality, integrity, and availability [2].

A classic concept of building fault-tolerant systems consists of replicating data on several servers. Erasure codes can improve the availability of distributed storage by splitting up the data into n blocks, encoding them redundantly using m blocks, and distributing the blocks over various servers [4]. As was shown in [5], the use of erasure codes reduces "mean time of failures by many orders of magnitude compared to replication systems with similar storage and bandwidth requirements." This approach can also be used to build large-scale storage installations that require fault-protection beyond RAID-5 in the case of multiple disk failures [6].

There are many ways of generating erasure codes. A standard approach is the use of the Reed–Solomon (RS) codes [7]. These codes were applied, among others, to provide a reliable data access in the well-known persistent data store, namely OceanStore [8]. The main disadvantage of this approach is a relatively large computational cost because all operations are implemented over the Galois field $GF(2^w)$ arithmetic, which is traditionally not supported by microprocessors, where

$$2^w \geq n + m. \tag{10.1}$$

All operations, such as addition, multiplication, or division, have to be performed in the Galois field $GF(2^w)$, which in the case of multiplication or division leads to a significant growth of computational cost. The computational cost of RS codes grows with the value of n [9] (and m, as well).

The development of high-performance multicore architectures opens a way to take advantages of RS erasure codes, since performance delivered by this architectures is no longer an obstacle to the utilization of RS codes in practical data storage systems [3, 10–12]. In this chapter, we focus on investigating how to map systematically the RS erasure codes on two multicore architectures: Cell/B.E. [13] processors, and graphics processing units (GPUs) [14]. The computational power of Cell/B.E., coupled with its security features, makes it a suitable platform to implement algorithms aimed at improving data confidentiality, integrity, and availability [2, 11]. Also, basic features of multicore GPUs [14, 15], such as utilization of a large number of relatively simple processing units operating in the SIMD (single instruction multiple data) manner as well as hardware-supported multithreading, enable the efficient implementation of this type of computations. A tremendous step toward a wider acceptation of GPUs in general-purpose computations was the development of Nvidia CUDA [15, 16] and OpenCL [17, 18] software environments, which allow programmers to implement algorithms on existing and future GPUs much easier.

The material of this chapter is organized as follows. Related works are outlined in Section 10.2. Details of the RS algorithm are introduced in Section 10.3. The proposed methodology for mapping the RS codes on the Cell/B.E. architecture as well as the performance results achieved are presented in Section 10.4. In Section 10.5, we discuss mapping the RS encoding algorithm on GPU architectures. Section 10.6 introduces methods that allow improvement of the algorithm performance, and concludes with presentation of performance results obtained on Tesla C1060 and Tesla M2070-Q GPUs in Section 10.7. Finally, Section 10.8 gives the conclusions and future directions of work.

10.2 RELATED WORKS

In the context of the high computational cost of RS codes, an interesting alternative for erasure codes is the so-called Tornado codes, known also as the *digital fountain codes* (DFC) [19]. These codes seem to feature a lower computation cost since their implementation can be reduced to a series of bitwise XOR operations. However, in the case of decoding, they do not require n available fragments, as in the case of RS codes, but $f \times n$ fragments, where $f > 1$ is an *overhead factor*, and f is close to 1 only when n tends to infinity. Therefore, in the case of values of n and m that are applicable in many real data storage systems, there could be a problem of significant overheads. For instance, when $n = 50$ and $m = 50$, the best known DFC code tolerates on average only $m/f = 36.025$ faults [4].

The Tornado codes are a special case of an entire class of solutions known as the *low-density parity-check* (LDPC) codes [20, 21], which are also applied in designing distributed data storage systems [22], and they constitute a promising alternative for the RS codes. However, as was shown by experiments [4, 9], this potential advantage of LDPC codes does not always work in practice when the value of n is rather small. In particular, the results of the performed experiments revealed that the performance of RS codes was not worse for the encoding ratio $r = n/(n + m) = 1/2$ than that of LDPC codes if $n \leq 50$. This relationship depends on the ratio between the performance of a network and the performance of processing units used for encoding/decoding. For a constant network performance, increasing the performance of processing units shows the advantage of RS codes.

This conclusion is especially important nowadays when multicore architectures begin to emerge in every area of computing [23]. An important step in the direction of improving the performance of RS codes has been done recently, when a Cauchy version of these codes was proposed in [24]. This new class of codes (known as *CRS* codes) does not require performing any multiplication using the Galois field arithmetic; a series of bitwise XOR operations is executed instead. Implementations of CRS codes on GPU multicores are presented in [25, 26].

A convincing example of efficient usage of RS codes to build a reliable storage for HPC applications in clouds is described in [3]. Compared to traditional approaches that rely on block replication, this work demonstrates that even using conventional CPU multicores it becomes possible to achieve about 50% higher throughput while reducing network bandwidth and storage utilization by a factor of 2 for the same targeted reliability level. These results are confirmed both by modeling and by real-life experimentation on hundreds of compute nodes.

The growing popularity of erasure coding can be also easily seen by the number of libraries developed in the last decade that implement a variety of different erasure codes. The performance comparison of selected open-source implementations of erasure coding is performed in [6], including both the classic RS and Cauchy RS codes. The conclusion is that the efficient exploitation of modern multicore architectures in such libraries is one of the key challenges to build high-performance, reliable storage systems based on erasure coding. This challenge is undertaken by a high-performance practical library, Gibraltar [10], which performs RS coding on graphics processors in a manner suitable for storage arrays. The performance of this library is compared with that of a widely available CPU implementation provided by the Jerasure library [6]. Its practicality is also demonstrated through a usage example.

10.3 REED–SOLOMON CODES AND LINEAR ALGEBRA ALGORITHMS

Applying EC codes to increase reliability of distributed data management systems can be described in the following way [7]. A file F of size $|F|$ is partitioned into n blocks (stripes) of size B words each, where

$$B = |F|/n. \tag{10.2}$$

Each block is stored on one of n data devices $D_0, D_1, \ldots, D_{n-1}$. Also, there are m checksum devices $C_0, C_1, \ldots, C_{m-1}$. Their contents are derived from contents of data devices, using an encoding algorithm. This algorithm has to allow for restoring the original file from any n (or a bit more) of $n + m$ storage devices $D_0, D_1, \ldots, D_{n-1}$, $C_0, C_1, \ldots, C_{m-1}$, even if m of these devices failed, in the worst case.

The application of the RS erasure codes includes [7, 27] two stages: (i) encoding and (ii) decoding. At the encoding stage, an input data vector $\mathbf{d}_n = [d_0, d_1, \ldots, d_{n-1}]^T$, containing n words each of size w bits, is multiplied by a special matrix

$$\mathbf{F}_{(n+m)\times n} = \begin{bmatrix} \mathbf{I}_{n\times n} \\ \mathbf{F}^*_{m\times n} \end{bmatrix}. \tag{10.3}$$

Its first n rows correspond to the identity matrix, while the whole matrix is derived as a result of transforming an $(n + m) \times n$ Vandermonde matrix, with elements defined over $GF(2^w)$. As a result of the encoding procedure, we obtain an $(n + m)$ column vector

$$\mathbf{e}_{n+m} = \mathbf{F}_{(n+m)\times n}\, \mathbf{d}_n = \begin{bmatrix} \mathbf{d}_n \\ \mathbf{c}_m \end{bmatrix}, \tag{10.4}$$

where

$$\mathbf{c}_m = \mathbf{F}^*_{m\times n}\, \mathbf{d}_n. \tag{10.5}$$

Therefore, the encoding stage can be reduced to performing many times the matrix–vector multiplication (10.5), where all operations are carried out over $GF(2^w)$, and the matrix $\mathbf{F}^*_{m \times n}$ corresponds to the last m rows of the matrix $\mathbf{F}_{(n+m) \times n}$.

The decoding stage consists in deleting those rows of the matrix $\mathbf{F}_{(n+m) \times n}$ that correspond to failed nodes—these can be both data nodes or checksum nodes. For the sake of simplicity, let us assume that the maximum possible number of nodes failed is m. Then we compute the inverse matrix (e.g., by Gaussian elimination) for the obtained matrix $\phi_{n \times n}$. The existence of the inverse matrix follows from the construction of the matrix $\mathbf{F}_{(n+m) \times n}$ on the basis of the Vandermonde matrix, which guarantees the linear independence of an arbitrary combination consisting of n rows of the matrix $\mathbf{F}_{(n+m) \times n}$. The reconstruction of failed elements (words) of the vector $\mathbf{d}_n$ is thus based on applying the following expression:

$$\mathbf{d}_n = \phi_{n \times n}^{-1} \times \mathbf{e}_n^*, \tag{10.6}$$

where the column $\mathbf{e}_n^*$ consists of entries of the original vector $\mathbf{e}_{n+m}$ located in nodes that did not fail. The decoding procedure ends with determining those entries of the checksum vector $\mathbf{c}_m$ that correspond to failed nodes.

In our investigations, we focus on mapping only the first stage, namely encoding, since our main objective is to determine opportunities given by applying innovative multicore architectures to accelerate computations required to implement the classic version of the RS codes. It follows from the above assumption that there is no need to consider the decoding phase, since it differs from the encoding phase only by an additional procedure of computing the inverse matrix of size $n \times n$, which is performed just once in order to reconstruct a given file after the failure.

Indeed, under the assumption that the Gaussian elimination is used to compute the inverse matrix $\phi_{n \times n}^{-1}$, the complexity of performed computations is estimated as $O(y^2 n)$ [7], since the elimination can be executed only for those rows of the matrix $\phi_{n \times n}$ that correspond to failed nodes. The number of such nodes is just $y = 1, \ldots, m$. This implies not only the low complexity of the inversion procedure for relatively small values of m, which are of our primary interest but also the independence of the discussed complexity from the file size. So, for sufficiently large files, efficiency aspects of entire computations depend in practice on the efficiency of operation (10.5).

10.4 MAPPING REED–SOLOMON CODES ON CELL/B.E. ARCHITECTURE

10.4.1 Cell/B.E. Architecture

This innovative heterogeneous multicore chip is significantly different from conventional multiprocessor or multicore architectures. The Cell/B.E. integrates nine processor elements (cores) of two types: the power processor element (PPE) is optimized for control tasks, while the eight synergistic processor elements (SPEs) provide an execution environment optimized for data-intensive computation. Each SPE supports vector processing on 128-bit words, implemented in parallel by two pipelines. Each SPE includes 128 vector registers, as well as a private local store for fast instruction and data access. The EIB bus connects all the cores with a high-performance communication subsystem. Also, the Cell/B.E. offers an advanced, hardware-based security architecture [2]. Instead of relying on software-implemented approaches, the Cell/B.E. was designed with the goal of providing hardware-based security features which are less vulnerable than software solutions.

10.4.2   Basic Assumptions for Mapping

In our investigation, we focus on mapping the following expression:

$$\mathbf{C}_{m \times B} = \mathbf{F}^*_{m \times n} \mathbf{D}_{n \times B} \tag{10.7}$$

which is obtained from (10.5) taking into consideration the necessity to process not a single vector $\mathbf{d}_n$ but B such vectors. An expression of the same kind is used at the decoding stage.

In the basic expression (10.7), parameters n and m play the crucial role as regards possible versions of the mapping we are interested in. Let us consider the ClusteriX distributed computing infrastructure [11]. It consists of 12 PC-Linux clusters located across Poland, and connected by dedicated 1 Gb/s channels provided by the PIONIER optical network. When we take the characteristics of the ClusteriX infrastructure as the basis, it is necessary to apply the following two schemes: (i) n, $m = 4$, which corresponds to eight storage nodes, out of which maximum four can be inaccessible; (ii) $n = 8$, $m = 4$, which corresponds to 12 storage nodes, out of which maximum 4 can be inaccessible.

It should be noted that, even in the first case, in which features double the capacity of the storage space (since $r = n/(n + m) = 1/2$), applying erasure codes allows us to achieve the tolerance for up to four faults, while using the classic replication requires us to expand the storage space $m + 1 = 5$ times.

The considered expression (10.7) represents a special case of multiplying rectangular matrices, where the basic operations are (i) multiplication over the Galois field $GF(2^w)$, and (ii) addition over $GF(2^w)$, which reduces to the XOR operation performed bit by bit.

Hence, we focus on providing the most efficient implementation of multiplication. For our purposes, it is sufficient (condition (10.1)) to assume $w = 8$, which gives 1-byte words. Then we can apply [7, 11] the look-up table technique for implementing multiplications of the form $c = f * d$ efficiently, based on the following formula:

$$c = gfilog(gflog(f) + gflog(d)). \tag{10.8}$$

Here, *gflog* and *gfilog* denote, respectively, the logarithms and antilogarithms defined over $GF(2^w)$. Their values are stored in two tables, whose length does not exceed 256 bytes. Following our previous work [11], the efficient implementation of table look-ups required by (10.8) is based on utilization of *shufb* permutation instruction, which performs 16 simultaneous byte table look-ups in a 32-entry table. Larger tables are addressed using a binary-tree process on a series of 32-entry table look-ups, when successive bits of the table indices are used as a selector (using *selb* instruction) to choose the correct subtable value.

The Cell/B.E. architecture enables us to apply parallel processing at three levels. In order from the highest to the lowest ones, they are (i) eight SPE cores running independently, and communicating via the EIB bus; (ii) vector processing in each SPE, whose instructions allow processing 16 bytes of data simultaneously; (iii) executing instructions by two pipelines (*even* and *odd*) in parallel.

Achieving the high performance of computing requires the exploitation of all three levels as much as possible. In the case of computing expression (10.7), this is obtained in the following way:

1. Parallelization at the highest level does not cause major problems. For this purpose, it is sufficient to decompose the matrix $\mathbf{D}_{n \times B}$ into eight smaller submatrices, where the ith submatrix contains columns from $a_i = p \times i$ to $b_i = p \times (i + 1) - 1$, where $i = 0, 1, \ldots, 7, p = B/8$.

2. Efficient vectorization of computations requires the adaptation of processed data to the length of SPE vector registers, which is equal to 128 bits. This means, with the given word length equal to $w = 8$ bits, the necessity of further decomposition of previously obtained submatrices—now into submatrices with 16-byte rows. Then expression (10.7), implemented in a vector way on one SPE core, has the following form:

$$\mathbf{C}_{m \times 16} = \mathbf{F}^*_{m \times n} \mathbf{D}_{n \times 16}. \tag{10.9}$$

It is clear that we need to have n registers for storing the matrix $\mathbf{D}$, m registers for the matrix $\mathbf{C}$, and some registers for the matrix $\mathbf{F}^*$. Also, at least 16 registers for logarithms and antilogarithms (in total at least 32 registers) are necessary.

3. In order to increase the utilization of two pipelines available in each SPE core, it is essential to consider the possibility of executing a series of optimizations of the code which corresponds to computing formula (10.9), after its prior vectorization. In the considered case, a form of the matrix $\mathbf{F}^*_{m \times n}$ provides additional opportunities for such optimizations.

10.4.3   Vectorization Algorithm and Increasing Its Efficiency

Below we present the proposed vectorization algorithm for the row-wise format of storing the input matrix $\mathbf{D}_{n \times 16}$, and the output matrix $\mathbf{C}_{m \times 16}$ of checksums. The algorithm describes the way of computing an arbitrary row $\mathbf{c}_i$ of the checksum matrix in n steps, on the basis of rows $\mathbf{d}_j$ of the input matrix:

Algorithm 10.1

```
vectorization algorithm for Reed-Solomon encoding {
      for i = 0,1,...,m-1 do {
          cᵢ = [0,0,...,0]
          for j = 0,1,...,n-1 do
              cᵢ := cᵢ ⊕ f*ᵢ,ⱼ ⊙ dⱼ
      }
}
```

where

- vector $\mathbf{f}^*_{i,j}$ is obtained by copying the entry (byte) $f^*_{i,j}$ of the matrix $\mathbf{F}^*_{n \times mj}$ onto all 16 entries (bytes) corresponding to a vector register of SPEs;

- ⊙ is the element-by-element multiplication of two vectors, implemented over $GF(2^8)$ using tables of logarithms and antilogarithms according to formula (10.8), where the size of each table is not greater than 256 bytes, while ⊕ denotes the element-by-element addition of two vectors, with the result determined by the bitwise XOR operation.

The properties of the Cell/B.E. architecture enable efficient realization of look-up operations in 256-byte tables as a series of operations performed concurrently for all 16 elements of vectors. This means that computing rows of the matrix $\mathbf{C}_{m \times 16}$ according to Algorithm 10.1 is indeed performed as a series of operations executed on 16-byte vectors.

In order to increase the efficiency of the vectorization algorithm, it is essential to consider the form of the matrix $\mathbf{F}^*_{m \times n}$. The aim is to increase the computational performance by a better use of two pipelines of the SPE, taking into account restriction on the number of registers. Particularly, for the first of the two combinations of parameters m and n selected in Section 10.4.2, we have

$$
\mathbf{F}^*_{4 \times 4} = \begin{bmatrix} 0x01 & 0x01 & 0x01 & 0x01 \\ 0x01 & 0xd9 & 0x5c & 0xac \\ 0x01 & 0x5c & 0x46 & 0x7b \\ 0x01 & 0x46 & 0x8f & 0xc8 \end{bmatrix}. \tag{10.10}
$$

The form of matrices $\mathbf{F}^*_{4 \times 4}$ and $\mathbf{F}^*_{4 \times 8}$ allows us to apply the following ways of increasing efficiency of computations (already vectorized):

1. By taking into account values of elements in the row with the index $i = 0$ of the matrix $\mathbf{F}^*_{m \times n}$, we can avoid performing multiplication in Algorithm 10.1 for the row $\mathbf{c}_0$ of the matrix $\mathbf{C}_{m \times 16}$. Moreover, only units occur at the beginning of each row of the matrix $\mathbf{F}^*_{m \times n}$. Hence, for other rows of the matrix $\mathbf{C}_{m \times 16}$ we can eliminate multiplication in the first step ($j = 0$) of computing values of Algorithm 10.1.

2. Since entries of the matrix $\mathbf{F}^*_{m \times n}$ are constant, it is not necessary to refer to the table of logarithms for vectors $\mathbf{f}^*_{i,j}$ — it is sufficient to fill registers corresponding to vectors $\mathbf{f}^*_{i,j}$ with logarithms of corresponding elements of the matrix $\mathbf{F}^*_{n \times m}$ instead. The number of these registers can be decreased up to 7 or 18 in the case of matrices $\mathbf{F}^*_{4 \times 4}$ and $\mathbf{F}^*_{4 \times 8}$, respectively, as we have to store only the vectors $\mathbf{f}^*_{i,j}$ which correspond to nonrepeating values $f^*_{i,j}$ of the matrix $\mathbf{F}^*_{m \times n}$.

10.4.4 Performance Results

In Table 10.1, we present the performance results achieved by us for three different variants of implementing the encoding procedure in the case of the classic RS codes. The table shows the number of clock cycles necessary to process by a single SPE core either 1 ($L_B = 1$) or 10 ($L_B = 10$) data packages of size $n \times 16$ bytes each, where $n = 4$. The implementation variants, which were tested for various compiler options that control the code optimization (from O1 to O3), correspond either to the basic variant of Algorithm 10.1 (variant 1) or to the usage of different manual optimizations (variants 2 and 3).

The analysis of results included in Table 10.1 allows us to arrive at the following conclusions:

1. The best performance is achieved for the second variant. As the proposed mapping allows us to use all eight SPE cores in parallel, this variant enables achieving the maximum processing bandwidth equal to $b^{RSC}_8 = 9.58$ GB/s, which follows from the following formula:

$$b^{RSC}_8 = (8 \times 3.2 \times L_B \times n \times 16)/L_C \text{ [GB/s]}. \tag{10.11}$$

2. Such a high value of the maximum bandwidth of processing the RS codes in cell processors means that in real circumstances the computing bandwidth is no longer a constraint for the entire system performance. For example, in the ClusteriX infrastructure, this performance is constrained by the maximum bandwidth provided by the wide-area PIONIER network (10 Gb/s), as well as by the maximum bandwidth of the external processor bus (8 GB/s for the PCIe 2.0 specification).

TABLE 10.1 Performance Results (Number of Clock Cycles) for Different Variants of Implementing the Encoding Procedure for the Classic Version of the Reed–Solomon Codes

Compiler Option	Variant 1		Variant 2		Variant 3	
	1 Block	10 Blocks	1 Block	10 Blocks	1 Block	10 Blocks
O1	223	2118	201	2078	214	2211
O2	215	1990	198	1710	215	1770
O3	215	1990	198	1710	215	1770

10.5   MAPPING REED–SOLOMON CODES ON MULTICORE GPU ARCHITECTURES

The CUDA programming environment [16] makes it possible to develop parallel applications for both the Windows and Linux operating systems, giving access to a programming interface in the C language. However, the utilization of GPUs in an everyday practice is still limited. The main reason is the necessity of adapting applications and algorithms to a target architecture in order to match its internal characteristics. This section deals with the problem of how to perform such an adaptation efficiently for the encoding stage in the classic version of RS codes.

The CUDA software architecture includes two modules dedicated, respectively, to a general-purpose CPU and a graphic processor. This allows the utilization of GPU as an application accelerator when a part of the application is executed on a standard processor while another part is assigned to GPU as the so-called kernel. The allocation of GPU memory, data transfers, and kernel execution are initialized by the CPU. Each data item used in the GPU needs to be copied from the main memory to the GPU memory; each of these transfers is a source of latency, which affects the resulting performance negatively [25]. These performance overheads can be reduced in CUDA using the stream processing mechanism. It allows overlapping kernel computations with data transfers between the main memory and the GPU memory using the asynchronous CUDA API, which immediately returns from CUDA calls before their completion. Another key feature of modern GPUs is their hierarchical memory organization, which includes several levels with different volumes and access times. First of all, GPUs are equipped with the *global memory* accessible by all the threads (read and write). However, access to this relatively large memory is rather expensive. Other types of GPU memory, accessible for all the threads running on a graphics card, are *constant memory* and *texture memory*. Their access time is shorter, but threads are allowed only to read from these memories. Within a particular CUDA block, threads share the fast *shared memory*, which is used for communication and synchronization among threads across the block. Finally, after being initialized, each thread obtains access to a pool of *registers*.

10.5.1   Parallelization of Reed–Solomon Codes on GPU Architectures

The starting point for the parallelization of RS encoding is Algorithm 10.1. The width of registers in the Cell/B.E. architectures (16 bytes) was the reason for splitting the input and output matrices $\mathbf{D}_{n \times B}$ and $\mathbf{C}_{m \times B}$ into submatrices of size $n \times 16$ and $m \times 16$ bytes, respectively. For GPUs, this limitation is no longer valid. Therefore, the whole matrices

$$\mathbf{D}_{n \times B} = [\mathbf{d}_0, \mathbf{d}_1, \dots, \mathbf{d}_{n-1}], \quad \mathbf{C}_{m \times B} = [\mathbf{c}_0, \mathbf{c}_1, \dots, \mathbf{c}_{m-1}] \qquad (10.12)$$

can be utilized, where vectors $\mathbf{d}_j$ and $\mathbf{c}_i$ correspond to rows of matrices $\mathbf{D}_{n \times B}$ and $\mathbf{C}_{m \times B}$, respectively. The resulting algorithm is presented in Algorithm 10.2.

Algorithm 10.2

```
basic algorithm for Reed-Solomon encoding on GPU {
    C = [0,0,...,0]
    for j = 0,1,...,n - 1 do {
        for k = 0,1,...,B - 1 do {
            for i = 0,1,...,m - 1 do
                cᵢ,ₖ := cᵢ,ₖ ⊕ f*ᵢ,ⱼ ⊙ dⱼ,ₖ
        }
    }
}
```

Unlike Algorithm 10.1, the order of loops corresponding to indices i and j is changed in the above algorithm. These indices are responsible for the management of access to elements of matrices $\mathbf{D}_{n\times B}$ and $\mathbf{C}_{m\times B}$. Such a change gives us the possibility to split the algorithm into n stages which are implemented using the stream processing mechanism that aims at overlapping transfer of matrix $\mathbf{D}_{n\times B}$ with computations on GPU. As will be shown later, the adopted variant of access to elements of this matrix is especially important in the case where the number of data devices is greater than the number of checksum devices ($n > m$).

In comparison with Algorithm 10.1, an additional loop with index k is introduced in Algorithm 10.2. The k-loop directly corresponds to computations performed in parallel by GPU threads. Consequently, in Algorithm 10.2 it becomes possible to separate a part that can be executed in parallel as the GPU kernel is shown in Algorithm 10.3.

Algorithm 10.3

```
GPU kernel {
    for i = 0,1,...,m - 1 do
        cᵢ,ₖ* := cᵢ,ₖ ⊕ f*ᵢ,ⱼ ⊙ dⱼ,ₖ
    }
}
```

In this way, the whole computations are divided into n stages, and each of them is responsible for encoding in parallel a fragment of the input file. Such a decomposition allows us to preserve the continuity of data stored in the arrays $\mathbf{D}_{n\times B}$ and $\mathbf{C}_{m\times B}$, as well as to adapt the pattern of the GPU global memory access to the structure of the stored data.

In this work, we assume that both the encoded file and checksums have to be located in the GPU global memory, which gives the following constraint:

$$B \times (n + m) < S_{\text{GM}} \quad \text{[byte]}, \tag{10.13}$$

where S_{GM} stands for the size of the global memory. Taking into account that B is given by formula (10.2), it is easy to determine the maximum size $|F|_{\text{max}}$ of an input file F that can be encoded using the proposed algorithm:

$$|F|_{\text{max}} = S_{\text{GM}} * \frac{n}{n + m} \quad \text{[byte]}. \tag{10.14}$$

As a result, in the case of Tesla C1060 GPU, equipped with 4 GB of global memory, it is possible to encode files with the size of up to 2 GB for $n, m = 4$, and up to 2.66 GB for $n = 8, m = 4$. For larger files, it is necessary to apply an additional decomposition of input files in such a way that the obtained fragments can be encoded separately.

10.5.2 Organization of GPU Threads

Besides memory limitations, there are other constraints that should be taken into account when mapping numerical algorithms on GPU architectures. One of the most important is the number of threads created by a GPU kernel. In the case of Algorithm 10.3, this number depends on the size of encoded file and the number of data elements processed by each GPU.

Initially, we assume that a single GPU thread is assigned to each element (or byte) of vector $\mathbf{d}_j$. In this case, B treads will be created. At the same time, the maximum number T_{max} of threads executed by a certain GPU varies by GPU generations. For example, in the case of Tesla C1060, $T_{max} = 33,553,920$ threads (up to 65,535 blocks, each of them consisting of up to 512 threads). This means that such a GPU is able to encode a bit less than 32 MB of data (for one stage), while for n stages this bound is extended to 127,998 MB for $n = 4, m = 4$, and 255,996 MB for $n = 8, m = 4$. Assuming the NVIDIA's Fermi GPU architecture, which allows the creation up to 1024 threads in each block, the maximum size of the encoded files increases by twice. To remove this constraint, the number of data elements assigned to each GPU thread is determined dynamically. In this case, the number of threads created for each kernel invocation is as follows:

$$T_{\text{count}} = \frac{B}{e_T}, \quad e_T = \left\lceil \frac{|F|}{n * T_{max}} \right\rceil = \left\lceil \frac{B}{T_{max}} \right\rceil, \tag{10.15}$$

where e_T denotes the number of elements in the vector $\mathbf{d}_j$ that are assigned to each GPU thread, and $\lceil x \rceil$ is the least integer greater than or equal to x. In practice, the number of created threads must be additionally rounded up to the nearest multiple of the number of threads created in each block.

The key operation of Algorithm 10.3 is multiplication over the Galois field $GF(2^8)$. Its efficient implementation is based on expression (10.8). For this aim, 256-entry tables with logarithms and antilogarithms should be stored in the constant (or texture) memory, in order to provide fast access to entries of these tables.

The matrix $\mathbf{D}_{n \times B}$, which consists of n data vectors $\mathbf{d}_j$, is stored as a 1D array $\mathbf{D}_{n * B}$ with the size of $n * B$ bytes (each array entry corresponds to 1 byte). The checksum matrix $\mathbf{C}_{m \times B}$ is stored in a similar way. Both matrices are stored in the GPU global memory. Such a data organization allows us to optimize the performance of access to the global memory. This is achieved using the coalesced memory access [16], when neighbouring threads access neighbouring cells in memory, with the arrays $\mathbf{D}$ and $\mathbf{C}$ stored in contiguous areas. The resulting basic version of GPU kernel, written in CUDA, is presented in Algorithm 10.4.

Algorithm 10.4

```
_global_ void RS_coding(unsigned char *c,
                        const unsigned char *d,
                        const unsigned int B,
                        const unsigned int j,
                        const unsigned int e_th)
{
  const int offset = gridDim.x * blockDim.x;
  const int th_id = blockIdx.x * blockDim.x + threadIdx.x;
  for (unsigned int ep = 0; ep < e_th; ep++){
    unsigned int k = ep * offset + th_id;
    for (int i=0; i<m; i++)
      c[B*i+k] ^= alogTable[logTable[d[B*j+k]] + logTable[f[i][j]]];
  }
}
```

10.6 METHODS OF INCREASING THE ALGORITHM PERFORMANCE ON GPUS

10.6.1 Basic Modifications

To optimize the encoding performance for the basic kernel shown in Algorithm 10.4, a series of code modifications are applied, allowing us first of all to minimize the number of memory references and delays of data accesses. Among the applied modifications, the most important are as follows:

1. replacement of m references (`logTable[d[B*j+k]]`) to the table of logarithms with a single reference;
2. *loop unrolling* applied for the inner loop;
3. implementation of access to the table of logarithms using the constant or texture memory, depending on pattern of access to this table.

A significant effect is achieved through replacement of one of references to the table of logarithms, stored in the constant memory, with reference implemented through the texture memory. This decision is the result of the way in which threads read entries from the table of logarithms. The constant memory allows for the minimization of access time only in the case when all the threads within successive 16 threads (*half_warp*) read the same memory cell. The majority of memory references in the code presented in Algorithm 10.4 satisfy this condition. The only exception is the reference (`logTable[d[B*j+k]]`), where indices of table entries depend on indices of neighboring threads. At the same time, this reference can be efficiently implemented through the texture memory. Algorithm 10.5 presents the resulting kernel `RS_coding_v1()` obtained from the basic one after the modifications described above.

Algorithm 10.5

```
_global_ void RS_coding_v1(unsigned char * c,
                          const unsigned char * d,
                          const unsigned int B,
                          const unsigned int j,
                          const unsigned int e_th)
{
   const int offset = gridDim.x * blockDim.x;
   const int th_id = blockIdx.x * blockDim.x + threadIdx.x;
   for (unsigned int ep = 0; ep<e_th; ep++){
    unsigned int k = ep * offset + th_id;
    const unsigned char tmp = tex1D(logTable_tex, d[j * B+k]);
    c[k]      ^= alogTable[(unsigned char)(tmp+0xff)];
    c[k+=B]   ^= alogTable[(unsigned char)(tmp+logTable[f[1][j]])];
    c[k+=B]   ^= alogTable[(unsigned char)(tmp+logTable[f[2][j]])];
    c[k+=B]   ^= alogTable[(unsigned char)(tmp+logTable[f[3][j]])];
   }
}
```

10.6.2   Stream Processing

According to Algorithm 10.3, the GPU implementation of RS encoding includes several steps:

- transfer of array $D_{n \times B}$ from the main memory to the GPU global memory;
- computing the checksum matrix $C_{m \times B}$ in GPU;
- transfer of array $C_{m \times B}$ from the GPU global memory to the main memory.

As a result, the total execution time t_E for the RS encoding can be expressed by the following sum:

$$t_E = t_D + t_{\text{kernel}} + t_C, \tag{10.16}$$

where

- t_D is the time of transferring the matrix $D_{n \times B}$ from host to GPU;
- t_{kernel} is the time of computing checksums in GPU;
- t_C is the time of transferring checksums from GPU to host.

The structure of data and properties of the considered algorithm allow us to utilize the mechanism of stream processing, when computations and transfers are implemented in parallel in order to reduce the encoding time t_E. At the same time, the stream processing can be implemented only for one of matrices $D_{n \times B}$ or $C_{m \times B}$. In our algorithm, the convenient organization of transfers is based on splitting the data into blocks of B bytes. In this case, the array $D_{n \times B}$, containing the encoded file, is transferred using n streams, while the array $C_{m \times B}$ of checksums is received from the GPU memory using m streams. Different variants of data decomposition for stream processing are illustrated in Fig. 10.1, where parts (a) and (b) correspond to the case

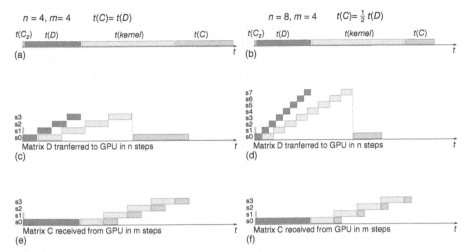

FIGURE 10.1 *Reducing encoding time using stream processing for different variants of data decomposition.*

without stream processing, for the two considered variants of parameters m and n. The rest of Fig. 10.1 illustrates the following cases: (i) using n streams for transferring the array $\mathbf{D}_{n \times B}$ from host to GPU, in n stages (parts (c) and (d)), and (ii) using m streams for transferring the array $\mathbf{C}_{m \times B}$ from GPU to host, in m stages (parts (e) and (f)).

If $m = n$, the encoding time is the same for both variants of data decomposition (Fig. 10.1c and e). At the same time, if $n \geq m$ (Fig. 10.1d, when $n = 8, m = 4$), the transfer of matrix $\mathbf{D}_{n \times B}$ using n streams allows us to decrease the encoding time, as compared with the transfer of matrix $\mathbf{C}_{m \times B}$ using m streams (Fig. 10.1f). It is the main reason why the order of loop indices is changed in Algorithm 10.2.

The benefits of using stream processing are shown in Fig. 10.2, where V_2 denotes the bandwidth achieved for the RS encoding on GPU with n streams, while the other bandwidths V_B, V_0, and V_1 are obtained for different versions of implementing the

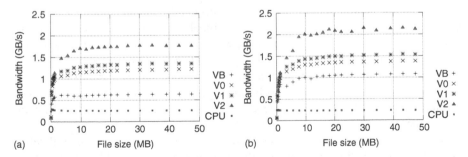

FIGURE 10.2 *Bandwidth achieved on Tesla C1060 GPU for different versions of implementing Reed–Solomon encoding, depending on size of encoded file. (a) First variant of coding with $n, m = 4$. (b) Second variant of coding with $n = 8$, $m = 4$.*

encoding algorithm without stream processing. Here, V_0 correspond to advantages of using the page-locked host memory with respect to the basic version characterized by V_B, while the bandwidth V_1 is obtained after the basic performance improvements described in Section 10.6.1. In all the cases, the achieved bandwidth is determined as the ratio of the input file size $|F|$ to the total execution time t_E of encoding.

The proposed mapping, coupled with the stream processing mechanism, allows us to encode data with the bandwidth of 1.7 GB/s (13.6 Gb/s) for $n, m = 4$, and 2.2 GB/s (17.6 Gb/s) for $n = 8$, $m = 4$. Note that the utilization of stream processing provides significant benefits for the file size greater than 2 MB.

10.6.3 Using Shared Memory

In the code presented in Algorithm 10.5, for each GPU thread there are 11 references that are implemented using the constant or texture memory: (i) $m = 4$ references to the 256-entry table alogTable[] of antilogarithms; (ii) $m = 4$ references to the 256-entry table logTable[] of logarithms; (iii) $m - 1 = 3$ references to the array $f_{m \times n}$ with size of 16 or 32 bytes, depending on values of parameters n and m, respectively.

In consequence, the whole block of 512 threads generates 5 632 references to a certain type of off-chip memory. The solution of this problem is to copy the tables of logarithms and antilogarithms to the shared memory in such a way that a single entry of each table is copied to the shared memory by a single GPU thread. As a result, the number of references to the constant (or texture) memory is decreased to 512 references, for each block of 512 threads.

Taking into account performance differences for different patterns of access to the constant and texture memories, we finally decided to place both the table of logarithms and table of antilogarithms in the texture memory. Then, all the 512 references within each block could be coalesced by groups of 16 references, and finally all the 512 references were implemented as 32 memory transactions. Note that this approach is not applicable to the array $f_{m \times n}$ because of relatively large overheads required to copy this fairly small array to the shared memory.

Algorithm 10.6 shows the resulting kernel RS_coding_v2() obtained from the code presented in Algorithm 10.6, using the proposed optimization of access to the GPU memory. The first 256 threads in each block are responsible for copying the table of logarithms to the shared memory, while the next 256 threads correspond to copying the table of antilogarithms. These threads access the tables of logarithms and antilogarithms through the texture memory. In order to guarantee that all data are copied to the shared memory, the barrier __syncthreads() is invoked. As a result, in the rest of kernel RS_coding_v2(), all threads read values located in the shared memory.

The resulting bandwidth V_3 is presented in Fig. 10.3. As expected, the utilization of shared memory allows us to reduce the time of access to the tables of logarithms and antilogarithms, which results in increasing the achieved encoding bandwidth up to 1.85 GB/s for $n, m = 4$, and up to 2.4 GB/s for $n = 8$, $m = 4$.

Algorithm 10.6

```
_global_ void RS_coding_v2(unsigned char *c,const unsigned char
* d, const unsigned int B, const unsigned int j, const unsigned
int e_th)
{
  _shared_ unsigned char SlogTable[256];
  _shared_ unsigned char SalogTable[256];
  int ti = threadIdx.x;
  const int th_id = blockIdx.x * blockDim.x + threadIdx.x;
  if (ti<256) {
    SlogTable[ti] = tex1D(logTable_tex,ti);
  } else {
    ti-=256;
    SalogTable[ti] = tex1D(alogTable_tex,ti);
  }
  _syncthreads();


  const int offset = gridDim.x * blockDim.x;
  for(unsigned int ep = 0; ep<e_th; ep++){
    unsigned int k = ep * offset + thid;
    const unsigned char tmp = SlogTable[D[k]];
    c[k]    ^= SalogTable[(unsigned char)(tmp+0xff)];
    c[k+=B]^= SalogTable[(unsigned char)(tmp+SlogTable[f[1][j]])];
    c[k+=B]^= SalogTable[(unsigned char)(tmp+SlogTable[f[2][j]])];
    c[k+=B]^= SalogTable[(unsigned char)(tmp+SlogTable[f[3][j]])];
  }
}
```

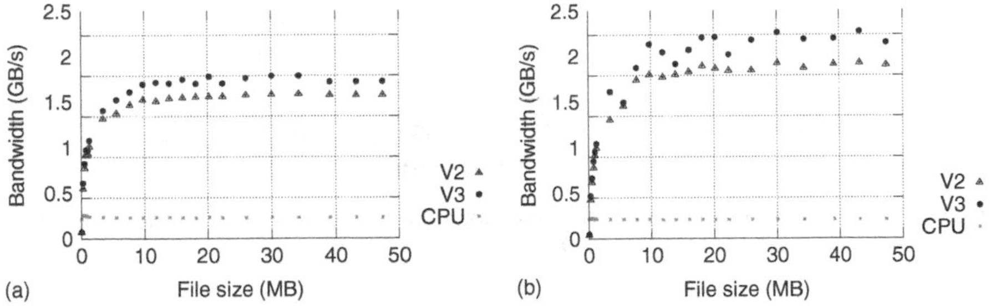

FIGURE 10.3 *Bandwidth achieved on Tesla C1060 GPU for Reed–Solomon encoding using stream processing and shared memory, depending on size of encoded file. (a) First variant of coding with $n, m = 4$. (b) Second variant of coding with $n = 8$, $m = 4$.*

10.7 GPU PERFORMANCE EVALUATION

10.7.1 Experimental Results

The performance experiments were carried out for two platforms containing GPUs of two different generations: (i) Tesla C1060 GPU and AMD PhenomII X4 3.12 GHz CPU, with the CUDA 2.2 software environment; (ii) Tesla M2070Q GPU (Fermi architecture) and Intel Xeon E5649 2.53 GHz CPU, with CUDA 3.0. For both

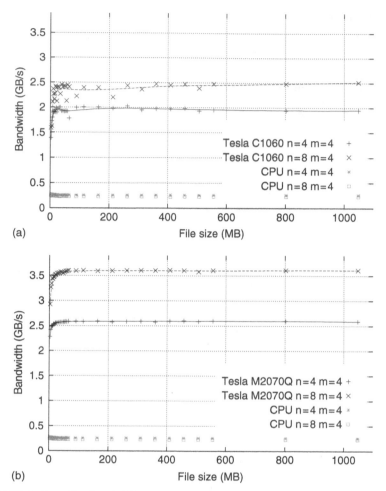

FIGURE 10.4 *Encoding bandwidth achieved depending on size of encoded file. (a) On Tesla C1060 GPU. (b) On Tesla M2070Q GPU.*

platforms, GPU and CPU were coupled through the PCIe x16 bus of the second generation, providing the maximum bandwidth of 8 GB/s.

Figure 10.4a shows the bandwidth achieved for the RS encoding on the first platform, for the file size not exceeding 1050 MB. It can be observed that, beginning with approximately 10 MB, this bandwidth is stabilized, and practically it does not depends on the file size. The utilization of the second platform (Fig. 10.4b) allows us to increase the bandwidth up to 2.6 GB/s (20.8 Gb/s) for $n, m = 4$, and up to 3.6 GB/s (28.8 Gb/s) for $n = 8$, $m = 4$.

In addition, Table 10.2 shows the comparison of performance results obtained on the Tesla M2070Q GPU and Intel Xeon E5649 2.53 GHz CPU, based on the West-mere microarchitecture. In the latter case, the Jerasure library [6] is used, which currently allows the utilization of a single core of CPU only. The speedup achieved

TABLE 10.2 Performance Comparison for Intel Xeon E5649 and Tesla M2070Q

| File Size [MB] | Variant 1 $n = 4, m = 4$ | | | Variant 2 $n = 8, m = 4$ | | |
	Intel Xeon Bandwidth [GB/s]	Tesla M2070Q Bandwidth [GB/s]	Ratio	Intel Xeon Bandwidth [GB/s]	Tesla M2070Q Bandwidth [GB/s]	Ratio
2.8	0.277	2.279	8.26	0.245	2.928	11.96
5.3	0.271	2.419	8.94	0.243	3.263	13.45
11.8	0.261	2.498	9.57	0.237	3.435	14.52
20.2	0.257	2.546	9.92	0.232	3.514	15.12
43.3	0.255	2.569	10.08	0.232	3.564	15.34
89.6	0.257	2.588	10.09	0.230	3.595	15.62
163.3	0.257	2.592	10.09	0.230	3.593	15.64
310.8	0.257	2.592	10.10	0.230	3.603	15.66
556.5	0.257	2.599	10.13	0.230	3.605	15.64
1048.0	0.257	2.589	10.01	0.231	3.609	15.65

for GPU over CPU varies from 8.26 to 10.01, for $n, m = 4$, and from 11.96 to 15.65, for $n = 8, m = 4$.

10.7.2 Performance Analysis using the Roofline Model

Computer architectures, as well as kernels of algorithms, have a different balance between computation and communication. Performance is a question of how well characteristics of a kernel map to characteristics of an architecture. In this context, an interesting approach to performance estimation and prediction is the roofline model [28]. This model shows inherent hardware limitations for a given kernel, as well as the potential benefit and priority of optimizations [29].

The roofline model is unique to each architecture. It relates processor performance to off-chip memory traffic. The model is based on the operational intensity parameter Q, meaning the amount of operations per byte of memory traffic (flops/byte). The attainable performance R_A (flops/s) is then upper-bounded by both the peak performance R_{max} (flops/s) and the product of the peak memory bandwidth V_{max} (bytes/s), and the operational intensity Q:

$$R_A = \min\{R_{max}, \; V_{max} * Q\} \; [\text{flops/s}]. \qquad (10.17)$$

Figure 10.5 presents the roofline model for the Tesla M2070Q GPU platform in the case of single-precision computations (without multiply-add operations). The graph shown in this figure is obtained by substituting the following values into (10.17): $R_{max} = 515$ Gflops/s, $V_{max} = 8$ Gbytes/s (access to the host memory through the PCIe bus is assumed as a critical factor limiting performance). A similar analysis can be performed for the Tesla C1060 GPU platform with $R_{max} = 312$ Gflops/s.

The model shows that the borderline values of operational intensity that separate memory-bound and compute-bound applications are $Q_B = 39$ Gflops/byte for Tesla C1060, and $Q_B = 64.38$ Gflops/byte for Tesla M2070Q.

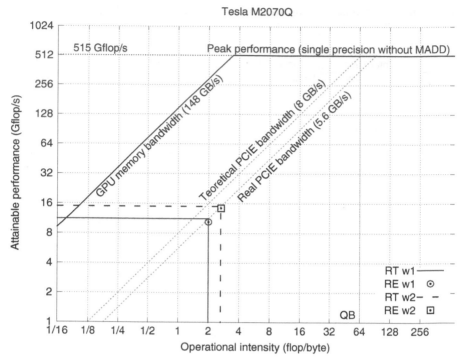

FIGURE 10.5 *Roofline model for Reed–Solomon encoding on Tesla M2070Q GPU.*

In the case of Algorithm 10.2, the total number L_{op} of performed operations depends on the size $|F|$ of an encoded file and the values of parameters n and m. In fact, since the operation of multiplication over the Galois field is implemented using the look-up table technique, when computing L_{op} we take into account only the XOR operation, so finally we have

$$L_{op} = |F| * m = n * B * m. \qquad (10.18)$$

Based on this estimation, it becomes possible to derive the operational intensity Q defined as ratio of L_{op} to the size S_d of processed data:

$$Q = \frac{L_{op}}{S_d} = \frac{n * B * m}{B * (n + m)} = \frac{n * m}{n + m}. \qquad (10.19)$$

Here, the estimation of S_d takes into account not only the transfer of input matrix $\mathbf{D}_{n \times B}$ from the host main memory to the GPU global memory but also copying the checksum matrix $\mathbf{C}_{m \times B}$ from GPU to the host. Equation (10.19) gives finally the following values of Q: (i) $Q_1 = 2$ flops/byte for n, $m = 4$, and (ii) $Q_2 = 2.66$ flops/byte for $n = 8$, $m = 4$. This means that the RS encoding is a memory-bound application.

For the Tesla M2070Q platform, the maximum real bandwidth V_{PCIe} of PCIe bus is measured in our experiments as $V_{\text{PCIe}} = 5.6$ GB/s. So it can be expected that in the best case—when the whole computations on GPU are hidden behind host–GPU communications—the RS encoding can be implemented with the performance R_T, which is expressed as

- $R_T = Q_1 * V_{\text{PCIe}} = 11.20$ Gflops/s for $n, m = 4$,
- $R_T = Q_2 * V_{\text{PCIe}} = 14.93$ Gflops/s for $n = 8, m = 4$.

These values determine the upper bound for the encoding performance, constrained by the real bandwidth of PCIe.

The maximum bandwidth V_{RS} for the RS encoding on GPU achieved in our experiments is given by $V_{\text{RS}} = 2.60$ GB/s for $n, m = 4$, and $V_{\text{RS}} = 3.60$ GB/s for $n = 8$, $m = 4$. Taking into account all bus transfers, which include also checksums, the GPU implements its computation with the bandwidth $V_{\text{RS}}^{\text{PCIe}} = 5.20$ GB/s for $n, m = 4$, and $V_{\text{RS}}^{\text{PCIe}} = 5.40$ GB/s for $n = 8, m = 4$. The RS encoding is then implemented with the maximally achieved performance R_E, expressed as

- $R_E = Q_1 * V_{\text{RS}}^{\text{PCIe}} = 10.40$ Gflops/s for $n, m = 4$,
- $R_E = Q_2 * V_{\text{RS}}^{\text{PCIe}} = 14.40$ Gflops/s for $n = 8, m = 4$,

which gives, respectively, 77% and 74% of R_T.

In the same way, the performance analysis for the Tesla C1060 platform is carried out. Here, the PCIe bus bandwidth is measured as $V_{\text{PCIe}} = 5.3$ GB/s. The comparison of performance results achieved for both platforms is presented in Table 10.3.

For Tesla C1060, the performance losses of 23.40% and 25.28%, depending on parameters n and m, are results of the fact that the stream processing mechanism (see Fig. 10.1c and d) does not allow us to fully overlap communications and GPU

TABLE 10.3 Comparison of Performance Results for Tesla C1060 and Tesla M2070Q

| | Tesla C1060 | | Tesla M2070Q | |
	Variant 1 $n = 4, m = 4$	Variant 2 $n = 8, m = 4$	Variant 1 $n = 4, m = 4$	Variant 2 $n = 8, m = 4$
P_{PCIe} [GB/s]	5.3	5.3	5.6	5.6
Q_i [flops/byte]	2	2.67	2	2.67
R_T [Gflops/s]	10.60	14.13	11.20	14.93
V_{RS} [GB/s]	2.03	2.64	2.60	3.60
$V_{\text{RS}}^{\text{PCIe}}$ [GB/s]	4.06	3.96	5.20	5.40
R_E [Gflops/s]	8.12	10.56	10.40	14.40
$\frac{R_E}{R_T} * 100$[%]	76.60	74.72	92.86	96.43

computations. In fact, in the proposed implementation, the time required for computations is longer than the time of transferring the matrix $\mathbf{D}_{n\times m}$. The percentage k of time of computations which are not overlapped with communications to the total execution time t_E is derived experimentally as

$$k = \frac{t_{\text{kernel}} - \frac{n-1}{n} * t_D}{t_E} * 100 \; [\%], \tag{10.20}$$

where the meaning of times t_{kernel}, t_D, and t_E are the same as in (10.16); these values are determined by measurements. As a result, we obtain $k = 24\%$ for $n, m = 4$, and $k = 25\%$ for $n = 8$, $m = 4$.

In the case of Tesla M2070Q GPU, which is based on the Fermi architecture, the measured time t_{kernel}, corresponding to GPU computations, is shorter than the time t_D required for transfer of matrix $\mathbf{D}_{n\times m}$. In consequence, the performance losses are now smaller—they are equal to 7.14% and 3.57%, depending on parameters n and m. The shortening of GPU computation time is the result of an improved internal architecture of GPU, which includes 448 CUDA cores instead of 240 cores in Tesla C1060. Another important feature of the Fermi architecture is the introduction of the L2 cache memory.

10.8 CONCLUSIONS AND FUTURE WORKS

Erasure codes can radically improve the availability of distributed storage in comparison with replication systems. In order to realize this thesis, efficient implementations of the most compute-intensive parts of the underlying algorithms should be developed. In this chapter, we investigated how to map systematically the RS erasure codes onto heterogeneous multicore architectures. We started with the Cell/B.E. architecture—an innovative solution which is significantly different from the conventional multicore architectures. In the most important part of the work, we focused on extending the methods developed for the cell multicore on heterogeneous computing platforms combining general purpose multicore CPUs and modern GPU accelerators. The resulting methods allowed us to adapt the underlying numerical algorithms to internal characteristics of these platforms. The investigation carried out in this work confirmed the advantage of using modern multicore architectures for the efficient implementation of the classic RS erasure codes.

In our future works, we plan to explore such perspective hybrid multicore architectures as APUs (accelerated processing units), where CPU and GPU are mixed in a single on-chip system. The important advantage of APUs is the possibility to eliminate time-consuming CPU–GPU transfers over the PCIe bus. An example of such an architecture is AMD Fusion, as well as NVIDIA Denver when the 64-bit ARM CPU is planned to be merged with an NVIDIA GPU. Another important direction of future work assumes the utilization of the OpenCL standard for parallel programming of hybrid CPU–GPU multicore systems. Contrary to the CUDA environment used in this work, OpenCL makes it possible to take advantage of GPUs of different vendors, for example, both NVIDIA and AMD.

ACKNOWLEDGMENTS

This work was supported by the COST Action IC0805 "Open European Network for High-Performance Computing on Complex Environments" and also by the Polish Ministry of Science and Higher Education under Grant No.648/N-COST/ 2010/0 COST IC0805.

The authors are grateful to Czestochowa University of Technology for granting access to IBM BladeCenter QS21 and Tesla C1060/M2070-Q platforms.

REFERENCES

1. V. Kher and Y. Kim, "Securing distributed storage: challenges, techniques, and systems," in *Proceedings of the 2005 ACM workshop on Storage Security and Survivability, StorageSS '05*, pp. 9–25. New York: ACM, 2005.

2. R. Wyrzykowski and L. Kuczynski, "Towards secure data management system for grid environment based on the Cell broadband engine," in *Lecture Notes in Computer Science*, vol. 4967, pp. 825–834, Berlin, Heidelberg: Springer-Verlag, 2008.

3. L. Bautista Gomez, B. Nicolae, N. Maruyama, F. Cappello, and S. Matsuoka, "Scalable Reed-Solomon-based reliable local storage for HPC applications on IaaS clouds," in *Lecture Notes in Computer Science*, Berlin, Heidelberg: Springer-Verlag, vol. 7484, pp. 313–324, 2012.

4. R. Collins and J. Plank, "Assessing the performance of erasure codes in the wide-area," in *Proceedings of 2005 International Conference on Dependable Systems and Networks—DSN'05*, Los Alamitos, CA, USA, pp. 182–187, IEEE Computer Society, 2005.

5. H. Weatherspoon and J. Kubiatowicz, "Erasure coding vs. replication: a quantitive comparison," in*Proceedings of IPTPS'02*, Cambridge, MA, USA, pp. 328–338, 2002.

6. J. Plank, J. Luo, C. Schuman, L. Xu, and Z. Wilcox-O'Hearn, "A performance evaluation and examination of open-source erasure coding libraries for storage," in *FAST-09: 7th USENIX Conference on File and Storage Technologies*, San Francisco, CA, USA, pp. 253–265, 2009.

7. J. Plank, "A tutorial on Reed-Solomon coding for fault-tolerance in RAID-like systems," *Software—Practice & Experience*, vol. 27, pp. 995–1012, 1997.

8. J. Kubiatowicz, D. Bindel, Y. Chen, S. Czerwinski, P. Eaton, D. Geels, R. Gummadi, S. Rhea, H. Weatherspoon, W. Weimer, C. Wells, and B. Zhao, "OceanStore: an architecture for global-scale persistent storage," in *Proceedings of Ninth International Conference on Architectural Support for Programming Languages and Operating Systems—ASPLOS 2000*, Cambridge, MA, USA, pp. 190–201, 2000.

9. J. Plank and M. Thomason, "A practical analysis of low-density parity-check erasure codes for wide-area storage applications," in *Proceedings of 2004 International Conference on Dependable Systems and Networks—DSN'04*, Los Alamitos, CA, USA, pp. 115–124, IEEE Computer Society, 2004.

10. M. L. Curry, A. Skjellum, H. Lee Ward, and R. Brightwell, "Gibraltar: a Reed-Solomon coding library for storage applications on programmable graphics processors," *Concurrency and Computation: Practice and Experience*, vol. 23, no. 18, pp. 2477–2495, 2011.

11. L. Kuczynski and R. Wyrzykowski, *Efficient Data Management in PC Meta-Clusters*. The Publishing Office of Czestochowa University of Technology, Czestochowa, Poland, 2011.

12. R. Wyrzykowski, L. Kuczynski, and M. Wozniak, "Towards efficient execution of erasure codes on multicore architectures," *Lecture Notes in Computer Science*, Berlin, Heidelberg: Springer-Verlag, vol. 7134, pp. 357–367, 2012.

13. T. Chen, R. Raghavan, J. Dale, and E. Iwata, "Cell broadband engine architecture and its first implementation: a performance view," *IBM Journal of Research and Development*, vol. 51, pp. 559–572, 2007.

14. K. Fatahalian and M. Houston, "A closer look at GPUs," *Communications of the ACM*, vol. 51, no. 10, pp. 50–57, 2008.

15. M. Wozniak, T. Olas, and R. Wyrzykowski, "Parallel implementation of conjugate gradient method on graphics processors," *Lecture Notes in Computer Science*, vol. 6067, pp. 125–135. Berlin, Heidelberg: Springer-Verlag, 2010.

16. NVIDIA Corporation, NVIDIA CUDA Programming Guide 2.0, 2008.

17. J. Stone, D. Gohara, and G. Shi, "OpenCL: a parallel programming standard for heterogeneous computing systems," *Computing in Science and Engineering*, vol. 12, pp. 66–73, 2010.

18. K. Rojek and L. Szustak, "Parallelization of EULAG model on multicore architectures with GPU accelerators," *Lecture Notes in Computer Science*, vol. 7204, pp. 391–400, Berlin, Heidelberg: Springer-Verlag, 2012.

19. D. MacKay, "Fountain codes," *IEE Proceedings*, vol. 152, no. 6, pp. 1062–1068, 2005.

20. R. Gallager, *Low-Density Parity-Check Codes*. Cambridge, MA: MIT Press, 1963.

21. V. Roca and C. Neumann, "Design, evaluation and comparison of four large block FEC codes, LDPC, LDGM, LDGM Staircase and LDGM Triangle, plus a Reed-Solomon small block FEC codes," Tech. Rep. 5225, INRIA Rhone-Alpes, Grenoble, France, 2004.

22. B. Gaidioz, B. Koblitz, and N. Santos, "Exploring high performance distributed file storage using LDPC codes," *Parallel Computing*, vol. 33, pp. 264–274, 2007.

23. S. Williams, L. Oliker, R. Vuduc, J. Shalf, K. Yelick, and J. Demmel, "Optimization of sparse matrix-vector multiplication on emerging multicore platforms," *Parallel Computing*, vol. 35, pp. 178–194, 2009.

24. J. Plank and L. Xu, "Optimizing Cauchy Reed-Solomon codes for fault-tolerant network storage applications," in *NCA-06: 5th IEEE International Symposium on Network Computing Applications*, Cambridge, MA, USA, pp. 173–180, 2006.

25. M. L. Curry, A. Skjellum, H. L. Ward, and R. Brightwell, "Accelerating Reed-Solomon coding in RAID systems with GPUs," in *Proceedings of IEEE International Symposium on Parallel and Distributed Processing IPDPS 2008*, pp. 1–6, Miami, FL, USA, 2008.

26. M. L. Curry, A. Skjellum, H. L. Ward, and R. Brightwell, "Arbitrary dimension Reed-Solomon coding and decoding for extended RAID on GPUs," in *Proceedings of ACM Petascale Data Storage Workshop (PDSW 08)*, (Austin, TX), 2008.

27. J. Plank and Y. Ding, "Note: correction to the 1997 tutorial on Reed-Solomon coding," *Software—Practice & Experience*, vol. 35, pp. 189–194, 2005.

28. S. Williams, A. Waterman, and D. Patterson, "Roofline: an insightful visual performance model for multicore architectures," *Communications of the ACM*, vol. 52, pp. 65–76, 2009.

29. R. Wyrzykowski, K. Rojek, and L. Szustak, "Model-driven adaptation of double-precision matrix multiplication to the cell processor architecture," *Parallel Processing*, vol. 38, pp. 260–276, 2012.

11

Heterogeneous Parallel Computing Platforms and Tools for Compute-Intensive Algorithms: A Case Study

Daniele D'Agostino, Andrea Clematis, and Emanuele Danovaro

IMATI CNR, Genoa, Italy

In this chapter we analyze the development of parallel programs for heterogeneous architectures, that is, workstation composed by multiple CPUs and accelerators, considering different programming models and tools, both commercial and freely available. In particular, we discuss the provided support and achievable performance for each of them with respect to some widely used, computationally intensive algorithms such as the convolution and the *N*-body algorithms. The aim is to provide a clear measure of the different efficiency figures with respect to the programming paradigm considered, the adopted tool, and the achievable peak performance.

High-Performance Computing on Complex Environments, First Edition.
Edited by Emmanuel Jeannot and Julius Žilinskas.
© 2014 John Wiley & Sons, Inc. Published 2014 by John Wiley & Sons, Inc.

11.1   INTRODUCTION

In 1965, Intel cofounder Gordon E. Moore affirmed that, over the history of computing hardware, the number of transistors on integrated circuits doubles approximately every year, and the trend would continue for at least 10 years [1]. This affirmation, recalibrated in "every two years" in 1975,[1] is still valid, but with a major change: every new generation of CPUs is more powerful than the previous one mostly because it provides more cores.

Multicore CPUs have been produced since 2005, when Intel's dual-core Pentium D 800 was released, followed by AMD's Athlon 64 X2. Presently, all important processor vendors have switched to multicore architectures, with great differences in terms of the homogeneity of these cores [2], as we will briefly describe in the following section.

Probably, the future supercomputers will be not just scaled versions of today's multicore processors but massively parallel systems with some heavyweight general-purpose cores, a number of lightweight integer/floating point units, and some specialized units equipped with general-purpose graphics processing units (GPGPUs or, in short GPUs) and field-programmable gate arrays (FPGAs) [3]. If we analyze the June 2011 edition of the TOP 500 list, only 19 systems (in particular those in position 2, 4, and 5) used GPUs as accelerators: 12 of them were equipped with nVidia chips, 5 with Cell processors, and 2 with ATI Radeon. On the contrary, Titan, the first system of the November 2012 edition, is equipped with GPUs, while the number of systems using accelerators or coprocessors increased up to 62. If we analyze the first two systems of the list, we find two very different architectural solutions: Titan provides 560,640 heterogeneous cores with a maximum result of the LINPACK benchmark of 17,590.0 tera floating point operations per second (TFlops), while the second system, Sequoia, is made up by 1,572,864 homogeneous CPU cores, providing 16,324.8 TFlops.

Two conclusions can be drawn from this. First, as recognized in [4], "This shift toward increasing parallelism is not a triumphant stride forward based on breakthroughs in novel software and architectures for parallelism; instead, this plunge into parallelism is actually a retreat from even greater challenges that thwart efficient silicon implementation of traditional uniprocessor architectures." Each new generation of CPU doubles the cores, but each single core has more or less the same compute capabilities: "The dilemma is that a large percentage of mission critical enterprise applications will not "automagically" run faster on multicore servers. In fact many will actually run slower."[2]

Furthermore, while the traditional homogeneous high-performance computing (HPC) solutions offer a well-known architecture, and this makes it easier to achieve performance figures very close to the theoretical peak, the efficient exploitation of the present more hierarchical and heterogeneous computing architectures requires

---

[1] http://news.cnet.com/2100-1001-984051.html
[2] Patrick Leonard, Rogue Wave Vice President for Product Development, http://software.intel.com/en-us/blogs/2007/03/14/the-multi-core-dilemma-by-patrick-leonard

an increased effort in the development of smart solution because, for example, the data movement among the memories of the different kinds of processors represents a new and major issue. This scenario was defined as "a true computing jungle" [5].

It is important to stress the fact that, from both the scientific and industrial points of view, the development, porting, and optimization of software is mostly considered an overhead that should be avoided or minimized when possible. So, "what if IT goes from a growth industry to a replacement industry? Instead of buying new computers, we are swapping in cores, but even then currently software cannot effectively make use of that speed. Therefore, there will be no advantage to buy a new computer."[3]

This issue was recently discussed in a workshop organized by the European Commission in the preparation of HORIZON 2020: "Software development has not evolved as fast as hardware capability and network capacity... Development and maintenance of software for advanced computing systems is becoming increasingly effort-intensive requiring dual expertise, both on the application side and on the system side."[4] The present frontier is therefore the development of programming models and tools enabling developers to balance the competing goals of productivity and implementation efficiency: "Writing programs that scale with increasing numbers of cores should be as easy as writing programs for sequential computers" [6].

Many research projects have aimed and continue to aim at providing a solution to this problem. For example, pattern-based parallel programming models, in particular using skeletons, promise several benefits such as a simplification of the code development and the easy portability and reusability of the solutions [7]. An example was the ASSIST programming environment [8, 9], originally developed in the framework of the GRID.it Italian national project. A complete survey is provided in [10].

Among the current projects, it is worth citing ParaPhrase,[5] "aiming to provide developers with parallel patterns for the creation of remappable component based applications;" the Hybrid for HPC (H4H) project,[6] "aiming at providing compute-intensive application developers with a highly efficient hybrid programming environment for heterogeneous computing clusters composed of a mix of classical processors and hardware accelerators;" and the Open Network for High-Performance Computing on Complex Environments (ComplexHPC)[7] EU COST Action, "aiming to coordinate European groups working on the use of heterogeneous and hierarchical systems for HPC, foster HPC efforts to increase Europe competitiveness and train new generations of HPC scientists."

Also, vendors have made significant efforts to assist developers in writing high-performance applications. This is also because such problems are not limited only to huge supercomputers: if we move toward a wider audience of scientists and IT developers, we can see that the same issues arise also with current workstations.

---

[3]Prof. Ed Lazowska, chair of the Computing Community Consortium, http://computingforsustainability .com/2008/04/03/posts-from-sicse-lazowska-suggests-green-it-as-next-space-race/
[4]http://cordis.europa.eu/fp7/ict/computing/documents/advanced_computing_ws_report.pdf
[5]http://paraphrase-ict.eu/
[6]http://www.h4h-itea2.org
[7]http://complexhpc.org/

In fact, it is possible to achieve up to 10 TFlops on a single machine equipped with multiple CPUs and accelerators, with a cost of less than $5000.

In this chapter, we analyze some of these programming models and tools, both commercial and freely available, in terms of the provided support and achievable performance with respect to some widely used compute-intensive algorithms such as the *N*-body and the convolution algorithms. The focus is on providing a clear measure of the different efficiency figures with respect to the programming paradigm considered, the adopted tool, and the achievable peak performance. We will see that it is quite easy to achieve an order of magnitude speed improvement for selected compute kernels with a limited effort, but also that developers have to know the specific features of every compute capability to achieve much higher performance.

11.2 A LOW-COST HETEROGENEOUS COMPUTING ENVIRONMENT

Current workstations can offer really amazing raw computational power, on the order of TFlops, on a single machine equipped with multiple CPUs and GPU devices. Such result can only be achieved with massive parallelism of the computational devices. For example, a workstation is usually equipped with a 1–4 multicore processor and up to four accelerators connected via a PCI express bus, as shown in Fig. 11.1.

Workstation CPUs are produced by Intel and AMD. Intel XEONs are characterized by 6-8-10 cores per CPU and the possibility to connect up to 8 CPUs on a single motherboard (up to 80 cores per board); each CPU usually has a shared cache (up to 30 MB). AMD Opterons are composed of two dies, each die has up to eight cores and 8 MB of cache. It is possible to install up to four Opterons (up to 64 cores on a single

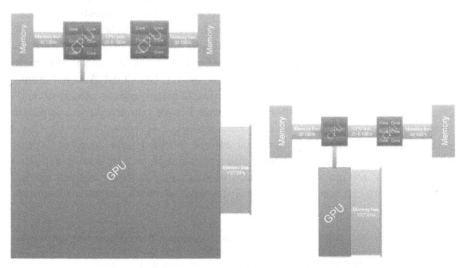

FIGURE 11.1 *Test computing environment. Note that GPU memory is represented as a very thin band, since it has (compared to main memory) a large aggregated bandwidth and small size. Left - Single precision. Right - Double precision.*

TABLE 11.1 Technical Characteristics of State-of-the-Art Workstation/Server CPUs

CPU Model Name	Price (US $)	Cores	Frequency (GHz)	Cache (MB)	GFlops (fp64)	GFlops (fp32)	CPU (GB/s)	Memory (GB/s)
Intel Xeon E5645	2x551	6	2.4	12	58	115	25.6	32.0
Intel Xeon E5-2650	2x1112	8	2.0	20	128	256	32.0	51.2
Intel Xeon E5-4610	4x1219	8	2.2	16	282	563	28.8	42.7
AMD Opteron 4386	2x348	8	3.1	12	198	397	25.6	42.7
AMD Opteron 6348	4x575	2x6	2.8	16	538	1075	25.6	51.2
AMD Opteron 6380	4x1088	2x8	2.5	16	640	1280	25.6	51.2

board). CPUs on the same board can communicate with a dedicated bus (QPI for Intel, HyperTransport for AMD); moreover, each CPU integrates DDR3 memory controller and PCI express controller, providing good scalability and extremely high aggregated bandwidth. One drawback of such architecture is that accessing memory connected to another CPU requires multiple transmission steps (from memory to CPU, from CPU to CPU one or more times) and thus increased latency.

Table 11.1 lists a few state-of-the-art CPUs from Intel and AMD, with number of cores, processor frequency, price, raw performance of a system with maximum number of CPUs installed, and bandwidth of communication buses to CPUs, memory, and PCI express. Note that peak performance requires the full exploitation of all the capabilities: all CPUs, all cores, and SIMD (single instruction multiple data) instruction in each core. In fact, recent CPUs offer an extended set of instructions (i.e., SSE1, ... ,SSE4, AVX) which are able to process up to eight single-precision or four double-precision values. The adoption of such SIMD instruction is often referred to as *vectorization.*

Accelerators based on GPUs are produced by nVidia and AMD. nVidia has three lines of products: consumer video cards (GTX), professional video cards (Quadro), and devices for HPC (Tesla). AMD has two lines: consumer video cards (Radeon) and professional video cards (FirePro). Here we focus on the consumer video cards which offer the best performance/price ratio. Key factors in analyzing a GPU accelerator are the theoretical maximum computing power (both in single and double precision), memory bandwidth, and supported languages (CUDA, OpenCL, OpenACC).

Table 11.2 lists the top GPUs from nVidia and AMD, with the number of cores, processor frequency, memory size, raw performance in double and single precision, and memory bandwidth.

As previously highlighted, amount of computational cores, memories, and communication bandwidth can be extremely heterogeneous. To this view of the system, there correspond different types of parallel cooperation among parallel processes: distributed memory for cooperation among nodes, shared memory for core cooperation, and SIMD parallelism inside CPUs and accelerators. The true challenge in using a similar system is the programming of parallel applications that are able to exploit in an efficient and effective manner the different levels and capabilities. This leads to the development of a large number of software libraries

TABLE 11.2   Technical Characteristics of Top Consumer GPUs from nVidia and AMD

Vendor	Model	Cores	Frequency (GHz)	Memory (GB)	GFlops (fp64)	GFlops (fp32)	Memory (GB/s)
nVidia	GTX Titan	2688	0.84	6.0	1480	4500	288.4
nVidia	GTX 690	2x1536	0.91	4.0	234	5622	2x192.0
nVidia	GTX 680	1536	1.00	4.0	129	3090	192.0
nVidia	GTX 590	2x512	1.21	3.0	311	2488	2x164.0
nVidia	GTX 580	512	1.54	1.5	198	1581	192.0
AMD	HD 7970	2048	1.05	3.0	1075	4301	288.0
AMD	HD 7950	1792	0.80	3.0	717	2867	240.0
AMD	HD 6970	1536	0.88	2.0	676	2703	176.0
AMD	HD 6950	1408	0.80	2.0	563	2253	160.0
AMD	HD 5870	1600	0.85	2.0	544	2720	153.6
AMD	HD 5850	1440	0.72	1.0	418	2088	128.0

supporting parallel programming, such as MPI, OpenMP, CUDA, OpenCL, and OpenACC.

The message passing interface (MPI) is a language-independent communications protocol used to program parallel computers. It supports communication among processes that model a parallel program running on a distributed memory system. Communications can be both point to point and collective. MPI's goals are high performance, scalability, and portability. MPI implementation can be clever enough to spot that it is being used in a shared memory environment and therefore optimizes its behavior accordingly. Designing programs around the MPI model (contrary to explicit shared memory models) may have advantages over NUMA (nonuniform memory access) architectures since MPI encourages memory locality.

The Open specifications for multi-processing (OpenMP) defines a set of compiler directives, library routines, and environment variables that can be used to specify shared memory parallelism in Fortran and C/C++ programs. Its approach, which is based on compiler directives, offers a simple and elegant paradigm for supporting core-level and CPU-level parallelism. Transition from sequential to parallel is extremely easy and smooth, since it supports a unified code for both serial and parallel applications: OpenMP constructs are treated as comments when sequential compilers are used. One drawback of OpenMP is that it currently runs efficiently only in shared-memory multiprocessor platforms; thus the main option for clusters remains MPI.

The compute unified device architecture (CUDA) is a parallel computing platform and programming model created by nVidia which gives developers access to the instruction set and memory of the parallel computational elements in nVidia GPUs. CUDA is accessible to software developers through CUDA-accelerated libraries, compiler directives (i.e., OpenACC), extensions to programming languages such as C/C++ and Fortran, and other interfaces, including OpenCL, Microsoft's Direct-Compute, and C++ AMP. In this chapter, we will focus on small kernels (functions that execute on GPUs) developed with CUDA SDK 5.0.

The Open Computing Language (OpenCL) is a framework proposed in 2008 by Apple for writing programs that execute across heterogeneous platforms consisting of CPUs, GPUs, and other processors. OpenCL includes a language (based on C99) for writing kernels (functions that execute on OpenCL devices) with some limitations and additions. It omits the use of function pointers, recursion, bit fields, variable-length arrays, and standard C99 header files. On the other site, the language is extended to easily use parallelism with vector types and operations, synchronization, and functions to work with work items/groups. It has memory region qualifiers (i.e., __global, __local, __constant, and __private), and many built-in functions are added as well. Compared to CUDA, the programmer is not able to directly use GPU-specific technologies, since one of the key features of OpenCL is portability (via its abstracted memory and execution model) but, if correctly tweaked, it performs no worse than CUDA [11].

The OpenACC application program interface describes a collection of compiler directives to specify loops and regions of code in standard C, C++, and Fortran to be offloaded from a host CPU to an attached accelerator, providing portability across operating systems, host CPUs, and accelerators. The directives and programming model, initially developed by PGI, Cray, and nVidia, with support from CAPS, allow programmers to create high-level host + accelerator programs without the need to explicitly initialize the accelerator, manage data or program transfers between the host and accelerator, or initiate accelerator startup and shutdown. All these details are implicit and are managed by the OpenACC API-enabled compilers and runtimes. The programming model allows the programmer to augment information available to the compilers, including specification of data local to an accelerator, guidance on mapping of loops on to an accelerator, and similar performance-related details. OpenACC members have worked as members of the OpenMP standard group to merge the OpenACC API with the OpenMP specification to create a common specification which extends OpenMP to support accelerators in a future release of OpenMP.[8] The main drawback of OpenACC is that so far it lacks open-source implementation,[9] but some projects aim at this [12]. In this chapter, we consider the use of the PGI compiler for OpenACC.

11.2.1 Adopted Computing Environment

Experiments described in the following sections have been performed on a node of our cluster, composed of a two-way motherboard running two Intel Xeon E5645 processors, 32 GB of RAM, and an nVidia GTX 580 GPU. Figure 11.1 shows the schema of this architecture: the two multicore CPUs and a GPU are depicted in blue, the 32 GB of main memory and 1.5 GB of GPU memory are depicted in green, and the several communication buses are depicted in orange. The area of the computing devices is proportional to theoretical maximum performance, as the width of the communication buses is proportional to their bandwidth. Left part of Fig. 11.1 refers

---

[8]http://www.openacc-standard.org/faq-page#n49
[9]http://www.openacc.org/node/57

FIGURE 11.2 *Computing resources exploited by different programming paradigms are shown darker. From left to right: single core: sequential application, multiple cores: MPI and OpenMP, GPU cores: CUDA, CPU and GPU cores: OpenCL and OpenACC.*

to single-precision floating point performance, while Right part of Fig. 11.1 refers to double-precision performance. Note that, in case of CPUs, on moving from single to double precision, the performance is halved. In case of GPU, the performance drops by a factor of 8.

Development and optimization tools available on our cluster are gcc version 4.4.7-3 (which is the most recent available for CentOS 6.3), Intel Cluster Studio XE 2013, PGI Accelerator C/C++ Server 12.10 (with OpenACC support), and CUDA SDK 5.0. In particular, gcc and Intel Cluster Studio have been adopted for sequential and OpenMP tests. MPI tests have been compiled with Intel Cluster Studio. PGI Accelerator has been adopted for OpenACC tests, while CUDA SDK has been used for CUDA and OpenCL tests on nVidia GTX 580 card. OpenCL tests on an additional Radeon HD 5850 card have been developed with AMD APP SDK 2.8. Note also that OpenCL can run both on CPU and GPU, but each computing resource requires its own OpenCL driver. We have not tested OpenCL on CPUs. Figure 11.2 shows the architectural capabilities exploited by the different paradigms.

11.3 FIRST CASE STUDY: THE *N*-BODY PROBLEM

Many physical phenomena involve, or can be simulated with, particle systems in which each particle interacts with all other particles according to the laws of physics. Examples include the gravitational interaction among the stars in a galaxy or for intergalactic matter, the Coulomb forces exerted by the atoms in a molecule for molecular dynamics applications, turbulent fluid flow studies, and many others. The challenge of efficiently carrying out the related calculations is generally known as the *N-body problem*, defined as follows: given an ensemble of *N* bodies in space whose interaction is governed by a potential function, the *N*-body problem is to calculate the force on each body in the ensemble that results from its interaction with all other bodies. Mathematically, given *N* bodies with mass m_i, initial position x_i, and initial velocity v_i, the *N*-body problem can be formulated as

$$U(x_i) = \sum_{j=0}^{N-1} F(x_i, x_j),$$

where $U(x_i)$ is a physical quantity at x_i, which can be obtained by summing the pairwise interactions with all the other particles of the system. In particular, the gravitational force exerted on the particle x_i is expressed as

$$F(x_i, x_j) = Gm_i m_j \frac{x_j - x_i}{\|x_j - x_i\|^3},$$

where G is the gravitational constant. Therefore, we have

$$U(x_i) = Gm_i \sum_{j=0}^{N-1} \frac{m_j(x_j - x_i)}{\|x_j - x_i\|^3}.$$

Normally, the denominator is rewritten as $(\|x_j - x_i\|^2 + \epsilon^2)^{\frac{3}{2}}$ to bound the force value for close objects, and the acceleration $a_i = \frac{U(x_i)}{m_i}$ is used to update the position of a body.

The solution of the N-body problem proceeds over time steps, each time computing the force on every body and thereby updating its position and other attributes. The All Pairs approach is the straightforward solution technique that evaluates the interactions between all the pairs of the N bodies. It requires $O(N^2)$ operations at each time step, and this makes the algorithm very popular for demonstrating the speedups achievable using different languages[10,11] or devices [13], therefore we focus on it. However, for actual applications, the All Pairs approach is used only for evaluating bodies that are interacting very closely. For others, more efficient hierarchical methods, which are based on the subdivision of the space and the clusterization of far objects, are adopted (14-18). These proposals differ in terms of both the computational cost and the accuracy[12] [19].

11.3.1 The Sequential N-Body Algorithm

In Algorithm 11.1, the sequential implementation of the All Pairs approach is shown. The main loop corresponds to the given number of time steps; in the second loop, at first the total force on each particle is computed as the sum of all gravitational attraction with all the other particles, obtained with the third loop; then each particle's position and velocity are updated as result of this force.

Hereafter, we will consider this code as the reference. In particular, the number of floating point operations (flops) for each iteration (i.e., considering the *for i* loop) is $(N * (N - 1) * 20) + (24 * N)$, and the total amount of flops operation per execution is *timesteps* $* ((N * (N - 1) * 20) + (24 * N))$. In this and in the following cases, we performed the tests considering *timesteps* $= 100$ and a number N of bodies of 100, 1000, and 10,000.

---

[10]NBabel, a gravitational N-body integrator in 1001 languages http://www.nbabel.org/
[11]The Computer Language Benchmarks Game http://benchmarksgame.alioth.debian.org/
[12]N-Body Methods Resources http://www2.epcc.ed.ac.uk/ mario/nbody.html

Algorithm 11.1

```
Main loop of the sequential N-body algorithm
for (k=0; k<timesteps; k++) {
  swap(oldbodies,newbodies);
  for (i=0; i<N; i++) {
    tot_force_i[X] = tot_force_i[Y] = tot_force_i[Z] = 0.0;
    for (j=0; j<N; j++) {
      if (j==i) continue;
      //20 floating point operations
      r[X] = oldbodies[j].pos[X] - oldbodies[i].pos[X];
      // analogous for r[Y] and r[Z]
      distSqr = r[X]*r[X] + r[Y]*r[Y] + r[Z]*r[Z] + EPSILON2;
      distSixth = distSqr * distSqr * distSqr;
      invDistCube = 1.0/sqrtf(distSixth);
      s = oldbodies[j].mass * invDistCube;
      tot_force_i[X] += s * r[X];
      // analogous for Y and Z
    }
    //24 flops
    dv[X] = dt * tot_force_i[X] / oldbodies[i].mass;
    newbodies[i].pos[X] += dt * ( oldbodies[i].vel[X] + dv[X]/2 );
    newbodies[i].vel[X] = oldbodies[i].vel[X] +dt * dv[X];
    // analogous for Y and Z
} }
```

For the sequential algorithm, we compared the performance achieved using both the gcc and the icc compilers. The resulting performance is shown as giga floating point operations per second (GFlops) in Table 11.3. A single core of our CPU is capable of a theoretical maximum of 9.6 GFlops, and right side of Table 11.3 reports the efficiency achieved. In particular, we considered the following four compilation commands:

icc icc -o nbody nbody.c -no-vec

icc with opt. icc -O3 -o nbody nbody.c

gcc gcc -o nbody nbody.c -lm

gcc with opt. gcc -O3 -o nbody nbody.c -lm -ftree-vectorize.

TABLE 11.3 **Performance of the Sequential *N*-Body Algorithm, in GFlops, Using the icc and gcc Compilers with and Without Optimizations Flags**

	Performance (GFlops)			Efficiency		
	$N=100$	$N=1000$	$N=10,000$	$N=100$	$N=1000$	$N=10,000$
icc	1.27	2.13	2.18	13.2%	22.2%	22.7%
icc with opt.	2.79	2.7	5.71	29.1%	28.1%	59.5%
gcc	0.34	0.6	0.61	3.5%	6.3%	6.4%
gcc with opt.	0.92	1.59	1.67	9.6%	16.6%	17.4%

We can see that icc outperforms gcc by up to 3.4 times. The first reason for this result is that icc is able to exploit, for the computation of the 1/sqrtf operation, the RSQRT instruction introduced by Intel with the streaming SIMD extensions 1 (SSE1). On the contrary, we were not able to get this translation in the assembler with gcc also using its architecture-specific optimization flags. The second reason is that gcc is not able to vectorize the most expensive loop, namely the innermost. The information is provided by gcc with the *ftree-vectorizer-verbose* report: *note: not vectorized: too many BBs in loop.*

11.3.2 The Parallel *N*-Body Algorithm for Multicore Architectures

As pointed out in Section 11.2, the full exploitation of the capabilities of a multicore processor workstation is achievable using both OpenMP and MPI, allowing developers to subdivide the work among the available cores.

While with the sequential algorithm we can consider the developer effort as independent of the compiler, here the choice of one of the two parallelization techniques involves a different set of modifications to the sequential code. OpenMP in fact requires only adding the following directive between lines 2 and 3:

```
#pragma omp parallel for private(j, r, distSqr,
        distSixth, invDistCube, s, tot_force_i, dv).
```

On the contrary, MPI requires the modification of the sequential code as shown in Algorithm 11.2. In particular, the *numprocs* parallel processes work in a data parallel manner, subdividing the *N* bodies of the main loop in equal chunks and exchanging the updated positions at the end of each iteration.

Algorithm 11.2

```
Main loop of the parallel algorithm using MPI
bnum = N % numprocs;
bstart=(N/numprocs*id)      + ((id>=bnum) ? bnum  :id);
bstop =(N/numprocs*(id+1)) + ((id>=bnum) ? bnum-1:id);
bnum = bstop-bstart+1;

MPI_Barrier(MPI_COMM_WORLD); //for timing purpose
for (k=0; k<num_steps; k++) {
  swap(oldbodies,newbodies);
  for (i=bstart; i<=bstop; i++) {...}
  MPI_Allgatherv(MPI_IN_PLACE, 0, MPI_DATATYPE_NULL, newbodies,...);
}
```

For the parallel algorithm for multicore architectures, we compared the performance achieved using the OpenMP and MPI implementations provided by Intel. The results are shown in Table 11.4. In particular, we used only the Intel compiler because of its better performance, with the following four compilation commands:

TABLE 11.4   Performance of the Parallel *N*-Body Algorithm for Multicore Architecture, in GFlops, Using the OpenMP and MPI Implementations Provided by Intel with and Without Optimizations Flags

Procs/threads	$N = 100$			$N = 1000$			$N = 10,000$		
	6	12	24	6	12	24	6	12	24
omp	2.54	2.56	1.72	11.44	19.49	5.66	12.36	19.69	15.53
omp with opt.	3.78	2.53	1.21	25.49	35.50	8.03	33.10	63.24	40.31
mpi	5.72	8.07	8.93	11.02	21.04	22.78	11.56	21.87	23.27
mpi with opt.	10.46	15.40	9.09	27.21	50.27	63.00	29.12	59.93	59.46

omp icc -openmp -o nbody nbody.c -no-vec

omp with opt. icc -openmp -O3 -o nbody nbody.c

mpi mpiicc -o nbody nbody.c -no-vec

mpi with opt. mpiicc -O3 -o nbody nbody.c.

The results show that the assumption that OpenMP on a single multicore system is faster than MPI does not always hold[13][20]. OpenMP makes the parallelization much simpler than MPI, but the MPI implementation can be clever enough to spot that it is being used in a shared memory environment and therefore optimizes its behavior accordingly.

Analyzing the behavior of the *omp with opt.* execution, we found that often the thread waits inside the *kmp_wait_sleep* OpenMP runtime. Potential causes are memory stalls [21], instruction starvation, branch misprediction, or long-latency instruction. An in-depth analysis of this behavior is outside the scope of this chapter, but it is useful to underline that (i) with only the insertion of a single directive it is possible to obtain a speed up of 11 in the largest case (N=10,000), and (ii) the lower effort in developing OpenMP code sometimes may require an in-depth tuning.

11.3.3   The Parallel *N*-Body Algorithm for CUDA Architectures

GPUs are the most common accelerators both in workstations and supercomputers. As mentioned earlier, presently it is possible to develop programs for such devices mainly using CUDA, OpenCL, and OpenACC. While the first two are equivalent and, in a certain way, comparable with the use of MPI in a multicore environment, OpenACC was designed following the same directive-based philosophy of OpenMP.

As with MPI and OpenMP, the use of CUDA or OpenACC involves a different set of modifications to the sequential code. A detailed description of the CUDA implementation of the *N*-body problem is presented in Chapter 31 of the GPU Gems 3.[14] The interested readers can refer to it, while the OpenACC version is presented in Algorithm 11.3.

---

[13] http://www.linux-mag.com/id/4608/ and http://www.linux-mag.com/id/7884/
[14] http://http.developer.nvidia.com/GPUGems3/gpugems3_ch31.html

Algorithm 11.3

```
Main loop of the parallel algorithm using OpenACC
#pragma acc data copy(bodies1[0:N], bodies2[0:N])
                    copyin(bodiesvel[0:N], bodiesm[0:N], dt)
for (k=0; k<num_steps; k++) {
  #pragma acc kernels loop independent
  for (i=0; i<num_bodies; i++) {
    tot_force_x = 0.0;...
    #pragma acc loop independent
                    reduction(+:tot_force_x,tot_force_y,tot_force_z)
    for (j=0; j<num_bodies; j++) { ... }
    ...
}
```

Considering the compute capabilities of the GTX580 device of our architecture, we tested only the largest case with $N=10,000$, obtaining very interesting results.

At first, the straightforward porting of the sequential algorithm leads to very close results both using the nVidia nvcc, which is based on a normal compiler for the code executed on the host while compiling the code to be executed on the device, and the PGI compiler, used with the following commands:

nvcc nvcc -o nbody_cuda nbody_cuda.cu

pgcc pgcc -ta=nvidia,time -o nbody_openacc nbody_openacc.c.

In particular, we got 167.71 GFlops with CUDA and 147.57 with OpenACC. But if we replace in both versions the computation of *distSixth* and *invDistCube* (see Listing 11.1) with the following:

```
distSixth = rsqrtf(distSqr);
invDistCube = distSixth * distSixth * distSixth;
```

the performance increase was up to 434.46 GFlops for the CUDA version, while with OpenACC we were not able to go beyond 211.80 GFlops also using the *fast-math* flag and the PGI C intrinsic functions. The reference performance value is provided by the highly optimized implementation described in the above-mentioned Chapter 31, provided as part of the CUDA SDK code samples, and it is equal to 597.11 GFlops.

An important remark is that CUDA devices with a compute capability ≥ 2.0 are equipped with a cache level also for the global memory space. This results in a lower importance for the use of the shared memory at the block level, while the coalesced access to the memory remains a key issue.

In conclusion, despite the MPI/OpenMP comparison, the skill of the developer remains a fundamental factor for achieving high performance: with three directives, it is possible to get a speed up of about 37, but the use of the lower level approach represented by CUDA allows the achievement of a speedup of 100.

11.4 SECOND CASE STUDY: THE CONVOLUTION ALGORITHM

As a second example, we considered the direct convolution of a one-dimensional (1D) signal. Given a 1D time-dependent signal $s(t)$, we often need to modify its frequency response. This can be done by converting it in the frequency domain by using a discrete Fourier transform (DFT), multiplying it against the desired frequency spectrum $F(X)$, and transforming it back with the inverse discrete Fourier transform (IDFT). An alternative approach is to transform the desired frequency spectrum in the time domain, obtaining $f(x)$, and to apply it directly to the original signal with the following discrete convolution:

$$s'(k) = \sum_{i=0}^{N-1} f(i)s(k+i).$$

Applying a filter $f = \{f_0, \dots, f_{N-1}\}$ composed by N coefficients to a signal s requires N multiplications and N additions for each output value.

Algorithm 11.4

```
Main loop of the sequenti alalgorithm for the 1-D Convolver
for (k=0; k<inputValues; k++) {
  out[k] = 0.0;
  for (i=0; i<N; i++) {
    //2 flops
    out[k] = out[k] + input[k+i] * filter[i];
  }
}
```

11.4.1 The Sequential Convolver Algorithm

A naive sequential implementation of a convolver is shown in Algorithm 11.4. The main loop computes the iterations for a given number of *inputValues*. The number of floating point operations (flops) for each iteration (i.e., considering the *for i* loop) is $2 * N$, and the total number of flop operation per execution is *inputValues* $* 2 * N$. A signal having a sampling frequency of 100 kHz convolved with a filter composed by 20,000 coefficients requires 4 GFlops/s of the input/output signal. In this case and in the following cases, we performed the tests considering *inputValues* and number of coefficients N of 10,000, 100,000, and 1,000,000 and using both single-precision and double-precision floating point values (fp32 and fp64).

For the sequential algorithm, we compared the performance achieved using both the gcc and the icc compilers. The resulting performance values are shown as GFlops in Table 11.5. A single core of our CPU is capable of a theoretical maximum of 9.6 GFlops, and the right side of Table 11.5 reports the efficiency achieved. In particular, we considered the following four compilation commands:

icc icc -o FIR-naive FIR-naive.c -no-vec

icc with opt. icc -O3 -o FIR-naive FIR-naive.c

TABLE 11.5   Performance of the Sequential Convolver Algorithm, in GFlops, Using the icc and gcc Compilers with and Without Optimizations Flags

	Performance (GFlops)			Efficiency		
	N=10K	N=100K	N=1M	N=10K	N=100K	N=1M
	Single precision (fp32)					
icc	2.53	2.54	2.55	26.3%	26.4%	26.6%
icc with opt.	5.58	5.76	5.96	58.2%	60.0%	62.1%
gcc	0.40	0.40	0.40	4.1%	4.1%	4.1%
gcc with opt.	1.78	1.77	1.77	18.5%	18.5%	18.5%
	Double precision (fp64)					
icc	2.15	2.16	2.21	44.8%	45.1%	46.0%
icc with opt.	2.71	2.70	2.79	56.5%	56.3%	58.1%
gcc	0.39	0.39	0.39	8.2%	8.2%	8.2%
gcc with opt.	1.69	1.68	1.70	35.2%	35.1%	35.4%

gcc gcc -o FIR-naive FIR-naive.c

gcc with opt. gcc -O3 -o FIR-naive FIR-naive.c -ftree-vectorize.

11.4.2   The Parallel Convolver Algorithm for Multicore Architectures

We tried to fully exploit the capabilities of present multicore processor systems using the OpenMP specifications, which also in this case requires a minimum effort from the developer: it is in fact sufficient to add *#pragma omp parallel for* before both line 1 and 3. Moreover, in this case we compared the performance achieved using the cores of only one or both of the available CPUs, using the following four compilation commands:

icc icc -openmp -o FIR-OpenMP FIR-OpenMP.c -no-vec

icc with opt. icc -openmp -O3 -o FIR-OpenMP FIR-OpenMP.c

gcc gcc -fopenmp -o FIR-OpenMP FIR-OpenMP.c

gcc with opt. gcc -fopenmp -O3 -o FIR-OpenMP FIR-OpenMP.c -ftree-vectorize.

The resulting performance values are shown in Table 11.6. A single CPU (using all six cores) is capable of a theoretical maximum of 57.6 GFlops, which rises to 115.2 GFlops in case of two CPUs, and the right side of Table 11.6 reports the achieved efficiency. With one CPU, the icc compiler outperforms gcc by a factor of 1.6 in single precision and 1.1 in double precision. Using two CPUs, with icc we have a small improvement, while with gcc the performance drops by a factor of 1.8 in single precision and 1.4 in double precision. However, also in this case, the performance values are rather low, in particular using the cores of both the CPUs.

TABLE 11.6 Performance of the OpenMP Convolver Algorithm, in GFlops, Using the icc and gcc Compilers with Optimizations Flags, on One or Two Multicore CPUs

	CPU	Performance (GFlops)			Efficiency		
		N=10K	N=100K	N=1M	N=10K	N=100K	N=1M
		Single precision (fp32)					
icc	1	22.52	29.82	29.2	39.1%	51.8%	50.7%
gcc	1	15.36	17.31	17.65	26.7%	30.1%	30.7%
icc	2	18.26	31.75	14.86	15.9%	27.6%	12.9%
gcc	2	6.96	9.91	11.1	6.0%	8.6%	9.6%
		Double precision (fp64)					
icc	1	13.71	12.38	15.23	47.6%	43.0%	52.9%
gcc	1	11.50	13.30	12.93	39.9%	46.2%	44.9%
icc	2	9.37	16.53	20.77	16.3%	28.7%	36.1%
gcc	2	6.76	10.04	9.82	11.7%	17.4%	17.1%

11.4.3 The Parallel Convolver Algorithm for GPU Architectures

In this section, we provide a comparison among the CUDA 5.0 programming environment, the nVidia OpenCL implementation (available in CUDA 5.0), and AMD OpenCL implementation available in AMD APP SDK 2.8 using also an AMD card available on another system of the laboratory. In particular, one of the key issues in exploiting the massive parallel processors available on GPUs is the efficient memory access. To stress this aspect, we developed four CUDA/OpenCL kernels: The first, listed in the first part of Algorithm 11.5, directly accesses the data available on the device global memory, which can easily fit the whole dataset. In the following, this approach will be referred to as "global." In the second part of Algorithm 11.5, we want to exploit data locality, so data are copied to a local memory (in CUDA it is called *shared*, since it is shared among the scalar cores belonging to the same streaming multiprocessor). Unfortunately, the local memory can fit only a small subset of the whole dataset, so we have to split the computation into small chunks. Each chunk takes care of copying the data to the local memory, that is, each thread in a warp takes care of copying only one value, with coalesced memory accesses. In the following, this approach will be referred to as "local."

In Algorithm 11.6, we access the memory by reading/writing small vectors of four values. This can improve the bandwidth compared to direct access to single values. In the following, this approach will be referred as "vector." We also tried a kernel that adopts local memory and vector access. It will be referred to as "local + vector."

OpenCL kernels are a direct translation of CUDA core. The only two differences are explicit reference to the MAD function, which can perform a multiplication and an addition in a single clock, and repetition of lines 8 and 26 in Algorithm 11.5 in order to unroll the *for* loops, because the #pragma clauses are only supported in CUDA.

Table 11.7 shows the performance obtained by executing the foue kernels for $N = 1,000,000$ and using CUDA 5.0 and OpenCL 1.2 on an nVidia GTX 580, and

Algorithm 11.5

```
CUDA kernel - 1-D Convolver - global and shared memory accesses
// *** GLOBAL MEMORY ACCESS *** //
tTot = TNUM * gridDim.x // total threads
tId = TNUM*blockIdx.x+tIdx.x; // this thread number
float fOut;
for (int i = 0; i < inLen - filterLen; i = i + tTot ) {
  fOut = 0.0;
  for (int j = 0; j < filterLen; j++) {
    fOut += input[i + tId + j]*filter[j];
  }
  _syncthreads();
  output[i + tId] = fOut;
}
// *** SHARED MEMORY ACCESS *** //
_shared_myData s_indata[2*TNUM], s_filter[TNUM];
for (int i = 0; i < inLen - filterLen; i = i + tTot) {
  fOut = 0.0;
  for (int j = 0; j < filterLen; j += TNUM) {
    //copy global to shared memory, for threads
    s_filter[tIdx.x] = filter[j + tIdx.x];
    s_indata[tIdx.x] = input[i + tId + j];
    s_indata[tIdx.x + TNUM] = input[i + tId + j + TNUM];
    _syncthreads();
    #pragma unroll 8
    for (int k = 0; k < TNUM; k++) {
      fOut += s_indata[k + tIdx.x] * s_filter[k];
    }
  }
  _syncthreads();
  output[i + tId] = fOut;
}
```

with OpenCL 1.2 on an AMD Radeon HD 5850. Note that the theoretical maximum performance and memory bandwidth of the cards are quite different: nVidia GTX 580 can reach 1.58 TFlops in single precision and 198 GFlops in double precision, with a memory bandwidth of 192 GB/s; Radeon HD 5850 can reach 2.09 TFlops in single precision and 418 GFlops in double precision, with a memory bandwidth of 128 GB/s.

We can clearly see how a simple access to global memory results in a heavy bottleneck, and therefore developers have to carefully tune this aspect in the kernel. This is especially true with single-precision computation. In CUDA, we can get a speed up factor of 3.1 using local memory and 5.2 using vectorization. The two techniques can be combined with a further small improvement, but even the best result presents an efficiency of only 48%. In double precision, the theoretical performance of our GTX 580 is only one-eighth of the single-precision case, and thus computational power becomes the bottleneck for this application: in fact, local, vector, or local + vector presents an efficiency $\geq 75\%$.

In single precision, OpenCL performance is extremely close to that of CUDA in case of the local and vector kernel. The local + vector OpenCL kernel offers a

Algorithm 11.6

```
CUDA kernel for the solution of the 1-D Convolver - vector memory
access
tTot = TNUM * gridDim.x // total threads
tId = TNUM*blockIdx.x+tIdx.x; // this thread number
float4 i0, i1, f, fOut;
for (int i = 0; i < inLen - filterLen; i = i + tTot )
  fOut.x = fOut.y = fOut.z = fOut.w = 0.0;
  i0 = input[i + tId];
  #pragma unroll 8
  for (int j = 0; j < filterLen;)
    f = filter[j++];
    i1 = input[i + tId + j];
    fOut.x += f.x*i0.x + f.y*i0.y + f.z*i0.z + f.w*i0.w;
    fOut.y += f.x*i0.y + f.y*i0.z + f.z*i0.w + f.w*i1.x;
    fOut.z += f.x*i0.z + f.y*i0.w + f.z*i1.x + f.w*i1.y;
    fOut.w += f.x*i0.w + f.y*i1.x + f.z*i1.y + f.w*i1.z;
    f = filter[j++];
    i0 = input[i + tId + j];
    fOut.x += f.x*i1.x + f.y*i1.y + f.z*i1.z + f.w*i1.w;
    fOut.y += f.x*i1.y + f.y*i1.z + f.z*i1.w + f.w*i0.x;
    fOut.z += f.x*i1.z + f.y*i1.w + f.z*i0.x + f.w*i0.y;
    fOut.w += f.x*i1.w + f.y*i0.x + f.z*i0.y + f.w*i0.z;

  _syncthreads();
  output[i + tId] = fOut;
```

10% improvement with respect to that with CUDA one. In double precision, OpenCL offers slightly better results, with a record efficiency of 93%.

Test on the Radeon HD 5850 highlights the architectural differences: local memory effect is minimal, while vectorization is of paramount relevance. The combined effect

TABLE 11.7   Performance of the GPU Convolver Algorithm, in GFlops, Using CUDA and OpenCL on nVidia and AMD Cards with Four Different Memory Access Approaches, with $N=1M$

	CUDA nVidia		OpenCL nVidia		OpenCL AMD	
	Perf.	Effic.	Perf.	Effic.	Perf.	Effic.
Single precision (fp32)						
global	114.94	7.3%	216.92	13.7%	73.37	3.5%
local	364.63	23.1%	361.20	22.8%	169.16	8.1%
vector	617.45	39.1%	594.89	37.6%	472.30	22.6%
local + vector	765.83	48.4%	839.22	53.1%	422.66	20.2%
Double precision (fp64)						
global	97.76	49.5%	104.69	53.0%	61.88	14.8%
local	157.47	79.7%	177.20	89.7%	63.83	15.3%
vector	149.00	75.4%	168.50	85.3%	290.73	69.6%
local + vector	149.50	75.6%	183.92	93.1%	165.56	39.6%

(local + vector) is often worse than with vector alone. Using vectors for memory access is the way to go in case of AMD GPUs. In general, OpenCL support to vectors is wider than in CUDA (OpenCL supports vectors composed by 2, 3, 4, 8, and 16 elements). Single-precision performance is clearly limited by memory bandwidth, with efficiency limited to 22.6% in the best case. This is mainly due to the lower memory bandwidth (128 vs. 192 GB/s) and the higher raw computational power (2 vs. 1.5 TFlops). In double precision, the raw computational power is one-fifth of that of the single precision case, so we get a better balance with memory bandwidth. In fact, we get 290 GFlops, for an efficiency of 69.6%. Given the small benefit (if any) associated with local memory access, we tested direct access to host memory, without any penalty, in case of vector memory access; this suggests the presence of an efficient caching policy, for global and host memory.

11.5 CONCLUSIONS

Recent heterogeneous architectures are extremely powerful, and parallel problems can benefit a tremendous speedup from accelerators, up to 140 times in the convolver experiments, from the best sequential results to the best OpenCL implementation. Nonetheless, the developer has to take extreme care in the selection of the right architecture and tool to use.

As an example, in the sequential N-body case, icc outperformed gcc by a factor of 3.4, without any effort from the developer. Moreover, the adoption of a multi-CPU architecture can lead to NUMA issues and impact performance: in the parallel convolver for multicore architectures case, the performance with OpenMP using a single CPU is better than using both the CPUs. The MPI implementation, characterized by better data locality, allows a reduction of this aspect, providing higher performance, but also more changes in the sequential code.

The implementations for GPU accelerators require the greatest effort from the developer point of view, but they present very high performance figures. Different architectures impose *ad hoc* optimizations, in particular with respect to memory access (vector I/O on both architectures, and shared memory for nVidia cards). Moreover, specialized functions (such as MAD or RSQRT) can double or triple the performance only by explicitly exploiting them. It is worth noting that we focused on use cases that allow the exploitation of both the CPU and the GPU, but there are problems (mainly those working on irregular data structures) that are difficult to port on GPUs, or where the porting benefit is minimal.

To sum up, with a recent heterogeneous workstation, such as the considered one, developers are able to exploit considerable compute capabilities, but the achievement of at least 50% of the maximum theoretical performance requires good knowledge of architecture-specific features such as the extended set of instructions available (i.e., SSE and AVX for CPUs), data locality techniques, and efficient memory access patterns, besides the availability of tools providing an efficient vectorization, which most of the times are not freely available.

ACKNOWLEDGMENTS

This work was supported by the COST Action IC0805 "Open European Network for High-Performance Computing on Complex Environments" and the Italian Flagship Project InterOmics funded by MIUR.

REFERENCES

1. G. E. Moore, "Cramming more components onto integrated circuits," *Electronics*, vol. 38, no. 8, pp. 114–117, 1965.
2. J. J. Dongarra and A. J. van der Steen, "High performance computing systems: status and outlook," *Acta Numerica*, vol. 21, pp. 379–474, 2012.
3. C. Brown, H.-W. Loidl, and K. Hammond, "Paraforming: forming parallel haskell programs using novel refactoring techniques," in *Proceedings of the 12th International Conference on Trends in Functional Programming, TFP'11*, pp. 82–97. Berlin, Heidelberg: Springer-Verlag, 2012.
4. K. Asanovic, R. Bodik, B. C. Catanzaro, J. J. Gebis, P. Husbands, K. Keutzer, D. A. Patterson, W. L. Plishker, J. Shalf, S. W. Williams, and K. A. Yelick, "The landscape of parallel computing research: a view from Berkeley," tech. rep., EECS Department, University of California, Berkeley, 2006. Technical Report No. UCB/EECS-2006-183.
5. F. J. Seinstra, J. Maassen, R. V. van Nieuwpoort, N. Drost, T. van Kessel, B. van Werkhoven, J. Urbani, C. Jacobs, T. Kielmann, and H. E. Bal, "Jungle computing: distributed supercomputing beyond clusters, grids, and clouds," in *Grids, Clouds and Virtualization, Computer Communications and Networks* (M. Cafaro and G. Aloisio, eds.), Springer-Verlag, Springer: London, 2011.
6. K. Asanovic, R. Bodik, J. Demmel, T. Keaveny, K. Keutzer, J. Kubiatowicz, N. Morgan, D. Patterson, K. Sen, J. Wawrzynek, D. Wessel, and K. Yelick, "A view of the parallel computing landscape," *Communications of the ACM*, vol. 52, no. 10, pp. 56–67, 2009.
7. M. Cole, "Bringing skeletons out of the closet: a pragmatic manifesto for skeletal parallel programming," *Parallel Computing*, vol. 30, no. 3, pp. 389–406, 2004.
8. M. Aldinucci, M. Danelutto, M. Vanneschi, and C. Zoccolo, "Assist as a research framework for high-performance grid programming environments," in *Grid Computing: Software Environments and Tools* (J. C. Cunha and O. F. Rana, eds.), pp. 230–256, Springer-Verlag, Springer: London, 2006.
9. P. Ammirati, A. Clematis, D. D'Agostino, and V. Gianuzzi, "Using a structured programming environment for parallel remote visualization," in *Euro-Par 2004 Parallel Processing, Lecture Notes in Computer Science* (M. Danelutto, M. Vanneschi, and D. Laforenza, eds.), vol. 3149, pp. 477–486. Berlin Heidelberg: Springer, 2004.
10. H. González-Vélez and M. Leyton, "A survey of algorithmic skeleton frameworks: high-level structured parallel programming enablers," *Software Practice & Experience*, vol. 40, no. 12, pp. 1135–1160, 2010.
11. J. Fang, A. L. Varbanescu, and H. Sips, "A comprehensive performance comparison of CUDA and OpenCL," in *Proceedings of the 2011 International Conference on Parallel Processing, ICPP '11*, pp. 216–225. Washington, DC: IEEE Computer Society, 2011.
12. R. Reyes, I. López-Rodríguez, J. J. Fumero, and F. de Sande, "accULL: an OpenACC implementation with CUDA and OpenCL support.," in *Euro-Par, Lecture Notes in Computer Science* (C. Kaklamanis, T. S. Papatheodorou, and P. G. Spirakis, eds.), vol. 7484, pp. 871–882, Springer: Berlin, Heidelberg, 2012.

13. D. P. Playne, M. Johnson, and K. A. Hawick, "Benchmarking GPU devices with N-body simulations," in *Proceedings 2009 International Conference on Computer Design, CDES'09*, (Las Vegas, USA), pp. 150–156, 2009.

14. J. Barnes and P. Hut, "A hierarchical O(N log N) force-calculation algorithm," *Nature*, vol. 324, pp. 446–449, 1986.

15. J. P. Singh, W.-D. Weber, and A. Gupta, "SPLASH: Stanford parallel applications for shared-memory," *SIGARCH Computer Architecture News*, vol. 20, no. 1, pp. 5–44, 1992.

16. J. Salmon, "Parallel N log N N-body algorithms and applications to astrophysics," in *Compcon Spring '91. Digest of Papers*, San Francisco, California, pp. 73–78, 1991.

17. F. Zhao and S. Johnsson, "The parallel multipole method on the connection machine," *SIAM Journal on Scientific and Statistical Computing*, vol. 12, no. 6, pp. 1420–1437, 1991.

18. P. Mills, L. S. Nyland, J. Prins, and J. H. Reif, "Prototyping N-body simulation in proteus," in *Proceedings of the 6th International Parallel Processing Symposium, IPPS '92*, pp. 476–482. Washington, DC: IEEE Computer Society, 1992.

19. G. Blelloch and G. Narlikar, "A practical comparison of N-body algorithms," in *Parallel Algorithms, Series in Discrete Mathematics and Theoretical Computer Science*, vol. 30, American Mathematical Society, Providence, RI, 1997.

20. D. A. Mallón, G. L. Taboada, C. Teijeiro, J. Touri no, B. B. Fraguela, A. Gómez, R. Doallo, and J. C. Mouri no, "Performance evaluation of MPI, UPC and OpenMP on multicore architectures," in *Proceedings of the 16th European PVM/MPI Users' Group Meeting on Recent Advances in Parallel Virtual Machine and Message Passing Interface*, pp. 174–184. Berlin, Heidelberg: Springer-Verlag, 2009.

21. Z. Liu, B. Chapman, T.-H. Weng, and O. Hernandez, "Improving the performance of OpenMP by array privatization," in *Proceedings of the OpenMP Applications and Tools 2003 International Conference on OpenMP Shared Memory Parallel Programming, WOMPAT'03*, pp. 244–259. Berlin, Heidelberg: Springer-Verlag, 2003.

12

Efficient Application of Hybrid Parallelism in Electromagnetism Problems

Alejandro Álvarez-Melcón and Fernando D. Quesada

Technical University of Cartagena, Cartagena, Spain

**Domingo Giménez, Carlos Pérez-Alcaraz,
José-Ginés Picón, and Tomás Ramírez**

University of Murcia, Murcia, Spain

Some computational problems in electromagnetism have high computational cost, which makes it is necessary to solve them efficiently in today's computational systems. This chapter studies the efficient solution of electromagnetism problems based on integral equation formulations in clusters of CPU + GPU nodes.

12.1 INTRODUCTION

With the appearance of multicore and many-core systems, the complexity of the computational systems has greatly increased in various ways. Examples of this complexity

High-Performance Computing on Complex Environments, First Edition.
Edited by Emmanuel Jeannot and Julius Žilinskas.
© 2014 John Wiley & Sons, Inc. Published 2014 by John Wiley & Sons, Inc.

are the increase in the number of cores and of memory levels in large cc-NUMA systems, or the combination of components of different architectures in clusters of multicores with graphics processing unit (GPU) cards.

Computationally demanding problems in science and engineering require efficient solutions in these complex computational systems, and it is necessary to combine parallel programming paradigms at different levels and in different computational systems.

Numerous computationally demanding problems arise in computational electromagnetism, and so parallelism has been traditionally applied in this field [1–4]. This chapter considers the efficient application of hybrid multilevel parallel programming techniques to electromagnetism problems based on integral equation formulations [5]:

- We consider first, at a low level, the application of hybrid parallelism for the computation of Green's functions in rectangular waveguides [6, 7], which are used as basic components in the analysis of microwave circuits using integral equation formulations. MPI + OpenMP, OpenMP + CUDA, and MPI + OpenMP+ CUDA routines are developed for 1D and 2D problems [8], and the use of heterogeneous clusters built up by nodes with different numbers of cores, computational speed ups, and GPU cards is analyzed.

- At a higher level, the combination of two-level OpenMP and multithread routines in cc-NUMA systems is applied to accelerate a tool called *MEATSS* (Microstrip Electromagnetic Analysis Tool for Space Systems) [9, 10]. This is a software tool for the analysis of microstrip circuits with finite dielectric substrates, using a volume integral equation technique (VIE), solved with the method of moments (MoM) [11].

In both cases, we consider the application of autotuning techniques to obtain efficient routines, independently of the expertise of the final user. The techniques used here can be applied to other problems, in electromagnetism or other scientific applications [12–16], thus contributing to a better use of today's advanced computational systems in computationally demanding problems.

The chapter is organized as follows. First, the application of hybrid parallelism for the computation of 2D Green's functions in uniform rectangular waveguides is studied. Next, the combination of two-level OpenMP and multithread LAPACK-style routines in cc-NUMA systems to accelerate MEATSS is analyzed. Finally, the application of autotuning techniques to the two problems is considered. The chapter finishes with the conclusions and the discussion of some possible extensions of the work.

12.2 COMPUTATION OF GREEN'S FUNCTIONS IN HYBRID SYSTEMS

The analysis of waveguide microwave circuits using integral equation formulations requires the computation of 1D or 2D Green's functions inside parallel plates or rectangular waveguides, respectively [17]. The study of real problems involves the calculation of the Green's functions for a huge number of pairs of source–observation points. This calculation is usually very time consuming, especially because of the large number of images needed in the series [18]. Depending on the problem size, the best parallelism paradigm or combination of paradigms changes. In this context, MPI + OpenMP, OpenMP + CUDA, and MPI + OpenMP + CUDA [19–21] routines are developed to accelerate the calculation of 1D and 2D waveguide Green's functions [8].

The scheme of the 2D hybrid algorithm for multiple pairs of source–observation points is shown in Algorithm 12.1. p MPI processes are started, the Green's functions to be computed are equally distributed into the processes, and $h + g$ threads run inside each process. Threads 0 to $h - 1$ work on the CPU (we call them OpenMP threads), while threads h to $h + g - 1$ calculate the Green's functions in the GPU by calling *CUDA kernels* (GPU threads). Thus, the work statically assigned to the processes is dynamically distributed between the cores and the GPUs in the system, with coarse-grained parallelism in the cores and fine-grained parallelism in the GPU.

Algorithm 12.1

```
GF-2D (m,n,nmod,mimag,nimag,p,h,g) {
    for each MPI process Pk, 0 ≤ k < p:
        omp_set_num_threads(h + g)
        #pragma omp parallel for schedule(dynamic,1)
        for i = km/p to (k+1)m/p - 1
            node=omp_get_thread_num()
        if node < h
            Compute with OpenMP thread
        else
            Call to CUDA kernel
}
```

Table 12.1 shows the different routines developed, depending on the number of computational components of each type (number of MPI processes, OpenMP threads, and CUDA kernels). Different combinations of the parameters give different types of parallelism, so the routine can be adapted to the particular system where the problem is to be solved.

12.2.1 Computation in a Heterogeneous Cluster

The different routines shown in Table 12.1 can be combined in different ways when working in a heterogeneous cluster. If there are n nodes numbered from

TABLE 12.1 Routines for the Computation of 2D Green's Functions, Depending on the Number of MPI Processes (p), OpenMP Threads (h), and CUDA Kernels (g)

$p \backslash h + g$	$1 + 0$	$h + 0$	$0 + g$	$h + g$
1	SEQ	OMP	CUDA	OMP+CUDA
p	MPI	MPI+OMP	MPI+CUDA	MPI+OMP+CUDA

1 to n, the number of processes, threads, and CUDA kernels in each node can change, and we have an array for each: $p = (p_1, p_2, \dots, p_n)$; $h = (h_1, h_2, \dots, h_n)$; and $g = (g_1, g_2, \dots, g_n)$, with p_i being the number of processes in node i, and h_i, g_i the numbers of OpenMP and GPU threads inside processes in node i.

The values of these parameters can be selected so that the number of processes assigned to each node is proportional to the computational capacity of the node, and, therefore, the number of pairs of points for which the node computes the Green's functions. Furthermore, the relative computational capacity of the nodes in the cluster is not constant; it changes with the problem size, thus causing the optimum values of the parameters in the node (h_i and g_i) to change, making it preferable in some nodes to use only threads in the CPU, or in the GPU, or a combination of both. In this way, we get a heterogeneous distribution of the work among the nodes, but it is possible to extend the heterogeneity within a node. For example, a group of processes can be assigned to each node. If q_i is the number of different groups of processes assigned to node i, then the number of processes in each group is $p_{i,j}$, with $1 \leq j \leq q_i$, and the total number of processes in node i is $\sum_{j=1}^{q_i} p_{i,j}$. The number of OpenMP and GPU threads in a process depends on the group, and a process in group j of node i will have $h_{i,j}$ and $g_{i,j}$ OpenMP and GPU threads.

The number of parameters to work with and to select to tune the program to the problem size and the computational system has now greatly increased, making it much more difficult to obtain a satisfactory selection of the parameters, and it becomes necessary to have an autotuning engine to select the appropriate values. In contrast, the number of parameters can be maintained at reasonable values if we consider that executions are usually launched only to the CPU or the GPU. In a cluster of four nodes, the parameters to be selected would be $(p_{1,1}, p_{1,2}, p_{2,1}, p_{2,2}, p_{3,1}, p_{3,2}, p_{4,1}, p_{4,2})$ for the processes, and the corresponding $h_{i,j}$ and $g_{i,j}$ for the threads, one with value zero. The two configurations running in node 1 would be $p_{1,1} \times (h_{1,1} + 0)$ and $p_{1,2} \times (0 + g_{1,2})$, which means some of the processes will run only OpenMP threads and others only CUDA kernels. It is also possible to combine OpenMP and GPU threads in the same process, but normally this is not the best approach and can be discarded to reduce the search space for the best configuration.

12.2.2 Experiments

Experiments to determine the optimum number of MPI processes, OpenMP threads, and CUDA kernels have been carried out in three basic computational systems and in homogeneous and heterogeneous clusters built up with those nodes:

- *Saturno* is a NUMA system with four Intel hexa-core NEHALEM-EX EC E7530 nodes, and a total of 24 cores, 1.87 GHz, 32 GB of shared memory. There is an NVIDIA Tesla C2050, CUDA Compute Capability 2.0, with 14 symmetric multiprocessors (SMP) of 32 cores, a total of 448 CUDA cores, 2.8 GB and 1.15 GHz.

- *Marte* and *Mercurio* are AMD Phenom II X6 1075T (hexa-core), 3 GHz, 15 GB (*Marte*), and 8 GB (*Mercurio*), private L1 and L2 caches of 64 and 512 KB, and L3 of 6 MB shared by all the cores. Each machine has an NVIDIA GeForce GTX 590 with two devices, CUDA Compute Capability 2.0, each with 16 SMP of 32 cores, a total of 512 CUDA cores in a device, 1.2 GHz. The total amount of memory in each GPU is 1.5 GB.

- *Luna* is an Intel Core 2 Quad Q6600, 2.4 GHz, 4 GB, with an NVIDIA GeForce 9800 GT, CUDA Compute Capability 1.1, with 14 SMP of 8 cores, a total of 112 CUDA cores, 0.5 GB, and 1.5 GHz.

With these systems, we can experiment with different configurations so that the versatility and validity of the programs developed are tested. In shared memory, we can test from small multicores (*Luna*) to medium-size NUMA systems (*Saturno*). Different types of GPUs are also available, including two devices in a card (*Marte* and *Mercurio*), and the three types of parallelism (shared memory, message-passing, and single instruction multiple data in GPU) can be studied in a small homogeneous cluster (*Marte* + *Mercurio*),[1] and the heterogeneous cluster composed of *Saturno* + *Marte* + *Mercurio* + *Luna* can be used for heterogeneous runs. The four nodes are connected through a 100 Mb/s network. With such a variety of systems, different parallelization strategies must be studied to obtain programs that run efficiently in the different systems or in homogeneous (*Marte* + *Mercurio*) or in heterogeneous (*Saturno* + *Mare* + *Mercurio* + *Luna*) clusters. For some problem sizes or particular inputs, it may be preferable to use only CPU or GPU computation in only one node, but in other cases an appropriate combination of the different components may produce a greater reduction in the execution time. So CPU and GPU parallelism have been combined to use all the potential computational system on hand offers, and fine- and coarse-grained approaches are considered. Mixed parallelism combining the two strategies and the three programming paradigms is also studied.

Figure 12.1 compares the execution time of 2D Green's functions in the three systems when CPUs or GPUs are used. The figure shows the quotient of the execution time of the CPU version ($p \times (h + 0)$) with respect to that of the GPU version ($p \times (0 + g)$). In each system, the CPU version uses a number of threads equal to the number of cores in the system: 4 in *Luna*, 24 in *Saturno*, and 6 + 6 in *Marte* + *Mercurio*, which are taken together as a homogeneous cluster. In the GPU version, three kernels are called for each GPU card (two cards in *Marte* + *Mercurio*). It is possible to develop more optimized GPU versions, but the parameterized approach used here allows us to use the same code in the different systems and to obtain the optimum number of kernels for each system. Although the optimum number of kernels varies with the computational system, with three kernels satisfactory performances have been obtained in the three systems. Consequently, this number of kernels is used for comparison, which is made for different numbers of images in the series (100, 1000, 10,000, 100,000) and pairs of source–observation points ($10 \times 10, 25 \times 25, 50 \times 50, 75 \times 75$). For large problem sizes, it is preferable to use the GPU, but

---

[1] We consider it homogeneous given that the only difference is in the memory capacity

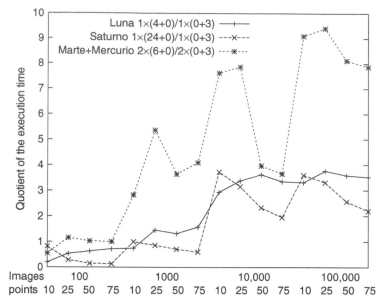

FIGURE 12.1   *Quotient of the execution time when using the same number of threads as cores with respect to that with the GPU with three kernel calls.*

the speed up achieved and the point at which GPU computation is preferable to CPU computation greatly varies with the system, depending on the number of cores and the relative speed of the CPUs and GPUs in it. For big problems, the speed up achieved with the GPU is around 8 in *Marte + Mercurio* and around 3 in *Luna* or *Saturno*.

The selection of the optimum values for p, h, and g produces lower execution times. Figure 12.2 shows the quotient of the execution time of the GPU version with three kernels with respect to the lowest execution time obtained experimentally for the different values of p, h, and g. The advantage of using the optimum values varies with the problem size and the computational system. The speed up achieved is approximately 2 for the largest problems, indicating that an important reduction in the execution time can be obtained if the optimum values of the parameters are selected, for which it is necessary to use some autotuning technique.

Since the best option in a single node and for large problems is to use just the GPU with several kernels, and three kernels is a good option for all the nodes, a good option could be to solve the problem with the three nodes *Saturno, Marte,* and *Mercurio* with three CUDA kernels in each node, and not to use *Luna*, because its GPU is slower and the assignment of processes to *Luna* would produce additional communications which are not compensated by the inclusion of a slow GPU. Figure 12.3 shows the quotient of the execution time obtained with the two GPUs in *Marte + Mercurio* $(0 \times (0 + 0) + 1 \times (0 + 3) + 1 \times (0 + 3) + 0 \times (0 + 0))$ or the three GPUs using also that of *Saturno* $(1 \times (0 + 3) + 1 \times (0 + 3) + 1 \times (0 + 3) + 0 \times (0 + 0))$ with respect to the lowest execution time obtained from experiments when varying the number of processes and of OpenMP and GPU threads in each node in the whole system. This

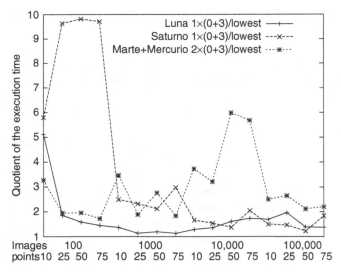

FIGURE 12.2 *Quotient of the execution time of the GPU version with three kernels with respect to the lowest execution time obtained experimentally.*

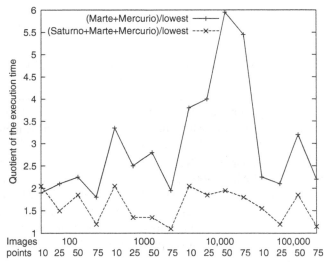

FIGURE 12.3 *Quotient of the execution time of the GPU version with three kernels with respect to the lowest time in experiments in the whole system.*

low experimental time may be the minimum possible with the system. We see that the use of the heterogeneous cluster gives lower times than those obtained with the two nodes composing the homogeneous cluster, and the execution time with this simple heuristic use of the heterogeneous cluster is not far (between 0% and 100% worse) from the lowest execution time we could obtain if a perfect oracle for the selection of the parameters were available.

12.3   PARALLELIZATION IN NUMA SYSTEMS OF A VOLUME INTEGRAL EQUATION TECHNIQUE

A software tool called *MEATSS* was developed for the analysis of finite microstrip structures using the VIE technique, solved with the MoM. In this case, the free-space Green's functions are used in the formulation. Therefore, there are no computational issues associated with the calculation of the Green's functions. Consequently, parallelism is introduced at the MoM level.

We use NUMA systems with shared memory but with a large memory hierarchy, which makes it difficult to achieve the maximum theoretical speed up [22]. A good approach to accelerate the computation in cc-NUMA systems is to use two-level parallelism [10]: OpenMP for independent computations corresponding to different frequencies, and the implicit multithread parallelism of the Intel Math Kernel Library (MKL) for the solution of the resulting complex, symmetric, and dense systems of equations. Two linear algebra routines (zsysv and zgesv, implemented in MKL[2]) for the solution of symmetric complex linear systems resulting from the MoM formulation are considered. The zsysv routine is used for symmetric matrices, while zgesv solves general problems, with a computational cost of twice that of zsysv [23], but with a better scalability, which makes it competitive in large cc-NUMAs.

12.3.1   Experiments

Experiments have been carried out in medium NUMA and cc-NUMA systems:

- As mentioned, *Saturno* is a NUMA system with four nodes with a total of 24 cores. The memory is organized hierarchically; there are several possible memory locations to store the data when solving the problem, and the memory access cost varies depending on the data allocation.
- *Ben* and *Bscsmp* are larger cc-NUMA systems—an HP Integrity Superdome SX2000 and an SGI Altix 4700, respectively. Both have a total of 128 cores of the Intel Itanium-2 dual-core processor, *Bscsmp* of the series Montecito (8 MB cache of L3), and *Ben* of the series Montvale (18 MB cache of L3), each at 1.6 GHz and with 1.5 TB shared memory. The memory hierarchy is larger than in *Saturno*, so the use of two-level parallelism will produce better results in these systems.

The LAPACK implementation is that of the Intel MKL toolkit, version 10.2 in *Saturno* and *Ben*, and 11.1 in *Bscsmp*. The better scalability of the general linear system routines is observed in Fig. 12.4, which compares the execution time of double precision (dsysv and dgesv) and complex double (zsysv and zgesv) routines, for matrix sizes 1024 and 2048, when varying the number of cores in *Saturno* and

---

[2]http://software.intel.com/en-us/intel-mkl/

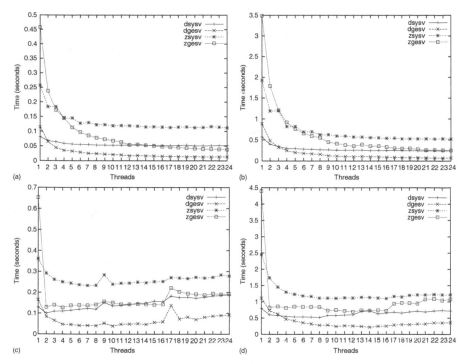

FIGURE 12.4 *Comparison of the execution time of linear system routines. (a) Matrix size 1024, in Saturno. (b) Matrix size 2048, in Saturno. (c) Matrix size 1024, in Bscsmp. (d) Matrix size 2048, in Bscsmp.*

Bscsmp. In *Saturno*, only one execution has been carried out for each problem size and number of cores, while in *Bscsmp* the number of experiments for each size and number of cores is 4, and the minimum of these has been taken. This is because *Saturno* was used in the stand-alone mode, while in *Bscsmp* the experiments were conducted with more users in the system. Some conclusions can be drawn:

- The execution time of the gesv routines is higher than those of the corresponding sysv routines for a small number of cores, but when this number increases the general routines are faster than the routines for symmetric matrices. Furthermore, the number of cores at which the preferred routine changes increases with the matrix size, and varies according to the computational system and for real and complex routines.

- When the number of cores is large, the execution time of the sysv routines does not decrease, showing that these routines have very bad scalability. This is more apparent in larger cc-NUMA systems, and in *Bscsmp* the execution time of the routines increases for a large number of cores, it being preferable not to use the whole system for the solution of the problem.

- The behavior of the routines is more irregular in the cc-NUMA system, where the correspondence between data allocation and cores is less clear. The irregular behavior shown in the figure for *Bscsmp* (the great reduction with two cores in zgesv and some peaks) is also shown where we consider the mean of the execution times and not the minimum time. So, this behavior seems to be produced by the system characteristics and the library used.

- The optimum number of cores does not coincide in large systems with the maximum available. Table 12.2 compares the behavior of sysv and gesv routines for the two matrix sizes and the two systems in Fig. 12.4. The table shows the number of cores at which gesv outperforms sysv (ge<sy), the optimum number of cores for sysv and gesv (op_sy and op_ge), the speed up of the execution time when using the optimum number of cores with respect to that with the maximum number of cores (max/opt), and the speed up of gesv with respect to sysv when the optimum number of cores is used in each routine (sy/ge). In *Saturno*, the optimum number of cores is 24 (the number of available cores) in most cases, but in *Bscsmp* this is far from the maximum number of cores experimented with (32). Thus, in large cc-NUMA systems it may be preferable to work with two-level routines to better exploit the system and further reduce the execution time [24].

- The table shows the speed up obtained when using the optimum number of cores with respect to the use of the maximum number in the cases in which those numbers do not coincide. An important reduction of the execution time is obtained if the number of cores is chosen satisfactorily in large systems. Also, the correct selection of the routine gives an important reduction of the execution time, which is shown in the last column of the table, which represents the speed up of the general routines with respect to the symmetric routines when the optimum number of cores is selected in the two routines. This motivated the use of some autotuning technique to select the number of cores and the basic routine [22].

TABLE 12.2 Comparison of the Behavior of sysv and gesv Routines, in *Saturno* and *Bscsmp*

Size-type	ge<sy	op_sy	max/opt	op_ge	max/opt	sy/ge
			Saturno			
1024-Double	3	9	1.1	24		2.5
1024-Complex	5	24		24		2
2048-Double	4	24		24		3
2048-Complex	7	24		24		2
			Bscsmp			
1024-Double	3	2	2	8	2	3
1024-Complex	2	8	1.3	2	1.8	2
2048-Double	4	6	1.4	14	2	2.5
2048-Complex	2	10	1.5	14	1.5	1.5

In the MEATSS software, several systems corresponding to different frequencies are solved and multithread linear algebra routines can be combined with OpenMP in a two-level parallelism code. Algorithm 12.2 shows a hybrid code in which the computation of a number of frequencies is assigned to a group of *ntomp* OpenMP threads (established in line 3). Inside each thread, the linear system is solved with an MKL routine with *ntmkl* threads (established in line 4). Nested parallelism is enabled (line 1), and the dynamic selection of threads by MKL is disabled (line 2) because it does not work properly in combination with nested parallelism [22]. The maximum speed up achieved with this two-level code in *Ben* was 35 using 64 cores, which is far from the maximum achievable (128). In any case, it is much better than the speed up of 6 obtained with the use of the multithread implementation of zsysv in MKL.

Algorithm 12.2

```
OpenMP+MKL MEATSS {
  1:               mop_set_nested(1)
  2:               mkm_set_dynamic(0)
  3:               omp_set_num_threads(ntomp)
  4:               mkl_set_numt_hreads(ntmkl)
  5:               for i = 0 to num_freq
  6:                       fillmatrix(i, init_freq, step)
  7:               #pragma omp parallel for private(i)
  8:               for i = 0 to num_freq
  9:                       solvesystem(i)
 10:               for i = 0 to num_freq
 11:                       circuitalparameters(i, init_freq, step)
}
```

To illustrate the advantage of the hybrid parallelism, Table 12.3 compares the execution time for the computation of 128 frequencies with 64 cores in *Ben* when zsysv or zgesv is used in solvesystem in Algorithm 12.2, for three meshes with different complexities. They correspond to the simple microstrip structure shown in Fig. 12.5, which has been generated with Gid,[3] and the system sizes for simple, medium, and complex meshes are 733, 3439, and 5159. The lowest time for each mesh and basic routine is highlighted. The use of nested parallelism with two MKL threads gives better times in some cases. In others, it is preferable to use OpenMP parallelism and, due to the reduced number of MKL threads leading to optimum times, it is preferable to use the routine zsysv. Anyway, for the solution of larger problems in larger cc-NUMA systems, it would be interesting to explore the use of hybrid parallelism with the two basic routines, to determine the preferred routine and the number of OpenMP and MKL threads depending on the problem size and the number of cores.

[3]http://www.gidhome.com/

TABLE 12.3   Execution Time (in Seconds) for the Computation of 128 Frequencies with Hybrid OpenMP + MKL Parallelism, in *Ben* for Meshes of Different Complexity

Mesh Complexity	ntomp-ntmkl		
	64-1	32-2	16-4
	zsysv		
Simple	3.08	**2.22**	2.85
Medium	**48.53**	63.66	97.65
Complex	**114.68**	152.91	241.79
	zgesv		
Simple	4.94	**4.93**	6.12
Medium	96.49	**81.36**	89.04
Complex	222.01	**171.42**	193.46

FIGURE 12.5   *3D geometry used in the experiments.*

12.4   AUTOTUNING PARALLEL CODES

The development of efficient parallel codes does not ensure that the codes will be used well and that the lowest execution times in a particular system will always be obtained. The high complexity of today's hybrid, heterogeneous, and hierarchical parallel systems makes it difficult to obtain general conclusions for the different computational systems available, and for the different types of parallelism (shared memory, message-passing, GPGPU). This means that the efficiency of the codes depends on a number of algorithmic parameters, and so it is difficult to estimate their best values leading to the lowest execution time for any computational architecture. A good selection of the values of the parameters could be made by an expert user in the problem, in a particular system, and taking into account the particularities of the programs used to solve it. Such an *expert* user does not exist in general, and an alternative is to develop codes with some autotuning engine. This technique ensures an execution close to the optimum, irrespective of the particular problem to be solved and of the characteristics of the system in which it is being solved. Autotuning techniques have been used in recent years to accelerate parallel codes in different fields [12, 13, 25–27], and especially in linear algebra routines [28–32], which are the basic components in many scientific computations.

Autotuning techniques can be based on theoretical modeling of the execution time of the routines or on the empirical study of the routines through exhaustive testing. The two techniques are briefly illustrated in the following sections with the two hybrid implementations presented.

12.4.1 Empirical Autotuning

The optimum execution time of the hybrid Green's function routine depends on a number of parameters (p, h, and g, or, in general, p_i, h_i, and g_i, $1 \leq i \leq n$, in a cluster with n nodes) which should be included in a theoretical model of the execution time. Some attempts have been made, but no satisfactory results have been obtained to date. The main difficulty is in the complexity of the computational system (hybrid, heterogeneous, hierarchical), which makes it difficult to develop a satisfactory theoretical model. An alternative for empirical autotuning is to run some test executions during the installation of the routine in a particular system. This information is then used at running time when a particular problem is being solved.

We consider the homogeneous cluster formed by *Marte + Mercurio*. The routine is run at installation time for a set of selected sizes, called the *installation set*, and for the different possible combinations of the parameters to be tuned. As the nodes have the same computational capacity, the same number of processes, threads, and CUDA kernels are used in the two nodes. Because the number of cores in a node is 6, p ranges from 1 to 6 and h from 0 to 6, and because the preferred number of CUDA kernels is not very large, g has been established in the range from 0 to 6, with $h + g \geq 1$. The installation time would therefore be very large, due to the high numbers of executions needed. An alternative is to conduct some guided search in the installation [24], for example, experimenting with all the values of the parameters for the smallest problem in the *installation set*, and making a local search in the parameters for each problem size, starting from the optimum combination of parameters for the previous problem in the set. The optimum values estimated are stored to be used at running time.

To illustrate how the method works, Table 12.4 compares the execution time when this autotuning technique is used (autotuning) with the lowest execution time from a large set of experiments (lowest). The sizes used in the installation are {100, 10,000} for the number of images in the series and {10, 50} for

TABLE 12.4 Comparison of the Execution Time When Using the Empirical Autotuning Methodology with the Experimental Lowest Execution Time, in *Marte + Mercurio*

Images-Points	1000-25	100,000-25	1000-100	100,000-100
Autotuning	0.155	5.012	1.706	87.814
Lowest	0.114	5.012	1.656	79.453
Deviation	35.96%	0%	3.02%	10.52%

TABLE 12.5   Values of the Parameters that Give the Lowest Experimental Execution Time for Different Numbers of Images and Points, in *Saturno + Marte + Mercurio + Luna*

Images/Points	10	25	50	75
100	*M* 1 ×(6+0)	*S* 1 ×(24+0)	*S* 1×(24+0)	*S* 1 ×(24+0)
1000	*S* 1×(24+0)	*S* 1×(24+0)	*S* 1 ×(24+0)	*S* 1 ×(24+0)
10,000	*L* 1 ×(0+3)	*MM* 1 ×(0+3)	*M* 1 ×(0+3)	*M* 1 ×(0+3)
100,000	*MM* 1 ×(0+3)	*M* 1 ×(0+3)	*M* 1 ×(0+3)	*M* 1 ×(0+3)

the number of source–observation points. The table compares the times for a *validation set* with images {100, 100,000} and points {25, 100}. The deviation (|autotuning-lowest|/lowest) is not high for large problems, so we can consider that the autotuning approach gives satisfactory results.

An empirical installation can also be conducted in a heterogeneous system. The values of the parameters that give the lowest execution time are shown in Table 12.5, where, for example, the *installation set* contains as number of images {100, 1000, 10,000, 100,000} and as points {10, 25, 50, 75}. In the table, the characters *S*, *M*, and *L* refer to *Saturno*, *Marte*, and *Luna*, and *MM* refers to *Marte+Mercurio*, and in this case 1 × (0 + 3) indicates one process and three kernels in each node. We observe that for small sizes the preferred option is to use *Saturno* with all its cores, and for big problems it is better to use the GPU of *Marte*. Only in two cases, the best option is to use two nodes, possibly due to the cost of communications introduced when using MPI (the nodes are connected through an Ethernet network at 100 Mb/s) and to the cost of initialization of the GPUs in different nodes. The entry in which *Luna* is the best option can be explained by the faster start up of its GPU, which compensates for its low computational capacity.

We use a *validation set* with numbers of images {500, 5000, 50,000, 200,000} and of points {15, 35, 60, 100}. For each pair images–points, the problem would be solved with the values of the parameters in the table generated in the installation (Table 12.5) in the entry closest to the actual problem size; for example, for 500 images and 15 points, the problem would be solved in *Marte* with six OpenMP threads, which is the entry in (100, 10). Table 12.6 compares the execution times for the sizes in the *validation set* when this autotuning technique is used with the lowest times obtained experimentally. For each entry in the table, only one value is shown when the optimum value coincides with that obtained with autotuning. When they are different, the experimental time obtained with autotuning and the lowest time are shown, as well as the configuration that gives the lowest time. The optimum values of the parameters have not been selected in 7 of the 16 cases, but the total execution time of all the entries when the autotuning technique is used is approximately 20% higher than that of the fastest executions, which is not big, and makes empirical autotuning an interesting option. But in this case the number of parameters to experiment with is larger than in single nodes or in a small homogeneous cluster, which makes the use of some guided search more interesting in order to reduce the number of experiments and consequently the installation time. At present, we have no satisfactory technique for a guided search in this case. The large number of parameters makes it very easy

TABLE 12.6 Values of the parameters that give the lowest experimental execution time for different numbers of images and points, in *Saturno + Marte + Mercurio + Luna*

Images/Points	15	35	60	100
500	0.210 0.0823 *S* 1×(24+0)	0.190	0.456	1.66
5000	0.380	1.38 1.27 *MM* 1×(0+3)	3.49 1.85 *MM* 1×(0+3)	9.56 3.26 *M* 1×(0+3)
50,000	3.22 1.28 *M* 1×(0+3)	6.93 2.24 *M* 1×(0+3)	4.45	10.6
200,000	3.30 1.75 *M* 1×(0+3)	5.03	12.8	33.9

to fall into local minima and obtain values far from the optimum. We are investigating the application of some restarting local search or metaheuristic approaches [33–35].

12.4.2 Modeling the Linear Algebra Routines

In Fig. 12.4, we see that the preferred basic routine for solving the symmetric linear system depends on the problem size and on the number of cores in the computational system. The automatic selection of the preferred routine helps to reduce the execution time of MEATSS.

The sequential execution time of the routines considered has order $O(n^3)$, so terms in n^3, n^2, and n might appear in the theoretical model. For the parallel version, if h is the number of threads, the highest cost (n^3) should be divided by h, but the other terms should be multiplied by h. Thus, we consider the combinations $\{n^3, n^2, n, 1\} \times \{h, 1, 1/h\}$. However, for the term n^3 we consider only $\frac{n^3}{h}$. Nor are the lowest order terms ($n/h, h, 1, 1/h$) included in the model. The execution time is then modeled as

$$T(n, h) = k_1 \frac{n^3}{h} + k_2 n^2 h + k_3 n^2 + k_4 \frac{n^2}{h} + k_5 nh + k_6 n. \tag{12.1}$$

Thus, an adjustment based on a minimum square technique can be used to estimate the values of the coefficients k_i for a particular routine in a particular system. Figure 12.6 compares in *Saturno* the experimental and modeled execution time for matrix sizes 1536 (Fig. 12.6a) and 2560 (Fig. 12.6b). We can see that the estimation is satisfactory, especially for big matrix sizes, and so the theoretical model can be used to select the optimum routine and the number of MKL threads.

Two-level OpenMP + MKL parallelism can be used in such a way that the number of OpenMP and MKL threads changes during the execution to have all the cores (or the number of cores selected) working in the computation. The scheme in Algorithm 12.2 changes to that in Algorithm 12.3. On varying the number of MKL threads

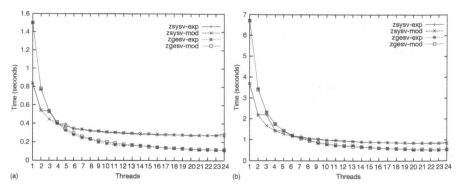

FIGURE 12.6   *Comparison of the modeled and experimental execution time of* `zsysv` *and* `zgevs, in Saturno. (a) Matrix size 1536. (b) Matrix size 2560.*

Algorithm 12.3

```
OpenMP+MKL MEATSS ADAPTIVE {
        inifrec=0
        finfrec=0
        nfres = f
        for ntmkl = 1 to cores
            if cores multiple of ntmkl
                ntomp = cores div ntmkl
                omp_set_num_threads(ntomp)
                mkl_set_num_threads(ntmkl)
                inifrec=finfrec+1
                finfrec = inifrec + nfres div ntomp * ntomp - 1
                #pragma omp parallel for private(i)
                for i = inifrec to finfrec
                    solvesystem(i)
                nfres = nfres- (finfrec - inifrec + 1)
}
```

($ntmkl$) from 1 to the number of cores, the maximum number of frequencies that can be equitably distributed between $ntomp = cores/ntmkl$ OpenMP threads is solved with $ntmkl$ MKL threads working in the solution of each system. The number of threads changes in successive steps, and the preferred MKL routine can be selected with an autotuning technique, which can be empirical or modeling based. Table 12.7 shows the frequencies computed at each step of the algorithm and the number of OpenMP and MKL threads and the routine selected, for a problem with medium complexity and 317 frequencies when the 128 cores of *Ben* are used.

12.5   CONCLUSIONS AND FUTURE RESEARCH

The combination of several parallelism paradigms allows the efficient solution of electromagnetic problems in today's computational systems, which are hybrid,

TABLE 12.7 Frequencies Computed at Each Step of Algorithm 12.3
and Number of OpenMP and MKL Threads and the Routine Selected,
for Medium Complexity and 317 Frequencies in *Ben*

Frequencies	*ntomp*	*ntmkl*	Routine
1–256	64	2	zsysv
257–288	32	4	zsysv
289–304	16	8	zgevs
305–312	8	16	zgevs
313–316	4	32	zgevs
317–317	1	128	zgevs

heterogeneous, and hierarchical. Significant improvements were reported for two problems related to integral equation formulations.

The calculation of Green's functions inside waveguides has been adapted for heterogeneous clusters with CPUs and GPUs with different speeds. The routines we have so far are homogeneous in the sense that the MPI processes receive approximately the same amount of data, and different numbers of OpenMP threads or CUDA kernels can be started inside each process depending on the relative speed of the different components in the system. It is also possible to develop heterogeneous routines or routines with a pool of tasks and a master–slave scheme, which may be preferable for a self-adaptation to the heterogeneity of the system.

For the solution of very large linear systems arising in VIE formulations, it will be necessary to extend the approach presented here by combining OpenMP and MKL parallelism to more levels of parallelism (MPI + OpenMP + GPU) with efficient use of the linear algebra routines (both multithread and multi-GPU) and out-of-core techniques. We are working in this direction to facilitate the solution of huge systems appearing in the study of the electromagnetic field in antennas [4, 36].

It has been shown that autotuning techniques can be incorporated into hybrid parallelism routines to solve computationally demanding electromagnetism problems, so non-parallelism experts can solve their problems efficiently in today hybrid, heterogeneous, and hierarchical computational systems. Empirical and modeling-based autotuning techniques have been shown for the two problems studied and in different computational systems, and satisfactory results obtained, but additional research is necessary to obtain better models for hybrid CPU + GPU parallelism and better installation techniques with which the installation time in current and future heterogeneous systems can be reduced.

ACKNOWLEDGMENTS

This work was supported by the COST Action IC0805 "Open European Network for High-Performance Computing on Complex Environments," the Spanish Ministry of Education through TIN2012-38341-C04-03 and TEC2010-21520-C04-04, and Feder funding. The authors gratefully acknowledge the Supercomputing Center of the Scientific Park of Murcia and the Barcelona Supercomputing Center, which have given access to their systems and provided assistance.

REFERENCES

1. U. Jakobus, I. Sulzer, and F. M. Landstorfer, "Parallel implementation of the hybrid MoM/Green's function technique on a cluster of workstations," in *IEE 10th International Conference on Antennas and Propagation*, Edinburgh, UK, pp. 182–185, 1997.
2. Y. Zhang, T. K. Sarkar, H. Moon, A. De, and M. C. Taylor, "Solution of large complex problems in computational electromagnetic using higher order basis in MoM with parallel solvers," in *IEEE Antennas and Propagation Society International Symposium*, Honolulu, Hawaii, pp. 5620–5623, 2007.
3. H. Guo, X. Xue, X. Wang, W. Tong, and W. Ni, "An implementation of parallel MLFMA on a cluster of computers with distributed memory," in *9th International Conference for Young Computer Scientists*, Hunan, China, pp. 1379–1383, 2008.
4. B. Kolundzija, M. Tasic, D. Olcan, D. Zoric, and S. Stevanetic, "Full-wave analysis of electrically large structures on desktop PCs," in *Computational Electromagnetics Workshop—CEM*, Izmir, Turkey, pp. 122–127, 2011.
5. A. Álvarez-Melcón, F. D. Quesada-Pereira, D. Giménez, C. Pérez-Alcaraz, T. Ramírez, and J.-G. Picón, "On the development and optimization of hybrid parallel codes for Integral Equation formulations," in *7th European Conference on Antennas and Propagation*, Gothenburg, Sweden, 2013.
6. F. Capolino, D. R. Wilton, and W. A. Johnson, "Efficient computation of the 2-D Green's function for 1-D periodic structures using the Ewald method," *IEEE Transactions on Antennas and Propagation*, vol. 53, no. 9, pp. 2977–2984, 2005.
7. F. J. Pérez, F. D. Quesada, D. Cañete, A. Álvarez, and J. R. Mosig, "A novel efficient technique for the calculation of the Green's functions in rectangular waveguides based on accelerated series decomposition," *IEEE Transactions on Antennas and Propagation*, vol. 56, no. 10, pp. 3260–3270, 2008.
8. C. Pérez-Alcaraz, D. Giménez, A. Álvarez-Melcón, and F. D. Quesada-Pereira, "Parallelizing the computation of Green functions for computational electromagnetism problems," in *26th IEEE International Parallel and Distributed Processing Symposium—Workshops*, Shanghai, China, pp. 1370–1377, 2012.
9. C. P. Vicente Quiles, F. Q. Pereira, J. S. G. Díaz, and M. Mattes, "New Investigations of RF Breakdown in Microwave Transmission Lines: Selection of Critical Structures," tech. rep., ASAT/ESA, Ref. AO/1-5086/06/NL/GLC, Valencia, Spain, 2007.
10. J.-G. Picón, "Optimización y paralelización del software para el cálculo de campos electromagnéticos MEATSS, (In Spanish)." End of studies project, Technical University of Valencia, September 2012.
11. W. C. Gibson, *The Method of Moments in Electromagnetics*. London: Chapman & Hall/CRC, 2008.
12. S. Jerez, J.-P. Montávez, and D. Giménez, "Optimizing the execution of a parallel meteorology simulation code," in *23rd IEEE International Parallel and Distributed Processing Symposium—Workshops*, Rome, Italy, 2009.
13. L. Seshagiri, M.-S. Wu, M. Sosonkina, Z. Zhang, M. S. Gordon, and M. W. Schmidt, "Enhancing adaptive middleware for quantum chemistry applications with a database framework," in *24th IEEE International Parallel and Distributed Processing Symposium—Workshops*, Atlanta, Georgia, 2010.

14. L.-G. Cutillas-Lozano, J.-M. Cutillas-Lozano, and D. Giménez, "Modeling shared-memory metaheuristic schemes for electricity consumption," in *Distributed Computing and Artificial Intelligence—9th International Conference*, Salamanca, Spain, pp. 33–40, 2012.

15. G. Bernabé, J. Cuenca, and D. Giménez, "Optimization techniques for 3D-FWT on systems with manycore GPUs and multicore CPUs," in *International Conference on Computational Science*, Barcelona, Spain, 2013.

16. M. Boratto, P. Alonso, D. Giménez, M. Barreto, and K. Oliveira, "Auto-tuning methodology to represent landform attributes on multicore and multi-GPU systems," in *International Workshop on Programming Models and Applications for Multicores and Manycores*, Shenzhen, China, pp. 125–132, 2013.

17. D. G. Duffy, *Green's Functions with Applications*, Studies in Advanced Mathematics, London: Chapman & Hall/CRC, 2001.

18. F. Capolino, D. R. Wilton, and W. A. Johnson, "Efficient computation of the 2-D Green's function for 1-D periodic layered structures using the Ewald method," in *IEEE Antennas and Propagation Society International Symposium*, San Antonio, Texas, pp. 194–197, 2002.

19. R. Chandra, R. Menon, L. Dagum, D. Kohr, D. Maydan, and J. McDonald, *Parallel Programming in OpenMP*. Burlington, Massachusets: Morgan Kauffman, 2001.

20. M. Snir and W. Gropp, *MPI. The Complete Reference*, Second ed.. Cambridge, Massachusets: The MIT Press, 1998.

21. J. Nickolls, I. Buck, M. Garland, and K. Skadron, "Scalable parallel programming with CUDA," *Queue*, vol. 6, no. 2, pp. 40–53, 2008.

22. J. Cuenca, L.-P. García, and D. Giménez, "Improving linear algebra computation on NUMA platforms through auto-tuned nested parallelism," in *20th Euromicro International Conference on Parallel, Distributed and Network-Based Processing*, Garching, Germany, pp. 66–73, 2012.

23. G. Golub and C. F. V. Loan, *Matrix Computations*. Baltimore, Maryland: The John Hopkins University Press, third ed., 1996.

24. J. Cámara, J. Cuenca, D. Giménez, and A. M. Vidal, "Empirical autotuning of two-level parallel linear algebra routines on large cc-NUMA systems," in *10th IEEE International Symposium on Parallel and Distributed Processing with Applications*, Leganés, Spain, pp. 843–844, 2012.

25. M. Frigo and S. G. Johnson, "FFTW: an adaptive software architecture for the FFT," *IEEE International Conference on Acoustics, Speech and Signal Processing*, vol. 3, pp. 1381–1384, 1998.

26. D. González, F. Almeida, L. Moreno, and C. Rodríguez, "Toward the automatic optimization mapping of pipeline algorithms," *Parallel Computing*, vol. 29, no. 2, pp. 241–254, 2003.

27. M. Püschel, J. M. F. Moura, B. Singer, J. Xiong, J. R. Johnson, D. A. Padua, M. M. Veloso, and R. W. Johnson, "Spiral: a generator for platform-adapted libraries of signal processing algorithms," *International Journal of High Performance Computing Applications*, vol. 18, no. 1, pp. 21–45, 2004.

28. R. C. Whaley, A. Petitet, and J. Dongarra, "Automated empirical optimizations of software and the ATLAS project," *Parallel Computing*, vol. 27, no. 1–2, pp. 3–35, 2001.

29. E.-J. Im, K. A. Yelick, and R. W. Vuduc, "Sparsity: optimization framework for sparse matrix kernels," *International Journal of High Performance Computing Applications*, vol. 18, no. 1, pp. 135–158, 2004.

30. S. Hunold and T. Rauber, "Automatic tuning of PDGEMM towards optimal performance," in *11th International Euro-Par Conference, Lisboa, Portugal, Lecture Notes in Computer Science*, vol. 3648, pp. 837–846, 2005.

31. J. Dongarra, G. Bosilca, Z. Chen, V. Eijkhout, G. E. Fagg, E. Fuentes, J. Langou, P. Luszczek, J. Pjesivac-Grbovic, K. Seymour, H. You, and S. S. Vadhiyar, "Self-adapting numerical software (SANS) effort," *IBM Journal of Research and Development*, vol. 50, no. 2–3, pp. 223–238, 2006.

32. T. Katagiri, K. Kise, H. Honda, and T. Yuba, "ABCLib_DRSSED: a parallel eigensolver with an auto-tuning facility," *Parallel Computing*, vol. 32, no. 3, pp. 231–250, 2006.

33. F. Glover and G. A. Kochenberger, *Handbook of Metaheuristics*. Boston, MA: Kluwer Academic Publishers, 2003.

34. J. Hromkovič, *Algorithmics for Hard Problems*. Heidelberg: Springer, second ed., 2003.

35. J. Dréo, A. Pétrowski, P. Siarry, and E. Taillard, *Metaheuristics for Hard Optimization*. Heidelberg: Springer, 2005.

36. B. Kolundzija, D. Olcan, D. Zoric, and S. Maric, "Accelerating WIPL-D numerical EM kernel by using graphics processing units," in *10th International Conference on Telecommunication in Modern Satellite Cable and Broadcasting Services (TELSIKS)*, Nis, Serbia, vol. 2, pp. 413–419, 2011.

PART V

CPU + GPU Coprocessing

13

Design and Optimization of Scientific Applications for Highly Heterogeneous and Hierarchical HPC Platforms Using Functional Computation Performance Models

David Clarke

University College Dublin, Dublin, Ireland

Aleksandar Ilic

Technical University of Lisbon, Lisbon, Portugal

Alexey Lastovetsky and Vladimir Rychkov

University College Dublin, Dublin, Ireland

Leonel Sousa

Technical University of Lisbon, Lisbon, Portugal

Ziming Zhong

University College Dublin, Dublin, Ireland

High-Performance Computing on Complex Environments, First Edition.
Edited by Emmanuel Jeannot and Julius Žilinskas.
© 2014 John Wiley & Sons, Inc. Published 2014 by John Wiley & Sons, Inc.

High-performance computing (HPC) platforms are getting increasingly heterogeneous and hierarchical. The main source of heterogeneity in many individual computing nodes is due to the utilization of specialized accelerators such as GPUs alongside general-purpose CPUs. Heterogeneous many-core processors will be another source of intra-node heterogeneity in the near future. As modern HPC clusters become more heterogeneous, due to increasing number of different processing devices, hierarchical approach needs to be taken with respect to memory and communication interconnects to reduce complexity. During recent years, many scientific codes have been ported to multicore and GPU architectures. To achieve optimum performance of these applications on CPU/GPU hybrid platforms, software heterogeneity needs to be accounted for. Therefore, the design and implementation of data-parallel scientific applications for such highly heterogeneous and hierarchical platforms represents a significant scientific and engineering challenge. This chapter presents the state of the art in the solution of this problem based on the functional performance models of computing devices and nodes.

13.1   INTRODUCTION

Highly heterogeneous and hierarchical high-performance computing (HPC) platforms, namely hardware-accelerated multicore clusters, are widely used in HPC because of better power efficiency and performance/price ratio. Introduction of multicores in HPC has resulted in significant refactoring of existing parallel applications. For general-purpose computing on graphics processing units (GPUs), new programming models, such as CUDA and OpenCL, have been proposed. A large number of algorithms and specific applications have been successfully ported to GPUs, delivering substantial speedup over their optimized CPU counterparts. Transition to hybrid CPU/GPU architectures is challenging in the aspects of efficient utilization of the heterogeneous hardware and reuse of the software stack. In existing programming and execution environments for hybrid platforms, such as OpenCL, StarPU [1], and CHPS [2], the problem of efficient cross-device data partitioning and load balancing still remains.

We target data-parallel scientific applications, such as linear algebra routines, digital signal processing, computational fluid dynamics, and so on. They are characterized by divisible computational workload, which is directly proportional to the size of data and dependent on data locality. Computation kernels optimized for multicore and GPU platforms are available for these applications. To execute such applications efficiently on hybrid multicore and multi-GPU platforms, the workload has to be distributed unevenly between highly heterogeneous computing devices. Our target architecture is a dedicated heterogeneous CPU/GPU cluster, characterized by a stable performance in time and a complex hierarchy of heterogeneous computing devices. We consider such platform as a distributed-memory system, and therefore apply data partitioning, a load-balancing method widely used on distributed-memory supercomputers.

Data partitioning algorithms, including those already proposed for hybrid platforms, rely on performance models of processors. In [3], *a priori* found constants, representing the sustained performance of the application on CPU/GPU, were used to partition data. In [4], a similar constant performance model (CPM) was proposed, but it was built adaptively, using the history of performance measurements. The fundamental assumption of the data partitioning algorithms based on CPMs is that the absolute speed of processors/devices does not depend on the size of a computational task. However, it becomes less accurate when (i) the partitioning of the problem results in some tasks fitting into different levels of memory hierarchy, or (ii) processors/devices switch between different codes to solve the same computational problem.

An analytical predictive model was proposed in [5]. In contrast to others, this model is application-specific: the number of parameters and the predictive formulas for the execution time of processors/devices are defined for each application. This approach requires a detailed knowledge of the computational algorithm, in order to provide an accurate prediction. In [5], it was also acknowledged that the linear models might not fit the actual performance in the case of resource contention and, therefore, data partitioning algorithms might fail to balance the load.

In the work presented in this chapter, we apply data partitioning based on functional performance models (FPMs), which was originally designed and proved to be accurate for heterogeneous clusters of uniprocessor machines [6]. The FPM represents the processor speed as a function of the problem size. It is built empirically and integrates many important features characterizing the performance of both the architecture and the application. This model can be used with any data-parallel application and is applicable in the situations (i) and (ii). In this chapter, we target CPU/GPU clusters, which consist of heterogeneous devices with separate memory and different programming models. Here we extend the FPM, originally designed for uniprocessors, to these platforms, and demonstrate how to design and optimize parallel scientific applications using FPM-based data partitioning.

Although hardware accelerators are significantly faster than traditional multicores, the computing power of the mulitcores should not be ignored. To obtain maximum performance from a parallel scientific application on an accelerated heterogeneous platform, the workload needs to be distributed over the hierarchy of the devices. Evaluation of device performance is complicated by resource contention and device-specific limitations (e.g., limited GPU memory). Furthermore, multiple computation kernels optimized for different devices and based on different programming models need to be used simultaneously.

In previous work [7], we proposed a method for building FPMs of multicore nodes, which took into account resource contention. The FPMs built this way were used for inter-node data partitioning. In this chapter, we present how to apply this approach to a hierarchical system that consists of several multicore sockets coupled with GPUs.

A GPU is controlled by a host process that handles data transfer between the host and device, and instructs the GPU to execute kernels. In this work, we measure the speed of the host process and build the performance model for the GPU coupled with its dedicated core, which includes the contributions from the kernel running on GPU and from the memory transfers. In general, this model can be defined only for the range of problem sizes that fit the local memory of the GPU. It can be extended to infinity for out-of-core applications, which can handle a large amount of data stored in low-speed memory [8].

FPMs are hardware- and application-specific and are built by empirically bench-marking the kernel. Building accurate models for the full range of problem sizes is expensive. This approach is not suitable for applications that will be run for a small number of times on a given platform, for example, in grid environments, where different processors are assigned for different runs of the application. Such applications should be able to optimally distribute computations between the processors of the executing platform assuming that this platform is different and *a priori* unknown for each run of the application. In [9], we proposed an algorithm that efficiently builds only the necessary parts of the speed functions (partial FPMs) to the required level of accuracy in order to achieve load balancing. In this chapter, we present an adaptation of this algorithm to hierarchical platforms [10].

In order to demonstrate how to design and optimize scientific applications for highly heterogeneous and hierarchical HPC platforms using functional computation performance models, we modify the parallel matrix multiplication to be used with FPM-based data partitioning. We show how to extract and benchmark the computation kernel of the application on different devices. The kernel will call the hardware-specific optimized code for each device (BLAS GEMM). We design a hierarchical data partitioning scheme that allows nested parallelism, and apply FPM-based data partitioning algorithms. This method was developed as a collaborative effort between the University College Dublin (Ireland) and the Technical University of Lisbon (Portugal), funded by the Complex HPC COST action IC0805.

This chapter is structured as follows: In Section 13.2, we review related work and conclude that data partitioning algorithms are more suited for balancing data-parallel scientific applications on heterogeneous platforms, but they may fail on highly heterogeneous hierarchical platforms if simplistic performance models are used. However, data partitioning based on the FPM, described in Section 13.3, can be applied successfully on such platforms. The main contribution of work described in this chapter is the adaptation of the FPM-based data partitioning to hybrid CPU/GPU nodes and clusters. We demonstrate how to design a scientific application to make use of FPM-based data partitioning on a heterogeneous hierarchical platform. More specifically, we use the well-known parallel matrix multiplication application, which is presented in Section 13.4. Building performance models for such an application on heterogeneous devices is challenging. In Sections 13.5–13.7, we present a solution for a hybrid multi-CPU/GPU node. Building full FPMs can be expensive, and hierarchical platforms add extra complexity to this, thereby prohibiting the use of full models. Fortunately, we have developed an efficient method that builds the models to a sufficient level of accuracy in the relevant range of problem sizes (partial FPM) as summarized in Section 13.8. Partial FPMs were originally designed for heterogeneous uniprocessors; another contribution of this chapter is the application of partial FPMs to hierarchical platforms. In Section 13.9, we design a hierarchical version of the matrix multiplication application for hybrid clusters. In this application, we use hierarchical data partitioning scheme and partial FPMs of devices and nodes.

13.2 RELATED WORK

In this section, we review a number of algorithms for load-balancing parallel scientific and engineering problems on heterogeneous platforms. The older algorithms referenced were designed for either heterogeneous networks of workstations or shared-memory supercomputers. The newer algorithms target hybrid CPU/GPU platforms.

Static algorithms, for example, those based on data partitioning [3, 5, 6, 11], use *a priori* information about the parallel application and platform. This information can be gathered either at compile time or at runtime. Static algorithms are also known as *predicting-the-future algorithms* because they rely on accurate performance models as input to predict the future execution of the application. Static algorithms are particularly useful for applications where data locality is important because they do not require data redistribution. However, these algorithms are unable to balance on nondedicated platforms, where load changes with time, and for applications with nondeterministic workload. *Dynamic* algorithms, such as task queue scheduling and work stealing [12–17], balance the load by moving fine-grained tasks between processors during the calculation. Dynamic algorithms do not require *a priori* information about execution but may incur significant communication overhead on distributed-memory platforms due to data migration. Dynamic algorithms often use static data partitioning for their initial step to minimize the amount of data redistributions needed. For example, in the state-of-the-art load-balancing techniques for multinode, multicore, and multi-GPU platforms, the performance gain is mainly due to better initial data partitioning. It was shown that even the static distribution based on simplistic performance models (single values specifying the maximum performance of a dominant computational kernel on CPUs and GPUs) improves the performance of traditional dynamic scheduling techniques by up to 250% [18].

In this chapter, we focus on parallel scientific applications where computational workload is directly proportional to the size of data and dependent on data locality. The general scheme of such applications can be summarized as follows: (i) all data is partitioned over the processors, (ii) some independent calculations are carried out in parallel, and (iii) some data synchronization takes place. Our target architecture is a dedicated heterogeneous distributed-memory HPC platform, such as heterogeneous clusters, interconnected clusters, and multicores with GPU and FPGA accelerators. These HPC platforms have the following features: (i) the performance of the application is stable in time and is not affected by varying system load; (ii) there is a significant overhead associated with data migration between computing devices; (iii) optimized architecture-specific libraries implementing the same kernels may be available for different computing devices. On these platforms, for most scientific applications, static load-balancing algorithms outperform dynamic ones because they do not involve data migration. Therefore, for this type of applications, we find that centralized static algorithms, such as data partitioning, are the most appropriate.

Most of the state-of-the-art data partitioning algorithms [3, 4, 11, 19–22] make the assumption that the speed of a process does not change with problem size, and hence are based on CPMs. In [4], the authors make redistribution decisions based on the average of recorded times of the previous iterations. In [3], the authors acknowledge performance changes with problem size, but for their partitioning calculations they use single-value sustained performance of computational kernel on devices. In [11], a linear model of time is used, which is equivalent to a constant speed.

The fundamental assumption of the conventional CPM-based algorithms is that the absolute speed of the processors does not depend on the size of the computational task. This assumption is typically satisfied when medium-sized scientific problems are solved on a heterogeneous network of workstations. However, it becomes much less accurate in the following situations: (i) the partitioning of the problem results in some tasks either not fitting into the available memory of the assigned device and hence causing out-of-core computations or fully fitting into faster levels of its memory hierarchy; (ii) some processing devices involved in computations are not traditional general-purpose processors (say, accelerators such as GPUs or specialized cores). In this case, the relative speed of a traditional processor and a nontraditional one may differ for two different sizes of the same computational task even if both sizes fully fit into the available memory; and (iii) different devices use different codes to solve the same problem locally.

The above situations become more and more common in modern and especially perspective high-performance heterogeneous platforms. As a result, the applicability of the traditional CPM-based distribution algorithms becomes more restricted. Indeed, if we consider two really heterogeneous processing devices P_i and P_j, then the more different they are, the smaller will be the range R_{ij} of sizes of the computational task where their relative speeds can be accurately approximated by constants. In the case of several different heterogeneous processing devices, the range of sizes where CPM-based algorithms can be applied will be given by the intersection of these pairwise ranges, $\cap_{i,j=1}^{p} R_{ij}$. Therefore, if an HPC platform includes even a few significantly heterogeneous processing devices, the area of applicability of CPM-based algorithms may become quite small or even empty. For such platforms, new algorithms are needed that would be able to optimally distribute computations between processing devices for the full range of problem sizes.

The FPM has proven to be more realistic than the CPM, because it integrates many important features, such as the hardware and software heterogeneity, the heterogeneity of memory structure, the effects of paging, and so on [6]. FPMs can be used for data partitioning between devices within a CPU/GPU node [8]; we present how this can be done in Section 13.7. Moreover, we also proposed several FPM-based load-balancing approaches for multicore CPU and multi-GPU environments, which are capable of exploiting the system's capabilities at multiple levels of parallel execution [23, 24]. For a cluster of hybrid nodes, hierarchical partitioning can be advantageous because it works well in scheduling divisible workload. For example, hierarchical scheduling was shown to be efficient for load balancing on homogeneous [25] and heterogeneous [12] hybrid clusters. In this chapter, we will demonstrate how FPMs can be used for hierarchical data partitioning.

13.3 DATA PARTITIONING BASED ON FUNCTIONAL PERFORMANCE MODEL

The FPM [6] is application- and hardware-specific. It is associated with a process executing the application on the particular piece of hardware. Under the FPM, the speed of each process is represented by a continuous function of the problem size. The speed is defined as the number of computation units performed by the process per second. The *computation unit* is the smallest amount of work that can be given to a process. All units require exactly the same number of arithmetic calculations and have the same input and output data storage requirements. The computation unit can be defined differently for different applications. The compute time for a fixed amount of computation units on a given process must remain constant.

Performance models consist of a series of speed measurements taken over a range of problem sizes. The speed is found experimentally by measuring the execution time. This can be done by benchmarking the full application for each problem size. However, since computationally intensive applications often perform the same core computation multiple times in a loop, a benchmark made of one such core computation will be representative of the performance of the whole application. We call this *core computation*, which performs much less computations but is still representative of the application, a *kernel*. If the nature of the application allows, FPMs can be built more efficiently by only benchmarking the kernel.

The problem of data partitioning using FPMs was formulated in [6] as follows: A total problem size n is given as the number of computation units to be distributed between p ($p < n$) processes $P_1, \ldots, P_p$. The speed of each process is represented by a positive continuous function of the problem size $s_1(x), \ldots, s_p(x) : s_i(x) = x/t_i(x)$, where $t_i(x)$ is the execution time of processing x units on the processor i. Speed functions are defined at $[0, n]$. The output of the algorithm is a distribution of the computation units, $d_1, \ldots, d_p$, so that $d_1 + d_2 + \cdots + d_p = n$. Load balancing is achieved when all processors execute their work at the same time, that

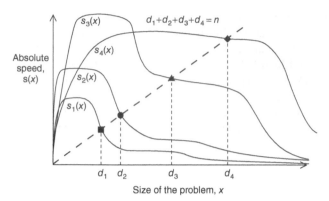

FIGURE 13.1 *Optimal data distribution. The number of computation units is geometrically proportional to the speeds of the processors.*

is, $t_1(d_1) \approx t_2(d_2) \approx \cdots \approx t_p(d_p)$. This can be expressed as

$$
\begin{cases}
\dfrac{d_1}{s_1(d_1)} \approx \dfrac{d_2}{s_2(d_2)} \approx \cdots \approx \dfrac{d_p}{s_p(d_p)}, \\[2mm]
d_1 + d_2 + \cdots + d_p = n.
\end{cases} \tag{13.1}
$$

The solution of these equations, $d_1, \ldots, d_p$, can be represented geometrically by the intersection of the speed functions with a line passing through the origin of the coordinate system. This is illustrated in Fig. 13.1 for $p = 4$.

The geometrical algorithm solving this data partitioning problem was proposed in [6] and can be summarized as follows: Any line passing through the origin and intersecting the speed functions represents an optimum distribution for a particular problem size. Therefore, the space of solutions of the data-partitioning problem consists of all such lines. The two outer bounds of the solution space are selected as the starting point of the algorithm. The upper line U represents the optimal data distribution $d_1^u, \ldots, d_p^u$ for some problem size $n_u < n$, $n_u = d_1^u + \cdots + d_p^u$, while the lower line L gives the solution $d_1^l, \ldots, d_p^l$ for $n_l > n$, $n_l = d_1^l + \cdots + d_p^l$. The region between two lines is iteratively bisected by new lines B_k. At iteration k, the problem size corresponding to the new line intersecting the speed functions at the points $d_1^k, \ldots, d_p^k$ is calculated as $n_k = d_1^k + \cdots + d_p^k$. Depending on whether n_k is less than or greater than n, this line becomes a new upper or lower bound. By making n_k close to n, this algorithm finds the optimal partition of the given problem $d_1, \ldots, d_p$: $d_1 + \cdots + d_p = n$. Figure 13.2 illustrates the work of the bisection algorithm. Correctness proof and complexity analysis of this algorithm are presented in [6].

In the following section, we present a typical computationally intensive parallel application, and define its computation unit and kernel.

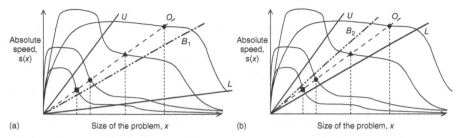

FIGURE 13.2 *Two steps of the iterative geometrical data partitioning algorithm. The dashed line O represents the optimal solution. (a) Upper U and lower L represent the outer bounds of the solution space. Line (B_1) represents the first bisection. (b) Line B_1 becomes L. Solution space is bisected by line B_2, which, at the next step, will become U. Through this method, the partitioner converges on the solution.*

13.4 EXAMPLE APPLICATION: HETEROGENEOUS PARALLEL MATRIX MULTIPLICATION

In this section, we describe a column-based heterogeneous modification [26] of the two-dimensional (2D) blocked matrix multiplication [27]. It will be used in subsequent sections to demonstrate how to design parallel scientific applications for heterogeneous hierarchical platforms, using the proposed data partitioning algorithms.

Parallelism in this application is achieved by slicing the matrices, with a one-to-one mapping between slices and processes. For efficiency and scalability, the application uses 2D slicing of the matrices. The general solution for finding the optimum matrix partitioning for a set of heterogeneous processors has been shown to be NP-complete [20]. By applying a column-based matrix partitioning restriction, an algorithm with polynomial complexity can be used to find optimum partitioning [28]. In this algorithm, each process is responsible for calculations associated with a rectangular submatrix. These rectangles are arranged into columns, and the area of the rectangles is proportional to the speed of the device upon which the process is running (Fig. 13.3a). A communication minimizing algorithm [20] uses this column-based partitioning and finds the shape and ordering of these rectangles such that the total volume of communication for parallel matrix multiplication is minimized.

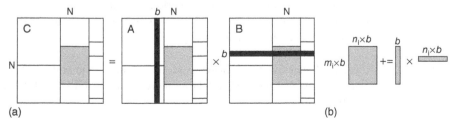

FIGURE 13.3 *Heterogeneous parallel column-based matrix multiplication. (a) One step of the algorithm. (b) Computational kernel.*

The application performs the matrix multiplication $C = A \times B$. Without loss of generality, we will work with square $N \times N$ matrices and we assume that N is a multiple of the blocking factor b. Dense matrices A, B, and C are partitioned into p submatrices A_i, B_i, C_i, each of height bm_i and width bn_i, where p is the number of processes, and m_i and n_i are the height and width of submatrices in blocks (Fig. 13.3b). The application consists of N/b iterations, with a column of blocks (the pivot column) of matrix A being communicated horizontally, and a row of blocks (the pivot row) of matrix B being communicated vertically. The pivot column and row move horizontally and vertically, respectively, with each iteration. If process i, with submatrix A_i, forms part of the pivot column, then it will send its part of the pivot column horizontally. If process i with submatrix B_i forms part of the pivot row, then it will send its part of the pivot row vertically. At each iteration, all processes will receive into a buffer $A_{(b)}$ of size $bm_i \times b$ and $B_{(b)}$ of size $b \times bn_i$. Then the following GEMM operation is performed by all processes in parallel: $C_i = C_i + A_{(b)} \times B_{(b)}$. This forms the computation kernel of the application.

For this kernel, we define the computation unit as an update of a $b \times b$ block of C_i. The amount of computations to update the whole ith rectangle is equal to its area measured in these units $d_i = m_i \times n_i$. The communication minimizing algorithm [20] arranges the processes into columns and sets the rectangles' dimensions (m_i, n_i) using the optimal areas of the rectangles $d_1, \ldots, d_p$ provided as input. The computational kernel is representative of the execution of one iteration of the application on a given processor while being independent of the performance of the processors neighbors.

While porting this application to hierarchical multicore multi-GPU platforms, we face the following challenges:

- On a hybrid node, parallel processes interfere with each other because of sharing resources. The speed of individual devices cannot be measured independently. However, the devices can be divided into groups so that there is no significant interference between the groups. The FPM of a group of devices can be defined. For example, on a multisocket node, a model of a socket can be built instead of the models of individual CPU cores.
- Interactions between CPUs and GPUs include data transfers between the host and GPU over PCI Express, launching of GPU kernels, and other operations. The effect on performance by these interactions is included in the FPM by designing an appropriate kernel for benchmarking.
- In order to achieve load balancing between hybrid nodes, the partitioning algorithm has to account for the hierarchy of processing devices and, hence, FPMs need to be defined for each level of hierarchy.

We address these challenges in the following sections and demonstrate how to use FPM-based data partitioning on hierarchical multicore and multi-GPU platforms, using the example application.

13.5 PERFORMANCE MEASUREMENT ON CPUS/GPUS SYSTEM

Here we apply the approach proposed in previous work [7] to measure the performance of multiple cores in a system by taking into account the resource contention between parallel processes. Each GPU is assumed to be controlled by a dedicated CPU core, which instructs the kernel execution on the GPU and handles the data transfers between them; therefore, we measure the combined performance of the GPU with its dedicated core, which includes the contributions from the kernel running on GPU and the memory transfers.

Our experimental system is a hybrid multicore and multi-GPU node of NUMA architecture, consisting of four sockets of six-core AMD processors with 16 GB memory each and accelerated by two different GPUs (Table 13.1). We used the GEMM kernel from ACML and CUBLAS for CPU and GPU, respectively.

Our approach to performance measurement on heterogeneous multicore and multi-GPU system can be summarized as follows. (i) Since automatic rearranging of the processes provided by the operating system may result in performance degradation, processes are bound to cores. (ii) Processes are synchronized to minimize the idle computational cycles, aiming at the highest floating point rate for the application. Synchronization also ensures that the resources will be shared between the maximum number of processes, generating the highest memory traffic. (iii) To ensure the reliability of the measurement, experiments are repeated multiple times until the results are statistically reliable.

First, we measured the execution time of the kernel on a single core and multiple CPU cores. We observed that the speed of a core depended on the number of cores executing the kernel on the same socket, because they compete for shared resources. However, the performance of the core was not affected by the execution of the kernel on other sockets, because of the NUMA architecture and a large memory. Therefore, we could accurately measure the time and, hence, the speed of a socket executing the same kernel simultaneously on its cores. This approach realistically reflects the performance of parallel applications designed for multicores.

Next, we experimented with the kernel on a GPU, with one core being dedicated to the GPU and other cores on the same socket being idle. Since the kernel does not provide data transfer between the host and device, we implemented sending/receiving

TABLE 13.1 Specifications of the Hybrid System *ig.icl.utk.edu*

	CPU (AMD)	GPUs (NVIDIA)	
		GF GTX680	Tesla C870
Architecture	Opteron 8439SE	GF GTX680	Tesla C870
Core clock	2.8 GHz	1006 MHz	600 MHz
Number of cores	4 × 6 cores	1536 cores	128 cores
Memory size	4 × 16 GB	2048 MB	1536 MB
Mem. bandwidth		192.3 GB/s	76.8 GB/s

of matrices and measured the combined execution time on the dedicated core. Communication operations with GPU take a large proportion of the whole execution time for most applications [29]; therefore, the time measured this way realistically reflects the performance of the kernel. This approach allows us to measure the speed of a single GPU.

Finally, we simultaneously executed the GEMM kernels on both a GPU and the cores located on the same socket. The cores, except for the one dedicated to the GPU, executed the ACML kernel. The dedicated core and the GPU executed the CUBLAS kernel. The amounts of work given to the CPUs and the GPU were proportional to their speeds obtained from the previous experiments for a single core and for a single GPU. This may not be a very accurate distribution of workload but is realistic, which reflects the hybrid parallel applications. We measured the execution time on all cores and observed that the performance of the GPU dropped by 7–15% because of resource contention, while the CPU cores were not so much affected by the GPU process. In this experiment, we exploited the distributed-memory feature of the hybrid architecture. That is, having received the data from the host memory, the GPU performed the computations in its local memory, and the dedicated core did not compete with other cores for resources. This observation allows us to measure the speed of multiple cores and GPUs independently with some accuracy.

13.6 FUNCTIONAL PERFORMANCE MODELS OF MULTIPLE CORES AND GPUS

We build the FPMs of the parallel matrix multiplication application described in Section 13.4 for multiple cores and GPUs, respectively, using the representative computational kernel of the application. Since the speed of the kernel for a given matrix area x does not vary with the nearly square shapes of submatrices [26], we build the speed functions by timing the kernel with the submatrices of size $\sqrt{x} \times \sqrt{x}$.

Speed Functions of Multiple Cores: $s_c(x)$. These functions approximate the speed of a socket executing the ACML kernels simultaneously on c cores, with the problem size (matrix area) x/c on each core.

Speed Functions of GPUs: $g_1(x), g_2(x)$. Each function approximates the combined performance of a GPU and its dedicated core, while the GPU executing the CUBLAS kernel, with the problem size (matrix area) x.

Figure 13.4a shows the FPMs of a socket, $s_5(x)$ and $s_6(x)$, executing the ACML kernel on five and six cores simultaneously. The maximum performance of the socket is observed when all cores are involved in computations. It does not increase linearly with the number of active cores, because of resource contention. Additionally, the performance depends on the blocking factor b, an application parameter. To exploit optimizations implemented in the ACML kernel, which take into account memory hierarchy of a multicore architecture, we experimented with $b = 640$.

In Fig. 13.4b, the speed functions built for different modifications of the kernel on GeForce GTX680 are presented. The speed was measured on a dedicated core, while other cores stayed idle. In version 1, the pivot column $A_{(b)}$ and row $B_{(b)}$ and the

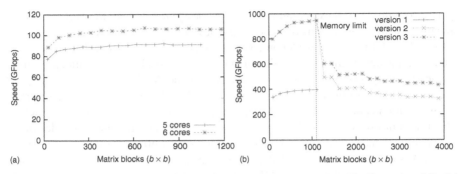

FIGURE 13.4 *(a) Speed functions of a socket, $s_5(x)$ and $s_6(x)$, with blocking factor $b = 640$. (b) Speed functions of GeForce GTX680 ($b = 640$) built for kernels accumulating the intermediate results in the host memory (version 1); in device memory with out-of-core extension (versions 2); with overlapping of communications and computations (version 3).*

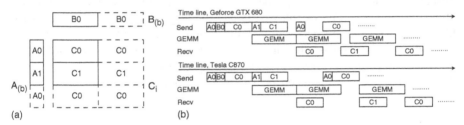

FIGURE 13.5 *(a) Out-of-core implementation of the kernel on GPU. (b) Concurrent data transfers and kernel executions on GPUs.*

submatrix C_i are stored in the host memory. Before the execution of GEMM on the device, the pivot column and row are transferred to the device. After the execution, the updated submatrix is transferred back from the device. Therefore, the speed of the first version includes all transfers between the host and device memory.

In the application, the kernel is executed multiple times with different pivot columns and rows, updating the same submatrix C_i. Therefore, the submatrix can be stored in the device memory, accumulating the intermediate results. The transfer of C_i can be excluded from the kernel and from the speed measurements. In *version 2*, submatrix C_i is stored and intermediate results are accumulated in the device until the device memory is exceeded. As shown in Fig. 13.4b, the performance doubles when problem sizes fit in the GPU memory. After that, it splits the pivot column $A_{(b)}$ and row $B_{(b)}$ and the submatrix C_i into rectangles that fit the device memory and performs the CUBLAS GEMM multiple times to update these rectangles serially (Fig. 13.5a). This implementation requires multiple transfers of the rectangles of the submatrix C_i to and from the device memory, which explains the performance drop in the range of large problem sizes.

In *version 3*, which is another out-of-core implementation of the kernel, we use the concurrency feature of NVIDIA GPUs on top of version 2. This feature enables us to perform multiple CUDA operations simultaneously and, hence, to overlap communications with computations on the host and device. In addition, modern generations of NVIDIA GPUs, such as GeForce GTX680, support concurrent data transfers to and from the device memory. As shown in Fig. 13.5a, five buffers are allocated in the device memory, using its maximum capacity: A0 and A1 for rectangles of the pivot column $A_{(b)}$; B0 for the pivot row $B_{(b)}$; and C0 and C1 for the submatrix C_i. Overlapping communications and computations in the out-of-core version of the kernel are illustrated in Fig. 13.5b. In the beginning of each column, the first rectangles of the pivot column and row and the submatrix are sent to the buffers A0, B0, and C0. While GEMM is executed with these buffers, the next rectangles of the pivot column and the submatrix are sent to A1 and C1. Next, three operations are overlapped. (i) The rectangle of the submatrix updated during the previous execution of GEMM is transferred from C0 to the host memory. (ii) GEMM is executed with the new rectangles of the pivot column and the submatrix, using the buffers A1, B0, and C1. (iii) The next rectangles of the pivot column and the submatrix are sent to A0 and C0. On the Tesla C870, which supports only one DMA engine, the latter operation is performed after (i) is complete (Fig. 13.5b). We can see from Fig. 13.4b that the performance of GeForce GTX680 improves by around 30% when using overlapping. Based on our experiments, the speed function shapes of Tesla C870 are similar to those of GeForce GTX680. However, there is less performance improvement from overlapping because Tesla C870 does not support concurrent data transfers.

13.7 FPM-BASED DATA PARTITIONING ON CPUS/GPUS SYSTEM

Table 13.2 shows the execution time of the heterogeneous matrix multiplication application [26] measured on different configurations of the hybrid system. The experiments were performed for square matrices with blocking factor $b = 640$. The first column shows the matrix size $n \times n$ in square blocks of 640×640. Column 2 shows the application execution time for the homogeneous matrix distribution between 24 CPU cores. Column 3 shows the execution time on GeForce GTX680 and a dedicated core. The last column shows the execution time for the heterogeneous matrix distribution between 22 CPU cores and 2 GPUs, with the remaining 2 CPU cores being dedicated to GPUs. The distribution was obtained from the FPM-based data partitioning algorithm with the speed functions of two GPUs, $g_1(x)$, $g_2(x)$, two sockets with five active cores, $2 \times s_5(x)$, and two sockets with six active cores, $2 \times s_6(x)$. GeForce GTX680 outperforms 24 CPU cores when the problem fits in the device memory. When the problem exceeds the device memory, CPUs perform better. FPMs capture these variations and, therefore, the FPM-based data partitioning algorithm successfully distributes computations for all problem sizes, and the application delivers high performance.

   In this section, we presented how to model performance of devices and how to use these models to find the optimal data partitioning within a node. On hardware-accelerated multicore clusters, there is a two-level hierarchy consisting of nodes and devices. To enable FPM-based data partitioning in this case, we need to

TABLE 13.2 Execution Time of Parallel Matrix Multiplication

Matrix (blks)	CPUs (s)	GTX680 (s)	Hybrid-FPM (s)
40 × 40	99.5	74.2	26.6
50 × 50	195.4	162.7	77.8
60 × 60	300.1	316.8	114.4
70 × 70	491.6	554.8	226.1

introduce the model of a node. This model has to represent the optimal performance of the node, which is achieved by balancing the load between its internal devices. For each point in the node model, it is necessary to build the models of devices and perform data partitioning. Hence, the cost of building the node model may be prohibitively high.

One method of building the FPMs efficiently is to estimate them at runtime, only in some region, with a sufficient degree of accuracy [9]. We refer to these estimates as the *partial FPMs*. In the following section, we give a brief description of this method, which was originally designed for heterogeneous uniprocessor clusters of workstations. Then, in Section 13.9, we use the partial models to reduce the cost of building the two-level hierarchical models. We redesign the example application to use hierarchical data partitioning based on partial models of devices and nodes.

13.8 EFFICIENT BUILDING OF FUNCTIONAL PERFORMANCE MODELS

FPMs are hardware- and application-specific and are built empirically by benchmarking the kernel for a range of problem sizes. The accuracy of the model depends on the number of experimental points used to build it. Despite the kernel being lightweight, building the full model can be very expensive. The applicability of FPMs built for the full range of problem sizes is limited to parallel applications executed many times on stable-in-time heterogeneous platforms. In this case, the time of construction of the full FPMs can become very small compared to the accumulated performance gains during the multiple executions of the optimized application. However, this approach is not suitable for applications that will be run a small number of times on a given platform, for example, in grid environments, where different processors are assigned for different runs of the application, or in hierarchical platforms, where the performance of a node depends not only on the workload assigned to the node but also on the distribution of this workload between the processing devices on the node. Such applications should be able to optimally distribute computations between the processors of the executing platform assuming that this platform is different and *a priori* unknown for each run of the application.

Partial estimates of the full speed functions can be built dynamically at application runtime to a sufficient level of accuracy to achieve load balancing [9, 30]. We refer to these approximations as partial FPMs. The partial FPMs are based on a few points connected by linear segments and estimate the real functions in detail only in the relevant regions: $\bar{s}_i(x) \approx s_i(x)$, $1 \leq i \leq p$, $\forall x \in [a, b]$. Both the partial models and the regions are determined at runtime.

The algorithm to build the partial FPMs is iterative and alternates between (i) benchmarking the kernel on each process for a given distribution of workload and (ii) repartitioning the data. At each iteration, the current distribution $d_1, \ldots, d_p$ is updated, converging to the optimum, while the partial models $\bar{s}_1(x), \ldots, \bar{s}_p(x)$ become more detailed. Initially, the workload is distributed evenly between all processes. Then the algorithm iterates as follows:

1. The time to execute the kernel for the current distribution is measured on each process. If the difference between timings is less than some ε, the current distribution solves the load-balancing problem and the algorithm stops.
2. The speeds are calculated from the execution times, and the points (d_i, s_i) are added to the corresponding partial models $\bar{s}_i(x)$ (Figs 13.6b, d, f).
3. Using the current partial estimates of the speed functions, the FPM-based partitioning algorithm calculates a new distribution (Figs 13.6a, c, e).

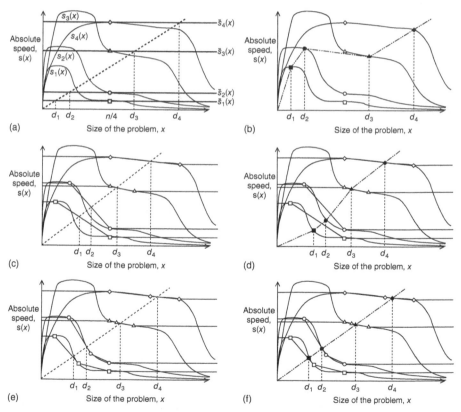

FIGURE 13.6 *Steps of the partial FPM-based data partitioning algorithm illustrated using four heterogeneous processors.*

This algorithm allows efficient load balancing and is suitable for use in self-adaptable applications, which run without *a priori* information about the heterogeneous platform. In the next section, we use the partial FPMs for data partitioning on hierarchical platforms.

13.9 FPM-BASED DATA PARTITIONING ON HIERARCHICAL PLATFORMS

In this section, our target platform is a two-level hierarchical heterogeneous cluster of CPU/GPU compute nodes. This distributed platform can be described as having q nodes, $Q_1, \dots, Q_q$, where a node Q_i has p_i devices, $P_{i1}, \dots, P_{ip_i}$. The problem to be solved by this algorithm is to partition a matrix between these nodes and devices with respect to the performance of each of these processing elements. The hierarchical partitioning algorithm is iterative and converges toward an optimum distribution that balances the workload. It consists of two iterative algorithms, *internode partitioning algorithm* (INPA) and *interdevice partitioning algorithm* (IDPA). The IDPA algorithm is nested inside the INPA algorithm [10].

As a demonstration of how to optimize scientific applications on the target platform, we take the heterogeneous parallel matrix multiplication application described in Section 13.4 and make the following modifications. Since the platform has two levels of hierarchy, we create a two-level partitioning scheme. The matrix is partitioned between the nodes (Fig. 13.7a) and then subpartitioned between the devices within each node (Fig. 13.7b). This gives the application nested parallelism.

There is a total of W computation units to be distributed, where $W = (N/b) \times (N/b)$. The INPA partitions the total matrix into q submatrices to be processed on each heterogeneous computing node. The submatrix owned by node Q_i has an area equal to $w_i \times b \times b$, where $w_1 + \cdots + w_q = W$. The functional performance model partitioning algorithm (FPM-PA), from Section 13.3, uses experimentally built speed functions to calculate a load-balanced distribution $w_1, \dots, w_q$. The shape and ordering of these submatrices is calculated by the *communication minimizing algorithm* (CMA) [20]. The CMA uses column-based 2D arrangement of nodes and outputs the heights bm_i and widths bn_i for each of the q nodes, such that $m_i \times n_i = w_i$, $bm = b \times m$, and $bn = b \times n$ (Fig. 13.8a). This 2D partitioning algorithm uses a column-based arrangement of processors. The values of m_i and n_i are chosen such that the column widths sum up to N and the heights of submatrices in a column sum to N.

The IDPA iteratively measures, on each device, the time of execution of the application-specific core computational kernel with a given size while converging to a load-balanced interdevice partitioning. It returns the kernel execution time of the last iteration to the INPA. IDPA calls the FPM-PA to partition the submatrix owned by Q_i into vertical slices of width d_{ij}, such that $d_{i1} + \cdots + d_{ip} = bn_i$ (Fig. 13.8b) to be processed on each device within the node. Device P_{ij} will be responsible for doing matrix operations on $bm_i \times d_{ij}$ matrix elements.

We now present an outline of a parallel application using the proposed hierarchical partitioning algorithm. The partitioning is executed immediately before execution

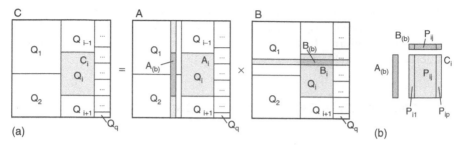

FIGURE 13.7   *Parallel matrix multiplication algorithm. (a) Two-dimensional blocked matrix multiplication between the nodes. (b) One-dimensional matrix multiplication within a node.*

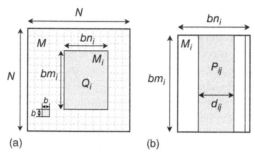

FIGURE 13.8   *Two-level matrix partitioning scheme. (a) Two-dimensional partitioning between the nodes. (b) One-dimensional partitioning between devices in a node.*

of the parallel algorithm. The outline is followed by a detailed description of the individual algorithms.

INPA $\left(\text{IN: } N, b, q, p_1, \ldots, p_q \text{ OUT: } \{m_i, n_i, d_{i1}, \ldots, d_{ip}\}_{i=1}^q\right)$ {

    WHILE inter-node imbalance

        CMA $\left(\text{IN: } w_1, \ldots, w_q \text{ OUT: } (m_1, n_1), \ldots, (m_q, n_q)\right)$;

    On each node i (IDPA):

        WHILE inter-device imbalance

            On each device j: **kernel** $\left(\text{IN: } bm_i, bn_i, d_{ij} \text{ OUT: } t_{ij}\right)$;

            FPM-PA $\left(\text{IN: } p_i, bn_i, p_i \text{ FPMs OUT: } d_{i1}, \ldots, d_{iq}\right)$;

        END WHILE

    FPM-PA $\left(\text{IN: } q, W, q\text{FPMs OUT: } w_1, \ldots, w_q\right)$;

    END WHILE

}

Parallel application $\left(\text{IN: } \{m_i, n_i, d_{i1}, \ldots, d_{ip}\}_{i=1}^q, \ldots\right)$

Internode Partitioning Algorithm (INPA). Run in parallel on all nodes with distributed memory. Inputs: square matrix size N, number of nodes q, number of devices in each node $p_1, \ldots, p_q$ and block size b.

1. To add initial small point to the model, each node, in parallel, invokes the IDPA with an input $(p_i, bm_i = 1, bn_i = 1)$. This algorithm returns a time which is sent to the head node.
2. The head node calculates speeds from these times as $s_i(1) = 1/t_i(1)$ and adds the first point, $(1, s(1))$, to the model of each node.
3. The head node then computes the initial homogeneous distribution by dividing the total number of blocks, W, between processors $w_i = W/q$.
4. The CMA is passed $w_1, \ldots, w_q$ and returns the internode distributions $(m_1, n_1), \ldots, (m_q, n_q)$ which are scattered to all nodes.
5. On each node, the IDPA is invoked with the input (p_i, bm_i, bn_i) and the returned time t_i is sent to the head node.
6. IF $\max\limits_{1 \le i,j \le q} \left| \dfrac{t_i(w_i) - t_j(w_i)}{t_i(w_i)} \right| \le \varepsilon_1$ THEN the current internode distribution solves the problem. All interdevice and internode distributions are saved and the algorithm stops;
   ELSE the head node calculates the speeds of the nodes as $s_i(w_i) = w_i/t_i(w_i)$ and adds the point $(w_i, s_i(w_i))$ to each node-FPM.
7. On the head node, the FPM-PA is given the node-FPMs as input and returns a new distribution $w_1, \ldots, w_q$. GOTO 4

Interdevice Partitioning Algorithm (IDPA). This algorithm is run on a node with p devices. The input parameters are p and the submatrix sizes bm, bn. It computes the device distribution $d_1, \ldots, d_p$ and returns the time of last benchmark.

1. To add an initial small point to each device model, the *kernel* with parameters $(bm, bn, 1)$ is run in parallel on each device and its execution time is measured. The speed is computed as $s_j(1) = 1/t_j(1)$ and the point $(1, s_j(1))$ is added to each device model.
2. The initial homogeneous distribution $d_j = bn/p$, for all $1 \le j \le p$ is set.
3. In parallel on each device, the time $t_j(d_j)$ to execute the kernel with parameters (bm, bn, d_j) is measured.
4. IF $\max\limits_{1 \le j \le p} \left| \dfrac{t_i(d_i) - t_j(d_j)}{t_i(d_i)} \right| \le \varepsilon_2$ THEN the current distribution of computations over devices solves the problem. This distribution $d_1, \ldots, d_p$ is saved and $\max_{1 \le j \le p} t_j(d_j)$ is returned;
   ELSE the speeds $s_j(d_j) = d_j/t_j(d_j)$ are computed and the point $(d_j, s_j(d_j))$ is added to each device-FPM.
5. The FPM-PA takes bn and device-FPMs as input and returns a new distribution $d_1, \ldots, d_p$. GOTO 3

Functional Performance Model Partitioning Algorithm (FPM-PA). This FPM partitioning algorithm is presented in detail in Section 13.3.

Communication Minimizing Algorithm (CMA). This algorithm is specific to the communication pattern of application and the topology of the communication network. It takes as input the number of computation units, w_i, to assign to each processing element and arranges them in such away, (m_i, n_i), as to minimize the communication cost. For example, for matrix multiplication, $\mathbf{A} \times \mathbf{B} = \mathbf{C}$, the total volume of data exchange is minimized by minimizing the sum of the half perimeters $H = \sum_{i=1}^{q} (m_i + n_i)$. A column-based restriction of this problem is solved in [20].

The Grid'5000 experimental test bed proved to be an ideal platform to test our application. We used 90 dedicated nodes from three clusters from the Grenoble site. Twelve nodes from the Adonis cluster included NVIDIA Tesla GPUs, and the rest were approximately homogeneous. In order to increase the impact of our experiments, we chose to utilize only some of the CPU cores on some machines (Table 13.3). Such an approach is not unrealistic because it is possible to book individual CPU cores on this platform. For the local *dgemm* routine, we used high-performance vendor-provided BLAS libraries, namely Intel MKL for CPU and CUBLAS for GPU devices. Open MPI was used for internode communication and OpenMP for interdevice parallelism. The GPU execution time includes the time to transfer data to the GPU. For these experiments, an out of core algorithm is not used when the GPU memory is exhausted. All nodes are interconnected by a high-speed InfiniBand network which reduces the impact of communication on the total execution time: for $N = 1.5 \times 10^5$, all communications (including wait time due to any load imbalance) took 6% of total execution time. The full FPMs of nodes, Fig. 13.9, illustrate the range of heterogeneity of our platform.

An appropriate block size of $b = 128$ proved to be a good balance between achieving near-peak performance of optimized BLAS libraries while providing sufficient granularity for load balancing [10]. In order to demonstrate the effectiveness of the proposed FPM-based partitioning algorithm, we compare it against three other partitioning algorithms. All four algorithms invoke the *communication minimization algorithm* and are applied to an identical parallel matrix multiplication application. They differ on how load-balancing decisions are made.

TABLE 13.3 Experimental Hardware Setup Using 90 Nodes from Three Clusters from Grenoble, Grid'5000[a]

Cores:	0	1	2	3	4	5	6	7	8	Nodes	CPUs	GPUs	Hardware
Adonis	2	1	1	1	1	1	2	3	0	12	48	12	2.4 GHz, 24 GB
Edel	0	6	4	4	4	8	8	8	8	50	250	0	2.3 GHz, 24 GB
Genepi	0	3	3	3	3	4	4	4	4	28	134	0	2.5 GHz, 8 GB
Total										90	432	12	Intel Xeon

[a] All nodes have eight CPU cores, but to increase heterogeneity only some of the CPU cores are utilized as tabulated below. One GPU was used with each node from the Adonis cluster; 10 have Tesla T10 and 2 have Tesla C2050 GPUs. A CPU core is devoted to control GPU. For example, we can read that six Edel nodes used just one CPU core. All nodes are connected with InfiniBand 20G & 40G

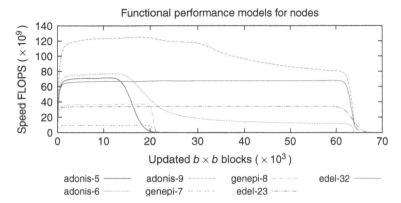

FIGURE 13.9 *Full FPMs for a number of nodes from Grid'5000 Grenoble site. Problem size is in number of b × b blocks of matrix C updated by a node. For each data point, it was necessary to build device models, find the optimum interdevice distribution, and then measure the execution time of the kernel with this distribution.*

- *Multiple-CPM Partitioning* uses the same algorithm as proposed above, with Step 7 of the INPA and Step 5 of the IDPA replaced with $w_i = W \times \frac{s_i}{\sum_q s_i}$ and $d_j = bn \times \frac{s_j}{\sum_p s_j}$, respectively, where s_i and s_j are constants. This is equivalent to the approach used in [21, 22, 31].
- *Single-CPM Partitioning* does one iteration of the above multiple-CPM partitioning algorithm. This is equivalent to the approach used in [20, 32].
- *Homogeneous Partitioning* uses an even distribution between all nodes: $w_1 = w_2 = \cdots = w_q$ and between devices in a node: $d_{i1} = d_{i2} = \cdots = d_{ip_i}$.

Figure 13.10 shows the speeds achieved by the parallel matrix multiplication application when the four different algorithms are applied. It is worth emphasizing that the performance results related to the execution on GPU devices take into account the time to transfer the workload to/from the GPU. The speed of the application with the *homogeneous distribution* is governed by the speed of the slowest processor (a node from Edel cluster with one CPU core). The *single-CPM* and *multiple-CPM* partitioning algorithms are able to load-balance for N up to 60,000 and 75,000 respectively, but this is only because the speed functions in these regions are horizontal. In general, for a full range of problem sizes, the simplistic algorithms are unable to converge to a balanced solution. By chance, for $N = 124,032$, the multiple-CPM algorithm found a reasonably good partitioning after many iterations, but in general this is not the case. Meanwhile, the *FPM-based partitioning* algorithm reliably found good partitioning for matrix multiplication involving in excess of 0.5 TB of data.

13.10 CONCLUSION

In this chapter, we proposed several techniques to efficiently exploit the capabilities of modern heterogeneous systems equipped with multicore CPUs and several

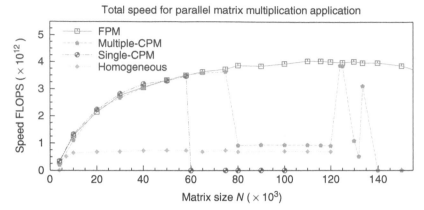

FIGURE 13.10   *Absolute speed for a parallel matrix multiplication application based on four partitioning algorithms, measured on 90 heterogeneous nodes consisting of 432 CPU cores and 12 GPUs from three dedicated clusters.*

GPU devices for scientific computations. We investigated the process of efficient design and optimization of scientific applications not only at the level of a single CPU/GPU computing node but also in highly heterogeneous and hierarchical HPC clusters. In contrast to other related works in this area, we based our approaches on functional performance modeling, which integrates many important features characterizing the performance of the platform and the application, such as contention on shared resources, high-performance disparity of architecturally different devices, limited memory of the accelerators, or scenarios when different devices use different codes to solve the same computational problem.

For a single hybrid CPU/GPU node, we presented the performance measurement methods and analyzed the efficiency of different implementations of parallel matrix multiplication, chosen as a case study. We defined and built FPMs of heterogeneous processing elements on a typical multicore and multi-GPU node. We showed that FPMs can facilitate performance evaluation of scientific applications on these hybrid platforms, and data partitioning algorithms based on accurate FPMs can deliver significant performance improvements when compared to the one obtained at the level of a single device.

To adapt parallel applications to hybrid heterogeneous clusters, we proposed a hierarchical data partitioning algorithm, which optimally distributed computation workload at two levels of the platform's hierarchy, namely, between nodes and between devices within each node. The presented approach is based on FPMs of processing elements which are efficiently built at runtime and realistically capture the high level of platform heterogeneity. The efficiency of the proposed algorithm was assessed on a real platform consisting of 90 highly heterogeneous nodes in three computing clusters and compared with the equivalent approaches based on traditional data partitioning algorithms. The results demonstrate that the presented algorithm minimizes the overall communication volume and provides efficient load-balancing decisions for very large problem sizes, while similar approaches were not able to find the adequate balancing solutions.

ACKNOWLEDGMENTS

This work was supported by the COST Action IC0805 "Open European Network for High-Performance Computing on Complex Environments," the Science Foundation Ireland (Grant 08/IN.1/I2054), and the Portuguese National Foundation of Science and Technology (PIDDAC program and SFRH/BD/44568/2008 fellowship). Experiments were carried out on Grid'5000 developed under the INRIA ALADDIN development action with support from CNRS, RENATER, and several Universities, as well as other funding bodies (see https://www.grid5000.fr).

REFERENCES

1. C. Augonnet, S. Thibault, R. Namyst, and P. Wacrenier, "StarPU: a unified platform for task scheduling on heterogeneous multicore architectures," *Euro-Par 2009*, Delft, The Netherlands, pp. 863–874, 2009.
2. A. Ilic and L. Sousa, "Collaborative execution environment for heterogeneous parallel systems," in *IPDPS Workshops and Phd Forum (IPDPSW)*, Atlanta, Georgia, USA, pp. 1–8, 2010.
3. M. Fatica, "Accelerating Linpack with CUDA on Heterogenous Clusters," in *GPGPU-2*, pp. 46–51. New York: ACM, 2009.
4. C. Yang, F. Wang, Y. Du, et al., "Adaptive optimization for petascale heterogeneous CPU/GPU computing," in *Cluster'10*, Heraklion, Crete, Greece, pp. 19–28, 2010.
5. Y. Ogata, T. Endo, N. Maruyama, and S. Matsuoka, "An efficient, model-based CPU-GPU heterogeneous FFT library," in *IPDPS 2008*, Miami, Florida, USA, pp. 1–10, 2008.
6. A. Lastovetsky and R. Reddy, "Data partitioning with a functional performance model of heterogeneous processors," *International Journal of High Performance Computing Applications*, vol. 21, pp. 76–90, 2007.
7. Z. Zhong, V. Rychkov, and A. Lastovetsky, "Data partitioning on heterogeneous multicore platforms," in *Cluster 2011*, Austin, Texas, USA, pp. 580–584, 2011.
8. Z. Zhong, V. Rychkov, and A. Lastovetsky, "Data partitioning on heterogeneous multicore and multi-GPU systems using functional performance models of data-parallel applications," in *Cluster 2012*, Beijing, China, pp. 191–199, 2012.
9. A. Lastovetsky and R. Reddy, "Distributed data partitioning for heterogeneous processors based on partial estimation of their functional performance models," in *EuroPar/HeteroPar 2009*, LNCS, vol. 6043, pp. 91–101, Springer: Berlin, Heidelberg, 2010.
10. D. Clarke, A. Ilic, A. Lastovetsky, and L. Sousa, "Hierarchical partitioning algorithm for scientific computing on highly heterogeneous CPU + GPU clusters," in *Euro-Par 2012*, LNCS, vol. 7484, pp. 489–501, Springer: Berlin, Heidelberg, 2012.
11. C.-K. Luk, S. Hong, and H. Kim, "Qilin: exploiting parallelism on heterogeneous multiprocessors with adaptive mapping," in *MICRO-42*, New York, USA, pp. 45–55, 2009.
12. A. Ilic and L. Sousa, "On realistic divisible load scheduling in highly heterogeneous distributed systems," in *PDP 2012*, pp. 426–433, IEEE, ACM, New York, USA, 2012.
13. R. Blumofe and C. Leiserson, "Scheduling multithreaded computations by work stealing," *Journal of the ACM*, vol. 46, no. 5, pp. 720–748, 1999.

14. J. Quintin and F. Wagner, "Hierarchical work-stealing," *Euro-Par 2010-Parallel Processing*, Ischia, Italy, pp. 217–229, 2010.

15. M. D. Linderman, J. D. Collins, H. Wang, et al., "Merge: a programming model for heterogeneous multi-core systems," *SIGPLAN Notices*, vol. 43, pp. 287–296, 2008.

16. C. Augonnet, S. Thibault, and R. Namyst, "Automatic calibration of performance models on heterogeneous multicore architectures," in *EuroPar'09*, Delft, The Netherlands, pp. 56–65, 2009.

17. G. Quintana-Ortí, F. D. Igual, E. S. Quintana-Ortí, and R. A. van de Geijn, "Solving dense linear systems on platforms with multiple hardware accelerators," *SIGPLAN Notices*, vol. 44, pp. 121–130, 2009.

18. F. Song, S. Tomov, and J. Dongarra, "Enabling and scaling matrix computations on heterogeneous multi-core and multi-GPU systems," in *ICS'12*, pp. 365–376, ACM, New York, USA, 2012.

19. M. Cierniak, M. Zaki, and W. Li, "Compile-time scheduling algorithms for heterogeneous network of workstations," *Computer Journal*, vol. 40, pp. 356–372, 1997.

20. O. Beaumont, V. Boudet, F. Rastello, and Y. Robert, "Matrix multiplication on heterogeneous platforms," *IEEE Transactions on Parallel Distributed Systems*, vol. 12, no. 10, pp. 1033–1051, 2001.

21. I. Galindo, F. Almeida, and J. Badía-Contelles, "Dynamic load balancing on dedicated heterogeneous systems," in *EuroPVM/MPI 2008*, pp. 64–74, Springer: Berlin, Heidelberg, 2008.

22. J. Martínez, E. Garzón, A. Plaza, and I. García, "Automatic tuning of iterative computation on heterogeneous multiprocessors with ADITHE," *Journal of Supercomputing*, vol. 58, no. 2, pp. 151–159, 2011.

23. A. Ilic and L. Sousa, "Scheduling divisible loads on heterogeneous desktop systems with limited memory," in *Euro-Par/HeteroPar 2011*, pp. 491–501, Springer: Berlin, Heidelberg, 2011.

24. A. Ilic and L. Sousa, "Simultaneous multi-level divisible load balancing for heterogeneous desktop systems," in *ISPA 2012*, pp. 683–690, IEEE, Washington, DC, USA, 2012.

25. J. Dongarra, M. Faverge, T. Herault, J. Langou, and Y. Robert, "Hierarchical QR factorization algorithms for multi-core cluster systems," *Arxiv preprint arXiv:1110.1553*, 2011.

26. D. Clarke, A. Lastovetsky, and V. Rychkov, "Column-based matrix partitioning for parallel matrix multiplication on heterogeneous processors based on functional performance models," in *Euro-Par 2011: Parallel Processing Workshops*, *LNCS*, vol. 7155, pp. 450–459, Springer: Berlin Heidelberg, 2012.

27. J. Choi, "A new parallel matrix multiplication algorithm on distributed-memory concurrent computers," *Concurrency: Practice and Experience*, vol. 10, no. 8, pp. 655–670, 1998.

28. A. Kalinov and A. Lastovetsky, "Heterogeneous distribution of computations solving linear algebra problems on networks of heterogeneous computers," *Journal of Parallel and Distributed Computing*, vol. 61, no. 4, pp. 520–535, 2001.

29. C. Gregg and K. Hazelwood, "Where is the data? Why you cannot debate CPU vs. GPU performance without the answer," in *ISPASS'11*, Austin, Texas, USA, pp. 134–144, 2011.

30. D. Clarke, A. Lastovetsky, and V. Rychkov, "Dynamic load balancing of parallel computational iterative routines on platforms with memory heterogeneity," in *Euro-Par/HeteroPar 2010*, pp. 41–50, Springer: Berlin Heidelberg, 2011.

31. A. Legrand, H. Renard, Y. Robert, and F. Vivien, "Mapping and load-balancing iterative computations," *IEEE Transactions on Parallel and Distributed Systems*, vol. 15, no. 6, pp. 546–558, 2004.

32. S. Hummel, J. Schmidt, R. N. Uma, and J. Wein, "Load-sharing in heterogeneous systems via weighted factoring," in *SPAA96*, pp. 318–328, ACM, New York, USA, 1996.

14

Efficient Multilevel Load Balancing on Heterogeneous CPU + GPU Systems

Aleksandar Ilic and Leonel Sousa

Technical University of Lisbon, Lisbon, Portugal

In this chapter, we propose several algorithms for efficient balancing of divisible load applications in order to fully exploit the capabilities of heterogeneous multicore CPU and multi-GPU environments for collaborative processing. The proposed algorithms allow achieving simultaneous load balancing at different execution levels, namely across execution subdomains defined by different types of processing devices, between devices in each subdomain, and at the level of a single accelerator. The proposed strategies also deal with the efficient overlap of computation and communication, with respect to the amount of supported concurrency and limited memory at the accelerator. Moreover, the proposed algorithms build several partial performance models during the application runtime using a minimal set of approximation points and while converging toward the optimal multilevel load distribution. The proposed approaches were experimentally evaluated in different desktop systems with multicore CPUs and several GPUs, for different applications.

High-Performance Computing on Complex Environments, First Edition.
Edited by Emmanuel Jeannot and Julius Žilinskas.
© 2014 John Wiley & Sons, Inc. Published 2014 by John Wiley & Sons, Inc.

Experimental results show the ability of the algorithms to provide significant performance improvements with low scheduling overhead when compared to the state-of-the-art scheduling approaches.

14.1 INTRODUCTION: HETEROGENEOUS CPU + GPU SYSTEMS

Modern desktop systems are true heterogeneous platforms capable of sustaining remarkable computational power. The overall enhancement of processing capabilities of commodity desktop systems can be generally attributed to architectural improvements and employment of both general-purpose processors (CPUs) and programmable accelerators/coprocessors, such as graphics processing units (GPUs). By coalescing their execution space, it is possible to further stretch the limits of parallel processing on the off-the-shelf computers and to unlock synergetic performance which is significantly higher than the one obtained at the level of a single device. Driven by this potential, the emergent trends in computer architecture are moving toward merging the functionalities of both CPU and GPU devices on a single die, such as AMD Fusion or Intel Ivy Bridge. However, efficient exploitation of the overall system and device capabilities for collaborative execution is not an easy task.

Besides the advance of the technology applied during the manufacturing process, the performance of modern CPUs is improved by increasing the number of processing cores on a single die. The computational power of multicore CPUs is usually exploited by relying on the coarse-grain parallelization techniques, supported in the programming frameworks such as OpenMP or PThreads. On the other hand, accelerators, such as GPUs, are usually built around different architectural principles, and they might deliver performance that greatly surpasses that attainable in multicore CPUs [1]. For example, modern GPUs incorporate hundreds of "simple" cores, where the computations are performed in parallel by groups of these cores. In order to exploit the capabilities of GPU architecture, it is usually required to perform compute-intensive and highly data-parallel computations, supported on fine-grained parallelization that is achieved by relying on different programming models and tools, such as NVIDIA CUDA or OpenCL.

Merging the execution space of architecturally different devices in heterogeneous CPU + GPU environments imposes additional challenges for collaborative processing (when computations of a single application are simultaneously performed on all devices). First of all, it is required to efficiently parallelize the application for each particular device architecture in the system (multicore CPU or GPU) according to device characteristics and by relying on different programming models and tools. Furthermore, per-device codes need to be developed to allow efficient collaborative processing and they need to be subsequently integrated into a unified cross-device execution environment. Although it is possible to alleviate the programmability issues in CPU + GPU platforms by relying on proposed programming frameworks, such as OpenCL, OpenACC, StarPU [2], or StarSs [3], a full control over the execution environment and the incorporated devices can only be achieved by relying on vendor-specific programming models and tools. For these reasons, we focus here on direct integration of highly optimized vendor-specific codes in a custom OpenMP + CUDA unified execution environment based on CHPS [4]. However, the proposed solutions are not bound to any specific execution environment; that is, they are general enough to be implemented in any platform that allows unification of the execution space between multicore CPUs and accelerators.

14.1.1 Open Problems and Specific Contributions

In heterogeneous environments with multicore CPUs and several accelerators, such as GPUs, the accelerators usually operate as coprocessors to the multicore CPU (host), that is, they are not stand-alone and independent devices. For example, all GPU memory (de)allocations, as well as the explicit data transfers between the host and the GPU global memory, must be performed before and after the execution on the GPU device. These data transfers, as well as GPU kernel invocations, are initiated by the host CPU and are conducted over bidirectional interconnection buses (i.e., PCI Express), usually with asymmetric bandwidth. The data transfers between host and GPU memory can be performed concurrently with GPU kernel execution, as long as they belong to different *GPU streams*.[1] In fact, even transfers in different directions can be performed concurrently depending on the number of direct memory access (DMA) engines in specific accelerator architecture (e.g., a single DMA engine in NVIDIA Tesla architecture does not allow concurrent data transfers, while in Fermi and Kepler architectures it is possible to overlap transfers in both directions).

In order to fully exploit the computational power of multicore CPUs and several accelerators for collaborative cross-device execution, there are three levels of parallel processing that must be carefully taken into account: (i) simultaneous execution across all available CPU cores and accelerators; (ii) parallel processing within each "controlling" host core–accelerator execution pair; and (iii) concurrency at the level of a single accelerator. In this chapter, we specifically focus on efficient load-balancing and scheduling algorithms for discretely divisible load (DL) applications in collaborative multicore CPU and multi-GPU systems at these three levels. The DL model [5] represents computations that can be arbitrarily divided into several load fractions, which are further processed independently with no precedence constraints. Hence, the main scheduling problem addressed here is how to distribute the application load across heterogeneous devices (i.e., to determine the exact load size to be processed on each device) such that the cross-device execution is as balanced as possible and the minimum execution time is attained, at all three levels of concurrency.

Focusing on the *first level* of parallel execution, distributing the loads in heterogeneous platforms with multicore CPUs and several GPUs is not an easy task, since their

---

[1] A GPU stream is a sequence of commands that execute in order. The commands are issued by the host and refer to data transfers and GPU kernel invocations. Different streams may execute their commands out of order with respect to one another or concurrently [1].

performance may differ by orders of magnitude. This difference does not only come from different computational resources and architectural concepts but also from the ability of each device hardware to efficiently execute the parallelized codes according to application-specific characteristics and demands. This mainly refers to the fact that devices with architectures rely on different implementations when collaboratively performing the same application or when the application uses several implementations for different load sizes (even at the level of a single accelerator).

Since the accelerators are physically separate devices, whose employment is directly orchestrated by the CPU host, the *second level* of parallel execution refers to efficient simultaneous execution between the "controlling" CPU core and the accelerator. A common practice in heterogeneous desktop computing is to underuse the compute potential of a single CPU core by devoting it to control the execution of an accelerator (GPU). In fact, the devoted core just issues the commands required to commence on-accelerator execution, but most of the time it is idle, waiting for the accelerator to finish with the processing. However, in current desktop environments, it is possible to establish the concurrent execution between the devoted core and accelerator via asynchronous calls, where the control is returned to the core before the execution on the accelerator is completed. Hence, during the idle periods, the core might be successfully employed to perform certain portions of the collaborative computation that can be overlapped with the execution on the accelerator. However, the amount of computation to be given to the core and accelerator must be carefully chosen, such that both devices finish their computations at the same time. This example serves as the major motivation for the research conducted herein, but the proposed methods are applicable to a wider range of scheduling problems and environments. To that extent, we refer to an execution subdomain which consists of a subset of available compute devices, as a *processing group*.

The *third level* of execution concurrency occurs at the level of a single accelerator, that is, GPU device, where host-initiated data transfers and on-device kernel executions can be overlapped in time. In order to efficiently exploit this level of concurrency, one needs to take into account both computational performance of a GPU device and asymmetric bidirectional bandwidth of communication lines (i.e., from host to device and from device to host), when determining the amount of data to be processed in different *GPU streams*. The load portions assigned to each *GPU stream* should be decided such that the minimum execution time on a single GPU device is attained by efficiently overlapping computation and communication across different *GPU streams* (in respect to the supported concurrency). Furthermore, in contrast to the multicore CPU execution which may benefit from virtually extended dynamic random access memory (DRAM) space (paging), the amount of data that can be stored on the GPU is strictly limited by the available space in its global memory, thus it must also be considered when deciding on the load size to be assigned. However, the amount of global memory to be allocated depends on the application memory requirements. A common practice in the literature is to characterize the memory requirements of the application with the amount of input and output data, that is, the data size to be transferred from/to the host. This is usually not sufficient to describe the behavior of real application and to allow proper utilization of the scarce GPU global memory, and therefore the application memory requirements must be expressed such that the additional memory allocated during the application execution is also considered.

In brief, in this chapter we propose a DL scheduling and load-balancing approach capable of fully exploiting the capabilities of heterogeneous multicore CPU and multi-GPU environments for collaborative processing at three different levels of parallel execution. For brevity, we separate the presentation of the proposed approach into two load-balancing algorithms targeting different levels of concurrency in order to clearly show the benefits of the proposed strategies at different levels, as well as to simplify the presentation of the algorithms. However, the proposed algorithms can be easily integrated into a unified DL balancing approach.

14.2 BACKGROUND AND RELATED WORK

Because of its practical importance, in the previous decades DL scheduling principles were applied to a wide variety of scientific problems and different types of distributed networks [5]. However, the extensive DL-related literature mainly targets "traditional" CPU-only distributed systems [5], and thus their contributions can only be partially applied for DL balancing in heterogeneous multicore CPU and multi-GPU systems. On the other hand, in modern desktop/server environments, efficient exploitation of the computational power of CPU and GPU devices for collaborative processing is still an area of ongoing research. In this section, we provide an overview of the state-of-the-art approaches for scheduling and load balancing in both (i) traditional CPU-only distributed systems and (ii) multicore CPU and multi-GPU environments.

14.2.1 Divisible Load Scheduling in Distributed CPU-Only Systems

Driven by the fact that modern multicore CPU and multiaccelerator systems can be perceived as heterogeneous star-shaped networks (since the accelerators are mainly coprocessors to the host CPU positioned at the star center), we specifically focus here on the existing DL-based research studies that target scheduling DLs on CPU-only distributed star networks.

Following the usual DL nomenclature [5], previously referred levels of concurrency in heterogeneous CPU + GPU systems can be roughly mapped as follows: (i) the *first level* of concurrency (where the load chunks are distributed across all heterogenous devices) is commonly referred to as *one-round* distribution strategy; (ii) the *second level* of parallel execution (between the "controlling" core and the accelerators) is usually addressed via employment of the master for execution; and (iii) the *third level* of parallelism (pipelined execution with overlapped computation and communication on a single accelerator with limited memory) is slightly connected to the *multiround* (*multi-installment*) strategy for distributed platforms with limited memory. It is worth emphasizing that this mapping is conducted in strictly theoretical terms, and it does not imply the direct mapping of DL scheduling strategies.

For example, *multiround* strategy in CPU-only distributed systems generally refers to the load partitioning that allows as soon as possible activation of the processors by pipelining the execution across all processing devices. This is mainly due to a common *single-port* communication in traditional distributed systems, where the master can only communicate with a single worker at a time [6], and only a very limited number of studies consider that the data (processed on the workers) is needed to be communicated back to the master, that is, results collection [7]. On the other hand, for *multiport* communication [8], the asymmetric bandwidth of bidirectional communication lines is usually not considered, which cannot be disregarded in CPU + GPU systems for efficient scheduling at the *third level* of concurrency. When dealing with limited memory, a common approach is to ensure that the dispatched loads fit into the limited size of the worker's input buffer/memory (usually expressed in the number of load chunks that can be stored) [6, 9]. Hence, it is implicitly assumed that the memory requirements linearly increase with the number of chunks, which can be realistic only for certain application types. For the *second level* of concurrency, the studies in traditional DL-based scheduling usually do not explicitly consider the employment of the master for computation [6–10].

The widespread popularity of DL balancing approaches in traditional distributed systems is mostly due to their analytical tractability. However, this analytical tractability is usually achieved by adopting some unrealistic assumptions about the application-specific computational performance of devices and the bandwidth of communication buses. For example, the time taken to compute a certain number of load chunks (x_i) on a single i worker is usually modeled as an affine function of the number of chunks and the relative processing speed of the device (s_i). It means that in a *linear cost model*, it is assumed that $x_i s_i$ units of time are required to execute x_i chunks, whereas the time to compute is modeled as $a_i + x_i s_i$ in the *affine cost model* (a_i is the "computational" latency). A similar approach is also conducted for communication modeling. Hence, both the relative processing speed and the relative bandwidth of the communication channel are assumed to be constant (i.e., they do not vary with the number of processed chunks). We refer here to this modeling principle and load-balancing approaches as constant performance modeling (CPM) approaches. Since in nondedicated systems the performance parameters may vary as a result of continuous and stochastic workload fluctuations, several adaptive DL balancing algorithms are proposed, where the load distributions are adjusted according to the current state of the platform. CPM-based adaptive load-balancing approaches [10, 11] usually alter the load distributions by recalculating the relative processor speeds, typically after each performed iteration. In particular, for each worker i, the time taken to process the currently assigned load size (x_i) is recorded (t_i) and used for estimating its relative performance, such that $s_i = x_i/t_i$. When the processor speeds are not *a priori* known, in the first iteration (*initial phase*), the total workload size N is usually equidistantly partitioned across p devices, such that each device processes N/p load chunks. In subsequent iterations, the relative speeds are recalculated and new load distributions are decided (*iterative phase*), such that each worker i is assigned with the load portion of a size $x_i = N \cdot s_i / \sum_{j=1}^{p} s_j$. Although adaptivity might lessen the impacts of unrealistic CPM, the adaptive CPM-based approaches might still not be able to provide adequate load distributions, especially in systems with high memory heterogeneity [12, 13].

In order to overcome the limitations imposed by CPM, the authors in [12, 14–16] propose several load-balancing algorithms based on a more realistic *functional performance modeling* (*FPM*). In contrast to the CPM, where the relative performance is assumed to be constant, in the FPM the relative performance (speed) of each worker i is modeled as a continuous function of the number of chunks x, that is, $s_i(x) = \frac{x}{t_i(x)}$, where $t_i(x)$ is the processing time of x chunks. The speed functions are application specific and defined at the interval $[0, N]$, where N is the total number of chunks. The shape of the performance speed is assumed to be monotonically increasing and concave until a certain point, after which it is monotonically decreasing [15]. Hence, any straight line passing through the origin of the coordinate system intersects the performance curve only at one point, where the intersections represent the distributions capable of achieving optimal load balancing (in the real domain). The main problem targeted with the FPM [12, 14–16] is the distribution of independent chunks over a unidimensional arrangement of p heterogeneous processors, that is, *one-round* distribution without explicit communication modeling. Following the optimality principle [5], the shortest parallel processing time is attained when all processors finish executions at the same time, such that

$$\frac{x_1}{s_1(x_1)} = \frac{x_2}{s_2(x_2)} = \cdots = \frac{x_p}{s_p(x_p)}; \quad \sum_{i=1}^{p} x_i = N. \tag{14.1}$$

Since the load distribution vector $(\bar{x}_1, \bar{x}_2, \ldots, \bar{x}_p)$ must consist of strictly integer values, the solution to (14.1) is found with a two-step algorithm. The first part of the algorithm seeks for the solution in the real domain, and approximates the load distributions by rounding down to the nearest integer, while in the second step (i.e., *refinement*) the remaining loads are redistributed to the processing devices. In detail, the first step of the algorithm commences by defining the upper and lower bounds of the solution search space, and converges toward the optimal distribution by bisecting the angle between these two boundaries and by assigning the bisection as one of the search limits in each iteration [15]. After the distribution that satisfies (14.1) is found, the algorithm proceeds to the *refinement* step, where processor loads are iteratively incremented until assigning the total problem size (N) to all processors. This algorithm is referred to here as the *single-level load-balancing algorithm* (*SLBA*).

FPM-based adaptive load-balancing strategies [12, 16] are usually capable of providing better distributions of loads across a heterogeneous set of processors by realistically capturing the performance variations in the execution platforms. Moreover, the FPM-based approaches might be even used to construct partial FPMs of each processor during the application runtime, that is, $\bar{s}_i(x) \approx s_i(x)$ for each i worker. In detail, the partial FPM $\bar{s}_i(x)$ is built by relying on the execution history in k previous iterations, where the approximation points for relative speeds $\bar{s}_i^k$ are calculated with a set of already performed $\bar{x}_i^k$ loads and the time t_i^k taken to perform them. Then, the partial FPM $\bar{s}_i(x)$ is obtained by applying piecewise linear approximation on a set of these points. In the *initial phase* of the FPM-based adaptive load-balancing algorithm, an equidistant data partitioning of a total problem size N across p workers, that is, $\bar{x}_i^1 = N/p$, is performed. The *iterative phase* consists of two steps: (i) updating of of the partial FPMs and (ii) determination of the new load distributions by applying the *SLBA* algorithm to the newly approximated FPMs. It is worth emphasizing that the quality of load-balancing decisions highly depends on how close the partial estimations $\bar{s}_i(x)$ are to the full models $s_i(x)$. In certain cases, a large number of iterations are required to construct the accurate partial FPMs and to determine the load balancing, since the *one-round* nature of *SLBA* allows obtaining at most one approximation point per iteration (for each device).

In general, for nondedicated platforms, the *iterative phase* of both CPM- and FPM-based adaptive load-balancing algorithms needs to be applied in each iteration. However, for systems where performance parameters do not significantly vary with time, the *iterative phase* can be stopped as soon as the load balancing is achieved, in order to reduce the scheduling overheads. It is usually designated as the *termination criterion*, which, for a certain iteration l, can be calculated as

$$\max_{1 \le i,j \le p} \left| \frac{t_i^l - t_j^l}{t_i^l} \right| \le \varepsilon, \tag{14.2}$$

where ε represents a predefined value for the relative accuracy of the solution. A relaxed optimality criterion is expressed in (14.2), where the time t_i^l taken to process loads on each i worker is compared, and, if the maximum relative difference satisfies the predefined ε value, the *iterative phase* of the algorithm is not invoked in subsequent iterations. In fact, the load distributions obtained in the lth iteration are considered as the ones that are capable of providing the adequate level of load balancing, and thus they are used for all further iterations.

14.2.2 Scheduling in Multicore CPU and Multi-GPU Environments

Current state-of-the-art scheduling and load-balancing approaches for collaborative CPU + GPU processing mainly tackle the issues at the *first level* of concurrency. Although the performance benefits at the other two levels of concurrency are widely acknowledged, they are usually attained either for application-specific purposes or without making any exact decisions about the load size processed in each *GPU stream* for efficient overlapping. Most of the proposed CPU + GPU DL balancing solutions [17–24] usually determine the load distributions by (i) building and fitting the full performance models with extensive experimental evaluation, (ii) performing an exhaustive search over the set of possible cross-device distributions, (iii) targeting only the *first level* of concurrency, (iv) relying on unrealistic CPM, and (v) applying any combination of the previously mentioned techniques. In detail, the approach proposed in [18] performs the load partitioning during the program compilation by relying on the application-specific performance models for each device. However, the procedure of building these performance models is very demanding, since they are constructed by fitting a large set of experimentally obtained points with affine functions (for each device and for each application). A similar, but even more demanding, approach is proposed in [17], where the authors advocate the use of a purely static data partitioning method, by detecting a predefined set of features in the OpenCL kernels during the program compilation. The extracted features are further used to determine the load distributions by analyzing a hierarchy of models to map features to devices. The feature-based models are experimentally obtained during the offline training process which also exhaustively examines all possible combinations of load distributions across all available devices. Furthermore, the authors in [19] also rely on extensive offline profiling to determine the program-specific constant "ratio"[2] to describe the performance disparity between CPU and GPU devices, which is further used to determine the cross-device load distributions. The potential benefits of applying the OpenMP-like parallelism for loop scheduling in heterogeneous CPU + GPU environments are analyzed in [20], where several (adaptive) CPM-based strategies are proposed on the basis of a similar "ratio."

Several CPM-based adaptive load-balancing approaches have also been analyzed in CPU + GPU environments [21–23]. The work proposed in [23] relies on a direct implementation of the previously referred adaptive CPM-based algorithm [11] by considering the constant performance to determine the load balancing in the *iterative phase*, while approaches in [21, 22] differ in the *initial phase*. In detail, in [22], extensive offline experiments are conducted to define the constant performance ratio, while in the *initial phase* from [21] the per-device loads are exponentially increased during several runs to discover the regions of constant performance for each device. In fact, the authors in [21] acknowledge that describing the device performance with a single constant might not be sufficient to guarantee the efficient cross-device execution (especially when the performance constants are obtained with a small number of chunks which are not capable of fully utilizing the capabilities of the GPU). However, it is worth emphasizing that, even when the approach of discovering the constant performance ranges is applied, it still does not resolve the previously described drawbacks of CPM-based adaptive load balancing. On the other hand, scientific studies that apply the FPM-based load balancing approaches to heterogeneous CPU + GPU platforms are surprisingly quite rare [13, 24, 25]. The authors in [24] analyze the impact of shared resource contention and apply the *SLBA* algorithm when implementing out-of-core parallel matrix multiplication. Therefore, they mainly address the *first level* of concurrency in the CPU + GPU systems, while the overlap of computation and communication is achieved by dispatching two independent one-round distributions to separate *GPU streams*.

14.3 LOAD BALANCING ALGORITHMS FOR HETEROGENEOUS CPU + GPU SYSTEMS

In this section, two load-balancing algorithms are presented that target efficient collaborative processing in heterogeneous multicore CPU and multi-GPU environments

---

[2]The "ratio" usually refers to a constant value obtained by dividing the time taken to execute the same problem on different devices, that is, CPU and GPU.

at different levels of parallel execution, namely (i) the *multi-level simultaneous load-balancing algorithm* (MSLBA) for efficient DL balancing at the first and the second level of parallel processing (i.e., across execution subdomains defined with several processing devices, and between devices in each subdomain), and (ii) *algorithm for multi-installment processing with multidistributions* (AMPMD), which deals with efficient execution at the first and the third level of concurrency by overlapping computation and communication at the accelerator in respect to the supported concurrency and limited memory, while balancing the execution across the devices.

According to the basic architectural principle of heterogeneous desktop/server systems, where the CPU (host) is responsible for orchestrating the execution on all processing devices (workers), let $D = (A, (P, E))$ be a heterogeneous star-shaped system, where the total load N of a DL application A needs to be distributed and processed in a system (P, E), as depicted in Fig. 14.1. The heterogeneous system consists of a set of $k + w$ processing devices P, where $(p_1, \ldots, p_k)$ subset represents k CPU cores, and w accelerators are designated as a subset of "distant workers" $(p_{k+1}, \ldots, p_{k+w})$. The term "distant worker" is used here to designate a processing device, such as GPU, connected to the master via a communication link. E is a set of w communication links $(e_{k+1}, \ldots, e_{k+w})$ that connect the master to each distant worker. The system heterogeneity is considered through the different processing speeds for the workers (i.e., CPU cores and accelerators), and different bandwidths of master–worker communication links. Precisely, each link is modeled as an asynchronous bidirectional full-duplex communication channel with asymmetric bandwidth in different transfer directions.

14.3.1 Multilevel Simultaneous Load Balancing Algorithm

In order to tackle the issues related to the efficient simultaneous processing at the first and the second level of concurrency, that is, across all heterogeneous devices and within each processing group, let Γ be a set of q processing groups $G_i = (P_i, E_i) \subset (P, E)$ $(1 \leq i \leq q)$ representing different execution subdomains. Each G_i processing group comprises a subset of k_i CPU cores and w_i distant workers from the P set,

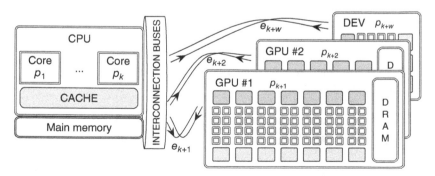

FIGURE 14.1   *Heterogeneous desktop system.*

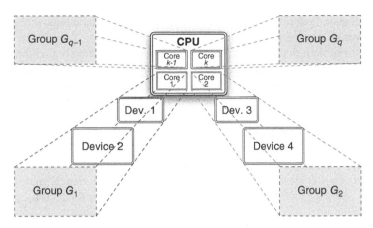

FIGURE 14.2 *Processing groups.*

whereas E_i subset represents the communication links to/from w_i distant workers. Figure 14.2 presents possible arrangement of processing elements in a typical heterogeneous desktop system with q processing groups: for example, *Group G_1* represents the execution subdomain defined with *Core 1*, *Device 1*, and *Device 2*.

Initially, the total load N of the divisible application $\mathcal{A}$ is stored at the master, and it can be split into load fractions (chunks) of an arbitrary size x. In order to realistically capture the performance disparity in heterogeneous desktop systems, the *total performance* of each processing device j (i.e., CPU core or distant worker) is modeled with a continuous relative performance function $\psi_{t_j}(x)$ of the number of chunks, where $1 \leq j \leq k + w$. The continuity of the performance function is required because of the fact that the proposed methods are based on the FPM approach, where the optimal load distribution lies in intersections of continuous performance curves with a straight line passing through the origin of the coordinate system (Section 14.2). Since the efficient execution at the *third level* of concurrency is separately considered in Section 14.3.2, the previously referred *total performance models* for distant workers encapsulate not only the time to process the load but also the time needed to transfer the data from/to the master; that is, the relative performance of distant workers is calculated as the ratio between the number of chunks and the total time taken to distribute and process the load, as well as to return the results to the host. Hence, if the full $\psi_{t_j}(x)$ device performance model is considered, it needs to be constructed with a full range of load sizes (i.e., from 1 to the total application workload of N), which is a very time-consuming process. In order to reduce this time, the approach proposed here relies on partial estimations of the total performance functions that are built during the application runtime, that is, $\overline{\psi}_{t_j}(x) \approx \psi_{t_j}(x)$.[3] More specifically, for each load assigned to a device, the processing and communication time is recorded,

[3]In order to simplify the presentation of the algorithms, we refer here to the partial models without the overline symbol.

and the calculated relative speed is used to improve the partial model with piecewise linear approximation on a set of previously obtained points.

The first problem that we tackle here is how to simultaneously find the load distributions at the first two levels of concurrency, that is, across heterogeneous devices within each G_i processing group, and across G_i processing groups from the Γ set, such that the overall parallel execution is performed in the shortest possible time. Hence, the proposed MSLBA approach partitions the total application load N into fractions $\alpha = \{\alpha_1, \ldots, \alpha_q\}$ to be processed in parallel across a set of $(G_1, \ldots, G_q)$ processing groups (where each G_i group is assigned with α_i loads), and, at the same time, for each G_i group it determines the β_i distribution vector to achieve load balancing across all devices within a single processing group. Hence, the determined $\beta_i = \{\beta_{i,1}, \ldots, \beta_{i,k_i}, \ldots, \beta_{i,k_i+w_i}\}$ distribution is used to assign $\beta_{i,j}$ loads to each device j in a G_i group, such that $\sum_{j=1}^{k_i+w_i} \beta_{i,j} = \alpha_i$.

In order to simultaneously determine α and β_i distributions, we construct not only the partial estimations of the total performance models for each device but also the partial estimations of the total performance models for each G_i processing group, that is, $\psi_{g_i}(x, \beta)$. Namely, the group performance model $\psi_{g_i}(x, \beta)$ is a continuous function of two parameters: (i) the total load x processed on all devices in parallel within a processing group, and (ii) β load distribution for which the performance is obtained. In detail, after the α_i and $\beta_{i,j}$ loads are processed within a G_i group, and the total cross-device parallel processing time, t_i is assessed (the maximum time taken to process $\beta_{i,j}$ loads in parallel on j devices), a single point is added to the group performance model $((\alpha_i, \beta_i), \alpha_i/t_i)$. Hence, the total performance model $\psi_{g_i}(x, \beta)$ of a group is a linear piecewise approximation on a set of these points. It is worth noting that a single group performance point reflects not only the total number of chunks but also the cross-device load distribution.

The MSLBA simultaneously achieves multilevel load balancing across processing groups and across devices in each group by dynamically building the partial estimations of the group performance models with the minimum number of points. The algorithm consists of two phases: namely determination of the initial multilevel distributions, and the refinement procedure. Both phases correspond to the two SLBA steps [15], and they need to be serially performed to achieve multilevel load balancing [25]. In brief, in addition to defining the upper and lower bounds of the solution search space by seeking the two straight lines passing through the origin of the coordinate system, the first part of the algorithm also builds the partial estimations of the total group models $\psi_{g_i}(x, \beta)$ according to the number of available processing devices, their current partial performance models $\psi_{t_j}(x)$, and the type of intersection with the straight line [25]. It further converges toward the optimal distributions by bisecting the angle between these two boundaries and by assigning the bisection line as one of the search limits in each iteration, while improving the partial estimations of the group models. It is worth emphasizing that due to the applied rounding down procedure, the unassigned loads after the first phase of the algorithm are iteratively assigned to the devices within the processing groups until the total problem size N is distributed such that the minimum parallel processing time is attained [25]. Finally, the obtained solution $(\alpha_i, \beta_i = \{\beta_{i,j}\})$ represents the load-balancing distribution vector consisting of the number of chunks to be assigned to a group i with devices j. It is worth emphasizing that MSLBA encapsulates all the functionality of the SLBA algorithm and can be considered as its generalization, where SLBA is a special case when each processing group consists of a single device.

14.3.2 Algorithm for Multi-Installment Processing with Multidistributions

The AMPMD deals with the efficient simultaneous execution at the first and the third level of concurrency. First, it is decided how many load chunks has to be sent to each device to ensure cross-device load balancing. Second, in order to reduce the impact of inevitable delays when distributing and retrieving the load, each individual load (assigned to a distant worker) needs to be subpartitioned into many smaller chunks, in order to (i) overlap computation and communication between independent subpartitions; (ii) efficiently use the asymmetric bandwidth of bidirectional communication links; (iii) respect the amount of supported concurrency at the distant worker; and (iv) fit into the limited device memory.

Besides the previously referred partial total performance models $\psi_{t_i}(x)$ for each distant worker i in the system, the AMPMD relies on additional three partially built performance models which include computational performance of the distant workers and explicit modeling of asymmetric communication bandwidth. In detail, for each load fraction x processed on a device or communicated over a link for a certain time t, the relative performance x/t is calculated and used to build different partial performance models by piecewise linear approximation. Namely, $\psi_{c_i}(x)$ represents the partially built relative computation performance of each device i as a function of the load size x. Bidirectional full-duplex asymmetric bandwidth of each e_i link from E is modeled with $\sigma_{t_i}(x)$ and $\sigma_{o_i}(x)$ functions (where the index t reflects the communication direction from the master to a distant worker, and the index o from a distant worker to the master). Moreover, $M = \{m_{k+1}, \ldots, m_{k+w}\}$ is the set of parameters describing the available memory at each distant worker. In contrast to the current state-of-the-art approaches, the application memory requirements are characterized by the input, output, and execution memory requirement functions, $\mu_i(x)$, $\mu_o(x)$, and $\mu_c(x, P)$, respectively. The execution memory requirement $\mu_c(x, P)$ is expressed as a function of the load size x and device type P, in order to represent the high level of heterogeneity in modern desktop systems where different implementations of the same problem might have different memory requirements.

The first part of the problem, considered in the AMPMD, is how to divide the total load N into fractions $\alpha = \{\alpha_1, \ldots, \alpha_k, \ldots, \alpha_{k+w}\}$ to be simultaneously processed on a set of master cores and distant workers p_i $(1 \le i \le k + w)$, such that the assigned loads are processed in the shortest possible time. Load partitioning at this level of parallel processing can be conducted either by relying on the previously presented MSLBA algorithm or by applying SLBA to the total performance models for each device in the system. The second part of the DL balancing problem considered here is how to subpartition a load fraction α_i assigned to a distant worker i $(k + 1 \le i \le k + w)$ into smaller β_j

load chunks and several $\beta_{j,l}$ subload distributions according to (i) the relative performance models of computation, ψ_{c_i}, and asymmetric full-duplex network links, $\sigma_{1_i}, \sigma_{o_i}$; (ii) the amount of concurrency supported by the p_i; and (iii) the limited worker's memory m_i and application memory requirements $\mu_i(x)$, $\mu_o(x)$, and $\mu_c(x, P)$, such that the processing is finished in the shortest time. Hence, the α_i load is further partitioned into subload distributions $\beta = \{\beta_j\}, 1 \le j \le |\beta|$, each of them consisting of subload fractions $\beta_j = \{\beta_{j,l}\}, 1 \le l \le |\beta_j|$, such that the total sum of load fractions is equal to α_i. It is required to serially perform β_j distributions with overlapped execution of $\beta_{j,l}$ fractions in each of them. For systems with limited memory, it must also be ensured that, for each β_j distribution, the sum of input, output, and execution memory requirements of each subfraction $\beta_{j,l}$ fits into the available memory size m_i of the distant worker p_i. In fact, each subdistribution may consume the whole available memory, which is released between consecutive and independent β_j distributions.

Figure 14.3 depicts the optimal overlap of three load fractions in a single load distribution for distant workers with different amounts of concurrency supported. The linear programming formulation of the problem in Fig. 14.3a states the necessary conditions for optimal overlap between subsequent load fractions in a β_j subdistribution, where $t_\delta(\beta_j)$ represents the total processing time of β_j. The subdistribution maximum relative performance, $\psi_\delta(\beta_j)$, is defined as the optimality criterion, because of its ability not only to select the distribution that efficiently uses both the computation power of the distant worker p_i, ψ_{c_i}, and asymmetric bandwidth of the e_i network link, σ_{1_i} and σ_{o_i}, but also to minimize the impact of the intrinsic communication overheads in the first, $\beta_{j,1}/\sigma_{1_i}(\beta_{j,1})$, and the last load fraction, $\beta_{j,|\beta_j|}/\sigma_{o_i}(\beta_{j,|\beta_j|})$.

$$\text{MAXIMIZE} \quad \psi_\delta(\beta_j) = \frac{\sum_{l=1}^{|\beta_j|} \beta_{j,l}}{t_\delta(\beta_j)} \quad \text{SUBJECT TO:}$$

$$\sum_{l=1}^{|\beta_j|} \beta_{j,l} \le \alpha_i; \quad \sum_{l=1}^{|\beta_j|} (\mu_i(\beta_{j,l}) + \mu_c(\beta_{j,l}, p_i) + \mu_o(\beta_{j,l})) \le m_i \quad (14.3)$$

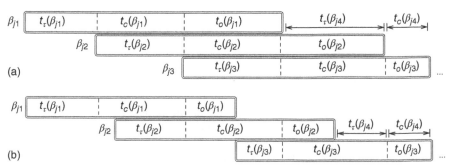

FIGURE 14.3 *Different amounts of overlapping concurrency. (a) Complete communication–computation concurrency. (b) Overlap of a single communication with computation.*

$$\frac{\beta_{j,1}}{\psi_{c_i}(\beta_{j,1})} \geq \frac{\beta_{j,2}}{\sigma_{1_i}(\beta_{j,2})}; \quad \frac{\beta_{j,3}}{\psi_{c_i}(\beta_{j,3})} \geq \frac{\beta_{j,2}}{\sigma_{o_i}(\beta_{j,2})} \tag{14.4}$$

$$\frac{\beta_{j,2}}{\psi_{c_i}(\beta_{j,2})} \geq \frac{\beta_{j,1}}{\sigma_{o_i}(\beta_{j,1})}; \quad \frac{\beta_{j,2}}{\psi_{c_i}(\beta_{j,2})} \geq \frac{\beta_{j,3}}{\sigma_{1_i}(\beta_{j,3})} \tag{14.5}$$

$$\frac{\beta_{j,l}}{\sigma_{1_i}(\beta_{j,l})} \leq \frac{\beta_{j,l-1}}{\psi_{c_i}(\beta_{j,l-1})}; \quad \frac{\beta_{j,l}}{\psi_{c_i}(\beta_{j,l})} \geq \frac{\beta_{j,l-1}}{\sigma_{o_i}(\beta_{j,l-1})}; \quad \forall l \in \{4, |\beta_j|\}. \tag{14.6}$$

It can be observed that the number of subdistributions and load fractions depend not only on the system capabilities and the amount of supported concurrency but also on the application's computation and communication characteristics. In the general case, it may not even be possible to satisfy all the above-mentioned conditions. Hence, we propose here an algorithm that finds a suboptimal β distribution from a closed set $\beta^* = \{\beta^{(n)}\}_{n=1}^{|\beta^*|}$, where $\sum_{j=1}^{|\beta^{(n)}|} \sum_{l=1}^{|\beta_j^{(n)}|} \beta_{j,l}^{(n)} = \alpha_i, \forall n \in \{1, |\beta^*|\}$, and $\sum_{l=1}^{|\beta_j^{(n)}|} (\mu_i(\beta_{j,l}^{(n)}) + \mu_c(\beta_{j,l}^{(n)}, p_i) + \mu_o(\beta_{j,l}^{(n)})) \leq m_i, \forall n, j$, such that

$$\beta = \beta^{(r)}; \quad \psi_t(\beta^{(r)}) = \max\{\psi_t(\beta^{(n)})\}_{n=1}^{|\beta^*|}; \quad \psi_t(\beta^{(n)}) = \alpha_i / t_t(\beta^{(n)}), \tag{14.7}$$

where $t_t(\beta^{(n)})$ is the total processing time of a $\beta^{(n)}$ distribution on the distant worker, and $\psi_t(\beta^{(n)})$ its total relative performance. Therefore, in order to construct the set β^*, we first determine the initial optimal load distribution with three load fractions satisfying (14.3) and (14.5), which are subsequently extended in a six-step procedure to satisfy the remaining conditions and to determine the schedule with maximum relative performance (further details regarding the algorithm's functionality and adaptive iterative approach can be found in [13]).

14.4 EXPERIMENTAL RESULTS

The efficiency of the proposed load-balancing algorithms was validated in several heterogeneous desktop environments equipped with different architectures of CPU and GPU devices. During the experimental evaluation, collaborative CPU + GPU execution was conducted with two mostly used scientific applications as the test cases, that is, dense matrix multiplication and fast Fourier transform (FFT), by relying on vendor-provided high-performance libraries (Intel MKL for CPU and NVIDIA CUBLAS/CUFFT for GPU devices) and without any *a priori* knowledge to ease performance modeling of the system resources.

14.4.1 MSLBA Evaluation: Dense Matrix Multiplication Case Study

The efficiency of the proposed MSLBA algorithm was assessed in a multiaccelerator desktop environment with a quad core Intel Core i7 950 processor (CPU) and two NVIDIA GeForce GPUs from different architectures, that is, Fermi GTX580

(GPU0) and Tesla GTX285 (GPU1). The execution was organized in four processing groups, where CPU Core0 and GPU0 belong to the processing Group 0, CPU Core1 and GPU1 form Group 1, whereas the last two groups contain one of the remaining CPU cores. Double-precision (DP) floating-point (FP) dense matrix multiplication with column-based 1D parallelization was selected ($A_{M \times K} \times B_{K \times N} = C_{M \times N}$), which requires transferring matrix A and columns of B and C matrices to/from the GPUs [4].

In order to show the effectiveness of the proposed MSLBA algorithm when achieving simultaneous multilevel load balancing and partial group performance modeling, matrix multiplication of a size $M = N = K = 8400$ was performed in the previously referred four processing group execution setup. Since performance models of neither the groups nor devices were known *a priori*, an iterative MSLBA-based routine was performed, which allows building the partial device performance models with one point per iteration. In detail, the iterative routine starts by assigning P devices with N/P loads for initial device performance modeling. In each subsequent iteration, MSLBA is used to build partial group performance models according to the current partial performance models of devices and to decide on load distributions across different execution subdomains.

By relying on the MSLBA, four iterations were required to achieve multilevel load balancing, that is, to determine per-group and per-device distributions across all execution subdomains (between processing groups and devices within each group). Figure 14.4a shows the obtained partial group performance models in the final (fourth) iteration. The dotted lines represent device full models obtained with the extensive experimental testing on each device in the system, while the dashed lines are the full models of processing groups constructed by performing exhaustive search over the full device models [25]. The MSLBA decisions were taken according to the partial performance models built by applying the piecewise linear approximation on a set of obtained points (Fig. 14.4a). The GPU performance models encapsulate the time to process and to transfer matrices to/from the host, and it can be noticed that none of considered GPUs was capable of executing a complete problem size because of the limited memory. In total, 111 points were obtained for group performance modeling: 58 points for modeling Group 0 performance, 45 points for Group 1, and 4 points for Groups 2 or 3. It is worth emphasizing that, by relying on exhaustive modeling procedures for group performance [25], it is required to determine a total of 16,808 approximation points to converge toward the same load distributions (8400 points for Groups 0 and 1). Besides achieving load balancing at each execution level, the MSLBA also results in the overall execution time reduction of almost 4 times when compared to the initial homogeneous distribution. In terms of the achieved performance, with the proposed MSLBA approach around 309 Gflops/s were achieved in the considered system, whereas the SLBA approach [15] was capable of discovering a total of 285 Gflops/s for the same problem size. Finally, the MSLBA is also a light-weight solution by imposing 0.9 ms per iteration of scheduling overheads.

In order to show the scalability of the proposed approach, matrix multiplication was performed for different problem sizes in the same execution setup. The obtained

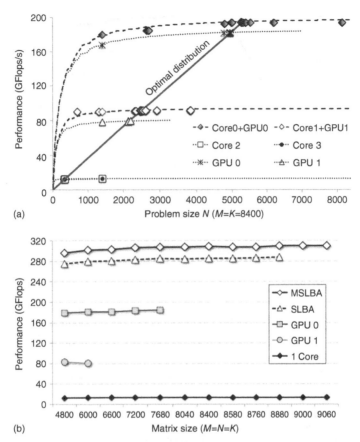

FIGURE 14.4 *MSLBA efficiency for matrix multiplication [25]. (a) Multilevel load balancing and partial performance modeling in the final (fourth) iteration. (b) Scalability analysis.*

results are presented in Fig. 14.4b, where the performance achieved with MSLBA is compared with that of SLBA and of a single device, that is, GPU0, GPU1, and CPU Core. In detail, MSLBA was capable of providing performance improvements for all problem sizes, which resulted in an average improvement of 22 Gflops/s when compared to SLBA. This improvement reflects the ability of MSLBA to employ all CPU cores for execution, while in SLBA a single CPU core must be devoted to control the GPU execution. Moreover, with MSLBA it was possible to perform problem sizes that are not executable either on a single GPU device (above 7680 for GPU0 and 6000 for GPU1) or with SLBA (above 8880) due to the limited memory of GPUs.

14.4.2 AMPMD Evaluation: 2D FFT Case Study

The proposed AMPMD approach was evaluated in a desktop system with an Intel Core 2 Quad Q9550 CPU, and an NVIDIA GeForce 285 GTX GPU, where only a single transfer can be successfully overlapped with computation at the time. The

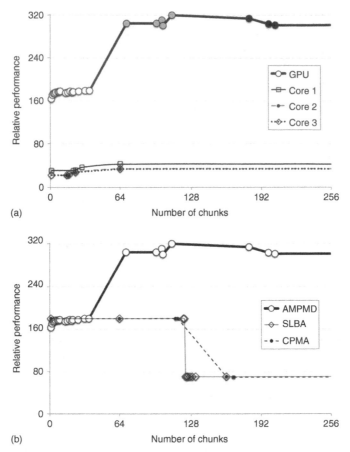

FIGURE 14.5 *AMPMD efficiency for 2D batch FFT [13]. (a) Total performance models in the final (fourth) iteration. (b) Comparison with the state-of-the-art approaches.*

collaborative execution was conducted with two forward and inverse 2D batch DP FP complex FFT of size 256 times 512×512, divisible in the first dimension.

By applying the AMPMD, the load balancing was achieved in four iterations, and the obtained per-device performance models (in the final iteration) are presented in Fig. 14.5a. As can be observed, the determined distribution ($\alpha = \{205, 21, 15, 15\}$ and $\beta = \{\{14, 26, 36, 16, 7, 3\}, \{14, 26, 36, 16, 7, 3, 1\}\}$) was capable of not only providing load balancing and efficient overlapping but also outperforming the directly used (single-load nonoverlapped) CUFFT implementation on the GPU for about 4.3 times (on average 4.5 times across all four iterations) [13]. In total, the GPU performance is modeled with 53 points in only four application runs, that is, 25 approximation points (Fig 14.5b) and 28 accuracy points. The accuracy points represent repeated load fractions or subdistributions, which do not increase the overall number of approximation points, but rather contribute by improving the modeling accuracy.

In order to provide a better insight into the efficiency of the AMPMD, a comparison with two iterative state-of-the-art approaches was conducted, namely SLBA [15] and adaptive CPM-based DL balancing approach (CPMA) [11]. As previously stated, the performance models in the CPMA are represented as constants obtained from the last application run, whereas the SLBA relies on building the FPMs to decide on load balancing. Figure 14.5 presents the comparison of total GPU performance models ψ_t obtained with different approaches in the iteration when load balancing is achieved (if possible). Using the SLBA, 10 iterations were required to converge to a steady load distribution, but even then the obtained distribution did not achieve load balancing, as the refinement procedure is applied on the performance model with instantaneous change in the relative performance. Furthermore, the CPMA neither achieves load balancing nor converges to the final distribution, as after eight iterations it arrives at the state where it oscillates between two distributions [12] because of its unawareness of a complete performance curve shape.

For SLBA and CPMA approaches, the total number of approximation points obtained for GPU performance is equal to the number of iterations, that is, 10 for SLBA, and 8 for CPMA (where 6 points are actually contributing, and the last two are repeated), compared to 53 points obtained with the proposed AMPMD approach. Considering the time taken to determine the load balancing, the SLBA requires 4.3 times more time to determine the steady-state distribution, whereas the CPMA takes about 3.2 times more time to arrive to a "ping-pong" state. In terms of performance, in the final iteration, the AMPMD load-balancing approach achieves more than 2 times better performance when compared to a steady-state SLBA distribution (when executing the complete problem in the same execution environment), and about 2.2 times better performance than the best distribution found with CPMA.

14.5 CONCLUSIONS

In this chapter, we presented two DL-balancing approaches for efficient collaborative processing in heterogeneous multicore CPU and multi-GPU environments at different levels of parallel execution, namely (i) MSLBA for efficient DL balancing across different execution subdomains defined with several processing devices, and across all processing devices within each subdomain, and (ii) AMPMD, which allows efficient overlapping of computation and communication at the single device level in respect to the supported concurrency and limited device memory, while balancing the execution across all other devices in the system. The proposed approaches rely on realistic FPMs of computational performance of processing devices and bidirectional asymmetric bandwidth of communication lines, as well as on partial performance models built for each execution subdomain. The partial estimations of the performance models are built during the application execution while converging towards the load distributions that guarantee as balanced an execution as possible across different execution domains. The proposed algorithms also automatically discover the minimum set of points required to build the partial estimations of the performance curves, which are further used to determine the load distributions.

The efficiency of the proposed approaches was validated in different heterogeneous desktop systems with different architectures of multicore CPUs and GPU devices. Two of the most commonly used scientific applications were used as the case studies, namely dense matrix multiplication and 2D batch FFT. Experimental results have shown that the presented algorithms were capable of delivering significant performance improvements when compared to the state-of-the-art scheduling approaches. Moreover, for test cases, the proposed approaches showed the capability to outperform what is thought to be the optimal implementation for about 4 times, whereas the current state-of-the-art solutions were incapable of determining the load-balancing distribution. Finally, by employing the proposed algorithms not only more accurate performance models were constructed significantly faster but also the overall application performance was improved.

ACKNOWLEDGMENTS

This work was supported by national funds through FCT—Fundação para a Ciência e a Tecnologia, under projects PEst-OE/EEI/LA0021/2013, PTDC/EEI-ELC/3152/2012, and PTDC/EEA-ELC/117329/2010, and the COST Action IC0805 "Open European Network for High-Performance Computing on Complex Environments."

REFERENCES

1. NVIDIA, *NVIDIA CUDA Compute Unified Device Architecture Programming Guide,* Santa Clara, CA: NVIDIA, 2013.
2. C. Augonnet, S. Thibault, R. Namyst, and P.-A. Wacrenier, "StarPU: a unified platform for task scheduling on heterogeneous multicore architectures," *Concurrency and Computation: Practice and Experience*, vol. 23, no. 2, pp. 187–198, 2011.
3. E. Ayguadé, R. M. Badia, F. D. Igual, J. Labarta, R. Mayo, and E. S. Quintana-Ortí, "An extension of the StarSs programming model for platforms with multiple GPUs," in *Proceedings of the Euro-Par 2009 Parallel Processing*, pp. 851–862, Springer-Verlag, Berlin, Heidelberg, 2009.
4. A. Ilic and L. Sousa, "Collaborative execution environment for heterogeneous parallel systems," in *Proceedings of the IPDPSW 2010*, pp. 1–8, IEEE Computer Society, Washington, DC, USA, 2010.
5. B. Veeravalli, D. Ghose, and T. G. Robertazzi, "Divisible load theory: a new paradigm for load scheduling in distributed systems," *Cluster Computing*, vol. 6, pp. 7–17, 2003.
6. O. Beaumont, A. Legrand, L. Marchal, and Y. Robert, "Independent and divisible tasks scheduling on heterogeneous star-shaped platforms with limited memory," in *Proceedings of the PDP 2005*, pp. 179–186, IEEE Computer Society, Lugano, Switzerland, 2005.
7. A. Ghatpande, H. Nakazato, O. Beaumont, and H. Watanabe, "SPORT: an algorithm for divisible load scheduling with result collection on heterogeneous systems," *IEICE Transactions on Communications*, vol. 91, no. 8, pp. 2571–2588, 2008.

8. O. Beaumont, N. Bonichon, and L. Eyraud-Dubois, "Scheduling divisible workloads on heterogeneous platforms under bounded multi-port model," in *Proceedings of the IPDPS 2008*, pp. 1–7, IEEE Computer Society, Miami, FL, USA, 2008.

9. J. Berlińska and M. Drozdowski, "Heuristics for multi-round divisible loads scheduling with limited memory," *Parallel Computing*, vol. 36, no. 4, pp. 199–211, 2010.

10. H. González-Vélez and M. Cole, "Adaptive statistical scheduling of divisible workloads in heterogeneous systems," *Journal of Scheduling*, vol. 13, no. 4, pp. 427–441, 2010.

11. I. Galindo, F. Almeida, and J. M. Badía-Contelles, "Dynamic load balancing on dedicated heterogeneous systems," in *Recent Advances in Parallel Virtual Machine and Message Passing Interface*, pp. 64–74, Springer-Verlag, Berlin, Heidelberg, 2008.

12. D. Clarke, A. Lastovetsky, and V. Rychkov, "Dynamic load balancing of parallel computational iterative routines on highly heterogeneous HPC platforms," *Parallel Processing Letters*, vol. 21, no. 02, pp. 195–217, 2011.

13. A. Ilic and L. Sousa, "Scheduling divisible loads on heterogeneous desktop systems with limited memory," in *Proceedings of the Euro-Par 2011*, pp. 491–501, Springer-Verlag, Berlin, Heidelberg, 2012.

14. A. Lastovetsky and R. Reddy, "Data partitioning for multiprocessors with memory heterogeneity and memory constraints," *Scientific Programming*, vol. 13, no. 2, pp. 93–112, 2005.

15. A. Lastovetsky and R. Reddy, "Data partitioning with a functional performance model of heterogeneous processors," *International Journal of High Performance Computing Applications*, vol. 21, no. 1, pp. 76–90, 2007.

16. A. Lastovetsky and R. Reddy, "Distributed data partitioning for heterogeneous processors based on partial estimation of their functional performance models," in *Proceedings of the Euro-Par 2009 Parallel Processing Workshops*, pp. 91–101, Springer-Verlag, Berlin, Heidelberg, 2010.

17. D. Grewe and M. F. O'Boyle, "A static task partitioning approach for heterogeneous systems using OpenCL," in *Proceedings of the CC 2011*, pp. 286–305, Springer-Verlag, Berlin, Heidelberg, 2011.

18. C.-K. Luk, S. Hong, and H. Kim, "Qilin: exploiting parallelism on heterogeneous multiprocessors with adaptive mapping," in *Proceedings of the MICRO 2009*, pp. 45–55, ACM, New York, USA, 2009.

19. K. Shirahata, H. Sato, and S. Matsuoka, "Hybrid map task scheduling for GPU-based heterogeneous clusters," in *Proceedings of the CloudCom 2010*, Indianapolis, Indiana, USA, pp. 733–740, 2010.

20. T. R. Scogland, B. Rountree, W.-c. Feng, and B. R. de Supinski, "Heterogeneous task scheduling for accelerated OpenMP," in *Proceedings of the IPDPS 2012*, pp. 144–155, IEEE Computer Society, Washington, DC, USA, 2012.

21. Z. Wang, L. Zheng, Q. Chen, and M. Guo, "CAP: co-scheduling based on asymptotic profiling in CPU+ GPU hybrid systems," in *Proceedings of the PMAM 2013*, pp. 107–114, ACM, New York, USA, 2013.

22. C. Yang, F. Wang, Y. Du, J. Chen, J. Liu, H. Yi, and K. Lu, "Adaptive optimization for petascale heterogeneous CPU/GPU computing," in *Proceedings of the CLUSTER 2010*, pp. 19–28, IEEE Computer Society, Washington, DC, USA, 2010.

23. A. Acosta, R. Corujo, V. Blanco, and F. Almeida, "Dynamic load balancing on heterogeneous multicore/multi-GPU systems," in *Proceedings of the HPCS 2010*, pp. 467–476, IEEE Computer Society, Washington, DC, USA, 2010.

24. Z. Zhong, V. Rychkov, and A. Lastovetsky, "Data partitioning on heterogeneous multi-core and multi-GPU systems using functional performance models of data-parallel applications," in *Proceedings of the CLUSTER 2012*, pp. 191–199, IEEE Computer Society, Washington, DC, USA, 2012.

25. A. Ilic and L. Sousa, "Simultaneous multi-level divisible load balancing for heterogeneous desktop systems," in *Proceedings of the ISPA 2012*, pp. 683–690, IEEE Computer Society, Washington, DC, USA, 2012.

15

The All-Pair Shortest-Path Problem in Shared-Memory Heterogeneous Systems

Hector Ortega-Arranz, Yuri Torres, Diego R. Llanos, and Arturo Gonzalez-Escribano

Universidad de Valladolid, Valladolid, Spain

This chapter deals with the all-pair shortest path problem for sparse graphs combining parallel algorithms and parallel-productivity methods in heterogeneous systems. As this problem can be divided into independent single-source shortest path subproblems, we distribute this computation space into different processing units, namely CPUs and graphical processing units (GPUs), that are usually present in modern shared-memory systems. Although the powerful GPUs are significantly faster than the CPUs, the combined use of the two leads to better execution times. Furthermore, two different policies have been used for the scheduling issue, namely an equitable scheduling, where the workspace is equitably divided between all computational units independently of its nature, and a work-stealing scheduling, where a computational unit steals a new task when it has finished its previous work.

15.1 INTRODUCTION

Many problems that arise in real-world networks require the computation of shortest paths and their distances from any source to any destination point. Some

High-Performance Computing on Complex Environments, First Edition.
Edited by Emmanuel Jeannot and Julius Žilinskas.
© 2014 John Wiley & Sons, Inc. Published 2014 by John Wiley & Sons, Inc.

examples include traffic simulations [1], databases [2], internet route planners [3], sensor network [4], or even the computation of graph features such as betweenness centrality [5]. Algorithms to solve shortest path problems are computationally costly, so, in many cases, commercial products implement heuristic approaches to generate approximate solutions, instead. Although heuristics are usually faster and do not need large amounts of data storage or precomputation, they do not guarantee the optimal path.

The all-pair shortest path (APSP) problem is a well-known problem in graph theory whose objective is to find the shortest paths between any pair of nodes. Given a graph $G = (V, E)$ and a function $w(e) : e \in E$ that associates a weight to the edges of the graph, it consists in computing the shortest paths for all pair of nodes $(u, v) : u, v \in V$. The APSP problem is a generalization of the classical problem of optimization, namely the single-source shortest path (SSSP), which consists in computing the shortest paths from just one source node s to every node $v \in V$. If the weights of the graph range only in positive values, $w(e) \geq 0 : e \in E$, we are dealing with the so-called nonnegative single-source shortest path (NSSP) problem.

There are two ways to solve the APSP problem. The first solution is to execute $|V|$ times an NSSP algorithm selecting a new node as source in each iteration. The classical algorithm that solves the NSSP problem is Dijkstra's algorithm [6]. The second solution is to execute an algorithm that globally solves the APSP problem using dynamic programming, such as the Floyd–Warshall algorithm [7, 8]. The former approach is used for sparse graphs, whereas the latter is more efficient for dense graphs.

In this chapter, we deal with the APSP problem for sparse graphs by combining parallel algorithms and parallel-productivity methods in heterogeneous systems. The first level of parallelism we use is the parallelization of Dijkstra's algorithm. The naïve Dijkstra's algorithm is a greedy algorithm whose efficiency is based on ordering the previously computed results. This feature makes its parallelization a difficult task. However, there are certain situations where parts of this ordering can be permuted without leading to wrong results or performance losses. The second level of parallelism exploited is the execution of $|V|$ simultaneous parallel algorithms. As the APSP problem can be divided into independent NSSP subproblems, we distribute the computation space into different processing units.

An emerging method of parallel computation includes the use of hardware accelerators such as GPUs. Their powerful capability has triggered their widespread use in speeding up high-level parallel computations. High-level languages for parallel-data computation, such as CUDA [9] and OpenCL [10], make the general-purpose programming easy for these heterogeneous systems with GPUs. The applications of GPGPU (general-purpose graphics processing computing) computing to accelerate problems related to shortest path problems have increased during the past years. Some GPU-implemented solutions to the NSSP problem have been previously developed [11–13] using some modifications of Dijkstra's algorithm. The latter algorithm is the parallel implementation which we have used as the first level of parallelism for the GPU units in our heterogeneous system.

The new generation of high-performance computing (HPC) tends to assemble different kinds of multicore CPUs and many-core GPUs in the same heterogeneous computing system. The goal of heterogeneous environments is to jointly exploit all computational capabilities of devices with different hardware resource configurations. The different nature of these heterogeneous computational units (HCUs) makes it necessary to implement the same algorithm in different ways in order to derive the maximum benefit of each underlying architecture. However, although each HCU has its own optimized code implementation, usually some of them solve a problem faster than others because of their different resource sets. In order to palliate this imbalance and to maximally exploit the heterogeneous systems, different methods of load balancing can be applied. One of these techniques is to assign more work to the most powerful HCU in our case the GPUs—and the remaining work to the conventional CPUs.

Load balancing is one of the challenging problems and has a tremendous impact on the performance of parallel applications, especially in heterogeneous environments. The objective of load-balancing methods is to distribute the workload proportionally according to the computational power of the devices. This way, these methods allow avoiding overloads on some devices while others are idle. However, in order to obtain good performance by exploiting heterogeneous systems, the programmer needs to manually implement these load-balancing methods.

In this chapter, we present parallel solutions for the APSP problem for heterogeneous systems composed of GPUs and CPU cores, which implement two different load-balancing methods. The used GPU devices have two latest architectures released by CUDA (Fermi and Kepler). Our experimental results show that the use of a heterogeneous environment for the APSP problem improves the execution time by up to 65% compared to the fastest GPU execution used as baseline.

The rest of this chapter is organized as follows. Section 15.2 introduces some basic concepts and notations related to graph theory, and briefly describes both the sequential Dijkstra's algorithm and the parallel version used. Section 15.3 introduces some details for both Fermi and Kepler CUDA architectures. Section 15.4 describes an introduction to the heterogeneous systems and how the load-balancing techniques try to improve their performance in distributing the work load. Section 15.5 explains in depth our Dijkstra GPU implementation using the ideas presented in [14] and our heterogeneous implementations with different load-balancing methods. Section 15.6 presents the experimental methodology and used platform, and the input sets considered. Section 15.7 discusses the results obtained. Finally, Section 15.8 summarizes the conclusions derived.

15.2 ALGORITHMIC OVERVIEW

15.2.1 Graph Theory Notation

We will first present some graph theory concepts and notations related to the shortest path problem. A graph $G = (V, E)$ is composed of a set of vertices V, also called *nodes*, and a set of edges E, also called *arcs*. Every vertex v is usually depicted as a point in the graph. Every edge e is usually depicted as a line that connects two and only two vertices. An edge is a tuple (u, v) that represents a link between vertices u and v. The number of edges connected to a vertex v is called the *degree* of v. In an *undirected graph*, all edges can be traversed in both directions, whereas an edge (u, v) of a *directed graph* only can be traversed from u to v. There is a weight function $w(u, v)$ associated to each edge, which represents the cost of traversing the edge.

A *path* $P = \langle s, \dots, u, \dots, v, \dots, t \rangle$ is a sequence of vertices connected by edges, from a source vertex s to a target vertex t. The *weight* of a path, $w(P)$, is the sum of all the weights associated with the edges involved in the path. The *shortest path* between two vertices s and t is the path with the minimum weight among all possible paths between s and t. Finally, the minimum distance between s and t, $d(s, t)$ or simply $d(t)$, is the weight of the shortest path between them. We denote by $\delta(s, t)$, or simply $\delta(t)$, a temporal tentative distance between s and t during the computation of $d(t)$.

15.2.2 Dijkstra's Algorithm

The basic solution for the NSSP is Dijkstra's algorithm [6]. This algorithm constructs minimal paths from a source node s to the remaining nodes, exploring adjacent nodes following a proximity criterion.

The exploration process is known as *edge relaxation*. When an edge (u, v) is relaxed from a node u, we say that node v has been *reached*. Therefore, there is a path from the source through u to reach v with a tentative shortest distance. Node v will be considered *settled* when the algorithm has found the shortest path from the source node s to v. The algorithm finishes when all nodes are settled.

The algorithm uses an array, D, that stores all tentative distances found from the source node s to the rest of the nodes. At the beginning of the algorithm, every node is unreached and no distances are known, so $D[i] = \infty$ for all nodes i, except for the current source node $D[s] = 0$. Note that both reached and unreached nodes are considered unsettled nodes.

The algorithm proceeds as follows:

1. (Initialization) The algorithm starts on the source node s, initializing the distance array $D[i] = \infty$ for all nodes i and $D[s] = 0$. Node s is considered as the *frontier node* f ($f \leftarrow s$) and it is settled.
2. (Edge relaxation) For every node v adjacent to f that has not been settled, a new distance from the source is found using the path through f, with value $D[f] + w(f, v)$. If this distance is lower than previous value $D[v]$, then $D[v] \leftarrow D[f] + w(f, v)$.
3. (Settlement) The node u with the lowest value in D is taken as the new frontier node ($f \leftarrow u$). After this, current frontier node f is now considered as settled.
4. (Termination criteria) If all nodes have been settled, the algorithm finishes. Otherwise, the algorithm proceeds to Step 2.

In order to recover the path, every node reached stores its predecessor, so at the end of the query phase the algorithm just runs back from the target through the stored predecessors till the source node is reached. The *shortest path tree* of a graph from source node s is the composition of every shortest path from s to the remaining nodes.

15.2.3   Parallel Version of Dijkstra's Algorithm

Dijkstra's algorithm, in each iteration i, calculates the minimum tentative distance of the nodes belonging to the unsettled set, U_i. The node whose tentative distance is equal to this minimum value can be settled and becomes the frontier node. Its outgoing edges are traversed to relax the distances of the adjacent nodes.

In order to parallelize Dijkstra's algorithm, we need to identify which nodes can be settled and used as frontier nodes at the same time. The idea of inserting into the frontier set, F_{i+1}, all nodes with this minimum tentative distance in order to process them simultaneously was implemented for GPUs in [11]. A more aggressive enhancement was introduced in [14], and later implemented for GPUs in [13], augmenting the frontier set with nodes with larger tentative distances. The algorithm computes in each iteration i, for each node of the unsettled set, $u \in U_i$, the sum of (i) its tentative distance, $\delta(u)$, and (ii) the minimum cost of its outgoing edges, $\Delta_{\text{node } u} = \min\{w(u,z) : (u,z) \in E\}$. Afterward, it calculates the minimum of these computed values. Finally, those nodes whose tentative distances are lower than or equal to this minimum value can be settled, becoming the frontier set.

15.3   CUDA OVERVIEW

GPUs started as image processing devices. Over the years, GPUs have improved in performance, architectural complexity, and programmability. Currently, these devices are widely used for general-purpose computing (GPGPU) [15] because of the performance improvements achieved on multiple kinds of parallel applications.

CUDA (compute unified device architecture) [9] is the parallel computing architecture developed by Nvidia Company for general-purpose applications. CUDA simplifies the GPGPU programming by means of high-level API and a reduced set of instructions.

Fermi [9] is the second generation of CUDA architectures, launched in early 2010, and the latest generation of CUDA architecture is Kepler [16], released in early 2012. Table 15.1 summarizes the main characteristics of Fermi and Kepler. Each new architecture generation has increased the number of SPs (streaming processors) and the maximum number of threads per SM (streaming multiprocessor). The main change introduced by Fermi is a transparent L1/L2 cache hierarchy which has been maintained in Kepler. However, the sizes and configuration possibilities are different. The global memory is organized in several banks. The number of banks has been decreased on Fermi and Kepler. Finally, the main feature introduced by Kepler is the next generation of streaming multiprocessor (SMX) with 192 single-precision CUDA cores, 4 different warp schedulers, and 2 dispatch units.

TABLE 15.1   Summary of CUDA Architecture Parameters (Fermi and Kepler)

Parameter	Fermi	Kepler
SPs (per-SM)	32	192
Maximum number of blocks (per SM)	8	16
Maximum number of threads (per SM)	1536	2048
Maximum number of threads (per block)	1024	1024
L2 cache	768 KB	$\geq$512 KB
L1 cache (per SM)	0/16/48 KB	0/16/32/48 KB
Size of global memory transaction	32/128 B	32/128 B
Global memory banks	5–6	4

15.4   HETEROGENEOUS SYSTEMS AND LOAD BALANCING

Heterogeneous computing [17] tries to jointly exploit different kinds of computational units, such as GPUs, field-programmable gate arrays (FPGAs), and CPU cores. Compared to traditional symmetric CPUs, this computing paradigm offers higher peak performance while being both energy and cost efficient. However, programming for heterogeneous environments is a tedious task and has a long learning curve. The authors in [18] show the importance and the high interest of heterogeneous environments and how a heterogeneous environment can improve significantly certain kind of parallel problems.

Load-balancing methods for heterogeneous systems try to distribute the work load between the computing units to exploit all available hardware resources. There are several load-balancing methods not only for the traditional system but also for heterogeneous systems. A brief classification is presented in the following.

In [19], the authors create dependence graphs in order to classify as dependent or independent the application tasks. More independent tasks are launched to GPU devices in order to reduce the costly data transfers between the PCI-express bus.

In [20], a model to estimate the possible execution time of each task (number of instructions and input data size) is presented, and, thus, to decide which hardware would be the best for each case. The size of each single task is fixed at the time of compilation. In [21], the author calculates the data transfer time between the different devices (GPUs and CPUs), and creates a model in order to reduce inter-GPU and CPU–GPU communication. In [22], the authors collect all the information of each GPU hardware. By means of CUDA API and a model created by the authors, they select a good device for a given task.

For a given set of tasks with preset sizes, in [23], the authors assign bigger tasks to more powerful devices. On the other hand, for a specific problem, [24] assign tasks with similar sizes to the same device in order to equilibrate the communication imbalance factor.

A static load balancing appears when all tasks are available to schedule before any real computation starts. From the previously mentioned works, [21] and [25] present static load-balancing techniques. The opposite is the dynamic load balancing. Now, the tasks are not known until midway through the execution, and new ones can appear. From the previously mentioned works, [23, 24, 26, 27] present a dynamic load-balancing scheme.

15.5 PARALLEL SOLUTIONS TO THE APSP

This section describes both the single GPU parallel implementation, which is used as baseline, and the different heterogeneous approaches implemented to solve the APSP problem.

15.5.1 GPU Implementation

We have used the implementation described in [13] for the GPU units of our heterogeneous system. It is an adaptation of the sequential Dijkstra's algorithm described in Section 15.5.2 to the CUDA architecture (Algorithm 15.1) following the parallel enhancements of [14]. It is composed of three kernels and executes the internal operations of the Dijkstra vertex loop:

- The *relax kernel* (invoked in line 3 of Algorithm 15.1) decreases the tentative distances for the remaining unsettled nodes of the current iteration i through the outgoing edges of the frontier nodes $f \in F_i$. A GPU thread is associated with each node in the graph. Those threads assigned to frontier nodes, $f \in F_i$, traverse their outgoing edges, relaxing the distances of their unsettled adjacent nodes.

- The *minimum kernel* (line 4 of Algorithm 15.1) computes the minimum tentative distance of the nodes that belong to the U_i set. To do so, the advanced *reduce3* method of the CUDA SDK [28] has been modified to accomplish this operation. Our *minimum kernel* is adapted in order to (i) add the corresponding $\Delta_{node\ v}$ value to $\delta(v)$, and (ii) compare its new assigned values to obtain the minimum one. The resulting value of the *minimum kernel* is the Δ_i.

- The *update kernel* (line 5 of Algorithm 15.1) settles those nodes from U_i whose tentative distances are lower than or equal to Δ_i. This task is carried out by extracting them from the unsettled set following the iteration, U_{i+1}, and putting them to the frontier set F_{i+1} following iteration. Each single GPU thread checks, for its corresponding node v, whether $(U(v)\ \ and\ \ \delta(v) \leq \Delta_i)$. If so, the thread assigns v to F_{i+1} and deletes v from U_{i+1}.

Algorithm 15.1

```
GPU implementation of Dijkstra's algorithm {
  (01)      <<<initialize>>>(U,F,δ);
  (02)      while (Δ ≠ ∞) {
  (03)          <<<relax>>>(U,F,δ);
  (04)          Δ = <<<minimum>>>(U,δ);
  (05)          <<<update>>>(U,F,δ,Δ);
  (06)      }
}
```

The nodes are numbered from 0 to $n - 1$. Besides the basic structures to hold nodes, vertices, and their weights, three vectors are defined:

- vector U, which stores in $U[v]$ whether node v is an unsettled node;
- vector F, which stores in $F[v]$ whether node v is a frontier node; and
- vector δ, which stores in $\delta[v]$ the tentative distance from the source to node v.

15.5.2   Heterogeneous Implementation

The solution of the APSP through the V-NSSP approach allows us to divide the problem into $|V|$ independent tasks. Numbering the nodes of the graph from 0 to $|V| - 1$, the task t_i solves the NSSP problem which has the node i as the source.

15.5.2.1   Equitable Scheduling   A simple way to apply load balancing to a heterogeneous system is to equitably distribute the work without taking into account the computational capabilities of the devices. This kind of technique usually leads to easy implementations, but at the expense of having a temporal cost equal to the time that the worst device takes to compute its work. Equitable scheduling can be classified as a static load-balancing technique at compilation time.

Our equitable scheduling (ES) approach statically divides the workspace between the computing threads, giving to each one the same number of tasks. If nc represents the number of computing threads, id the thread identifier, and $nt = |V|/nc$ the number of tasks per thread, this approach makes each thread responsible for computing the tasks from $id \cdot nt$ to $id \cdot nt + nt - 1$. If this task division is not exact, each of the first threads takes one of the remaining tasks until there is no more work to do.

15.5.2.2   Work-Stealing Scheduling   Work stealing is one of the most important techniques of load balancing. It is commonly employed to accomplish dynamic work scheduling between any kind of hardware devices. All hardware devices of a heterogeneous system can steal a task from the global task queue. Note that the access to the global task queue must be implemented with some kind of synchronization in order to avoid that two or more devices steal the same task. Usually, this synchronization involves a bottleneck in the execution times. Work-stealing scheduling can be classified as a dynamic load-balancing technique at runtime.

Our work-stealing scheduling (WS) approach allows an idle thread that has finished its previous work to steal the following task t_i. This task is immediately eliminated from the queue at the moment it is taken. Then, the thread computes the corresponding NSSP problem with node i as source. Finally, when the thread ends its work, it comes back to the global task queue in order to take another one, repeating the process till there is no more pending work. The synchronization of task-stealing has been implemented using an atomic region. That means that only one thread can take the following work at any moment.

Algorithm 15.2

```
Work-stealing implementation {
(01)        #parallel                              /* Parallel region */
(02)        if (idThread < numGPUs){               /* For GPUs */
(03)            selectGPU(idThread);               /* GPU selection */
(04)            atomic{ t = steal_work(taskQueue) };
(05)            while( t != NULL ){
(06)                launch_GPU_Kernel(t);
(07)                atomic{ t = steal_work(taskQueue) };
(08)            }//while
(09)        }else{                                 /* For CPU-cores */
(10)            atomic{ t = steal_work(taskQueue) };
(11)            while( t != NULL ){
(12)                launch_CPU_Kernel(t);
(13)                atomic{ t = steal_work(taskQueue) };
(14)        }//else
(15)        #end parallel
}
```

Algorithm 15.2 is the pseudocode of the work-stealing technique to solve the APSP problem. Lines (2) and (9) indicate that the first threads are assigned to GPU devices and the rest to CPU cores. The *taskQueue* stores the list of all tasks, and the *atomic{}* primitive creates an exclusion region to avoid simultaneous stealing of the same task from different idle threads.

15.6 EXPERIMENTAL SETUP

We will first describe the methodology used for our experiments, the input set problems, and the load-balancing techniques evaluated.

15.6.1 Methodology

We have compared our heterogeneous implementations against the single-GPU implementation, which we have denominated as baseline, in order to evaluate the performance gain of using heterogeneous systems for the particular APSP problem. The algorithm implemented for GPU devices is an adaptation of the ideas in [14] for the CUDA architecture presented in [13]. Moreover, the sequential version of this algorithm is used for the CPU devices.

Furthermore, several instances with different numbers of OpenMP threads, for both load-balancing methods presented, have been executed in order to determine the best configuration. These instances have been tested with graphs of 1×2^{20} nodes solving the complete APSP problem. Additionally, we have used for our experiment graphs whose number of nodes ranges from 1×2^{20} to 11×2^{20}. However, because of the large amount of computations needed to solve the APSP in these graphs, we have bounded the problem to a *512-source-nodes-to-all* in order to reduce the global execution time. For the selection of these source nodes, we have used the random function *srand48()* from the C libraries.

15.6.2 Target Architectures

The evaluated heterogeneous system is composed of different computational units which are grouped into two categories:

- for the shared-memory CPU system, the host machine is an Intel(R) Core(TM) i7 CPU 960 3.20 GHz, 64-bits compatible, with a global memory of 6 GB DDR3, with two GPUs;
- the GPU system has two GPU devices of different architectures:
  - a GeForce GTX 680 (Kepler) Nvidia GPU device, and
  - a GeForce GTX 480 (Fermi) Nvidia GPU device.

The evaluated baseline implementation is executed in the same shared-memory host machine of the previously described heterogeneous system, but it only uses one GPU device as the computational unit, which is a GeForce GTX 680 (Kepler) GPU device.

Regarding the software used, the host machine runs on a UBUNTU Desktop 10.10 (64 bits) operating system, and the experiments have been launched using CUDA 4.2 toolkit and the 295.41 64-bit driver.

15.6.3 Input Set Characteristics

The input set is composed of a collection of graphs randomly generated by a graph-creation tool used by [11] in their experiments. They have been created by adding seven adjacent predecessors to each node of the graph. Afterward, they have inverted the graphs in order to store the node successors sequentially. These graphs are represented through adjacency lists, the nodes are numbered from 0 to $|V| - 1$, and the edge weights are integers that randomly range from 1 to 10.

The node distribution of this kind of graphs shows an irregular behavior for the computational time of the APSP problem in terms of each NSSP subproblem. The iterations of the first nodes of the graph need more computational time to solve its NSSP problem than the final ones. Figure 15.1 shows, using intervals of 32 nodes, how the time needed is considerably reduced as long as the baseline implementation gets closer to the final nodes. Because of the nature of the problem, there are no inter-NSSP dependences and communication in the complete APSP computation.

15.6.4 Load-Balancing Techniques Evaluated

Both load-balancing techniques described, namely equitable scheduling and work stealing, have been implemented with respect to different number of OpenMP threads. Several instances with different numbers of threads have been evaluated against the baseline implementation.

We have tagged each instance, depending on which load-balancing technique is implemented, with the label "E" for equitable scheduling instances and "W" for work-stealing scheduling instances, followed by a number that represents the number of OpenMP threads used (Table 15.2). Thus, the evaluated instances "E_3" and "W_8" are the implementation of equitable scheduling with three threads and the implementation of WS scheduling with eight threads, respectively.

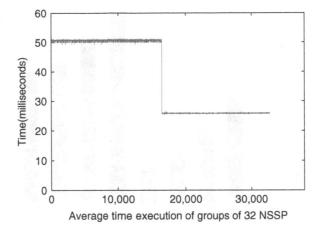

FIGURE 15.1 *Temporal cost of the different source nodes in the graph for the Kepler GPU.*

TABLE 15.2   Experimental Instances

Legend	Description
G_1	Single GPU thread (Kepler)
E_2 / W_2	2 GPU threads (Fermi & Kepler)
E_3 / W_3	2 GPU threads + 1 CPU threads
E_4 / W_4	2 GPU threads + 2 CPU threads
E_6 / W_6	2 GPU threads + 4 CPU threads
E_8 / W_8	2 GPU threads + 6 CPU threads
E_{14} / W_{14}	2 GPU threads + 12 CPU threads
E_{16} / W_{16}	2 GPU threads + 14 CPU threads

The first two threads are always assigned to the two GPU hardware devices, one for each graphic accelerator. The rest of the threads are executed in the CPU cores. Therefore, the instances "E_2" and "W_2" only use the GPUs' resources with the corresponding load-balancing technique.

15.7   EXPERIMENTAL RESULTS

In this section, we present the experimental results obtained for the execution of the complete APSP with $|V| = 1 \times 2^{20}$ and the 512-source-to-all for graphs for which the number of nodes ranges from 1×2^{20} to 11×2^{20}.

15.7.1   Complete APSP

15.7.1.1   Equitable Scheduling   Figure 15.2a presents the execution times of the equitable scheduling technique for instances with different numbers of OpenMP threads. The performance of the baseline approach (G_1) is significantly improved

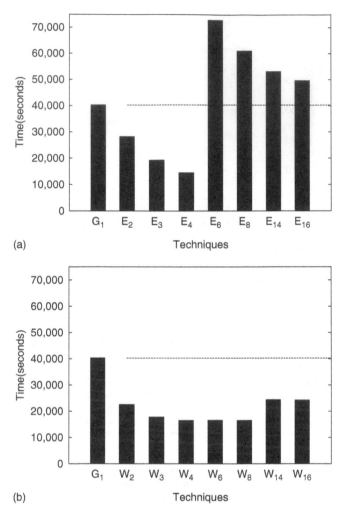

FIGURE 15.2   Execution times of scheduling policies. (a) Equitable. (b) Work stealing.

when a second GPU device is used (E_2). However, a 2× speedup is not reached because the architectures of the used GPUs are different. This means that the total execution time corresponds to that of the less powerful GPU device. Nonetheless, E_2 presents a 30% improvement in performance against the baseline.

The use of one and two CPU cores (E_3 and E_4) helps in decreasing this critical execution time because the number of subproblems (SSSP problems) that the critical GPU has to resolve is reduced. The instance E_4 shows a 65% performance improvement. The more the number of threads launched, the less the amount of computation given to each device. Nevertheless, because of the irregular nature of the graph (see the distribution time in Fig.15.1), there is a threshold beyond which the equitable partition overloads the CPU cores with too much work. This occurs when the most costly tasks, which were assigned to GPUs before, are assigned to CPU cores. For this reason, the total execution time of the approach E_6 is significantly increased, even surpassing the baseline time. Furthermore, as more threads are launched from this point, the total time of execution is reduced. This occurs because the number of tasks per computational unit is less and all devices are used, but the time still surpasses the baseline times.

15.7.1.2 Work-Stealing Scheduling Figure 15.2b shows the execution time results of the work-stealing technique for instances with different numbers of OpenMP threads. The performance of the baseline approach (G_1) is significantly improved by any experimental instance that uses the work-stealing method (W_i). The instance that uses only two GPUs has a 44% performance improvement against the baseline. As we increase the number of OpenMP threads, more hardware devices are used, thereby reducing the execution times. Although the most costly tasks are also taken by the CPU cores, while they are computing their subproblem, the GPUs are continuously stealing tasks. The fastest execution times is for the W_4 instance, leading to a 60% performance improvement. However, when the number of launched threads exceeds the number of heterogeneous computational units (W_{14} and W_{16}), the execution of threads that belong to the same CPU core is concurrent. This behavior leads to slight penalty times, reaching a performance improvement of 40% against the baseline.

15.7.2 512-Source-Node-to-All Shortest Path

15.7.2.1 Equitable Scheduling Figure 15.3a presents the execution times for instances for the equitable scheduling implementation and different OpenMP launched threads. The best performance is obtained with the E_2 configuration, leading to a 45% performance improvement against the baseline.

The heterogeneous approaches with CPU cores ($E_{\{3,...,16\}}$) have worse execution times than the baseline because of memory access bottlenecks. This is because the CPUs take the costly tasks due to the random nature of the selection of the 512 nodes. However, as in the complete APSP scenario, this time is reduced when more threads are launched.

15.7.2.2 Work-Stealing Scheduling Figure 15.3b shows the work-stealing implementation for different OpenMP launched threads. As in the APSP scenario, the execution time of any work-stealing instance ($W_{\{2,...,16\}}$) is better than the baseline (G_1). The instance of two threads that only use GPU devices, W_2, has a very good performance against the baseline (46% performance improvement). Inserting an additional CPU core to the heterogeneous system, W_3, leads to an even better performance improvement of 47%. However, adding more than one CPU core to the heterogeneous system, $W_{\{4,...,16\}}$, leads to slightly worse execution times compared to the best.

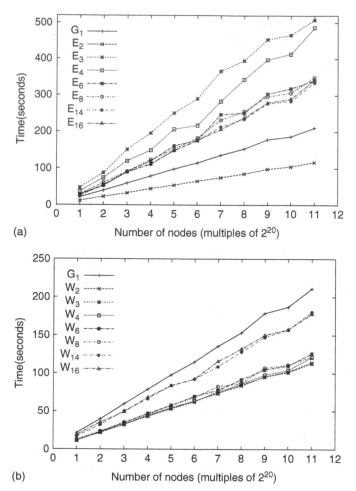

FIGURE 15.3   *Execution times for 512 nodes for different scheduling. (a) Equitable. (b) Work stealing.*

15.7.3 Experimental Conclusions

The best execution time for the complete APSP scenario is achieved with an equitable scheduling implementation, E_4, leading to a 65% performance improvement compared to the baseline G_1. However, the approaches that closely follow this improvement are those that use a work-stealing implementation, ($W_{\{3,...,8\}}$), instead of other equitable scheduling instances with similar thread configuration.

For the 512-source-to-all scenario, the best results are reached with a work-stealing implementation, W_3, with a 47% improvement compared to G_1. The equitable scheduling approach loses performance against the baseline for all thread configurations excepting the version that only uses GPUs, E_2.

These results show that (i) the equitable scheduling can be tuned up to achieve the best performance times avoiding critical code regions but it is very sensitive to changes of the input graph, and (ii) the work-stealing implementations have a more robust performance than equitable scheduling because they are less dependent on the nature of the graph.

15.8 CONCLUSIONS

We have presented solutions of the APSP problem for heterogeneous systems composed of GPUs and CPU cores using equitable and work-stealing load-balancing techniques. These solutions could achieve a performance improvement Of up to 65% compared to the baseline single-GPU solution. Moreover, the results of our experiments have shown that the work-stealing implementation with the same number of OpenMP threads could give good performance for both tested scenarios. However, the equitable scheduling implementation that involves CPU cores did not show any significant performance improvement if the nature of the graph was not taken into account.

Our first conclusion is that the joint use of very different computational power devices is useful in improving the total execution time compared to the fastest GPU implementation. Second, the previous study of the nature of the input problem allows us to better map the costliest tasks to the most powerful devices. For our case, the equitable scheduling that maps all costly tasks to the GPUs and leaves light ones to the CPU cores leads to the best performance. Finally, the application of the work-stealing technique results in a more robust implementation against the equitable scheduling because it is less sensitive to the nature of the input problem.

ACKNOWLEDGMENTS

The authors would like to thank P. Martín, R. Torres, and A. Gavilanes for letting us use the source code and input sets of the graph-creation tools described in [11]. This research was partly supported by the Spanish Government (TIN2007-62302, TIN2011-25639, CENIT OCEANLIDER, CAPAP-H networks TIN2010-12011-E, and TIN2011-15734-E), Junta de Castilla y León, Spain (VA094A08, VA 172A12-2), the HPC-EUROPA2 project (project number: 228398) with the support of the European Commission—Capacities Area—Research Infrastructures Initiative, and the ComplexHPC COST Action.

REFERENCES

1. J. Barceló, E. Codina, J. Casas, J. L. Ferrer, and D. García, "Microscopic traffic simulation: a tool for the design, analysis and evaluation of intelligent transport systems," *Journal of Intelligent & Robotic Systems*, vol. 41, pp. 173–203, 2005.
2. L. Chang, J. X. Yu, L. Qin, H. Cheng, and M. Qiao, "The exact distance to destination in undirected world," *The VLDB Journal*, vol. 21, no. 6, pp. 869–888, 2012.
3. G. Rétvári, J. J. Bíró, and T. Cinkler, "On shortest path representation," *IEEE/ACM Transactions on Networking*, vol. 15, pp. 1293–1306, 2007.
4. F. Huc, A. Jarry, P. Leone, and J. Rolim, "Brief announcement: routing with obstacle avoidance mechanism with constant approximation ratio," in *Proceedings of the 29th*

ACM SIGACT-SIGOPS Symposium on Principles of Distributed Computing, PODC '10, pp. 116–117. New York: ACM, 2010.

5. D. Gkorou, J. Pouwelse, D. Epema, T. Kielmann, M. J. van Kreveld, and W. J. Niessen, "Efficient approximate computation of betweenness centrality," in *16th Annual Conference of the Advanced School for Computing and Imaging (ASCI 2010)*, Veldhoven, 2010.

6. E. W. Dijkstra, "A note on two problems in connexion with graphs," *Numerische Mathematik*, vol. 1, pp. 269–271, 1959.

7. R. W. Floyd, "Algorithm 97: shortest path," *Communications of the ACM*, vol. 5, no. 6, pp. 345–345, 1962.

8. S. Warshall, "A theorem on boolean matrices," *Journal of the ACM*, vol. 9, no. 1, pp. 11–12, 1962.

9. D. B. Kirk and W. W. Hwu, *Programming Massively Parallel Processors: A Hands-on Approach*. Burlington, WI: Morgan Kaufmann, 2010.

10. J. Stone, D. Gohara, and G. Shi, "OpenCL: a parallel programming standard for heterogeneous computing systems," *Computing in Science Engineering*, vol. 12, no. 3, pp. 66–73, 2010.

11. P. Martín, R. Torres, and A. Gavilanes, "CUDA solutions for the SSSP Problem," in *Computational Science—ICCS 2009, LNCS* (G. Allen, J. Nabrzyski, E. Seidel, G. van Albada, J. Dongarra, and P. Sloot, eds.), vol. 5544, pp. 904–913, Berlin / Heidelberg: Springer, 2009. DOI: 10.1007/978-3-642-01970-8_91.

12. P. Harish, V. Vineet, and P. J. Narayanan, "Large Graph Algorithms for Massively Multi-threaded Architectures," Tech. Rep. IIIT/TR/2009/74. Hyderabad, India, Centre for Visual Information Technology, International Institute of Information Technology, 2009.

13. H. Ortega-Arranz, Y. Torres, D. R. Llanos, and A. Gonzalez-Escribano, "A New GPUbased Approach to the Shortest Path Problem," in *High Performance Computing and Simulation (HPCS)*, 2013, International Conference on, pp. 505–512, Helsinki, 2013.

14. A. Crauser, K. Mehlhorn, U. Meyer, and P. Sanders, "A parallelization of Dijkstra's shortest path algorithm," in *Mathematical Foundations of Computer Science 1998, LNCS* (L. Brim, J. Gruska, and J. Zlatuška, eds.), vol. 1450, pp. 722–731. Berlin / Heidelberg: Springer, 1998. DOI: 10.1007/BFb0055823.

15. G. C. de Verdière, "Introduction to GPGPU, a hardware and software background," *Comptes Rendus Mécanique*, vol. 339, no. 2–3, pp. 78–89, 2011.

16. NVIDIA, *NVIDIA CUDA Programming Guide 4.2: Kepler*. Santa Clara, CA: NVIDIA, 2012.

17. A. R. Brodtkorb, C. Dyken, T. R. Hagen, J. M. Hjelmervik, and O. O. Storaasli, "State-of-the-art in heterogeneous computing," *Journal Scientific Programming*, vol. 18, no. 1, pp. 1–33, 2010.

18. S. Singh, "Computing without processors," *Communications of the ACM*, vol. 54, pp. 46–54, 2011.

19. E. Hermann, B. Raffin, F. Faure, T. Gautier, and J. Allard, "Multi-GPU and multi-CPU parallelization for interactive physics simulations," in *Proceedings of the 16th International Euro-Par Conference on Parallel Processing: Part II, Euro-Par'10*, pp. 235–246. Berlin, Heidelberg: Springer-Verlag, 2010.

20. A. Leung, O. Lhoták, and G. Lashari, "Automatic parallelization for graphics processing units," *Proceedings of the 7th International Conference on Principles and Practice of Programming in Java PPPJ 09*, p. 91–100, Calgary, 2009.

21. N. R. Satish, *Compile Time Task and Resource Allocation of Concurrent Applications to Multiprocessor Systems*. PhD thesis, EECS Department, University of California, Berkeley, 2009.

22. A. Binotto, C. Pereira, and D. Fellner, "Towards dynamic reconfigurable load-balancing for hybrid desktop platforms," in *2010 IEEE International Symposium on Parallel Distributed Processing, Workshops and Phd Forum (IPDPSW)*, pp. 1–4, Atlanta, 2010.

23. S. Tzeng, A. Patney, and J. D. Owens, "Task Management for Irregular-Parallel Workloads on the GPU," in *Proceedings of the Conference on High Performance Graphics*, HPG'10, Saarbrucken, pp. 29–37, Aire-la-Ville, Switzerland, Switzerland: Eurographics Association, 2010.

24. P. Yao, H. An, M. Xu, G. Liu, X. Li, Y. Wang, and W. Han, "CuHMMer: a load-balanced CPU-GPU cooperative bioinformatics application," in *HPCS'2010*, pp. 24–30, Caen, 2010.

25. E. Burrows and M. Haveraaen, "A hardware independent parallel programming model," *Journal of Logic and Algebraic Programming*, vol. 78, pp. 519–538, 2009.

26. D. Cederman and P. Tsigas, "On sorting and load balancing on GPUs," *ACM SIGARCH Computer Architecture News*, vol. 36, no. 5, pp. 11–18, 2008.

27. C.-K. Luk, S. Hong, and H. Kim, "Qilin: exploiting parallelism on heterogeneous multiprocessors with adaptive mapping," in *Proceedings of the 42nd Annual IEEE/ACM International Symposium on Microarchitecture, MICRO 42*, pp. 45–55. New York: ACM, 2009.

28. M. Harris, *Optimizing Parallel Reduction in CUDA*. Santa Clara, CA: NVIDIA, 2008.

PART VI

Efficient Exploitation of Distributed Systems

16

Resource Management for HPC on the Cloud

Marc E. Frincu and Dana Petcu

West University of Timisoara, Timisoara, Romania

This chapter starts by presenting an overview on existing resource management systems and scheduling algorithms for high-performance computing for clouds. Next, we describe a prototype framework for building autonomous resource management systems. This is aimed at allowing administrators to enhance their own solutions with autonomous behavior by relying on the API and the communication protocol we offer. The current version only supports self-healing, but we intent to extend its capabilities to those of a fully autonomous system.

16.1 INTRODUCTION

High-performance computing (HPC) has appeared as a result of the increasing demand for processing speed. It allows the use of supercomputers and parallel processing in order to solve complex problems that would otherwise require unreasonable amounts of time on ordinary machines. Moreover, the Globus project showed that grid computing can be successfully used to harness the power of large-scale distributed systems, thus proving that HPC can go beyond the single supercomputer restriction as well as being offered to a larger community of researchers enrolled in virtual organizations.

High-Performance Computing on Complex Environments, First Edition.
Edited by Emmanuel Jeannot and Julius Žilinskas.
© 2014 John Wiley & Sons, Inc. Published 2014 by John Wiley & Sons, Inc.

Recently, cloud computing has emerged as the *de facto* pay-per-use paradigm, allowing the use of a large amount of resources on an on-demand basis. Citing IDC,[1] the cloud business is ever increasing, and estimates give a worldwide revenue of US$72.9 billion by 2015 of which one out of seven dollars spent on software or storage will be through public/private clouds. Hence it is likely that the HPC community will benefit from clouds as well. The odds are even better if we look at the almost unlimited storage and instantly available and scalable computing resources clouds can offer to users. Moreover, through the availability of cluster-based services, the access to HPC facilities is now possible to individual users in a matter of seconds.

Clouds offer a wide array of features, including on-demand provisioning, customized virtual machine (VM) images, and service-level guarantees. Depending on the level of abstraction, the access to these can be eased to the point of using web interfaces for uploading the input files for the application. The three main levels usually found in clouds are infrastructure as a service (IaaS), platform as a service (PaaS), and software as a service (SaaS). IaaS offers only low-level access to the infrastructure for handling VMs or storage. PaaS adds a level of abstraction over it and provides OS-like services for handling application design, development, and deployment. It also features modules for monitoring, scalability, security, etc. In other words, it offers the client a complete software stack to manage the cloud-oriented application. Finally, SaaS provides clients with actual cloud applications based on existing PaaS.

When HPC and cloud merge, they give birth to high-performance cloud computing (HPC2) [1], which essentially means applying cloud-based environments to HPC architectures. This lets HPC systems to be more flexible and cost efficient.

However, contrary to web applications that have quickly gained ground on most clouds, HPC2 has some specific demands, which makes its adoption somewhat difficult. HPC applications are usually tailored for a specific hardware and software stack. While the latter can be easily surpassed by bundling the right type of VM image, the former might require special configurations hard to find in most cloud providers. We refer here to CPU, memory, communication, and storage specifications. Among these, the most problematic is the communication aspect since the high speed requirements of HPC applications cannot be usually met in regular clouds.

Furthermore, most HPC applications are batch applications, many of them performing parameter sweeps. Especially for them, it is important to find the correct resource configuration and allocation for a given application and a set of user objectives. This requires the use of sophisticated scheduling and scaling mechanisms. In addition, long running experiments require sustainability in order to reduce the chances of having a 3-day experiment crash just before its completion. Hence a self-healing mechanism combined with a high-availability enforcement for both cloud service and the application on it is essential.

Since cloud systems are constantly expanding—the prospect of the intercloud [2] is currently addressed by both academia and industry—and user intervention becomes less efficient, the resource management systems (RMSs) will eventually

---

[1] http://www.idc.com/prodserv/idc_cloud.jsp

need to become autonomous systems. Autonomous systems are systems that are self-optimizing, self-configuring, self-healing , and self-protecting. Given the above, we notice that most self-characteristics are absent from existing RMSs (cf. Section 16.3). The reason could be that cloud-based technologies are still emerging and it will take some time before standards are proposed, accepted, and implemented.

In this chapter, we investigate the main cloud and HPC2 platforms and propose a prototype autonomous framework.

The rest of the chapter is structured as follows: Section 16.2 discusses the main application types used in HPC, while Section 16.3 presents some general PaaS solutions as well as specific on-demand HPC offers. A comparison between their offerings in term of scaling, scheduling, self-healing, high availability, and ability to handle multiple clouds is also given. The section ends with some representative work in the area of HPC scheduling. Next, in Section 16.4, a brief overview of some existing scheduling algorithms dealing with HPC-related applications and objectives is presented. In Section 16.5, a proposal for an autonomous RMS is suggested. The self-properties are discussed from the point of view of an RMS, and two use cases are given for the available prototype. Section 16.6 concludes the chapter with a brief recap and future research directions.

16.2   ON THE TYPE OF APPLICATIONS FOR HPC AND HPC2

HPC is suited for many types of applications, including parallel and dependent (workflows) jobs.

In the case of scientific workflow jobs, we notice that areas such as astronomy require complex chains made of mixed parallel and sequential jobs whose numbers depend on the size of the input data. This includes examples such as Montage [3] and CSTEM [4].

The most often encountered applications are either computation- or data-intensive. The computationally intensive ones are generally based on MPI (message passing interface) jobs.

The data-intensive ones are based on slicing techniques and a few communications between slice processors (e.g., the ones that are matching well the computational patterns of MapReduce). On one hand, MPI jobs require data sharing and the processing of large amounts of datasets, while, on the other hand, MapReduce jobs usually split the dataset and handle each chunk in parallel before merging back the results. Consequently, they require little or no communication at all between the parallel nodes.

It can be noticed that, although both are parallel applications, their requirements are very different. For instance, MapReduce requires a dedicated cluster and an optimized distributed file system, for example, Hadoop [5]. Also, its jobs need to be adapted to HPC environments because, usually on an HPC cluster, users must specify the required number of nodes and execution time [6]. With MapReduce jobs, these values usually vary depending on the number of map and reduce jobs.

Considering communication factors alone and assuming an ordinary cloud infrastructure running a MapReduce application, we can devise a procedure similar to the one followed on a grid since it does not require any strong restrictions on the network characteristics. Yet, the MPI job will exhibit large delays from the network, as most cloud providers do not offer high-speed interconnects such as InfiniBand. While Amazon's EC2 Cluster Instance offers a 10-Gb Ethernet, it is still insufficient for some classes of data-intensive MPI applications. In this context, the importance and the impact of InfiniBand-based communication have been recently emphasized in [1], where a novel IaaS architecture supporting multitenancy and using virtualized Infiniband is advanced.

Therefore, despite the fact clouds and HPC have been designed for different kinds of jobs, there are cases—for example, the MapReduce jobs—in which both can solve the same problem in comparative terms. For these, the EC2 environment, for instance, has been used from its early days. Other more network-sensitive jobs such as those falling in the MPI category need special dedicated clouds for HPC. With the recent interest in cloud computing, it is not surprising that some offers have already begun to emerge (cf. Section 16.3.2).

16.3 HPC ON THE CLOUD

Because of the control level offered by IaaS, it has been the preferred approach for exposing HPC to the public. However, system administration knowledge is needed to set the environments, reducing thus the number of potential users. We consider that the future in HPC2 is related to PaaS, which requires less administration knowledge since the environment for the HPC community is already set by the platform, leaving the users to handle application development and submission alone.

Therefore, we investigate next some of the main PaaS providers and emphasize on their ability to schedule, scale—either horizontally in terms of number of instances or vertically in terms of instance capacity, self-heal, and achieve high availability. These are some of the most advertised properties of existing PaaS for clouds. They also hint at what the current state of the art is regarding the ability of these systems to self-manage.

16.3.1 General PaaS Solutions

16.3.1.1 The Google App Engine (GAE) [7] has been one of the PaaS pioneer solutions. It supports several languages such as Java, Python, or Go. Limiting to Java, the environment is quite restrictive: it sets limits on application start-up times, response times, and there is no control/access to the operating system, and so on. Dynamic horizontal scaling is allowed by monitoring the number of requests a given instance receives. Vertical scaling is also possible but only by manually changing the instance type. In terms of service-level agreements (SLAs), GAE promises a 95.95% uptime and a compensation in the form of money transfer from 1 month to the next if the SLA has been broken. Studies comparing GAE and Amazon EC2 [8] have shown that, for short HPC parallel tasks (e.g., under 1 h), the former offers lower provisioning overhead and costs. Nonetheless, a performance bottleneck is seen in the form of middleware overhead and resource quotas.

16.3.1.2   *The Amazon Elastic Beanstalk*   [9] is based on the EC2 infrastructure and the S3 to host application archives. Support for numerous languages is offered, including for Java, .Net, or PHP. It allows horizontal elastic scaling based on load indicators, and offers simple built-in monitoring. Vertical scaling is also possible by manually allocating larger instance types. Self-healing is possible using the simple queue service or by setting up alarms in case the number of VMs drops below a threshold and implementing policies to react accordingly. Compared to GAE, it allows a detailed control over the environment: setting Tomcat parameters, access to the VM image and OS, and so on. Also, one of its main limitations lies in its "one-server-one-VM" policy. By contrast, GAE allows multiple applications on a single machine.

16.3.1.3   *CloudFoundry*[2]   is an open-source PaaS from VMware, allowing seamless cloud portability on infrastructures including AWS, OpenStack, Rackspace, vSphere, and so on. Supported languages include Java, Ruby, Node.js, Python, PHP, and others. It allows only manual horizontal scaling without any support for automatic elasticity. Self-healing is achieved through a HealthManager, which receives periodic heartbeats or change notification on the deployed application instances.

16.3.1.4   *Microsoft Azure*[3]   is a PaaS with support for various languages such as ASP.NET, PHP, or Node.js. It allows the handling of VM, Web sites, or other cloud/mobile services on Microsoft data centers around the world. Various SLAs for cloud services (99.95% external connectivity and 99.9% detection success of failed instances), storage (99.9% success in processing requests), SQL (Structured Query Language) databases (99.9% availability per month), and others are offered. Based on fabric controllers, Azure is able to detect and recover from software and hardware failures automatically by relying on monitoring agents. The fabric controllers also permit automatic horizontal scaling based on load indicators.

16.3.1.5   *dotCloud*[4]   is a PaaS offering the entire stack of technologies for handling a cloud-based application. Applications written in PHP, Node.js, or Python are supported. dotCloud allows load balancing, self-healing, and horizontal/vertical scale based on demand. The main drawback is that, except load balancing, all these features are handled via the command line by the client.

16.3.1.6   *Heroku*[5]   is a PaaS initially designed for Ruby. Nowadays, it supports Node.js, Java, Python, Scala, and Clojure. It allows application to scale horizontally using either the API or the command line. Automatic scaling is only available for web applications. Some level of availability can be achieved if the platform decides to distribute the application on different geographic locations.

[2]http://www.cloudfoundry.com/ (accessed March 18th, 2013)
[3]http://go.microsoft.com/?linkid=9682907&clcid=0x409 (accessed March 18th, 2013)
[4]https://www.dotcloud.com/ (accessed March 18th, 2013)
[5]http://www.heroku.com (accessed March 18th, 2013)

16.3.1.7 Jelastic[6] is a PaaS allowing clients to deploy cloud-enabled Java and PHP applications. It allows automatic load balancing and vertical scaling. The latter is achieved through the use of cloudlets (1 cloudlet = 128 MB RAM and 200 MHz CPU core), which basically indicate the amount of resources an application consumes. Horizontal scaling can be done via the user interface. Still, the maximum number of web servers a client can scale to is limited to 8. High availability is also possible through session replication. Major IaaS platforms such as EC2 and Google can be used to deploy the Jelastic platform.

16.3.1.8 OpenShift[7] is a free PaaS provided by RedHat. It supports multiple languages such as Java, Ruby, Node.js, Python, PHP, or Perl. It features automatic horizontal scaling by actively monitoring application load and high availability through replication. It also allows choosing the cloud infrastructure, making it a multicloud platform.

16.3.1.9 Rackspace[8] is a PaaS for deploying PHP and ASP.NET applications. It allows automatic horizontal scaling and high availability using load balancers.

16.3.1.10 mOSAIC [10] is an open-source and deployable PaaS,[9] to which we have recently contributed. It supports Java, Python, Erlang, and Node.js. It is designed to ensure portability on top of IaaS (including Amazon Web Services, OpenStack, OpenNebula, Eucalyptus, vCloud, OnApp, Flexiscale, etc.). It features vertical scaling and is currently undergoing modifications to include features for HPC2. Its initial resource management procedures are expected to be improved as discussed in the following sections.

In Table 16.1, we present a side-by-side comparison of the features of the above-mentioned PaaSs.

Considering the previous overview, the following remarks can be made:

- Most solutions offer inbuilt load balancing. This means that, as far as the client is concerned, demand will be evenly split between existing application instances. Nevertheless, there is no support for complex scheduling strategies. Although for web servers this is unnecessary, there are other cloud-based applications where, depending on user objectives, simple load balancing becomes deficient. For instance, data-intensive jobs require locality-aware scheduling, and budget-constrained jobs require selecting only certain resources so that the cost does not exceed the allocated budget.

- Horizontal scaling is widely supported with limited vertical scale present. This means that, although users have the possibility to scale their applications in terms of the amount of resources, they cannot change the instance characteristics on the fly. This can be an issue since there are applications—for example,

---

[6]http://jelastic.com/ (accessed March 18th, 2013)
[7]https://openshift.redhat.com/app/ (accessed March 18th, 2013)
[8]http://www.rackspace.co.uk/ (accessed March 18th, 2013)
[9](codes are available at https://bitbucket.org/mosaic)

TABLE 16.1   PaaS Comparison

Name	Load Balancing	Horizontal Scale	Vertical Scale	Self-Healing	High Availability	Multiple Clouds
AWS Beanstalk		Inbuilt/manual	Manual	Manual	99.95%	Yes
Cloud Foundry	Inbuilt	Manual		Inbuilt		Yes
dotCloud	Inbuilt	Manual	Manual	Manual	Manual	
GAE		Inbuilt			99.95%	
Heroku		Inbuilt/manual			Manual	
Jelastic	Inbuilt	Manual	Inbuilt		Inbuilt	Yes
mOSAIC		Manual	Inbuilt		Manual	Yes
MS Azure		Inbuilt		Inbuilt	99.95%	Yes
OpenShift	Inbuilt	Inbuilt			Inbuilt	Yes
Rackspace	Inbuilt	Inbuilt			Manual	Yes

thread-based applications—that could be better suited for vertical scaling. In addition, the management can become problematic if a large amount of resources is deployed.

- The ability of a system to recover from failures, that is, self-healing, is part of the more general self-management property of autonomous systems. Healing is usually achieved through monitoring the state of each application and acting accordingly in case it fails. Monitoring is generally achieved by handling heartbeats, that is, presence notification messages, sent by each application to the monitor. In case a heartbeat fails to reach the monitor within a given threshold, the application is considered unavailable and a new one is started. Besides Amazon Beanstalk, CloudFoundry, and MS Azure, no other PaaS offers an inbuilt healing mechanism. Others like dotCloud and Amazon Beanstalk allow clients to receive failure notifications and recover applications from within their code or user interfaces.

- High availability ideally means offering 99.9999% uptime (31 s downtime per year). As noticed, only a few providers guarantee 99.95% (around 4.5 h of downtime per year) through their SLA, and others simply state they support it either inbuilt or manually through replication. Since clouds are not failure proof and HPC experiments can take several days, it is important for instances and applications to be highly available. Furthermore, as failures can hit entire data centers (e.g., hurricanes, floods), multiple-cloud support for the PaaS is necessary in order to ensure availability of services. This can be done by the provider through multiple regional sites (e.g., Amazon regions) or by relying on federations and cross-cloud resource management tools (e.g., the intercloud concept).

- Multiple-cloud support is essential for maintaining high availability and allowing user to pick the best provider in terms of SLA. The fact that all but three PaaSs offer this feature is an indicator of the trend toward the intercloud.

16.3.2   On-Demand Platforms for HPC

Several on-demand platforms for HPC have recently been proposed. All of them are either at the IaaS or SaaS level, but we investigate them nonetheless since they provide the first generation of genuine HPC2. Generally, they do not offer any monitoring, scaling, self-healing, or high availability, and leave the client in charge of handling the available instances.

16.3.2.1 Penguin On-Demand[10] is a joint project between various top universities in the United States and Penguin Computing, aimed at offering HPC on demand. It offers a pay-per-use access to CPU/GPU cores and high-speed networks. Based on user demand, the capacity can be elastically scaled. The main advantage is that it offers access to nonvirtualized resources, and hence does not have to deal with the overhead induced by virtualization. As indicated on the Web site, it is closer to an SaaS. Yet, we list it here since it represents one of the few projects dealing with on-demand HPC.

16.3.2.2 R-HPC[11] offers three products: dedicated systems (R-Edge), on-demand HPC computing with technical support (R-Fusion), and pay-per-use customizable HPC resources (R-Cloud). R-cloud is an IaaS providing both a shared cluster, in which users are billed by the job, and virtual private clusters, in which access is billed on a 24/7 basis.

16.3.2.3 Amazon Cluster Instances[12] represents Amazon's response to their initial limitation of doing efficient HPC2. They propose an IaaS classic cluster CPU instance (cc2.8xlarge) made up of 88 compute units (each having 2× eight-core processors), 244 GB of memory, and 10 Gb links; cluster GPU instances comprising of 33.5 compute units, 2 NVIDIA M2050 GPUs, 22 GB memory, and 10 Gb links; and high I/O instances having 35 compute units and 2 SSD volumes of 1024 GB each with 10 Gb links. According to the provider's Web site, a 1064 instance CPU cluster achieved 240.09 TeraFLOPS, placing it at the 42nd position in November 2011's Top500 list.

The cluster instances have been widely studied and benchmarked. For instance, in [11], a thorough comparison study between the cc2.8xlarge and the old cc1.4xlarge (44 compute units with 2× quad-core processors) cluster instances is given. Results indicate that, when using NAS parallel benchmarks and representative HPC codes, the new instances provide poorer scalability for collective-based communication-intensive applications and are usually less cost effective.

A study on the efficiency of cc1.4xlarge instances against parallel fluid simulations, which require large bandwidths as all parallel processes communicate simultaneously, is presented in [12]. The conclusion is that, for this particular application type, good speedup and scaling is obtained for up to 8 CPU/GPU instances.

[10]http://www.penguincomputing.com/services/hpc-cloud/pod (accessed March 18th, 2013)
[11]http://www.r-hpc.com/ (accessed March 18th, 2013)
[12]http://aws.amazon.com/hpc-applications/ (accessed March 18th, 2013)

Beyond that limit, the Ethernet network becomes a bottleneck. Overall, Amazon's HCP cluster instances seem fit for moderately sized computational fluid dynamics that is encountered in most industrial engineering applications.

16.3.2.4 Cyclone[13] is an on-demand cloud computing service for technical applications. It provides two models, one for IaaS—where users run their own applications—and the other for SaaS—where a set of open-source applications and commercial software is offered. The environment is not virtualized.

As can be seen, each provider offers its own platform. This makes it hard to broker HPC2 services. In [13], a unified framework for exposing HPC applications as SaaS is proposed. The solution relieves users from the burden of managing the installation and administration of HPC applications by offering a framework relying on an HPC library for accessing EC2 resources. To prove its functionality, the authors deploy, on a cc2.8xlarge cluster instance, an MPI application for gene sequencing which would otherwise require up to 3 weeks on a single machine.

16.4 SCHEDULING ALGORITHMS FOR HPC2

The scheduling algorithm is the main decision maker concerning job-to-resource mappings in any RMS. Concerning HPC2 alone, we notice that there is a particular interest for the scheduling problem in areas such as energy consumption, parallel job scheduling (MPI and MapReduce), and multitenant scheduling. All these are problems specific to the HPC community, and prove that HPC2 has been gaining an increasing attention over the last few years.

In [14], a failure-tolerant framework and an algorithm for MPI applications are presented. The framework relies on the sensors that come bundled with many modern processors. A rule-based approach allows for alerts to be emitted when a failure is likely to occur. These are handled by daemons installed on each physical machine. Three policies are considered in order to minimize the impact of a failure: (i) leasing another instance, (ii) eliminating the unhealthy node, and (iii) notifying the administrator to take a decision. Results show that the proposed technique significantly reduces the wall clock execution time compared to other techniques involving benchmarks. However, since the daemons are installed on the physical machines themselves, the framework cannot efficiently deal with external or unpredictable instant failures such as power disruptions.

An algorithm for making MapReduce jobs compatible with HPC systems (cf. Section 16.2) is described in [6]. Since map—and afterward reduce—jobs usually run in parallel without any significant intercommunication, there is no specific need for specialized scheduling. Still, since on HPC systems users usually have to specify the time and the needed resources, the proposed algorithm computes these numbers based on the number of map and reduce jobs.

---

[13]http://www.sgi.com/products/hpc_cloud/cyclone/ (accessed March 18th, 2013)

MaxJobPerf is a power-constrained scheduling algorithm for parallel jobs proposed in [15]. The algorithm relies on an integer linear programming model, which makes it unsuitable for online scheduling because the time to solve it grows exponentially with the number of jobs. Essentially, the algorithm determines which job to run at which frequency by taking advantage of a technique called *dynamic voltage frequency scaling*. Results reveal that it outperforms other algorithms and manages to considerably reduce job wait time.

In [16], another energy-aware scheduling algorithm is proposed that is also capable of exploiting the heterogeneity of the data centers. It relies on multiple computing factors such as energy cost, carbon emission rate, workload, and CPU power efficiency. The algorithm addresses the problem from a provider point of view by trying to maximize revenue while minimizing carbon emission. Tests run on real parallel traces show that the algorithm is capable of reducing emissions while maintaining the profit.

An offline algorithm for scheduling multitenant workflows on HPC2 is presented in [17]. The method tries to take advantage of any gaps—due to communication costs and dependencies—in the schedule. Two methods are compared: one in which an entire job group is considered when searching for a gap, and the other where a job group is partitioned and each partition is evaluated against existing gaps. Despite the results showing that the second version gives better results in terms of makespan and resource utilization, the experimental test bed is limited and further tests are needed to prove the robustness of the algorithm.

16.5   TOWARD AN AUTONOMOUS SCHEDULING FRAMEWORK

As mentioned in Section 16.1, autonomous systems need to expose four main self-management properties, namely self-optimizing, self-configuring, self-healing, and self-protecting. From an RMS point of view, these properties can be described as follows:

- *Self-Configuration*: RMS benefits from being tailored for a specific purpose, namely that of scheduling jobs on resources based on several user and provider objectives. A self-configuring RMS should be able—based on a limited amount of information regarding the characteristics of the jobs, resources, and the user requirements—to set up suitable instance of itself in order to oversee the upcoming schedules. For instance, in the case of a multicloud scenario in which a job should take advantage of offers from several providers (e.g., some for storage and others for execution), the RMS should be able to automatically configure a broker and several schedulers for each IaaS together with appropriate scheduling policies. Naturally, during runtime any of the initial parameters could change, and so the self-configuring can take place at any moment during the RMS's life.

- *Self-Optimization*: Although clouds offer somewhat stable resources, accessing them depends on the Internet fabric. Furthermore, different jobs have different properties and user objectives. Thus, an RMS should be able to adapt the scheduling policy it uses to the current environment based either on past knowledge or on on-the-spot decisions.

- *Self-Healing*: The relatively safe environment of clouds does not mean that resources cannot fail. As seen in Table 16.1, even large providers such as Amazon, Google, and Microsoft do not offer high availability beyond 99.95%. In human terms, this translates to roughly 4.5 h of unavailability per year. Yet, this does not include unpredictable events such as natural disasters which can render an entire data center inoperable for several days or weeks in a row. The ability to self-heal and the deployed application are thus essential in any RMS. In order to achieve this, the system must consider factors such as geographical spread regions, offered SLA, past information regarding incidents, or user feedback.

- *Self-Protecting*: It usually means that the RMS should be able to defend itself and the applications from outside attacks. While clouds offer contained environments in which each tenant only has access to his/her own resources and it is much easier to prevent an attack from spreading to others, the RMS can be a target itself. The communication mechanism is especially vulnerable since it carries the commands for the RMS decisions. A compromised message could corrupt anything from job schedules and monitoring data to self- decisions. Certificate-based communication and the use of secure HTTP could help improve these scenarios. In addition to these, clouds have brought to attention the issue of legality of the actions. The choice of placing a data or executing a job is no longer merely a decision based on user objectives but a matter of obeying the legislation of the country the data center resides in. Consequently, the RMS must ensure that the user data/jobs obey these restrictions and that looser legislations do not allow for user-sensitive information to be compromised by external parties.

In what follows, we present a prototype for a modular autonomous scheduling framework for cloud systems. It must be noted that in the following we use the term *platform* to denote a running instance of the framework and the term *framework* to refer to the generic solution.

16.5.1 Autonomous Framework for RMS

The framework is intended to offer self-management to clients wishing to enhance their RMS with autonomous features. The modular architecture (Fig. 16.1) allows for any of the RMS-specific modules (i.e., scheduling, analyzer, negotiator, executor, and monitor) to be replaced by any software that can be adapted to communicate with the framework through the offered message queuing system (MQS).

The framework comprises several modules:

- The *healing* module is responsible for the self-healing of all the platform modules.
- The *configuration* module sets up the initial platform deployment based on user requirements concerning targeted providers and application type.

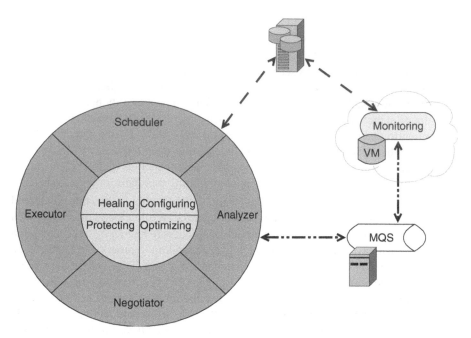

FIGURE 16.1   *General architecture of the proposed framework.*

- The *optimization* module adapts the scheduling strategies based on current environmental parameters including job characteristics and platform status.
- The *protection* module oversees that all intraplatform messages are digitally signed and unaltered and checks to see that the user requirements in terms of data safety are met by the providers.
- The *monitoring* module is in charge of monitoring the status of the VM and of the underlying network.
- The *MQS* handles all the communication between the platform components. It provides a set of message exchanges that can be used by client-picked solutions to communicate with the rest of the framework.
- The *storage* deposits data regarding the platform status, submitted jobs, and the necessary recovery files.
- The *RMS* modules comprise the *scheduler* (responsible for assigning jobs to resources), *analyzer* (responsible for analyzing the state of the environment and deciding on whether to change the scheduling policy or not), *resource negotiator* (responsible for brokering several clouds), and *task executor* (responsible for the actual job execution). Each of these modules can be defined through the framework API, or existing solutions can be used instead.

To maximize availability, each of the above components can be placed on a separate physical resource (PR). Hence, in case any component fails, the rest will continue executing. Communication between various parts is ensured by the MQS, which in

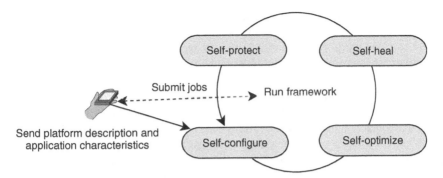

FIGURE 16.2 *Self-management cycle.*

our case is represented by RabbitMQ, which is an implementation of the AMQP standard. Message queues follow a publish–subscribe policy and have the advantage of being persistent even in case the communication end points fail. In this case, the messages are stored until a new subscriber binds to the queue and continues to consume the stored messages. To further ensure redundancy, a distributed file system such as Hadoop is responsible for storing any files related to the platform, and custom images needed by the clients need to execute jobs.

Modules can be grouped together as agents. An agent acts as the entity that governs a specific part of the platform. For instance, each cloud provider can be governed by one agent. An agent can comprise at most one module type for each of the RMS modules.

A prototype is available under the GPL license.[14] The current version supports self-healing for modules built using the exposed API as well as for external software under the condition that it uses the framework's communication protocol. A detailed overview on its structure and some tests regarding the time to recover from errors is given in [18].

16.5.2 Self-Management

The core of the framework is given by the *self-management* modules. They allow any application written using the framework API or tailored to use the exposed MQS to act as an autonomous entity. The entire cycle is described in Fig. 16.2.

16.5.2.1 Self-Configuring The initial deployment is done by the client using the provided deployment scripts. There, the client can specify a list of available resources for the platform modules and the application types intended to be executed using the platform. The location of the platform recovery archives, custom images, and certificates is also mentioned in the deployment scripts.

Through these scripts, the self-configuration module will take care of the installation, and the client will be able to monitor the status of its platform through

---

[14] https://bitbucket.org/mfrincu/autonomous-scheduling-platform

logs. Based on several indicators such as the number of requested providers, the self-configuration module will decide on the number of RMS modules to start and where to place them. In addition, taking into account the application type and user objectives, an appropriate scheduling policy will be selected.

16.5.2.2 Self-Healing The *healing* module is responsible for the accurate execution of the autonomous RMS. In particular, it is responsible for the self-healing capacity, which is achieved by monitoring the *heartbeats* received from the registered modules. As soon as a heartbeat fails to be acknowledged within a predetermined threshold, the module is considered unavailable and a new one is started. To avoid cases in which the unresponsive module is simply overloaded or some network issues occur, the *healing* module will send a shutdown signal to the unresponsive module. Healing modules also monitor themselves through the same heartbeat mechanism. Figure 16.3 gives an overview of this process.

Each module acts as a state machine in which the current state is dictated by the interaction with a *healing* module it is registered to. A newly deployed module can be in any of the following two states, *READY_FOR_RUNNING* and *PAUSED*, depending on the intent: use the module immediately or later, for example, as an idle backup for a failed one. A module in the *READY_FOR_RUNNING* state will send a request to the healer to check for similar modules registered to it. This is done in order to avoid having multiple competitive modules at the same time for an arbitrary agent. If no similar module has been found, the status is set to *RUNNING* and the module can proceed with its normal execution. Periodically, it will send a *heartbeat* to the healing module it is registered to, to notify its existence. If a module fails to send this message within a predefined interval, the *healing* module will consider it as *NOT_RESPONDING* and try to start a new one instead. A new module can be started in two ways: either a similar *PAUSED* one is started, or a newly one is deployed based on the platform recovery files stored in Hadoop.

16.5.2.3 Self-Optimization During the platform's life cycle, many properties, including the cloud environment, the characteristics of the submitted jobs, and even the user objectives, can vary. Since it has been proven that the efficiency of

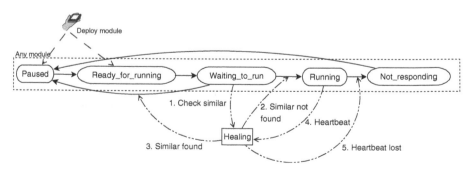

FIGURE 16.3 Self-healing workflow.

the schedule depends on these factors [19, 20], any autonomous RMS for clouds requires a module for optimizing the scheduling policy based on the latest data on the environment and on past experience. In the proposed framework, the monitoring modules running on the allocated resources periodically transmit information to the RMS schedule analyzer. This information includes data on the load and CPU/memory/bandwidth availability. Data on the job characteristics (e.g., estimated execution time, deadlines, objectives to be met) are sent automatically to the same schedule analyzer at job submission time. Once the information is processed, it decides on the next policy to be used.

16.5.2.4 *Self-Protection*

Clouds break the geographical boundaries between countries. In doing so, they are not restricted to a single jurisdiction, and thus users must be aware of where they place possibly sensitive or restricted data. An autonomous RMS targeting the intercloud should be able, based on information from the users, to decide where to place data and how to partition its processing so that no laws are broken. This decision must be incorporated into the scheduling algorithm since it is the entity responsible with VM-to-PR, job-to-VM, and data-to-job assignments.

In addition to the legal aspect, there is still the open issue of malicious attacks. Although possessing a multitenant environment, clouds have the advantage of isolating users from each other. This means that any attack will be restricted to the use(s) of the platform. To counteract this kind of situation, the platform ensures that all intraplatform messages are digitally signed and contain only valid data. In this way, situations in which messages to recreate falsely failed modules or creation of an unreasonably large number of VMs due to fake jobs is automatically taken care of.

Another vulnerable point is represented by the user application and the data itself, but solving any intrusion on this side is left to the user to deal with.

16.5.3 Use Cases

We have envisioned two use cases for the proposed platform. First, we consider a hybrid cloud (Fig. 16.4) in which a client deploys an application on the local cloud and only uses external resources when it runs out of VMs. Second, we assume that the application is deployed arbitrarily on any cloud resources (Fig. 16.5) based on the policies implemented by the *scheduler* and *negotiator* modules.

In both use cases, self-optimization is taken care of by the scheduling *analyzer* module, self-healing is handled by the *healing* module, self-protection is assumed to be embedded in the communication and *scheduling* modules, and, finally, self-configuration is to be taken care of by the deployment scripts.

16.5.3.1 *Hybrid Cloud*

The hybrid-cloud scenario considers that a client has access to a private HPC cloud which she/he uses for submitting jobs. However, since HPC jobs may require vast amount of resources, a secondary cloud is used. This can be either a public or another private cloud whose resources can be accessed on demand based on existing agreements. To achieve this, the client could deploys the

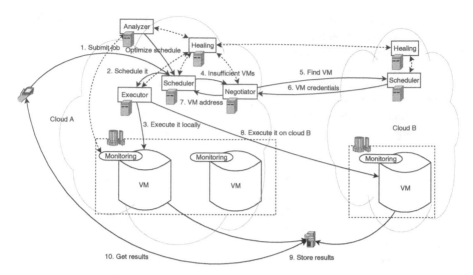

FIGURE 16.4 *Platform use case — hybrid cloud.*

autonomous RMS platform as in Fig. 16.4. For the private cloud, the platform would set up three modules for scheduling incoming jobs analyzing the current environment: one module for executing them on allocated VMs; one module for negotiating with the external cloud for new VMs; and, finally, one module for taking care of the platform health. On the external cloud, only two modules for scheduling and for healing are installed, as this cloud acts only as external VM provisioner.

A typical job submission would proceed as follows: First, the user would submit jobs to the local *scheduler*. In turn, this would try to allocate VMs and place the jobs on them according to some scheduling policies decided by the *analyzer* based on data from the *monitors* running on the already deployed VMs. If there are no more VMs that can be allocated, the *scheduler* would send a bid request to the *negotiator*. This would ask the platform *scheduler* attached to the external cloud whether it can obtain the needed VMs from the cloud's own internal RMS—not part of our platform. If affirmative, the credentials for the VMs are transferred back to the *negotiator*. These will be used by the local *scheduler* to assign new jobs directly to the external VMs. Finally, all output data are placed on a distributed file system to be queried by the user.

As can be noticed, in this scenario the *scheduler* deployed on the external cloud only acts as a liaison to the proprietary scheduler used on it. Its sole purpose is to interface the autonomous RMS to the external RMS so that communication can be achieved.

A scenario can be easily imagined in which multiple external clouds are used and, based on indicators such as price and SLA, the best one will be picked after one or several rounds of bids.

16.5.3.2 *Intercloud* By expanding the hybrid-cloud scenario, we can imagine a scenario in which the decision on where to put the tasks is taken by the *negotiator*

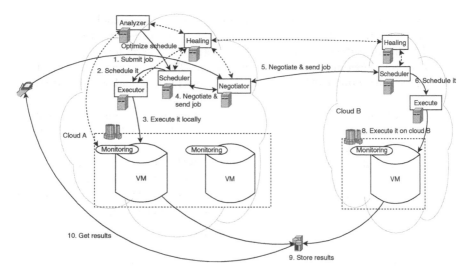

FIGURE 16.5 *Platform use case – intercloud.*

which, based on jobs from users and bid results from external clouds, will decide the best placement choice (Fig. 16.5). The properties of each new job are sent to the *schedulers* deployed across clouds. Each *scheduler* would decide, based on its own scheduling policy, a placement for it and send back the results to the *negotiator*. According to some decision criteria, it would then select the cloud in which to execute the job.

It can be seen that in this scenario the central role shifts from the *scheduler* to the *negotiator.*

Contrary to the hybrid-cloud use case, the intercloud seems more suited for scenarios where users do not have the benefit of a private cloud. Concerning the platform deployment, this case involves having all RMS modules deployed across every cloud (for simplicity, in Fig. 16.5 cloud B is shown without the *analyzer* and intraplatform communication links). This means extra complexity especially for the self-healing and self-optimization mechanisms.

Moreover, in this scenario, cloud A does not have direct access to VMs from cloud B. The jobs will be sent directly by the *negotiator* to each cloud.

16.6 CONCLUSIONS

This chapter addressed the issue of HPC on clouds. Special emphasis was given to the RMSs for such systems. We have shown that, irrespective of the large variety of PaaS and SaaS available for HPC2, there are still some open issues concerning self-management. Even though self-healing has been addressed to some extent by providers such as Amazon Beanstalk, CloudFoundry, dotCloud, and MS Azure, to date there is no widely available, truly autonomous solution. Besides, the scheduling policies offered by most providers cannot be customized, and vertical scaling is lacking in most offers. However, we have noticed a general tendency toward the intercloud, with most platforms ready for this step. This is especially important in a context in which renting HPC resources from various places could be more affordable than buying, upgrading, or running an HPC cluster.

Our contribution consisted in proposing a working autonomous RMS prototype. We presented the main features such a platform would require from a self-{healing, protecting, optimizing, configuring} perspective. Two use cases for it were proposed. They targeted (i) the needs of clients owning small HPC clusters to extend their use by harnessing resources from outside, and (ii) the users wanting to take advantage of HPC without having to buy an expensive data center. The prototype currently allows self-healing from both platform modules developed using the framework API and external software capable of interfacing with the proposed communication protocol.

Future work is targeted toward enhancing the framework with the rest of the self-functionality.

ACKNOWLEDGMENT

This work was partially supported by the European Commission FP7 programme under Project No. FP7-REGPOT-CT-2011-284595-HOST, which has been initiated based on the collaborations established in the frame of the EC-COST Action IC0805 ComplexHPC.

REFERENCES

1. V. Mauch, M. Kunze, and M. Hillenbrand, "High performance cloud computing," *Future Generation Computer Systems*, vol. 29, no. 6, pp. 1408–1416, 2013.
2. D. Bernstein, E. Ludvigson, K. Sankar, S. Diamond, and M. Morrow, "Blueprint for the intercloud—protocols and formats for cloud computing interoperability," in *Fourth International Conference on Internet and Web Applications and Services, 2009, ICIW '09*, Venice/Mestre, Italy, pp.–328–336, 2009.
3. E. Deelman, G. Singh, M.-H. Su, J. Blythe, Y. Gil, C. Kesselman, G. Mehta, K. Vahi, G. B. Berriman, J. Good, A. Laity, J. C. Jacob, and D. S. Katz, "Pegasus: a framework for mapping complex scientific workflows onto distributed systems," *Scientific Programming*, vol. 13, no. 3, pp. 219–237, 2005.
4. A. Doğan and F. Özgüner, "Biobjective scheduling algorithms for execution time-reliability trade-off in heterogeneous computing systems," *Computer Journal*, vol. 48, no. 3, pp. 300–314, 2005.
5. K. Shvachko, H. Kuang, S. Radia, and R. Chansler, "The Hadoop distributed file system," in *Proceedings of the 2010 IEEE 26th Symposium on Mass Storage Systems and Technologies (MSST), MSST '10*, pp. 1–10. Washington, DC: IEEE Computer Society, 2010.

6. M. V. Neves, T. Ferreto, and C. De Rose, "Scheduling mapreduce jobs in HPC clusters," in *Proceedings of the 18th International Conference on Parallel Processing, Euro-Par'12*, pp. 179–190. Berlin, Heidelberg: Springer-Verlag, 2012.

7. M. Malawski, M. Kuz?niar, P. Wo?jcik, and M. Bubak, "How to use Google App Engine for free computing," *Internet Computing, IEEE*, vol. 17, no. 1, pp. 50–59, 2013.

8. R. Prodan, M. Sperk, and S. Ostermann, "Evaluating high-performance computing on Google App Engine," *Software, IEEE*, vol. 29, no. 2, pp. 52–58, 2012.

9. J. Vliet, F. Paganelli, S. Van Wel, and D. Dowd, *Elastic Beanstalk*. Sebastopol, CA: Real Time Bks, O'Reilly Media, 2011.

10. D. Petcu, G. Macariu, S. Panica, and C. C. aciun, "Portable cloud applications—from theory to practice," *Future Generation Computer Systems*, vol. 29, no. 6, pp. 1417–1430, 2013.

11. R. R. Expósito, G. L. Taboada, S. Ramos, J. Touriño, and R. Doallo, "Performance analysis of HPC applications in the cloud," *Future Generation Computer Systems*, vol. 29, no. 1, pp. 218–229, 2013.

12. P. Zaspel and M. Griebel, "Massively parallel fluid simulations on Amazon's HPC cloud," in *First International Symposium on Network Cloud Computing and Applications (NCCA)*, Toulouse, France, pp. 73–78, 2011.

13. A. K. Wonga and A. M. Goscinskia, "A unified framework for the deployment, exposure and access of HPC applications as services in clouds," *Future Generation Computer Systems*, vol. 29, no. 6, pp. 1333–1344, 2013.

14. I. P. Egwutuoha, S. Chen, D. Levy, B. Selic, and R. Calvo, "A proactive fault tolerance approach to High Performance Computing (HPC) in the cloud," in *Cloud and Green Computing (CGC), 2012 Second International Conference on*, Xiangtan, China, pp. 268–273, 2012.

15. M. Etinski, J. Corbalan, J. Labarta, and M. Valero, "Parallel job scheduling for power constrained HPC systems," *Parallel Computing*, vol. 38, no. 12, pp. 615–630, 2012.

16. S. K. Garg, C. S. Yeo, A. Anandasivam, and R. Buyya, "Environment-conscious scheduling of HPC applications on distributed cloud-oriented data centers," *Journal of Parallel and Distributed Computing*, vol. 71, no. 6, pp. 732–749, 2011.

17. H.-J. Jiang, K.-C. Huang, H.-Y. Chang, D.-S. Gu, and P.-J. Shih, "Scheduling concurrent workflows in HPC cloud through exploiting schedule gaps," in *Proceedings of the 11th International Conference on Algorithms and Architectures for Parallel Processing—Volume Part I, ICA3PP'11*, pp. 282–293. Berlin, Heidelberg: Springer-Verlag, 2011.

18. M. E. Frincu, N. M. Villegas, D. Petcu, H. A. Muller, and R. Rouvoy, "Self-healing distributed scheduling platform," in *Proceedings of the 11th IEEE/ACM International Symposium on Cluster, Cloud and Grid Computing, CCGRID '11*, pp. 225–234. Washington, DC: IEEE Computer Society, 2011.

19. M. Frincu, S. Genaud, and J. Gossa, "Comparing provisioning and scheduling strategies for workflows on clouds," in *27th IEEE International Parallel and Distributed Processing Symposium—Workshops (IPDPS-Workshops'13)*, IEEE, Boston, USA, 2013.

20. E. Michon, J. Gossa, and S. Genaud, "Free elasticity and free CPU power for scientific workloads on IaaS Clouds," in *18th IEEE International Conference on Parallel and Distributed Systems (ICPADS'12)*, pp. 85–92, IEEE, Singapore, 2012.

17

Resource Discovery in Large-Scale Grid Systems

Konstantinos Karaoglanoglou and Helen Karatza

Aristotle University of Thessaloniki, Thessaloniki, Greece

A grid involves a multiplicity of resources that are heterogeneous in nature, encompassing a vast range of technologies. The full and efficient use of these resources requires effective resource discovery mechanisms that are able to overcome the complicity and dynamicity of such systems. Discovering the appropriate resources is considered to be challenging and difficult, thus intensifying the need for effective resource discovery mechanisms in grid systems.

17.1 INTRODUCTION AND BACKGROUND

17.1.1 Introduction

A grid is a type of distributed system that enables the sharing, selection, and aggregation of geographically distributed "autonomous" resources dynamically at runtime depending on their availability, capability, performance, cost, and users' quality Of service (QoS) requirements. Grid technologies support the sharing and coordinated use of diverse resources in dynamic virtual organizations (VOs) that is, the creation, from geographically and organizationally distributed components, of virtual computing systems that are sufficiently integrated to deliver the desired QoS [1].

It is obvious that the basis of grid technology is the concept of resource sharing. The shared resources in a grid infrastructure could vary from networks, clusters of

High-Performance Computing on Complex Environments, First Edition.
Edited by Emmanuel Jeannot and Julius Žilinskas.
© 2014 John Wiley & Sons, Inc. Published 2014 by John Wiley & Sons, Inc.

computers, memory space or storage capacity, computational power (CPU time or CPU cycles), data repositories, files, attached peripheral devices, sensors, software applications, online instruments and data, all connected usually through the Internet, and a middleware software layer that provides basic services for security, monitoring, resource management, and so on [2].

By examining the information from grid literature sources, it is apparent that, in order to characterize and describe a grid, multidimensional factors need to be addressed. The main grid characteristics, described in [3], are the following:

- *Large Scale:* A grid must be able to deal with a number of resources ranging from just a few to millions. This raises serious problems, such as the scalability of the system and the potential performance degradation due to the system's size increase.
- *Geographical Distribution:* Grid resources are usually located at distant places.
- *Heterogeneity:* A grid system is comprised of heterogeneous resources with different capabilities and technical characteristics.
- *Resource Sharing:* Grid resources are shared among the infrastructure, allowing distant organizations (i.e., users) to access them.
- *Multiple Administrations:* Each sharing organization may establish different security and administrative policies of how its owned resources will be accessed and used within the grid infrastructure. This makes the network security problem an even more challenging task, taking into account all the different policies.
- *Resource Coordination:* Grid resources must be coordinated in order to provide aggregated computing capabilities.
- *Transparent Access:* Apart from its complex architecture, a grid should be seen, from an operating aspect, as a single virtual machine.
- *Dependable Access:* A grid must ensure the delivery of services under established QoS requirements.
- Consistent access: A grid must be built with standard devices, protocols, and interfaces, hiding its heterogeneous nature but allowing its scalability.
- *Pervasive Access:* A grid should be able to operate in environments prone to resource failures, granting access to all the available resources by adapting its behavior, in order to attain the maximum performance from the shared resources.

17.1.2   Resource Discovery in Grids

A critical issue in grid systems is how to manage all these types of resources and how to provide access to remote resources either to execute a job or to have access to the resources' data. In order to access a grid resource, a request for it is created somewhere in the system. For satisfying the request, it is essential to discover the most appropriate resource. If the resource located is not the most suitable one, then the request cannot be properly satisfied, thus threatening the well-functioning of the system. A resource discovery mechanism , provided by the grid infrastructure, should be able to discover efficiently an appropriate resource for such requests [4].

The difficulties for the deployment of effective discovery mechanisms mainly emerge from the technical aspects that characterize a grid system. A grid involves a multiplicity of resources that are heterogeneous in nature and will encompass a vast range of technologies. Despite being a challenge, resource discovery is crucial for the functioning of such demanding systems. The benefits expected to be provided from an effective resource discovery mechanism are numerous, including the efficient mapping of resources, better knowledge of the resource availability, and, finally, the maximized usage of resources.

17.1.3   Background

One of the popular approaches for the resource discovery in grids, also analyzed in this chapter, is the so-called matchmaking framework . Several research papers make use of this framework attempting to add new aspects, in order to cover a wider range of the resource discovery challenges. The matchmaking concept is mainly based on the existence of requestors and providers that advertise their characteristics and requirements in classified advertisements. A matchmaking service is responsible of finding a match between the advertisements and the relevant entities of the match. The matchmaking framework is often combined with semantic web concepts. These approaches implement semantics, ontologies, and matchmaking rules to define resources. For the efficient and effective correspondence among the various devices on grid systems, resources' semantic descriptions must possess a frequency matching that aims at eliminating all the platform compatibility issues [5–7].

Another notable approach to the resource discovery problem, which is loosely based on the matchmaking approach, is the semantic communities approach [8, 9]. The main target in this approach is to create grid communities based on policies of similar interests, allowing community nodes to learn of each other without relying on a central meeting point.

Finally, a noteworthy research direction suggests the incorporation of existing peer-to-peer (P2P) resource discovery protocols in grid environments [10, 11]. Although grid and P2P systems emerged from different communities in order to serve different needs and to provide different functionalities, both systems constitute successful resource sharing paradigms [12]. Though P2P networks are not strictly grid systems, several P2P approaches are relevant and applicable in grid environments, and the most noteworthy are presented in this chapter.

17.2   THE SEMANTIC COMMUNITIES APPROACH

17.2.1   Grid Resource Discovery Using Semantic Communities

In [13], a community-based model is proposed to discover resources in dynamic, large-scale, and distributed grid environments. The motivation and basis behind the semantic communities mechanism is the observation that grids are similar to human social networks. Both grid communities and human communities are comprised of members that are engaged in the sharing, communication, and promotion of common interests. The formation of grid communities is basically a clustering policy for grid nodes.

The semantic communities system's architecture, proposed by the authors of [13], is comprised of two layers (Fig. 17.1). The bottom layer is the physical node layer, with its edges representing nodes that share physical connections. The top layer of the unstructured network depicts communities classified in different semantic categories. A node may join several communities, and therefore communities can overlap. Communities are built in a decentralized adaptive manner, allowing nodes with similar interests to acquire knowledge of each other without relying on a central meeting point. Each node maintains a community routing table, which represents the node's knowledge of the communities in the network. A routing table includes three columns:

- the domain name,
- the community that controls that domain,
- and representative nodes serving as a contact list.

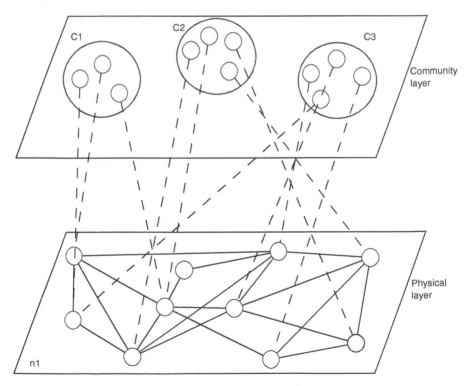

FIGURE 17.1   *System architecture.* Source: [13].

When a node joins the network, it connects to an existing node and downloads its routing table. Then, the newly joined node tries to find its interested communities from the downloaded community routing table. If the node discovers the interested community, it joins the community by connecting to the contact nodes. If the joining node is not able to discover its interested community, it will create a community and propagate this information to all its neighbors.

As nodes join and leave the system, we emphasize that it is important to maintain the community overlays. The main task of maintenance is to keep the community routing table up to date, so that nodes can locate relevant communities in a valid and correct way. Updating a node's information about other communities occurs by periodically probing remote neighbors and maintaining only the active neighbors in its routing table. In order to exchange information, nodes use gossip. When a node has information to share, it sends the information to a number of randomly chosen neighbors. Eventually, all nodes will gain complete information about the availability of other nodes in the system due to gossiping. Finally, another important task of community maintenance is merging communities that share the same interests. When a node discovers two communities with the same domain name, it is obliged to proceed in unifying their community id.

The presented architecture suggests a decentralized technique for identifying groups of nodes with common interests and building overlays that depict those shared interests. It appears to achieve higher search efficiency and scalability than previously proposed flooding-based or history-based search schemes. Moreover, the system inherits many desirable features of unstructured overlays, such as robustness and self-organization.

17.2.2 Grid Resource Discovery Based on Semantically Linked Virtual Organizations

A framework for sharing and discovering resources on an unprecedented scale and for geographically distributed groups is presented in [14]. Incorporating the semantic link network (SLN) model [15, 16] and acknowledging the similarities between grid and social networks, the proposed discovery framework utilizes the phenomenon of query transferring through locally available knowledge in acquaintances, achieving the construction of a semantic-small-world structure.

The authors of [14] suggest the separation of the ontology knowledge into two parts: the terminological box (T-Box) and the assertion box (A-Box). The T-Box is a finite set of terminological axioms, which includes all axioms for concept definition and descriptions of domain structure. The A-Box is a finite set of assertional axioms, which includes a set of axioms for the descriptions of concrete data and relations. The separation of the two boxes is suggested in order to enable better knowledge indexing and support the scalability of the system. For the purposes of accessing several ontologies and exchanging information in a meaningful and semantically appropriate manner, the notion of semantic links is proposed. A semantic link between two ontologies, as defined in [17], could be one of the following:

- Equal-to, denoted by $Pi - \text{equ} \rightarrow Pj$, meaning that Pi is semantically equal to Pj. The equal-to link is reflexive, symmetric, and transitive.
- Similar-to, denoted by $Pi - (\text{sim, sd}) \rightarrow Pj$, meaning that Pi is semantically similar to Pj to the degree sd.
- Reference, denoted by $Pi - \text{ref} \rightarrow Pj$, meaning that Pi refers semantically to Pj.
- Implication, denoted by $Pi - \text{imp} \rightarrow Pj$, meaning that Pi semantically implies Pj. The implication link is transitive.
- Subtype, denoted by $Pi - \text{st} \rightarrow Pj$, meaning that Pj is semantically a part of Pi. The subtype link is transitive.
- Sequential, denoted by $Pi - \text{seq} \rightarrow Pj$, meaning that the content of Pj is the successor of the content of Pi in a context.

Another important aspect of the framework in [14] is how to measure the semantic similarity between two objects. First, it is suggested to extract the class and property labels from the T-Box ontology, and maintain them into the ontology signature set (OSS). Taking into consideration that a semantic meaning may be represented by different labels in different ontologies, while it is also possible that the same label in different ontologies has different meanings, the above approach of simply extracting the OSS is not considered sufficient. An extension of the OSS occurs by extending each concept with its semantic meanings, creating groups of synonyms and hypernyms. After the extension, the authors emphasize the necessity of excluding the unrelated terms by keeping only the words with the most appropriate meanings, based on the subsumption relation. The subsumption relation suggests that a concept's semantic meaning should be consistent with its super-class's meaning. If this is not the case, the meaning is removed as inconsistent.

In order to compute semantic similarity of two objects, the following scenario is considered. A and B are two peers, and their extended OSSs are $S(A)$ and $S(B)$, respectively. The semantic similarity between peer A and peer B is defined as $sim(A, B)$ and is computed by

$$\frac{|S(A) \cup S(B)|}{|S(A) \cup S(B)| + \alpha |S(A) - S(B)| + \beta |S(B) - S(A)|},$$

where $\cup$ denotes set intersection, $-$ is set difference, $||$ represents set cardinality, and α and β are parameters that provide for differences in focus on the different components.

With the similarity measure specified, the following definition is introduced: node A and node B are semantically equivalent if their semantic similarity measure, $sim(A, B)$, equals 1 (implying $sim(B, A)=1$ as well). Node A is semantically related to node B if $sim(A, B)$ exceeds the user-defined similarity threshold t ($0 < t \leq 1$). Node A is semantically unrelated to node B if $sim(A, B) < t$.

The resource distance vector (RDV) routing algorithm is used for the construction and update of the nodes' routing tables, supporting the efficient forward of resource discovery queries. The following scenario describes the process of a node joining the cluster and constructing its routing table, based on the RDV routing algorithm, analyzed in [14]. Assuming that node C is willing to join the network, it should first connect to an existing node, for instance A. Node C, then, should send its resource indices to A. Acting in the same manner, A should inform C of all the resources that it has knowledge of. A merges its local and neighbor vectors into one vector and sends it to C. C receives the merged vector from A, and subsequently adds one hop to each element of the vector. C also adds an additional row in its routing table. After A receives C's resource information, it updates its routing table and, finally, informs its neighbors of the update.

The discussed framework is designed for large-scale heterogeneous grids, where nodes automatically organize themselves based on their semantic properties to form a semantically linked overlay network. Moreover, the framework includes a routing algorithm to enable efficient information retrieval within the semantically linked system. According to the authors, the framework has been proven to be effective in scalability, efficiency, robustness, and overhead.

17.3   THE P2P APPROACH

17.3.1   On Fully Decentralized Resource Discovery in Grid Environments Using a P2P Architecture

Acknowledging the fact that grid environments are comprised of large and heterogeneous collections of remote resources, and that these resources are identified by a set of desired attributes characterized by various degrees of dynamism, the authors of [18] propose and evaluate a set of request-forwarding algorithms in a fully decentralized architecture. This set of algorithms is designed to accommodate heterogeneity (in both sharing policies and resource types) and dynamism.

A restatement of the resource discovery problem is attempted in order to follow a P2P approach for discovering resources in grid environments. A grid is a collection of resources shared by different organizations, with different sharing policies. The authors claim that the attempt to enforce uniform participation rules to all the resources within the system would drastically limit participation. A solution would be to allow every participating organization to control access to information about its local shared resources. Every participant in the VO has one or more servers that store and provide access to local resources controlled. These servers are called *nodes* or *peers*. A node may control information about one or multiple resources, depending on the number of resources it shares within the infrastructure. Although the discussed P2P approach assumes that the sets of resources published are disjoint, there may be multiple resources with identical descriptions and technical characteristics.

The basic P2P approach in grid resource discovery assumes that users send requests to a local node. If the node maintains the matching resource descriptions locally, it is responsible for responding to the request; otherwise it forwards the request to another node. Intermediate nodes forward the request based on a time-to-live strategy until its expiration or matching resources are found. If a node maintains information about a forwarded request, it sends it directly to the node that initially started the forwarding.

Within this modeling system, the presented resource discovery algorithm depends on two mechanisms: the membership protocol that provides information about other participating nodes, and a request forwarding strategy in order to determine to which nodes requests should be forwarded. Regarding the membership protocol, the frequently encountered P2P soft-state membership protocol is used. Membership lists are updated through periodic "I'm alive" messages exchanged by neighboring nodes. Membership information can also be extended with more knowledge of the system's availability. When a node receives a message from a previously unknown node, the node can add the new address to its membership list.

The request-forwarding strategy determines to which node a request will be forwarded. Nodes are not only capable of adding new node addresses to their membership lists but can also store various information about their peers, such as information about requests previously forwarded successfully. The request-forwarding strategies, proposed in [18], are the following:

- The simple random strategy suggests the forwarding of a request randomly to a node, with no information about the transaction stored on nodes.

- The combination of experience-based and the random strategy suggests that nodes acquire knowledge by monitoring requests satisfied by other nodes. A request is forwarded to the peer that satisfied similar requests previously. If no knowledge about previous requests is available, the request is forwarded to a randomly chosen node.

- The "best neighbor" algorithm monitors the number of satisfactory answers received from each peer, without maintaining information about the type of requests answered. A request is forwarded to the peer who answered the largest number of requests.

- Finally, the combination of experience-based and the best neighbor strategies suggests that when no relevant knowledge exists, the request is forwarded to the best neighbor, namely the peer who answered the largest number of requests.

The inherent problems of grid architectures are the trade-offs between communication costs and performance. To better understand these trade-offs and to evaluate the different strategies for resource discovery, extensive performance evaluation tests have been conducted with encouraging results, showing that the future of this research area would be promising. And, indeed, it is. The research work presented here is one of the first regarding incorporation of P2P protocols into grid systems. Since then, a whole lot of research work has been done in this research area, with designs and evaluations of different membership protocols and new request-forwarding strategies.

17.3.2   P2P Protocols for Resource Discovery in the Grid

The work introduced in [19] is based on the fact that a P2P approach would be suitable for dynamically distributed searching in a large-scale grid environment. It proposes two P2P protocols for resource discovery: the query resource discovery mechanism (QRDM), and the seeking resource discovery mechanism (SRDM). Both protocols are based on the main characteristics of P2P systems, namely decentralization and self-organization. The main difference between the two proposed P2P grid resource discovery mechanisms is that the SRDM performs a dissemination of resource information, whereas the QRDM only tries to discover the resource requested by the user.

The authors claim that the pure content-based text search that is used in P2P systems is not sufficient for discovering resources in the grid. Locating files in P2P systems is easily achieved using file names, but file-sharing is only a small portion of the resources shared within a grid system. Grid resource discovery mechanisms need to rely on information about the desired resources, which is in the form of metadata, the data about data, improving the accuracy and efficiency of resource discovery. Metadata describing grid resources should be updated at regular intervals, requiring the checking of system resources, such as scheduled jobs and system load.

The grid environment is modeled by a graph $G = (N, E)$. N is the set of nodes in the network: $N = \{n_1, n_2, n_3, \ldots \}$. The edges in the graph are the communication links between nodes and are denoted by $E = \{e(n_1), e(n_2), e(n_3), \ldots \}$. Let $L(n_1)$ be a list of nodes known to n_1. $l(n_1)$ is the set of nodes to which a node n_1 is connected. Each node maintains a set of resources that are made available to the users. The list of resources maintained at each node is denoted by $\Gamma(n_1)$.

Figure 17.2 shows a graph composed of six nodes: $N = \{n_1, n_2, n_3, n_4, n_5, n_6\}$. Each node is allowed to make connections with two or three nodes. There is an edge from n_1 to n_2 if node n_1 knows node n_2. Based on the above, the authors conclude the following:

- $(n_1) = \{n_2, n_3, n_4, n_5, n_6\}$,
- $l(n_1) = \{n_2, n_3 \in L(n_1)\}$,
- $e(n_1) = \{(n_1, n_3), (n_1, n_2) \in E\}$.

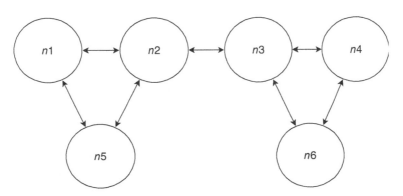

FIGURE 17.2 *Example of a P2P network.* Source: [19]).

The QRDM, analyzed in [19], operates as follows:

1. Initially, each node is connected to a number of neighboring nodes. These neighbors are stored in the node's routing table $l(n_1)$.
2. A user connects to his local node, n_1, requesting resources. The node searches its metadata $\Gamma(n_1)$ and responds if the resource exists on this node. If the recipient node does not have any information in its metadata about the requested resources, it encapsulates the request into a message and forwards the message to a randomly chosen node. The nodes forward the message until either the resource is found or the time-to-live of the message reaches zero.
3. If the requested resource is discovered, a reply message is sent back to the original node either directly or via each node that forwarded the request.
4. Once the node that initiated the request receives a reply, the user is allowed to access the resource.

The SRDM, also analyzed in [19], operates as follows:

1. Each node maintains a document that represents the descriptions of resources that are available for other nodes. Each node also maintains a repository for the documents of other nodes.
2. Each node will send a message at regular intervals. Messages are sent randomly to one of the nodes in the routing table. A node that has not received a message previously is always given priority over the nodes which received messages.
3. When a message arrives at a node, the time-to-live for this message is decremented. Description documents of the message and documents at the node's repository are merged. The intermediate nodes keep forwarding the message until expiration.
4. When the time-to-live reaches zero, the message is sent back to its originating node. There it updates the node's repository with the description documents it collected during its journey. The process continues from step 2.
5. When a user initiates a request, the node checks its store of documents and, if a matching resource is found, it sends a request directly to the node that controls this resource. If the resource is not found, the node sends a message with an increased time-to-live and starts searching for the requested resource.

In this work, the authors suggest that a P2P approach would be suitable for dynamic distributed searching in a large-scale grid environment. Two P2P protocols for resource discovery are proposed: the QRDM and the SRDM, based on the main characteristics of P2P systems, namely decentralization and self-organization. The authors' main concern and point of attention includes providing, to the proposed mechanisms, the procedures that would allow the P2P protocols to make a trade-off between the size of the network and efficiency in finding resources without flooding the system with query messages.

17.4 THE GRID-ROUTING TRANSFERRING APPROACH

17.4.1 Resource Discovery Based on Matchmaking Routers

The presented resource discovery framework based on matchmaking routers [20, 21] operates in a decentralized manner taking into consideration a large number of heterogeneous resources with distributed ownership. Using semantic-based descriptions of resources and requests, the matchmaking routers are responsible for providing a set of resources that can satisfy a specific request and then directing the request to one of these resources [22].

Assuming that at a point of time a request is created in one of the matchmaking routers, the router should be able to provide an appropriate matching resource. The matchmaking process in the resource discovery framework has to obey certain rules. The matchmaking rules determine the set of candidate resources that can satisfy a specific request. The basic matchmaking rules in the framework, introduced in [22], are the following:

- The architecture and operating system characteristics of the request must match those of the resource.
- The minimum disk size required by the request must be smaller than or equal to the available disk size of the resource.
- The minimum memory space required by the request must be smaller than or equal to the available memory space of the resource.

The two developed approaches for the proposed grid resource discovery framework take into consideration the concept of the best suitability (best fit) and the factor of distance when there is more than one resource capable of satisfying a specific request.

In Fig. 17.3, a grid system comprised of five matchmaking routers and four different types of resources is presented. At some point of time, a request is created in Router 1. This request requires a resource with the following characteristics: Intel architecture, Linux operating system, 30,000 MB disk size, 1024 MB memory space. The resource discovery mechanism should be able to provide an appropriate resource capable of satisfying the request. Figure 17.3 also presents the descriptions of characteristics of the four different types of resources available in the system.

The matchmaking router (in this case Router 1), based on the matchmaking rules, is responsible of providing the set of resources capable of satisfying the request. From the four different types of resources available in the system, only two are appropriate for the request's requirements. These are resources of Type 3 and resources of Type 4.

After gathering the set of the appropriate resources for the request, the resource discovery mechanism has to direct efficiently the request to one of those resources. Assuming that the directing of the request happens with the "best fit" approach, the matchmaking router 1 has to decide which of the two resources is most suited for satisfying the request. In this case, the best fit resource is the

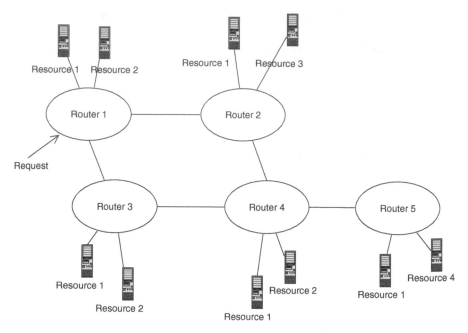

Request: Intel, Linux, 30,000, 1024
Resource 1: SGI, IRIX6, 25,000, 128
Resource 2: Intel, Linux, 25,000, 512
Resource 3: Intel, Linux, 40,000, 2048
Resource 4: Intel, Linux, 35,000, 1024

FIGURE 17.3   *Sample grid system.* Source: [22].

resource of type 4. So, the request is forwarded to Router 5, where the resource of type 5 exists locally. Satisfying the request occurs in a total distance of 4 hops.

Assuming that directing of the request happens with the minimum distance approach, the process for satisfying the request is the following: After gathering the set of the resources appropriate for the request, matchmaking Router 1 has to decide which one of the two resources will satisfy the request. Based on the information maintained in its Routing Table, the matchmaking Router 1 decides to forward the request to the nearest resource. Distance from Router 1 to resource of type 3 is 2 hops, which is smaller than the distance to resource of type 4, which is equal to 4 hops. So, resource of type 3 is selected for satisfying of the request.

Both approaches, namely minimum distance and best fit, present extremely good performance results, showing their effectiveness in discovering the appropriate resource. The minimum distance approach guarantees satisfying a request in the smallest number of hops. The best fit approach guarantees discovering the most suited approach for the request resource without producing unacceptable results in terms of distance in hops.

17.4.2 Acquiring Knowledge in a Large-Scale Grid System

In [23, 24], a resource discovery scheme is introduced, based on locality and vicinity, which manages to satisfy requests created in the system and to efficiently direct these requests to the appropriate resources capable of satisfying them. Moreover, the proposed resource discovery scheme, while satisfying requests, supports the participant groups of resources in order to obtain a better knowledge of the resource availability in the grid. As the satisfying of requests progresses, the groups gain more and more information about the availability of resources, even for resources that are located relatively far in the system.

The grid concept is defined as the coordinated resource sharing and problem solving among VOs of resources. By expanding the grid-router model and complying with the grid concept of forming VOs, the VO-based depiction of grid systems is presented in Fig. 17.4. Each VO includes a number of local resources, and the router maintains the VOs' physical connection with the other VOs in the system. The resources of each

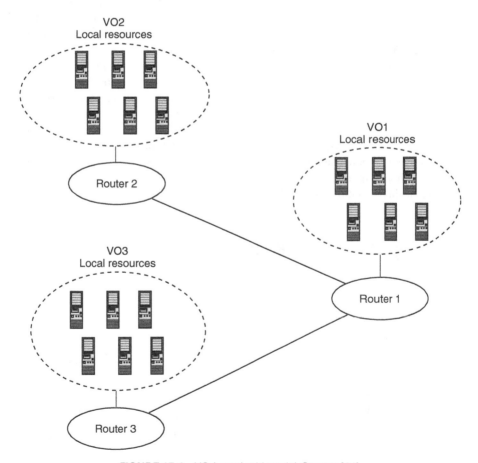

FIGURE 17.4 *VO-based grid model.* Source: [24].

VO are the group of shared elements in the grid infrastructure dedicated to the system waiting to satisfy remote requests.

The router of each VO in the VO-based grid system maintains a routing table with size equal to the number of resources, which the VO has knowledge of. Each data element in that table is the minimum distance measured in hops from that VO's router to the specific resource that the VO is aware of. When a request for a specific resource is created in a VO of the system, information available in the VOs' routing tables depicts the path the request has to follow in order to get to the desired resource.

A VO's routing table is organized into three sections: local resources, neighbors' resources, and remote resources. The local resources section maintains information about the resources this specific VO controls locally. The section neighbors' resources maintains information about the resources that are controlled by neighboring VOs, that is, by VOs that share a physical and direct connection with this specific VO. Finally, the remote resources section contains the distances in hops to known resources controlled by other VOs in the system.

In the case example of resource discovery, first discussed in [23], VOs maintain information about their local resources and also about the local resources in their close vicinity. The sample grid system for presenting the resource discovery scheme is based on Fig. 17.5. Each VO is aware of the local resources it controls and also its neighbors' resources. This information is maintained in the routing tables. A request is created for resource of Type 6 in VO1. The resource is not controlled locally, so the request has to be forwarded to another VO of the system which locally controls resource of Type 6.

Router 1, now, is responsible for locating a resource of Type 6 somewhere in the system. First, it creates a query for resource of Type 6 and forwards it to its neighbors (Routers 1 and 2). Since no response is received, Router 1 increases the radius of the query by 1 hop. The query, now, is in Router 4, and an entry regarding resource of type 6 exists in its routing table in the neighbors' resources subsection with a distance

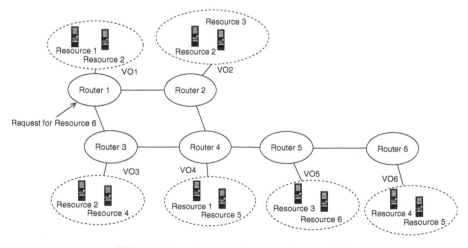

FIGURE 17.5   *Sample grid system.* Source: [23].

of 2 hops. Because of the existence of resource of type 6 in the close vicinity of VO4, the query suffered the forwarding process in a distance of only 2 hops.

Router 4, based on the neighbors' resources subsection, produces an answering query in the form of a backward counter-response. Starting from Router 4, the counter-response passes through all the relevant routers/VOs, updating their information maintained in their routing tables regarding resource of type 6. The request, now, is able to follow a credible path through the system, until it reaches VO6, in order to get satisfied.

By basing resource discovery on locality and vicinity, obvious advantages are achieved in the distance of the queries and the distance of the responses. The queries are not forced to travel the whole distance until they get to a VO that controls locally the relevant resource. The same can be said for response forwarding also. When executed in a large grid system with different topologies and architectures, these advantages become even more obvious and significant.

In conclusion, the discovery scheme suggests that each VO maintains information about its local resources and also of its neighbors' resources, that is, resources in its close vicinity. The goal is for the VOs to acquire better perception of the grid resource availability. When a request is created in a system's VO, and this request cannot get satisfied from a local or neighboring resource, a process of query forwarding is initiated. When the query reaches a VO that controls the desired resource, a counter-response follows a backward path to the VO that originally created the query. In this backward path, all the relevant VOs that participated in the query forwarding update their information in the routing tables regarding the newly discovered resource. As the system continues to satisfy requests, the VOs manage to acquire a better, almost complete, knowledge regarding the actual resource availability in the system.

17.5 CONCLUSIONS

In this chapter, we discussed issues concerning resource discovery mechanisms and strategies in large-scale grid systems. First, we presented the theoretical background regarding the architecture of grid systems and the challenges when deploying resource discovery mechanisms for such systems. Also, we have provided popular well-known resource discovery mechanisms and analyzed them in order to present the different types of approaches in the resource discovery research area. In particular, this chapter analyzed the following resource discovery approaches: the semantic communities approach, the incorporation of P2P discovery protocols into grid systems, and, finally, strategies based on the grid routing–transferring approach.

The semantic communities approach enables efficient resource discovery in grids. By clustering nodes into communities and taking into consideration their semantic properties, the structure helps prune the search space and reduce the cost of the search. The system also exhibits many desirable properties because it supports complex queries and is fully decentralized and scalable. The P2P approaches suggest the use of existing P2P discovery techniques into grid systems, in order to achieve a trade-off between the size of the network and efficiency in finding resources, without flooding the system with query messages. Finally, resource discovery mechanisms, based on the grid routing–transferring model, suggest a combination of matchmaking and routing techniques, as well as methods for acquiring a close-to-complete knowledge of the available resources and disseminating the available information in large-scale grid systems.

ACKNOWLEDGMENT

This work was supported by the COST Action IC0805 "Open European Network for High-Performance Computing on Complex Environments."

REFERENCES

1. I. Foster, C. Kesselman, and S. Tuecke, "The anatomy of the grid: enabling scalable virtual organizations," *International Journal of High Performance Computing Applications*, vol. 15, no. 3, pp. 200–222, 2001.
2. I. Foster, C. Kesselman, J. Nick, and S. Tuecke, "The physiology of the grid: an open grid services architecture for distributed systems integration," in *Open Grid Service Infrastructure WG, Global Grid Forum*, 2002.
3. M. Bote-Lorenzo, Y. Dimitriadis, and E. Gomez-Sanchez, "Grid characteristics and uses: a grid definition," in *Postproceedings of the First European Across Grids Conference (ACG'03), Lecture Notes in Computer Science*, vol. 2970, pp. 291–298. Santiago de Compostela, Spain: Springer-Verlag, 2004.
4. R. Buyya and S. Venugopal, "A gentle introduction to grid computing and technologies," *Computer Society of India Communications*, vol. 29, pp. 9–19, 2005.
5. H. Tangmunarunkit, S. Decker, and C. Kesselman, "Ontology-based resource matching in the grid–the grid meets the semantic web," in *Proceedings of the 2nd International Semantic Web Conference*, pp. 706–721, Sanibel Island, FL, USA, 2003.
6. A. Vidal, J. Braga, F. Kon, and S. Kofuji, "Defining and exploring a grid system ontology," in *The 4th International Workshop on Middleware for Grid Computing*, p. 16. New York: ACM press, 2006.
7. S. Castano, A. Ferrara, S. Montanelli, and G. Racca, "Matching techniques for resource discovery in distributed systems using heterogeneous ontology descriptions," in *Proceedings of the International Conference on Information Technology: Coding and Computing (ITCC?04)*, vol. 1, pp. 360–366, Las Vegas, Nevada, USA, 2004.
8. C. Zhu, Z. Liu, W. Zhang, W. Xiao, Z. Xu, and D. Yang, "Decentralized grid resource discovery based on resource information community," *Journal of Grid Computing*, vol. 2, pp. 261–277, 2005.
9. T. Somasundaram, R. Balachandar, V. Kandasamy, R. Buyya, R. Raman, N. Mohanram, and S. Varun, "Semantic based grid resource discovery and its integration with the grid service broker," in *ADCOM 2006: Proceedings of 14th International Conference on Advanced Computing and Communications*, pp. 84–89, Mangalore, India, 2006.
10. D. Talia, P. Trunfio, J. Zeng, and M. Hogqvist, "A DHT-based peer-to-peer framework for resource discovery in grids," Tech. Rep. TR-0048, Institute on System Architecture, CoreGRID—Network of Excellence, 2006.

11. S. Basu, S. Banerjee, P. Sharma, and S. Lee, "Nodewiz: Peer-to-peer resource discovery for grids," in *5th International Workshop on Global and Peer-to-Peer Computing (GP2PC) in conjunction with CCGrid*, vol. 1, pp. 213–220, Palo Alto, CA, USA, 2005.
12. P. Trunfio, D. Talia, P. Fragopoulou, H. Papadakis, M. Mordacchini, M. Pennanen, K. Popov, V. Vlassov, and S. Haridi, "Peer-to-peer models for resource discovery on grids," Tech. Rep. TR-0028, Institute on System Architecture, CoreGRID—Network of Excellence, 2006.
13. J. Li and S. Vuong, "Grid resource discovery using semantic communities," in *Proceedings of the 4th International Conference on Grid and Cooperative Computing*, (Beijing, China), pp. 657–667, 2005.
14. J. Li, "Grid resource discovery based on semantically linked virtual organizations," *Future Generation Computer Systems, Elsevier*, vol. 26, no. 3, pp. 361–373, 2010.
15. H. Zhuge, R. Jia, and J. Liu, "Semantic link network builder and intelligent semantic browser," *Concurrency—Practice and Experience*, vol. 16, no. 14, pp. 1453–1476, 2004.
16. H. Zhuge, Y. Sun, R. Jia, and J. Liu, "Algebra model and experiment for semantic link network," *International Journal of High Performace Computing*, vol. 3, no. 4, pp. 227–238, 2005.
17. H. Zhuge, J. Liu, L. Feng, and C. He, "Semantic-based query-routing and heterogeneous data integration in peer-to-peer semantic link networks," in *International IFIP Conference on Semantics of a Networked World: ICSNW 2004*, pp. 91–107, Paris, France, 2004.
18. A. Iamnitchi and I. Foster, "On fully decentralized resource discovery in grid environments," in *International Workshop on Grid Computing 2001*, (Denver, CO), pp. 51–62, 2001.
19. N. Al-Dmour and W. Teahan, "Peer-to-peer protocols for resource discovery in the grid," in *The IASTED International Conference on Parallel and Distributed Computing and Networks (PDCN)*, (Innsbruck Austria), pp. 319–324, 2005.
20. W. Li, Z. Xu, F. Dong, and J. Zhang, "Grid resource discovery based on a routing-transferring model," in *Grid 2002, Lecture Notes in Computer Science*, vol. 2536, pp. 145–156. Berlin / Heidelberg: Springer, 2002.
21. S. Tangpongprasit, T. Katagiri, H. Honda, and T. Yuba, "A time-to-live based reservation algorithm on fully decentralized resource discovery in grid computing," *Parallel Computing*, vol. 31, pp. 529–543, 2005.
22. K. Karaoglanoglou and H. Karatza, "Resource discovery in a grid system based on matchmaking-routers," in *Proceedings of the 12th Panhellenic Conference on Informatics, PCI*, pp. 73–77. Samos, Greece: IEEE Computer Society, 2008.
23. K. Karaoglanoglou and H. Karatza, "Acquiring knowledge in a grid system via a resource discovery scheme," *International Journal of Modeling, Simulation, and Scientific Computing (IJMSSC), World Scientific*, vol. 2, no. 1, pp. 1–28, 2011.
24. K. Karaoglanoglou and H. Karatza, "Directing requests and acquiring knowledge in a large-scale grid system," in *2012 International Symposium on Performance Evaluation of Computer and Telecommunication Systems, SPECTS 2012*, (Genoa, Italy), 2012.

PART VII

Energy Awareness in High-Performance Computing

18

Energy-Aware Approaches for HPC Systems

Robert Basmadjian

Passau University, Passau, Germany

Georges Da Costa

Toulouse University, Toulouse, France

**Ghislain Landry Tsafack Chetsa
and Laurent Lefevre**

INRIA, LIP Laboratory, Ecole Normale Superieure of Lyon, Lyon, France

Ariel Oleksiak

Poznan Supercomputing and Networking Center, Poznan, Poland

Jean-Marc Pierson

Toulouse University, Toulouse, France

Optimization of complex HPC systems is no more only a raw performance matter. Because of increase of ecological and cost awareness, energy performance is now a primary focus. From models to runtimes, a vast field of research offers insight into the links between energy and raw performance.

High-Performance Computing on Complex Environments, First Edition.
Edited by Emmanuel Jeannot and Julius Žilinskas.
© 2014 John Wiley & Sons, Inc. Published 2014 by John Wiley & Sons, Inc.

18.1 INTRODUCTION

With the *race to exascale*, one of the major concern for actors involved in the development and operation of high-performance computing (HPC) systems is no longer the number of PFlops (petaflops) their system can achieve per second, but how many PFlops they can achieve per watt. This novel method of evaluating supercomputers' performance places a great emphasis on their energy consumption. This emphasis can be justified by the fact that computer chips seem to have hit a wall, meaning that we cannot make them go any faster. Consequently, supercomputer designers just have to add more chips to increase the computing power. But this approach has a significant impact on energy usage.

However, tremendous efforts are being undertaken by HPC operators from multiple levels to make supercomputers greener. This is evidenced by the Green500 list;[1] its latest issue shows that the recent supercomputers are getting greener. The rise of graphics processors in massive server clusters and the acquisition of low-power memories are probably the main reasons for their sudden improvement in energy efficiency. Just to give a global picture, in 2009 Samsung claimed that more than 95 TWh/year or US$6–7 billion/year could potentially be saved if the memory in all 32 Mu servers worldwide could be replaced with their Samsung Green DDR3 memory chip.

Similar efforts are being carried out regarding all other HPC subsystems, from the processor to the network to the storage subsystems. However, significant efforts still need to be made if today's supercomputers want to meet the 20-MW constraint for exascale.

Bellow is a non exhaustive list of directions for improving the energy efficiency of HPC systems form a software perspective:

- new and fitted programming models,
- smart failure management for applications,
- optimized data management, and
- improved runtimes.

There is a common belief that a considerable share of energy consumed by HPC systems during their operations could potentially be saved if user applications were programmed differently. Put another way, throughout their life cycle, user applications exhibit behaviors whose understanding allows the implementation of power reduction schemes which can significantly reduce the amount of energy they consume at runtime. This has been proven true by the literature [1–6].

From what precedes, making HPC applications more energy friendly requires (i) rewriting most of the existing applications with energy constraints in mind, and (ii) coding new applications with the same constraints. These alternatives may not always be possible. Rewriting some HPC applications is so costly that most people

---

[1] http://green500.org

find paying the electrical bill worth it (there is no evidence; however, this issue has been in people's mind for a while, but to our knowledge no one has proposed an energy-efficient version of an HPC application so far), whereas application developers usually do not pay much attention to how much energy their applications will consume. The main reason for this is that power-saving schemes are platform-specific. For example, let us consider the dynamic voltage and frequency scaling (DVFS) technology. It allows scaling the processor's frequency according to the workload in some cases. So integrating DVFS into a program source code assumes that the developers know all the potential platforms that will run their applications, which does not make sense.

It is more convenient to improve energy efficiency at runtime. Contrary to application-level improvements, this has the potential to cover large classes of applications, some of which the source code may not be accessible, on a large variety of hardware.

To achieve an energy-efficient runtime, a fine-grained knowledge on the hardware and application is necessary. This knowledge is necessary in order for the runtime to evaluate the possible gain of applying leverages.

A server's power consumption is complex to evaluate and measure [7], as it embeds multiple subcomponents having non linear power consumption models. At the design stage, care is also given to other power-consuming elements, including the cooling, light and network systems. This make sense; for example, a considerable share of the energy consumed by the computing infrastructure, between 20% and 30%, is attributed to the cooling system. However, the cooling system beyond the scope of this chapter which addresses on software modifications throughout the life cycle of the HPC infrastructure.

Applications are also complex structures. Alongside the spatial structure of hardware, applications have a temporal structure. Runtime must take into account this structure to make decisions adapted to each phase of applications.

In the following, we will first provide a detailed explanation of server power consumption in Section 18.2; then we will describe in Section 18.3 application, phase detection, and identification. Finally, we will show in Section 18.4 the available leverages in HPC systems.

18.2 POWER CONSUMPTION OF SERVERS

In [8], Rivoire establishes a comparison among many different energy models. Two categories are defined: comprehensive models, and high-level models called *black-box models*. Comprehensive CPU models were proposed in [9, 10]. These models are very accurate in terms of CPU power consumption and rely on specific details of the CPU microarchitecture. High-level models are more general, and do not take into account specific low-level details of the operation and characteristics of the modeled infrastructure. Nevertheless, it increases the portability of the model and the simulation speed. These simple models sacrifice the accuracy of computation, but do not require a very detailed knowledge of the architecture of the processors used.

In Section 18.2.1, we introduce the most relevant energy-related attributes of a server in the form of UML (unified modeling language) class diagram. Then, based on these attributes, in Section 18.2.2 we give the power consumption prediction models.

18.2.1 Server Modeling

Figure 18.1 demonstrates the UML class diagram of servers depicting their most relevant energy-related dynamic and static attributes. The former denotes the fact that the attribute needs to be kept up to date by monitoring systems. By static attributes we mean that those whose value remains constant; most of the time, the values of static attributes are obtained from the manufacturers' data sheet.

The server class is an abstraction of a generic server computing system whose subclasses, including tower server, rackable server and blade server classes, are distinguished by their physical form factor.

Typically, a server has a mainboard and runs baseline software components (e.g., native operating system). The mainboard provides most of the core hardware components of the system: central processing units (CPU class), random access memories (RAMStick), network interface cards (NICs), hardware RAIDs (HardwareRAID), and storage units (HardDisk). Its *memoryUsage* attribute denotes the total usage (in gigabytes) of all the attached memory modules.

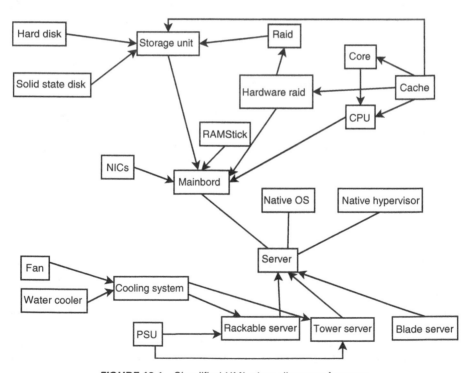

FIGURE 18.1 *Simplified UML class diagram of servers.*

In modern processors, a `CPU` is commonly composed of more than one `core`. Each core can have its own `cache`, depending on the cache *level* (e.g., Level 1). It is also possible that certain cores share the same cache (e.g., Level 3). The most relevant energy-related attributes of the `CPU` class are as follows:

1. *Architecture*: indicates the processor's vendor (e.g., Intel, AMD, etc.); it is relevant because it translates into different power consumption behaviors;
2. *CPU Usage*: gives the utilization rate (load) of the processor;
3. *DVFS*: used to indicate whether energy-saving mechanisms (e.g., Intel Speed-Step) are enabled or not;
4. *Lithography*: denotes the size of the processor in nanometers;
5. *Transistor Number*: presents the number of transistors expressed in the order of millions.

Each `core` operates at a certain *frequency* (in gigahertz) and *voltage*(in volt). *coreLoad* expresses the utilization rate of the corresponding core. The `RAMStick` class has several attributes relevant to power consumption estimation:

1. *Voltage*: indicates the supply voltage at which the memory module operates; it is highly dependent on the memory *type* (e.g., DDR3);
2. *Size*: denotes the size of the memory module (in gigabytes);
3. *Frequency*: shows the memory module's operational frequency (in megahertz);
4. *Vendor*: presents the manufacturer (e.g., KINGSTON, HYNIX);
5. *Buffer Type*: type of buffer technology (e.g., fully buffered).

`Hard disk` class' energy-related attributes are the following: *maxReadRate* and *maxWriteRate* respectively indicate the maximum read and write rates of the disk, which are computed in terms of transferred data size per second (MB/s). *readRate* and *writeRate* respectively indicate, in MB/s, the actual read and write rate of the disk. *powerIdle* is the power consumed by the hard disk when it is inactive.

`Tower servers` and `rackable servers` are equipped with their own `power supply units` (PSUs) and `fans`. The most relevant energy-related attribute of a `PSU` is the *efficiency*, which indicates (in percentage) the amount of loss for the power supplied to server components. Attributes of the class `fan` include: *depth* which denotes the fan's depth in meters; *maxRPM* and *powerMax* which denote the fan's maximum nominal number of rotations per minute and power consumption respectively; finally, the *actualRPM* attribute denotes its actual instantaneous rotation speed.

18.2.2 Power Prediction Models

In this section, we first introduce the idle power consumption of a server and then present its dynamic power.

18.2.2.1 Idle Power Consumption Basically, the idle power of a server does not fluctuate significantly (e.g., ± 1 W) and strongly depends on its hardware configuration (e.g., number of processors, memory modules). Over the last years, there have been several efforts to reduce the idle power consumption of servers. Those efforts usually combine software solutions (e.g., C-states for the processor) with intelligent hardware designs.

Processor. Based on Joule's and Ohm's laws [11], the power consumption of a processor can be expressed by

$$P = I \times V, \tag{18.1}$$

where P denotes the power (W), I represents the electric current (A), and V indicates the voltage (V).

With the advent of multicore processors, a processor is in the idle state when all of its constituent cores are also inactive. Consequently, (18.1) can be rewritten for each core as follows

$$P_i = I_i \times V_i. \tag{18.2}$$

Furthermore, the idle power consumption of each core i depends on its number of transistors. Hence, (18.1) can also be adapted to express the idle power of transistors (in the order of million):

$$P_{ji} = I_{ji} \times V_{ji}, \tag{18.3}$$

where I_{ji} and V_{ji} denote, respectively, the current and voltage of the jth transistor of the core i.

Basically, the processors' operating voltage lies between 0 and 2 V. Findings provided in [12] reveal a linear relationship between the current and the supply voltage when the processor operates within the above mentioned voltage range. Hence, the current leakage I_{ji} of transistors is modeled using the curve-fitting methodology by means of a second-order polynomial:

$$I_{ji} = \alpha V_{ji}^2 - \beta V_{ji} + \gamma, \tag{18.4}$$

where $\alpha = 0.114312$, $\beta = 0.22835$, and $\gamma = 0.139204$ are the coefficients.

Let t_i denote the total number of transistors (in the order of millions) of a core i; then its power consumption is given by

$$P_i = \sum_{j=1}^{t_i} I_{ji} \times V_{ji}. \tag{18.5}$$

Recently, several energy-saving mechanisms (e.g., Intel SpeedStep [13] and AMD Cool'n'Quiet[2]) have been introduced in order to reduce the power consumption of

[2]*AMD Cool'n'Quiet Technology* http://www.amd.com/us/products/technologies/cool-n-quiet/Pages/cool-n-quiet.aspx

processors. In using equation (18.5), power saving mechanisms affect the power consumption of a core i as follows:

$$Pr_i = \delta_i \times P_i, \tag{18.6}$$

where δ_i is the reduction factor in the power consumption P_i of core i, and Pr_i represents the reduced power consumption of a core i. Note that δ_i can vary depending upon the corresponding energy-saving mechanisms, where each of such mechanisms has its own particular behavior. For a different modeling of δ_i, the interested readers can refer to [14]. However, it is worth pointing out that for AMD processors both frequency and voltage scaling play a major role in reducing the power consumption, whereas for Intel processors only the voltage is an important factor. Hence, the idle power consumption of a multicore processor provided with n cores is the arithmetic sum of the static power of each of its constituent cores:

$$P_{\text{CPU}} = \sum_{i=1}^{n} Pr_i. \tag{18.7}$$

Memory. Similar to the processor, the memory's power consumption can be expressed as

$$P = I \times V. \tag{18.8}$$

As mentioned previously, it was shown in [12] that there is a linear relationship between the supplied voltage V (between 0 and 2 V) and the current I. Since the modern memory module technologies (e.g., DDR2, DDR3) operate within the above-mentioned range, the current I can be given by

$$I = c \times V, \tag{18.9}$$

where the constant c is either 0.00043 for DDR2 or 0.00013 for DDR3. The idle power consumption of a memory module for a given *frequency f* (MHz) and size s (GB) can be expressed as

$$P(f, s) = c \times V^2. \tag{18.10}$$

In order to reflect the impact of frequency as well as the size of a memory module, (18.10) can be rewritten as

$$P = s \times f \times c \times V^2. \tag{18.11}$$

Given a set of n memory modules, their idle power consumption is given by

$$P_{\text{RAM}} = \sum_{i=1}^{n} s_i \times f_i \times c \times V_i^2, \tag{18.12}$$

where $s_i, f_i,$ and V_i denote, respectively, the size, frequency, and voltage of a specific memory module i, and c is a constant whose value is given above.

Hard Disk. The hard disk's *idle mode* (e.g., no operation) consists of the follow-ing three states:[3] *idle*, *standby*, and *sleep*. Furthermore, the power consumption of standby and sleep states is quite identical, and it is on average 10% of the idle state power consumption. The main reason for such a behavior is that, during the standby and sleep states, the disk's mechanical parts are stopped. The *idle mode* power con-sumption of the hard disk is given by

$$P_{HDD} = y \times P_{idle}(\alpha + 0.1 \times \beta + 0.1 \times \gamma), \tag{18.13}$$

where $y \in [0, 1]$ denotes the probability that the disk is in idle mode, and P_{idle} is the idle state power consumption provided by the manufacturer's data sheet. Values of y can be found in Section 18.2.2.2. The parameters $\alpha, \beta, \gamma \in [0, 1]$ indicate, respec-tively, the probability that the disk is in the idle, standby, and sleep states. To derive the values of α, β, and γ, such that $\alpha + \beta + \gamma = 1$, the following probabilistic approach can be adopted:

1. If $0 < y \leq 0.3$, then $\alpha = 0.9$, and $\beta = \gamma = 0.05$.
2. If $0.3 < y \leq 0.6$, then $\alpha = 0.5$ and $\beta = \gamma = 0.25$.
3. If $0.6 < y \leq 1$, then $\alpha = 0.1$ and $\beta = \gamma = 0.45$.

From above equations, one can observe that the more the disk stays in idle mode (i.e., $y \simeq 1$), the higher the probability that it will remain in standby and sleep states. Note that whenever the state transition of the disk is accurately detected, then the parameters α, β, and γ can appropriately be configure so as to always zero two of them.

Mainboard. The idle power consumption of the mainboard is the sum of the power consumption of its constituent components:

$$P_{Mainboard} = \sum_{i=1}^{l} P_{CPU_i} + P_{RAM} + \sum_{j=1}^{m} P_{NIC_j} + \sum_{k=1}^{n} P_{HDD_k} + c, \tag{18.14}$$

where P_{CPU}, P_{RAM}, and P_{HDD} are given, respectively, by (18.7), (18.12), and (18.13), whereas c is a constant related to the mainboard's own power draw. Thus, the value of c can be configured through the *powerIdle* attribute of the Mainboard class either from the manufacturer's data sheet or by means of observations. Finally, P_{NIC} denotes the idle power consumption of the network interface cards, whose value can be found in the manufacturer's specifications.

18.2.2.2 *Dynamic Power Consumption*   Unlike the idle power of servers, the dynamic one significantly fluctuates depending on running applications along with their workloads. As in the case of the idle power, there have been several efforts to reduce the dynamic power consumption of servers by means of energy-saving mech-anisms (e.g., DVFS) in combination with the hardware.

---

[3]The hard disk changes its state sequentially from idle to standby and then to sleep.

Processor. Based on the CMOS circuits' [15] power draw, the dynamic power consumption of a core i is given by the following utilization-based model:

$$P'_i = V_i^2 \times f_i \times C_{\text{eff}} \times \frac{L_i}{100}, \tag{18.15}$$

where P'_i denotes the dynamic power (W) of a core i having a utilization L_i, V_i and f_i indicate, respectively, the voltage and frequency of the corresponding core i, and C_{eff} presents the effective capacitance.

Given an n-core processor ($n > 1$) with no specific energy-saving mechanisms enabled, its dynamic power consumption is given by

$$P'_{\text{CPU}} = \sum_{i=1}^{n} P'_i. \tag{18.16}$$

In [16], the authors show that the power consumption of a multicore processor is not a simple sum of those of its constituent cores as suggested by equation (18.16). Consequently, they decompose a multicore processor into three component levels: (i) chip, (ii) die, and (iii) core level, and model the power consumption of each of the corresponding component. Furthermore, they show that (18.16) usually overestimates the power consumption, and propose a model that takes into account both resource-sharing and energy-saving mechanisms. Refer to [16] for further details.

Memory. Basically, the dynamic power consumption of the memory results from access (there is always only one active operating rank per channel regardless of the number of memory modules or module ranks in the system). Such a power is always constant during access regardless of the operation type (e.g. read, write, etc.) and can be expressed as:

$$P'_{\text{RAM}} = \gamma \times \beta, \tag{18.17}$$

where $\beta = 7$ W, 17 W, and 10 W for DDR2 unbuffered, DDR2 fully buffered, and DDR3 unbuffered memory modules, respectively, whereas $\gamma \in [0, 1]$ denotes the probability that a memory access is performed. Such a parameter is useful for systems when the application profile of accessing the memory module is not known in advance. The following technique can be adopted to set values for γ:

1. If the processor is in the idle state performing no activity, then it can be equally assumed that the memory modules are also in the idle state: that is, $\gamma = 0$.
2. If the processor is performing some computations (utilization of more than 1%), then a probabilistic approach can be adopted in modeling γ, such that the more the total memory in use, the higher the probability that a memory access is performed:

$$\gamma = \frac{memoryUsage}{\sum_{i=1}^{n} s_i}$$

such that s_i and n as defined in (18.12), and *memoryUsage* is introduced in Section 18.2.1.

Hard Disk. It was shown in [17] that the power to perform read or write operations on the hard disk drive is on average 1.4 times more than the idle state power consumption, whereas the start-up power consumes on average 3.7 times more than for the idle state:

$$P'_{HDD} = x \times 1.4 \times P_{idle} + z \times 3.7 \times P_{idle}, \tag{18.18}$$

where $x, z \in [0, 1]$ denote, respectively, the probability that the disk is in accessing and start-up modes, such that $x + y + z = 1$, and P_{idle} and y are introduced in Section 18.2.2.1. Values of x, y, and z can be computed as follows:

1. If the average operation size (MB/s) of reads and writes per second is zero (i.e., *readRate* or *writeRate* = 0), then it can be assumed that the disk is in idle mode ($x = z = 0$ and $y = 1$).
2. If the average number of read/write operations per second is not zero, we adopt a probabilistic approach in modeling the mode changes such that

   - If *readRate* or *writeRate* > 0, then $x = \frac{readRate + writeRate}{maxReadRate + maxWriteRate}$,
   - If *writeRate* = 0, then $x = \frac{readRate}{maxReadRate}$,
   - If *readRate* = 0, then $x = \frac{writeRate}{maxWriteRate}$,

   where $y = 0.9 \times (1 - x)$ and $z = 0.1 \times (1 - x)$.

Mainboard. As for the idle part, the dynamic power consumption of the mainboard is given by

$$P'_{Mainboard} = \sum_{i=1}^{l} P'_{CPU_i} + P'_{RAM} + \sum_{j=1}^{m} P'_{NIC_j} + \sum_{k=1}^{n} P'_{HDD_k}, \tag{18.19}$$

where P'_{CPU}, P'_{RAM}, and P'_{HDD} are given, respectively, by (18.16), (18.17), and (18.18), and P'_{NIC} denotes the dynamic power consumption of the network interface card whose value is at most 5% of the idle power consumption.

18.2.2.3 Total Power Consumption

Fan. Based on the literature,[4] the power consumption of a fan is expressed as

$$P = d_p \times q, \tag{18.20}$$

[4]http://www.engineeringtoolbox.com/fans-efficiency-power-consumption-d_197.html

where P represents the power consumption (W), d_p indicates the total pressure increase in the fan (Pa or N/m^2), and q denotes the air volume flow delivered by the fan (m^3/s). Consequently, (18.20) can be rewritten as

$$P = \frac{F}{A} \times \frac{V}{t}, \tag{18.21}$$

where F, A, V, and t denote, respectively, the force (N), area (m^2), volume (m^3), and time (s). Since the ratio of the volume V to the area A presents the depth d (m), then (18.21) can be expressed as

$$P = \frac{F \times d}{t}. \tag{18.22}$$

It was shown in [14] that F is proportional to the square of the RPM (revolutions per minute) of the motor:

$$F = c_{\text{Fan}} \times \text{RPM}^2. \tag{18.23}$$

Hence, the power consumption of a fan having a depth d and an actual instantaneous revolution per minute RPM is given by

$$P_{\text{Fan}} = \frac{c_{\text{Fan}} \times \text{RPM}^2 \times d}{3600}, \tag{18.24}$$

such that c_{Fan} is a constant for a given fan can be computed as

$$c_{\text{Fan}} = \frac{3600 \times P_{\text{fanmax}}}{\text{RPM}_{\text{max}}^2 \times d}, \tag{18.25}$$

where P_{fanmax} and RPM_{max} denote, respectively, the maximum power consumption and RPM of a fan whose values can be extracted, in addition to the depth d, from the manufacturer's data sheet.

Power Supply Unit. The *efficiency* is the main indicator of the power consumption of a PSU. Consequently, it is not surprising that manufacturers provide the efficiency range of their PSU w.r.t. a given load. Given an *efficiency* of e, the power consumption of the PSU is estimated as follows:

$$P_{\text{PSU}} = (100 - e)\frac{P_{\text{Mainboard}} + P'_{\text{Mainboard}} + P_{\text{Fan}}}{n \times e}, \tag{18.26}$$

where $P_{\text{Mainboard}}$, $P'_{\text{Mainboard}}$, and P_{Fan} are as introduced in (18.14), (18.19), and (18.24), respectively, whereas n denotes the number of PSUs and e their efficiency (assuming that it is identical for all the installed PSUs).

Total Power. Given a server composed of a mainboard, fans, and power supply units, as depicted in Fig. 18.1, then

1. For *blade*-type servers, the power consumption is

$$P_{\text{Blade}} = P_{\text{Mainboard}} + P'_{\text{Mainboard}}. \tag{18.27}$$

2. For *tower-* or *rackable*-type servers, the power consumption is given by

$$P_{\text{Tower\_Rackable}} = P_{\text{Mainboard}} + P'_{\text{Mainboard}} + \sum_{i=1}^{l} P_{\text{Fan}} + \sum_{j=1}^{m} P_{\text{PSU}}, \tag{18.28}$$

where $P_{\text{Mainboard}}$, $P'_{\text{Mainboard}}$, P_{Fan}, and P_{PSU} are, respectively, given by (18.14), (18.19), (18.24), and (18.26).

18.3 CLASSIFICATION AND ENERGY PROFILES OF HPC APPLICATIONS

In the HPC world, the details of applications are often discarded. Most applications are considered identical and to use 100% of the servers resources. Actually, it is far from being the case.

For instance, in Fig. 18.2, all the benchmarks run with 100% load. However, their power profiles are different. This suggests that having the load and memory access profiles is insufficient for an effective evaluation of the power consumed by an application. For example, Integer Sort (IS) and Fast Fourier Transform (FT) have the same average resource utilization for the CPU and the memory, but there is a difference of 16 W in their power consumption on the same hardware. The two just mentioned

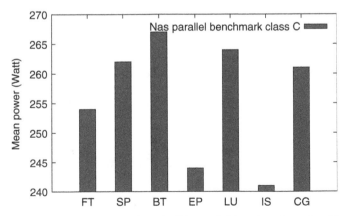

FIGURE 18.2 *Mean power consumption of NAS parallel benchmark on Sun Fire X2200 M2 with AMD Opteron 2218 processors.*

applications (IS and FT) from the NAS parallel benchmark (NPB [18]) suite have different patterns of access to the memory and the network subsystems. We believe that the difference in their total energy consumption can be attributed to the fact that they have different memory and network profiles.

Depending on the behavior of the application, several policies are often possible. Nevertheless, similar applications can be treated in the same way. The similarity criterion is often relative and may not always be the same. For example, applications can be said to be similar if they have the same resource utilization pattern (i.e., the same behavior in terms of resource utilization). Considering that many scientific applications often exhibit different behaviors (also known as phases) throughout their life cycle, in the following, a phase can be either an application (if it only has a single behavior) or a specific phase of an application.

As just mentioned, comparing two applications or telling whether they are similar or not can be very difficult. Several authors propose to analyze applications offline. In [19], the authors introduce metrics to characterize parallel applications. Motivated by the need for choosing the appropriate platform for a given application, authors rely upon static code analysis to classify applications. This approach offers the benefit of not being platform dependent; however, it does not allow online applications/phase classification or phase detection. A similarity-based taxonomy approach is proposed in [20], but the authors do not place emphasis on how applications are differentiated. Approaches described in [19, 20] show that parallel applications can be classified in a limited number of classes.

In [21], the authors manually analyzed the communication patterns of 27 applications from different HPC benchmarks based on the MPI communication library. Their purpose was to study the possible deterministic communication patterns in order to exploit them in fault-tolerance algorithms. Code analysis is time consuming and does not allow for runtime analysis. However, it proves the potential and value of communication pattern discovery. The authors of [22] propose a tool for assessing the code quality of HPC applications which turns to static pattern analysis, while [23] propose Modular Assembler Quality Analyzer and Optimizer (MACAO) to tune the performance of OpenMP codes.

In [19], the authors present an integrated performance monitor (IPM). IPM tool allows MPI application profiling and workload characterization. It allows postmortem analysis of the application behavior to understand the computation and communication phases. Vampir [24], Tau [25], and Sun Studio [26] are other examples of such performance analysis tools. In [27], the authors use Periscope to automatically detect memory access patterns, after the program ends. Similarly, Scalasca [28] searches for particular characteristic event sequences in event traces automatically. From low-level event traces, it classifies the behavior and quantifies the significance of the events by searching for patterns of inefficient behaviors. It relies on a number of layers to create an instrumented code, to collect and measure via measurement libraries linked with the application, and to trace the running application to finally analyze a report produced after the run. The authors of [29] use an I/O stress test benchmark, namely IOR, to reproduce and predict I/O access patterns. Analysis of the results shows that a simple test bed can be used for the characterization of more complex applications, but a manual tuning of the benchmark is required, which leads to impractical usage. In [30], the authors examined and compared two input/output access pattern classification methods based on learning algorithms. The first approach used a feed-forward neural network previously trained on benchmarks to generate qualitative classifications. The second approach used Markov models trained from previous executions to create a probabilistic model of input/output accesses.

Works done in [5, 31] use online techniques to detect applications execution phases, characterize them, and accordingly set the appropriate CPU frequency. They rely on hardware monitoring counters to compute runtime statistics such as cache hit/miss ratio memory access counts, retired instructions counts, and so on, which are then used for phase detection and characterization. Policies developed in [5, 31] tend to be designed for single-task environments. As the infrastructure in HPC systems tends to be a shared environment, usually the monitoring infrastructure must gather information at different levels: process/application/virtual machine level, and not only at the host level. Online recognition of communication phases in MPI application was investigated by Lim *et al.* [4]. Once a communication phase is recognized, the authors apply the CPU DVFS to save energy. They intercept and record the sequence of MPI calls during the execution of the program and consider a segment of the program code to be reducible if there are highly concentrated MPI calls or if an MPI call is long enough. The CPU is then set to run at the appropriate frequency when the reducible region is recognized again.

18.3.1 Phase Detection

A classical methodology relies on the concept of execution vector (EV), which is similar to power vectors (PVs), as shown in [32]. An EV is a column vector whose entries are system's metrics including hardware performance counters, network byte sent/received, and disk read/write counts. For convenience, those metrics will be referred to as *sensors*. On the one hand, sensors related to hardware performance counters provide insights into access rates of system's registers over a given time interval. Typically, information collected from those registers include: the number of instructions, last level cache accesses and misses, and branch misses and predictions. On the other hand, sensors related to the network and disk monitor network and disk activities respectively. The sampling rate corresponding to the time interval after which each sensor is read depends on the granularity. While a larger sampling rate may hide information regarding the system's behavior, a smaller sampling rate may incur a non-negligible overhead. A sampling rate of 1 s is often a good trade-off. EVs are also time-stamped with the time at which they were sampled.

By definition, the Manhattan distance between two points in an *n*-dimensional space is the distance between them if a grid-like path is followed. It offers the advantage that it does not depend on the translation of the coordinate system with respect to a coordinate axis, that is, it weighs more heavily the differences in each dimension. In order to detect system's phase changes at runtime, the Manhattan distance between consecutive execution vectors is used as the resemblance or similarity criterion. This

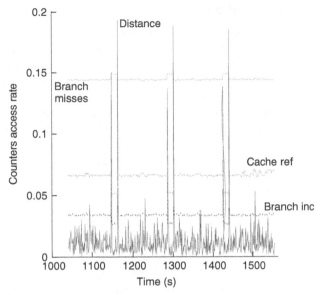

FIGURE 18.3 *Phase identification using the similarity between consecutive execution vectors as the phase identification metric. This is a zoomed-in view of the traces collected on one node when the system was running molecular dynamics simulation; "distance" represents the variation of the distance between consecutive execution vectors.*

similarity is used to cluster EVs along the execution time line as follows: two consecutive EVs along the execution time line belong to the same group or are similar if the Manhattan distance between them is lower than a fixed similarity threshold. The similarity threshold can be a fixed or variable percentage of the maximum known distance between all consecutive execution vectors.

For example, given a fixed similarity threshold of 10%, two consecutive EVs belong to the same group if the Manhattan distance between them is less than 10% of the similarity threshold.

Considering that the behavior of the system is relatively stable during a phase (a phase is a time period during which the behavior of the system is stable) and assuming that this stability is translated into EVs sampled during that phase, a phase is defined as any behavior delimited by two successive Manhattan distances exceeding the similarity threshold. Therefore, considering Fig. 18.3 (where the *x*-axis represents the execution time line and using MDS[5] as an example) along with a similarity threshold of 50% and assuming that the maximum Manhattan distance between two consecutive EVs along the execution time-line is 0.2, seven phases separated by six micro-phases or transition phases (0.1 is 50% of 0.2; referring to the definition of a phase, phases are delimited by distances greater than 0.1) can be detected. These phases correspond to variations reported in the access rate of the plotted performance counters.

[5] http://ringo.ams.sunysb.edu/index.php/MD_Simulation:_Protein_in_Water

18.3.2   Phase Identification

The need to reuse system reconfiguration information for recurring phase is essential for many cases (e.g., to avoid the characterization overhead). This probably justifies the many phase identification techniques one can find in the literature. The cost associated with phase identification may depend on the methodology employed. Data collected during a phase are often too large to efficiently represent and compare in hardware; to overcome that limitation, a phase is usually represented by a few pieces of information. How this is achieved basically depends on the phase detection mechanism. Here, a phase is represented with a special EV known as the *representative vector* of that phase. It is actually the arithmetic average of all EVs collected during that phase.

A phase being represented with a single vector, identifying two phases with each other boils down to comparing their representative vectors. However, the cost associated with this increases with the number of archived phases, which can lead to performance degradation during runtime.

For phase identification to guide reuse of system reconfiguration information, one can associate each phase with a label that implicitly indicates the subsystem (including the processor, the memory, storage, and network) that was mainly used during the phase. For example, compute-intensive phases are likely to stress the processor more than the storage subsystem, in which case the phase can be labeled as *compute intensive*. In an environment where energy efficiency matters, this can help determine which subsystem can be switched off to save energy. Referring to HPC workloads, five labels can be defined: *compute intensive*, *memory intensive*, *mixed*, *network intensive*, and *I/O intensive*. They are self-explanatory with the exception of "mixed." Briefly, workloads/phases labeled as "mixed" are both memory and compute intensive, which means that they alternate between-memory intensive and compute-intensive behaviors; however, the granularity at which this occurs is low to the point into which they cannot be considered as phases.

Another approach consists in using a decision tree like in [33]. In this work, the authors use a decision tree (Fig. 18.4). It is a tree-shaped diagram that determines a course of action. Each branch of the decision tree represents a possible phase class. The tree structure shows how one choice leads to the next. The decision tree can be produced by multiple algorithms that identify various ways of splitting a dataset into classes. Their representation of the acquired knowledge in a tree form is intuitive and easy to understand by humans. What is more, the learning and classification steps of decision tree induction are simple and fast.

These classifications produce classes of applications that share the same resource consumption profiles. Using those classification and models, it is possible to estimate the power profile of an application. Taking into account time in addition to power enables evaluating energy consumed by an application. Having an application that consumes power at a steady state has a different impact compared to an application that consumes power in a random way, even though the two applications have the same total energy and the same duration. Their different ways to consume energy lead to different starting times of fans and to different final temperatures of the elements.

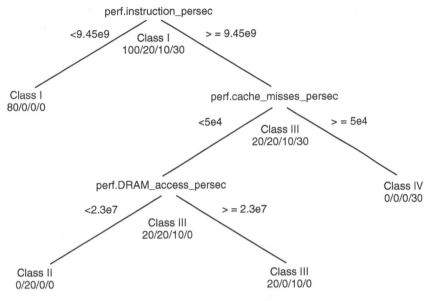

FIGURE 18.4   *Classification tree for AMD Opteron 275.*

Once the complete status is available, at the same time from the hardware and from the application or phase point of view, green leverages can be applied.

18.4 POLICIES AND LEVERAGES

There is a large body of work addressing the issue of power consumption in HPC systems. These work can roughly be divided into offline and online approaches. Offline approaches necessitating human intervention involve several steps, including source code instrumentation for performance profiling, execution with profiling, determination of the appropriate CPU frequency for each phase, and source code instrumentation for inserting DVFS instructions.

Offline methods usually use a two-level approach:

- profiled test runs and/or source code instrumentation;
- source code modification to add leverages or power saving capabilities.

For offline approaches, Freeh *et al*. [34] exploit PMPI to time MPI calls to insert DVFS scheduling calls based on duration, while Cameron *et al*. [35] profile MPI communications to create scenarios that will be followed when running application at full scale. Kimura *et al*. [1] instrumented program source code to insert DVFS directives according to the program's behavior in order to reduce the program's energy consumption without significant performance degradation.

Online approaches use the methods described in the previous section to detect program execution phases and apply DVFS accordingly. Several authors [5, 31] characterize phases and set the appropriate CPU frequency accordingly.

Tracking communications in an MPI program can also allow applying power saving capabilities. In [4], the authors intercept and record the sequence of MPI calls during program execution and consider a segment of the program code to be reducible if there are highly concentrated MPI calls or if an MPI call is long enough. The CPU is then set to run at the appropriate frequency when the reducible region is recognized again.

Power saving schemes presented above are effective in the sense that they permit the reduction of application's energy consumption without significant performance degradation; however, those techniques are not scalable. In addition, they can hardly be used by a nonexpert because they require a deep understanding of the applications.

More recently, [36, 37] showed that the energy consumption (the energy used when operating) of HPC systems can significantly be reduced through system reconfiguration mechanisms such as using DVFS to scale the processor's frequency down/up according to the workload. Those work can be seen as instances of the generic methodology presented in this chapter. Phase identification is the ability to identify recurring phases or, more generally, to identify phases with each other. It is a desirable property for phase detection techniques because it can be used in tuning algorithms to reuse previously found optimal configurations for recurring phases.

Phase identification is often used in conjunction with phase prediction. The earlier a phase is detected, the more the reconfiguration will save energy.

Table 18.1 summarizes the possible reconfiguration decisions that can be taken given a specific workload/phase label. Decisions are selected so as to guarantee that they do not result in significant performance degradation; they rely on the fact that some specific workloads might not need certain resources. Note that some elements in the table are counterintuitive: switching on memory banks when running I/O intensive workloads is indeed efficient. An increase in the RAM size reduces the dependency on the disk, which in turn improves the overall performance. If the system has several disks, some can be switched off instead of sending them to sleep; the reverse operation is performed if necessary when running I/O intensive workloads. Also notice that the disk (respectively, the NIC) automatically changes to active when it is accessed.

18.5 CONCLUSION

HPC systems require energy during their full life cycle from design and production to transportation to usage and recycling/dismanteling. This chapter focused on the usage aspect of HPC and how adapted and optimized software solutions could improve energy efficiency. Measuring and understanding energy consumption and energy efficiency improvements are challenging tasks that can generate some misunderstandings [38]. This chapter proposed some solutions for modeling the power consumption of servers. This allows designing power prediction models for better decision making. Meanwhile, due to the complexity of applications and their

TABLE 18.1 Phase Labels and Associated Energy Reduction Schemes

Phase Label	Possible Reconfiguration Decisions
Compute intensive	Switch off memory banks; send disks to sleep; scale the processor up; put NICs into LPI mode
Memory intensive	Scale the processor down; decrease disks or send them to sleep; switch on memory banks
Mixed	Switch on memory banks; scale the processor up; send disks to sleep; put NICs into LPI mode
Communication intensive	Switch off memory banks; scale the processor down; switch on disks
I/O intensive	Switch on memory banks; scale the processor down; increase disks, increase disks (if needed)

nonconstant usage of resource, runtime support based on phase detection and phase identification were presented. These approaches allow the deployment and usage of a set of available green leverages, permitting energy reduction.

ACKNOWLEDGEMENTS

This work was partially supported by the COST (European Cooperation in Science and Technology) framework, under Action IC0804 (Energy Efficiency in Large Scale Distributed Systems), and under Action IC0805 (Open European Network for High-Performance Computing on Complex Environments).

REFERENCES

1. H. Kimura, T. Imada, and M. Sato, "Runtime energy adaptation with low-impact instrumented code in a power-scalable cluster system," in *10th IEEE/ACM International Conference on Cluster, Cloud and Grid Computing (CCGrid)*, pp. 378–387, IEEE, Melbourne, Australia, Washington, DC, USA, 2010.
2. N. Kappiah, V. W. Freeh, and D. K. Lowenthal, "Just in time dynamic voltage scaling: exploiting inter-node slack to save energy in MPI programs," in *Proceedings of the 2005 ACM/IEEE Conference on Supercomputing*, p. 33, IEEE Computer Society, Washington, DC, USA, 2005.
3. B. Rountree, D. K. Lownenthal, B. R. de Supinski, M. Schulz, V. W. Freeh, and T. Bletsch, "Adagio: making DVS practical for complex HPC applications," in *Proceedings of the 23rd International Conference on Supercomputing*, pp. 460–469, ACM, Tampa, FL, Florida, 2009.
4. M. Y. Lim, V. W. Freeh, and D. K. Lowenthal, "Adaptive, transparent frequency and voltage scaling of communication phases in MPI programs," in *Proceedings of the ACM/IEEE SC 2006 Conference*, pp. 14–14, IEEE, 2006.
5. K. Choi, R. Soma, and M. Pedram, "Fine-grained dynamic voltage and frequency scaling for precise energy and performance tradeoff based on the ratio of off-chip access to on-chip computation times," *IEEE Transactions on Computer-Aided Design of Integrated Circuits and Systems*, vol. 24, no. 1, pp. 18–28, 2005.

6. R. Ge, X. Feng, and K. W. Cameron, "Performance-constrained distributed DVS scheduling for scientific applications on power-aware clusters," in *Proceedings of the 2005 ACM/IEEE Conference on Supercomputing*, p. 34, IEEE Computer Society, Washington, DC, USA, 2005.

7. M. E. M. Diouri, M. F. Dolz, O. Glück, L. Lefèvre, P. Alonso, S. Catalán, R. Mayo, E. S. Quintana-Ortí, "Solving some mysteries in power monitoring of servers: take care of your Wattmeters!," in *Energy Efficiency in Large Scale Distributed Systems conference (EE-LSDS)*, Viena, Austria, Berkeley, CA, USA, 2013.

8. S. Rivoire, P. Ranganathan, and C. Kozyrakis, "A comparison of high-level full-system power models," in *Proceedings of the 2008 Conference on Power Aware Computing and Systems*, vol. 3, USENIX Association, Berkeley, CA, USA, 2008.

9. R. Joseph and M. Martonosi, "Run-time power estimation in high performance microprocessors," in *Proceedings of the 2001 International Symposium on Low Power Electronics and Design*, pp. 135–140, ACM, Washington, DC, USA, 2001.

10. C. Isci and M. Martonosi, "Runtime power monitoring in high-end processors: Methodology and empirical data," in *Proceedings of the 36th Annual IEEE/ACM International Symposium on Microarchitecture*, pp. 93–104, IEEE Computer Society, 2003.

11. R. L. Meade and R. Diffenderfer, *Foundations of Electronics, Circuits and Devices*. Clifton Park, NY: Thomson Delmar Learning, 2003.

12. H. J. Van Der Bijl, "Theory and operating characteristics of the thermionic amplifier," *Proceedings of the Institute of Radio Engineers*, vol. 7, no. 2, pp. 97–128, 1919.

13. P. Raghuvanshi, "Adaptive CPU clock management," 2007. US Patent 7,219,245.

14. R. Basmadjian, F. Niedermeier, and H. De Meer, "Modelling and analysing the power consumption of idle servers," in *Sustainable Internet and ICT for Sustainability (SustainIT), 2012*, pp. 1–9, IEEE, Pisa, Italy, 2012.

15. A. P. Chandrakasan and R. W. Brodersen, "Minimizing power consumption in digital CMOS circuits," *Proceedings of the IEEE*, Madrid, Spain, vol. 83, no. 4, pp. 498–523, 1995.

16. R. Basmadjian and H. de Meer, "Evaluating and modeling power consumption of multi-core processors," in *Third International Conference on Future Energy Systems: Where Energy, Computing and Communication Meet (e-Energy)*, pp. 1–10, IEEE, New York, USA, 2012.

17. R. Basmadjian, N. Ali, F. Niedermeier, H. de Meer, and G. Giuliani, "A methodology to predict the power consumption of servers in data centres," in *Proceedings of the 2nd International Conference on Energy-Efficient Computing and Networking*, pp. 1–10, ACM, 2011.

18. D. H. Bailey, E. Barszcz, J. T. Barton, D. S. Browning, R. L. Carter, L. Dagum, R. A. Fatoohi, P. O. Frederickson, T. A. Lasinski, R. S. Schreiber, et al., "The NAS parallel benchmarks summary and preliminary results," in *Proceedings of the 1991 ACM/IEEE Conference on Supercomputing, Supercomputing'91*, Albuquerque, NM, pp. 158–165, IEEE, 1991.

19. K. Fürlinger, N. J. Wright, and D. Skinner, "Performance analysis and workload characterization with ipm," in *Tools for High Performance Computing 2009*, pp. 31–38, Springer, 2010.

20. K. Asanovic, R. Bodik, J. Demmel, T. Keaveny, K. Keutzer, J. Kubiatowicz, N. Morgan, D. Patterson, K. Sen, J. Wawrzynek, et al., "A view of the parallel computing landscape," *Communications of the ACM*, vol. 52, no. 10, pp. 56–67, 2009.

21. F. Cappello, A. Guermouche, and M. Snir, "On communication determinism in parallel HPC applications," in *Proceedings of 19th International Conference on Computer Communications and Networks (ICCCN)*, Zurich, Switzerland, pp. 1–8, IEEE, 2010.

22. T. Panas, D. Quinlan, and R. Vuduc, "Tool support for inspecting the code quality of HPC applications," in *Proceedings of the 3rd International Workshop on Software Engineering for High Performance Computing Applications*, p. 2, IEEE Computer Society, Washington, DC, USA, 2007.

23. D. Barthou, A. C. Rubial, W. Jalby, S. Koliai, and C. Valensi, "Performance tuning of x86 OpenMP codes with Maqao," in *Tools for High Performance Computing 2009*, pp. 95–113, Springer, 2010.

24. W. E. Nagel, A. Arnold, M. Weber, H.-C. Hoppe, and K. Solchenbach, *VAMPIR: Visualization and Analysis of MPI Resources*. Citeseer, 1996.

25. S. S. Shende and A. D. Malony, "The TAU parallel performance system," *International Journal of High Performance Computing Applications*, vol. 20, no. 2, pp. 287–311, 2006.

26. M. Itzkowitz and Y. Maruyama, "HPC profiling with the Sun Studio performance tools," in *Tools for High Performance Computing 2009*, pp. 67–93, Springer, 2010.

27. M. Gerndt and E. Kereku, "Automatic memory access analysis with periscope," in *Computational Science—ICCS 2007*, pp. 847–854, Springer, 2007.

28. M. Geimer, F. Wolf, B. J. Wylie, D. Becker, D. Böhme, W. Frings, M.-A. Hermanns, B. Mohr, and Z. Szebenyi, "Recent developments in the scalasca toolset," in *Tools for High Performance Computing 2009*, pp. 39–51, Springer, Austin, Texas, USA, 2010.

29. H. Shan, K. Antypas, and J. Shalf, "Characterizing and predicting the I/O performance of HPC applications using a parameterized synthetic benchmark," in *Proceedings of the 2008 ACM/IEEE conference on Supercomputing*, p. 42, IEEE Press, 2008.

30. T. M. Madhyastha and D. A. Reed, "Learning to classify parallel input/output access patterns," *IEEE Transactions on Parallel and Distributed Systems*, Washington, DC, USA, vol. 13, no. 8, pp. 802–813, 2002.

31. C. Isci, G. Contreras, and M. Martonosi, "Live, runtime phase monitoring and prediction on real systems with application to dynamic power management," in *Proceedings of the 39th Annual IEEE/ACM International Symposium on Microarchitecture*, pp. 359–370, IEEE Computer Society, 2006.

32. C. Isci and M. Martonosi, "Identifying program power phase behavior using power vectors," in *IEEE International Workshop on Workload Characterization, WWC-6*, pp. 108–118, IEEE, 2003.

33. M. Jarus, A. Oleksiak, T. Piontek, and J. Weglarz, "Runtime power usage estimation of HPC servers for various classes of real-life applications," *Future Generation Computer Systems*, to appear, 2013.

34. V. W. Freeh and D. K. Lowenthal, "Using multiple energy gears in MPI programs on a power-scalable cluster," in *Proceedings of the Tenth ACM SIGPLAN Symposium on Principles and Practice of Parallel Programming*, New York, USA, pp. 164–173, ACM, 2005.

35. K. W. Cameron, R. Ge, and X. Feng, "High-performance, power-aware distributed computing for scientific applications," *Computer*, Singapore, vol. 38, no. 11, pp. 40–47, 2005.

36. G. L. T. Chetsa, L. Lefrvre, J.-M. Pierson, P. Stolf, and G. Da Costa, "A runtime framework for energy efficient HPC systems without a priori knowledge of applications," in *IEEE 18th International Conference on Parallel and Distributed Systems (ICPADS)*, pp. 660–667, IEEE, New York, USA, 2012.

37. G. L. T. Chetsa, L. Lefevre, J.-M. Pierson, P. Stolf, and G. Da Costa, "Beyond CPU frequency scaling for a fine-grained energy control of HPC systems," in *IEEE 24th International Symposium on Computer Architecture and High Performance Computing (SBAC-PAD)*, pp. 132–138, IEEE, Chicago, IL, USA, 2012.

38. A.-C. Orgerie, L. Lefevre, and J.-P. Gelas, "Demystifying energy consumption in grids and clouds," in *2010 International Green Computing Conference*, pp. 335–342, IEEE, 2010.

19

Strategies for Increased Energy Awareness in Cloud Federations

Gabor Kecskemeti

University of Innsbruck, Innsbruck, Austria

Attila Kertesz, Attila Cs. Marosi, and Zsolt Nemeth

MTA SZTAKI Computer and Automation Research Institute, Budapest, Hungary

This chapter first identifies three scenarios that current energy-aware cloud solutions cannot handle as isolated IaaSs, but their federative efforts offer opportunities to be explored. These scenarios are centered around (i) multi-data-center cloud operator, (ii) commercial cloud federations, and (iii) academic cloud federations. Based on these scenarios, we identify energy-aware scheduling policies to be applied in the management solutions of cloud federations. These policies are exemplified through our earlier work which introduced the federated cloud management architecture to provide a unified interface over multiple cloud providers.

19.1 INTRODUCTION

Cloud computing encompasses many aspects of sharing software and hardware solutions, including computing and storage resources, application runtimes, and complex

High-Performance Computing on Complex Environments, First Edition.
Edited by Emmanuel Jeannot and Julius Žilinskas.
© 2014 John Wiley & Sons, Inc. Published 2014 by John Wiley & Sons, Inc.

application functionalities. The cloud paradigm changed the way people look at computing infrastructures. First, one does not need to be an expert in infrastructure administration, operation, and maintenance even if large-scale systems are utilized. Second, the elasticity of infrastructure as a service (IaaS) clouds allow these systems to better follow the users' actual demands. However, there is also an adverse effect: the virtual nature of these systems detaches users from several operational issues such as energy-efficient usage, which has been addressed previously in the context of parallel and distributed systems and largely remains unnoticed.

The cloud computing technology has made a qualitative breakthrough, as it is present in many consumer appliances from mobile phones to television sets, and, thus, a quantitative explosion, too. The illusion of infinite resources toward the consumers, however, raises severe issues with energy consumption; the higher levels of quality and availability require irrational energy expenditures. According to some experts, the consumed energy of resources spent for idling represents a considerable amount [1]. Current trends are claimed to be clearly unsustainable with respect to resource utilization, CO_2 footprint, and overall energy efficiency. It is anticipated that, since further growth is hampered by energy consumption furthermore, competitiveness of companies are and will be strongly tied to these issues.

Several European data centers maintain infrastructures similar to IaaS cloud systems and provide some (quasi-)dynamic services to their users (e.g., virtual server hosting or virtual private server offerings). Even in this case, addressing—the currently neglected—energy-related issues (e.g., improving energy and environmental performance of their data centers) could increase the competitiveness of these data centers even in a noncloud scenario.

Energy awareness is a highlighted research topic, and there are efforts and solutions for processor-level, component-level, and data-center-level energy efficiency. For instance, new energy-efficient approaches were proposed to automate the operation of data centers behind clouds [2], so that they could help rearrange the virtualized load from various users. Thus, smaller-sized physical infrastructure is sufficient for the actual demand, and momentarily unused capacities can be switched off. Nevertheless, these approaches are applicable to single data centers only.

Nowadays, cloud providers operate geographically distributed data centers as demands such as disaster recovery and multisite backups have become widespread. Recent solutions hide the diversity of multiple clouds and form a unified federation on top of them. Therefore, today's large systems are composed of multiple service providers *per se* that need new approaches to ensure their overall energy-aware operation, on one hand. On the other hand, there is an unexplored potential for energy-aware operation in federated and interoperable clouds. Our work is targeted at examining what new aspects of energy awareness can be exploited in federative schemes.

This chapter first identifies three scenarios that current energy-aware cloud solutions cannot handle as isolated IaaS, but their federative efforts offer opportunities to be explored. These scenarios are centered around (i) multi-data-center cloud operator, (ii) commercial cloud federations, and (iii) academic cloud federations. Based on these scenarios, we identify energy-aware scheduling policies to be applied in the management solutions of cloud federations. Among others, these policies should consider the behavior of independent administrative domains and the frequently contradicting goals of the participating clouds and federation-wide energy consumption.

Our earlier work introduced the federated cloud management architecture to provide a unified interface over multiple cloud providers [3]. This architecture consists of three main components: meta-brokering (intercloud scheduling), cloud brokering (intracloud scheduling), and a generic virtual machine (VM) image repository. In this chapter, regarding the meta-brokering component, we propose a new scheduling policy that minimizes the overall energy consumption of a federation while maintaining its performance. Concerning the cloud brokering component, we offer new heuristics for VM management, such as early destruction, which maintains the energy-efficient serving of service calls within a global limit and aggressively shuts down idling or surplus VMs.

This chapter is organized as follows. First, relevant research is reviewed in Section 19.2. Afterward, Section 19.3 discusses three scenarios to highlight the issues that impede the energy-aware operation of current systems. Section 19.4 discusses the identification of the necessary cloud extensions that enable energy-conscious federations, and extends the federated cloud management architecture with multilevel and energy-aware scheduling strategies. Finally, Section 19.5 provides our conclusion and suggests some future research directions.

19.2 RELATED WORK

Cloud federation refers to a mesh of cloud providers that are interconnected based on open standards to provide a universal decentralized computing environment, where everything is driven by constraints and agreements in a ubiquitous, multiprovider infrastructure. Until now, the cloud ecosystem has been characterized by the steadily rising hundreds of independent and privately managed heterogeneous cloud providers offering various services to their clients.

Buyya *et al.* [4] suggest a federation-oriented, just-in-time, opportunistic, and scalable application services provisioning environment called *InterCloud*. They envisioned utility-oriented federated IaaS systems that are able to predict application service behavior for intelligent infrastructures with down- and upscaling abilities. They list research issues of flexible service-to-resource mapping, user- and resource-centric quality of service (QoS) optimization, integration with in-house systems of enterprises, and scalable monitoring of system components. They present a market-oriented approach to offer InterClouds, including cloud exchanges and brokers that bring together producers and consumers. Producers offer domain-specific enterprise clouds that are connected and managed within the federation with their cloud coordinator component. Celesti *et al.* [5] propose an approach for establishing federations considering generic cloud architectures according to a three-phase model, representing an architectural solution for federation by means of a cross-cloud federation manager (CCFM), that is, a software component in charge of executing the three main functionalities required for a federation. In particular, the component explicitly manages (i) the discovery phase in which information about other clouds are received and sent, (ii) the matchmaking phase performing the best choice of the provider according to some utility measure, and (iii) the authentication phase creating a secure channel between the federated clouds.

Marshall *et al.* proposed an IaaS cloud solution to elastically extend physical clusters with cloud resources [6]. They created a so-called elastic site manager on top of Nimbus, which interfaces directly with local cluster managers; three different policies were examined for elastic site addition. Rochwerger *et al.* [7] introduced the Reservoir project and its federated IaaS cloud management model, and proposed that commercial cloud providers could also temporarily lease excess capacities during high-demand periods. They investigated the following problems faced by federated cloud solutions: (i) dynamic service elasticity, (ii) admission control, (iii) policy-driven placement optimization, (iv) cross-cloud virtual networks, (v) cross-cloud monitoring, and (vi) cross-cloud live migration. Bernstein *et al.* [8] defined two use case scenarios that exemplify the problems of multi-cloud systems such as (i) VM mobility, where they identify the networking, the specific cloud VM management interfaces, and the lack of mobility interfaces as the three major obstacles, and (ii) storage interoperability and federation scenario in which storage provider replication policies are subject to change when a cloud provider initiates subcontracting.

Lucas-Simarro *et al.* [9] proposed different scheduling strategies for optimal deployment of services across multiple clouds based on various optimization criteria. The examined scheduling policies including budget, performance, load balancing, and other dynamic conditions but neglected energy efficiency, which is the aim of our investigation.

Regarding energy efficiency in a single cloud, Cioara *et al.* [2] introduced an energy-aware scheduling policy to consolidate power management using reinforcement learning techniques to bring back the service center in an energy-efficient state. Cardosa *et al.* [10] presented a novel suite of techniques for placement and power consolidation of VMs in data centers taking advantage of the min–max and shares features inherent in virtualization technologies, such as VMware and Xen. These features let one specify the minimum and maximum amount of resources that can be allocated to a VM, and provide a share-based mechanism for the hypervisor to distribute spare resources among contending VMs. Lee *et al.* [11] discussed service request scheduling in clouds based on achievable profits. They proposed a pricing model using processor sharing for composite services in clouds. Berral *et al.* [12] presented a framework to address energy efficiency using an intelligent consolidation methodology, which applies various techniques such as machine learning on scheduling algorithms to improve server workload predictions, power-aware consolidation algorithms, and turning off spare servers and thereby saving energy in a data center. However, their approach was limited to a private data center, and did not consider hybrid clouds with engineering approaches such as federation. Feller *et al.* [13, 14] proposed energy management algorithms and mechanisms of a novel holistic energy-aware VM management framework called *Snooze* for private clouds. Their solution uses power meters to monitor energy usage of cloud resources, and estimates the resource usage of VMs. Their mechanisms address VM placement, relocation, and migration by keeping VMs on as few nodes as possible. This solution is able to dynamically consolidate the workload of a software/hardware heterogeneous large-scale cluster composed of resources using the virtualization. Also, IBM has proposed pMapper [15], which is a power-aware application placement controller in the context of an environment with heterogeneous virtualized server clusters. The placement component of the application management middleware takes into account the power and migration costs in addition to the performance benefit while placing the application containers on the physical servers. These approaches focus on consolidating power usage mostly within a single cloud. On the other hand, our goal is to consolidate power usage within a cloud federation by redistributing VM calls and utilizing federation-wide VM management policies.

Service level agreement (SLA) management is also an important issue in clouds. An autonomic SLA violation detection solution was presented in [16] by Emeakaroha *et al.*, which can be used to minimize user interaction. We also try to minimize user involvement in energy-efficient service provisioning over multiple clouds by the use of SLAs.

In this chapter, we propose different approaches for enabling an energy-aware cloud federation with various resource sharing strategies (e.g., energy-aware scheduling policies to affect carbon emissions). We also investigate how service integrations among different providers can be performed with the application of these strategies, in order to enable enhanced reliability, scalability, and utilization to broaden the market for smaller providers by bursting and enabling outsourcing toward such providers that could not sell their entire capacity previously.

19.3 SCENARIOS

19.3.1 Increased Energy Awareness Across Multiple Data Centers within a Single Administrative Domain

As small cloud providers and cloud startups are becoming more popular, they soon face user demands that cannot be satisfied with their current infrastructures. These user demands range from occasional needs for an extremely large amount of resources (compared to the provider's own infrastructure) to the need for multisite VM deployment options that allow disaster recovery. Providers thus are deemed to increase the size of their infrastructure by introducing multiple data centers on various locations and offering unprecedented amount of resources. Unfortunately, the increase in infrastructure size also increases resource heterogeneity. Hence, these providers have to deal with inhomogeneities by novel VM placement and scheduling strategies. Current IaaS solutions offer these strategies, allowing providers to focus their attention to nontechnical issues such as the increased operating cost of their data centers.

19.3.1.1 Facing the Increased Energy Consumption Energy consumption is a major component of the operating cost. Despite its significance, current IaaS clouds barely provide energy-aware solutions. Providers are restricted to reduce their consumption at the hardware level—independently from the IaaS. These reductions range from the use of more energy-efficient computer components to the upgrade of their heating, ventilation, and air conditioning (HVAC) systems to increase their power usage efficiency (PUE). Although these improvements are crucial, the energy consumption could also be significantly reduced by software means in overprovisioned IaaS systems where more physical resources are available at the provider side than actually requested by the users. Overprovisioning is a key behavior at smaller sized providers that offer services for users with occasional peaks in resource demands. We consider a provider small if the number of its customers with such requirements does not reach approximate uniform distribution throughout the year. To reduce their energy costs, these providers should minimize their overprovisioning while maintaining a flexible attitude toward their customers without violating the previously agreed service level. Energy consumption could be reduced with software techniques focusing on intra- and interdata-center issues.

First, let us consider intradata-center issues. State-of-the-art techniques that reduce overprovisioning range from basic ones, such as switching on/off unused parts of the infrastructure, to more elaborate ones, such as the use of load migration between resources to reduce resource usage fragmentation. Although some significant research efforts were devoted to the investigation of these techniques, they are not adopted by IaaS solutions (and as a consequence by cloud providers). Even nowadays, the adoption curve is still in its early stages because of several issues: for example, (i) computers that frequently switch on and off have a smaller mean time between failures (MTBF); (ii) switching on and off introduces considerable amount of delays in infrastructure provisioning; (iii) migration support by underlying technologies is weak; (iv) frequently the cost of migration is high; (v) migration might cause disruptions in service level; and (vi) providers usually do not apply software energy meters that could continuously monitor their infrastructure's consumption and thus support decisions toward overprovisioning reduction.

Next, energy awareness raises further issues if the provider has multiple data centers. The intradata-center techniques are often not applicable in interdata-center situations (i.e., operations between data centers on distant geographic locations). In such situations, the cost of migration significantly rises and frequently causes service level degradations for the affected customers. Also, providers often have a wide variety of energy sources to choose from for each of their data centers. This variety of choices is often temporal, and each energy source has a different price and CO_2 emission for a given amount of consumed energy. For example, recent wind activity could significantly change a data center's implicit CO_2 emission if a wind turbine is amongst its energy sources. Despite the fact that even providers with a single data center could introduce additional usage policies to drive their users toward greener operations, these policies may lead to significant SLA changes (e.g., offering resources only for such time periods when wind turbines are the main energy source for the data center). When multiple data centers are at the disposal of the provider, these centers open new possibilities for the provider to maintain the service level while still increasing energy efficiency of the user loads. These possibilities include cross-data-center energy-aware VM placement strategies and scheduling prioritization of data centers with green energy surplus.

19.3.1.2 Increasing Green Operations of Interdata-Center Constructs

The diverse locations of the available data centers of a provider increase the likelihood of having one or more data centers with available energy sources that are free of CO_2 emission. In such cases, customers with no specific requirements on resource location could be directed and hosted in these data centers (e.g., the IaaS scheduler could prioritize the greener data centers). As some green energy sources are quite unpredictable, the IaaS is advised to continuously check for better provisioning options even after a customer is directed to a particular data center. If the variety of potential energy sources tends to be less green, the data center's future resource schedule must be proactively rearranged. For example, if the agreed service level is not violated, the IaaS may migrate some workload.

A consumption profile defines how a particular resource behaves energy-wise under specific types of load, and this information may offer differentiated solutions in energy awareness. Even with a strong central administration (i.e., hardware purchases are controlled for all the data centers of the provider by a single authority), the multitude of data centers increases the heterogeneity in the offered resources. For example, despite the administrative efforts, small differences in newly bought hardware are inevitable. A seemingly minuscule difference in the used resources (e.g., processor stepping) could lead to significant changes in the energy consumption profiles of the data centers. IaaS solutions could reduce the overall energy consumption of the provider's infrastructure more efficiently by taking into consideration these consumption profiles across all the provider's data centers. Therefore, to reduce the overall energy consumption of the entire cloud system, VM placement policies have to be enhanced with awareness of available consumption profiles.

Although both CO_2 emission and diversification of energy sources are important for increased greenness of larger scale cloud providers, these details are not accessible and not even offered for use by the IaaS solutions today. Fortunately, because of the strength of their central administration (i.e., all of their data centers are within the same administrative domain), these providers have a chance to enforce emission and consumption profile collection. Therefore, a natural next step would be to allow them to increase the greenness of their operations by offering the collected data to be used by IaaS solutions. The availability of these data allows future IaaS solutions to make energy-conscious decisions even without the user's consent.

19.3.1.3 The View of the Energy-Conscious User

Nowadays, more and more users are getting energy conscious and try to integrate green aspects into their requirements toward the cloud infrastructure providers. More and more providers advertise their green practices, but they offer minimal control over the greenness of the resources granted for a particular consumer. Currently, users could assume that, during the fulfillment of their requests, the provider has the least amount of energy consumed when its dynamic pricing scheme (e.g., spot prices at Amazon Elastic

Compute Cloud[1]) indicates the smallest price/resource. This approach, however, is not applicable to providers who do not have dynamic pricing, while it also leads to false concepts, because the pricing scheme might reflect other factors than energy consumption. For those users who plan to ensure some level of energy consumption reduction on an arbitrary cloud infrastructure, an alternative approach could be the optimization of their applications (even on the source code level if necessary) with energy awareness in mind (e.g., use of [17]). This approach is, however, not practical in most of the user scenarios, and does not even solve the root cause of excessive energy consumption. Therefore, there is a need for some novel techniques that could provide measures or estimates for greenness and energy awareness. Through the use of these techniques, energy conscious users should be able to determine the circumstances when their tasks will have the least effect on the environment or on the overall consumption of the provider.

19.3.2 Energy Considerations in Commercial Cloud Federations

In the previous section we have discussed how a single cloud provider could increase its energy efficient behavior, while also introducing the way energy-conscious users should approach these providers. However, multiple cloud providers add further challenges to the picture, regarding the improvement of energy consumption and greenness.

19.3.2.1 Challenges for Cloud Infrastructure Providers within A Federation
Federations can be formed in various ways, but commercial cloud providers are obviously driven by clear financial benefits. These providers prefer to be the primary contacts to their users, so commercial federations will mostly be formed by those cloud providers with a large enough user base. These larger providers will make contracts with some smaller ones to serve as an outsourcing target in case the users of the large provider request some special kind or amount of resources. Although these contracts will not bring the smaller providers within the same administrative domain, they simplify the interfacing between two providers and define the service level that is necessary for the larger provider to fulfill its SLA requirements.

With the help of these contracts, the large providers can introduce new policies that determine outsourcing to their contractual partners. The initial decision of the large provider is based purely on its partners' prices. However, with the introduction of green policies, this initial simple policy might change.

- As legislation proceeds towards cloud providers, large providers will soon face CO_2 quotas. With these quotas, the decisions made by large providers are not simply based on local and partner prices but also include the price of their carbon credits (or their actual price in emission trading systems). This step does not inherently reduce the emissions while performing user requests, as

---

[1]http://aws.amazon.com/ec2/

the smaller provider might have different operating costs or could just value its available carbon credits more cheaply. Therefore, in case the users ask for specific guarantees in terms of CO_2 emissions, smaller providers must share their CO_2 emissions for their offered resources. We assume that the number of such users will rise over time as CO_2 quotas are introduced more widely (i.e., more and more infrastructure users have their own CO_2 emission caps which should include the emitted CO_2 even at the cloud provider side).

- Even before the legislation reaches the providers, they can start experimenting and offering green options to their users. As a result, large providers can see the demand for green resources without immediate investments. In such environments, the federated partners could even compete on the level of greenness offered to the large provider.

However, in both cases the providers have to trust each other regarding the reported CO_2 emissions. Thus, there is an increasing need for third parties (e.g., auditors as envisioned by the European Commission in [18]) to independently assess the energy and CO_2 efficiency of a particular infrastructure. This third-party infrastructure evaluation increases the provider's credibility, and enables the construction of new decision-making tools that use the public evaluation records (if they are offered to the general public).

19.3.2.2 *Pursuing Energy Awareness by Users of Cloud Federations*

Although federations created by large providers could enable a simple way for users to reduce their ecological footprint, the decisions made by a large provider are not necessarily the most beneficial for users. Thus, users might try to make decisions themselves. This is especially important when there are providers worth considering but not present in federations. Therefore, a user may have the incentive to create a different kind of federation based on providers a particular user has access to. However, to construct such a federation, the users have to face several issues that were previously hidden by large providers. These issues range from the differences between the applied IaaS solutions by the accessible providers to the inability of interoperation between the various providers' participating in the user's federation. To overcome these issues, users frequently turn toward third-party federative solutions which are capable of hiding the differences of the providers underneath but allow users to optimally reach them. Currently, these federative solutions are barely aimed at energy awareness.

The previously envisioned interfaces to publish CO_2 emissions and third-party estimates for greenness allow the creation of basic energy consumption and CO_2 emission profiles for providers, data centers, or even individual cloud resources (that are provisioned to the user). These profiles pave the way for new and more energy-conscious federative solutions which allow their users to construct federations of infrastructure clouds on a way that optimizes not only the performance or the reliability of the user's tasks but also their energy consumption and CO_2 emissions.

19.3.3 Reduced Energy Footprint of Academic Cloud Federations

Academic cloud infrastructures are offered without profit to fellow academics. These infrastructures usually do not consider energy efficiency and green operations as priorities. Also, compared to commercial providers, academic cloud infrastructures are relatively small. Academics tend to use infrastructures in bursts (causing likely overloaded infrastructures in certain periods of the year). Thus, they frequently find infrastructure limitations (e.g., temporal underprovisioning), even though these infrastructures are often underutilized. To be more energy efficient, when the resources are barely utilized, academic IaaS should switch to an energy-saving virtual and physical machine management strategy. To reduce the effects of under-provisioning during computing bursts, academics could use federations over the currently existing small islands of academic clouds. Both previously mentioned federation approaches are used within academic clouds. A few academic providers offer bursting capabilities, which outsource some of the resource requests to other academic clouds on the users' request. On the other hand, user-oriented federations are also supported with similar or the same federative solutions mentioned in the previous section. Unfortunately, because of their nonprofit nature, academic providers do not have the incentive to reduce their carbon footprint or energy consumption. This is also the case for their users.

Since users will soon start using the federative solutions widely, energy efficiency could be enforced by the software accomplishing federations (federative/outsourcing solutions). If other circumstances are identical or indifferent, this software should prefer the more energy-efficient cloud operators and base its decision in favor of a provider using third-party estimates for greenness. With this approach, users will end up with more energy-efficient/green resources without knowing it. At the provider side, this could result in significantly less load on less energy-aware academic clouds. The loss of demand for these providers would indicate that they should either increase their greenness or retire their infrastructure.

19.4 ENERGY-AWARE CLOUD FEDERATIONS

As we learned in [18], reducing the carbon footprint of European countries is a must and expected by the European Commission, as well as to increase the number and size of European cloud providers. By federating these providers, more competitive initiatives can be founded that can be sophisticatedly managed to meet these expectations. The general goal of the management layer in a cloud federation is to distribute load among the participating cloud providers, to enhance user satisfaction by filtering out underperforming providers, and to schedule and execute service calls with minimized energy consumption within the selected IaaS system. To achieve this, we proposed an architecture called *federated cloud management* (FCM—as introduced in [3]). In this holistic approach, a two-level brokering solution is used: a meta-brokering component is used to direct service calls to providers, and then a cloud-brokering component is used to map these calls onto an optimized number of VMs.

In order to address green aspects, that is, energy consumption and CO_2 emissions, enhanced call scheduling algorithms should be developed. These approaches may focus on different aspects. At the meta-brokering layer, relying on an enhanced monitoring system within the federation, service executions can be directed to data centers of providers consuming less energy, having higher CO_2 emission quotas, or have produced less amount of CO_2 expected within some timeframe. In this way, the issues raised in the second and third scenarios can be managed in practice.

At the cloud-brokering layer, if the energy consumption parameters of a cloud *suddenly change*, there should be strategies to limit or move around calls and even (if necessary) VMs federation-wise. The changes here may mean the introduction of new hardware, or just switching on or off some parts of the data centers, or changing the number of VMs. Realigning calls may not have immediate effects; however, migration of VMs across the federation is also an energy-consuming operation that needs to be measured and considered when decisions are made (thus this operation should not happen only in case of really drastic changes). The *system should prefer* data centers where the difference between the highest load and the average load is small because a VM has the smallest impact on those resources [19]. In Section 19.4.3, we introduce strategies to be followed by a cloud broker (CB) acting in this layer, which can solve energy utilization problems mentioned in all three scenarios.

19.4.1 Availability of Energy-Consumption-Related Information

In order to provide a solution that is able to handle the previously introduced scenarios, we extend our FCM concept [3] to energy awareness by taking into account energy consumption metrics for decision making at both levels. We introduce the following model into FCM.

Energy use of a computer system is usually expressed as the energy necessary for a certain unit of work to be performed, which is defined and measured differently at various levels. There are component (processor, node, network) and facility (e.g., a whole data center) related metrics that differ in granularity, detail, and precision of observation. Commonly, they can be characterized as the energy devoted to carry out certain activity (workload), where the workload may be an instruction, a certain type and number of instructions, transactions, queries, storing or transferring a certain amount of data, and so on, expressed as an $\frac{energy}{workload}$ ratio. Commonly, both Energy and Workload are normalized to unit time, and hence

$$\frac{energy}{workload} = \frac{\dfrac{energy}{time}}{\dfrac{workload}{time}} = \frac{power}{performance},$$

where performance may be expressed as MIPS, FLOPS, MFLOPS, BPS, and other well-known quantities. Energy efficiency, on the other hand, is a quantity that should be higher if the same amount of work is done using less energy, or more work is done using the same energy. For this purpose, energy efficiency of a computer system can be characterized as $\frac{workload}{energy}$ or $\frac{performance}{power}$ [19], although this definition is not entirely precise because efficiency should be the ratio of two energy quantities and hence dimensionless.

In our case, we have to select the right metrics carefully. Our work is aimed at a federated cloud system, and hence it is pointless to take into consideration the energy used for each instruction; also, cumulative metrics of a whole data center would not give the necessary details for decision making. Since the cloud infrastructure is service-oriented, we consider the $\frac{service}{energy}$ or $\frac{service\ throughput}{power}$ fraction as our definition for energy efficiency.

In our FCM architecture, we try to improve energy awareness by optimizing (i) the number of VMs per provider, and (ii) direct service calls to these VMs. Each service is associated with a virtual appliance stored in a repository. Appliances are automatically transferred and deployed at a provider's IaaS when needed. In order to maintain an "energy saving state" of the whole federation, we keep the values of the above-introduced *call throughput per power* (*ctpp*) $\frac{service\ throughput}{power}$ $\left[\frac{1}{W}\right]$ of all participating providers within an interval. Later, we will see how this metric is dependent on the number of VMs and the number of service calls.

19.4.2 Service Call Scheduling at the Meta-Brokering Level of FCM

Regarding the energy-efficient management of cloud federations at the meta-brokering level, the user calls have to be balanced over the cloud providers (and their datacenters) participating in the federation based on their energy consumption parameters. Therefore, the meta-broker component [20] of FCM forwards the service calls to providers having the lowest *ctpp* value. The exact number of physical and virtual machines serving the actual load of requests for the user services should be intelligently managed locally by cloud brokers of the corresponding cloud infrastructure providers (discussed in detail in the next section).

Let $m(ctpp(i, t))$ denote the average service call throughput per unit of power for a service type i. Therefore in the simplest case the "energy-balancing" algorithm chooses a provider j, for a given new service call for service i, from N participating providers based on the *ctpp* measure with the following formula: $E_{tot}[j] * m(ctpp(i, t))[j]$. Once the call arrives at a cloud broker that manages the selected provider, it tries to execute the call in a way that the overall energy consumption of the provider stays optimal.

Another important issue is the reduction of CO_2 emissions. In order to minimize this measure among the providers of a federation, one should find a way to measure the CO_2 emissions and modify the algorithm. A more aggressive rebalancing strategy could also be used within the federation by migrating VMs from overloaded providers to less loaded ones. If we consider migrations to adapt to changing conditions during deployment and execution phases at the data centers, we also have to consider the estimated costs of migrations from one provider to another. In this work, we refrain from discussing algorithms considering migrations; instead, we focus on energy-aware VM management strategies detailed in the next section.

19.4.3 Service Call Scheduling and VM Management at the Cloud-Brokering Level of FCM

A cloud broker (CB) manages VMs and dispatches the received service calls in a single cloud of a provider. If the green aspects of the architecture are prioritized, the CB should apply VM management strategies more aggressively toward energy awareness. Incoming service calls are queued first, but served only if (i) they pass a threshold for waiting time (T_q^{up}) or (ii) the energy usage for serving the same type of service calls exceeds the energy required for creating and terminating the VM by a given factor. VMs are terminated immediately when no service calls are queued for them.

We introduce the service efficiency factor $\alpha(i, t)$ as a measure of efficiency for serving queued service calls per service type in the CB. It is formulated as follows:

$$\alpha(i, t) = \frac{\text{Energy for creating or terminating VMs}}{\text{Energy for running services}}$$

$$= \frac{vmc(i, t) * (E_{\text{creat}} + E_{\text{term}})}{scc(i, t) * \dfrac{1}{m(ctpp(i, t))}}$$

$$= \frac{vmc(i, t) * m(ctpp(i, t)) * (E_{\text{creat}} + E_{\text{term}})}{scc(i, t)} \left[\frac{1 * \dfrac{1}{[J]} * ([J] + [J])}{1} \right],$$

where $vmc(i, t)$ denotes the number of VMs, $scc(i, t)$ represents the total number of service calls in the CB for a given service i at time t, and E_{creat} and E_{term} denote the energy required for starting and terminating VMs in the cloud. Note that the value of α is calculated for each service type and should be recalculated as $scc(i, t)$ or $vmc(i, t)$ changes over time. Hence, $\alpha(i, t)$ is defined as

$$\alpha(i, t) = \begin{cases} 0 & \text{if } scc(i, t) = 0, \\ \dfrac{vmc(i, t) * m(ctpp(i, t)) * (E_{\text{creat}} + E_{\text{term}})}{scc(i, t)} & \text{if } scc(i, t) > 0. \end{cases}$$

In certain cases, these functions may be replaced by constants for the sake of simplicity: for example, we may assume $scc = scc(i_0, \tau_0)$ and $vmc = vmc(i_0, \tau_0)$ for the decision making at $t = \tau_0$, or simply replace them by constants independent of i and t; thus, α is defined as

$$\alpha(i, t, vmc, scc) = \begin{cases} 0 & \text{if } scc = 0, \\ \dfrac{vmc}{scc} * m(ctpp(i, t)) * (E_{\text{creat}} + E_{\text{term}}) & \text{if } scc > 0. \end{cases}$$

Let α_i denote $\alpha(i, t)$, α_i^{up} denote an upper threshold, and α_i^{low} denote a lower threshold for α_i at τ_0. These thresholds represent an upper and a lower efficiency barrier for service types at a CB instance and should be determined by the administrators. Let vmc_i denote $vmc(i, t)$ and scc_i denote $scc(i, t)$ at τ_0:

$$\alpha_i = \alpha(i, \tau_0),$$

$$\alpha_i(vmc, scc) = \alpha(i, t_0, vmc, scc),$$

$$\alpha^{up} \geq \max_{1 \leq i \leq z}(\alpha_i),$$

$$\alpha^{low} \geq \min_{1 \leq i \leq z}(\alpha_i),$$

$$vmc_i = vmc(i, \tau_0),$$

$$scc_i = scc(i, \tau_0).$$

Let $\Theta = \{\theta_1, \theta_2, \dots, \theta_z\}$ be a permutation of $\{1, 2, \dots, z\}$ so that

$$\begin{cases} \alpha_{\theta_i} \leq \alpha_{\theta_j} & \text{if } i < j, \\ T_{q,\theta_i} \geq T_{q,\theta_j} & \text{if } i < j \text{ and } \alpha_{\theta_i} = \alpha_{\theta_j}. \end{cases}$$

That is, we define an order of services so that α values are in increasing order and waiting times in decreasing order should the α values be equal. We say that Θ is a CB instance represented as an ordered set of z type of services. Let $w_{ctpp}(i, t)$ denote the reciprocal of $m(ctpp(i, t))$, and let $w_{ctpp}(i)$ denote $w_{ctpp}(i, t)$ at τ_0:

$$w_{ctpp}(i, t) = \begin{cases} \dfrac{1}{m(ctpp(i, t))} & \text{if } m(ctpp(i, t)) \neq 0 \\ 0 & \text{else} \end{cases} \qquad [J],$$

$$w_{ctpp}(i) = w_{ctpp}(i, \tau_0) \qquad [J].$$

Let $\hat{\gamma}$ denote the current total and γ^{up} the maximum energy as a function of call throughput of all the VMs managed by the CB at τ_0:

$$\hat{\gamma} = \sum_{i=1}^{z} vmc_i * w_{ctpp}(i) \qquad [J],$$

$$\gamma^{up} \geq \max_{1 \leq i \leq z}(w_{ctpp}(i)) \qquad [J]. \qquad (19.1)$$

The value of γ^{up} is determined by the administrators and it is a characteristic of the cloud the CB is accessing. It represents the maximum energy consumption limit allowed to be consumed by the cloud: the definition (cf. 19.1) only states that, if it is set (> 0), then the cloud should be able to execute at least one service call of each available service type.

The mapping of queued service calls to available VMs is also the responsibility of the CB; however, in this work we focus on VM management. We assume that (i) a VM is handling a single service call at a time; (ii) a VM is only able to serve

Algorithm 19.1

```
ERG-gamma {
    stopCond(k) {
        return(αₖ > αᵘᵖ ∨ γ̂ > γᵘᵖ ∨ sccₖ = 0) ∧ vmcₖ > 0
    }
    startCond(k) {
        return tₒ(k) > 0 ∧ (γ̂ + wₒₜₚₚ(k) ≤ γᵘᵖ) ∧ αₖ < αˡᵒʷ
    }
    for i = z → 1
    {
        while stopCond(θᵢ)
        {
            stopVM(θᵢ)
        }
    }
    for i = 1 → z
    {
        while startCond(θᵢ)
        {
            startVM(θᵢ)
        }
    }
}
```

a single type of service; and (iii) the time required for VM startup and termination is insignificant compared to service call execution times. We propose an example algorithm (called *ERG-gamma*, cf. Algorithm 19.1) based on the metrics defined in this section to demonstrate their usability. This algorithm is evaluated periodically, and for the following we assume it is evaluated at τ_0 and Θ is recalculated only before the execution of the algorithm, not continuously.

Algorithm 19.1 (*ERG-gamma*) shows an example how to satisfy γ^{up}, α^{up}, and α^{low} constraints by first stopping service instances with the highest α when required. The stop condition function (*stopCond(i)*) states that an instance must be terminated if the upper limits (α^{up} and γ^{up}) are reached, or if there are no more service calls for the service (scc_i). This ensures that the limits are honored and instances with no service requests are terminated. New instances for a service type i are started if there are any service calls waiting ($t_q(i)$), the global energy limit (γ^{up}) allows their execution, and the service efficiency factor is below the threshold.

This approach enables the cloud administrators to define an interval ($[\alpha^{low}, \alpha^{up}]$) for setting the service efficiency of their infrastructure and an overall limit for all services running combined. This allows maintaining the energy-efficient serving of service calls within a global limit and also aggressively shutting down idling or surplus VMs. Administrators may choose the interval based on their knowledge of their system to conform to internal or third-party requirements regarding energy awareness.

19.5 CONCLUSIONS

Current cloud infrastructure solutions are very rigid and do not exhibit the flexibility and configurability potential to address energy consumption reductions. To be competitive, infrastructures are required to set up their available hardware to be offered publicly (similar to the already available commercial public cloud infrastructures) in a flexible and configurable way. Thus, there is a need for sophisticated infrastructure management techniques instantly applicable for providers in federations to reduce their overall carbon footprint. On the other hand, there is an unexplored potential for energy-aware operation in federated and interoperable clouds. Our work is targeted at examining what new aspects of energy awareness can be exploited in federative schemes.

In this chapter, we identified three scenarios that current energy-aware cloud solutions cannot handle as isolated IaaS, but their federative efforts offer opportunities to be explored. These scenarios include multidata-center cloud operator, commercial cloud federations, and academic cloud federations. Based on these scenarios, we identified energy-aware scheduling policies to be applied in the management solutions of cloud federations. We applied these approaches in an FCM architecture which provides a unified interface over multiple cloud providers. In its high-level meta-brokering component, we proposed a new scheduling policy that minimizes the overall energy consumption of a federation while maintaining its performance, and in the cloud-brokering component, we discussed new heuristics for energy-aware VM management such as early destruction, which maintains the energy-efficient serving of service calls within a global limit and aggressively shuts down idling or surplus VMs.

In future research, we plan to investigate methods, for example, fuzzy and pliant control methods, for better determining and handling of the upper and lower thresholds (α^{up} and α^{low}), involve consumption profiles in the calculations, and establish prediction methods for power management. Also we plan to refine our model using these approaches to include nonlinearity instead of the current simplistic linear approach for determining the service efficiency factor itself.

ACKNOWLEDGMENTS

This work was partially supported by the European Community's Seventh Framework Programme FP7/2007-2013 under Grant RI-283481 (SCI-BUS), by the Institute for Computer Science and Control of the Hungarian Academy of Sciences (MTA SZTAKI) under Grant 121183 (SZTAKI Cloud), and by the EU COST Action IC0805 "Open European Network for High-Performance Computing on Complex Environments."

REFERENCES

1. L. Lefèvre and A.-C. Orgerie, "Towards energy aware reservation infrastructure for large-scale experimental distributed systems," *Parallel Processing Letters*, vol. 19, no. 03, pp. 419–433, 2009.
2. T. Cioara, I. Anghel, I. Salomie, G. Copil, D. Moldovan, and A. Kipp, "Energy aware dynamic resource consolidation algorithm for virtualized service centers based on

reinforcement learning," in *10th International Symposium on Parallel and Distributed Computing (ISPDC)*, Cluj Napoca, Romania, pp. 163–169, IEEE, Washington, DC, USA, 2011.

3. G. Kecskemeti, A. Kertesz, A. Marosi, and P. Kacsuk, "Interoperable resource management for establishing federated clouds," in *Achieving Federated and Self-Manageable Cloud Infrastructures: Theory and Practice* (M. Villari, I. Brandic, and F. Tusa, eds.), Chapter 2, Hersey, PA, USA, pp. 18–35, IGI Global, 2012.

4. R. Buyya, R. Ranjan, and R. N. Calheiros, "Intercloud: utility-oriented federation of cloud computing environments for scaling of application services," in *Algorithms and Architectures for Parallel Processing*, Busan, Korea, pp. 13–31, Springer, Berlin Heidelberg, Germany, 2010.

5. A. Celesti, F. Tusa, M. Villari, and A. Puliafito, "How to enhance cloud architectures to enable cross-federation," in *IEEE 3rd International Conference on Cloud Computing (CLOUD)*, Miami, FL, USA, pp. 337–345, IEEE, Washington, DC, USA, 2010.

6. P. Marshall, K. Keahey, and T. Freeman, "Elastic site: using clouds to elastically extend site resources," in *Proceedings of the 10th IEEE/ACM International Conference on Cluster, Cloud and Grid Computing*, Melbourne, Australia, pp. 43–52, IEEE Computer Society, Washington, DC, USA, 2010.

7. B. Rochwerger, D. Breitgand, A. Epstein, D. Hadas, I. Loy, K. Nagin, J. Tordsson, C. Ragusa, M. Villari, S. Clayman, E. Levy, A. Maraschini, P. Massonet, H. Muñoz, and G. Tofetti, "Reservoir-when one cloud is not enough," *Computer*, vol. 44, no. 3, pp. 44–51, 2011.

8. D. Bernstein, E. Ludvigson, K. Sankar, S. Diamond, and M. Morrow, "Blueprint for the intercloud-protocols and formats for cloud computing interoperability," in *4th International Conference on Internet and Web Applications and Services, ICIW'09*, pp. 328–336, IEEE, 2009.

9. J. L. Lucas-Simarro, R. Moreno-Vozmediano, R. S. Montero, and I. M. Llorente, "Scheduling strategies for optimal service deployment across multiple clouds," *Future Generation Computer Systems*, Amsterdam, The Netherlands, vol. 29, no. 6, pp. 1431–1441, 2013.

10. M. Cardosa, M. R. Korupolu, and A. Singh, "Shares and utilities based power consolidation in virtualized server environments," in *IFIP/IEEE International Symposium on Integrated Network Management, IM'09*, Long Island, NY, USA, pp. 327–334, IEEE, Piscataway, NJ, USA, 2009.

11. Y. C. Lee, C. Wang, A. Y. Zomaya, and B. B. Zhou, "Profit-driven service request scheduling in clouds," in *Proceedings of the 10th IEEE/ACM International Conference on Cluster, Cloud and Grid Computing*, Melbourne, Australia, pp. 15–24, IEEE Computer Society, Washington, DC, USA, 2010.

12. J. L. Berral, Í. Goiri, R. Nou, F. Julià, J. Guitart, R. Gavaldà, and J. Torres, "Towards energy-aware scheduling in data centers using machine learning," in *Proceedings of the 1st International Conference on Energy-Efficient Computing and Networking*, Passau, Germany, pp. 215–224, ACM, New York, USA, 2010.

13. E. Feller, C. Rohr, D. Margery, and C. Morin, "Energy management in IaaS clouds: a holistic approach," in *IEEE 5th International Conference on Cloud Computing (CLOUD)*, Honolulu, HI, USA, pp. 204–212, IEEE, Washington, DC, USA, 2012.

14. E. Feller, L. Rilling, C. Morin, R. Lottiaux, and D. Leprince, "Snooze: a scalable, fault-tolerant and distributed consolidation manager for large-scale clusters," in *Proceedings of the 2010 IEEE/ACM International Conference on Green Computing and Communications & International Conference on Cyber, Physical and Social Computing*, Hangzhou, China, pp. 125–132, IEEE Computer Society, Washington, DC, USA, 2010.

15. A. Verma, P. Ahuja, and A. Neogi, "pMapper: power and migration cost aware application placement in virtualized systems," in *Middleware 2008*, Leuven, Belgium, pp. 243–264, Springer, New York, NY, USA, 2008.
16. V. C. Emeakaroha, M. A. Netto, R. N. Calheiros, I. Brandic, R. Buyya, and C. A. De Rose, "Towards autonomic detection of SLA violations in cloud infrastructures," *Future Generation Computer Systems*, vol. 28, no. 7, pp. 1017–1029, 2012.
17. Z. Herczeg, D. Schmidt, Á. Kiss, N. Wehn, and T. Gyimóthy, "Energy simulation of embedded XScale systems with XEEMU," *Journal of Embedded Computing*, vol. 3, no. 3, pp. 209–219, 2009.
18. L. Schubert, K. G. Jeffery, and B. Neidecker-Lutz, *The Future of Cloud Computing: Opportunities for European Cloud Computing Beyond 2010: Expert Group Report*. European Commission, Information Society and Media, http://ec.europa.eu/information_society/newsroom/cf/dae/document.cfm?doc_id=1168, 2010.
19. D. Tsirogiannis, S. Harizopoulos, and M. A. Shah, "Analyzing the energy efficiency of a database server," in *Proceedings of the 2010 ACM SIGMOD International Conference on Management of Data*, Indianapolis, Indiana, USA, pp. 231–242, ACM, New York, USA, 2010.
20. A. Kertész and P. Kacsuk, "GMBS: a new middleware service for making grids interoperable," *Future Generation Computer Systems*, vol. 26, no. 4, pp. 542–553, 2010.

20

Enabling Network Security in HPC Systems Using Heterogeneous CMPs

Ozcan Ozturk

Bilkent University, Ankara, Turkey

Suleyman Tosun

Ankara University, Ankara, Turkey

As technology scales, the International Technology Roadmap for Semiconductors projects that the number of cores will drastically increase to satisfy the performance requirements of future applications. Performance improvements brought by multi-core architectures have already been used in network security processors either using homogeneous chip multiprocessors (CMP) or through custom system-on-a-chip (SoC) designs. However, homogeneous CMPs provide only one type of core to match various application requirements, thereby not fully utilizing the available chip area and power budget. On the other hand, the heterogeneous CMP is a better option for a network security processor with programming needs ranging from encryption/decryption to content processing, as it allows the processor to better match the execution resources of application needs. This chapter explores the possibility of using heterogeneous CMPs for network and system security. More specifically, we propose an integer linear programming (ILP)-based methodology to mathematically analyze and provide heterogeneous CMP architectures and task

High-Performance Computing on Complex Environments, First Edition.
Edited by Emmanuel Jeannot and Julius Žilinskas.
© 2014 John Wiley & Sons, Inc. Published 2014 by John Wiley & Sons, Inc.

distributions that can reduce the energy consumption of the system. Our results indicate that the proposed approach generates better results when compared to a homogeneous counterpart.

20.1 INTRODUCTION

Network security has become a key problem with the increase in the number of Internet users and network traffic. Possible Internet threats and attacks include (i) viruses and worms that infect a computer, (ii) distributed denial of service (DDoS) attacks such as a UDP (user datagram protocol) storm, (iii) trojans that aim data destruction, remote access, or security software disable, (iv) spyware to take partial control of the computer, and (v) spam in many forms such as spam e-mail, chat spam, or blog spam. To overcome these security threats, network security has become increasingly complex with the diversity and number of different security applications. Applications widely used for security include antivirus software, spyware systems, firewalls, intrusion detection systems, antispam systems, and DDoS systems. Network security systems provide more complex security features while sustaining the required throughput for the increasing network bandwidth.

Ideal network security can be provided by real-time data packet inspection using the aforementioned security system tools. The performance of the underlying architecture is crucial for accomplishing such real-time data packet inspection. Traditional single-processor network systems are not sufficient to fully inspect the packets with the increased number of inspection demands and the density of the network traffic. Recently, CMP architectures have been proposed to address the processing requirements of network security systems because CMP technology offers higher performance, scalability, and energy efficiency.

CMPs become an increasingly attractive option for obtaining high performance and low power consumption since it has become an increasingly difficult task to obtain more performance out of single-processor designs. As a result, CMPs are widely available in the market and have been used as an attractive option for overcoming the barriers in processor design. As technology scales, the International Technology Roadmap for Semiconductors projects that the number of cores will drastically increase to satisfy the performance requirements of future applications [1].

One of the most important benefits of a CMP over a traditional single-processor design is the power consumption reduction by reduced clock frequency. Other benefits of CMPs include (i) scalability provided using many dimensions of parallelism such as thread-level parallelism, loop-level parallelism, and instruction-level parallelism; (ii) cost of design and ease of verification, which in turn reduces the time to market and lowers the chip costs; (iii) better area utilization of the available silicon as the cores share common logic; and (iv) faster and cheaper on-chip communication.

In the network security domain, a CMP will be able to provide many advantages over a traditional single-processor design because there are multiple tasks. If the network security system is not fast enough, either packet transmission will slow down or packet inspection will be performed partially. For example, consider a network security processor that ensures security features in real time while processing information. In such a system, the network security processor will need to perform multiple tasks such as firewall, virtual private network (VPN), internet protocol (IP) security, content processing, and cryptography simultaneously [2, 3]. A single processor will not be powerful enough, whereas a CMP-based network security processor will process the packets fast enough while providing the security features, which requires parallel processing.

There are many open issues that need to be addressed in the context of network security CMPs. For example, data mapping, communication optimization, and task partitioning play important roles in a general-purpose CMP design which also applies to network security processors.

- *Data Mapping:* On-chip memory area should be managed carefully because accessing off-chip memory presents large performance penalties even if a small fraction of memory references go off-chip. Moreover, frequent off-chip memory accesses can increase the overall power consumption dramatically.

- *Communication Optimization:* Communication between the cores in the CMP should be performed carefully because the bandwidth between the CMP nodes is limited. Careful data placement and effective communication protocol is key to reducing the communication overheads.

- *Task Partitioning:* Ensuring security while processing the content of the packets requires effective task partitioning. Task partitioning is a well-known problem for multiple processor environments, but it needs a fresh look for network security CMPs as there are additional constraints/requirements and opportunities. For example, certain security-related tasks can be performed on different packets simultaneously, providing parallel processing. On the other hand, one needs to be careful in distributing the security tasks because this may cause a lot of interprocessor data communication.

Performance improvements brought by CMP architectures have already been realized in network security processors either using homogeneous CMPs or through custom system-on-a-chip (SoC) designs. However, homogeneous CMPs provide only one type of core to match various application requirements, thereby not fully utilizing the available chip area and power budget. On the other hand, heterogeneous CMP is a better option for a network security processor with programming needs ranging from firewall and encryption/decryption to content processing, as it allows the processor to better match execution resources of application needs.

Security tasks require a variety of resources such as computational power, memory space, and bandwidth. Compared to a packet inspection unit, a cryptography engine requires more processing power, whereas the former requires more memory space and bandwidth compared to the latter. General-purpose CMPs provide the same type of processor for various security applications. This mapping allocates unnecessary resources to certain types of applications, which increases the power consumption. On the contrary, network security tasks can be mapped onto the appropriate processor in the heterogeneous CMP to meet the performance requirement while minimizing power consumption and development complexity. To strike the right balance, one should be careful in choosing the type of processors and memory components.

This chapter explores the possibility of using heterogeneous CMPs for network and system security. We compare heterogeneous CMPs with homogeneous counterparts and provide experimental evaluation of using both on network security systems. The remainder of this chapter is structured as follows: Section 20.2 explains the related work on CMPs and their use in network security. The details of heterogeneous NoC (network-on-chip)-based CMP architecture and an overview of our approach are given in Section 20.3. Section 20.4 discusses the heterogeneous CMP-based network security processor design and advantages. An experimental evaluation is presented in Section 20.5. Conclusions are provided in Section 20.6.

20.2   RELATED WORK

We present the related work in two parts. First, we summarize the related work on heterogeneous processors in general and their benefits. Second, we explore the related studies on CMP network security processors.

Heterogeneous CMPs have been introduced to provide a wide variety of processing resources to effectively use the available chip area while ensuring enough processing power. Benefits provided by heterogeneous CMPs are discussed from many angles in [4, 5]. In [6], the authors present a model-based exploration method to support the design flow of heterogeneous CMPs. They implement cost models for the design space exploration using several cost parameters such as performance and throughput. The work presented in [7] explores the effects of heterogeneity on commercial applications using a hardware prototype.

On the software side, OpenMP directives are extended [8] to address the heterogeneity in CMPs. Several optimization techniques are extended to utilize advanced architecture features of the target system. In [9], the authors present a multithreaded code generation method that tries to reduce the number of interprocessor communications. They primarily try to reduce the number of messages exchanged, thereby reducing the total communication between the cores. In [10] a method is proposed to parallelize the JPEG compression algorithm on a heterogeneous CMP. Task partitioning with replication is applied on heterogeneous CMPs in [11]. Specifically, the authors employ replication up to a certain threshold in order to improve system reliability. In [12], the authors explore the power–performance efficiency of hyperthreaded heterogeneous CMP servers, and propose a scheduling algorithm to reduce the overall power consumption of a server while not affecting the performance. Becchi and Crowley [13] explore the benefits of heterogeneous CMPs using a dynamic assignment policy that assigns the threads between the cores. One of the early heterogeneous CMP architectures proposed [14] chooses the appropriate core for a task and reduces the energy–delay product by doing so.

From a hardware perspective, [15] explores the processor design problem for a heterogeneous CMP from scratch, as processors designed for homogeneous architectures do not sufficiently map to the heterogeneous domain. They study the effects of processor design in terms of area or power efficiency. A compiler-driven tightly coupled VLIW (very long instruction word) processor is presented in [16]. It is a superscalar processor on a single chip, to improve the performance of single threaded applications while supporting multithreaded applications. More specifically, they use a high-performance VLIW core to run high ILP applications, whereas a superscalar core is used to exploit multithreaded applications. In [17] signal processing architectures at the system level are employed for heterogeneous CMPs, while [18] present a heterogeneous CMP with same instruction set architectures (ISAs) working on different voltage levels and frequencies.

Network security processors have been widely studied in the context of security coprocessor implementations [19–21]. In [19], the authors present a security processor to accelerate cryptographic processing such as RSA, Advanced Encryption Standard (AES), and random number generation. CryptoManiac [20] presents a coprocessor for cryptographic workloads. On the other hand, a generic network security processor for security-related protocols is presented in [21]. With the emerging CMP architectures, CMP security processors have also been introduced. Commercial products to provide network security using CMP architectures are already in the market. Octeon [2] introduced by Cavium has multiple MIPS64 cores, which is used for traffic control, content, and security processing. Similarly, SonicWALL [22] has been proposed to provide a faster packet processing platform through data packet inspection on a CMP architecture. Endian Firewall Macro X2 [3] provides network protection and content inspection with Intel CMP architecture. CMP architectures are used for other security systems [23]. A parallel intrusion detection system by using CMP architecture has been proposed. In [24], the authors present the performance improvement in DDoS defense by using CMP architectures. Deep packet inspection using parallel Bloom filters is discussed in [25].

There have been prior attempts to use task allocation on a network processor using pipelining [26–28]. Shoumeng et al. [26] propose a genetic algorithm-based task assignment for network processors. They assign different packet processing tasks to the network processors in a pipelined manner. Similarly, a task allocation scheme for CMP architectures is proposed in [27], where the selective replication of some modules is made to increase the number of tasks running parallel. The authors in [28] introduce GreedyPipe, a heuristic-based task scheduling algorithm on CMP-based network processors in a pipelined manner. A randomized rounding (RR) based solution for task mapping and scheduling is presented in [29]. Our approach is different from these prior efforts, as we try to optimize the energy consumption of a network processor using a heterogeneous CMP architecture.

20.3   OVERVIEW OF OUR APPROACH

20.3.1   Heterogeneous CMP Architecture

Despite the many advantages of CMPs over uniprocessor architectures, one of the key questions raised by many researchers is the effectiveness of CMPs [4, 5]. One aspect of this problem is due to the infancy of the software solutions targeting such architectures. Current programs, compilers, and software architecture techniques, in general, rely on the fact that there is only one core running on the background [30]. Hence, it becomes very difficult to effectively use the underlying processing power. There are some initial attempts to target this problem, but these techniques are still in their infancy [30].

On the other hand, from a hardware point of view, the homogeneity inherent to CMPs is another source of limitation in extracting the best utilization from these architectures. To overcome the limitations due to the homogeneous behavior of CMPs, heterogeneous (asymmetric) CMPs have been proposed [31, 32]. For example, IBM's Cell Processor is a heterogeneous CMP composed of one PPU (power processing unit) and eight SPUs (synergistic processing unit) [31, 32]. In this architecture, PPU is used as the main coordinator, whereas SPUs perform SIMD (single instruction multiple data) processing on mass data.

Even though complex cores provide higher single-thread performance, they consume more area and power compared to their simpler counterparts. Every application has a different processing need and a memory requirement. Even one single application has different requirements throughout its execution. A network security application may exploit a high level of ILP where a powerful core will be a better match, whereas a simpler core will suffice for a different application with lower ILP. Choosing the best match for an application will reduce the power consumption. However, homogeneous CMPs provide only one type of core to match all these various requirements. The ability to dynamically switch between different cores and power down unused cores is the key in heterogeneous CMPs. It allows the processor to better match execution resources with application needs, which in turn enables different workloads from high to low. It was shown that a representative heterogeneous processor using two core types achieves as much as 63% performance improvement over an equivalent-area homogeneous processor [4, 5]. Hence, heterogeneous multiprocessors achieve better coverage of a spectrum of load levels.

In our proposed approach, NoC-based heterogeneous CMP architecture is exposed to the ILP solver. We assume that a heterogeneous NoC-based CMP is a two-dimensional mesh topology, where each node of this mesh consists of a network switch/router, a processor, and a memory hierarchy.

20.3.2   Network Security Application Behavior

Network security applications have different resource requirements such as computational power, memory space, or bandwidth. For example, in a network security system, a packet inspection unit will require more memory space and higher bandwidth compared to a cryptography engine. On the other hand, a cryptography engine will require more processing power to perform multiple encryption/decryption tasks. Previously proposed CMP architectures use general-purpose CMPs which provide the same type of processor for a wide spectrum of security applications. This mapping allocates unnecessary resources to certain applications, thereby increasing the overall power consumption. On the contrary, network security tasks can be mapped onto the appropriate processor in the heterogeneous CMP to meet the performance requirement while minimizing power consumption and development complexity.

Consider a network processor that has two main components, content processing and security processing. The content processing unit performs packet inspection which manipulates packets coming from the physical layer. This process involves multiple tasks including data compression, classification, header modification, and framing. Similarly, security processing involves encryption, decryption, user authentication, and key management. Individual tasks can be mapped onto cores of a given CMP architecture with various performance values. Table 20.1 gives the performance values of different components of a security unit with different processors [19, 20]. This table is obtained using AES encryption/decryption with a 128-bit key, and RSA engine with 1024 bits and HMAC using SHA1. The reported results are within acceptable ranges, where the overall power consumption at 83 MHz is reported to be 383.5 mW. As can be seen from this table, processor requirements may vary depending on the underlying functionality.

20.3.3 High-Level View

Figure 20.1 illustrates a high-level view of our approach. First, we extract the computational resource requirements of different tasks in a network processor either by actual system measurements or through simulation. This collected information includes energy and execution latency values for each task on all processor types. This information is subsequently passed to the ILP solver, which determines the best processor matching the needs of the task to meet the performance deadlines while keeping the power consumption at the lowest rate. The ILP tool is provided with a pool of processors to choose from, where our goal in selecting the processor for each task is to minimize the energy consumption. Note that each processor can exhibit different characteristics in terms of performance, energy, temperature, area, and communication bandwidth supported.

TABLE 20.1 Performance Values of Security Engines with Different Processors

Task	Processor	Throughput
AES engine	100 MHz	1.28 Gb/s
	83 MHz	1.06 Gb/s
	58 MHz	0.39 Gb/s
RSA engine	250 MHz	80.7 Kb/s
	83 MHz	66.9 Kb/s
HMAC-SHA1	89 MHz	140 Mb/s
	83 MHz	130.5 Mb/s
RNG	200 MHz	6.40 Gbps
	83 MHz	2.66 Gb/s

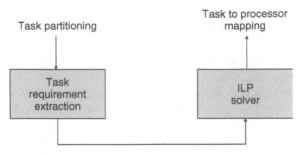

FIGURE 20.1   *High-level view of our approach.*

20.4   HETEROGENEOUS CMP DESIGN FOR NETWORK SECURITY PROCESSORS

20.4.1   Task Assignment

A widely used application model on a CMP-based network processor is to implement a pipeline where each packet is processed by multiple processors performing different tasks [26–28]. In this approach, packet processing tasks are assigned to a stage of the pipeline. Each of these stages is processed by a different processor of the CMP. We do not consider the task partitioning problem in this work; rather, we assume that a set of ordered tasks has already been implemented as a pipeline in the network processor.

As shown in Fig. 20.1, we first need to extract the task processing requirements for a given network system. We use profiling information to identify the computational requirements of each given task in the pipeline. While this part of the system has not been completely automated yet, we are able to generate close estimates and use them in our ILP formulation for preliminary tests.

In this representation, shown in Fig. 20.2, the execution of the network system is viewed as a series of *tasks* preformed on the packets. Once the task partitioning is known, we can execute each task on the available processor types. As a result, we

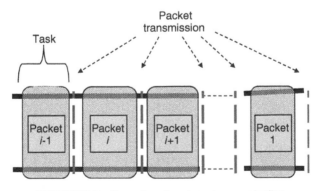

FIGURE 20.2   *Example network processor pipeline.*

obtain energy and execution latency values for each task on all processor types in our pool. Our ILP-based optimization approach operates on these values and selects the most suitable processor to run the task on. The goal of our ILP formulation, explained in the next section, is to select the processor type for each task to minimize the overall energy consumption.

20.4.2 ILP Formulation

Our goal in this section is to present an ILP formulation of the problem of minimizing the energy consumption of a given network security system by determining the optimal processor types that can be used in a heterogeneous CMP. Table 20.2 gives the constant terms used in our ILP formulation. We used the *Xpress-MP* [33], a commercial tool, to formulate and solve our ILP problem, though its choice is orthogonal to the focus of this chapter. In our baseline ILP formulation, we assume that our design is not limited with any area constraint, that is, we can allocate any type of processor to each task. Our goal with this ILP formulation is to select the most suitable processor for individual tasks.

Assume that we are given N number of tasks, t_i, where $1 \leq i \leq N$. Our approach uses 0–1 variables to select a processor for a given task among the processor pool, and at the end returns the overall task to processor mapping. In our design, we assume that we have a pool of processors $Proc_1, \ldots, Proc_P$, where frequency of $Proc_i$ is higher than that of $Proc_j$ if $i > j$. More specifically, $Proc_P$ is the fastest processor with the highest area requirements, whereas $Proc_1$ has the lowest frequency and area. Execution latency of a task is expressed by $L_{t,p}$, which indicates the latency of executing task t on processor p. As explained earlier, latency information has been extracted using simulators and through actual implementations.

We use the $M_{t,p}$ variable to indicate that task t will be running on processor type p. More specifically,

- $M_{t,p}$ indicates whether task t is running on processor type p.

TABLE 20.2 Constant Terms Used in our ILP Formulation; These are Either Architecture-Specific or Program-Specific

Constant	Definition
N	Number of tasks
P	Number of processor types
$L_{t,p}$	Execution latency of task t on processor type p
$E_{t,p}$	Energy consumption of task t on processor type p
Area	Area allocated for processors
$Area_p$	Area needed for processor p
α	Weight of energy in the total cost
β	Weight of throughput in the total cost

Similarly, T_{max} is a variable that indicates the maximum execution latency of a given task. This can be expressed as

$$T_{max} = \max_t L_{t,P}, \quad \forall t \text{ with Proc}_P. \tag{20.1}$$

As explained earlier, we assume that network processor is implemented to process the packets in a pipelined manner. Network pipeline performance is usually measured by the throughput it achieves, which can also be expressed as the number of packets processed per second. Pipeline throughput is limited by the maximum latency among all the tasks. We can find the maximum latency among the tasks by comparing their latencies on Proc_P, as it is the fastest processor in the processor pool.

After describing the variables, we next give our constraints. Our first constraint is regarding the unique assignment of a task, that is, a task can be assigned to a single processor:

$$\sum_{i=1}^{P} M_{t,i} = 1, \quad \forall t. \tag{20.2}$$

In the above equation, i corresponds to the processor type and iterates over all the combinations. When executed on a slower processor, a task may have a longer execution latency compared to T_{max}, which potentially can reduce the pipeline throughput. In order to prevent such cases, we need to make sure that maximum allocated time for any task is limited by T_{max}.

$$\sum_{i=1}^{P} M_{t,i} \times L_{t,i} \leq T_{max}, \quad \forall t. \tag{20.3}$$

Meanwhile, we aim at reducing the energy consumption. To achieve this, we select an energy-efficient processor that does not degrade the pipeline throughput.

$$TE_t = \sum_{i=1}^{P} M_{t,i} \times E_{t,i}, \quad \forall t. \tag{20.4}$$

In this expression, TE_t indicates the energy consumption of task t or the corresponding pipeline stage to process one packet. This energy will depend on the processor mapped to the task and the energy value of that processor.

Having specified the necessary constraints in our ILP formulation, we next give our objective function. We define our cost function as the sum of the task energies, which is given by Energy_{total}. Consequently, our objective function can be expressed as

$$\min \quad (\text{Energy}_{total} = \sum_{i=1}^{N} TE_i). \tag{20.5}$$

To summarize, our processor selection problem can be formulated as "minimize Energy_{total} under constraints (20.1) through (20.4)." It is important to note that this ILP formulation is very flexible, as it can accommodate different number of processors and tasks.

20.4.3 Discussion

Note that, in our ILP formulation, we employ performance and energy as constraints, whereas area, temperature, communication bandwidth, and other possible constraints are left out. For example, depending on the area constraint, it may not be possible to accommodate a certain processor mixture. Our ILP formulation, presented earlier, does not cover this constraint and similar ones. However, the ILP problem can easily be modified to include such constraints. Area constraint can be added by simply adding the areas of processors that are being used for tasks.

$$\text{Area} \geq \sum_{i=1}^{N} \sum_{j=1}^{P} M_{i,j} \times \text{Area}_j. \tag{20.6}$$

The right-hand side of the expression given above sums up the areas of the processors that are being used, and this sum should be less than the total area available. Note that we are not doing an exact placement within the available area, which would require further analysis.

To include area as one of the constraints, we also need to modify (20.1), which is used to find $T_{\max}$. This comes from the fact that we no longer know whether Proc_P will fit into the available silicon area with the rest of the processors. Our new $T_{\max}$ expression will consider all processors and all possible mappings. This can be achieved directly using (20.2) and removing (20.1) from the constraint set.

After removing (20.1), one can observe that the ILP tool will select the lowest frequency processors for all the tasks since our objective is to minimize the energy consumption. This will obviously increase the execution latency, which is very critical for network systems. To prevent such problems, we can use a weighted approach where we use both energy and throughput in our objective function. More specifically

$$\min \quad (\alpha \times \text{Energy}_{\text{total}} + \beta \times T_{\max}). \tag{20.7}$$

The first part of the above expression captured with a weight of α emphasizes energy, whereas the second part given with a weight of β stresses on the performance. Note that $T_{\max}$ gives the maximum latency of any one task in our pipeline. Assigning a very large value to β compared to α will try to first reduce the $T_{\max}$ value as much as possible. When $T_{\max}$ reaches the maximum value, then the ILP tool will exploit the energy reduction opportunities.

Note that so far we did not assume any limit on the number of processors in any processor type. Our ILP formulation can easily be modified to include processor count as a constraint as well; however, because of space limitation we do not go into details.

One can also optimize the placement of the processors within the CMP to minimize the associated communication overhead. Although not presented here, our formulation can easily be modified to reflect such a goal. For example, we can incorporate coordinates to processors and reduce the communication distances between the subsequent tasks. In our future studies, we plan to explore the aforementioned objectives.

20.5   EXPERIMENTAL EVALUATION

20.5.1   Setup

We tested our approach with 10 different network security system scenarios. We assume that, for each network system, there are multiple tasks required to be performed in a pipelined manner, as given in Section 20.4.1. As explained earlier, we assume that task assignment is already available, and we only select the processor type to run each of these tasks. The available processor types and their characteristics are listed in Table 20.3. The second column gives the IPC value of each processor type, while the third column shows the average energy consumption, and the last column shows the area required for the processor. Note that the values given in this table represent normalized values based on Alpha cores.

On the other hand, Table 20.4 lists the tasks along with their execution latency and energy consumption values. Note that the execution latency and energy values are obtained by running the given task on processors P_1–P_4. To compare the energy reduction brought by a heterogeneous CMP over a homogeneous CMP using multiple pipelines, we randomly selected 10 different subsets of the tasks in Table 20.5. The second column of the table lists the selected tasks. We performed experiments with four different optimization schemes for each pipeline in our experimental suite:

- *HM:* In this approach, we implement a homogeneous CMP using the same type of processors. We implement this approach within our ILP framework by adding

TABLE 20.3   Processors Used in Our Heterogeneous CMP and Their Characteristics

Processor	IPC	Energy	Area
P_1	1	3.73	1
P_2	1.3	6.88	2
P_3	1.87	10.68	8
P_4	2.14	46.44	40

TABLE 20.4   Tasks Used in This Study

Task	P_1		P_2		P_3		P_4	
	Latency	Energy	Latency	Energy	Latency	Energy	Latency	Energy
T_1	0.50	1.87	0.38	2.65	0.27	2.86	0.23	10.85
T_2	1.40	5.22	1.08	7.41	0.75	8.00	0.65	30.38
T_3	1.60	5.97	1.23	8.47	0.86	9.14	0.75	34.72
T_4	0.80	2.98	0.62	4.23	0.43	4.57	0.37	17.36
T_5	2.00	7.46	1.54	10.58	1.07	11.42	0.93	43.40
T_6	1.20	4.48	0.92	6.35	0.64	6.85	0.56	26.04
T_7	2.10	7.83	1.62	11.11	1.12	11.99	0.98	45.57
T_8	0.20	0.75	0.15	1.06	0.11	1.14	0.09	4.34

Execution latency and energy consumption values are obtained by running tasks on processors $P_1, \dots, P_4$.

TABLE 20.5 Pipelines Tested

Pipeline	Tasks
$Pipeline_1$	T_1, T_3, T_4, T_6, T_8
$Pipeline_2$	T_2, T_3, T_4, T_5
$Pipeline_3$	T_1, T_4, T_6, T_7, T_8
$Pipeline_4$	T_2, T_5, T_7
$Pipeline_5$	T_3, T_6, T_7
$Pipeline_6$	T_2, T_4, T_6, T_7
$Pipeline_7$	T_1, T_2, T_4, T_7
$Pipeline_8$	T_1, T_3, T_5, T_6
$Pipeline_9$	$T_1, T_2, T_3, T_4, T_5, T_6, T_7, T_8$
$Pipeline_{10}$	T_1, T_3

an additional constraint that forces all processors to be the same type:

$$M_{t_1,p} = M_{t_2,p}, \quad \forall t_1, t_2, p. \tag{20.8}$$

This constraint makes sure that, if task t_1 is assigned to a certain processor type p, then the rest of the tasks should also be mapped to the same processor type.

- *HT:* This is the first ILP-based heterogeneous CMP strategy discussed in this chapter (Section 20.4.2).

- *HM+:* This is very much similar to HM except that it enforces the area constraint given in Section 20.4.3.

- *HT+:* This is an extension to the HT scheme wherein area constraints are also applied. This strategy is discussed in Section 20.4.3 in detail. Note that we set the default area available for the processors as 200 units. All the listed tasks in the pipelines need to be implemented within this area limit. Later, we also modify the default area to test the sensitivity of our approach. The ILP solution times for our approaches range from 0.5 to 15 s, with an average of 3 s, across all the test cases.

20.5.2 Results

We first evaluate and compare our approach HT to HM scheme for pipelines given above in Fig. 20.3. Each bar represents the normalized energy consumption of our approach (HT) with respect to the HM case. As can be seen from the graph (Fig. 20.3), on average, our approach reduces the energy consumption by 41% over the HM case.

We also performed experiments with area constraints enforced. As has been stated earlier, for the default case we assumed abundant area. The graph in Fig. 20.4 shows the experimental results for the HM+ and HT+ approaches. Each bar corresponds to the percentage reductions of HT+ over the HM+ case, respectively. We observe that the reductions vary between 7% and 48%. On average, our approach yields a 37% reduction in the energy consumption over the HM+ approach.

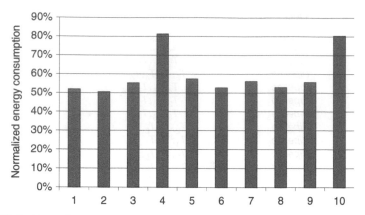

FIGURE 20.3 Normalized energy consumption in our ILP-based HT approach over the HM approach.

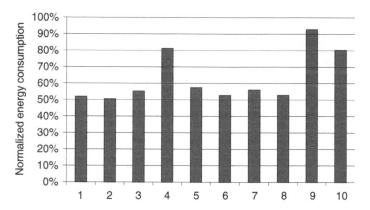

FIGURE 20.4 Normalized energy consumption with the HT+ approach over the HM+ case.

Recall that the pipelines given in Table 20.5 use a fixed area constraint of 200 in the default case. The graph in Fig. 20.5 shows the percentage reductions with different area constraints. In this figure, we specifically test the sensitivity of our approach to the area constraint.

As can be seen from this chart, energy savings are higher with a larger processor area. This follows from the fact that, with increased area, HM+ uses the fastest processor to increase the throughput. However, this also increases the wasted energy on the noncritical tasks using the same power-hungry processor. However, HT+ selects a power-efficient processor for the noncritical tasks while using a fast processor for the critical ones. One can also observe from these results that the reduction brought using HT+ approach over the HM+ case is 26%, on average.

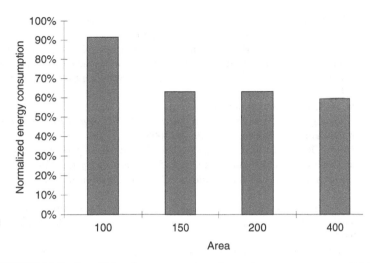

FIGURE 20.5 *Sensitivity of our approach to the total processor area available.*

20.6 CONCLUDING REMARKS

Growing importance of security within networking devices makes it imperative to consider techniques to optimize performance and power consumption of security tasks in network processors. Motivated by this observation, this chapter proposed and experimentally evaluated an ILP-based approach to use heterogeneous CMPs in network security processors. The goal was to use the most suitable processor for a given task as much as possible, thereby saving energy while not reducing the throughput. We tested our approach using synthetic task sets. Our experimental results indicate that heterogeneous CMPs reduce the energy consumption dramatically compared to homogeneous CMPs. We also found that the solution times taken by our approach were within tolerable limits for all the cases tested.

ACKNOWLEDGMENTS

This work was supported in part by Open European Network for High-Performance Computing on Complex Environments, the TUBITAK Grant 112E360, and a grant from Turk Telekom under Grant 3015-04.

REFERENCES

1. ITRS, "International technology roadmap for semiconductors."
2. "Octeon by Cavium," in http://www.cavium.com/OCTEON_MIPS64.html, 2014.
3. Endian, "Endian firewall macro x2," in http://www.endian.com/en/products, 2008.

4. R. Kumar, D. M. Tullsen, N. P. Jouppi, and P. Ranganathan, "Heterogeneous chip multiprocessors," *Computer*, vol. 38, no. 11, pp. 32–38, 2005.

5. R. Kumar, D. M. Tullsen, P. Ranganathan, N. P. Jouppi, and K. I. Farkas, "Single-ISA heterogeneous multi-core architectures for multithreaded workload performance," in *ISCA '04: Proceedings of the 31st Annual International Symposium on Computer Architecture*, p. 64, 2004.

6. H. Blume, H. T. Feldkaemper, and T. G. Noll, "Model-based exploration of the design space for heterogeneous systems on chip," *Journal of VLSI Signal Processing Systems*, München, Germany, vol. 40, no. 1, pp. 19–34, 2005.

7. S. Balakrishnan, R. Rajwar, M. Upton, and K. Lai, "The impact of performance asymmetry in emerging multicore architectures," in *ISCA '05: Proceedings of The 32nd Annual International Symposium on Computer Architecture*, Madison, Wisconsin, USA, pp. 506–517, 2005.

8. F. Liu and V. Chaudhary, "Extending OpenMP for heterogeneous chip multiprocessors," in *Proceedings of International Conference on Parallel Processing*, Kaohsiung, Taiwan, p. 161, 2003.

9. L. Brisolara, S.-i. Han, X. Guerin, L. Carro, R. Reis, S.-I. Chae, and A. Jerraya, "Reducing fine-grain communication overhead in multithread code generation for heterogeneous MPSoC," in *SCOPES '07: Proceedings of the 10th International Workshop on Software & Compilers for Embedded Systems*, pp. 81–89. New York, NY: ACM, 2007.

10. S. L. Shee, A. Erdos, and S. Parameswaran, "Heterogeneous multiprocessor implementations for JPEG: a case study," in *CODES+ISSS '06: Proceedings of the 4th International Conference on Hardware/Software Codesign and System Synthesis*, pp. 217–222. New York, NY: ACM, 2006.

11. S. Gopalakrishnan and M. Caccamo, "Task partitioning with replication upon heterogeneous multiprocessor systems," in *RTAS '06: Proceedings of the 12th IEEE Real-Time and Embedded Technology and Applications Symposium*, pp. 199–207. Washington, DC: IEEE Computer Society, 2006.

12. R. Grant and A. Afsahi, "Power-performance efficiency of asymmetric multiprocessors for multi-threaded scientific applications," *IEEE International Parallel and Distributed Processing Symposium*, p. 344, 2006.

13. M. Becchi and P. Crowley, "Dynamic thread assignment on heterogeneous multiprocessor architectures," in *CF '06: Proceedings of the 3rd Conference on Computing Frontiers*, Ischia, Italy, pp. 29–40, 2006.

14. R. Kumar, K. I. Farkas, N. P. Jouppi, P. Ranganathan, and D. M. Tullsen, "Single-ISA heterogeneous multi-core architectures: the potential for processor power reduction," in *MICRO 36: Proceedings of the 36th Annual IEEE/ACM International Symposium on Microarchitecture*, San Diego, CA, p. 81, 2003.

15. R. Kumar, D. M. Tullsen, and N. P. Jouppi, "Core architecture optimization for heterogeneous chip multiprocessors," in *PACT '06: Proceedings of the 15th International Conference on Parallel Architectures and Compilation Techniques*, Seattle, Washington, pp. 23–32, 2006.

16. J. Yan and W. Zhang, "Hybrid multi-core architecture for boosting single-threaded performance," *SIGARCH Computer Architecture News*, vol. 35, no. 1, pp. 141–148, 2007.

17. P. Lieverse, P. V. D. Wolf, K. Vissers, and E. Deprettere, "A methodology for architecture exploration of heterogeneous signal processing systems," *Journal of VLSI Signal Processing Systems*, vol. 29, no. 3, pp. 197–207, 2001.

18. S. Ghiasi, T. Keller, and F. Rawson, "Scheduling for heterogeneous processors in server systems," in *CF '05: Proceedings of the 2nd Conference on Computing Frontiers*, Ischia, Italy, pp. 199–210, 2005.

19. C.-P. Su, C.-H. Wang, K.-L. Cheng, C.-T. Huang, and C.-W. Wu, "Design and test of a scalable security processor," in *ASP-DAC '05: Proceedings of the 2005 Conference on Asia South Pacific Design Automation*, Shanghai, China, pp. 372–375, 2005.

20. L. Wu, C. Weaver, and T. Austin, "CryptoManiac: a fast flexible architecture for secure communication," in *ISCA '01: Proceedings of the 28th Annual International Symposium on Computer Architecture*, Göteborg, Sweden, pp. 110–119, 2001.

21. C.-H. Wang, C.-Y. Lo, M.-S. Lee, J.-C. Yeh, C.-T. Huang, C.-W. Wu, and S.-Y. Huang, "A network security processor design based on an integrated SOC design and test platform," in *DAC '06: Proceedings of the 43rd Annual Conference on Design Automation*, Anaheim, CA, USA, pp. 490–495, 2006.

22. DELL SonicWALL, "The advantages of a multi-core architecture in network security appliances," in http://www.sonicwall.com, 2008.

23. D. Tian and Y. Xiang, "A multi-core supported intrusion detection system," in *NPC '08: Proceedings of the 2008 IFIP International Conference on Network and Parallel Computing*, pp. 50–55, 2008.

24. A. Chonka, W. Zhou, K. Knapp, and Y. Xiang, "Protecting information systems from DDoS attack using multicore methodology," in *CITWORKSHOPS '08: Proceedings of the 2008 IEEE 8th International Conference on Computer and Information Technology Workshops*, Shanghai, China, pp. 270–275, 2008.

25. S. Dharmapurikar, P. Krishnamurthy, T. S. Sproull, and J. W. Lockwood, "Deep packet inspection using parallel bloom filters," *IEEE Micro*, Sydney, Australia, vol. 24, no. 1, pp. 52–61, 2004.

26. Y. Shoumeng, Z. Xingshe, W. Lingmin, and W. Haipeng, "GA-based automated task assignment on network processors," in *Proceedings of the 11th International Conference on Parallel and Distributed Systems (ICPADS'05)*, Fuduoka, Japan, pp. 112–118, 2005.

27. A. Mallik, Y. Zhang, and G. Memik, "Automated task distribution in multicore network processors using statistical analysis," in *ANCS '07: Proceedings of the 3rd ACM/IEEE Symposium on Architecture for Networking and Communications Systems*, Orlando, Florida, pp. 67–76, 2007.

28. S. Datar and M. A. Franklin, *Task Scheduling of Processor Pipelines with Application to Network Processors*. Department of Computer Science and Engineering, Washington University in St. Louis, St. Louis, Missouri, USA, 2003.

29. L. Yang, T. Gohad, P. Ghosh, D. Sinha, A. Sen, and A. Richa, "Resource mapping and scheduling for heterogeneous network processor systems," in *ANCS '05: Proceedings of the 2005 ACM Symposium on Architecture for Networking and Communications Systems*, Princeton, New Jersey, USA, pp. 19–28, 2005.

30. "Corezilla: build and tame the multicore beast," in *Proceedings of the 44th Annual Conference on Design Automation*, 2007.

31. B. Flachs, S. Asano, S. Dhong, P. Hotstee, G. Gervais, R. Kim, T. Le, P. Liu, J. Leenstra, J. Liberty, B. Michael, H. Oh, S. Mueller, O. Takahashi, A. Hatakeyama, Y. Watanabe, and N. Yano, "A streaming processing unit for a CELL processor," in *Digest of Technical Papers from Solid-State Circuits Conference*, San Diego, CA, USA, Vol. 1, San Francisco, CA, USA, 2005, pp. 134–135.

32. D. Pham, S. Asano, M. Bolliger, M. Day, H. Hofstee, C. Johns, J. Kahle, A. Kameyama, J. Keaty, Y. Masubuchi, M. Riley, D. Shippy, D. Stasiak, M. Suzuoki, M. Wang, J. Warnock, S. Weitzel, D. Wendel, T. Yamazaki, and K. Yazawa, "The design and implementation of a first-generation CELL processor," in *Digest of Technical Papers from Solid-State Circuits Conference*, San Francisco, CA, USA, Vol. 1, 2005, pp. 184–592.

33. FICO, "Xpress-MP," http://www.dashoptimization.com/pdf/Mosel1.pdf, 2002.

PART VIII

Applications of Heterogeneous High-Performance Computing

21

Toward a High-Performance Distributed CBIR System for Hyperspectral Remote Sensing Data: A Case Study in Jungle Computing

Timo van Kessel

VU University, Amsterdam, The Netherlands

Niels Drost and Jason Maassen

Netherlands eScience Center, Amsterdam, The Netherlands

Henri E. Bal

VU University, Amsterdam, The Netherlands

Frank J. Seinstra

Netherlands eScience Center, Amsterdam, The Netherlands

Antonio J. Plaza

University of Extremadura, Caceres, Spain

High-Performance Computing on Complex Environments, First Edition.
Edited by Emmanuel Jeannot and Julius Žilinskas.
© 2014 John Wiley & Sons, Inc. Published 2014 by John Wiley & Sons, Inc.

Despite the immense performance of modern computing systems, many scientific problems are of such complexity and scale that a wide variety of computing hardware must be employed concurrently. Moreover, as the required hardware often is not available as part of a single system, scientists often are forced to exploit the computing power of a very diverse distributed system. As many different types of hardware are available nowadays, this results in a complex hierarchical collection of heterogeneous computing hardware, which we refer to as a *jungle computing system*. Using such a collection of hardware all at once (let alone efficiently) is a difficult problem.

An example application domain that brings forth very diverse hardware requirements is that of content-based image retrieval (CBIR) for hyperspectral remote sensing data. Whereas algorithms to process remote sensing data are often already computationally complex, instruments for earth observation generate immense amounts of (distributed) data. As a result, to process this data within reasonable time, there is a need to exploit as much available computing power as possible.

In this chapter, we present a prototype for a CBIR system for remotely sensed image data. We focus on hyperspectral data, a type of remote sensing data characterized by very high resolution in the spectral domain. We show that our prototype system can easily be adapted to match the configuration of a jungle computing system, and is able to process and search the contents of several repositories efficiently.

21.1   INTRODUCTION

Many scientific problems are of such complexity and scale that solutions are obtained only using a wide variety of computing hardware—all at once. To effectively exploit the available processing power, a thorough understanding of the complexity of such systems is essential.

Despite the fact that there is an obvious need for programming solutions that allow scientists to obtain high performance and distributed computing both efficiently and transparently, real solutions are still lacking [1, 2]. Worse even, the high-performance and distributed computing landscape is currently undergoing a revolutionary change. Traditional clusters, grids, and cloud systems are more and more equipped with state-of-the-art many-core technologies (e.g., graphics processing units or GPUs [3, 4]). Although these devices often provide orders-of-magnitude speed improvements, they make computing platforms more heterogeneous and hierarchical—and vastly more complex to program and use.

Further complexities arise in everyday practice. Given the ever-increasing need for computing power, and because of additional issues including data distribution, software heterogeneity, and so on, scientists are commonly forced to apply multiple clusters, grids, clouds, and other systems concurrently—even for single applications. In this chapter, we refer to such a simultaneous combination of heterogeneous, hierarchical, and distributed computing resources as a *jungle computing system* [5].

Constellation [6] is a lightweight software platform, specifically designed to implement applications able to run on jungle computing systems. Constellation aims to efficiently run applications on complex combinations of distributed, heterogeneous, and hierarchical computing hardware. In addition, Constellation makes retargeting applications to completely different computing environments straightforward.

Constellation assumes that applications consist of multiple distinct activities with certain dependencies between them. These activities can be implemented independently using the tools, and targeted at the architecture, that suit them best. Multiple implementations of an activity may be created to support different hardware architectures (e.g., in C, C++/MPI, CUDA) or problem instances. Existing external codes can also be used. This approach to application development vastly reduces the programming complexity. Instead of having to create a single application capable of running in a complex, distributed, and heterogeneous environment, it is sufficient to create (or reuse) several independent activities targeted at smaller and simpler homogeneous environments. Traditional high-performance computing (HPC) tools and libraries such as MPI [7] or CUDA[1] can be used to create each of the separate activities.

Remote sensing of the Earth is a research field in which problems are of such a complexity that the use of jungle computing systems becomes indispensable.[2] For instance, the NASA Jet Propulsion Laboratory's Airborne Visible Infrared Imaging Spectrometer (AVIRIS) [10] is able to record the visible and near-infrared spectrum of the reflected light of an area several kilometers long (depending on the duration of the flight) using hundreds of spectral bands. The resulting "image cube" is a stack of images (Fig. 21.1), in which each pixel (vector) has an associated spectral signature or "fingerprint" that uniquely characterizes the underlying objects. The resulting data often comprise several gigabytes per flight.

The amount of data generated by such instruments tends to grow as new instruments are deployed. This is caused not only by an increasing number of instruments that are operational but also by the fact that modern instruments are able to produce much more complex images by increasing both the image resolution and the number of spectral bands that are captured. In addition, more advanced instruments are being developed that will produce even more data. At present, the data generated by hyperspectral instruments is stored at several locations. To make things worse, some of these data might be replicated over multiple repositories. In short, analyzing all data generated by modern and future instruments is a hard problem.

To analyze all these data, there is a need for a system that enables researchers to search in all these repositories in a sensible way. For this purpose, content-based image retrieval (CBIR) intends to retrieve, from real data stored in distributed databases, information that is relevant to a query [11]. This is particularly important in large data repositories, such as those available in remotely sensed hyperspectral imaging [12]. In [8], we described how spectral information can be extracted out of hyperspectral images to create a CBIR system suitable for the remote sensing community. In this system, spectral endmembers are extracted from an image that is used as a *query image*, and are compared with the spectral endmembers of the

---

[1] http://www.nvidia.com/cuda.html.

[2] Many other of such domains exists, such as computational astrophysics [9], climate modeling, etc.

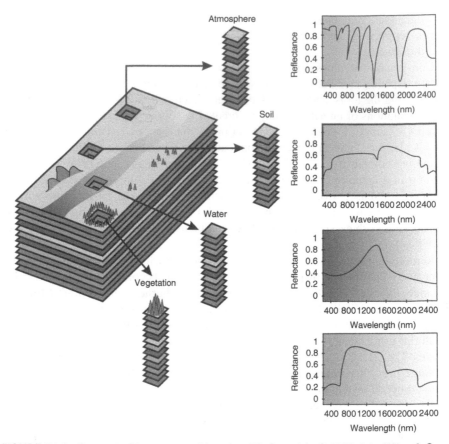

FIGURE 21.1 *Concept of hyperspectral imaging [8]. Copyright © 2009 John Wiley & Sons, Ltd. Reprinted by permission of John Wiley & Sons, Inc.*

hyperspectral images in a database to determine a similarity score. The most similar images are then returned as the result of the query.

In this chapter, we will discuss how the Constellation programming system can be used to design a flexible system for CBIR of hyperspectral remote sensing data for jungle computing systems. We argue that the system is easily adaptable to the specific circumstances of the jungle environment. Finally, we show that a prototype implementation of our system offers good performance in a real-world jungle environment.

This chapter is organized as follows: In Section 21.2, we introduce the remote sensing problem and discuss the hyperspectral imaging techniques that are required for hyperspectral image retrieval. Section 21.3 introduces the jungle computing paradigm. Section 21.4 introduces Ibis and Constellation, the software platform that enables the creation of applications for jungle computing systems. Section 21.5 describes our design of a prototype CBIR system for hyperspectral remote sensing data using the Constellation platform. An evaluation of the prototype system is given in Section 21.6, followed by our conclusions in Section 21.7.

21.2   CBIR FOR HYPERSPECTRAL IMAGING DATA

One of the main problems involved in hyperspectral data exploitation is spectral unmixing [13], as many of the pixels collected by imaging spectrometers such as AVIRIS are highly mixed in nature due to spatial resolution and other phenomena. For instance, it is very likely that the pixel labeled as "vegetation" in Fig. 21.1 is actually composed of several types of vegetation canopies interacting at subpixel levels. Similarly, the "soil" pixel may comprise different types of geological features. As a result, spectral unmixing is a very important task for hyperspectral data exploitation, since the spectral signatures collected in natural environments are invariably a mixture of the pure signatures of the various materials found within the spatial extent of the ground instantaneous field view of the imaging instrument. Among several techniques designed to deal with the inherent complexity of hyperspectral images in a supervised manner [13, 14], linear spectral unmixing follows an unsupervised approach which aims at inferring pure spectral signatures, called *endmembers*, and their material fractions, called *abundances*, at each pixel of the scene.

21.2.1   Spectral Unmixing

Let us assume that a remotely sensed hyperspectral image with n bands is denoted by $\mathbf{I}$, in which a pixel of the scene is represented by a vector $\mathbf{x} = [x_1, x_2, \ldots, x_n] \in \mathbb{R}^N$, where $\mathbb{R}$ denotes the set of real numbers in which the pixel's spectral response x_k at sensor channels $k = 1, \ldots, n$ is included. Under the linear mixture model assumption [15, 16], each pixel vector in the original scene can be modeled using the following expression:

$$\mathbf{x} \approx \mathbf{Ea} + \mathbf{n} = \sum_{i=1}^{p} \mathbf{e}_i a_i + \mathbf{n}, \tag{21.1}$$

where $\mathbf{E} = \{\mathbf{e}_i\}_{i=1}^{p}$ is a matrix containing p pure spectral signatures (endmembers), $\mathbf{a} = [a_1, a_2, \ldots, a_p]$ is a p-dimensional vector containing the abundance fractions for each of the p endmembers in $\mathbf{x}$, and $\mathbf{n}$ is a noise term. Solving the linear mixture model involves (i) identifying a collection of $\{\mathbf{e}_i\}_{i=1}^{p}$ endmembers in the image, and (ii) estimating their abundance in each pixel $\mathbf{x}$ of the scene. These processing steps are described in the following sections.

21.2.1.1   Endmember Extraction   First, a set of $\mathbf{E} = \{\mathbf{e}_i\}_{i=1}^{p}$ endmember signatures are extracted from the input dataset. For this purpose, we consider the N-FINDR algorithm [17], which is one of the most widely used and successfully applied methods for automatically determining endmembers in hyperspectral image data without using *a priori* information. This algorithm looks for the set of pixels with the largest possible volume by *inflating* a simplex inside the data. The procedure begins with a random initial selection of pixels. Every pixel in the image must be evaluated in order to refine the estimate of endmembers, looking for the set of pixels that maximizes the volume of the simplex defined by selected endmembers. The corresponding volume is calculated for every pixel in each endmember position by replacing that endmember and finding the resulting volume. If the replacement results in a an increase of volume, the pixel replaces the endmember. This procedure is repeated in iterative manner until there are no more endmember replacements. The method can be summarized by a step-by-step algorithmic description which is given as follows:

1. *Feature Reduction*: Apply a dimensionality reduction transformation such as the principal component analysis (PCA) [18] to reduce the dimensionality of the data from n to $p - 1$, where p is an input parameter to the algorithm (number of endmembers to be extracted).

2. *Initialization*: Let $\{e_1^{(0)}, e_2^{(0)}, \ldots, e_p^{(0)}\}$ be a set of endmembers randomly extracted from the input data.

3. *Volume Calculation*: At iteration $k \geq 0$, calculate the volume defined by the current set of endmembers as follows:

$$V(e_1^{(k)}, e_2^{(k)}, \ldots, e_p^{(k)}) = \frac{\left| \det \begin{bmatrix} 1 & 1 & \cdots & 1 \\ e_1^{(k)} & e_2^{(k)} & \cdots & e_p^{(k)} \end{bmatrix} \right|}{(p-1)!}. \tag{21.2}$$

4. *Replacement*: For each pixel vector **x** in the input hyperspectral data, recalculate the volume by testing the pixel in all p endmember positions, that is, first calculate $V(\mathbf{x}, e_2^{(k)}, \ldots, e_p^{(k)})$, then calculate $V(e_1^{(k)}, \mathbf{x}, \ldots, e_p^{(k)})$, and so on, until $V(e_1^{(k)}, e_2^{(k)}, \ldots, \mathbf{x})$. If none of the p recalculated volumes is greater than $V(e_1^{(k)}, e_2^{(k)}, \ldots, e_p^{(k)})$, then no endmember is replaced. Otherwise, the combination with maximum volume is retained. Let us assume that the endmember absent in the combination resulting in the maximum volume is denoted by $e_i^{(k+1)}$. In this case, a new set of endmembers is produced by letting $e_i^{(k+1)} = \mathbf{x}$ and $e_l^{(k+1)} = e_l^{(k)}$ for $l \neq i$. The replacement step is repeated for all the pixel vectors in the input data until all the pixels have been exhausted.

21.2.1.2 Abundance Estimation

Once the set of endmembers $\mathbf{E} = \{e_i\}_{i=1}^{p}$ has been extracted, an unconstrained solution to (21.1) is simply given by the following expression [12]:

$$\mathbf{a} \approx (\mathbf{E}^T \mathbf{E})^{-1} \mathbf{E}^T \mathbf{x}. \tag{21.3}$$

However, two physical constraints are generally imposed in order to estimate the p-dimensional vector of abundance fractions $\mathbf{a} = [a_1, a_2, \ldots, a_p]$ at a given pixel **x**, these are the abundance nonnegativity constraint (ANC), that is, $a_i \geq 0$ for all $1 \leq i \leq p$, and the abundance sum-to-one constraint (ASC), that is, $\sum_{i=1}^{p} a_i = 1$ [16]. As indicated in [16], a fully constrained (i.e., ASC-constrained and ANC-constrained) estimate can be obtained in least-squares sense simultaneously.

Such fully constrained linear spectral unmixing estimate is generally referred to in the literature by the acronym FCLSU [16].

21.2.2 Proposed CBIR System

The proposed CBIR system for retrieval of hyperspectral imagery is based on the spectral unmixing methodology described in the earlier section. In this section, we describe the stages involved in a standard search procedure using the proposed CBIR system from an user's point of view as follows:

1. *Input Query*: The user first selects a portion or a full hyperspectral scene to be used as an input image **I**. Then, the system computes a feature vector associated to that portion given by the spectral signatures of endmembers $\mathbf{E} = \{\mathbf{e}_i\}_{i=1}^{p}$, derived using the N-FINDR algorithm, and their correspondent FCLSU-derived abundances summed across all the pixels in the considered portion. The number of endmembers to be extracted from the sample portion is automatically calculated using the hyperspectral signal identification by minimum error (HySime) method [19].

2. *Signature Comparison and Sorting*: The feature vector obtained in the previous stage, which comprises the p endmembers and their macroscopic abundances in the selected image portion **I**, is compared with the precomputed feature vectors of all the hyperspectral images in the database, using the following spectral signature matching algorithm (SSMA). Let $\{\mathbf{e}_i\}_{i=1}^{p}$ be a set of p endmembers extracted from the considered image **I**, and let $\{\mathbf{r}_j\}_{j=1}^{q}$ be a set of q endmembers extracted from a reference hyperspectral image **R** already available in the database (we assume that the database contains a large number of hyperspectral images). The idea now is to analyze if **R** should be retrieved as a hyperspectral image that is "sufficiently similar" with regard to **I**. It should be noted that the endmembers and their corresponding abundances are stored for each image dataset catalogued in the system, hence we use this information in order to decide about the similarity of the compared images. To accomplish this task, we use a spectral angle distance (SAD) based [15] similarity criterion which is implemented using the following steps:

   (a) *Initial Labeling*: Label all endmembers in the test set $\{\mathbf{e}_i\}_{i=1}^{p}$ as *unmatched*.

   (b) *Matching*: For each unmatched endmember in the test set $\{\mathbf{e}_i\}_{i=1}^{p}$, calculate the spectral angle between the test endmember and all endmembers in the reference set $\{\mathbf{r}_j\}_{j=1}^{q}$. If the pair $(\mathbf{e}_k, \mathbf{r}_l)$, with $1 \leq k \leq p$ and $1 \leq l \leq q$, results in the minimum obtained value of $\mathrm{SAD}(\mathbf{e}_k, \mathbf{r}_l)$, and the value is below threshold angle v_a, then label the endmembers $\mathbf{e}_k$ and $\mathbf{r}_l$ as "matched."

   (c) *Relative Difference Calculation*: For each matched endmember $\mathbf{e}_k$ resulting from the previous step, the identifiers of the M images which contain such endmember are extracted and ranked in descending order of spectral similarity.

3. *Display Results*: A mosaic made up of the first M images selected is assembled and then presented to the user as the search result.

21.3 JUNGLE COMPUTING

When the notion of grid computing was introduced over a decade ago; its foremost visionary aim (or "promise") was to provide *efficient and transparent (i.e., easy-to-use) wall-socket computing over a distributed set of resources* [20]. Since then, many other distributed computing paradigms have been introduced, including peer-to-peer computing [21], volunteer computing,[3] and—more recently—cloud computing [22]. These paradigms all share many of the goals of grid computing, eventually aiming to provide end users with access to distributed resources (ultimately even at a worldwide scale) with as little effort as possible.

These new distributed computing paradigms have led to a diverse collection of resources available to research scientists, including stand-alone machines, cluster systems, grids, clouds, desktop grids, and so on. Extreme cases in terms of computational power further include mobile devices at the low end of the spectrum and supercomputers at the top end.

If we take a step back, and look at such systems from a high-level perspective, then all of these systems share important common characteristics. Essentially, *all* of these systems consist of a number of basic computing nodes, each having local memories, and each capable of communicating over a local or wide-area connection. The most prominent differences are in the semantic and administrative organization, with many systems providing their own middleware, programming interfaces, access policies, and protection mechanisms [23].

Apart from the increasing diversity in the distributed computing landscape, the "basic computing nodes" mentioned above currently are undergoing revolutionary change as well. General-purpose CPUs at present have multiple computing cores per chip, with an expected increase in the years to come [24]. Moreover, special-purpose chips (e.g., GPUs) are now combined or even integrated with CPUs to increase performance by orders of magnitude [25].

With clusters, grids, and clouds thus being equipped with multicore processors and many-core "accelerators," systems available to scientists are becoming increasingly hard to program and use. Despite the fact that the programming and efficient use of many-core devices is known to be hard, this is not the only—or most severe—problem. With the increasing heterogeneity of the underlying hardware, the efficient mapping of computational problems onto the "bare metal" has become vastly more complex. Now more than ever, programmers must be aware of the potential for parallelism *at all levels of granularity*.

But the problem is even more severe. Given the ever-increasing desire for speed and scalability in many scientific research domains, the use of a single high-performance computing platform is often not sufficient. In part, the need to access multiple platforms concurrently from within a single application often is due to the impossibility of reserving a sufficient number of computing nodes at once in a single multiuser system. Moreover, additional issues such as the distributed nature of the input data, heterogeneity of the software pipeline being applied, and

---

[3]e.g., SETI@home, see also http://setiathome.ssl.berkeley.edu.

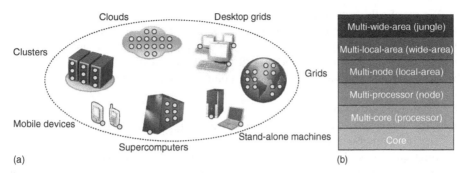

FIGURE 21.2 *Jungle computing system. (a) A "worst-case" jungle computing system as perceived by scientific end users, simultaneously comprising any number of clusters, grids, clouds, and other computing platforms. (b) Hierarchical view of a jungle computing system. [5]. © Springer-Verlag London Limited 2011. Reprinted with kind permission from Springer Science+Business Media B.V.*

ad hoc availability of the required computing resources further indicate a need for computing across multiple, and potentially very diverse, platforms. For all of these reasons, many research scientists (now and in the near future) are being forced to apply multiple clusters, grids, clouds, and other systems *concurrently*—even for executing single applications. We refer to such a simultaneous combination of heterogeneous, hierarchical, and distributed computing resources as a *jungle computing system* (Fig. 21.2).

Although the notion of jungle computing systems exposes *all* computing problems that scientists today can be (and often are) confronted with, we do not expect most (or even any) research scientists to have to deal with the "worst case" scenario depicted in Fig. 21.2. We do claim, however, that—in principle—*any* possible subset of this figure represents a realistic scenario. Hence, if we can define the fundamental methodologies required to solve the problems encountered in the worst case scenario, we ensure that our solution applies to all possible scenarios.

21.3.1 Jungle Computing: Requirements

Although jungle computing systems and grids are not identical (i.e., the latter being constituent components of the former), the generic aims of jungle computing are already defined by the "founding fathers of the grid." Foster *et al.* [20] indicate that one of the main aims of grid computing is to deliver *transparent* and potentially *efficient* computing, even at a world-wide scale. This aim extends to jungle computing as well.

It is well known that adhering to the general requirements of transparency and efficiency is a hard problem. Although rewarding approaches exist for specific application types (i.e., work-flow-driven problems [2, 26] and parameter sweeps [27]), solutions for more general applications types (e.g., involving irregular communication patterns) do not exist today. This is unfortunate, as advances in optical networking allow for a much larger class of distributed (jungle computing) applications to run efficiently [28].

We ascribe this rather limited use of grids and other distributed systems—or the lack of efficient and transparent programming models—to the intrinsic complexities of distributed (jungle) computing systems. Programmers often are required to use low-level programming interfaces that change frequently. Also, they must deal with system and software heterogeneity, connectivity problems, and resource failures. Furthermore, managing a running application is hard, because the execution environment may change dynamically as resources come and go. These problems limit the acceptance of the many distributed computing technologies available today.

The above-mentioned general requirements of transparency and efficiency are unequal quantities. The requirement of transparency decides whether an end user is capable of using a jungle computing system at all, while the requirement of efficiency decides whether the use is sufficiently satisfactory. In the following, we will therefore focus mainly on the transparency requirements. We will simply assume that—once the requirement of transparency is fulfilled—efficiency is a derived property that can be obtained amongst others by introducing "intelligent" optimization techniques, application domain-specific knowledge, and so on [5].

21.4 IBIS AND CONSTELLATION

The Ibis project [23] (see also www.cs.vu.nl/ibis/) aims to simplify the programming and deployment process of applications for jungle computing systems. The Ibis philosophy is that such applications should be developed on a local workstation and simply be launched from there. This write-and-go philosophy requires minimalistic assumptions about the execution environment, and sends most of the environment's software (e.g., libraries) along with the application. To this end, Ibis exploits Java virtual machine technology, and uses middleware-independent application programming interfaces that are automatically mapped onto the available middleware.

Ibis provides different programming abstractions, ranging from low-level message passing to high-level divide-and-conquer parallelism (Fig. 21.3). All programming abstractions are implemented on the same Java library, called the *Ibis portability layer* (IPL). Ibis also includes a deployment system, based on the JavaGAT (which provides file I/O, job submission, job monitoring, etc., in a middleware-independent manner) and on the Zorilla peer-to-peer system. The Ibis system is designed to run in a jungle computing environment that is dynamic and heterogeneous and suffers from connectivity problems. For example, Ibis solves connectivity problems automatically using the "SmartSockets" socket library.

A recent addition to the Ibis project is *Constellation*: a lightweight platform that is specifically designed for distributed, heterogeneous, and hierarchical computing environments [6]. Similar to most of the software developed in the Ibis project, Constellation itself is implemented in Java, which provides both portability and acceptable performance. Currently, we assume that a Constellation application (i.e., the glue code connecting the activities) is also a Java application. Although a Java class is used to represent an activity, the code performing the actual processing may be implemented using scripts, C, CUDA, MPI, and so on. In this section, we will give an overview of the programming model offered by Constellation.

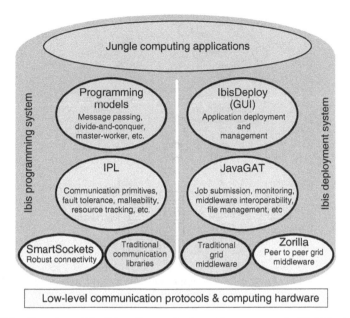

FIGURE 21.3 *Overview of the Ibis software stack and its components [5]. © Springer-Verlag London Limited 2011. Reprinted with kind permission from Springer Science+Business Media B.V.*

In Constellation, a program consists of a set of loosely coupled *activities* that communicate using *events*. The complexity of a program may vary from a simple bag of tasks to a complex workflow comprised of multiple interdependent activities. Figure 21.4 (top) shows a simple example using four activities. There, an initial activity (white) is started that submits three additional activities (gray and black).

Each activity represents a distinct action that needs to be performed by the application, for example, process a piece of data or run a simulation. As such, an activity usually represents a combination of code, parameters, and data. Each activity may consist of a script, sequential C, CUDA, a parallel application using OpenMP or MPI, and so on.

Constellation uses *executors* to represent hardware capable of running activities. An executor may represent a single core of a machine, a single machine with multiple cores, a specialized piece of hardware (e.g., a GPU), an entire cluster, and so on. The application is free to determine how the executors should represent the hardware.

Constellation assumes that a *glide-in* [29–31] approach is used to start the executors on the available hardware, for example, using IbisDeploy [23] or Zorilla [32]. In this chapter, we will not describe how the necessary resources are obtained. Instead, we assume that a heterogeneous set of resources capable of running the necessary executors is available.

In Fig. 21.4 (bottom), three executors are shown, one representing a multicore machine, one representing a machine containing a GPU, and one representing a small cluster of eight machines. Obviously, when such a heterogeneous set of executors is

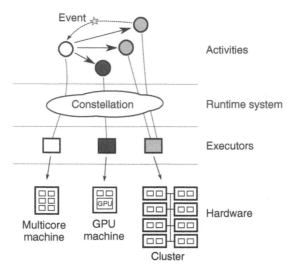

FIGURE 21.4 *Example of a Constellation application [6]. © 2011 Association for Computing Machinery, Inc. Reprinted by permission. http://doi.acm.org/10.1145/1996010.1996013.*

used, not every activity will be able to run on every executor. An activity consisting of GPU code will not run on an MPI cluster, nor will an MPI application run on a GPU. Therefore, it is essential for running the application that the activities end up on a suitable executor. For this purpose, Constellation uses the concept of *context*.

A context is an application defined label (or set of labels) that can be attached to both activities and executors. A label can describe data dependencies ("dataset X"), hardware capabilities ("GPU"), or problem size ("large"). When an activity and executor use the same label, they *match*; that is, the executor is assumed to offer the right context for running the activity. Constellation plays the role of matchmaker to ensure that each activity is forwarded to a suitable executor. In Fig. 21.4, this is illustrated by the different shades used for the activities and executors.

Although the concept of context matching is similar to the resource requirement matching used in traditional resource managers [29, 33], there is an important difference. Resource managers often use a predefined list of attributes describing both the hardware and software (e.g., libraries) that are available on a machine. A feature can only be used for matching if it was included in the list to begin with. In addition, complex combinations of attributes often are needed to describe a task's requirements, thereby making the matching procedure complicated and expensive.

In contrast, Constellation uses simple *application-defined* labels to describe what context an activity requires and an executor has to offer. Using application-specific knowledge, the distinctions between the different activities and executors are often easy to make. For example, for many applications, simple labels such as "GPU" or "dataset X" are sufficient to classify the executors. This makes context matching simple and fast, allowing fine-grained applications to be scheduled efficiently.

Events can be used for communication with activities. When an activity is created, it is assigned a globally unique ID. When sending an event to an activity, this ID can be used as a destination address. Events are mainly used for signaling between activities, for example, to indicate that certain data is available or that certain processing steps have finished. However, if necessary, they can also be used to transfer data between activities.

The complete set of activities does not have to be known in advance. During the application's lifetime, new activities may be submitted to the Constellation run time system (RTS), either by some external application or spawned dynamically by activities that are already running. Newly created activities are activated on a suitable executor to perform processing. When finished, the activity may decide to either terminate or suspend and wait for events. Whenever an activity receives an event, it is reactivated to allow it to process the event and perform additional processing, if necessary. When finished, the activity must again decide to terminate or suspend.

It is the task of the Constellation RTS to ensure that all activities in an application are run on suitable executors. In addition, load balancing is performed to maximize utilization of the available executors. In Constellation, a single *context-aware work stealing* algorithm is responsible for both. Whenever an executor becomes idle, it selects another executor and sends it a request for work that includes its context. The executor receiving the request can then perform context matching to find a suitable activity in its queues. If one is found, it is returned. Otherwise, the idle executor is notified that no work is available. This process is repeated until work is found.

21.5 SYSTEM DESIGN AND IMPLEMENTATION

In this section, we discuss how we have used Constellation to create a prototype system for CBIR of hyperspectral remote sensing data for jungle computing systems. In our CBIR system, two main processes can be identified: (i) extraction of the endmembers from the actual images, and (ii) the execution of queries on the endmember data.

These two processes are tied together by the *endmember store*. The endmember store consists of the actual store, a database containing endmember information, and one or more specialized *endmember store executors* that can access the store. In an endmember store, the endmember information of each image is placed next to the names of the repositories in which the related image is stored. In addition, any extra metadata information that can be useful for querying (e.g., the date and location on which an image is taken) can be stored in the endmember store as well.

The endmember store manages the endmember extraction process for all repositories assigned to it. In turn, the end user can perform queries on the data stored in all endmember stores known to the end user. In our system, several endmember stores can be present, each of them managing their own set of repositories.

Figure 21.5 shows the activities that are involved in both the endmember extraction and query execution process, and Fig. 21.6 shows the executors of the CBIR system that must execute those activities. The labels assigned to both the activities

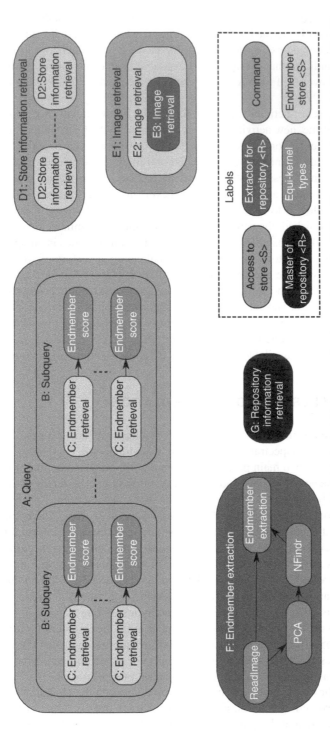

FIGURE 21.5 *Activities of the CBIR system and their labels. Activities can consist of one or more subactivities. The arrows show the data dependencies between activities.*

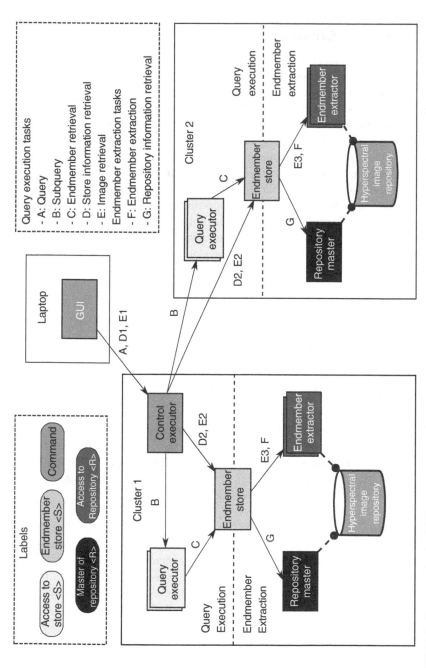

FIGURE 21.6 *Executors for the CBIR system, with the endmember store on the border between the endmember extraction and the query execution parts. The arrows show how the activities traverse the system to execute the query execution and endmember extraction tasks.*

and executors are used by the matchmaking mechanism of Constellation to assign each activity to a suitable executor, as explained in more detail in Section 21.5.4.

21.5.1 Endmember Extraction

In the process of endmember extraction, endmembers are calculated for each image in the repositories and placed in an endmember store. Next to the endmember store and the repositories themselves, this process also involves *endmember extractors*. The endmember extractors are executors capable of retrieving image data from a repository and execute the endmember extraction algorithm. Finally, a *repository master* executor is assigned to each repository. The task of a repository master is to monitor the contents of the repository it is assigned to.

To start the endmember extraction process, the endmember store first creates a *repository information retrieval activity* for each repository. In turn, this activity will start the repository monitoring process on the appropriate repository master executor. The repository master executor retrieves the information about the contents of the repository and sends it back to the endmember store using an event. When images are added to or removed from the repository later on, the repository master executor will notify the endmember store by sending additional events.

When the endmember store has received the information about the contents of the repositories, it creates endmember extraction activities for all images. The endmember extractors retrieve (using the Constellation job stealing mechanism) the activities that are suitable for their configuration and execute them, and finally they deliver the extracted endmembers to the endmember store.

21.5.2 Query Execution

As soon as the first endmembers are extracted and added to the endmember stores, queries can be executed on the contents of the endmember stores. All tasks involved in querying the stores are started by the user interface, but coordinated by the *control executor*, which acts as a proxy for the user interface. The user interface can start three operations: (i) retrieving the contents of all stores, (ii) executing a query, and (iii) retrieving an actual image from a repository.

21.5.2.1 Store Contents Retrieval The user interface can obtain a list of the contents of the stores by sending a *store information retrieval activity* to the control node. On receiving of such an activity, the control executor creates separate store information retrieval activities for each store. These activities will create a list of contents of a single store and send it back to the control executor by an event. In turn, the control node aggregates the results and sends them to the user interface.

21.5.2.2 Query Execution The user interface can execute a query by creating a *query activity*, which will be scheduled to the control node by the Constellation runtime system. To make the query easily distributable over several *query executors*, the control executor splits the query into *subquery activities*, each querying only a

small subset of the contents of the endmember stores. A subquery only contains query tasks for images that are processed by the same set of endmember stores.

Each subquery activity is assigned to an appropriate query executor by the matchmaking mechanism of Constellation. Next, the query executor creates comparison tasks for all images in the subquery. These comparison tasks consist of two steps: (i) retrieving the endmembers of the image out of the store, and (ii) calculating a similarity score between the image endmembers and the endmembers of the query image. When all comparisons are made, the images of the subquery are ordered by their score and sent back to the control node using an event.

The control node aggregates the results of all subqueries and orders the results by their scores. To conclude the query, an event containing a list of the best matching images is sent to the user interface.

21.5.2.3 *Image Retrieval*   To retrieve an actual image, the user interface creates an *image retrieval activity* that is be processed by the control node. In turn, the control node looks up which stores contain the endmembers of the image, as these stores know how to locate a repository that contains the image. Then the control executor creates a new image retrieval activity which will be assigned to an appropriate store executor. This store executor creates another image retrieval request which is taken to a suitable endmember extraction executor. Finally, the endmember extraction executor retrieves the image from the repository and sends it back to the user interface using an event.

21.5.3   Equi-Kernels

If we regard the activities in Fig. 21.5 in more detail, we identify two classes of activities. Most of the activities described above, namely the *control activities*, deal with moving other activities or data within Constellation to a suitable location (i.e., executor). A second class of activities, the *operational activities*, perform the actual operations involved in either the query process or endmember extraction process. These activities are equipped with labels expressing *equi-kernel types* required for the operations.

Operational activities execute operations by invoking the corresponding kernel on the executor it runs on. Depending on the hardware platform it represents, an executor will use the best suitable *equi-kernel* available for each of its kernel operations.

Equi-kernels are different implementations of the same kernel functionality. For example, the endmember extraction activity, which is a control activity, contains amongst others the PCA and N-FINDR (operational) activities. These activities invoke the PCA and N-FINDR kernels, respectively. For both these kernels, a CPU and GPU equi-kernel are available, implemented in C++ and CUDA, respectively. Therefore, an endmember extraction executor representing a CPU resource will load the equi-kernels containing the CPU code, whereas executors that represent a GPU will load the GPU equi-kernels instead.

In our system, we use equi-kernels that differ in the hardware platform that is used to implement the kernel operation. However, equi-kernels can also differ from each other in other ways. For example, they could use different heuristics to implement the same kernel functionality.

21.5.4 Matchmaking

The design of our CBIR system involves several types of executors, each with their own capabilities and roles in the overall system. Similarly, all subtasks involved in the CBIR process are represented by activities. To direct all activities to a suitable executor, we use the *labels* of the Constellation matchmaking system.

Each executor contains a label that describes its role. Additionally, a label describing the hardware represented by the executors is assigned as well. For example, an endmember extraction executor having access to repository "A" and representing a CPU core as well as a GPU will contain the following set of labels as its context: **[ExtractorForRepository< A>, GPU, CPU]**.

Similarly, each activity specifies on which type of executor it can run using the appropriate labels. For example, an endmember extraction activity for an image present in both repository "A" and "B" will have the label **[ExtractorForRepository<A>, ExtractorForRepository<B>]**, which expresses that it can be executed by any endmember extraction executor that has access to either repository "A" or "B."

In the same way, activities that represent a kernel operation carry a label that specifies the kernel type supported by that operation. The Constellation matchmaking mechanism allows executors to express their preference for a type of activity by ordering their labels accordingly. For example, an executor capable of running both CPU and GPU codes will contain the labels **[GPU, CPU]**, expressing that it prefers to execute activities that can use GPU equi-kernels. However, if such an activity is not present, it also accepts activities for which only CPU equi-kernels are available.

21.6 EVALUATION

The design for the CBIR system as described in the previous section fulfills most of the requirements for a jungle computing application. The Ibis platform already fully provides middleware independence, robust connectivity, and system-level fault tolerance, while it offers mechanisms to implement support for malleability and application-level fault tolerance. In addition, Constellation allows us to create a very flexible system that can easily adapt to all kinds of jungle environments.

First, it is very easy to exploit new resources by deploying extra executors on those new resources. Depending on the needs of the user and properties of the resources, the user can select the most appropriate executor.

Second, the matchmaking mechanism of Constellation and its labeling approach makes it very simple to configure the behavior of the CBIR system. For example, we could alter the label of the image retrieval activity in such a way that the image is retrieved by the repository master instead of the endmember extractor by changing a label of the image retrieval activity E3 (Fig. 21.5) to **[MasterOfRepository< A>]**.

Of course, the system designer has to take care not to alter the labels in such a way that activities will be assigned to executors that are unable to process the activity.

Third, the equi-kernel approach allows integration with external software while maintaining resource independence. For each operation, a special code for each platform can be included. By including a "default" equi-kernel for each operation as well, the CBIR system can transparently exploit special hardware and codes, without failing to operate when such hardware is not available.

21.6.1 Performance Evaluation

Now that we have established that our design for the CBIR system leads to a flexible solution suitable for jungle computing systems, we will validate the performance of our system. In these experiments, we use the DAS-4, which is a heterogeneous computing system consisting of six computing clusters spread over six universities and research institutes in The Netherlands. Table 21.1 lists the most important properties of the computing nodes for each cluster site.node configurations of all cluster site. Finally, all clusters are equipped with an 40 Gb/s Infiniband local network, and the DAS-4 clusters are connected to each other via a 10 Gb/s optical network.

In our experiments, we used a subset of the AVIRIS dataset of the 2010 Gulf Oil Spill Response.[4] This dataset consists of several *flight lines* of hyperspectral data, each of which can easily contain several tens of gigabytes of uncompressed data. As these flight lines are too large to process as a whole, they are split into image tiles of up to 512×512 pixels by our repository I/O kernels.

Our CBIR framework for remote sensing data executes two tasks, namely endmember extraction and query execution, largely independent of each other. We will first evaluate these tasks separately. For these experiments, we used the DAS-4 cluster located at VU University in Amsterdam. We also evaluated the CBIR system in a jungle environment. For this experiment, in addition to the DAS-4 cluster at the VU, we also used the DAS-4 clusters located at Leiden University, University of Amsterdam, TU Delft, and ASTRON.

21.6.1.1 Endmember Extraction In our first tests, we evaluated the performance of the endmember extraction process of the CBIR system. The main activity

TABLE 21.1 Node Configurations of the DAS-4 Clusters

Cluster	Nodes	CPU	Memory	Accelerators
VU Amsterdam	74	2 quad-core Intel E5620	24 GB	16x GTX480
Leiden University	16	2 quad-core Intel E5620	48 GB	
Univ. of Amsterdam	16	2 quad-core Intel E5620	24 GB	
TU Delft	32	2 quad-core Intel E5620	24 GB	8x GTX480
ASTRON	24	2 quad-core Intel E5620	24 GB	8x GTX580

[4]http://aviris.jpl.nasa.gov/html/gulfoilspill.html

of the endmember extraction phase is the endmember extraction activity. As already shown in Fig. 21.5, the endmember extraction activity consists of four kernel activities, each performing a single kernel operation:

1. `LoadImage`: Load an image from a repository into main memory;
2. `PCA`: The PCA dimensionality reduction Algorithm;
3. `N-FINDR`: The N-FINDR endmember extraction algorithm: Computes the end-members in the reduced image space;
4. `EndmemberExtraction`: Extracts the endmembers (that are found by the N-FINDR algorithm) from original image.

In addition to loading image data from the repository, the `LoadImage` kernel converts the image data to the correct format for use in our algorithm as well. For both PCA and N-FINDR kernels, we have a CPU and GPU implementation. The `EndmemberExtraction` kernel is a simple operation that extracts the endmembers found by the N-FINDR kernel from the original image data, and is not significant in the system performance.

We benchmarked the endmember extraction process for two scenarios:

- *Static Repositories:* A repository contains a constant number of images. No new images are added at runtime;
- *Streaming Data:* New image data is delivered to the system at runtime. The CBIR system processes the data immediately and adds the endmembers to the system as soon as possible.

Although the functionality is similar for both scenarios, the evaluation criteria differ. In case of a static repository, we are mainly interested in the time needed to process the entire repository. In case of streaming data, we are interested in how many resources are needed in order to "keep up" with the data stream. Next to these two scenarios, a third scenario could be formulated in which new data is added to an already existing repository. As this scenario essentially is a combination of two scenarios we described above, we will not discuss it any further.

For the static repository scenario, we used the NFS file system of the DAS-4 cluster as our repository. In this repository, we stored a 77 GB dataset consisting of 13 flight lines of oil spill data, resulting in 784 image tiles of up to 512 × 512 pixels. We measured the time our system used to extract the endmembers for all image tiles and store the endmember information in the endmember store. To emulate a data stream for the streaming data scenario, we used randomly generated data as input image data, eliminating the influence of the I/O speed of the DAS-4 NFS file system.

Table 21.2a shows the time required by the endmember extraction process to process all 784 image tiles of the static repository, using only CPU kernels. As the extraction executors operate completely independently of each other, we initially expected the performance of to scale close to linear with respect to the number of executors in the system. However, as more executors are used on a single node, we

TABLE 21.2 Static Repository: Time (in seconds) Needed to Extract the Endmembers of All 784 Image Tiles: (a) Only the CPU is Used; (b) One GPU Per Node Static Repository, and One GPU Per Node

		Executors per Node						Executors per Node		
		1	2	4	8			1	2	4	8
Nodes	1	7 951	4 680	4 048	3 581	Nodes	1	6 103	5 148	3 998	1 434
	2	3 555	2 546	2 190	796		2	2 998	2 283	1 957	816
	4	1 853	1 261	1 082	595		4	1 393	1 147	635	484
	8	971	683	643	683		8	777	503	491	517

| (a) | (b) |

can clearly see that the performance increase is not as large as expected. The main source of this decrease in performance is the LoadImage kernel: the execution times of the LoadImage kernel rises with the addition of extra executors.

When we increase the number of endmember extraction nodes in the system, we initially do get close-to-linear performance increase as expected. However, the benefits of increasing the number of executors for the endmember extraction process decrease quickly, and using more than 16 executors in total hardly improves overall performance any further. This indicates that we hit a bottleneck in our system. Most likely, the NFS file system used by our repository implementation is not able to keep up with the I/O requests made by the endmember extraction executors anymore. The best results were obtained using four nodes with eight executors each, leading to a speedup factor of 13.

Looking at the execution times in more detail, we can see that the LoadImage kernel behaves unpredictably and takes a relatively long time. For higher numbers of executors, we notice that loading the images from the repositories is the bottleneck of the entire endmember extraction pipeline. For one part, this can be attributed to the bandwidth of the repository to the computing nodes. However, we noticed that the I/O performance is affected by another factor as well: in the repositories, the image data is ordered using the "band interleaved per pixel" format, whereas the endmember extraction algorithm expects the data to be in the "band sequential" order. Therefore, the images are converted to the band sequential layout by the input kernel immediately. This conversion step, which is a matrix transposition, appeared to be significant as well. With up to eight endmember extractors in total, an entire I/O operation (including conversion) takes about 6 s for a 512×512 tile. However, when we increase the number of executors to 32, the I/O time increases to 13 s on average.

When we include one GPU executor per node (Table 21.2b), the time required to process all images is reduced significantly. In case of a single executor per node, we measure a reduction in execution time of 15–25%. This advantage quickly reduces when more (CPU) executors are added to each node. Although the GPU executor is significantly faster in computing the endmembers, the overall benefit of using the GPU is limited because of the large impact of the I/O on overall system performance.

For the PCA kernel, the GPU implementation is about 3 times faster than the CPU implementation, whereas for N-FINDR, the performance increases by up to a factor

TABLE 21.3   Streaming Data. Extraction Speed (Tiles/s). (a) With CPU Only. (b) With One GPU Per Node

		Executors per Node						Executors per Node		
		1	2	4	8			1	2	4	8
Nodes	1	0.0829	0.163	0.303	0.478	Nodes	1	0.797	0.787	0.884	0.834
	2	0.157	0.307	0.584	0.906		2	1.62	1.54	1.64	1.54
	4	0.358	0.639	1.14	1.82		4	2.89	3.01	3.15	3.13
	8	0.725	1.25	2.17	3.26		8	5.90	6.30	6.51	5.86

(a)   (b)

16 when GPUs are used. When multiple executors are deployed, we can see that the performance of the CPU kernel slightly degrades, probably due to sharing computing resources and memory bandwidth.

In the streaming data scenario, we can see that adding extra executors within a computing node results in improved performance even if more than 16 executors are used (Table 21.3a). This shows that, in the static repository scenario, performance was indeed limited by the I/O performance. Tables 21.3a and 21.3b show that the performance of the endmember extraction process now shows close to linear scalability in the number of nodes used.

With the I/O bottleneck eliminated, using GPUs in the endmember extraction leads to a significantly higher throughput. In this scenario, a single GPU executor reaches a higher throughput as an entire CPU node with eight executors. However, Table 21.3b shows that adding extra CPU executors to the nodes that already have a GPU executor does not lead to significant performance improvements.

21.6.1.2   *Query Execution*
Next we evaluated how fast our system is able to execute queries on the endmember data stored in the endmember stores. To that end, we performed queries on stores containing 10,000 and 100,000 elements, using several configurations of query executors (Table 21.4). Our query system is configured to retrieve the 30 most similar elements from the endmember store.

In our experiments with a single query executor and both 10,000 and 100,000 images in the endmember store, roughly 1 ms is needed on average to process a single image. The image comparison kernel itself needs about 0.6 ms to compare

TABLE 21.4   Query Speed: Time (in seconds) to Complete A Query: (a) 10,000 Images; (b) 100,000 Images

		Executors per Node						Executors per Node		
		1	2	4	8			1	2	4	8
Nodes	1	10.24	5.43	3.02	1.91	Nodes	1	100.74	50.83	26.09	14.37
	2	5.36	3.02	1.79	1.15		2	50.03	25.52	13.35	7.54
	4	2.98	1.89	1.12	0.84		4	24.72	12.92	6.96	4.12

(a)   (b)

endmember sets with each other. The remainder of the time is spent in sorting the results and overhead of the system runtime itself.

When 100,000 images are used, performance of our system scales linearly with the number of executors used up to about eight executors. In case a total of 32 executors spread over four nodes are used, a speedup of 24.5 is achieved compared to when using a single executor. In case of 10,000 images, scalability of the system is worse, and using 32 executors only leads to a speedup of 12.2.

With 32 executors distributed over four nodes, our system is capable of executing a query within 1 s in case of 10,000 images, and in about 4 s in case of 100,000 images in the endmember store.

21.6.1.3 *Jungle Deployment* Finally, we show that our system is capable of running in a jungle computing scenario by deploying it on five clusters (VU, UvA, Leiden, Delft, and Astron) of the DAS-4 system, using CPU nodes only. Over these cluster sites, we distributed 40 flight lines of hyperspectral imaging data, for a total of 221.9 GB of data (Table 21.5). The dataset on the VU cluster is the same as used for the static repository experiment.

On each cluster site, we deployed a separate node with a repository master, four nodes with four endmember extractors each, a single node containing the endmember store and a single store executor, and one node with eight query executors to query the endmember store. We deployed the control executor on a node on the DAS-4 cluster at the VU and the GUI on a local workstation.

It took 990 s (16:30 min) to complete the endmember extraction process on all image data, which is similar to the time needed to process the VU dataset in isolation (Table 21.2a), which is the largest dataset. This shows that the CBIR system did not introduce any new overheads when processing multiple repositories concurrently. A query on the full dataset (2464 image tiles) distributed over five endmember stores could be easily completed within 1 s, leading to a smooth and interactive querying experience over the distributed data.

By exploiting several clusters within a single jungle computing system, our CBIR system is able to process the contents of multiple repositories in parallel, without any additional overheads. At the same time, it enables the user to perform queries on the contents of multiple repositories interactively, completely hiding the complexities of the underlying system.

TABLE 21.5   Data Distribution

Cluster Site	Flight Lines	Tiles (512 × 512)	Data Size (GB)
VU Amsterdam	13	784	77.0
Leiden	9	491	38.2
UvA	3	288	24.5
Delft	7	351	30.2
Astron	8	550	52.0
Total	40	2464	221.9

21.7   CONCLUSIONS

In this chapter, we discussed the ever-increasing amounts of data generated by remote sensing instruments, and the challenges that the research domain of remote sensing has to face to process all these data. We argued that the application of jungle computing techniques can help in processing these huge amounts of data.

Next we introduced the Ibis/Constellation, a platform for creating flexible and efficient applications for jungle computing systems. We described how Ibis/Constellation can be used to build a system for CBIR for hyperspectral remote sensing data, which offers a search functionality on the contents of multiple distributed data repositories in a single system.

In this system, we can distinguish two independent processes, linked together by the endmember store. First, in the endmember extraction process, endmembers are extracted of each image present in a repository, and the endmembers are placed in an endmember store. Next, the query process is able to execute queries on the data that is stored in the endmember stores.

We showed that our prototype implementation of the CBIR system can be easily adapted to match the properties of a jungle computing system, and can exploit the available computing resources in an efficient way. Finally, we demonstrated that our prototype system can indeed provide query functionality on multiple distributed data repositories in a transparent and efficient way.

ACKNOWLEDGMENTS

This work was supported by COST Action IC0805 "Open European Network for High Performance Computing on Complex Environments," and partially funded by the Dutch national research program COMMIT.

REFERENCES

1. D. E. Wojick, W. L. Warnick, B. C. Carroll, and J. Crowe, "The digital road to scientific knowledge diffusion: a faster, better way to scientific progress?" *D-Lib Magazine*, vol. 12, no. 6, 2006.

2. I. Taylor, I. Wang, M. Shields, and S. Majithia, "Distributed computing with Triana on the grid," *Concurrency and Computation: Practice and Experience*, vol. 17, no. 9, pp. 1197–1214, 2005.

3. J. Maassen and H. E. Bal, "Smartsockets: solving the connectivity problems in grid computing," in *Proceedings of the 16th International Symposium on High Performance Distributed Computing, HPDC'07*, pp. 1–10. New York: ACM, 2007.

4. R. Medeiros, W. Cirne, F. Brasileiro, and J. Sauvé, "Faults in grids: why are they so bad and what can be done about it?" in *Proceedings of the 4th International Workshop on Grid Computing, GRID'03*, pp. 18–24. Washington, DC: IEEE Computer Society, 2003.

5. F. J. Seinstra, J. Maassen, R. V. van Nieuwpoort, N. Drost, T. van Kessel, B. van Werkhoven, J. Urbani, C. Jacobs, T. Kielmann, and H. E. Bal, "Jungle computing: distributed supercomputing beyond clusters, grids, and clouds," in *Grids, Clouds and Virtualization, Computer Communications and Networks* (M. Cafaro and G. Aloisio, eds.), pp. 167–197. London: Springer, 2011.

6. J. Maassen, N. Drost, H. E. Bal, and F. J. Seinstra, "Towards jungle computing with Ibis/Constellation," in *Proceedings of the 2011 Workshop on Dynamic Distributed Data-Intensive Applications, Programming Abstractions, and Systems, 3DAPAS'11,* pp. 7–18. New York: ACM, 2011. http://doi.acm.org/10.1145/1996010.1996013.

7. R. L. Graham, G. M. Shipman, B. W. Barrett, R. H. Castain, G. Bosilca, and A. Lumsdaine, "Open MPI: a high-performance, heterogeneous MPI," in *Proceedings of the Fifth International Workshop on Algorithms, Models and Tools for Parallel Computing on Heterogeneous Networks,* Barcelona, Spain, pp. 1–9, 2006.

8. A. J. Plaza, J. Plaza, and A. Paz, "Parallel heterogeneous CBIR system for efficient hyperspectral image retrieval using spectral mixture analysis," *Concurrency and Computation: Practice and Experience,* vol. 22, no. 9, pp. 1138–1159, 2010.

9. N. Drost, J. Maassen, M. A. J. van Meersbergen, H. E. Bal, F. I. Pelupessy, S. P. Zwart, M. Kliphuis, H. A. Dijkstra, and F. J. Seinstra, "High-performance distributed multi-model / multi-kernel simulations: a case-study in jungle computing," in *Proceedings of the 2012 IEEE 26th International Parallel and Distributed Processing Symposium Workshops & PhD Forum, IPDPSW'12,* pp. 150–162. Washington, DC: IEEE Computer Society, 2012.

10. R. O. Green, M. L. Eastwood, C. M. Sarture, T. G. Chrien, M. Aronsson, B. J. Chippendale, J. A. Faust, B. E. Pavri, C. J. Chovit, M. Solis, M. R. Olah, and O. Williams, "Imaging spectroscopy and the Airborne Visible/Infrared Imaging Spectrometer (AVIRIS)," *Remote Sensing of Environment,* vol. 65, no. 3, pp. 227–248, 1998.

11. A. W. M. Smeulders, M. Worring, S. Santini, A. Gupta, and R. Jain, "Content-based image retrieval at the end of the early years," *IEEE Transactions on Pattern Analysis and Machine Intelligence,* vol. 22, no. 12, pp. 1349–1380, 2000.

12. C.-I. Chang, *Hyperspectral Imaging: Techniques for Spectral Detection and Classification.* New York: Plenum Publishing Co., 2003.

13. A. Plaza, J. A. Benediktsson, J. W. Boardman, J. Brazile, L. Bruzzone, G. Camps-Valls, J. Chanussot, M. Fauvel, P. Gamba, A. Gualtieri, M. Marconcini, J. C. Tilton, and G. Trianni, "Recent advances in techniques for hyperspectral image processing," *Remote Sensing of Environment,* vol. 113, (Suppl. 1), no. 0, pp. S110–S122–, 2009. Imaging Spectroscopy Special Issue.

14. G. Camps-Valls and L. Bruzzone, "Kernel-based methods for hyperspectral image classification," *IEEE Transactions on Geoscience and Remote Sensing,* vol. 43, no. 6, pp. 1351–1362, 2005.

15. N. Keshava and J. Mustard, "Spectral unmixing," *IEEE Signal Processing Magazine,* vol. 19, no. 1, pp. 44–57, 2002.

16. D. C. Heinz and C.-I. Chang, "Fully constrained least squares linear spectral mixture analysis method for material quantification in hyperspectral imagery," *IEEE Transactions on Geoscience and Remote Sensing,* vol. 39, no. 3, pp. 529–545, 2001.

17. M. E. Winter, "N-FINDR: an algorithm for fast autonomous spectral end-member determination in hyperspectral data," *Proceedings of SPIE,* vol. 3753, pp. 266–275, 1999.

18. J. A. Richards and X. Jia, *Remote Sensing Digital Image Analysis: An Introduction.* Berlin: Springer, 2006.

19. J. Bioucas-Dias and J. Nascimento, "Hyperspectral subspace identification," *IEEE Transactions on Geoscience and Remote Sensing,* vol. 46, no. 8, pp. 2435–2445, 2008.

20. I. Foster, C. Kesselman, and S. Tuecke, "The anatomy of the grid: enabling scalable virtual organizations," *International Journal of High-Performance Computing Applications*, vol. 15, no. 3, pp. 200–222, 2001.

21. J. I. Khan and A. Wierzbicki, "Guest editor's introduction; foundation of peer-to-peer computing," *Computer Communications*, vol. 31, no. 2, pp. 187–189, 2008.

22. "Editorial: Cloud computing: Clash of the clouds," in *The Economist*, 2009, Retrieved from http://www.economist.com/node/14637206.

23. H. E. Bal, J. Maassen, R. V. van Nieuwpoort, N. Drost, R. Kemp, N. Palmer, G. Wrzesinska, T. Kielmann, F. Seinstra, and C. Jacobs, "Real-world distributed computing with Ibis," *Computer*, vol. 43, no. 8, pp. 54–62, 2010.

24. M. Reilly, "When multicore isn't enough: trends and the future for multi-multicore systems," in *Proceedings of the 12th Annual Workshop on High-Performance Embedded Computing (HPEC 2008)*, Lexington, MA, USA, 2008.

25. P. J. Lu, H. Oki, C. A. Frey, G. E. Chamitoff, L. Chiao, E. M. Fincke, C. M. Foale, S. H. Magnus, W. S. Mcarthur Jr., D. M. Tani, P. A. Whitson, J. N. Williams, W. V. Meyer, R. J. Sicker, B. J. Au, M. Christiansen, A. B. Schofield, and D. A. Weitz, "Orders-of-magnitude performance increases in GPU-accelerated correlation of images from the International Space Station," *Journal of Real-Time Image Processing*, vol. 5, no. 3, pp. 179–193, 2010.

26. B. Ludäscher, I. Altintas, C. Berkley, D. Higgins, E. Jaeger, M. Jones, E. A. Lee, J. Tao, and Y. Zhao, "Scientific workflow management and the Kepler system," *Concurrency and Computation: Practice and Experience*, vol. 18, no. 10, pp. 1039–1065, 2006.

27. D. Abramson, R. Sosic, J. Giddy, and B. Hall, "Nimrod: a tool for performing parametised simulations using distributed workstations," in *Proceedings of the Fourth IEEE International Symposium on High Performance Distributed Computing (HPDC'95)*, Washington, DC, USA, pp. 112–121, 1995.

28. K. Verstoep, J. Maassen, H. E. Bal, and J. W. Romein, "Experiences with fine-grained distributed supercomputing on a 10G testbed," in *Proceedings of the 2008 Eighth IEEE International Symposium on Cluster Computing and the Grid, CCGRID'08*, pp. 376–383. Washington, DC: IEEE Computer Society, 2008.

29. D. Thain, T. Tannenbaum, and M. Livny, "Distributed computing in practice: the Condor experience: research articles," *Concurrency and Computation: Practice and Experience*, vol. 17, no. 2-4, pp. 323–356, 2005.

30. I. Raicu, Y. Zhao, C. Dumitrescu, I. Foster, and M. Wilde, "Falkon: a Fast and Light-weight tasK executiON framework," in *Proceedings of the 2007 ACM/IEEE Conference on Supercomputing, SC'07*, Reno, NV, USA, pp. 1–12, 2007.

31. E. Walker, J. P. Gardner, V. Litvin, and E. L. Turner, "Personal adaptive clusters as containers for scientific jobs," *Cluster Computing*, vol. 10, no. 3, pp. 339–350, 2007.

32. N. Drost, R. V. van Nieuwpoort, J. Maassen, F. J. Seinstra, and H. E. Bal, "Zorilla: a peer-to-peer middleware for real-world distributed systems," *Concurrency and Computation: Practice and Experience*, vol. 23, no. 13, pp. 1506–1521, 2011.

33. B. Bode, D. M. Halstead, R. Kendall, Z. Lei, and D. Jackson, "The portable batch scheduler and the maui scheduler on linux clusters," in *Proceedings of the 4th Annual Linux Showcase & Conference—Volume 4, ALS'00*, p. 27. Berkeley, CA: USENIX Association, 2000.

22

Taking Advantage of Heterogeneous Platforms in Image and Video Processing

Sidi A. Mahmoudi
University of Mons, Mons, Belgium

Erencan Ozkan
Ankara University, Ankara, Turkey

Pierre Manneback
University of Mons, Mons, Belgium

Suleyman Tosun
Ankara University, Ankara, Turkey

Image and video processing algorithms present an important tool for various domains related to computer vision, such as pattern recognition, video surveillance, medical imaging, and so on. Because of the fast shift toward high definition on images and videos, the performances of these algorithms have beenseverely hampered. Indeed, they require more resources and memory to achieve their computations. In this chapter, we propose a development scheme that enables efficient exploitation of

High-Performance Computing on Complex Environments, First Edition.
Edited by Emmanuel Jeannot and Julius Žilinskas.
© 2014 John Wiley & Sons, Inc. Published 2014 by John Wiley & Sons, Inc.

parallel (GPU, graphics processing unit) and heterogeneous (multi-CPU/multi-GPU) platforms, in order to improve the performance of both image and video processing algorithms. This scheme enables an efficient scheduling of hybrid tasks and an effective management of heterogeneous memories. Based on this scheme, we develop heterogeneous implementations of several image and video processing algorithms. These implementations are exploited for accelerating two applications. The first one is a medical method of vertebra detection in X-ray images, while the second consists of real-time motion detection using a mobile camera. Experimental results show a global speedup ranging from 5 to 40 when processing different sets of high-definition images and videos in comparison with CPU implementations.

22.1 INTRODUCTION

During the past years, the architecture of central processing units (CPUs) has much evolved that the number of integrated computing units has been multiplied in order to achieve better performance. This evolution is reflected in both general (CPU) and graphic (GPU) processors, as well as in recent accelerated processors (APU) which combine CPU and GPU on the same chip.[1] Moreover, GPUs have a larger number of computing units, and their power far exceeds that of the CPUs. Indeed, the advent of GPU programming interfaces (API) has encouraged many researchers to exploit them for accelerating algorithms initially designed for CPUs.

In this context, image and video processing algorithms can be well adapted for acceleration on the GPU by exploiting its processing units in parallel, since they consist mainly of a common computation over many pixels. Moreover, these algorithms require a high consumption of computing power and memory. Therefore, the exploitation of graphic processors present an efficient solution for accelerating single image processing algorithms, as the output image can be directly visualized from GPU, using graphic libraries for image rendering, such as OpenGL.[2] However, in case of processing multiple images, two additional constraints occur: the first one is the inability to visualize many output images using only one video output that requires a transfer of results from the GPU to the CPU memory. The second constraint is the high computation intensity when processing large sets of images. On the other hand, the new standards, especially those involving high resolutions, cause that current implementations, even running on modern hardware, no longer meet the needs of real-time processing. A fast processing of these videos is required to ensure the treatment of 25 high-definition frames per second (25 fps), which means that each video frame has to be processed in less than 40 ms. To overcome these constraints, several GPU computing approaches have recently been proposed. Although they present a great potential of a GPU platform, hardly any is able to process high-definition images and video sequences efficiently. Thus, there was a need to develop a tool capable of addressing the outlined problem.

---

[1] AMD Fusion (APU). http://sites.amd.com/us/fusion/apu/Pages/fusion.aspx/.
[2] OpenGL. http://oss.sgi.com/projects/ogl-sample/registry/.

In this chapter, we propose a development scheme that enables full exploitation of parallel (GPU) and heterogeneous (multi-CPU/multi-GPU) architectures for improving the performances of image and video processing algorithms. This scheme enables us to select resources according to the types of applied algorithms and processed data. The proposed scheme allows also overlapping data transfers by kernel executions using the CUDA (compute unified device architecture) streaming technique within multiple GPUs. The exploitation of heterogeneous platforms is based on efficient scheduling of tasks using the runtime system StarPU [1]. Based on this scheme, we developed parallel and hybrid implementations of several algorithms such as contour and corner detection methods, motion detection, and tracking using optical flow estimation. These implementations are exploited in two applications. The first one is a medical method of vertebra detection and segmentation in X-ray images [2], while the second one is an application of camera motion estimation inside real-time video frames. This method uses both camera motion estimation and background subtraction to separate background and foreground in real-time video frames while the camera is moving.

The remainder of the chapter is organized as follows: Related works are described in Section 22.2. Section 22.3 presents the proposed development scheme for image processing on GPU, while Section 22.4 describes our development scheme for processing multiple images on heterogeneous architectures. Section 22.5 is devoted to presenting the proposed scheme for real-time video processing on GPU. These schemes are summarized in a general framework in Section 22.6. This section presents also two use cases of the presented model with a comparison between CPU, GPU, and hybrid implementations. Finally, Section 22.7 concludes and proposes further work.

22.2 RELATED WORK

We categorize two types of related works based on the exploitation of parallel and heterogeneous platforms for multimedia processing: one is related to image processing on GPU, and the other is devoted to video processing on GPU.

22.2.1 Image Processing on GPU

Most image processing algorithms dispose of sections that consist of similar computation over many pixels, which makes them well adapted for acceleration on GPU by exploiting its processing units in parallel. In this category, Yang *et al.* [3] implemented classic image processing algorithms on GPU with CUDA.[3] Castano *et al.* [4] presented an evaluation of different GPU implementations such as principal component analysis (PCA), as well as linear and nonlinear filtering. These implementations achieved accelerations ranging from 10 to 20 times compared to CPU implementations. The OpenVIDIA project [5] has implemented different computer vision algorithms running on graphic hardware such as single or multiple GPUs. There are also

---

[3]NVIDIA CUDA. http://www.nvidia.com/cuda.

some GPU works dedicated to medical imaging for parallel [2] and heterogeneous [6], [7] computation for vertebra detection and segmentation in X-ray images. Moreover, there are different works dealing with the exploitation of hybrid platforms. OpenCL[4] proposed a framework for writing programs that execute across hybrid platforms consisting of both CPUs and GPUs. Ayguadé *et al.* presented a flexible programming model for multicores [8]. StarPU [1] provided a unified runtime system for heterogeneous multicore architectures, enabling the development of effective scheduling strategies. However, the accelerations obtained within these implementations can be reduced when processing image databases with different resolutions. Indeed, an efficient exploitation of parallel and heterogeneous platforms requires an effective management of both CPU and GPU memories. Moreover, the treatment of low-resolution images cannot exploit effectively the high power of GPUs since few computations will be launched. This implies an analysis of the spatial and temporal complexities of algorithms before their parallelization on a GPU.

22.2.2   Video Processing on GPU

Video processing algorithms require generally a real-time treatment of images. We may find several methods in this category, such as understanding human behavior, event detection, camera motion estimation, and so on. These methods are generally based on motion tracking algorithms that can exploit several techniques such as optical flow estimation [9], the block matching technique [10], and scale-invariant feature transform (SIFT) [11] descriptors.

Currently, motion tracking methods present an active research topic in computer vision and video surveillance domains. These methods try to estimate the displacement and velocity of features in a given video frame with respect to the previous one. In this chapter, we focus more on optical flow methods since they present a promising solution for tracking even in noisy and crowded scenes or in the case of small motions. In the case of GPU-based optical flow motion tracking algorithms, one can find two kinds of related works. The first presents the so-called dense optical flow which tracks all video frame pixels without selecting features. In this context, Marzat *et al.* [12] have presented a GPU implementation of the Lucas–Kanade method used for optical flow estimation. The method was developed with CUDA to compute dense and accurate velocity field at about 15 fps with 640×480 video resolution. The authors in [13] proposed the CUDA implementation of the Horn–Schunck optical flow algorithm with a real-time processing of low-resolution videos (316×252). The second category consists of methods that enable the tracking of selected image features only. Sinha *et al.* [14] developed a GPU implementation of the Kanade-Lucas-Tomasi (KLT) feature tracker and the SIFT feature extraction algorithm [11]. This enabled the detection of 800 features from 640×480 video at 10 fps, which is around 10 times faster than the CPU implementation. This method can also track a thousand features in real time in a video of resolution 1024×768, which is approximately 20 times faster than the CPU version. However, despite their high speedups, none of the above-mentioned GPU-based implementations can provide real-time processing of high-definition videos.

[4]OpenCL. http://www.khronos.org/opencl.

22.2.3   Contribution

Our contribution is presented by two development schemes that enable an efficient exploitation of parallel and heterogeneous platforms. The first scheme is related to single and multiple image processing, which offers a full exploitation of the computing power of parallel and hybrid platforms. This scheme allows dynamic scheduling of tasks within multiple CPUs and GPUs; it also exploits the CUDA streaming technique for overlapping data transfers by kernel executions. The second scheme is devoted to real-time video processing on GPU, enabling an efficient management of GPU memories. This scheme allows fast visualization of results, thanks to the reutilization of buffers already existing on the GPU. Based on these two schemes, we developed parallel and heterogeneous implementations of several image and video processing algorithms such as feature (edges and corners) detection, silhouette extraction, and optical flow estimation. These implementations are exploited for improving the performance of a medical application of vertebra segmentation [2] and an application of real-time motion detection using a moving camera.

22.3   PARALLEL IMAGE PROCESSING ON GPU

As described in the previous section, graphic cards present an effective tool for accelerating image processing algorithms. This section is presented in four parts: the first one describes our development scheme for processing single and multiple images on a GPU. The second part is devoted to presenting the employed GPU optimization techniques. The third part describes our GPU implementations of edge and corner detection methods. The fourth part presents an analysis of the obtained results and an evaluation of the complexity of the implemented algorithms based on different metrics.

22.3.1   Development Scheme for Image Processing on GPU

The proposed scheme is based on CUDA for parallel constructs and OpenGL for visualization. This scheme consists of the three following steps: loading of input images, CUDA processing, and presentation of results [15].

1. *Loading of Images on GPU.* The input images are loaded on the GPU memory.
2. *CUDA Processing.* This step consists two phases:
   (a) Threads Allocation: This step consists of defining the number of threads of the GPU's grid, so that each thread can perform its processing on one or a group of pixels in parallel.
   (b) CUDA Processing: The CUDA functions (kernels) are executed N times using the N selected threads.
3. *Results Presentation:* Results can be presented using two different scenarios:
   (a) OpenGL Visualization: In the case of a single image processing, results (output image) can be directly visualized on a screen through the video output of the GPU. We propose to exploit the graphic library OpenGL enabling fast visualization, since it works with buffers already existing on the GPU.

(b) Transfer of Results: OpenGL visualization cannot be applied in the case of multiple image processing using one video output only. A transfer of the output images from GPU to CPU memory is required, which represents an additional cost for the application.

22.3.2   GPU Optimization

We employ different optimization techniques that depend mainly on the type of images (single or multiple) to treat the following:

- *Single Image Processing:* We propose to load the input image on texture memory for a fast access to pixels. Moreover, we load each pixel neighbors on shared memory for fast processing of the pixels using their neighbors' values [2].
- *Multiple Image Processing:* We exploit the GPU's shared memory for fast access of neighbors' values. We also exploit CUDA streams to overlap kernel executions by data transfers to/from the GPU. This enables us to treat each subset of images on its own stream. Each stream consists of three steps:
  — copying of the image subsets from the host to GPU memory;
  — computations performed by CUDA kernels;
  — copying of output images from the GPU to host memory.

22.3.3   GPU Implementation of Edge and Corner Detection

Based on the scheme described in Section 22.3, we propose the CUDA implementation of edge and corner detection methods, enabling both efficient results in terms of the quality of detected contours and corners and improved performance, as a result of the exploitation of GPU's computing units in parallel.

22.3.3.1   *Edge Detection on GPU*   We proposed a GPU implementation of the recursive contour detection method using the Deriche technique [16]. The noise truncature immunity and the reduced number of required operations make this method very efficient. However, it is hampered by the large increase in computing time when processing large sets of images. Our GPU implementation of this method is [2, 6] based on the parallelization of its four steps on the GPU.

22.3.3.2   *Corner Detection on GPU*   We developed the CUDA implementation of Bouguet's corner extraction method [17], based on the Harris detector [18]. Our GPU implementation is described in [19–21], and is based on parallelizing its four steps on the GPU.

22.3.4   Performance Analysis and Evaluation

Table 22.1 presents a comparison of the computing times between CPU and GPU implementations involving edge and corner detections. This table shows that the use

TABLE 22.1 Performance of Single Image Processing: Global Memory

Images	CPU	GPU GTX 280 (Global Memory)				Acc
	Time	Load	Kernels	OpenGL Vis.	Total Time	
256 × 256	7.88 ms	3.2 (39%)	4.1 (50%)	0.9 (11%)	8.2 ms	0.96
512 × 512	45 ms	3.4 (39%)	4.5 (51%)	0.9 (10%)	8.8 ms	5.11
1024 × 1024	141 ms	3.7 (30%)	6.3 (52%)	2.2 (18%)	12.2 ms	11.6
2048 × 2048	630 ms	5.6 (15%)	23.1 (61%)	9.0 (24%)	37.7 ms	16.7
3936 × 3936	2499 ms	14.4 (11%)	90.2 (69%)	27 (21%)	131.6 ms	18.9

TABLE 22.2 Performances of Single Image Processing: Texture and Shared Memories

Images	CPU	GPU GTX 280 (Tex. & Shared Memory)				Acc
	Time	Load	Kernels	OpenGL Vis	Total Time	
256 × 256	7.88 ms	3.1 (39%)	4.0 (50%)	0.9 (11%)	8 ms	0.99
512 × 512	45 ms	2.5 (35%)	3.7 (52%)	0.9 (13%)	7.1 ms	6.34
1024 × 1024	141 ms	2.5 (23%)	6.1 (56%)	2.2 (20%)	10.8 ms	13.1
2048 × 2048	630 ms	4.1 (12%)	22 (65%)	8.0 (23%)	34.1 ms	18.5
3936 × 3936	2499 ms	8.8 (8%)	82.5 (73%)	22 (19%)	113.3 ms	22.1

TABLE 22.3 Performances of Multiple Image Processing: Texure and Shared Memories

Images	CPU	GPU GTX 280 (Tex. & Shared Memory)				Acc
Nbr	Time	Load	Kernels	OpenGL Vis	Total time	
10	6 s	0.08 (11%)	0.50 (68%)	0.15 (21%)	0.73 s	8.2
50	30.3 s	0.3 (8%)	2.63 (72%)	0.73 (20%)	3.66 s	8.3
100	61.5 s	0.61 (9%)	4.84 (70%)	1.47 (21%)	6.92 s	8.9
200	136.1 s	1.30 (8%)	10.6 (68%)	3.70 (24%)	15.6 s	8.7

of GPU for single image processing enables a high acceleration (speedup of 18.9) as a result of the exploitation of the GPU's computing units and the fast visualization of results using OpenGL. Table 22.2 presents the interest of exploiting texture and shared GPU memories, which allows improving the performance (speedup of 22.1) compared to GPU solution using global memory. This acceleration is due to the fast access to pixel values within these memories. On the other hand, in case of processing multiple images, the improvement in performance is less (Table 22.3). The use of CUDA streaming technique enables a slight improvement in performance thanks to the overlapping of data transfers by kernel executions (Table 22.4). We note also that the GPU implementations are slower than the CPU ones when treating low-resolution images since we cannot exploit the GPU power sufficiently. Therefore, we propose to estimate the algorithm complexity using five parameters: parallel fraction, computation per pixel, computation per image, shared to global memory access ratio, and texture to global memory access ratio.

TABLE 22.4 Performances of Multiple Image Processing: CUDA Streaming

Images	CPU	GPU GTX 280 (CUDA streaming)				Acc
Nbr	Time	Load	Kernels	OpenGL Vis	Total time	
10	6 s	0.03 (5%)	0.49 (84%)	0.06 (10%)	0.58 s	10.34
50	30.3 s	0.12 (4%)	2.58 (85%)	0.33 (11%)	3.03 s	9.99
100	61.5 s	0.28 (5%)	4.79 (85%)	0.55 (10%)	5.62 s	10.95
200	136.1 s	0.50 (4%)	10.58 (85%)	1.32 (11%)	12.4 s	10.98

- *Parallel Fraction* (f): Amdahl proposed a law [22] that estimates the theoretical speedup using N processors. It supposes that f is the part of program that can be parallelized and $(1 - f)$ is the part that cannot be made in parallel. Indeed, high values of f can provide better performance, and vice versa.

- *Computation Per Pixel (Comp-Pixel):* The GPUs enable the acceleration of image processing algorithms by exploiting the GPU's computing units in parallel. These accelerations become more significant in case of applying intensive treatments since the GPU is specialized for parallel computation. The number of operations per pixel presents a relevant factor to estimate the computation intensity.

- *Computation Per Image (Comp-Image):* This parameter is computed with the multiplication of the image resolution by the computation per pixel (described above).

- *Shared to Global Memory Access Ratio (SM to GM):* The use of shared memory offers a faster access (read/write) to pixels in comparison with global memory. Thus, a high usage of shared memory provides better performance.

- *Texture to Global Memory Access Ratio (TM to GM):* The use of texture memory provides a faster reading (read only from GPU) of pixels compared to global memory.

Table 22.5 presents the measured metrics described above and the corresponding GPU accelerations. The parallel fraction f represents the percentage of parallelizable computing part relative to total time, while the remaining part $(1 - f)$ represents transfer (loading, visualization) operations. The computation per pixel is presented by the average number of operations between the steps of contour and corner detection. The ratio of shared (or texture) to global memory access is computed by dividing the number of access to shared (or texture) memory by the number of access to global memory. Table 22.5 shows significant accelerations once we have high values of metrics. Otherwise, the use of low-resolution images provides low values of f and low computations per image, and hence less performance. The use of shared and texture memories does not improve the performance significantly in this case since there are no sufficient treatments.

TABLE 22.5 Complexity Evaluation of Edge and Corner Detection on GPU

Images	f	Comp-Pixel	Comp-Image	SM to GM	TM to GM	Acc
256^2	57%	6.1	4.0×10^5	0.37	0.25	0.99
512^2	81%	6.1	1.6×10^6	0.37	0.25	6.34
1024^2	86%	6.1	6.4×10^6	0.37	0.25	13.1
2048^2	88%	6.1	2.6×10^7	0.37	0.25	18.5
3936^2	88%	6.1	9.4×10^7	0.37	0.25	22.1

22.4 IMAGE PROCESSING ON HETEROGENEOUS ARCHITECTURES

As described earlier, the GPU implementations have improved performance when processing single images (speedup of 22). But, in case of multiple image processing, we have less improvement of performance (speedup of 10). Therefore, we propose to exploit the full computing power of hybrid platforms, which offers a faster solution for multiple image processing. To this aim, we use the executive support StarPU [1], which provides a runtime for heterogeneous platforms. This section consists of three subsections: the first one is devoted to presenting the proposed scheme development for processing multiple images on heterogeneous platforms. The second part describes the employed scheduling strategy within multiple CPUs and GPUs. The last section presents the interest in exploiting the CUDA steaming technique in order to overlap data transfers by kernels executions.

22.4.1 Development Scheme for Multiple Image Processing

This section presents our proposed scheme for processing multiple images on hybrid architectures, following three steps: loading of the input images, hybrid processing, and presentation of results.

22.4.1.1 Loading of Input Images The first step consists of loading the input images in queues so that StarPU can apply treatments on these images.

22.4.1.2 Hybrid Processing After loading the input images, we can launch the CPU and GPU functions on heterogeneous processing units using StarPU. The latter consists of two main structures: the codelet and the task. The codelet enables defining the computing units that could be exploited (CPUs or/and GPUs) and the related implementations. The tasks apply this codelet on the set of images so that each task is created and launched to treat one image in the queue using CPU or GPU.

22.4.1.3 Results Presentation Once all tasks are completed, the results are copied in buffers using a specific function in StarPU, which enables the transfer of data from GPU to CPU memory.

22.4.2 Task Scheduling within Heterogeneous Architectures

In order to achieve efficient scheduling, we propose to estimate the duration of each task. Indeed, we provide codelets with a performance model assuming that, for similar sizes of images, the performance will be very close. StarPU will then check the record of the average time of the previous executions on different processing units, which will be used as estimation. The tasks are submitted asynchronously, and the DMDA (deque model data aware) scheduler is employed that uses both task execution performance models and data transfer times into account. Indeed, tasks using low-resolution images and applying light treatments will be launched on CPUs. Otherwise, tasks using high-resolution images and applying intensive treatments will be launched on GPUs.

22.4.3 Optimization Within Heterogeneous Architectures

For a better exploitation of the hybrid processing units, we propose to overlap data transfers within multiple GPUs using the CUDA streaming technique. Indeed, we propose to create four CUDA streams for each GPU, so that each one can overlap effectively data transfers by kernel executions. Our heterogeneous implementation will be composed of two steps only: loading of input images, and hybrid processing and results transfer.

1. Loading of input images: same as in Section 22.4.1.1.
2. Hybrid processing and results transfer: this step includes the phases of hybrid processing and results transfer (Sections 22.4.1.2 and 22.4.1.3) in order to benefit from overlapping data transfers by kernel executions.

The number of selected CUDA streams is 4 because it offers better performances. Figure 22.1 presents a comparison between CPU, GPU, and hybrid implementations involving edge and corner detection algorithms, applied on sets of high-resolution images. We note that the use of multiple CPUs and GPUs improved performance compared to multiple GPU solutions. This is due to the efficient scheduling and memory management, as well as to the overlapping of data transfers by kernel executions. Experimentations have been conducted using a Ubuntu 11.04 on several platforms:

- CPU: Dual core 6600, 2.40 GHz, memory: 2 GB;
- GPU: Tesla C1060, 240 CUDA cores, memory: 4 GB.

22.5 VIDEO PROCESSING ON GPU

As pointed out in the previous sections, a GPU presents an effective tool for accelerating both image and video processing algorithms. This section is presented in four parts: the first one describes our development scheme for video processing on GPU; the second part presents the employed GPU optimization techniques; the third part

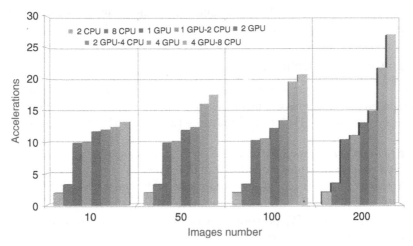

FIGURE 22.1 *Heterogeneous computing of edges and corners in multiple images* (2048 × 2048).

is devoted to describing our GPU implementations of several video processing algorithms such as silhouette extraction and optical flow estimation; and the fourth part presents an analysis of the obtained results.

22.5.1 Development Scheme for Video Processing on GPU

The proposed scheme is based on CUDA for parallel computing and OpenGL for visualization. This scheme consists of the three following steps:

1. *Loading of Video Frames on GPU:* We start with reading and decoding the video frames using OpenCV[5] library. We copy the current frame on a device (GPU) which processes it in the next step.
2. *CUDA Parallel Processing:* Before launching the parallel processing of the current frame, the number of GPU threads in the so-called blocks and grid has to be defined, so that each thread can perform its processing on one pixel or a group of pixels. This enables the program to treat the image pixels in parallel. Note that the number of threads depends on the number of pixels. Once the number and the layout of threads are defined, different CUDA functions (kernels) are executed sequentially, but each of them in parallel using multiple CUDA threads.
3. *OpenGL Visualization:* The current image (result) can be directly visualized on the screen through the video output of the GPU. Therefore, we use the OpenGL graphics library which allows fast visualization, as it can operate buffers already existing on GPU, and thus requires less data transfer between host and

[5] OpenCV. www.opencv.org.

device memories. Once the visualization of the current image is completed, the program goes back to the first step to load and process the next frames.

22.5.2   GPU Optimizations

The employed optimizations for video processing on the GPU are very similar to those applied for image processing on the GPU since a video is always presented by a succession of images. Therefore, we propose two main optimizations as follows:

1. *Exploitation of Texture and Shared memories:* This enables fast access to image pixels within the video using the texture memory. The neighboring pixels are loaded on shared memory for fast processing of the pixels using their neighbors' values.
2. *CUDA Streaming:* We propose to exploit CUDA streams in order to overlap kernel executions by image (frame) transfers to/from the GPU. Each stream consists of three instructions:
   (a) copying the current frame from host to GPU memory;
   (b) computations performed by CUDA kernels;
   (c) copying the current frame (already processed) from the GPU to host memory.

22.5.3   GPU Implementations

Based on the scheme described in Section 22.5.1, we propose the GPU implementation of silhouette extraction and optical flow estimation methods, which enables obtaining efficient results both in terms of the quality of detected and tracked motions and improved performance.

22.5.4   GPU-Based Silhouette Extraction

The computation of difference between frames presents a simple and efficient method for detecting the silhouettes of moving objects. Based on the scheme presented in Section 22.3.1, we propose the GPU implementation of this method using the three steps shown in the scheme. In this case, we start by loading the first two video frames on the GPU in order to compute the difference between them on the GPU during the CUDA parallel processing step. Once the first result (image) is displayed, we replace the first loaded image by the next video frame in order to apply the same treatment.

Figure 22.2 presents the obtained result of silhouette extraction on GPU. This figure shows two silhouettes extracted, which represent two moving persons. In order to improve the quality of the results, a threshold of 200 was used for noise elimination.

22.5.5   GPU-Based Optical Flow Estimation

Optical flow presents a distribution of the apparent velocities of movement of brightness pattern in an image. It enables the computation of the spatial displacements of

FIGURE 22.2 *GPU-based silhouette extraction.*

image pixels based on the assumption of the constant light hypothesis which supposes that the properties of consecutive images are similar in a small region. For more details about optical flow computation, we refer the reader to [17].

22.5.5.1 Process of Optical Flow Computation In the literature, several methods exist for estimating optical flow, such as the Horn–Shunck [23], Lucas–Kanade [24], block-matching techniques [10]. In this work, we propose the GPU implementation of the Lucas–Kanade algorithm, which is well known for its high efficiency, accuracy, and robustness. This algorithm can be summarized in six steps:

- *Step 1: Pyramid Construction:* In the first step, the algorithm computes a pyramid representation of images I and J, which represent two consecutive images from the video. The other pyramid levels are built in a recursive manner by applying a Gaussian filter. Once the pyramid is constructed, a loop is launched that starts from the smallest image (the highest pyramid level) and ends with the original image (Level 0). Its goal is to propagate the displacement vector between the pyramid levels. Note that this vector is initialized with 0 values and will be calculated during the next steps.
- *Step 2: Pixel Matching over Levels:* For each pyramid level (described in the previous step), the new coordinates of pixels (or corners) are calculated.
- *Step 3: Local Gradient Computation:* In this step, the matrix of the spatial gradient G is computed for each pixel (or corner) of the image I. This matrix of four elements (2×2) is calculated on the basis of the horizontal and vertical spatial derivatives. The computation of the gradient matrix takes into account the area (window) of pixels that are centered on the point to analyze (track). The size of the window depends on the image type and size.
- *Step 4: Iterative Loop Launch and Temporal Derivative Computation:* In this step, a loop is launched and iterated until the difference between the two successive optical flow measures (calculated in the next step), or iterations, is higher

than a defined threshold. Once the loop is launched, the computation of the temporal derivatives is performed using the image J (second image). This derivative is obtained by subtracting each pixel (or corner) of the image I (first image) from its corresponding corner in the image J (second image). This enables the estimation of the displacement, which is then propagated between successive pyramid levels.

- *Step 5: Optical Flow Computation:* The optical flow measure $\bar{b}$ is calculated using the gradient matrix (cf. Step 3) and the sum of temporal derivatives presented by the shift vector $\bar{b}$. Then, the measure of optical flow is calculated by multiplying the inverse of the gradient matrix G by the shift vector $\bar{b}$.

- *Step 6: Result Propagation and End of the Pyramid loop:* In this step, the current results are propagated to the lower level. Once the algorithm reaches the lowest pyramid level (original image), the pyramid loop (launched in the first step) is stopped. The vector $\bar{g}$ represents the final optical flow value of the analyzed corner. For more details about this method, we refer the reader to [17].

Upon matching and tracking pixels (corners) between frames, the result is a set of vectors as shown below:

$$\Omega = \{\omega_1, \ldots, \omega_n \quad | \quad \omega_i = (x_i, y_i, \upsilon_i, \alpha_i)\}, \tag{22.1}$$

where:

- x_i, y_i are the x and y coordinates of the feature i,
- υ_i represents the velocity of the feature i, and
- α_i denotes motion direction of the feature i.

22.5.5.2 *GPU Implementation* Based on the scheme presented in Section 22.3.1, we propose the GPU implementation of the Lucas–Kanade optical flow method by parallelizing its steps on the GPU. These steps are executed in parallel using the CUDA library such that each GPU thread applies its instructions (among the six steps) on one pixel or corner. Therefore, the number of selected GPU threads is equal to the number of pixels or corners. Since the algorithm looks at the neighboring pixels, for a given pixel, the images, or pyramid levels, are kept in the texture memory. This allows faster access within the two-dimensional spatial data. Other data, for example the arrays with computed displacements, are kept in the global memory, and are cached in the shared memory if needed. The software has been optimized for the Fermi architecture, and many low-level optimizations, such as the number of threads within a block or the actual location of different variables, were selected empirically. Moreover, the great advantage of the Fermi architecture is the L1/L2 cache which allows an efficient data fetch in case of recurring reads of consecutive elements from a cache line. Figure 22.3 presents the obtained results of optical flow computation on GPU, which enables an efficient tracking of corners previously detected.

FIGURE 22.3 *GPU-based optical flow computation using the Lucas–Kanade approach.*

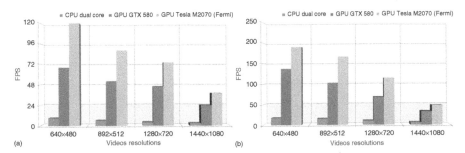

FIGURE 22.4 *Performances of GPU-based video processing. (a) Silhouette extraction on GPU. (b) Optical flow computation on GPU.*

22.5.6 Result Analysis

This section is devoted to presenting the performance of the above-mentioned GPU implementations. Notice that the quality of the results remains identical since the process has not changed. Only the architecture and the implementation did. Figure 22.4a presents the comparison between CPU and GPU implementations of silhouette extraction method, while Fig. 22.4b presents the performance of our GPU implementation of optical flow estimation. These performances are compared with a CPU solution developed with OpenCV. Notice that we have a real-time processing of high-definition videos thanks to the efficient exploitation of the high power of computing of the GPUs.

The proposed implementations are summarized in a general scheme for a better exploitation of parallel and heterogeneous architectures in Fig. 22.5. This scheme enables treating both images and videos effectively. For single image processing, we apply a complexity evaluation (Section 22.3.4) in order to effect sequential treatment for low-intensive methods and parallel treatments for high-intensive tasks. On the other hand, hybrid implementations are applied when treating multiple images by

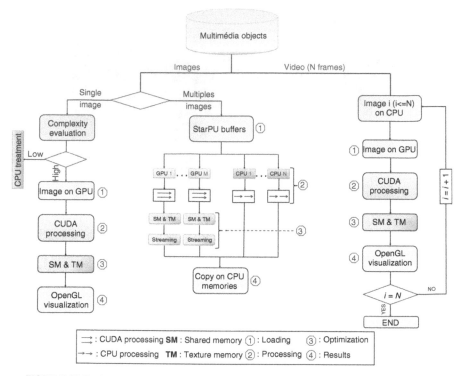

FIGURE 22.5   *Image and video processing on parallel and heterogeneous platforms.*

exploiting both CPUs and GPUs. In the case of video processing, we propose a GPU treatment based upon CUDA for parallel constructs and OpenGL for visualization. Figure 22.5 presents also the different optimization techniques that are applied for each scenario.

22.6   EXPERIMENTAL RESULTS

The proposed scheme in Fig. 22.5 is exploited in two applications: vertebra segmentation, and motion estimation with a moving camera.

22.6.1   Heterogeneous Computing for Vertebra Segmentation

The aim of this application is related to cervical vertebra mobility analysis on X-ray images. It consists of detecting vertebrae automatically. A sequential solution was developed in [2], based on several steps. This method is characterized by the large sets of high-resolution images to treat, with a low grey level variation. The computation time and noise immunity truncation present the most important requirements for this application. Based on our scheme, we propose a hybrid implementation of the most intensive steps (contour and corner detection) of the approach.

TABLE 22.6 Optimizations of Heterogeneous Computing of Edge and Corner Detection

Platforms	Basic Implementation	SM & TM Exploitation	Efficient Scheduling	CUDA Streaming
1 GPU/2 CPU	08.43×	9.26×	10.33×	11.65×
2 GPU/4 CPU	13.11×	14.20×	14.96×	15.81×
4 GPU/8 CPU	16.93×	19.79×	22.39×	28.06×

On one hand, the quality of vertebra extraction remains identical since the procedure has not changed; only the architecture and the implementation did. On the other hand, the exploitation of multi-CPU/multi-GPU architectures enabled the acceleration of the process of vertebra detection on X-ray images. This allowed the application of the proposed approach on large sets of medical images to have more precision for vertebra extraction.

The obtained accelerations are presented in Table 22.6. These optimizations are applied on the edge and corner detection steps, which are implemented heterogeneously. Indeed, the exploitation of texture and shared memories enabled the improvement of the performances (speedup of 19.79×) compared to basic hybrid implementation (16.93×). Multi-CPU/multi-GPU treatments are improved further (22.39×) when we employ efficient scheduling of tasks taking into account the transfer and computing times of the previous tasks. The overlapping of data transfers by kernel executions within multiple GPUs enables also the acceleration of the computation (28.06×). These results are obtained using a set of 200 X-ray images with a resolution of 1476 × 1680 each. These accelerations allowed us to obtain a gain of 85% (3.5 min) compared to the total time the application (4 min) using a set of 200 images with a resolution of 1472 × 1760.

22.6.2 GPU Computing for Motion Detection Using a Moving Camera

Motion detection algorithms are generally based on background subtraction, which is a widely used technique in the field of computer vision. Typically, a fixed background is given to the application and new frames are subtracted from this background to detect the motion. The difference will give the objects or motion when the frame is subtracted from the fixed background. This difference in the resulting binary image is called *foreground objects*. However, some scenarios present a dynamic background, which can change because of the movement of cameras. In this context, we propose an application for real-time background subtraction, which enables automatic background and foreground subtraction using a moving camera.

22.6.2.1 CPU Implementation This application can be summarized in two steps:

1. *Camera Motion Estimation:* This step is presented by three phases:
   (a) *Corner Detection:* The Harris corner detector is applied to extract good features to track and examine camera motion.

(b) *Optical Flow Computation:* The Lukas–Kanade optical flow method is applied to track the previously detected corners.

(c) *Camera motion inhibition:* The camera motion is estimated by computing the dominant values of optical flow vectors. This enables the extraction of the common area between each two consecutive images and focus only on motions related to objects in the scene.

2. *Motion Detection:* This step consists of detecting movements based on computing the difference between every two consecutive frames.

22.6.2.2 GPU Implementation In order to achieve a real-time treatment of high-definition videos, we developed a GPU implementation of the above-mentioned method by parallelizing the most intensive steps on GPU: corner detection, optical flow computation, and motion detection.

1. *Corner Detection:* This step is applied for each video frame. The GPU implementation of this phase is described in detail in Section 22.3.3.2.

2. *Optical Flow Computation:* This step consists of tracking the previously detected corners using our GPU implementation of the Lucas–Kanade optical flow method, described in Section 22.5.5.

3. *Motion Detection:* This step consists of computing (on GPU) the difference between every two consecutive frames as shown in Section 22.5.4. Notice that the GPU implementation is based on the scheme described in Section 22.3.1, following the steps of loading the video frames on GPU, CUDA parallel processing, and OpenGL visualization.

Figure 22.6a shows a scene of camera motion. The dotted and dashed line represents the first image, the dotted line represents the second frame, and the solid line shows the joint area of two frames. Once the camera motion is estimated, the

(a)   (b)

FIGURE 22.6   *(a) Camera motion estimation. (b) Motion detection.*

TABLE 22.7   GPU Performances of Motion Detection Using Mobile Camera

Resolution	CPU Dual-Core	GPU	Acceleration
512 × 512	5 fps	79 fps	15.80×
1280 × 720	2.9 fps	51 fps	17.59×
1920 × 1080	1.7 fps	35 fps	20.59×

joint area between two consecutive frames is determined by cropping the incoming and outgoing areas as seen in Fig. 22.6a. The white outline shows the common area between two consecutive frames. Figure 22.6b shows the resulting image of background subtraction. The white areas represent the difference around moving objects. Table 22.7 presents a comparison between CPU and GPU performances of the above-mentioned method. Notice that the use of GPU enabled a real-time processing for full HD videos (1920 × 1080), which is 20 times faster than the corresponding CPU version.

22.7   CONCLUSION

In this chapter, we proposed a model for image and video processing which exploits parallel and heterogeneous architectures. This model offers an efficient scheduling of jobs based on estimating the performance and the required transfer time for each previous task. Our model also enables overlapping data transfers by kernel executions within multiple GPUs. This solution was exploited for improving the performance of a medical application of vertebra detection, and an application of motion detection using a moving camera. Experimentation showed a global speedup ranging from 5 to 40, which is due to three main factors:

- *Low-level parallelization:* GPU parallel processing between pixels in the image. The video frames are also processed following the same process.
- *High-level parallelization:* Enabling the exploitation of both CPU and GPU cores simultaneously, so that each core treats a subset of images efficiently.
- *Efficient management of heterogeneous memories:* consists of exploiting the fast access GPU (texture and shared) memories, efficient scheduling of hybrid tasks, and overlapping of data transfers by kernels execution on multiple GPUs.

As future work, we plan to develop a smart system for real-time processing of high-definition videos in multiuser scenarios. The idea is to provide a dynamic platform enabling the facilitation and implementation of new advanced monitoring and control systems that exploit parallel and heterogeneous architectures, with minimum energy consumption. We also plan to improve the scheduling strategy by taking into account more parameters (number of operations, dependency factor, etc.), in order to have a better exploitation of resources.

ACKNOWLEDGMENT

This work was supported by the European COST action IC0805 "Open European Network for High-Performance Computing on Complex Environments."

REFERENCES

1. C. Augonnet, S. Thibault, R. Namyst, and P.-A. Wacrenier, "StarPU: a unified platform for task scheduling on heterogeneous multicore architectures," *Concurrency and Computation: Practice and Experience*, vol. 23, no. 2, pp. 187–198, 2011.
2. S. A. Mahmoudi, F. Lecron, P. Manneback, M. Benjelloun, and S. Mahmoudi, "GPU-based segmentation of cervical vertebra in X-Ray images," in *IEEE International Conference on Cluster Computing*, Crete, Greece, pp. 1–8, 2010.
3. Z. Yang, Y. Zhu, and Y. Pu, "Parallel image processing based on CUDA," *International Conference on Computer Science and Software Engineering*, vol. 3, pp. 198–201, 2008.
4. D. Castano-Diez, D. Moser, A. Schoenegger, S. Pruggnaller, and A. S. Frangakis, "Performance evaluation of image processing algorithms on the GPU," *Journal of Structural Biology*, vol. 164, no. 1, pp. 153–160, 2008.
5. J. Fung, S. Mann, and C. Aimone, "OpenVIDIA: Parallel GPU computer vision," in *Proceedings of ACM Multimedia*, Singapore, pp. 849–852, 2005.
6. F. Lecron, S. A. Mahmoudi, M. Benjelloun, S. Mahmoudi, and P. Manneback, "Heterogeneous computing for vertebra detection and segmentation in X-Ray images," *Journal of Biomedical Imaging*, vol. 2011, pp. 5:1–5:12, 2011.
7. S. A. Mahmoudi, F. Lecron, P. Manneback, M. Benjelloun, and S. Mahmoudi, "Efficient exploitation of heterogeneous platforms for vertebra detection in X-Ray images," in *Biomedical Engineering International Conference (Biomeic'12)*, (Tlemcen, Algeria), 2012.
8. E. Ayguadé, R. M. Badia, F. D. Igual, J. Labarta, R. Mayo, and E. S. Quintana-Ortí, "An extension of the StarSs programming model for platforms with multiple GPUs," in *Proceedings of the 15th International Euro-Par Conference on Parallel Processing, Euro-Par '09*, pp. 851–862–. Berlin, Heidelberg: Springer-Verlag, 2009.
9. A. del Bimbo, P. Nesi, and J. L. C. Sanz, "Optical flow computation using extended constraints," *IEEE Transactions on Image Processing*, vol. 5, no. 5, pp. 720–739, 1996.
10. B. Kitt, B. Ranft, and H. Lategahn, "Block-matching based optical flow estimation with reduced search space based on geometric constraints," in *13th International IEEE Conference on Intelligent Transportation Systems (ITSC)*, Funchal, Portugal, pp. 1104–1109, 2010.
11. D. G. Lowe, "Distinctive image features from scale-invariant keypoints," *International Journal of Computer Vision*, vol. 60, no. 2, pp. 91–110, 2004.
12. J. Marzat, Y. Dumortier, and A. Ducrot, "Real-time dense and accurate parallel optical flow using CUDA," in *International Workshop on Computer Vision and Its Application to Image Media Processing*, Tokyo, Japan, p. 105, 2008.
13. Y. Mizukami and K. Tadamura, "Optical flow computation on compute unified device architecture," in *14th International Conference on Image Analysis and Processing*, Modena, Italy, pp. 179–184, 2007.
14. S. N. Sinha, J.-M. Frahm, M. Pollefeys, and Y. Genc, "GPU-based video feature tracking and matching," in *Workshop on Edge Computing Using New Commodity Architectures*, Chapel Hill, North Carolina, 2006.

15. S. A. Mahmoudi, S. Frémal, M. Bagein, and P. Manneback, "Calcul intensif sur GPU: exemples en traitement d'images, en bioinformatique et en télécommunication," in *CIAE 2011: Colloque d'informatique, automatique et électronique*, Casablanca, Morocco, 2011.

16. R. Deriche, "Using Canny's criteria to derive a recursively implemented optimal edge detector," *International Journal of Vision, Boston*, vol. 1, no. 2, pp. 167–187, 1987.

17. J. Y. Bouguet, "Pyramidal implementation of the Lucas Kanade feature: Description of the algorithm," OpenCV Document, Intel, Microprocessor Research Labs, 2000.

18. C. Harris and M. Stephens, "A combined corner and edge detector," in *The 4th Alvey Vision Conference, vol. 15*, pp. 147–151, 1988.

19. S. A. Mahmoudi, P. Manneback, C. Augonnet, and S. Thibault, "Traitements d'images sur architectures parallèles et hétérogènes," *Technique et Science Informatiques, Nouvelles architectures parallèles, Algorithmes, modèles et Outils*, vol. 31/8-10-2012, pp. 1183–1203, 10/20102 2012.

20. S. A. Mahmoudi, P. Manneback, C. Augonnet, and S. Thibault, "Détection optimale des coins et contours dans des bases d'images volumineuses sur architectures multicœurs hétérogènes," in *20ème Rencontre francophone du Parallélisme, RenPar'20*, (Saint-Malo. France), 2011.

21. S. A. Mahmoudi and P. Manneback, "Efficient exploitation of heterogeneous platforms for images features extraction," in *3rd International Conference on Image Processing Theory, Tools and Applications (IPTA)*, pp. 91–96, 2012.

22. A. Grama, A. Gupta, G. Karypis, and V. Kumar, *Introduction to Parallel Computing*. Pearson Education Limited, second ed., Addison Wesley, 2003.

23. B. K. P. Horn and B. G. Schunck, "Determining optical flow," *Artificial Intelligence*, vol. 17, pp. 185–203, 1981.

24. B. D. Lucas and T. Kanade, "An iterative image registration technique with an application to stereo vision," in *Proceedings of the 7th International Joint Conference on Artificial intelligence—Volume 2, IJCAI'81*, pp. 674–679, 1981.

23

Real-Time Tomographic Reconstruction Through CPU + GPU Coprocessing

José Ignacio Agulleiro, Francisco Vazquez, and Ester M. Garzon

University of Almería, Almería, Spain

Jose J. Fernandez

National Centre for Biotechnology. National Research Council (CNB-CSIC), Madrid, Spain

Modern desktop computers are shipped with multicore processors and one or several GPUs (graphics processor units). If full exploitation of these computers is to be achieved, CPUs and GPUs have to tightly collaborate in the computation tasks. One inherent characteristic of these modern platforms is their heterogeneity, which raises the issue of workload distribution among the different processing elements. Adaptive load balancing techniques are thus necessary to properly adjust the amount of work to be done by each. We have tested an "on-demand" strategy, a well-known classical technique in the HPC (high-performance computing) field, whereby the different processing devices (GPUs, CPU cores) asynchronously request for a piece of work when they become idle. We have evaluated this strategy with its application to tomographic reconstruction. The results show that our scheme accommodates to the underlying heterogeneous platform and succeeds in keeping the system fairly well balanced. This CPU + GPU coprocessing strategy is directly applicable or extendable to many other scientific problems that rely on data parallelism. The combination

High-Performance Computing on Complex Environments, First Edition.
Edited by Emmanuel Jeannot and Julius Žilinskas.
© 2014 John Wiley & Sons, Inc. Published 2014 by John Wiley & Sons, Inc.

of this hybrid computing approach with CPU- and GPU-optimized solutions makes possible real-time tomographic reconstruction on a desktop computer.

23.1   INTRODUCTION

Electron tomography (ET), which combines electron microscopy with the power of three-dimensional (3D) imaging, has emerged as the leading technique for the structural analysis of unique complex biological specimens [1–4]. ET has made it possible to directly visualize the molecular architecture of organelles, cells, and complex viruses, and, in particular, has been crucial for recent breakthroughs in life sciences [5–11].

ET and computer-assisted tomography (CT) in medicine are alike. In ET, a set of images from a single individual specimen (so-called tilt series) is acquired at different orientations by means of an electron microscope. Those images represent projections (similar to "radiographs" in medicine) of the specimen. From those projection images, a 3D reconstruction is obtained using tomographic reconstruction algorithms [4]. Computer-automated data collection has been essential for the advent of ET as an important structural technique in cellular biology [1]. It allows automated specimen tilting, area tracking, focusing, and recording of images under low electron-dose conditions in order to preserve the specimen from radiation damage.

Recently, real-time ET systems have appeared on the scene [12–15]. These systems combine the computer-assisted image collection with the 3D reconstruction and provide the users not only with the acquired tilt series but also with a preliminary structure of the specimen. This rough structure allows users to easily evaluate the quality of the specimen and decide whether a more time-consuming processing and thorough analysis of the dataset is worthwhile. These systems also guide the users to select further target areas to be imaged. Real-time 3D reconstruction is typically performed on a tilt series with reduced resolution (2×, 4×) and using HPC techniques on multicore computers, clusters of workstations, or GPUs in order to obtain the volume in a matter of minutes [12–15].

HPC has turned out to be the key to cope with the highly demanding computational requirements of tomographic reconstruction algorithms [14], thereby allowing determination of the 3D structure of large volumes in reasonable computation time. However, from a practical point of view, starting up a parallel computing system in a laboratory of structural biology is not a trivial task because strong computer skills are needed not only for configuring and maintaining the system but also for users to launch parallel jobs.

On the other hand, modern standalone desktop computers are now equipped with powerful engines such as multicore processors and GPUs, which turn them into outstanding computing platforms [16]. They can be configured, managed, and used easily, thereby making them appropriate for structural biology laboratories. The implementations so far have been, however, purely focused on either GPUs [17] or CPUs [18]. We have developed a hybrid approach that collaboratively combines the GPUs and CPUs available in a computer, thus fully exploiting the power available in

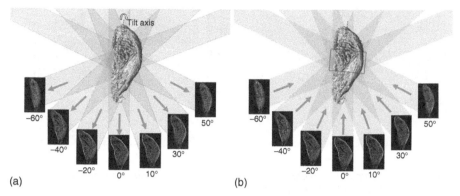

FIGURE 23.1 *Data acquisition geometry and 3D reconstruction in ET. (a) Single-tilt axis data acquisition geometry. (b) Conceptual scheme of 3D reconstruction by backprojection.*

the computer [19]. When it is combined with optimized implementations for CPUs and GPUs, real-time tomographic reconstruction on a desktop computer is possible.

This chapter is organized as follows: First, the fundamentals of tomographic reconstruction are presented. Second, the optimized implementations for CPUs and GPUs are then reviewed. The hybrid CPU + GPU coprocessing approach is then described. Next, the results are presented. The chapter finishes with concluding remarks.

23.2 TOMOGRAPHIC RECONSTRUCTION

In ET, the projection images are acquired from the specimen by following the so-called single-axis tilt geometry. Here, the specimen is tilted over a limited range, typically from −60° (or −70°) to +60° (or +70°), at small tilt increments (1°–2°). An image of the same object area is then recorded at each tilt angle (Fig. 23.1a). The set of acquired images is called a *tilt series* and usually contains a number of images in the range 60–200. Owing to the resolution requirements, the image size typically ranges between 1024 × 1024 and 4096 × 4096 pixels. For the purpose of real-time reconstruction, sizes of 512 × 512 to 1024 × 1024 are typically used, though. The reconstruction problem in ET is then to obtain the 3D structure of the specimen from the set of projection images.

Weighted backprojection (WBP) [20] is currently the standard algorithm in ET. Briefly, the method distributes the known specimen mass present in projection images evenly over the computed backprojection rays. When this process is repeated for a series of projection images recorded from different tilt angles, backprojection rays from the different images intersect and reinforce each other at the points where mass is found in the original structure. Therefore, the 3D mass of the specimen is reconstructed. Figure 23.1b shows a sketch of the backprojection process to 3D reconstruction from projections. The backprojection process involves an implicit low-pass filtering that makes reconstructed volumes blurred. In practice, in order to compensate the transfer function of the backprojection process, a previous high-pass filter

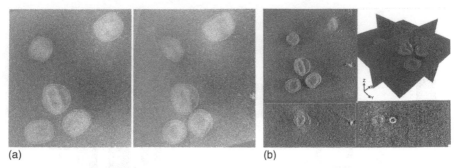

(a)   (b)

FIGURE 23.2   *Tomographic reconstruction of* Vaccinia virus. *(a) Some images of the tilt series.*
(b) Slices at different orthogonal axes of the tomogram.

(i.e., weighting) is applied to the projection images, hence the term *weighted back-projection*. The computation burden due to the filtering is negligible compared to backprojection. For a more in-depth description of the method, see [20].

Figure 23.2 shows an illustrative example with a sample of *Vaccinia virions*, which is the virus used as a vaccine against small pox [7]. Figure 23.2a shows some images (taken from the sample at 0° and 40° tilt) in the tilt series. Figure 23.2b presents some orthogonal slices of the 3D reconstruction, also known as the *tomogram*. In this example, the tomogram was computed from a tilt series of 61 images with the specimen tilted in the range [−60°, +60°].

Assuming voxels as the basis functions to represent the volume, the 3D reconstruction problem can be decomposed into a set of independent two-dimensional (2D) reconstruction subproblems corresponding to the 2D slices perpendicular to the tilt axis [14]. One such slice is sketched with a red square in Fig. 23.1b. The reconstruction of a 2D slice is computed from the corresponding set of 1D projections (so-called sinogram), using the same algorithm but now working in two dimensions. Figure 23.1b sketches 1D projections with red lines in the projection images. The 3D volume is then obtained by stacking the reconstructed 2D slices. This decomposition has been extensively used for the development of efficient HPC approaches to this problem (see in the following sections).

The 2D tomographic reconstruction process by WBP can be mathematically expressed in simple terms as the following formula:

$$s_j = \sum_{i=1}^{n} B_{j,i} W(p_i), \quad 1 \leq j \leq m, \tag{23.1}$$

where p denotes the set of experimental 1D projections (i.e., the sinogram) and s is the reconstructed slice, with size n and m, respectively. $n = n_{\text{tilts}} n_{\text{bins}}$, with n_{tilts} being the number of projection angles and n_{bins} the number of projection values obtained for every projection angle, and $m = m_x m_y$, with m_x and m_y being the number of voxels in the x and y dimensions of the slice, respectively. $W()$ represents the high-pass filtering operation involved in WBP. The coefficient $B_{j,i}$ of the matrix $\mathbf{B}$ is a weighting factor representing the contribution of the voxel j to the projection value i, and its value depends only on the geometry of the projections. This matrix is sparse, that is, many coefficients are zero since the contribution of every voxel is associated with a small subset of projection values. In particular, for a given tilt angle θ, a pixel (x, y) of the slice is projected to the point $r = x\cos(\theta) + y\sin(\theta)$ in the projection vector.

Algorithm 23.1 is a high-level description of the 3D reconstruction. The outer loop sweeps across the slices of the volume in order to perform the backprojection process, slice by slice. The body of this loop represents the WBP working in two dimensions. It consists of computing the point rf where the projection at angle a of the current pixel (x, y) of the slice is located (note that the variable weight represents one coefficient $B_{j,i}$). The density value to be backprojected is then computed by linear interpolation from the 1D projection $proj$. The set of $proj[s]$ denotes the 1D projections (i.e., the sinogram) corresponding to the current slice $slice[s]$.

Algorithm 23.1

3D reconstruction based on 2D-WBP.

```
{
        for s in Nslices
        {
            /*—Two-dimensional WBP—*/
            for a in Nangles
                for y in Nrows
                    for x in Ncols
                    {
                        rf = projected_point(x,y,a)
                        r = (int)rf
                        weight = r - rf
                        slice[s][y][x] = slice[s][y][x]
                                        + proj[s][a][r+1]*weight
                                        + proj[s][a][r]*(1-weight)
                    }
            /*—End of Two-dimensional WBP—*/
        }
}
```

23.3 OPTIMIZATION OF TOMOGRAPHIC RECONSTRUCTION FOR CPUs AND FOR GPUs

Tomographic reconstruction has long been studied with great interest from the HPC perspective. The single tilt axis geometry used in ET allows decomposition of the 3D reconstruction problem into a set of independent 2D reconstruction subproblems corresponding to the slices perpendicular to the tilt axis. The independent slices (or slabs of slices) of the volume can then be computed in parallel by the different processing elements using any reconstruction method. This data decomposition has often been exploited in the field [14]. Historically, there have been proposals for supercomputers [21], distributed systems [22, 23], and clusters [13, 24–27]. Most of these implementations have provided an effective reduction of computation time, approximately proportional to the number of processors used. Recently, the trend has turned toward GPUs, and a number of approaches have been presented [17, 28–32], including the use of multi-GPU strategies [33, 34], that have achieved outstanding speedup factors. In most of them, the multiple threads within the GPUs work at the level of individual voxels.

We have proposed a novel matrix approach of WBP for GPUs that outperforms previous strategies [17]. The 2D WBP procedure given by the analytic expression of WBP shown in (23.1) is directly implemented as a sparse matrix vector product (SpMV). The 3D reconstruction is then performed by a series of SpMV operations, where an important point behind this efficient implementation is the fact that the matrix B is invariable and shared for all the slices to be reconstructed. The other pillar of the good efficiency of the method is the development and use of sparse matrix data structures optimized for GPUs. We use the ELL-R scheme [35, 36], which consists of two arrays of dimension $m \times (2\, n_{\text{tilts}})$, where $m = m_x m_y$ is the number of rows of B and $2\, n_{\text{tilts}}$ is the maximum number of nonzeroes in the rows. The first array, B_{sp}, stores the nonzeroes, and the second, I, stores the original column index (i) in matrix B for each value in B_{sp}. An additional vector rl of dimension m keeps the actual number of nonzeroes in each row. The arrays B_{sp} and I store their elements in column-major order. As every thread in the GPU computes a row, this ensures optimal coalesced global memory access. Algorithm 23.2 shows how the SpMV operation is performed on the GPU using the ELL-R scheme (note that $s[x]$ denotes s_j in (23.1)). The reader is referred to [17] for details.

Algorithm 23.2

```
SpMV code on GPU using ELL-R scheme:s = B_sp p
{
        int x = blockIdx.x * blockDim.x + threadIdx.x;

        if (x < m)
        {
            int j, length;
            float svalue=0.0, value;

            length = rl[x];
            for(j=0; j<length; j++)
            {
                value = B_sp [j * m + x];
                col = I[j * m + x];
                svalue = svalue + value * p[col];
            }
            s[x] = svalue;
        }
}
```

On the other hand, on the CPU side we have developed a vectorized multithreaded approach that takes full advantage of the power in multicore computers [18, 37, 38]. Modern computers are usually shipped with one or more multicore processor chips,

Volume: pool of slabs of four slices

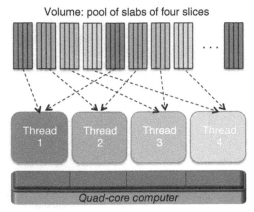

FIGURE 23.3   *Vectorized multithreaded approach for CPU tomographic reconstruction. Allocation of slabs to threads is coded with different grey levels.*

each comprising several powerful cores (e.g., dual-2, quad-4, hexa-6, octo-8). Moreover, the individual cores contain vector instructions, typically known as *SIMD* (single instruction, multiple data), which perform multiple computations with different data elements of the same kind simultaneously [39]. In particular, the SSE (streaming single instruction, multiple data extensions) instructions, present in all Intel and AMD processors, can perform four single-precision floating-point operations of the same type (addition, multiplication, etc.) with their corresponding four pairs of operands. Our strategy applies code optimization at the single-core level [40], and then takes advantage of two levels of parallelism that are available for the CPU programmer. First, vector processing is exploited through the SSE instructions to reconstruct four slices at a time [37]. Second, the program creates a number of threads, typically as many as the number of cores in the computer, that run concurrently in the system. The slices of the 3D volume to be reconstructed are grouped into slabs of four slices, and these slabs are asynchronously dispatched to the threads as soon as they are idle. The four slices in a slab are reconstructed simultaneously thanks to vector instructions. As far as basic single-core code optimization [40] is concerned, we have paid special attention to minimization of latencies and maximum exploitation of the functional units, and code reorganization and data structures to make the most of cache memory (see [37] for details). The performance of this CPU-based strategy approaches, or even outperforms, that of GPU solutions [18, 38]. Figure 23.3 shows a scheme of our vectorized multithreaded approach to CPU tomographic reconstruction.

23.4   HYBRID CPU + GPU TOMOGRAPHIC RECONSTRUCTION

CPU cores and GPUs present significant differences in their internal architecture, exploit different levels of parallelism, and work at different paces [16]. The architecture of a modern computer comprising multicore processors and GPUs is thus

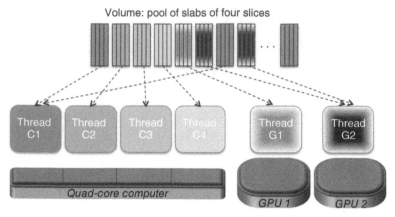

FIGURE 23.4   *Hybrid CPU + GPU computing on a computer equipped with multicore processors and multiple GPUs.*

heterogeneous. Then, proper distribution of the workload among the various processing elements is an issue if maximum exploitation is intended [41]. Therefore, there is need for an efficient mechanism to orchestrate the workload in order to maximize the use of the processing elements (CPU cores and GPUs) while minimizing latencies and waiting times. In the HPC field, load balancing has been a subject of research for long [41]. One dynamic load-balancing technique that has turned out to be effective consists in splitting the problem into tasks, which are assigned to the processing elements as they become idle (hence "dynamic") [41]. We use this strategy to dynamically distribute the workload among the CPU cores and the GPUs.

Our hybrid approach to tomographic reconstruction then works as follows: A pool of slabs (each slab containing four slices) to reconstruct is maintained. A number of threads run concurrently in the system at the CPU level (so-called C-threads). In addition, for each GPU in the system a specific thread (so-called G-threads) is created, which will be in charge of sending out the projection data (sinograms) to the GPU and receiving the reconstructed slices. As the threads become idle, they are assigned a new slab to reconstruct. When a slab is allotted to a C-thread, the calculations will be performed on one of the CPU cores, and the four slices in the slab will be computed simultaneously thanks to the vector instructions. In the case of the G-threads, the calculations will be carried out on the GPU using fine-grained parallelism at the level of the voxel. When a thread (either C- or G-) finishes its work, it requests another slab to reconstruct. This asynchronous dispatching of workload on demand is the implementation of the dynamic load-balancing technique referred to above. As the GPU normally makes the computations much faster than a single CPU core, a G-thread will be allotted more slabs than a C-thread. Moreover, faster GPUs will be assigned work more frequently than modest GPUs. Figure 23.4 shows an illustrative scheme of our hybrid CPU + GPU approach, which is valid for other scientific problems as well.

We have provided codes for users and developers. They can be downloaded from the following sites, respectively:

http://www.cnb.csic.es/%7ejjfernandez/tomo3dhybrid
http://www.cnb.csic.es/%7ejjfernandez/hybridcomputing

23.5 RESULTS

To evaluate our hybrid implementation and compare it with the CPU- and GPU-based ones, we have used an eight-core machine (two quad-core processors Intel Xeon E5640 at 2.66 GHz) equipped with two GPUs Nvidia Tesla C2050, each GPU with 448 cores at 1.15 GHz and 2.6 GB memory. We selected a tilt series of 122 images of 1024×1024 pixels to yield a 3D reconstruction of $1024 \times 1024 \times 256$, which is a representative size of real-time ET. All experiments were executed five times, and the average time was selected for analysis.

We have tested all the different CPU versions. We began from the original code, and followed with the progressively optimized versions by using the basic optimizations, vectorization, and multithreading with 2, 4, and 8 threads (denoted by 2T, 4T, and 8T, respectively). Table 23.1 presents the processing time (in seconds) required by the original version as well as the different optimized versions. The individual speedup factor achieved by each optimization is also presented. The basic optimizations succeed in accelerating the code by an impressive factor of 6.6, and vector processing achieved a remarkable factor of 3.7 out of a expected maximum of 4. This version (equipped with basic optimizations and vectorization, which takes 19.35 s to produce the reconstruction) is considered the best single-core CPU version (highlighted with a box in Table 23.1), and it will be used as a reference from now on. As far as multithreading is concerned, Table 23.1 shows that it exhibits a good speedup curve as a function of the number of cores though it slightly deviates from the linear behavior. In terms of the effective speedup with respect to the original CPU version (which took 468.74 s), the optimized vectorized multithreaded implementation reaches an outstanding speedup factor of 176.88, providing the reconstructed volume in just 2.65 s.

For the GPU versions, we used the matrix approach previously described and a multi-GPU strategy where both GPUs collaborate in the 3D reconstruction. CUDA (compute unified device architecture) was used for these implementations. It has to be pointed out that the weighting operation in the WBP reconstruction was carried out on the CPU cores because it proved to be more efficient in those computing engines than in the GPU thanks to the use of the optimized FFTW library [42]. Table 23.2 presents the results that were obtained, in particular the processing time (in seconds) and the speedup with regard to the best single-core CPU version. The use of two GPUs

TABLE 23.1 Results with the CPU-Based Implementations

Optimization:	Original	Basic optimizations	Vectorization	2T	4T	8T
Time:	468.74	71.23	19.35	9.79	4.99	2.65
Speedup:		6.58	3.68	1.98	3.88	7.30

TABLE 23.2   Results with the GPU-Based Implementations

Optimization	One GPU	Two GPUs
Time	4.79	2.72
Speedup	4.04	7.11

provided an acceleration factor of 7.11× with regard to the best single-core CPU version, which is slightly lower than the best one obtained with the multithreaded CPU implementations. In relative terms, the use of two GPUs instead of only one implies an improvement factor of 1.76×.

The results shown in Tables 23.1 and 23.2 confirm that multicore processors and GPUs can be considered as peers and both platforms can provide performance of similar magnitude. This has also been proved for other scientific problems [43].

Finally, we focused on the hybrid approach. We tested different configurations to determine which provided the maximum exploitation of the machine. We thus explored the hybrid strategy launching threads for all the CPU cores and all GPUs (i.e., eight C-threads and two G-threads, which is denoted by 8C + 2G). We also tested the hybrid approach launching G-threads for all the GPUs but keeping the total sum of threads no higher than the CPU cores available (i.e., 6C + 2G). Additional experiments were conducted in this study. For brevity, these results are not included here because, with fewer C-threads than the configurations tested here, the performance was poorer. To simulate a machine with only one GPU, we also launched the configurations 8C + 1G and 7C + 1G. The results—processing time (in seconds) and speedup factor with respect to the best single-core CPU implementation—are summarized in Table 23.3. The effective speedup factor ranges from 9× to 11×.

The results on the processing time with the hybrid approach show that the 3D volume would be ready for inspection in 1.75 s. This range of time undoubtedly demonstrates that the hybrid system is suitable for real-time tomographic reconstruction.

The results in Table 23.3 demonstrate that the collaborative combination of the CPUs and GPUs contribute to reducing the processing time and increasing the effective speedup compared to the pure CPU- or GPU-based solutions. In particular, the improvement factor with regard to the best multithreaded CPU implementation (8T in Table 23.1) ranges in [1.26×, 1.51×], whereas with regard to the GPU solutions it is around 2.3× for one GPU or 1.5× for two GPUs. Interestingly, all those results point out that for the sake of maximum performance it is better to keep the total number of threads running in the system no higher than the number of CPU cores in the

TABLE 23.3   Results with the Hybrid CPU + GPU Implementations

Optimization	8C + 1G	7C + 1G	8C + 2G	6C + 2G
Time	2.11	2.05	1.83	1.75
Speedup	9.17	9.44	10.57	11.06

TABLE 23.4   Workload Distribution in the Hybrid CPU + GPU Implementations

Optimization	8C + 1G	7C + 1G	8C + 2G	6C + 2G
Slices (CPU/GPU)	684/340	652/372	524/500	448/576
Percentage (CPU/GPU)	66.8/33.2	63.7/36.3	51.2/48.8	43.8/56.2

platform. That is, the configuration 7C + 1G is faster than 8C + 1G, whereas 6C + 2G outperforms 8C + 2G, when one or two GPUs are available, respectively. This restriction of the number of threads involves an improvement of 3–5% of the speedup.

Table 23.4 shows the distribution of workload for the computing elements, that is, how many slices have been reconstructed by the CPUs and by the GPUs. The workload is expressed in terms of the number of reconstructed slices and in percentage with respect to the total number of slices (i.e., 1024). It can be observed that, in the configuration 8C + 2G, the CPU cores are in charge of around 51.2% of the slices, whereas the remaining 48.8% are for the two GPUs. When the total number of threads is restricted (i.e., 6C + 2G), a redistribution of the workload toward the GPUs is seen (around 44% CPU, 56% GPUs), that is, each GPU gets around 3.5% more work than with the previous configuration. Something similar happens with the configurations 8C + 1G versus 7C + 1G. Interestingly, it can be observed that, when the number of threads is restricted (i.e., 6C + 2G or 7C + 1G), not only the G-threads get more workload but also the C-threads actually increase their burden as well, though at a lower rate (around 1.1% compared to the 3.5% of the G-threads).

As a summary, Fig. 23.5 shows the effective speedup achieved by all implementations tested here when compared with the best single-core CPU implementation (that was equipped with basic optimizations and vectorization). It clearly shows that the hybrid approach manages to make the most of the power latent in the computer, which is distributed among the CPU cores and GPUs. The best pure CPU-optimized and MultiGPU/GPU-based implementations reach an acceleration factor of slightly above 7×. The best hybrid approach then allows a good increase to achieve the level of 11×.

23.6   DISCUSSION AND CONCLUSION

This chapter presented a hybrid computing approach to tomographic reconstruction that combines GPUs and multicore processors to fully take advantage of the power of modern desktop computers. The ultimate aim was to provide 3D volumes at a speed suitable for real-time ET systems. These systems are meant to provide the users with the raw tilt series acquired during the data acquisition stage as well as a rough 3D reconstruction. This preliminary volume thus allows assessment of the quality of the sample and enables users to make decisions accordingly.

Our hybrid system relies on optimized versions focused on CPUs and GPUs. For CPUs, we made use of basic optimizations at a single-core level, followed by vectorization through SSE instructions, and finally multithreading. On the GPU side, the

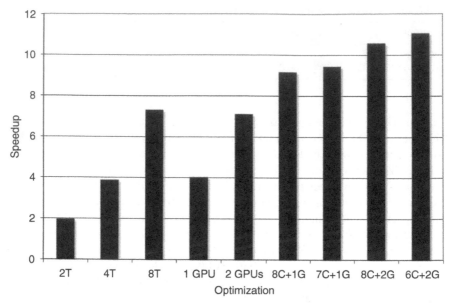

FIGURE 23.5 *Speed up of the optimizations versus the best single-core CPU code.*

optimal matrix implementation has been employed. Compared to the best single-core CPU version, our hybrid CPU + GPU approach to tomographic reconstruction was faster by 11× (which reaches an impressive figure of 268× when compared to the original CPU-based implementation). It thus provides 3D volumes in less than 2 s, which confirms its suitability for real-time systems. The fact that tomographic reconstruction linearly scales with the size of datasets makes this hybrid strategy valuable in the most general case.

One inherent characteristic of these modern platforms equipped with CPUs and GPUs is their heterogeneity. This turns distribution of the workload among the different processing elements into an issue. Adaptive load-balancing techniques are thus necessary to properly adjust the amount of work to be done by each computing element. Here we have chosen the "on-demand" strategy, a well-known technique in the HPC field, by which the different elements asynchronously request a piece of work to do when they become idle, thereby keeping the system reasonably balanced.

Our hybrid approach improves the performance by a factor in the range 1.5× to 2.3×, with regard to the best optimized CPU- or GPU-based strategies. Although these figures are relative to the system and implementations that were tested here, they are useful to illustrate the potential of the technique. In platforms with a higher number of GPUs, more powerful GPUs, or with better GPU implementations, our hybrid approach will be capable of adapting to the system by assigning more work to the GPUs. On the contrary, if modest GPUs or GPU implementations are used, it will allot more work to the multiple CPU cores in the system. Furthermore, this dynamic load-balancing technique may readily accommodate to a variety of heterogeneous platforms, for instance, when several GPUs with different computing capabilities are connected to a multicore computer.

The results we have obtained clearly point out that, for the sake of performance, it is important to limit the total number of threads running in the system to the number of CPU cores, regardless of the number of GPUs available. This limitation involves a further reduction of the processing time. This is due to the fact that even the threads that submit the work to the GPUs still need to do some work on the CPU (e.g., the transfer of data and results between CPU and GPU). Limitation of the total number of threads to the CPU cores available minimizes such competition.

The application of hybrid computing to jointly exploit CPUs and GPUs for different scientific problems is supposed to be straightforward, as has happened with GPU computing thus far. Therefore, the approach proposed here is expected to be valuable and of general applicability for the scientific computing community.

ACKNOWLEDGMENTS

This work was supported by grants TIN2008-01117, TIN2012-37483, JA-P10-TIC 6002, JA-P11-TIC7176, and EU COST Action IC0805.

REFERENCES

1. V. Lučić, F. Förster, and W. Baumeister, "Structural studies by electron tomography: from cells to molecules," *Annual Review of Biochemistry*, vol. 74, pp. 833–865, 2005.
2. J. J. Fernandez, C. O. S. Sorzano, R. Marabini, and J. M. Carazo, "Image processing and 3D reconstruction in electron microscopy," *IEEE Signal Processing Magazine*, vol. 23, no. 3, pp. 84–94, 2006.
3. A. P. Leis, M. Beck, M. Gruska, C. Best, R. Hegerl, W. Baumeister, and J. W. Leis, "Cryo-electron tomography of biological specimens," *IEEE Signal Processing Magazine*, vol. 23, no. 3, pp. 95–103, 2006.
4. J. J. Fernandez, "Computational methods for electron tomography," *Micron*, vol. 43, pp. 1010–1030, 2012.
5. O. Medalia, I. Weber, A. S. Frangakis, D. Nicastro, G. Gerisch, and W. Baumeister, "Macromolecular architecture in eukaryotic cells visualized by cryoelectron tomography," *Science*, vol. 298, pp. 1209–1213, 2002.
6. K. Grünewald, P. Desai, D. C. Winkler, J. B. Heymann, D. M. Belnap, W. Baumeister, and A. C. Steven, "Three-dimensional structure of herpes simplex virus from cryo-electron tomography," *Science*, vol. 302, pp. 1396–1398, 2003.
7. M. Cyrklaff, C. Risco, J. J. Fernandez, M. V. Jiménez, M. Esteban, W. Baumeister, and J. L. Carrascosa, "Cryo-electron tomography of vaccinia virus," *Proceedings of the National Academy of Sciences of the United States of America*, vol. 102, pp. 2772–2777, 2005.
8. D. Nicastro, C. Schwartz, J. Pierson, R. Gaudette, M. E. Porter, and J. R. McIntosh, "The molecular architecture of axonemes revealed by cryoelectron tomography," *Science*, vol. 313, pp. 944–948, 2006.

9. M. Beck, V. Lučić, F. Förster, W. Baumeister, and O. Medalia, "Snapshots of nuclear pore complexes in action captured by cryo-electron tomography," *Nature*, vol. 449, pp. 611–615, 2007.

10. W. He, M. S. Ladinsky, K. E. Huey-Tubman, G. J. Jensen, J. R. McIntosh, and P. J. Björkman, "FcRn-mediated antibody transport across epithelial cells revealed by electron tomography," *Nature*, vol. 455, pp. 542–546, 2008.

11. S. Li, J. J. Fernandez, W. F. Marshall, and D. A. Agard, "Three-dimensional structure of basal body triplet revealed by electron cryo-tomography," *EMBO Journal*, vol. 31, pp. 552–562, 2012.

12. R. H. M. Schoenmakers, R. A. Perquin, T. F. Fliervoet, W. Voorhout, and H. Schirmacher, "New software for high resolution, high throughput electron tomography," *Microscopy and Analysis*, vol. 19(4), pp. 5–6, 2005.

13. S. Q. Zheng, B. Keszthelyi, E. Branlund, J. M. Lyle, M. B. Braunfeld, J. W. Sedat, and D. A. Agard, "UCSF tomography: an integrated software suite for real-time electron microscopic tomographic data collection, alignment, and reconstruction," *Journal of Structural Biology*, vol. 157, pp. 138–147, 2007.

14. J. J. Fernandez, "High performance computing in structural determination by electron cryomicroscopy," *Journal of Structural Biology*, vol. 164, pp. 1–6, 2008.

15. S. Q. Zheng, J. W. Sedat, and D. A. Agard, "Automated data collection for electron microscopic tomography," *Methods in Enzymology*, vol. 481, pp. 283–315, 2010.

16. J. L. Hennessy and D. A. Patterson, *Computer Architecture: a Quantitative Approach.* Burlington, MA: Morgan Kaufmann, fifth ed., 2011.

17. F. Vazquez, E. M. Garzon, and J. J. Fernandez, "A matrix approach to tomographic reconstruction and its implementation on GPUs," *Journal of Structural Biology*, vol. 170, pp. 146–151, 2010.

18. J. I. Agulleiro and J. J. Fernandez, "Fast tomographic reconstruction on multicore computers," *Bioinformatics*, vol. 27, pp. 582–583, 2011.

19. J. I. Agulleiro, F. Vazquez, E. M. Garzon, and J. J. Fernandez, "Hybrid computing: CPU+GPU co-processing and its application to tomographic reconstruction," *Ultramicroscopy*, vol. 115, pp. 109–114, 2012.

20. M. Radermacher, "Weighted back-projection methods," in *Electron Tomography: Methods for Three-Dimensional Visualization of Structures in the Cells* (J. Frank, ed.), pp. 245–273. New York: Springer, second ed., 2006.

21. G. A. Perkins, C. W. Renken, J. Y. Song, T. G. Frey, S. J. Young, S. Lamont, M. E. Martone, S. Lindsey, and M. H. Ellisman, "Electron tomography of large, multicomponent biological structures," *Journal of Structural Biology*, vol. 120, pp. 219–227, 1997.

22. S. T. Peltier, A. W. Lin, D. Lee, S. Mock, S. Lamont, T. Molina, M. Wong, L. Dai, M. E. Martone, and M. H. Ellisman, "The Telescience Portal for advanced tomography applications," *Journal of Parallel and Distributed Computing*, vol. 63, pp. 539–550, 2003.

23. J. J. Fernandez, I. Garcia, J. M. Carazo, and R. Marabini, "Electron tomography of complex biological specimens on the Grid," *Future Generation Computer Systems*, vol. 23, pp. 435–446, 2007.

24. J. J. Fernandez, J. M. Carazo, and I. Garcia, "Three-dimensional reconstruction of cellular structures by electron microscope tomography and parallel computing," *Journal of Parallel and Distributed Computing*, vol. 64, pp. 285–300, 2004.

25. J. J. Fernandez, D. Gordon, and R. Gordon, "Efficient parallel implementation of iterative reconstruction algorithms for electron tomography," *Journal of Parallel and Distributed Computing*, vol. 68, pp. 626–640, 2008.

26. X. Wan, F. Zhang, and Z. Liu, "Modified simultaneous algebraic reconstruction technique and its parallelization in cryo-electron tomography," in *Proceedings of 15th International Conference on Parallel and Distributed Systems (ICPADS 2009)*, pp. 384–390, 2009.

27. P. C. Fritzsche, J. J. Fernandez, D. Rexachs, I. Garcia, and E. Luque, "Analytical performance prediction for iterative reconstruction techniques in electron tomography of biological structures," *International Journal of High Performance Computing Applications*, vol. 24, pp. 457–468, 2010.

28. D. Casta ño-Díez, H. Mueller, and A. S. Frangakis, "Implementation and performance evaluation of reconstruction algorithms on graphics processors," *Journal of Structural Biology*, vol. 157, pp. 288–295, 2007.

29. D. Casta ño-Díez, D. Moser, A. Schoenegger, S. Pruggnaller, and A. S. Frangakis, "Performance evaluation of image processing algorithms on the GPU," *Journal of Structural Biology*, vol. 164, pp. 153–160, 2008.

30. W. Xu, F. Xu, M. Jones, B. Keszthelyi, J. Sedat, D. Agard, and K. Mueller, "High-performance iterative electron tomography reconstruction with long-object compensation using graphics processing units (GPUs)," *Journal of Structural Biology*, vol. 171, pp. 142–153, 2010.

31. F. Vazquez, E. M. Garzon, and J. J. Fernandez, "Matrix implementation of simultaneous iterative reconstruction technique (SIRT) on GPUs," *Computer Journal*, vol. 54, pp. 1861–1868, 2011.

32. W. J. Palenstijn, K. J. Batenburg, and J. Sijbers, "Performance improvements for iterative electron tomography reconstruction using graphics processing units (GPUs)," *Journal of Structural Biology*, vol. 176, pp. 250–253, 2011.

33. S. Q. Zheng, E. Branlund, B. Kesthelyi, M. B. Braunfeld, Y. Cheng, J. W. Sedat, and D. A. Agard, "A distributed multi-GPU system for high speed electron microscopic tomographic reconstruction," *Ultramicroscopy*, vol. 111, pp. 1137–1143, 2011.

34. X. Wan, F. Zhang, Q. Chu, and Z. Liu, "High-performance blob-based iterative three-dimensional reconstruction in electron tomography using multi-GPUs," *BMC Bioinformatics*, vol. 13 (Suppl. 10):S4, 2012.

35. F. Vazquez, J. J. Fernandez, and E. M. Garzon, "A new approach for sparse matrix vector product on NVIDIA GPUs," *Concurrency and Computation: Practice and Experience*, vol. 23, pp. 815–826, 2011.

36. F. Vazquez, J. J. Fernandez, and E. M. Garzon, "Automatic tuning of the sparse matrix vector product on GPUs based on the ELLR-T approach," *Parallel Computing*, vol. 38, pp. 408–420, 2012.

37. J. I. Agulleiro, E. M. Garzon, I. Garcia, and J. J. Fernandez, "Vectorization with SIMD extensions speeds up reconstruction in electron tomography," *Journal of Structural Biology*, vol. 170, pp. 570–575, 2010.

38. J. I. Agulleiro and J. J. Fernandez, "Evaluation of a multicore-optimized implementation for tomographic reconstruction," *PLoS ONE*, vol. 7(11), p. e48261, 2012.

39. M. Hassaballah, S. Omran, and Y. B. Mahdy, "A review of SIMD multimedia extensions and their usage in scientific and engineering applications," *Computer Journal*, vol. 51, pp. 630–649, 2008.

40. K. R. Wadleigh and I. L. Crawford, *Software Optimization for High Performance Computing*. Upper Saddle River, NJ: Prentice Hall PTR, 2000.

41. B. Wilkinson and M. Allen, *Parallel Programming: Techniques and Applications Using Networked Workstations and Parallel Computers*. Englewood Cliffs, NJ: Prentice Hall, second ed., 2004.

42. M. Frigo and S. G. Johnson, "The design and implementation of FFTW3," *Proceedings of the IEEE*, vol. 93, pp. 216–231, 2005.

43. V. W. Lee, C. Kim, J. Chhugani, M. Deisher, D. Kim, A. D. Nguyen, N. Satish, M. Smelyanskiy, S. Chennupaty, P. H. R. Singhal, and P. Dubey, "Debunking the 100X GPU vs. CPU myth: an evaluation of throughput computing on CPU and GPU," *ACM SIGARCH Computer Architecture News*, vol. 38, pp. 451–460, 2010.

Index

High-Performance Computing on Complex Environments, First Edition.
Edited by Emmanuel Jeannot and Julius Žilinskas.
© 2014 John Wiley & Sons, Inc. Published 2014 by John Wiley & Sons, Inc.

WILEY SERIES ON PARALLEL AND DISTRIBUTED COMPUTING
Series Editor: Albert Y. Zomaya

Computing for Numerical Methods Using Visual C++ / Shaharuddin Salleh, Albert Y. Zomaya, and Sakhinah A. Bakar

Architecture-Independent Programming for Wireless Sensor Networks / Amol B. Bakshi and Viktor K. Prasanna

High-Performance Parallel Database Processing and Grid Databases / David Taniar, Clement Leung, Wenny Rahayu, and Sushant Goel

Algorithms and Protocols for Wireless and Mobile Ad Hoc Networks / Azzedine Boukerche (*Editor*)

Algorithms and Protocols for Wireless Sensor Networks / Azzedine Boukerche (*Editor*)

Optimization Techniques for Solving Complex Problems / Enrique Alba, Christian Blum, Pedro Isasi, Coromoto León, and Juan Antonio Gómez (*Editors*)

Emerging Wireless LANs, Wireless PANs, and Wireless MANs: IEEE 802.11, IEEE 802.15, IEEE 802.16 Wireless Standard Family / Yang Xiao and Yi Pan (*Editors*)

High-Performance Heterogeneous Computing / Alexey L. Lastovetsky and Jack Dongarra

Mobile Intelligence / Laurence T. Yang, Augustinus Borgy Waluyo, Jianhua Ma, Ling Tan, and Bala Srinivasan (*Editors*)

Advanced Computational Infrastructures for Parallel and Distributed Adaptive Applicatons / Manish Parashar and Xiaolin Li (*Editors*)

Market-Oriented Grid and Utility Computing / Rajkumar Buyya and Kris Bubendorfer (*Editors*)

Cloud Computing Principles and Paradigms / Rajkumar Buyya, James Broberg, and Andrzej Goscinski (*Editors*)

Energy-Efficient Distributed Computing Systems / Albert Y. Zomaya and Young Choon Lee (*Editors*)

Scalable Computing and Communications: Theory and Practice / Samee U. Khan, Lizhe Wang, and Albert Y. Zomaya (*Editors*)

The DATA Bonanza: Improving Knowledge Discovery in Science, Engineering, and Business / Malcolm Atkinson, Rob Baxter, Michelle Galea, Mark Parsons, Peter Brezany, Oscar Corcho, Jano van Hemert, and David Snelling (*Editors*)

Large Scale Network-Centric Distributed Systems / Hamid Sarbazi-Azad and Albert Y. Zomaya (*Editors*)

Verification of Communication Protocols in Web Services: Model-Checking Service Compositions / Zahir Tari, Peter Bertok, and Anshuman Mukherjee

High-Performance Computing on Complex Environments / Emmanuel Jeannot and Julius Žilinskas (*Editors*)